Microsoft® Office

Publisher 2007

Complete Concepts and Techniques

Gary B. Shelly

Thomas J. Cashman

Joy L. Starks

THOMSON

COURSE TECHNOLOGY

THOMSON COURSE TECHNOLOGY   25 THOMSON PLACE   BOSTON MA 02210

SHELLY
CASHMAN
SERIES®

Australia • Canada • Denmark • Japan • Mexico • New Zealand • Philippines • Puerto Rico • Singapore • South Africa • Spain • United Kingdom • United States

THOMSON
COURSE TECHNOLOGY

Microsoft Office Publisher 2007
Complete Concepts and Techniques

Gary B. Shelly

Thomas J. Cashman

Joy L. Starks

Executive Editor
Alexandra Arnold

Senior Product Manager
Reed Curry

Associate Product Manager
Klenda Martinez

Editorial Assistant
Jon Farnham

Senior Marketing Manager
Joy Stark-Vancs

Marketing Coordinator
Julie Schuster

Print Buyer
Julio Esperas

Director of Production
Patty Stephan

Senior Content Project Manager
Jennifer Goguen McGrail

Developmental Editor
Jill Batistick

Proofreader
Kim Kosmatka

Indexer
Liz Cunningham

QA Manuscript Reviewers
John Freitas, Serge Palladino,
Chris Scriver, Danielle Shaw,
Marianne Snow, Teresa Storch

Art Director
Bruce Bond

Cover and Text Design
Joel Sadagursky

Cover Photo
Jon Chomitz

Compositor
GEX Publishing Services

Printer
Banta Menasha

Microsoft® Office
Publisher 2007
Complete Concepts and Techniques

Contents

Preface	ix
To the Student	xiv

Microsoft Office **Publisher 2007**

CHAPTER ONE
Creating and Editing a Publication
Objectives	**PUB 1**
What Is Microsoft Office Publisher 2007?	**PUB 2**
Project — Flyer Publication	**PUB 3**
Overview	PUB 4
Starting Publisher	**PUB 4**
To Start Publisher	PUB 5
Using a Template to Create a Flyer	**PUB 6**
Selecting a Template	PUB 6
To Select a Template	PUB 7
Setting Publication Options	PUB 9
To Set Publication Options	PUB 9
The Publisher Window	**PUB 13**
The Workspace	PUB 13
Menu Bar and Toolbars	PUB 15
Resetting Menus and Toolbars	PUB 16
The Task Pane	PUB 16
To Close the Task Pane	PUB 17
Entering Text	**PUB 18**
Using Text Boxes	PUB 18
To Enter Text	PUB 19
To Zoom	PUB 21
To Zoom and Enter Text	PUB 21
To Display Formatting Marks	PUB 24
Wordwrap	PUB 24
To Wordwrap Text as You Type	PUB 25
To Enter Bulleted Items	PUB 26
To Enter Tear-off Text	PUB 27
Deleting Objects	**PUB 28**
To Delete an Object	PUB 28
Checking the Spelling	**PUB 29**
To Check Spelling as You Type	PUB 30
Saving the Project	**PUB 31**
To Save a Publication	PUB 31
Using Graphics	**PUB 34**
To Replace a Graphic Using the Clip Art Task Pane	PUB 34

Changing Publication Properties and Saving Again	**PUB 38**
To Change Publication Properties	PUB 38
To Save an Existing Publication with the Same File Name	PUB 40
Printing a Publication	**PUB 40**
To Print a Publication	PUB 40
Quitting Publisher	**PUB 41**
To Quit Publisher	PUB 41
Starting Publisher and Opening a Publication	**PUB 41**
To Open a Publication from Publisher	PUB 42
Correcting Errors	**PUB 44**
Types of Changes Made to Publications	PUB 44
To Delete the Tear-offs	PUB 44
Inserting a Text Box	PUB 45
To Insert a Text Box in an Existing Publication	PUB 46
To Format Text	PUB 47
Inserting a Hyperlink	PUB 49
To Insert a Hyperlink	PUB 49
Creating a Web Page from a Publication	**PUB 51**
To Run the Design Checker	PUB 51
To Save a Publication with a New File Name	PUB 52
Converting a Print Publication to a Web Publication	PUB 53
To Convert a Print Publication to a Web Publication	PUB 53
Publishing to the Web	PUB 55
To Publish to the Web	PUB 55
To Preview the Web Publication in a Browser	PUB 57
Closing the Entire Publication	PUB 57
Publisher Help	**PUB 58**
To Search for Publisher Help	PUB 58
Chapter Summary	**PUB 61**
Learn It Online	**PUB 62**
Apply Your Knowledge	**PUB 62**
Extend Your Knowledge	**PUB 65**
Make It Right	**PUB 66**
In the Lab	**PUB 67**
Cases and Places	**PUB 71**

CHAPTER TWO
Designing a Newsletter
Objectives	**PUB 73**
Introduction	**PUB 74**

Project — Newsletter	**PUB 74**
Overview	PUB 76
Benefits and Advantages of Newsletters	PUB 77
Using a Newsletter Template	**PUB 77**
To Choose a Newsletter Template and Change Options	PUB 78
To Set Page Options	PUB 82
Editing the Newsletter Template	**PUB 82**
Pagination	PUB 82
To Change and Delete Pages in a Newsletter	PUB 83
Editing the Masthead	**PUB 85**
Editing Techniques	PUB 85
To Edit the Masthead	PUB 85
Newsletter Text	**PUB 88**
Replacing Placeholder Text Using an Imported File	PUB 89
To Edit a Headline and Import a Text File	PUB 89
Continuing Stories Across Pages	PUB 92
To Import Text for the Secondary Story and Continue It on Page 2	PUB 92
To Format with Continued Notices	PUB 95
Editing Stories in Microsoft Word	**PUB 98**
To Edit a Story Using Word	PUB 98
Using the Color Scheme Colors	**PUB 102**
To Use the Color Scheme Colors	PUB 102
Selecting Text and Objects	PUB 104
Using Graphics in a Newsletter	**PUB 105**
To Replace a Graphic and Edit the Caption	PUB 106
To Insert a New Picture from Clip Art	PUB 110
Moving and Resizing Objects	PUB 111
To Move and Resize a Graphic	PUB 112
To Edit a Sidebar	PUB 113
Inserting a Pull Quote	PUB 116
To Insert a Pull Quote	PUB 117
Moving Text	PUB 121
To Move Text	PUB 122
Inserting Page Numbers	**PUB 124**
Headers and Footers	PUB 124
To Insert Page Numbers in the Footer	PUB 124
Checking a Newsletter for Errors	**PUB 126**
Spelling Errors	PUB 126
To Check the Newsletter for Spelling Errors	PUB 127
Checking the Newsletter for Design Errors	PUB 129
Creating a Template	**PUB 129**
To Access the Publisher Tasks Task Pane	PUB 130
Setting File Properties at the Time of Creation	PUB 131
To Create a Template with Property Changes	PUB 131
Printing a Two-sided Page	**PUB 134**
To Print a Two-Sided Page	PUB 134
Chapter Summary	**PUB 135**
Learn It Online	**PUB 136**
Apply Your Knowledge	**PUB 136**
Extend Your Knowledge	**PUB 138**
Make It Right	**PUB 139**
In the Lab	**PUB 141**
Cases and Places	**PUB 143**

CHAPTER THREE

Publishing a Tri-Fold Brochure

Objectives	**PUB 145**
Introduction	**PUB 146**
Project — Brochure	**PUB 146**
Overview	PUB 146
The Brochure Medium	**PUB 148**

Creating a Tri-Fold Brochure	**PUB 150**
Making Choices about Brochure Options	PUB 150
To Choose Brochure Options	PUB 150
Custom Color Schemes	**PUB 153**
To Open the Create New Color Dialog Box	PUB 153
To Change an Accent Color	PUB 154
To Save a New Color Scheme	PUB 156
Deleting Objects on Page 1	PUB 157
Replacing Text	**PUB 157**
To Edit Text in the Brochure	PUB 159
Font Styles	**PUB 162**
Applying a Style	PUB 162
To Insert a Text Box and Apply a Font Scheme Style	PUB 162
AutoCorrect Options	**PUB 164**
To Use the AutoCorrect Options Button	PUB 165
The Format Painter	**PUB 167**
To Use the Format Painter	PUB 168
Creating a New Style	**PUB 169**
To Open the Styles Task Pane	PUB 171
To Create a New Style	PUB 173
To Apply the New Style	PUB 175
Formatting Fonts and Paragraphs	**PUB 176**
Font Effects	PUB 176
Using a Font Effect	PUB 176
To Apply a Font Effect	PUB 177
Editing the Sign-up Form	PUB 178
To Edit the Sign-up Form	PUB 179
Formatting Paragraphs	**PUB 180**
Changing the Paragraph Spacing	PUB 180
To Change the Paragraph Spacing	PUB 181
Using Photographs in a Brochure	**PUB 183**
Inserting a Photograph from a File	PUB 184
Wrapping Text around Pictures	PUB 185
To Text Wrap	PUB 185
Replacing Graphics on Page 1	PUB 186
Creating a Logo from Scratch	**PUB 187**
Creating a Shape for the Logo	PUB 187
To Create a Shape for the Logo	PUB 188
To Fill a Shape with Color	PUB 189
To Edit AutoShape Lines	PUB 190
To Add Text to an AutoShape	PUB 192
To Fit Text	PUB 193
To Copy the Logo	PUB 194
To Reposition and Resize the Logos	PUB 195
Creating a Watermark with WordArt	**PUB 196**
To Access the Master Page	PUB 196
WordArt	**PUB 198**
Inserting a WordArt Object	PUB 198
To Insert a Word Object	PUB 199
To Format WordArt	PUB 200
Completing the Watermark	PUB 203
To Remove the Watermark from Page 1	PUB 203
To Make Text Boxes Transparent	PUB 204
Checking and Saving the Publication	PUB 204
Outside Printing	**PUB 205**
Previewing the Brochure Before Printing	PUB 205
Printing the Brochure	**PUB 206**
Printing Considerations	PUB 206
Paper Considerations	PUB 207
Color Considerations	PUB 207
Choosing a Commercial Printing Tool	PUB 208
To Choose a Commercial Printing Tool	PUB 209

Packaging the Publication for the Printing
    Service **PUB 210**
    Using the Pack and Go Wizard PUB 210
    To Use the Pack and Go Wizard PUB 210
    Using PostScript Files PUB 212
Quitting Publisher **PUB 212**
Chapter Summary **PUB 213**
Learn It Online **PUB 214**
Apply Your Knowledge **PUB 214**
Extend Your Knowledge **PUB 216**
Make It Right **PUB 217**
In the Lab **PUB 218**
Cases and Places **PUB 223**

E-MAIL FEATURE
Creating an E-Mail Letter Using Publisher
Objectives **PUB 225**
Introduction **PUB 226**
Project — E-Mail Message **PUB 226**
    Overview PUB 228
E-Mail Templates **PUB 228**
    Creating an E-Mail Message PUB 229
    To Open an E-Mail Template PUB 229
    To Customize the E-Mail Page Size PUB 230
Editing Text **PUB 231**
    Editing the Body of the E-Mail Letter PUB 231
Creating a Hyperlink **PUB 233**
    Editing the Hyperlink PUB 233
E-Mail Logos and Graphics **PUB 234**
    To Edit the Logo **PUB 234**
Backgrounds **PUB 235**
    To Add a Background PUB 235
Sending an E-Mail Letter **PUB 236**
    Using the Send E-Mail Command PUB 236
    To Preview and Send a Publication via E-Mail PUB 237
Sending Print Publications as E-Mail Messages **PUB 238**
Feature Summary **PUB 239**
In the Lab **PUB 240**

CHAPTER FOUR
Using Business Information Sets
Objectives **PUB 241**
Introduction **PUB 242**
Project — Business Information Sets **PUB 242**
    Overview PUB 244
Creating a Company Letterhead **PUB 245**
    Creating a Blank Publication PUB 246
    To Select a Blank Publication PUB 246
Creating a Business Information Set **PUB 247**
    Creating and Editing the Business
      Information Set PUB 247
    To Create a Business Information Set PUB 248
Using Margin and Ruler Guides **PUB 250**
    Changing the Margins PUB 251
    To Edit the Margin Guides PUB 251
    Using Rulers and Ruler Guides PUB 253
    To Move a Ruler PUB 253
    To Create a Ruler Guide PUB 254
Using Business Information **PUB 255**
    To Turn On Snapping PUB 255

    To Insert and Position Business Information
      Set Components PUB 256
    To Center a Text Box Relative to the Margins PUB 259
Editing Graphics **PUB 260**
    Creating the Clip Art Graphic PUB 261
    Cropping a Graphic PUB 262
    To Crop a Graphic PUB 262
    Cropping to a Nonrectangular Shape PUB 264
    To Crop to a Nonrectangular Shape PUB 264
    Rotating and Flipping Objects PUB 265
    To Flip an Object PUB 266
    Saving Edited Graphics PUB 267
    To Save Clip Art as a Picture PUB 267
Editing AutoShapes **PUB 268**
    Fill Effects PUB 268
    To Fill an AutoShape with a Picture PUB 269
    To Select a Line Color PUB 271
    Line/Border Styles PUB 272
    To Select a Line/Border Style PUB 272
    Shadows PUB 273
    To Add a Shadow PUB 274
    Creating the Rectangle Graphic PUB 274
    To Create a Gradient Fill Effect PUB 275
    Changing the Order PUB 278
    To Change the Order PUB 278
Using an Automatic Date **PUB 279**
    Inserting a Date in the Letterhead PUB 279
    To Insert an Automatic Date PUB 280
    Saving the Letterhead PUB 282
Using the Content Library **PUB 282**
    To Add to the Content Library PUB 283
    To Close a Publication Without Quitting
      Publisher PUB 284
    Read-Only Files PUB 284
Using Tables **PUB 286**
    Creating Tables PUB 286
    To Create a Table PUB 286
    Selecting Within Tables PUB 287
    To Select Portions of a Table PUB 288
    Formatting Tables PUB 289
    To Format the Table PUB 289
    Merge Cells and Cell Diagonals PUB 290
    To Create a Cell Diagonal PUB 291
    Entering Data PUB 292
    To Enter Data into a Table PUB 293
    Checking the Publication for Errors PUB 294
    Saving the Letter PUB 294
Business Cards **PUB 295**
    The Business Card Template PUB 295
    Editing the Business Card PUB 295
    Using the Select Objects Button PUB 296
    To Select Multiple Objects PUB 296
    To Insert from the Content Library PUB 297
    Using the Measurement Toolbar PUB 298
    To Position Objects Using the Measurement
      Toolbar PUB 299
    Saving and Printing the Business Card PUB 300
    Deleting Content PUB 300
    To Delete Content from the Content Library PUB 300
    To Delete the Business Information Set PUB 301

Quitting Publisher   **PUB 302**
Chapter Summary   **PUB 303**
Learn It Online   **PUB 303**
Apply Your Knowledge   **PUB 304**
Extend Your Knowledge   **PUB 306**
Make It Right   **PUB 307**
In the Lab   **PUB 308**
Cases and Places   **PUB 312**

CHAPTER FIVE

Merging Publications and Data
Objectives   **PUB 313**
Introduction   **PUB 314**
Project — Publisher Merge Features   **PUB 314**
  Overview   PUB 315
  To Edit the Letterhead Text Boxes   PUB 318
Using a Drop Cap   **PUB 320**
  To Create and Format a Drop Cap   PUB 320
Character Spacing   **PUB 322**
  Tracking Characters   PUB 323
  To Track Characters   PUB 323
  Kerning Character Pairs   PUB 324
  To Kern Character Pairs   PUB 324
Merging Data into Publications   **PUB 324**
  Creating a Publisher Address List   PUB 325
  To Create the Address List   PUB 326
  To Customize Address List Columns   PUB 327
  Entering Data into the Address List   PUB 330
  To Enter Data into the Address List   PUB 330
  To Create New Entries in the Address List   PUB 331
  To Save the Address List   PUB 332
  Creating the Form Letter   PUB 333
  To Start the Form Letter   PUB 333
  Connecting the Address List to the Form
    Letter   PUB 335
  To Connect the Address List   PUB 335
  To Filter Recipients   PUB 337
  Inserting Field Codes   PUB 338
  To Insert Grouped Field Codes   PUB 339
  To Insert Individual Field Codes   PUB 342
Working with Tabs and Markers   **PUB 343**
  Inserting a Tab Stop   PUB 345
  To Insert a Tab Stop   PUB 345
  To Enter Tabbed Text   PUB 346
Printing the Merged Document   **PUB 348**
  To Print Merged Pages   PUB 349
Creating Labels   **PUB 350**
  Label Print Settings   PUB 352
  To Change the Print Settings and Print Labels   PUB 353
Envelopes   **PUB 353**
Catalog Merge   **PUB 354**
  Creating the Westside Realty Catalog   PUB 355
  Starting the Catalog Merge   PUB 358
  To Start the Catalog Merge   PUB 358
  Connecting to a Catalog Data Source   PUB 358
  To Connect to a Catalog Data Source   PUB 359
  Inserting Catalog Fields   PUB 360
  Using the Catalog Merge Layout Toolbar   PUB 360
  Inserting Fields into the Catalog Merge Area   PUB 361
  Saving a Merged File   PUB 364

Calendars   **PUB 365**
  Inserting a Calendar   PUB 365
  To Insert a Calendar   PUB 365
  Resizing the Calendar and Entering Text   PUB 367
  To Edit the Calendar   PUB 368
Find and Replace   **PUB 370**
  Finding and Replacing Text   PUB 370
  To Find and Replace Text   PUB 370
Printing the Catalog   **PUB 372**
Saving the Catalog and Quitting Publisher   **PUB 373**
Chapter Summary   **PUB 373**
Learn It Online   **PUB 374**
Apply Your Knowledge   **PUB 374**
Extend Your Knowledge   **PUB 376**
Make It Right   **PUB 377**
In the Lab   **PUB 378**
Cases and Places   **PUB 383**

CHAPTER SIX

Creating an Interactive Web Site
Objectives   **PUB 385**
Introduction   **PUB 386**
Project — Interactive Web Site   **PUB 387**
  Overview   PUB 388
Creating a Web Site   **PUB 389**
  To Select Web Site Template Options   PUB 390
Editing the Home Page   **PUB 392**
  To Edit the Masthead and Heading   PUB 393
  Editing the Navigation Bar   PUB 394
  To Edit the Navigation Bar   PUB 394
Bookmarks   **PUB 399**
  Inserting a Bookmark   PUB 400
  To Insert a Bookmark   PUB 400
Web Graphics   **PUB 401**
  Inserting an Animated Graphic   PUB 401
  To Preview an Animated Graphic   PUB 401
  Using Empty Picture Frames   PUB 404
  To Create an Empty Picture Frame   PUB 404
  Alternative Text   PUB 406
  To Add Alternative Text   PUB 406
Setting Web Page Options   **PUB 407**
  To Edit Web Page Options   PUB 408
  Background Sound   PUB 409
  To Insert a Background Sound   PUB 409
  Saving the Web Site   PUB 410
  Making Changes on Page 2 of the Web Site   PUB 410
  To Go to a Bookmark   PUB 411
  Making Changes on Page 3 of the Web Site   PUB 412
  Saving the Web Site Again   PUB 414
Creating a Web Page from Scratch   **PUB 414**
  Inserting a New Page in a Web Publication   PUB 414
  To Insert a New Page in a Web Publication   PUB 415
  Editing Objects on the New Web Page   PUB 416
Form Controls   **PUB 418**
  Labels   PUB 419
  To Create Labels   PUB 420
  Textbox Form Controls   PUB 422
  To Insert Textbox Form Controls   PUB 422
  Textbox Form Control Properties   PUB 424
  To Edit Textbox Form Control Properties   PUB 424
  Text Area Form Controls   PUB 425

To Insert a Text Area Form Control   PUB 425
Text Area Form Control Properties   PUB 425
To Edit Text Area Form Control Properties   PUB 426
Checkbox Form Controls   PUB 427
To Insert Checkbox Form Controls   PUB 428
Checkbox Form Control Properties   PUB 429
To Edit Checkbox Form Control Properties   PUB 429
Option Button Form Controls   PUB 430
To Insert Option Button Form Controls   PUB 430
Option Button Form Control Properties   PUB 431
To Edit Option Button Form Control Properties   PUB 432
List Box Form Controls   PUB 433
To Insert a List Box Form Control   PUB 433
List Box Form Control Properties   PUB 433
To Edit List Box Form Control Properties   PUB 434
Submit Form Controls   PUB 436
To Insert Submit Form Controls   PUB 437
Form Properties   PUB 439
To Edit Form Properties   PUB 439
Hot Spots   **PUB 439**
Creating a Hot Spot   PUB 440
To Insert a Hot Spot   PUB 440
HTML Code Fragments   **PUB 440**
Creating a Scrolling Marquee   PUB 440
To Insert an HTML Code Fragment   PUB 441
To Preview and Test the Web Site   PUB 443
Visual Basic for Applications   **PUB 446**
Using the Visual Basic Editor   PUB 447
To Open the VBA Code Window   PUB 448
Entering Code Statements and Comments   PUB 449
To Program the BeforeClose Event   PUB 449
Security Levels   **PUB 450**
Setting Security Levels in Publisher   PUB 451
To Set a Security Level in Publisher   PUB 451
Checking and Saving the Publication   **PUB 452**
Checking for Spelling and Design Errors   PUB 452
Saving the Web Files   PUB 452
Testing the Web Site   PUB 453
Testing the Macro and Quitting Publisher   PUB 453
To Test the Macro and Quit Publisher   PUB 453
Chapter Summary   **PUB 454**
Learn It Online   **PUB 454**
Apply Your Knowledge   **PUB 455**
Extend Your Knowledge   **PUB 456**
Make It Right   **PUB 457**
In the Lab   **PUB 458**
Cases and Places   **PUB 464**

INTEGRATION FEATURE
Object Linking and Embedding
Objectives   **PUB 465**
Introduction   **PUB 466**
Project – Object Linking and Embedding   **PUB 466**
Overview   PUB 468
Starting Publisher   PUB 469
**Embedding an Excel Worksheet in a Publisher
    Publication**   **PUB 470**
Embedding an Excel Worksheet   PUB 470
To Embed an Excel Worksheet in a Publisher
    Publication   PUB 470

Editing an Embedded Worksheet   PUB 471
To Edit an Embedded Worksheet   PUB 471
Saving a Publication with an Embedded
    Worksheet   PUB 472
Starting Publisher and Excel   PUB 472
To Open a Publisher Publication and an Excel
    Workbook   PUB 473
**Linking an Excel Worksheet to a Publisher
    Publication**   **PUB 474**
Linking an Excel Worksheet   PUB 474
To Link an Excel Worksheet to a Publisher
    Publication   PUB 474
Saving a Publication with a Linked Worksheet   PUB 476
Quitting Excel   PUB 476
Editing a Linked Worksheet   **PUB 476**
To Edit a Linked Worksheet   PUB 477
Quitting Publisher and Saving the Publication   PUB 478
Feature Summary   **PUB 478**
In the Lab   **PUB 479**

Appendices

APPENDIX A
Project Planning Guidelines
Using Project Planning Guidelines   **APP 1**
Determine the Project's Purpose   APP 1
Analyze Your Audience   APP 1
Gather Possible Content   APP 2
Determine What Content to Present to Your
    Audience   APP 2
Summary   **APP 2**

APPENDIX B
Introduction to Microsoft Office 2007
What Is Microsoft Office 2007?   **APP 3**
Office 2007 and the Internet, World Wide Web,
    and Intranets   APP 4
Online Collaboration Using Office   APP 4
Using Microsoft Office 2007   **APP 4**
Microsoft Office Word 2007   APP 4
Microsoft Office Excel 2007   APP 5
Microsoft Office Access 2007   APP 5
Microsoft Office PowerPoint 2007   APP 6
Microsoft Office Publisher 2007   APP 6
Microsoft Office Outlook 2007   APP 6
Microsoft Office 2007 Help   **APP 7**
Collaboration and SharePoint   **APP 7**

APPENDIX C
Microsoft Office Publisher 2007 Help
Using Microsoft Office Publisher Help   **APP 9**
To Open the Publisher Help Window   APP 10
The Publisher Help Window   **APP 11**
Search Features   APP 11
Toolbar Buttons   APP 12

Searching Publisher Help APP 13
To Obtain Help Using the Type words to search
for Text Box APP 13
To Obtain Help Using the Help Links APP 15
To Obtain Help Using the Help Table of Contents APP 16
Obtaining Help while Working in Publisher APP 17
Use Help APP 18

APPENDIX D
Publishing Office 2007 Web Pages to a Web Server
Using Web Folders to Publish Office 2007
Web Pages APP 19
Using FTP to Publish Office 2007 Web Pages APP 20

APPENDIX E
Customizing Microsoft Office Publisher 2007
Changing Screen Resolution APP 21
To Change the Screen Resolution APP 21

Customizing the Publisher Toolbars and Menus APP 23
Resetting the Publisher Toolbars APP 23
To Reset the Publisher Toolbars APP 24
Editing Toolbars APP 25
To Edit Toolbars APP 25
Resetting the Publisher Menu Usage APP 27
To Reset the Publisher Menu Usage APP 27

APPENDIX F
Steps for the Windows XP User
For the XP User of this Book APP 28
To Start Publisher APP 28
To Save a Document APP 29
To Open a Publication APP 31

Index IND 1

Quick Reference Summary QR 1

Preface

The Shelly Cashman Series® offers the finest textbooks in computer education. We are proud of the fact that our series of Microsoft Office 4.3, Microsoft Office 95, Microsoft Office 97, Microsoft Office 2000, Microsoft Office XP, and Microsoft Office 2003 textbooks have been the most widely used books in education. With each new edition of our Office books, we have made significant improvements based on the software and comments made by instructors and students.

Microsoft Office 2007 contains more changes in the user interface and feature set than all other previous versions combined. Recognizing that the new features and functionality of Microsoft Office 2007 would impact the way that students are taught skills, the Shelly Cashman Series development team carefully reviewed our pedagogy and analyzed its effectiveness in teaching today's Office student. An extensive customer survey produced results confirming what the series is best known for: its step-by-step, screen-by-screen instructions, its project-oriented approach, and the quality of its content.

We learned, though, that students entering computer courses today are different than students taking these classes just a few years ago. Students today read less, but need to retain more. They need not only to be able to perform skills, but to retain those skills and know how to apply them to different settings. Today's students need to be continually engaged and challenged to retain what they're learning.

As a result, we've renewed our commitment to focusing on the user and how they learn best. This commitment is reflected in every change we've made to our Office 2007 books.

Objectives of This Textbook

Microsoft Office Publisher 2007: Complete Concepts and Techniques is intended for a six- to nine-week period in a course that teaches Publisher 2007 in conjunction with another application or computer concepts. The text may also be used in a 1-credit hour or trimester course. No experience with a computer is assumed, and no mathematics beyond the high school freshman level is required. The objectives of this book are:

- To offer an in-depth presentation of Microsoft Office Publisher 2007
- To expose students to practical examples of the computer as a useful tool
- To acquaint students with the proper procedures to create publications suitable for coursework, professional purposes, and personal use
- To help students discover the underlying functionality of Publisher 2007 so they can become more productive
- To develop an exercise-oriented approach that allows learning by doing

The Shelly Cashman Approach

Features of the Shelly Cashman Series Microsoft Office Publisher 2007 books include:

- **Project Orientation** Each chapter in the book presents a project with a practical problem and complete solution in an easy-to-understand approach.

- **Plan Ahead Boxes** The project orientation is enhanced by the inclusion of Plan Ahead boxes. These new features prepare students to create successful projects by encouraging them to think strategically about what they are trying to accomplish before they begin working.

- **Step-by-Step, Screen-by-Screen Instructions** Each of the tasks required to complete a project is clearly identified throughout the chapter. Now, the step-by-step instructions provide a context beyond point-and-click. Each step explains why students are performing a task, or the result of performing a certain action. Found on the screens accompanying each step, call-outs give students the information they need to know when they need to know it. Now, we've used color to distinguish the content in the call-outs. The Explanatory call-outs (in black) summarize what is happening on the screen and the Navigational call-outs (in red) show students where to click.

Q&A What is a maximized window?

A maximized window fills the entire screen. When you maximize a window, the Maximize button changes to a Restore Down button.

Other Ways

1. Click Italic button on Mini toolbar
2. Right-click selected text, click Font on shortcut menu, click Font tab, click Italic in Font style list, click OK button
3. Click Font Dialog Box Launcher, click Font tab, click Italic in Font style list, click OK button
4. Press CTRL+I

Toolbar Rows
The Standard and Connect Frames toolbars are preset to display on one row, immediately below the menu bar. The Publisher Tasks and Formatting toolbar are displayed below that. If the resolution of your display differs from that in the book, some of the buttons that belong on these toolbars may not appear. Use the **Toolbar Options button** to display these hidden buttons.

- **Q&A** Found within many of the step-by-step sequences, Q&As raise the kinds of questions students may ask when working through a step sequence and provide answers about what they are doing, why they are doing it, and how that task might be approached differently.

- **Experimental Steps** These new steps, within our step-by-step instructions, encourage students to explore, experiment, and take advantage of the features of the Office 2007 new user interface. These steps are not necessary to complete the projects, but are designed to increase the confidence with the software and build problem-solving skills.

- **Thoroughly Tested Projects** Unparalleled quality is ensured because every screen in the book is produced by the author only after performing a step, and then each project must pass Thomson Course Technology's Quality Assurance program.

- **Other Ways Boxes and Quick Reference Summary** The Other Ways boxes displayed at the end of most of the step-by-step sequences specify the other ways to do the task completed in the steps. Thus, the steps and the Other Ways box make a comprehensive reference unit. A Quick Reference Summary at the end of the book contains all of the tasks presented in the chapters, and all ways identified of accomplishing the tasks.

- **BTW** These marginal annotations provide background information, tips, and answers to common questions that complement the topics covered, adding depth and perspective to the learning process.

- **Integration of the World Wide Web** The World Wide Web is integrated into the Publisher 2007 learning experience by (1) BTW annotations that send students to Web sites for up-to-date information and alternative approaches to tasks; (2) a Quick Reference Summary Web page that summarizes the ways to complete tasks (mouse, shortcut menu, and keyboard); and (3) the Learn It Online section at the end of each chapter, which has chapter reinforcement exercises, learning games, and other types of student activities.

- **End-of-Chapter Student Activities** Extensive student activities at the end of each chapter provide the student with plenty of opportunities to reinforce the materials learned in the chapter through hands-on assignments. Several new types of activities have been added that challenge the student in new ways to expand their knowledge, and to apply their new skills to a project with personal relevance.

Organization of This Textbook

Microsoft Office Publisher 2007: Complete Concepts and Techniques consists of six chapters on Microsoft Office Publisher 2007, two special features, six appendices, and a Quick Reference Summary.

End-of-Chapter Student Activities

A notable strength of the Shelly Cashman Series Microsoft Office Publisher 2007 books is the extensive student activities at the end of each chapter. Well-structured student activities can make the difference between students merely participating in a class and students retaining the information they learn. The activities in the Shelly Cashman Series Office books include the following.

CHAPTER SUMMARY A concluding paragraph, followed by a listing of the tasks completed within a chapter together with the pages on which the step-by-step, screen-by-screen explanations appear.

LEARN IT ONLINE Every chapter features a Learn It Online section that is comprised of six exercises. These exercises include True/False, Multiple Choice, Short Answer, Flash Cards, Practice Test, and Learning Games.

APPLY YOUR KNOWLEDGE This exercise usually requires students to open and manipulate a file from the Data Files that parallels the activities learned in the chapter. To obtain a copy of the Data Files for Students, follow the instructions on the inside back cover of this text.

EXTEND YOUR KNOWLEDGE This exercise allows students to extend and expand on the skills learned within the chapter.

MAKE IT RIGHT This exercise requires students to analyze a publication, identify errors and issues, and correct those errors and issues using skills learned in the chapter.

IN THE LAB Three all new in-depth assignments per chapter require students to utilize the chapter concepts and techniques to solve problems on a computer.

CASES AND PLACES Five unique real-world case-study situations, including Make It Personal, an open-ended project that relates to student's personal lives, and one small-group activity.

Instructor Resources CD-ROM

The Shelly Cashman Series is dedicated to providing you with all of the tools you need to make your class a success. Information about all supplementary materials is available through your Thomson Course Technology representative or by calling one of the following telephone numbers: Colleges, Universities, and Continuing Ed departments, 1-800-648-7450; High Schools, 1-800-824-5179, and Career Colleges, Business, Government, Library and Resellers, 1-800-477-3692.

The Instructor Resources CD-ROM for this textbook include both teaching and testing aids. The contents of each item on the Instructor Resources CD-ROM (ISBN 1-4239-1233-0) are described on the following page.

INSTRUCTOR'S MANUAL The Instructor's Manual consists of Microsoft Word files, which include chapter objectives, lecture notes, teaching tips, classroom activities, lab activities, quick quizzes, figures and boxed elements summarized in the chapters, and a glossary page. The new format of the Instructor's Manual will allow you to map through every chapter easily.

LECTURE SUCCESS SYSTEM The Lecture Success System consists of intermediate files that correspond to certain figures in the book, allowing you to step through the creation of a project in a chapter during a lecture without entering large amounts of data.

SYLLABUS Sample syllabi, which can be customized easily to a course, are included. The syllabi cover policies, class and lab assignments and exams, and procedural information.

FIGURE FILES Illustrations for every figure in the textbook are available in electronic form. Use this ancillary to present a slide show in lecture or to print transparencies for use in lecture with an overhead projector. If you have a personal computer and LCD device, this ancillary can be an effective tool for presenting lectures.

POWERPOINT PRESENTATIONS PowerPoint Presentations is a multimedia lecture presentation system that provides slides for each chapter. Presentations are based on chapter objectives. Use this presentation system to present well-organized lectures that are both interesting and knowledge based. PowerPoint Presentations provides consistent coverage at schools that use multiple lecturers.

SOLUTIONS TO EXERCISES Solutions are included for the end-of-chapter exercises, as well as the Chapter Reinforcement exercises.

Instructor Resources

Instructor's Manual
(Lesson plan & teaching tips)

Syllabus

PowerPoint Presentations

Figure Files
(Illustrations from the text)

Solutions to Exercises

Test Bank & Test Engine

Data Files for Students

Additional Activities
for Students

| Exit | ? | Home |

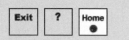
Student Edition Labs

TEST BANK & TEST ENGINE In the ExamView test bank, you will find our standard question types (40 multiple-choice, 25 true/false, 20 completion) and new objective-based question types (5 modified multiple-choice, 5 modified true/false and 10 matching). Critical Thinking questions also are included (3 essays and 2 cases with 2 questions each) totaling the test bank to 112 questions for every chapter with page number references, and when appropriate, figure references. A version of the test bank you can print also is included. The test bank comes with a copy of the test engine, ExamView, the ultimate tool for your objective-based testing needs. ExamView is a state-of-the-art test builder that is easy to use. ExamView enables you to create paper-, LAN-, or Web-based tests from test banks designed specifically for your Thomson Course Technology textbook. Utilize the ultra-efficient QuickTest Wizard to create tests in less than five minutes by taking advantage of Thomson Course Technology's question banks, or customize your own exams from scratch.

DATA FILES FOR STUDENTS All the files that are required by students to complete the exercises are included. You can distribute the files on the Instructor Resources CD-ROM to your students over a network, or you can have them follow the instructions on the inside back cover of this book to obtain a copy of the Data Files for Students.

ADDITIONAL ACTIVITIES FOR STUDENTS These additional activities consist of Chapter Reinforcement Exercises, which are true/false, multiple-choice, and short answer questions that help students gain confidence in the material learned.

Assessment & Training Solutions
SAM 2007
SAM 2007 helps bridge the gap between the classroom and the real world by allowing students to train and test on important computer skills in an active, hands-on environment.

   SAM 2007's easy-to-use system includes powerful interactive exams, training or projects on critical applications such as Word, Excel, Access, PowerPoint, Outlook, Windows, the Internet, and much more. SAM simulates the application environment, allowing students to demonstrate their knowledge and think through the skills by performing real-world tasks.

   Designed to be used with the Shelly Cashman series, SAM 2007 includes built-in page references so students can print helpful study guides that match the Shelly Cashman series textbooks used in class. Powerful administrative options allow instructors to schedule exams and assignments, secure tests, and run reports with almost limitless flexibility.

Student Edition Labs
Our Web-based interactive labs help students master hundreds of computer concepts, including input and output devices, file management and desktop applications, computer ethics, virus protection, and much more. Featuring up-to-the-minute content, eye-popping graphics, and rich animation, the highly interactive Student Edition Labs offer students an alternative way to learn through dynamic observation, step-by-step practice, and challenging review questions.

Online Content

Blackboard is the leading distance learning solution provider and class-management platform today. Thomson Course Technology has partnered with Blackboard to bring you premium online content. Instructors: Content for use with *Microsoft Office Publisher 2007: Complete Concepts and Techniques* is available in a Blackboard Course Cartridge and may include topic reviews, case projects, review questions, test banks, practice tests, custom syllabi, and more.

Thomson Course Technology also has solutions for several other learning management systems. Please visit http://www.course.com today to see what's available for this title.

Blackboard

CourseCasts Learning on the Go. Always Available…Always Relevant.

Want to keep up with the latest technology trends relevant to you? Visit our site to find a library of podcasts, CourseCasts, featuring a "CourseCast of the Week," and download them to your portable media player at http://coursecasts.course.com.

Our fast-paced world is driven by technology. You know because you are an active participant — always on the go, always keeping up with technological trends, and always learning new ways to embrace technology to power your life.

Ken Baldauf, a faculty member of the Florida State University (FSU) Computer Science Department, is responsible for teaching technology classes to thousands of FSU students each year. He knows what you know; he knows what you want to learn. He is also an expert in the latest technology and will sort through and aggregate the most pertinent news and information so you can spend your time enjoying technology, rather than trying to figure it out.

Visit us at http://coursecasts.course.com to learn on the go!

CourseNotes

Course Technology's CourseNotes are six-panel quick reference cards that reinforce the most important and widely used features of a software application in a visual and user-friendly format. CourseNotes will serve as a great reference tool during and after the student completes the course. CourseNotes for Microsoft Office 2007, Word 2007, Excel 2007, Access 2007, PowerPoint 2007, Windows Vista, and more are available now!

About Our New Cover Look

Learning styles of students have changed, but the Shelly Cashman Series' dedication to their success has remained steadfast for over 30 years. We are committed to continually updating our approach and content to reflect the way today's students learn and

experience new technology. This focus on the user is reflected in our bold new cover design, which features photographs of real students using the Shelly Cashman Series in their courses. Each book features a different user, reflecting the many ages, experiences, and backgrounds of all of the students learning with our books. When you use the Shelly Cashman Series, you can be assured that you are learning computer skills using the most effective courseware available. We would like to thank the administration and faculty at the participating schools for their help in making our vision a reality. Most of all, we'd like to thank the wonderful students from all over the world who learn from our texts and now appear on our covers.

To the Student . . . Getting the Most Out of Your Book

Welcome to *Microsoft Office Publisher 2007: Complete Concepts and Techniques*. You can save yourself a lot of time and gain a better understanding of the Office 2007 programs if you spend a few minutes reviewing the figures and callouts in this section.

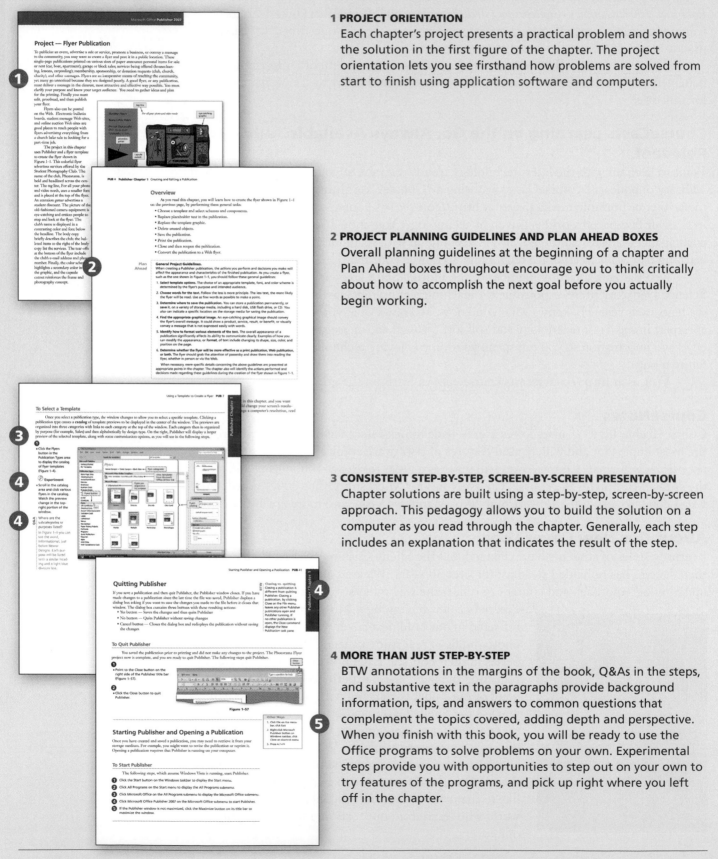

1 PROJECT ORIENTATION
Each chapter's project presents a practical problem and shows the solution in the first figure of the chapter. The project orientation lets you see firsthand how problems are solved from start to finish using application software and computers.

2 PROJECT PLANNING GUIDELINES AND PLAN AHEAD BOXES
Overall planning guidelines at the beginning of a chapter and Plan Ahead boxes throughout encourage you to think critically about how to accomplish the next goal before you actually begin working.

3 CONSISTENT STEP-BY-STEP, SCREEN-BY-SCREEN PRESENTATION
Chapter solutions are built using a step-by-step, screen-by-screen approach. This pedagogy allows you to build the solution on a computer as you read through the chapter. Generally, each step includes an explanation that indicates the result of the step.

4 MORE THAN JUST STEP-BY-STEP
BTW annotations in the margins of the book, Q&As in the steps, and substantive text in the paragraphs provide background information, tips, and answers to common questions that complement the topics covered, adding depth and perspective. When you finish with this book, you will be ready to use the Office programs to solve problems on your own. Experimental steps provide you with opportunities to step out on your own to try features of the programs, and pick up right where you left off in the chapter.

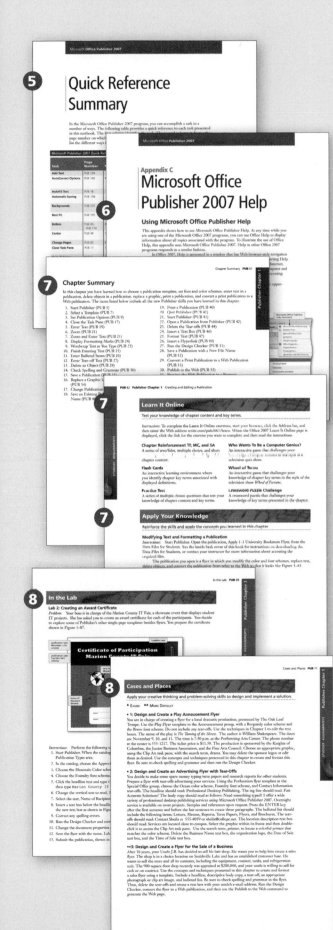

5 OTHER WAYS BOXES AND QUICK REFERENCE SUMMARY

Other Ways boxes that follow many of the step sequences and a Quick Reference Summary at the back of the book explain the other ways to complete the task presented, such as using the mouse, Ribbon, shortcut menu, and keyboard.

6 EMPHASIS ON GETTING HELP WHEN YOU NEED IT

The first project of each application and Appendix C show you how to use all the elements of Office Help. Being able to answer your own questions will increase your productivity and reduce your frustrations by minimizing the time it takes to learn how to complete a task.

7 REVIEW, REINFORCEMENT, AND EXTENSION

After you successfully step through a project in a chapter, a section titled Chapter Summary identifies the tasks with which you should be familiar. Terms you should know for test purposes are bold in the text. The Learn It Online section at the end of each chapter offers reinforcement in the form of review questions, learning games, and practice tests. Also included are exercises that require you to extend your learning beyond the book.

8 LABORATORY EXERCISES

If you really want to learn how to use the programs, then you must design and implement solutions to problems on your own. Every chapter concludes with several carefully developed laboratory assignments that increase in complexity.

1 | Creating and Editing a Publication

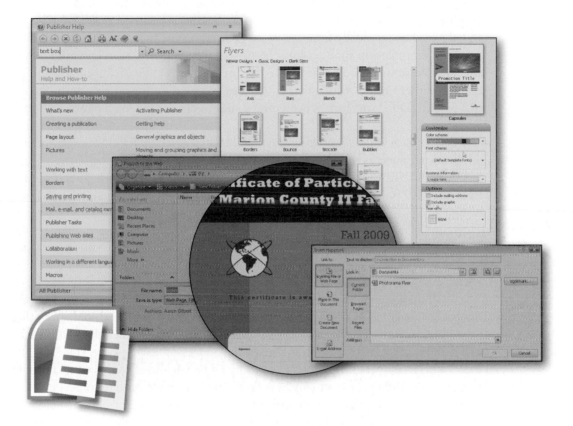

Objectives

You will have mastered the material in this chapter when you can:

- Start and quit Publisher
- Describe the Publisher window
- Choose Publisher template options
- Create a flyer from a template
- Replace Publisher template text
- Edit a synchronized object
- Delete objects
- Check spelling

- Save a publication
- Replace a graphic
- Print a publication
- Change publication properties
- Open and modify a publication
- Convert a print publication to a Web publication
- Use Publisher Help

1 | Creating and Editing a Publication

What Is Microsoft Office Publisher 2007?

Microsoft Office Publisher 2007 is a powerful desktop publishing (DTP) program that assists you in designing and producing professional, quality documents that combine text, graphics, illustrations, and photographs. DTP software provides additional tools over and above those typically found in word processing packages, including design templates, graphic manipulation tools, color schemes or libraries, advanced layout and printing tools, and Web components. For large jobs, businesses use DTP software to design publications that are camera ready, which means the files are suitable for outside commercial printing. In addition, DTP software is becoming a tool of choice for Web pages and interactive Web forms.

Microsoft Publisher is used by people who regularly produce high-quality color publications, such as newsletters, brochures, flyers, logos, signs, cards, and business forms. Saving publications as Web pages or complete Web sites is a powerful component in Publisher. All publications can be saved in a format that easily is viewed and manipulated using a browser.

Publisher has many features designed to simplify production and make publications look visually appealing. Using Publisher, you easily can change the shape, size, and color of text and graphics. You can include many kinds of graphical objects, including mastheads, borders, tables, images, pictures, charts, and Web objects in publications.

While you are typing, Publisher performs many tasks automatically. For example, Publisher detects and corrects spelling errors in several languages. Publisher's thesaurus allows you to add variety and precision to your writing. Publisher also can format text, such as headings, lists, fractions, borders, and Web addresses, as you type.

This latest version of Publisher has many new features to make you more productive. For example, Publisher has many new predefined templates and graphical elements designed to assist you with preparing publications and marketing strategies. Publisher also includes new e-mail, charting, and diagramming tools; uses themes so that you can coordinate colors, fonts, and graphics; and enables you to convert a publication to the PDF format. Publisher's tracking tools help determine the effectiveness of marketing mailings.

To illustrate the features of Publisher, this book presents a series of projects that create publications similar to those you will encounter in academic and business environments.

Project Planning Guidelines

The process of developing a publication that communicates specific information requires careful analysis and planning. As a starting point, establish why the publication is needed. Once the purpose is determined, analyze the intended audience and its unique needs. Then, gather information about the topic and decide what to include in the publication. Define a plan for printing, including color, type of paper, and number of copies. Finally, determine the publication design, layout, and style that will be most successful at delivering the message. After editing and proofreading, your publication is ready to print or upload to the Web. Details of these guidelines are provided in Appendix A. In addition, each project in this book provides practical applications of these planning considerations.

Project — Flyer Publication

To publicize an event, advertise a sale or service, promote a business, or convey a message to the community, you may want to create a flyer and post it in a public location. These single-page publications printed on various sizes of paper announce personal items for sale or rent (car, boat, apartment); garage or block sales; services being offered (housecleaning, lessons, carpooling); membership, sponsorship, or donation requests (club, church, charity); and other messages. Flyers are an inexpensive means of reaching the community, yet many go unnoticed because they are designed poorly. A good flyer, or any publication, must deliver a message in the clearest, most attractive and effective way possible. You must clarify your purpose and know your target audience. You need to gather ideas and plan for the printing. Finally you must edit, proofread, and then publish your flyer.

Flyers also can be posted on the Web. Electronic bulletin boards, student message Web sites, and online auction Web sites are good places to reach people with flyers advertising everything from a church bake sale to looking for a part-time job.

The project in this chapter uses Publisher and a flyer template to create the flyer shown in Figure 1–1. This colorful flyer advertises services offered by the Student Photography Club. The name of the club, Photorama, is bold and headlined across the center. The tag line, For all your photo and video needs, uses a smaller font and is placed at the top of the flyer. An attention getter advertises a student discount. The picture of the old-fashioned camera equipment is eye-catching and entices people to stop and look at the flyer. The club's name is displayed in a contrasting color and font below the headline. The body copy briefly describes the club; the bulleted items to the right of the body copy list the services. The tear-offs at the bottom of the flyer include the club's e-mail address and phone number. Finally, the color scheme highlights a secondary color in the graphic, and the capsule cutout reinforces the frame and photography concept.

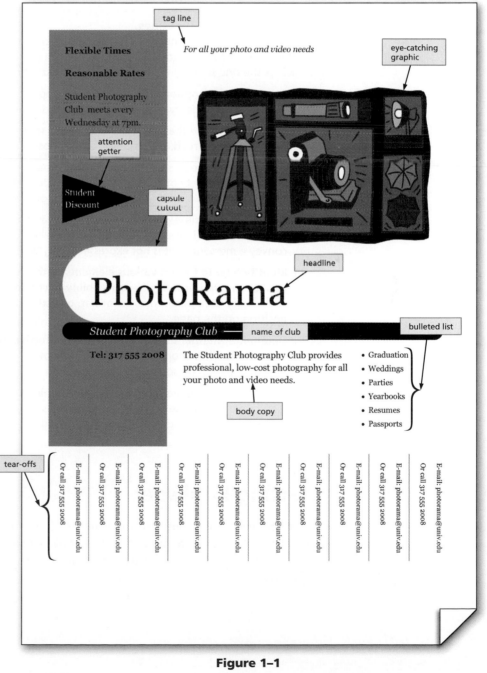

Figure 1–1

Overview

As you read this chapter, you will learn how to create the flyer shown in Figure 1–1 on the previous page, by performing these general tasks:

- Choose a template and select schemes and components.
- Replace placeholder text in the publication.
- Replace the template graphic.
- Delete unused objects.
- Save the publication.
- Print the publication.
- Close and then reopen the publication.
- Convert the publication to a Web flyer.

Plan Ahead

> **General Project Guidelines.**
> When creating a Publisher publication, the actions you perform and decisions you make will affect the appearance and characteristics of the finished publication. As you create a flyer, such as the one shown in Figure 1–1, you should follow these general guidelines:
>
> 1. **Select template options.** The choice of an appropriate template, font, and color scheme is determined by the flyer's purpose and intended audience.
>
> 2. **Choose words for the text.** Follow the less is more principle. The less text, the more likely the flyer will be read. Use as few words as possible to make a point.
>
> 3. **Determine where to save the publication.** You can store a publication permanently, or **save** it, on a variety of storage media, including a hard disk, USB flash drive, or CD. You also can indicate a specific location on the storage media for saving the publication.
>
> 4. **Find the appropriate graphical image.** An eye-catching graphical image should convey the flyer's overall message. It could show a product, service, result, or benefit, or visually convey a message that is not expressed easily with words.
>
> 5. **Identify how to format various elements of the text.** The overall appearance of a publication significantly affects its ability to communicate clearly. Examples of how you can modify the appearance, or **format**, of text include changing its shape, size, color, and position on the page.
>
> 6. **Determine whether the flyer will be more effective as a print publication, Web publication, or both.** The flyer should grab the attention of passersby and draw them into reading the flyer, whether in person or via the Web.
>
> When necessary, more specific details concerning the above guidelines are presented at appropriate points in the chapter. The chapter also will identify the actions performed and decisions made regarding these guidelines during the creation of the flyer shown in Figure 1–1.

Starting Publisher

If you are using a computer to step through the project in this chapter, and you want your screen to match the figures in this book, you should change your screen's resolution to 1024 × 768. For information about how to change a computer's resolution, read Appendix E.

To Start Publisher

The following steps, which assume Windows Vista is running, start Publisher, based on a typical installation. You may need to ask your instructor how to start Publisher for your computer.

Note: If you are using Windows XP, see Appendix F for alternate steps.

1

• Click the Start button on the Windows Vista taskbar to display the Start menu.

• Click All Programs at the bottom of the left pane on the Start menu to display the All Programs list.

• Click Microsoft Office in the All Programs list to display the Microsoft Office list (Figure 1–2).

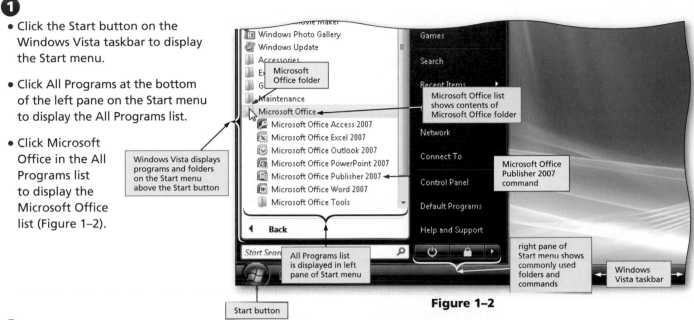

Figure 1–2

2

• Click Microsoft Office Publisher 2007 to start Publisher (Figure 1–3).

• If the Publisher window is not maximized, click the Maximize button next to the Close button on its title bar to maximize the window.

Q&A

What is a maximized window?

A maximized window fills the entire screen. When you maximize a window, the Maximize button changes to a Restore Down button.

Other Ways

1. Double-click Publisher icon on desktop, if one is present

2. Click Microsoft Office Publisher 2007 on Start menu

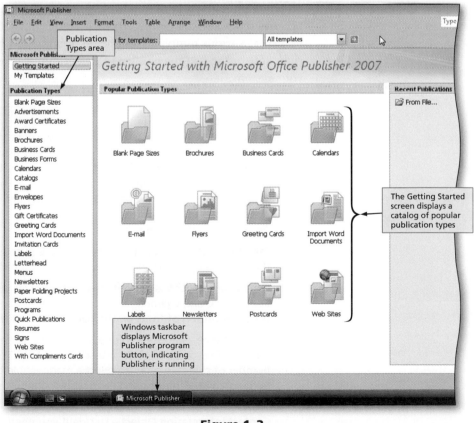

Figure 1–3

Using a Template to Create a Flyer

Publisher provides many ways to begin the process of creating and editing a publication. You can:

- Create a new publication from a design template
- Create a new publication or a Web page from scratch
- Create a new publication based on an existing one
- Open an existing publication

Choosing the appropriate method depends upon your experience with desktop publishing and how you have used Publisher in the past.

Because composing and designing from scratch is a difficult process for many people, Publisher provides templates to assist in publication preparation. Publisher has hundreds of templates to create professionally designed and unique publications. A **template** is a tool that helps you through the design process by offering you publication options and changing your publication accordingly. A template is similar to a blueprint you can use over and over, filling in the blanks, replacing prewritten text as necessary, and changing the art to fit your needs. In this first project, as you are beginning to learn about the features of Publisher, a series of steps is presented to create a publication using a design template.

Selecting a Template

In the Getting Started with Microsoft Office Publisher 2007 window (Figure 1–3 on the previous page), Publisher displays a list of publication types on the left side of the screen. **Publication types** are typical publications used by desktop publishers. The more popular types also are displayed in the center of the window. Each publication type is a link to display various templates and blank publications from which you may choose. On the right side of the window is a list of recent publications that have been created or edited on your system.

Select template options.
Publisher flyer templates are organized by purpose. A good flyer must deliver a message in the clearest, most attractive and effective way possible. The purpose is to communicate a single concept, notion, or product in a quick, easy-to-read format. The intended audience may be a wide, nonspecific audience, such as those who walk by a community bulletin board, or the audience may be a more narrowly defined, specialized audience, such as those who visit an auction Web site.
   Four primary choices must be made:

- **Template** – Choose a template that suits the purpose with headline and graphic placement that attracts your audience. Choose a style that has meaning for the topic.

- **Font Scheme** – Choose a font scheme that gives your flyer a consistent professional appearance and characterizes your subject. Make intentional decisions about the font style. Repetition of fonts on the page adds consistency to flyers.

- **Color Scheme** – Choose a color scheme that is consistent with your company, client, or purpose. Do you need color or black and white? Think about the plan for printing and the number of copies in order to select a manageable color scheme. Remember that you can add more visual interest and contrast by bolding the colors in the scheme; however, keep in mind that too many colors can detract from the flyer and make it difficult to read.

- **Contact Information Object** – Decide if you need a contact information tear-off. Is there something specific that may be difficult for your audience to remember? What kind of tear-off makes sense for your topic and message?

To Select a Template

Once you select a publication type, the window changes to allow you to select a specific template. Clicking a publication type causes a **catalog** of template previews to be displayed in the center of the window. The previews are organized into three categories with links to each category at the top of the window. Each category then is organized by purpose (for example, Sales) and then alphabetically by design type. On the right, Publisher will display a larger preview of the selected template, along with some customization options, as you will see in the following steps.

1

- Click the Flyers button in the Publication Types area to display the catalog of flyer templates (Figure 1–4).

🔍 **Experiment**

- Scroll in the catalog area and click various flyers in the catalog. Watch the preview change in the top-right portion of the window.

Q&A

Where are the subcategories or purposes listed?

In Figure 1–4 you can see the word, Informational, just below Newer Designs. Each purpose will be listed with a similar heading and a light blue division line.

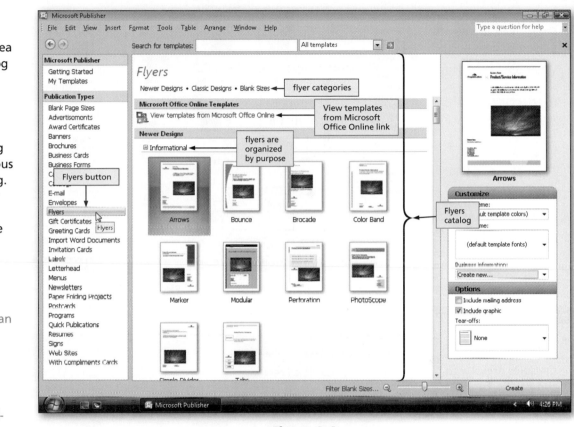

Figure 1–4

2

- Click the Classic Designs link at the top of the catalog to display flyer templates from the Classic Designs.

- Click the down scroll arrow until Special Offer flyers are displayed (Figure 1–5).

Q&A

What does the minus sign mean beside Special Offer?

You can click the minus sign to collapse the Special Offer group of templates so that the previews no longer display.

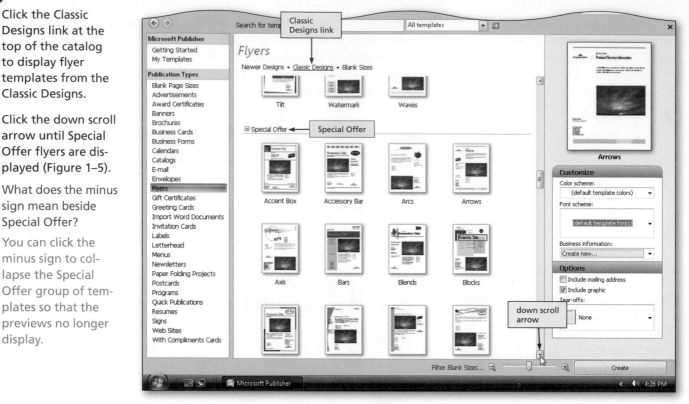

Figure 1–5

3

- Scroll down and then click the Capsules preview to choose the Capsules flyer template (Figure 1–6).

Q&A

Can I change the number of templates that display at one time on the screen?

Yes, you can click the Zoom Out or Zoom In button on the status bar to change the way the screen is displayed. If you zoom out to display more templates, the previews are smaller.

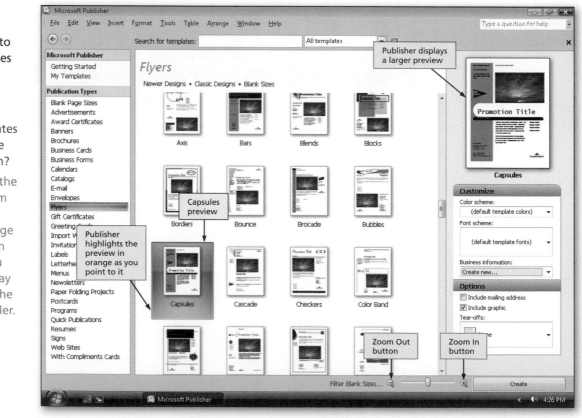

Figure 1–6

Setting Publication Options

Once you choose a publication from the catalog, Publisher will allow you to make choices about the color scheme, font schemes, and other components of the publication.

A **color scheme** is a defined set of colors that complement each other when used in the same publication. Each Publisher color scheme provides a main color and four accent colors. A **font scheme** is a defined set of fonts associated with a publication. A **font**, or typeface, defines the appearance and shape of the letters, numbers, and special characters. For example, a font scheme might be made up of one font for headings and another for body text and captions. Font schemes make it easy to change all the fonts in a publication to give it a new look. Within each font scheme, both a major font and a minor font are specified. Generally, a major font is used for titles and headings, and a minor font is used for body text.

Other options allow you to choose to include business information, a mailing address, a graphic, or tear-offs. As you choose customization options, the catalog and preview will reflect your choices.

BTW

Publisher Templates
Many additional templates can be downloaded from Microsoft Office Online. The View templates from Microsoft Office Online link, which can be used to view the online templates, is displayed near the top of the catalog, as shown in Figure 1–4 on page PUB 7.

To Set Publication Options

1

• Click the Color scheme box arrow in the Customize area to display the list of color schemes (Figure 1–7).

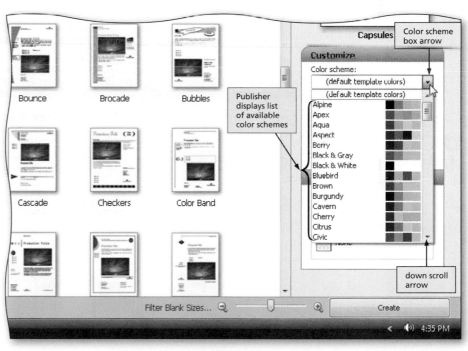

Figure 1–7

● Scroll down in the
list and then click
Sapphire to select
the Sapphire color
scheme (Figure 1–8).

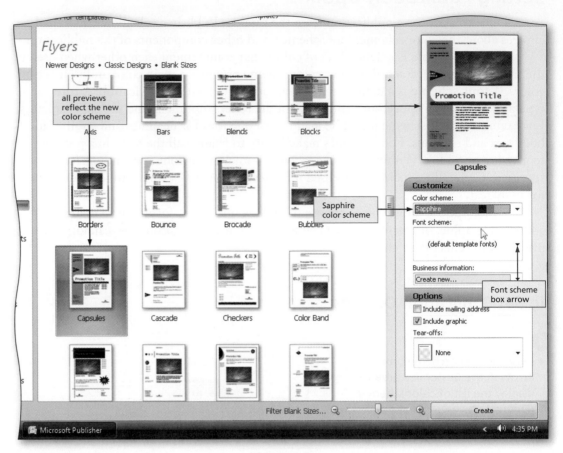

Figure 1–8

● Click the Font
scheme box arrow
in the Customize
area to display the
list of font schemes
(Figure 1–9).

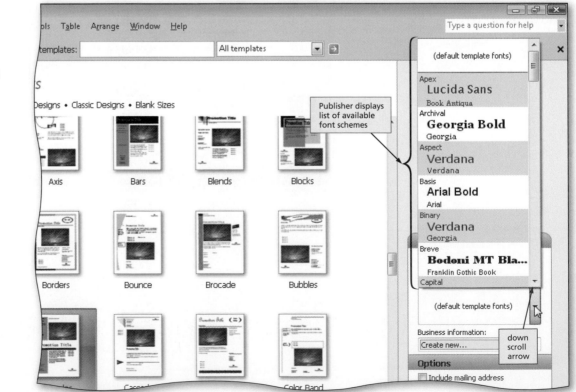

Figure 1–9

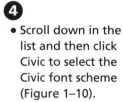

4

- Scroll down in the list and then click Civic to select the Civic font scheme (Figure 1–10).

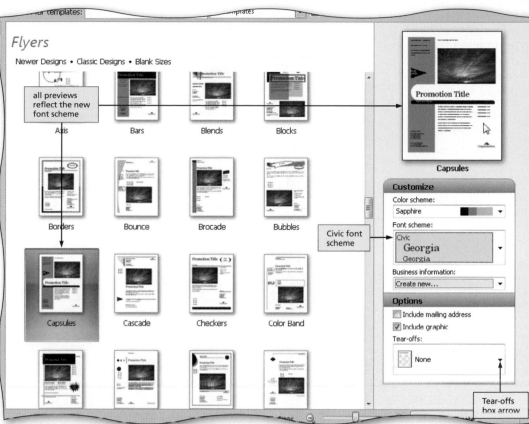

Figure 1–10

5

- Click the Tear-offs box arrow in the Options area to display a list of tear-offs (Figure 1–11).

Figure 1–11

6

- Click Contact information in the list to select tear-offs that will display contact information (Figure 1–12).

Q&A

What are the other kinds of tear-offs?

You can choose to display tear-offs for coupons, order forms, response forms, and sign-up forms.

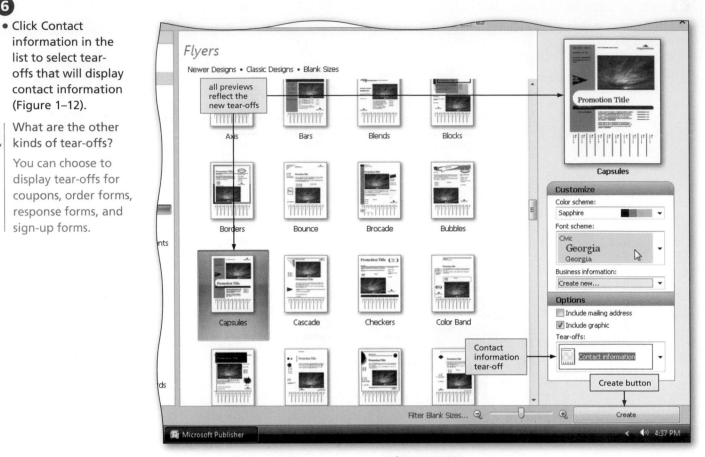

Figure 1–12

7

- Click the Create button on the status bar to create the publication using the selected template and options (Figure 1–13).

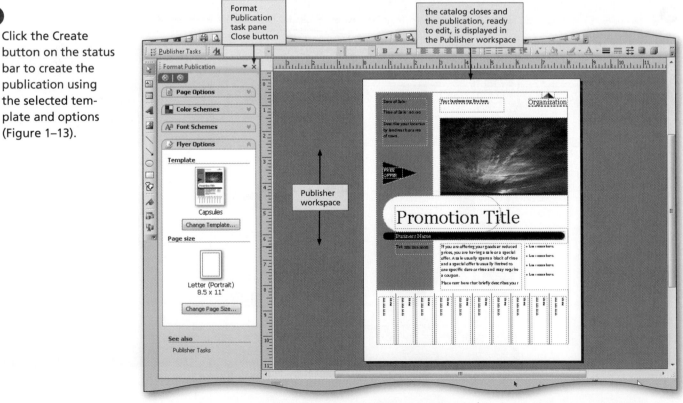

Figure 1–13

The Publisher Window

The Publisher window consists of a variety of components to make your work more efficient and your publication more professional. The following sections discuss these components.

The Workspace

The **workspace** contains several elements similar to the document windows of other applications, as well as some elements unique to Publisher. As you create a publication, the page layout, rulers, scroll bars, guides and boundaries, and status bar are displayed in the gray workspace (Figure 1–14). Objects can display on the page layout or in the gray workspace.

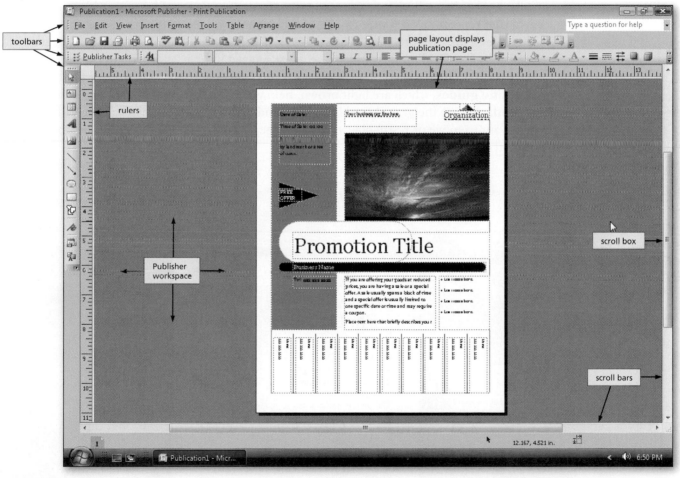

Figure 1–14

Page Layout The **page layout** contains a view of the publication page, all the objects contained therein, plus the guides and boundaries for the page and its objects. The page layout can be changed to accommodate multipage spreads. You also can use the Special Paper command to view your page layout, as it will be printed on special paper, or see the final copy after preparing your publication for a printing service.

Rulers   Two rulers outline the workspace at the top and left. A **ruler** is used to measure and place objects on the page. Although the vertical and horizontal rulers display at the left and top of the workspace, they can be moved and placed anywhere you need them. You use the rulers to measure and align objects on the page, set tab stops, adjust text frames, and change margins. Additionally, the rulers can be hidden to show more of the workspace. You will learn more about rulers in a later chapter.

Scroll Bars   By using **scroll bars**, you display different portions of your publication in the workspace. At the right edge of the publication window is a vertical scroll bar. At the bottom of the publication window is a horizontal scroll bar. On both the vertical and horizontal scroll bars, the position of the **scroll box** reflects the location of the portion of the publication that is displayed in the publication window.

Guides and Boundaries   Publisher's page layout displays the guides and boundaries of the page and its objects. Aligning design elements in relation to each other, both vertically and horizontally, is a tedious task; therefore, three types of **layout guides** create a grid that repeats on each page of a publication to define sections of the page and help you align elements with precision (Figure 1–15). **Margin guides** are displayed in blue at all four margins. **Grid guides**, which also are displayed in blue, assist you in organizing text pictures and objects into columns and rows to give a consistent look to your publication. **Baseline guides**, which are light brown, help you align text horizontally across text boxes. **Boundaries** are the gray, dotted lines surrounding an object. Boundaries are useful when you want to move or resize objects on the page. Boundaries and guides can be turned on and off using the View menu.

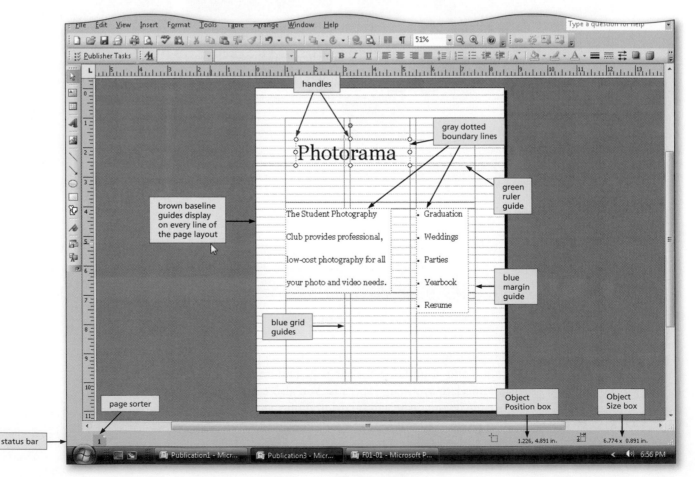

Figure 1–15

Status Bar Immediately above the Windows taskbar at the bottom of the Publisher window is the status bar. In Publisher, the **status bar** contains the page sorter, the Object Position box, and the Object Size box (Figure 1–15).

The **page sorter** displays a button for each page of your publication. The current page in a multipage document will display selected in orange in the page sorter. You may click any page to display it in the workspace or right-click to display the page sorter shortcut menu.

As an alternative to using the rulers, you can use the **Object Position** and **Object Size boxes** as guidelines for lining up objects from the left and top margins. The exact position and size of a selected object is displayed in inches as you create or move it. You may choose to have the measurement displayed in pica, points, or centimeters. If no object is selected, the Object Position box displays the location of the mouse pointer. Double-clicking the status bar will display the Measurements toolbar. You will learn more about the Measurements toolbar in a future project.

Objects **Objects** include anything you want to place in your publication, such as text, WordArt, tear-offs, graphics, pictures, bookmarks, bullets, lines, and Web tools. You click an object to **select** it; selected objects are displayed with **handles** at each corner and middle location of the object boundary. Many objects also display a green rotation handle connected to the top of the object or a yellow adjustment handle used to change the shape of some objects. A selected object can be resized, rotated, moved, deleted, or grouped with other objects. To select an object such as a picture, click the picture. The entire object is selected automatically. If you want to select a text box, however, you must click the boundary of the text box rather than the text inside. You will learn more about object manipulation later in the project.

Menu Bar and Toolbars

Publisher displays the menu bar at the top of the screen just below the title bar. Other toolbars display below the menu bar; another toolbar is displayed down the left side of the Publisher Window (Figure 1–16).

BTW

Toolbar Rows
The Standard and Connect Frames toolbars are preset to display on one row, immediately below the menu bar. The Publisher Tasks and Formatting toolbar are displayed below that. If the resolution of your display differs from that in the book, some of the buttons that belong on these toolbars may not appear. Use the **Toolbar Options button** to display these hidden buttons.

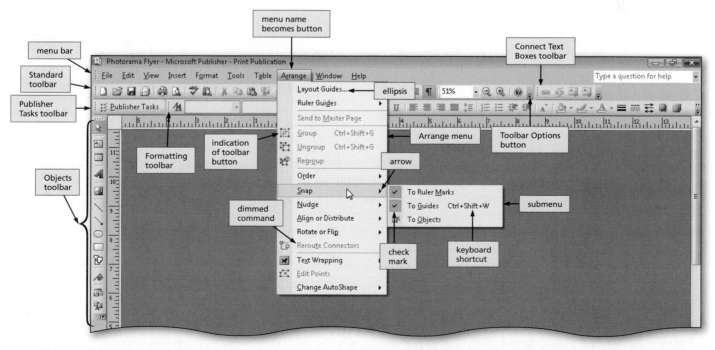

Figure 1–16

BTW

Positioning Toolbars
Initially Publisher displays **docked toolbars**, or ones that are attached to the edge of the Publisher window. Additional toolbars may be displayed either stacked below the Formatting toolbar or floating in the Publisher window. A **floating toolbar** is not attached to an edge of the Publisher window. You can rearrange the order of docked toolbars and can move floating toolbars anywhere in the Publisher window by dragging the move handle to the desired location. You will learn about other toolbars in future projects. If you do not see a toolbar in the window, click Toolbars on the View menu and then click the name of the toolbar you want to be displayed.

BTW

Toolbar Settings
Each time you start Publisher, the Publisher window is displayed the same way it was the last time you used Publisher. If the toolbar buttons are displayed on one row, then they will be displayed on one row the next time you start Publisher. Typically, four toolbars are displayed on two rows when you first install Publisher: the Standard toolbar, the Connect Frames toolbar, the Publisher Tasks toolbar, and the Formatting toolbar. You can display or hide toolbars by right-clicking any toolbar and clicking the appropriate check boxes, or by clicking Toolbars on the View menu.
      As you work through creating a publication, you will find that other toolbars will be displayed automatically as they are needed in order to edit particular types of objects in Publisher.

Menu Bar   The **menu bar** is a special toolbar displaying at the top of the window, just below the Publisher title bar. The menu bar lists the menu names. When you point to a **menu name** on the menu bar, the area of the menu bar containing the name displays a button. Publisher shades selected buttons in light orange.

When you click a menu name, Publisher displays a menu. A **menu** contains a list of commands to retrieve, store, print, and manipulate data in the publication (Figure 1–16 on the previous page). In the menu, if you point to a command with an arrow to its right, a **submenu** is displayed. An ellipsis (…) denotes that Publisher will display a dialog box when you click that menu command. **Keyboard shortcuts**, when available, are displayed to the right of menu commands. If a toolbar button exists for the command, it is displayed to the left of the menu command. A check mark displayed left of the menu command indicates the setting currently is being used. A **dimmed command** is displayed gray, or dimmed, instead of black, which indicates it is not available for the current selection.

Toolbars   **Toolbars** contain buttons and boxes that allow you to perform frequent tasks more quickly than when using the menu bar. For example, to print a publication, you can click the Print button on a toolbar instead of navigating through the File menu.

Each button on a toolbar has a picture on its face that helps you remember its function. In addition, when you move the mouse pointer over a button or box, the name of the button or box is displayed below it in a **ScreenTip**. Each button and box is explained in detail as it is used in the projects.

The **Standard toolbar** is displayed just below the menu bar. The **Connect Text Boxes toolbar** is displayed to the right of the Standard toolbar. Immediately below the Standard toolbar, on the second row, the **Publisher Tasks toolbar** provides access to the Publisher Tasks pane; the **Formatting toolbar** is displayed to its right. The **Objects toolbar** is displayed on the left edge of the Publisher window. Additional toolbars, such as the Measurements toolbar, the Picture toolbar, and WordArt toolbar, are object-specific, which means they are displayed only when you use that specific type of object.

Resetting Menus and Toolbars

Each project in this book begins with the menus and toolbars displaying as they did at the initial installation of the software. By default, Publisher shows full menus, listing all of their commands. You can display shorter menus, listing only the most recently used commands, by clicking Customize on the Tools menu and then turning off the full menu option. If you are stepping through this project on a computer, and you want your menus and toolbars to match the figures in this book, then you should reset your menus and toolbars. For more information about how to reset menus and toolbars, read Appendix E.

The Task Pane

A **task pane** is a special window with buttons, boxes, lists, and links to help you perform specific tasks, such as applying publication options or styles, inserting clip art or clipboard contents, or providing search and replace options (Figure 1–17). Publisher displays a task pane at startup, at other times when it is needed, or when you choose Task Pane from the View menu.

Similar to other windows, a task pane has a title bar with a Close button. Next to the Close button is an Other Task Panes button, which displays a list of available task panes when clicked. Below the title bar are the Back and Forward buttons which help you move among recently viewed task panes. Below that, each task pane's content differs; the content will be explained as each task pane is used.

The **Format Publication task pane** is displayed when you first create a page layout. It contains four choices that display options related to page, color, font, and the publication type, to help you format your publication.

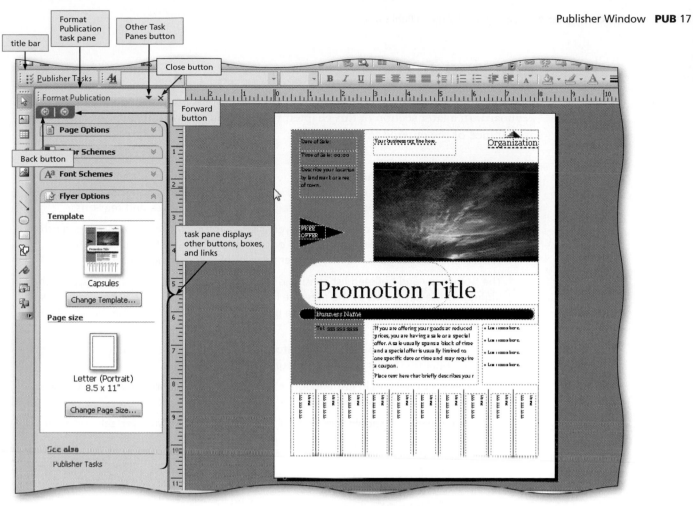

Figure 1–17

To Close the Task Pane

Because you have already made decisions on the template, font, and color schemes, you can close the task pane as shown in the following step.

1

• Click the Close button on the Format Publication task pane title bar to close the task pane (Figure 1–18).

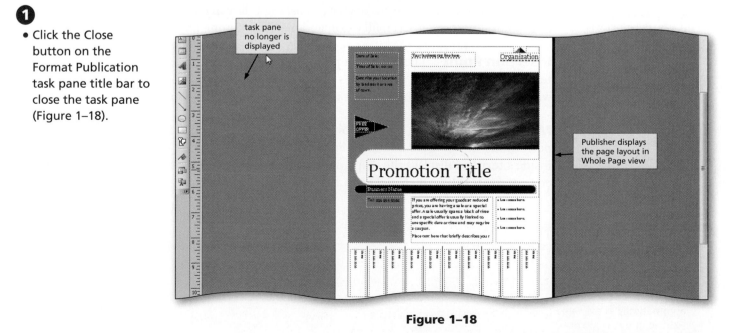

Figure 1–18

Entering Text

The first step in editing a publication template is to replace its text by typing on the keyboard. In a later section of this chapter, you will learn how to format, or change the appearance of the entered text.

> **Choose the words for the text.**
> The text in a flyer usually is organized into several areas: headline, body copy, bulleted lists, business name, informational text boxes, tag lines, attention getter, and tear-offs.
>
> - The headline is the largest text on the flyer. It conveys the product or service being offered, such as a car for sale or personal lessons, or the benefit that will be gained, such as a convenience, better performance, greater security, higher earnings, or more comfort.
>
> - The body copy and bulleted list consists of descriptive text below the headline, which highlights the key points of the message in as few words as possible. It should be easy to read and follow. While emphasizing the positive, the body text must be realistic, truthful, and believable.
>
> - Sometimes supplied by a database or information set, the business name, tag line, and informational text boxes need to be accurate and easy to read.
>
> - The tear-offs must contain just enough information to contact the flyer's creator or to turn around requested information.
>
> - Attention getter text should include information about a special offer, sale, price, or Web page.

Using Text Boxes

BTW

Flyer Templates
Some flyer templates include a headline text box whose font size is copyfitted, or self-adjusting. If you type too many words in the text box to fit at the current font size, Publisher will autofit the text and reduce the font size to make all the words fit in the box. Clicking AutoFit Text on the Format menu will display a submenu allowing you to change the way text is copyfitted in a text box.

Most of the templates in the design catalog come with text already inserted into text boxes. A **text box** is an object in a publication designed to hold text in a specific shape, size, and style. Text boxes also can be drawn on the page using the Text Box Button on the Objects toolbar. Text boxes can be formatted from the task pane, on the Formatting toolbar, or on the **shortcut menu** displayed by right-clicking the text box. A text box has changeable properties. A **property** is an attribute or characteristic of an object. Within text boxes, you can **edit**, or make changes to, the following properties: font, spacing, alignment, line/border style, fill color, and margins, among others.

Insertion Point   The **insertion point** is a blinking vertical bar that indicates where text will be inserted in a text box. As you type, the insertion point moves to the right, and when you reach the end of a line, it moves downward to the beginning of the next line.

Mouse Pointer   The **mouse pointer** changes shape, depending on the task you are performing in Publisher and the pointer's location on the screen. The mouse pointer inside a text box displays the shape of an I-beam. If the mouse pointer is positioned on the edge of the text box, it changes to a four-headed arrow.

To Enter Text

Flyers typically display a **headline**, or title, using the major font from the font scheme. A headline is designed to identify, with just a few words, the purpose of the flyer and to draw attention to the flyer. Text in the Business Name text box can be entered manually or filled in from information sets of data entered into the software. You will learn about information sets in a later chapter.

Two types of text selection are used in Publisher templates. **Placeholder text**, or text supplied by the template, is selected with a single click, allowing you to begin typing immediately. Other text, such as the business name, address, or tag line, is selected by pressing CTRL+A to select all of the text in the text box before you type. The following steps select and replace template text.

1

- Click the headline text to select it (Figure 1–19).

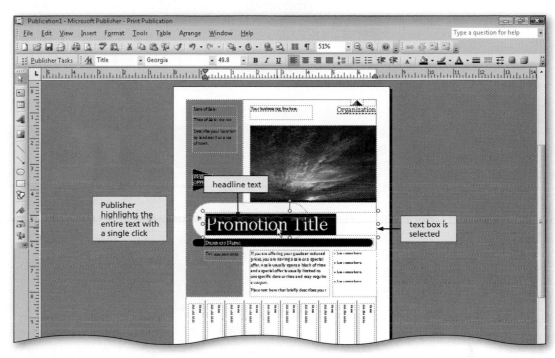

Figure 1–19

2

- Type Photorama as the headline text (Figure 1–20).

Q&A

What if I make an error while typing?

You can press the BACKSPACE key until you have deleted the text in error and then retype the text correctly.

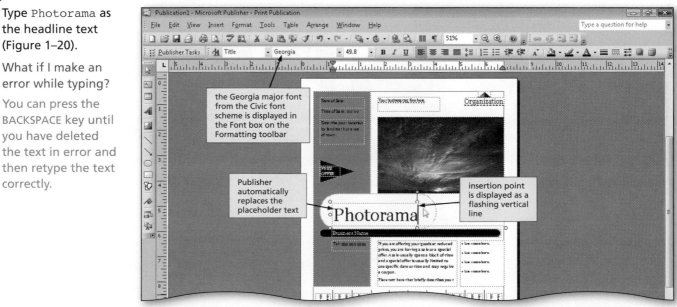

Figure 1–20

3

- Click the text in the Business Name text box to begin editing the text (Figure 1–21).

Q&A Why does the text have a red, wavy line underneath it?

Publisher is checking for spelling errors. The word, Photorama, is not in Publisher's dictionary. Publisher flags potential errors in the publication with a red wavy underline. Later in the project, you will learn how to use the spell checking features of Publisher to make the red, wavy line disappear.

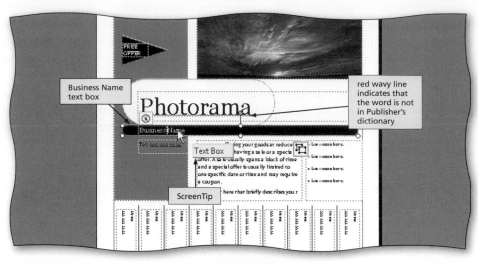

Figure 1–21

4

- Press CTRL+A on the keyboard to select all of the text in the Business Name text box (Figure 1–22).

Q&A What is the button that is displayed with the i on it?

That is a smart tag button. If you click it, Publisher offers to fill in the text for you with various options. **Smart tag buttons** display when you point to certain text boxes that are part of the business information set or when you click a logo.

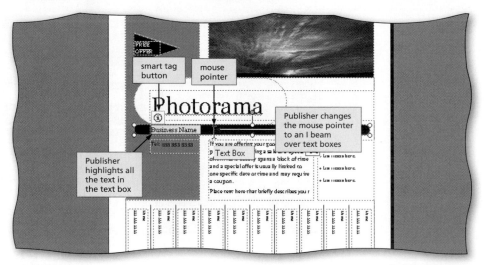

Figure 1–22

5

- **Type** Student Photography Club to replace the text (Figure 1–23).

Q&A Why does a blue dotted line display beneath the text?

The blue or purple dotted lines beneath text in your presentation indicate that a smart tag is available for that data.

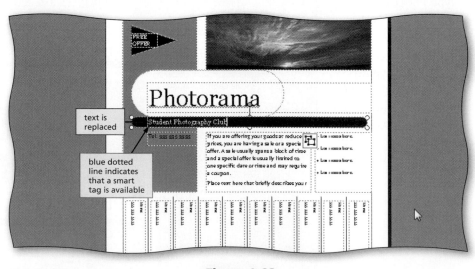

Figure 1–23

To Zoom

Sometimes the size of the text box or other Publisher object is small, and therefore, difficult to edit. Publisher provides several ways to **zoom in**, or increase the magnification of an object to facilitate viewing and editing.

Table 1–1 shows several zoom methods.

Table 1–1 Zoom Methods

Method	Result
Press the F9 key on the keyboard.	Selected object is displayed, centered in the workspace at 100% magnification.
Click the Zoom box arrow on the Standard toolbar. Click the desired magnification.	Objects are displayed at selected magnification.
Click the Zoom In button on the Standard toolbar.	Objects are displayed at a higher magnification.
Right-click object. Point to Zoom on shortcut menu. Click the desired magnification.	Objects are displayed at selected magnification.
On the View menu, point to Zoom. Click the desired magnification.	Objects are displayed at selected magnification.

Editing small areas of text is easier if you use zooming techniques to enlarge the view of the publication. When viewing an entire printed page, 8½-by-11 inches, the magnification is approximately 51 percent, which makes reading the small text difficult. You may press the F9 key to enlarge selected objects to 100 percent magnification. Pressing the F9 key a second time returns the layout to its previous magnification. Publisher also allows you to zoom using the **Zoom box** on the Standard toolbar. Clicking the Zoom box arrow displays a list of magnifications, such as Whole Page, Page Width, and various magnifications. Additionally, the **Zoom In button** on the Standard toolbar allows you to increase magnification. If you click an object before zooming in, Publisher displays the selected object magnified, in the center of the workspace, when you zoom.

To Zoom and Enter Text

The following steps zoom and enter text.

1

- Click the text in the text box located in the upper-left corner of the template to select it (Figure 1–24).

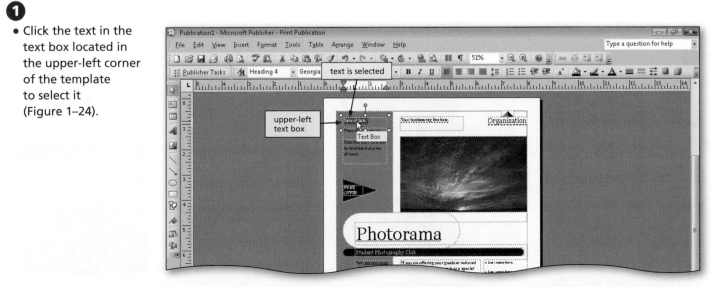

Figure 1–24

2

- Press the F9 key on the keyboard to zoom the text box to 100%. Type `Flexible Times` to replace the text (Figure 1–25).

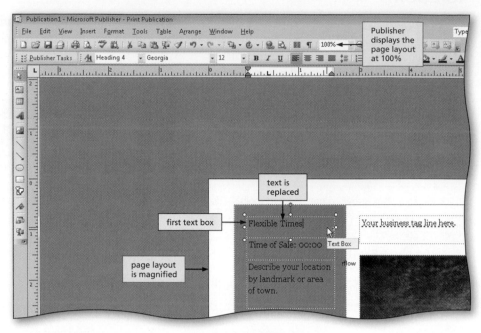

Figure 1–25

3

- Click the text, Time of Sale, to select it.

- Press and hold the SHIFT key while clicking the text, 00.00, to add it to the selection.

- To replace the text, type `Reasonable Rates` (Figure 1–26).

Q&A

Why did I have to hold down the SHIFT key while clicking?

Some templates have two sets of placeholder text in individual text boxes. You can press CTRL+A to select all of the text or SHIFT+CLICK to select each portion of placeholder text.

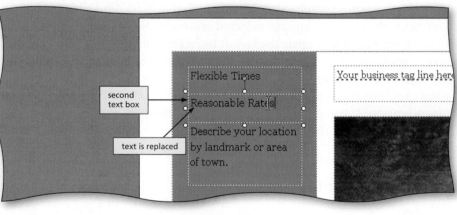

Figure 1–26

4

- To select the placeholder text in the Describe your location text box, click the text.

- Replace the placeholder text with the new text, `Student Photography Club meets every Wednesday at 7pm.` (Figure 1–27).

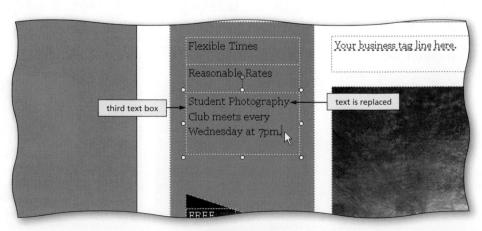

Figure 1–27

⑤

- Select the text in the text box that is displayed within the black triangle in order to replace it.

- Type Student Discount (Figure 1–28).

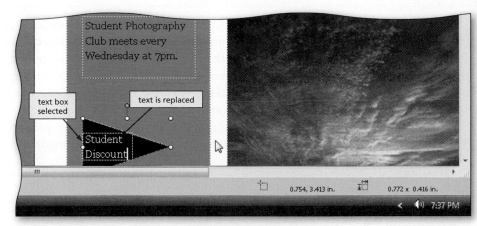

Figure 1–28

⑥

- Click the Zoom box arrow on the Standard toolbar (Figure 1–29).

Q&A

What is the best way to zoom to 100%?

If an object on the page is selected, pressing the F9 key toggles between a zoom of 100% and the previous zoom percentage. You also can choose 100% by clicking the Zoom box arrow and then clicking 100% in the list.

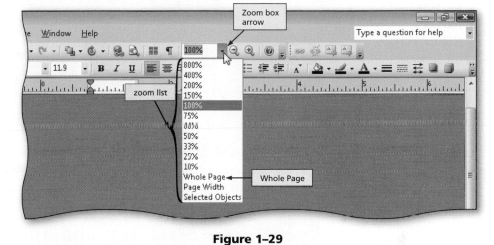

Figure 1–29

⑦

- Click Whole Page in the list to zoom to display the whole page (Figure 1–30).

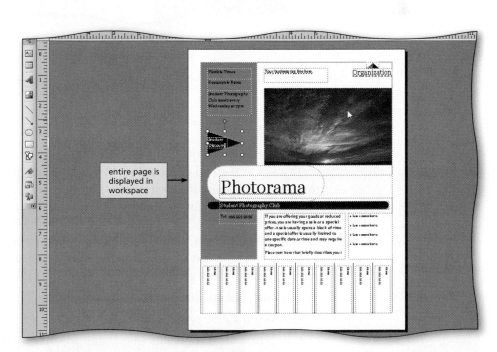

Figure 1–30

To Display Formatting Marks

To view where in a publication you pressed the ENTER key or SPACEBAR, you may find it helpful to display formatting marks. A **formatting mark**, sometimes called a **nonprinting character**, is a special character that Publisher displays on the screen, but one that is not visible on a printed publication. For example, the **paragraph mark** (¶) is a formatting mark that indicates where you pressed the ENTER key. A **raised dot** (·) shows where you pressed the SPACEBAR. An **end of field marker** (¤) is displayed to indicate the end of text in a text box. Other formatting marks are discussed as they appear on the screen.

Depending on settings made during previous Publisher sessions, your Publisher screen already may display formatting marks (Figure 1–31). The following step displays formatting marks, if they do not show already on the screen.

1

- If it is not selected already, click the Special Characters button on the Standard toolbar (Figure 1–31).

What if I do not want formatting marks to show on the screen?

If you feel the formatting marks clutter the screen, you can hide them by clicking the Special Characters button again. The publication windows presented in this book show the formatting marks.

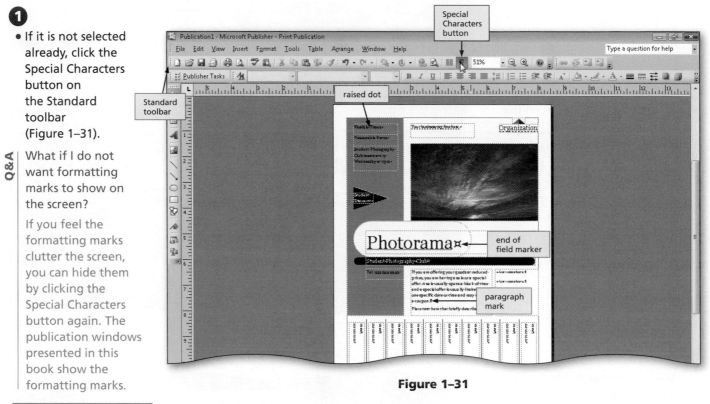

Figure 1–31

Other Ways

1. Press CTRL+SHIFT+Y

Wordwrap

Wordwrap allows you to type words in a text box continually without pressing the ENTER key at the end of each line. When the insertion point reaches the right margin of a text box, Publisher automatically positions the insertion point at the beginning of the next line. As you type, if a word extends beyond the right margin, Publisher also automatically positions that word on the next line along with the insertion point.

Publisher creates a new paragraph or hard return each time you press the ENTER key. Thus, as you type text in a text box, do not press the ENTER key when the insertion point reaches the right margin. Instead, press the ENTER key only in these circumstances:

- To insert blank lines in a text box
- To begin a new paragraph
- To terminate a short line of text and advance to the next line
- To respond to questions or prompts in Publisher dialog boxes, task panes, and other on-screen objects

To Wordwrap Text as You Type

The next step in creating the flyer is to type the body copy. The following step wordwraps the text in the body copy.

1

- Select the text in the center text box below the headline.

- Press the F9 key to zoom to 100%.

- Type The Student Photography Club provides professional, low-cost photography for all your photo and video needs. to replace the text (Figure 1–32).

Q&A

Why does my publication wrap on different words?

Differences in wordwrap relate to your printer. It is possible that the same publication could wordwrap differently if printed on different printers.

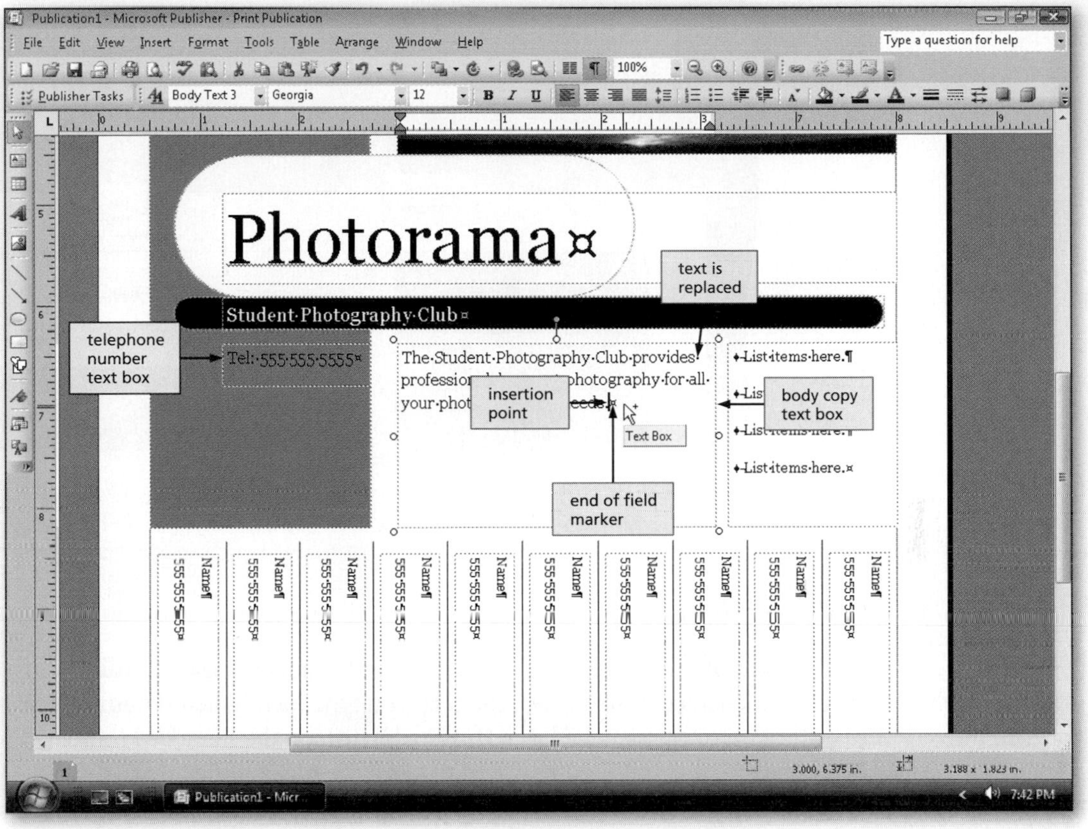

Figure 1–32

To Finish Entering Text

The following steps replace the text in the telephone number text box and the business tag line text box.

1 Select the text in the telephone text box.

2 Type Tel: 317 555 2008 to replace the text.

3 Zoom to Whole Page by pressing the F9 key on the keyboard.

4 Select the tag line text box at the top of the page.

5 Zoom to 100% by pressing the F9 key on the keyboard.

6 Select the text in the business tag line text box by pressing CTRL+A.

7 Type For all your photo and video needs (Figure 1–33 on the next page).

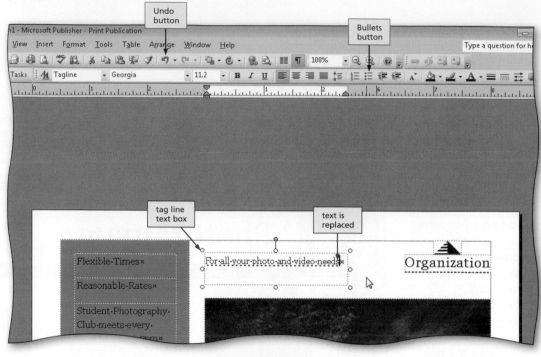

Figure 1–33

To Enter Bulleted Items

In the flyer, to the right of the body copy, is a text box with a bulleted list. A **bulleted list** is a series of paragraphs, each beginning with a bullet character. To replace the text, you type each bulleted item pressing the ENTER key at the end of each line. To turn bullets on or off, you click the **Bullets button** on the Standard toolbar (Figure 1-33).

The following steps create a bulleted list by replacing the placeholder text.

1

- Click the down scroll arrow until the bulleted list is displayed.

- Select the text in the bulleted list text box (Figure 1–34).

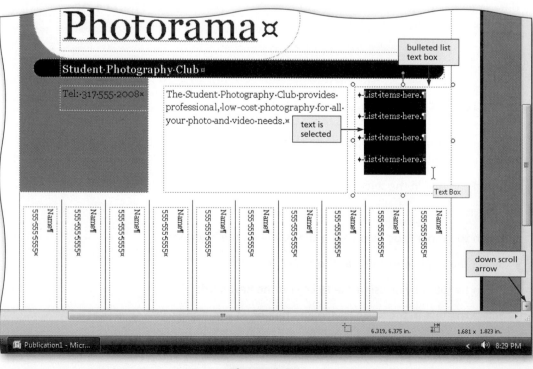

Figure 1–34

2

- Type `Graduations` and then press the ENTER key.

- Type `Weddings` and then press the ENTER key.

- Type `Passports` and then press the ENTER key.

- Type `Yearbooks` and then press the ENTER key.

- Type `Resumes` to complete the bullets (Figure 1–35).

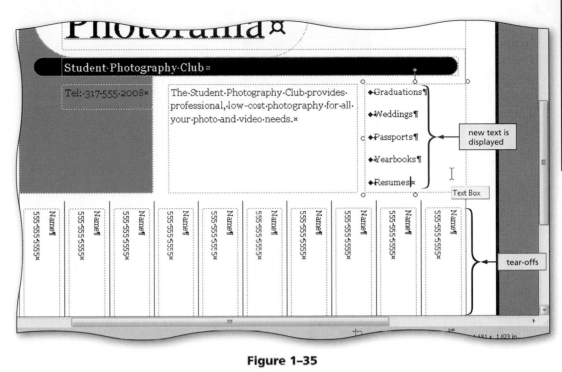

Figure 1–35

To Enter Tear-off Text

Across the lower portion of the flyer are contact information tear-offs. **Tear-offs** are small, ready-to-be scored text boxes with some combination of name, telephone, fax, e-mail, or address. Designed for customer use, tear-offs typically are perforated so a person walking by can tear off a tab to keep, rather than having to stop, find a pen and paper, and write down the name and telephone number. Traditionally, small businesses or individuals wanting to advertise something locally used tear-offs, but more recently, large companies are mass-producing advertising flyers with tear-offs to post at shopping centers, display in offices, and advertise on college campuses.

Publisher tear-offs contain replacement text and are **synchronized**, which means when you finish editing one of the tear-off text boxes, the others change to match it automatically. You may undo synchronization by clicking the **Undo button** on the Standard toolbar (Figure 1–33).

The following steps edit the tear-off text boxes.

1

- Click the text in one of the tear-off text boxes.

- Type `E-mail: photorama@univ.edu` and then press the ENTER key.

- Type `Or call 317 555 2008` to complete the tear-off (Figure 1–36).

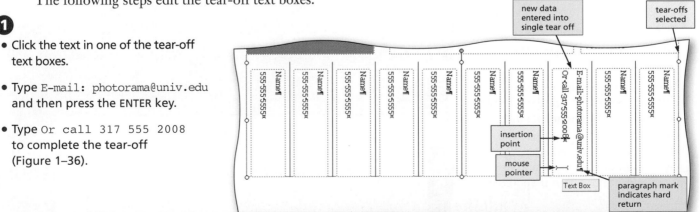

Figure 1–36

2

- Click outside of the text box to synchronize the other tear-offs (Figure 1–37).

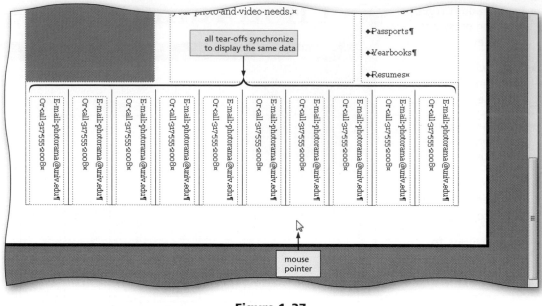

Figure 1–37

Deleting Objects

Templates may display objects in the page layout that you do not wish to use. In those cases, or when you change your mind about including an inserted object, you must **delete objects**.

To Delete an Object

In order to delete an object, it must be selected. To select objects that contain text, you must click the object's boundary; you select other objects by clicking anywhere in the object. In the following steps, the logo is deleted.

1

- Scroll to the upper portion of the page to display the logo.

- Click the boundary of the logo to select it (Figure 1–38).

Q&A

What if I want to delete only the text?

To delete text inside a text box, click inside the text box rather than on a text box boundary. Then, you can select the text and press the DELETE key. Inside text boxes, you can use other backspace and delete key combinations as you do in basic word processing.

Figure 1–38

2

- Press the DELETE key on your keyboard to delete the object (Figure 1–39).

Q&A My logo was not deleted. Why did only the text disappear?

You clicked the text instead of the boundary of the logo. Logos supplied by the template are a combination of a logo picture and logo text. To delete them, you must select the entire object by clicking its boundary.

Q&A What if I delete an object by mistake?

If you delete an object by mistake, you can click the Undo button on the Standard toolbar. The object will reappear in the original location.

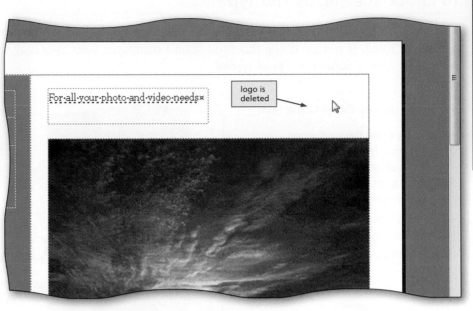

Figure 1–39

Checking the Spelling

As you type text in a publication, Publisher checks your typing for possible spelling errors. As mentioned earlier, Publisher flags the potential error in the publication window with a red wavy underline. A red wavy underline means the flagged text is not in Publisher's dictionary (because it is a proper name or misspelled). Although you can check the entire publication for spelling errors at once, you also can check these flagged errors as they appear on the screen.

To display a list of corrections for flagged text, right-click the flagged text. When you right-click a flagged word, for example, a list of suggested spelling corrections is displayed in the shortcut menu. A flagged word, however, is not necessarily misspelled. For example, many names, abbreviations, and specialized terms are not in Publisher's main dictionary. In these cases, you tell Publisher to ignore the flagged word. As you type, Publisher also detects duplicate words while checking for spelling errors. For example, if your publication contains the phrase, to the the store, Publisher places a red wavy underline below the second occurrence of the word, the.

To Check Spelling as You Type

In the following steps, the word, Photorama, is not in Publisher's dictionary. You will direct Publisher to ignore the word. If you are doing this project on a computer, your flyer may contain other misspelled words, depending on the accuracy of your typing.

1

- Scroll to display the headline text.

- Right-click the flagged word, Photorama, in the headline to display a shortcut menu that includes a list of suggested spelling corrections for the flagged word (Figure 1–40).

Q&A

What if Publisher does not flag my spelling errors with wavy underlines?

To verify that the Check spelling as you type features are enabled, point to Spelling on the Tools menu and then click Spelling Options. When the Spelling Options dialog box is displayed, ensure the 'Check spelling as you type' check box has a check mark. Also ensure the Hide spelling errors check box does not have a check mark. Click the OK button.

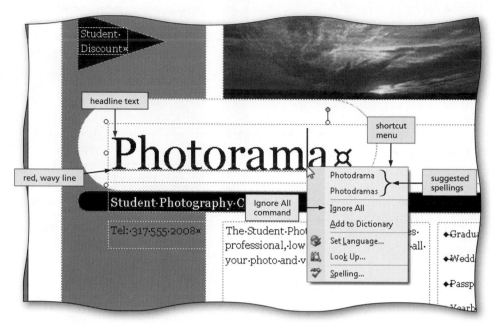

Figure 1–40

2

- Click Ignore All on the shortcut menu to direct Publisher to ignore the word, Photorama, which is not in its dictionary (Figure 1–41).

3

- Right-click any other words that display wavy lines to display a shortcut menu that includes a list of suggested spelling corrections for each flagged word.

- Choose the appropriate correct word on the shortcut menu.

Q&A

What if, when I right-click the misspelled word, my desired correction is not in the list on the shortcut menu?

You can click outside the shortcut menu to close the menu and then retype the correct word, or you can click Spelling on the shortcut menu to display the Spelling dialog box which will be discussed in a later chapter.

Figure 1–41

Saving the Project

While you are creating a publication, the computer stores it in memory. When you save a publication, the computer places it on a storage medium, such as a USB flash drive, CD, or hard disk. A saved publication is referred to as a **file**. A **file name** is the name assigned to a file when it is saved.

It is important to save a publication frequently for the following reasons:

- The publication in memory will be lost if the computer is turned off, or you lose electrical power while Publisher is open.

- If you run out of time before completing your project, you may finish your publication at a future time without starting over.

BTW

The .pub extension
Some Microsoft Office 2007 applications use a new, four-letter extension on file names; however, Publisher saves print publications in a file format with the three-letter extension, .pub. The **.pub extension** allows Publisher easily to open your formatted file and assign a recognizable icon to the shortcut on your disk.

Plan Ahead

> **Determine where to save the publication.**
> When saving a publication, you must decide which storage medium to use.
>
> - If you always work on the same computer and have no need to transport your projects to a different location, then your computer's hard drive will suffice as a storage location. It is a good idea, however, to save a backup copy of your projects on a separate medium in case the file becomes corrupted or the computer's hard disk fails.
>
> - If you plan to work on your projects in various locations or on multiple computers, then you should save your projects on a portable medium, such as a USB flash drive or CD. The projects in this book use a USB flash drive, which saves files quickly and reliably and can be reused. CDs are easily portable and serve as good backups for the final versions of projects because they generally can save files only one time

To Save a Publication

You have performed many tasks while creating this project and do not want to risk losing the work completed thus far. Accordingly, you should save the publication. The following steps save a publication on a USB flash drive using the file name, Photorama Flyer.

1

- With a USB flash drive connected to one of the computer's USB ports, click the Save button on the Standard Toolbar to display the Save As dialog box (Figure 1–42).

- If the Navigation pane is not displayed in the Save As dialog box, click the Browse Folders button to expand the dialog box.

- If a Folders list is displayed below the Folders button, click the Folders button to remove the Folders list.

Q&A

Do I have to save to a USB flash drive?

No. You can save to any device or folder. A **folder** is a specific location on a storage medium. You can save to the default folder or a different folder. You also can create your own folders, which is explained later in this book.

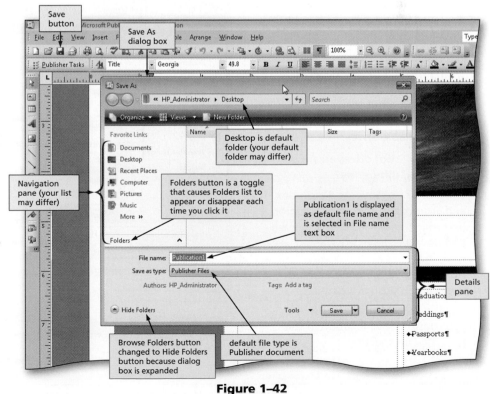

Figure 1–42

2

- Type Photorama Flyer in the File name text box to change the file name. Do not press the ENTER key after typing the file name (Figure 1–43).

Q&A What characters can I use in a file name?

A file name can have a maximum of 260 characters, including spaces. The only invalid characters are the backslash (\), slash (/), colon (:), asterisk (*), question mark (?), quotation mark ("), less than symbol (<), greater than symbol (>), and vertical bar (|).

Q&A What are file properties and tags?

File properties contain information about a file, such as the file name, author name, date the file was modified, size, and tags. A **tag** is a file property that contains a word or phrase about a file. You can organize and locate files based on their file properties.

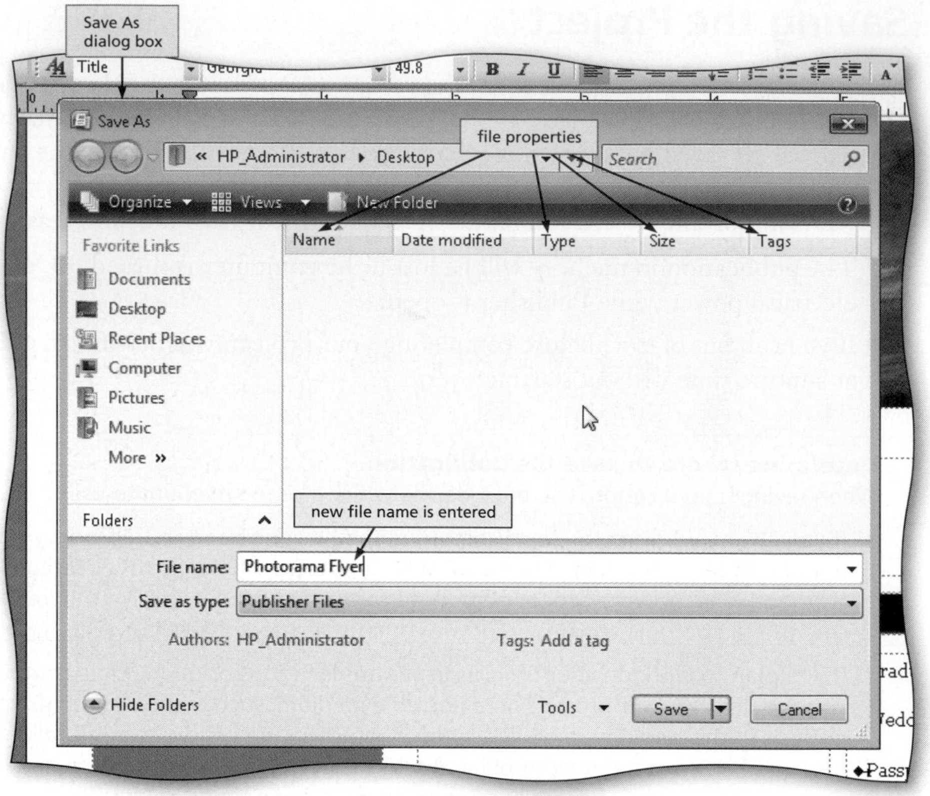

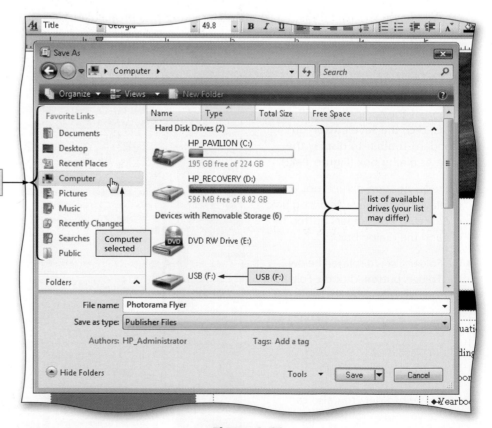

Figure 1–43

3

- If Computer is not displayed in the Favorite Links section, drag the top or bottom edge of the Save As dialog box until Computer is displayed.

- Click Computer in the Favorite Links section to display a list of available drives (Figure 1–44).

- If necessary, scroll until USB (F:) appears in the list of available drives.

Q&A Why is my list of drives arranged and named differently?

The size of the Save As dialog box and your computer's configuration determine how the list is displayed and how the drives are named.

Q&A How do I save the file if I am not using a USB flash drive?

Use the same process, but select your desired save location in the Favorite Links section.

Figure 1–44

4

- Double-click USB (F:) in the Computer list to open the USB flash drive, Drive F in this case, as the new save location (Figure 1–45).

Q&A What if my USB flash drive has a different name or letter?

It is very likely that your USB flash drive will have a different name and drive letter and be connected to a different port.

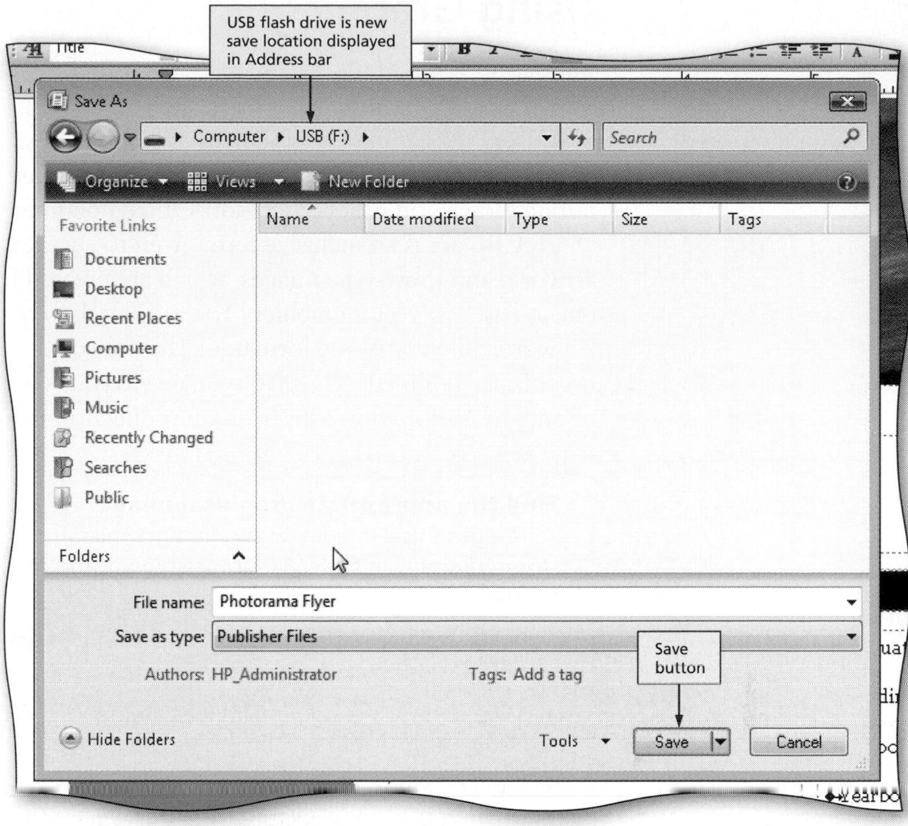

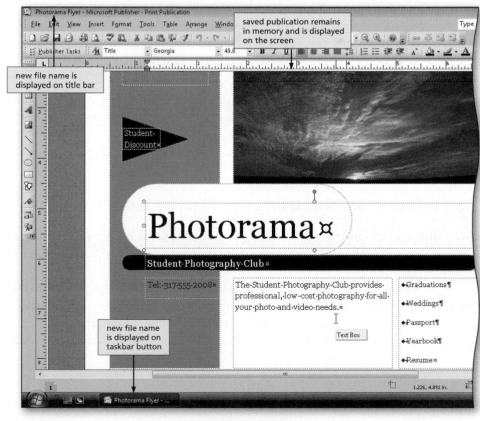

USB flash drive is new save location displayed in Address bar

File name: Photorama Flyer

Save as type: Publisher Files

Save button

Figure 1–45

5

- Click the Save button in the Save As dialog box to save the publication on the USB flash drive with the file name, Photorama Flyer (Figure 1–46).

Q&A How do I know that the project is saved?

While Publisher is saving your file, Windows briefly displays a busy mouse pointer, while it accesses the storage device. In addition, your USB drive may have a light that flashes during the save process. The title bar and task bar button display the new file name.

Other Ways

1. Click File on the menu bar, click Save As, type file name, click Computer, select drive or folder, click Save button

2. Press CTRL+S, type file name, click Computer, select drive or folder, click Save button

new file name is displayed on title bar

saved publication remains in memory and is displayed on the screen

Student Discount

Photorama

Student Photography Club

Tel: 317-555-2008

The Student Photography Club provides professional, low-cost photography for all your photo and video needs.

◆Graduations

◆Weddings

◆Passport

◆Yearbook

◆Resume

Text Box

new file name is displayed on taskbar button

Figure 1–46

Using Graphics

Files containing graphical images, also called **graphics**, are available from a variety of sources. Publisher includes a series of predefined graphics, such as drawings, photographs, sounds, videos, and other media files, called clips. A **clip** is a single media file, including art, sound, animation, or movies, that you can insert and use in print publications, Web publications, and other Microsoft Office documents.

Clip art is an inclusive term given to a variety of predefined graphics, such as images, artwork, and draw-type images, which are created from a set of instructions (also called object-based or vector graphics). You can search for graphics and clip art based on descriptive keywords, file name, file format, or clip collection. The **clip collection** is a hierarchical organization of media clips. You can create your own clip collections; import clip collections; or add, move, or copy clips from one collection to another.

<table>
<tr>
<td>Plan
Ahead</td>
<td>

Find the appropriate graphical image.

To use graphical images, also called graphics, in a Publisher publication, the image must be stored digitally in a file. Files containing graphical images are available from a variety of sources:

- Publisher includes a collection of predefined graphical images that you can insert in a publication.

- Microsoft has free digital images on the Web for use in a publication. Other Web sites also have images available, some of which are free, while others require a fee.

- You can take a picture with a digital camera and **download** it, which is the process of copying the digital picture from the camera to your computer.

- Appropriate images not only should refer to the context of the publication, but also should represent the reality of that context. If you are trying to sell something or describe a person or place, use a photograph. If you are describing a service or general object, you can use clip art. For example, if you are trying to sell a used car, try to use a real picture of the car. If you're describing cars in general, you can use clip art.

- With a scanner, you can convert a printed picture, drawing, or diagram to a digital file.

   If you receive a picture from a source other than yourself, do not use the file until you are certain it does not contain a virus. A **virus** is a computer program that can damage files and programs on your computer. Use an antivirus program to verify that any files you use are virus free.

</td>
</tr>
</table>

To Replace a Graphic Using the Clip Art Task Pane

Because this flyer is advertising photographic services, it is more appropriate to choose a graphic related to photography than the picture of the sunset supplied by the template. A graphic should enhance the message of the publication.

In Publisher templates, clip art and pictures commonly are placed within a picture frame. A **picture frame** is an invisible border that helps with placement and text wrapping.

The following steps retrieve an appropriate graphic using the **Clip Art task pane** to replace the supplied graphic. If you cannot access the graphic described, choose a suitable replacement from your system's clip art.

1

- If necessary, zoom to display the Whole Page.

- Click the graphic to select the picture frame.

- Click the graphic again to select the picture within the frame.

- Right-click the graphic to display its shortcut menu.

- Point to Change Picture to display the Change Picture submenu (Figure 1–47).

Q&A Why did the sizing handles turn gray with an x inside?

When the frame is selected, the sizing handles are white. When the picture within the frame is selected, Publisher changes the sizing handles so you know you are manipulating the picture rather than the frame.

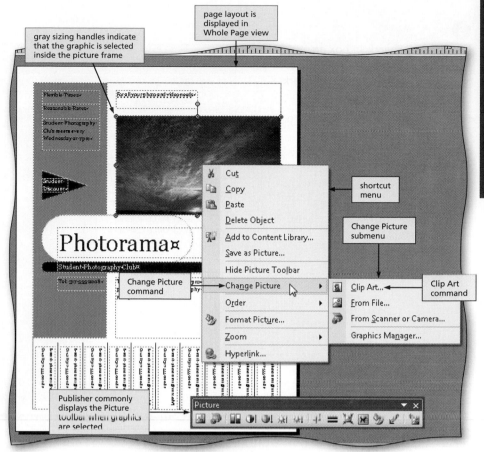

Figure 1–47

2

- Click Clip Art on the Change Picture submenu to display the Clip Art task pane.

- When the Clip Art task pane is displayed, if the Search for text box contains text, drag through the text to select it.

- Type photography in the Search for text box to enter a searchable key word (Figure 1–48).

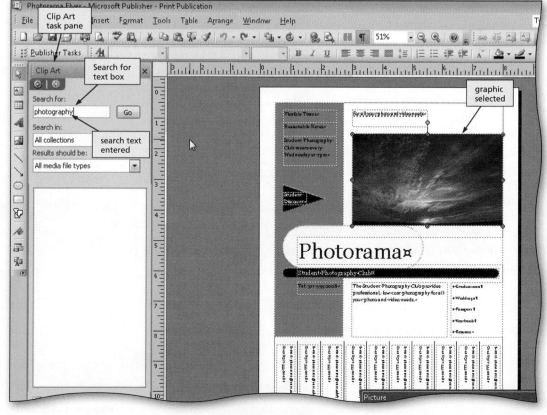

Figure 1–48

3

- Click the Search in box arrow and click the Everywhere check box so that it displays a check mark (Figure 1–49).

Q&A What if I am not connected to the Web?

If you are not connected to the Web, your Web collections check box will not be checked. Your search then would be limited to the clip art installed locally on your system.

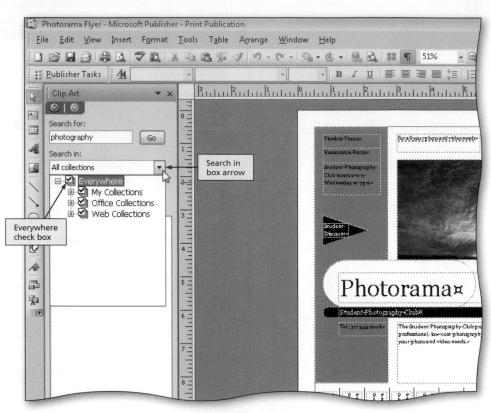

Figure 1–49

4

- Click the Search in box arrow again to close the list.

- Click the Results should be box arrow and ensure that the All media types check box displays a check mark (Figure 1–50).

Q&A What is the difference between the media types?

The Results should be box arrow displays four types of media to include in the search results: Clip Art, Photographs, Movies, and Sounds. Clip art includes all images that are not real photos, without animation or sound. Photographs are pictures of real objects. Movies include all clips that have any kind of animation or action. Sounds do not display a graphic, but play a sound if the speakers are turned on. Sounds and movies are used for Web publications.

Figure 1–50

5

- Click the Go button to begin the search for clip art (Figure 1–51).

Q&A

What are the links at the bottom of the Clip Art task pane?

You can click the link, Organize clips, to open the Microsoft Clip Organizer. You can use the Clip Organizer to browse through clip collections, add clips, or catalog clips in ways that make sense to you. For example, you can create a collection to group the clips you use most frequently, or let the Clip Organizer automatically add and catalog clips on your hard disk. The second link opens a Web browser and displays content from Microsoft Office Online. The third link offers tips from the Publisher Help system on finding clips.

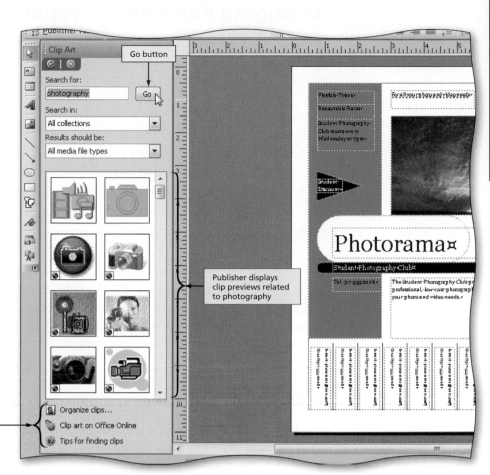

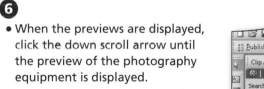

Figure 1–51

6

- When the previews are displayed, click the down scroll arrow until the preview of the photography equipment is displayed.

- Click the preview shown in Figure 1–52 or another one from your clip art collection to replace the current graphic.

7

- Click the close button in the Clip Art task pane title bar to close the task pane.

Other Ways

1. On Insert menu, point to Picture, click Clip Art, enter search criteria, click preview
2. Double-click non-grouped graphic, enter search criteria in Clip Art task pane, click preview

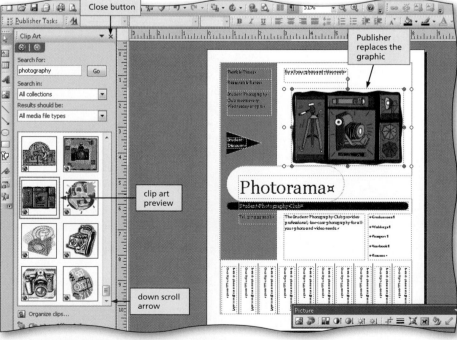

Figure 1–52

Changing Publication Properties and Saving Again

Publisher helps you organize and identify your files by using **publication properties**, which are the details about a file. Publication properties, also known as **metadata**, can include such information as the project author, title, or subject. **Keywords** are words or phrases that further describe the publication. For example, a class name or publication topic can describe the file's purpose or content.

Publication properties are valuable for a variety of reasons:

- Users can save time locating a particular file because they can view a publication's properties without opening the publication.

- By creating consistent properties for files having similar content, users can better organize their publications.

- Some organizations require Publisher users to add publication properties so that other employees can view details about these files.

Many different types of publication properties exist, but the more common ones used in this book are standard and automatically updated properties. **Standard properties** are associated with all Microsoft Office publications and include author, title, and subject. **Automatically updated properties** include file system properties, such as the date you create or change a file, and statistics, such as the file size.

To Change Publication Properties

The **Properties dialog box** contains boxes where you can view and enter publication properties. You can view and change information in this panel at any time while you are creating a publication. Before saving the flyer again, you want to add your name and class name as publication properties. The following steps use the Properties dialog box to change publication properties.

- Click File on the menu bar to display the File menu (Figure 1–53).

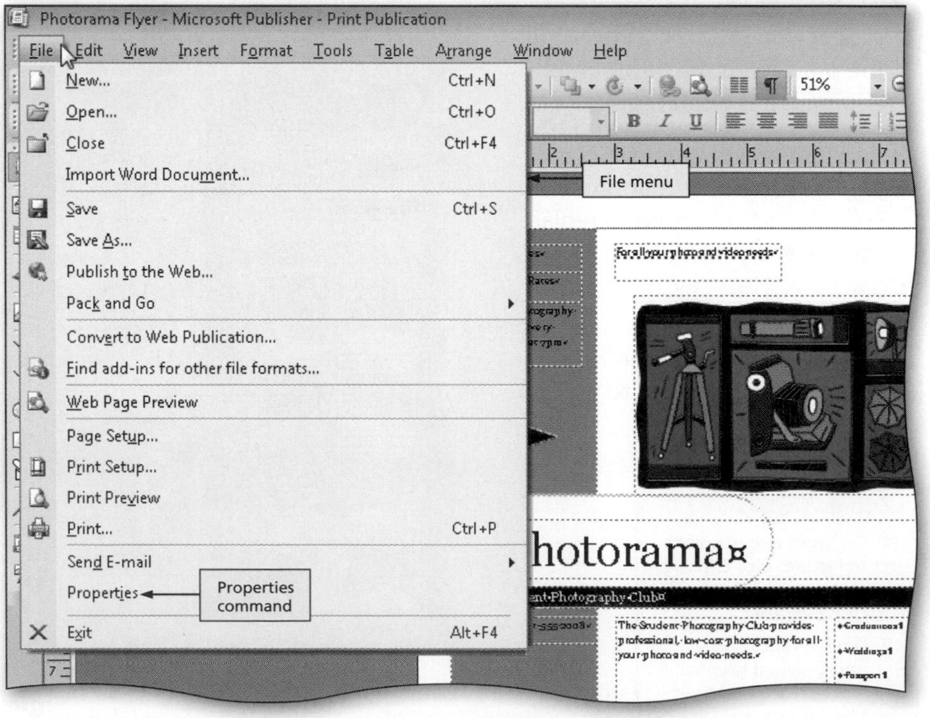

Photorama Flyer - Microsoft Publisher - Print Publication

File Edit View Insert Format Tools Table Arrange Window Help

New...   Ctrl+N
Open...   Ctrl+O
Close   Ctrl+F4
Import Word Document...
Save   Ctrl+S
Save As...
Publish to the Web...
Pack and Go
Convert to Web Publication...
Find add-ins for other file formats...
Web Page Preview
Page Setup...
Print Setup...
Print Preview
Print...   Ctrl+P
Send E-mail
Properties
Exit   Alt+F4

File menu

Properties command

Figure 1–53

2

- Click Properties to access the Properties dialog box (Figure 1–54).

Q&A Why are some of the publication properties in my Properties dialog box already filled in?

The person who installed Microsoft Office 2007 on your computer or network may have set or customized the properties.

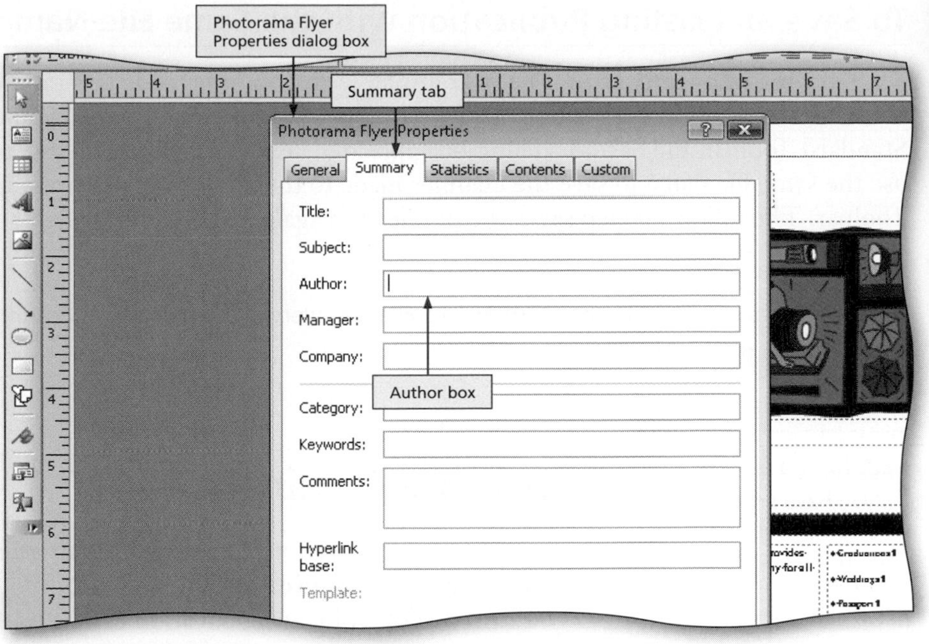

Figure 1–54

3

- Click the Subject text box; if necessary, delete any existing text, and then type your course and section as the Subject property.

- Click the Author text box, if necessary, and then type your name as the Author property. If a name already is displayed in the Author text box, delete it before typing your name.

- Click the Keywords text box; if necessary, delete any existing text, and then type Photography Club as the Keywords property (Figure 1–55).

Q&A What types of publication properties does Publisher collect automatically?

Publisher records such details as how long you worked at creating your project and how many times you revised the publication.

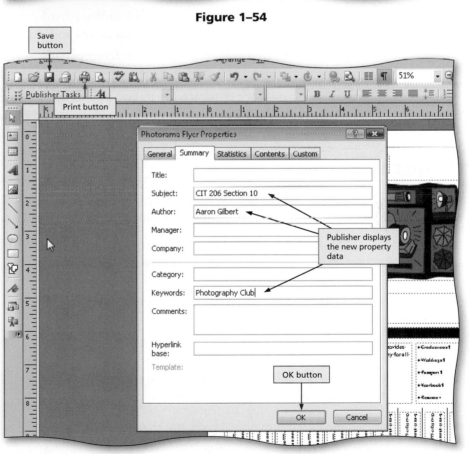

Figure 1–55

4

- Click the OK button in the Properties dialog box so that the dialog box no longer is displayed.

Q&A What other kinds of things can be done using the Properties dialog box?

You or your instructor can insert comments about the publication in the Comments box. On the Custom tab, you can assign other properties, such as editor, department, language, or publisher, and then enter text, date, yes/no, or a numeric value to these custom properties. For example, your instructor can grade your publication, typing his or her name in the Checked by category, and then assign a letter or numeric grade in the Project or Disposition category.

To Save an Existing Publication with the Same File Name

Saving frequently cannot be overemphasized. You have made several modifications to the publication since you saved it earlier in the chapter. When you first saved the publication, you clicked the Save button on the Standard Toolbar, the Save As dialog box appeared, and you entered the file name, Photorama Flyer. If you want to use the same file name to save the changes made to the publication, you again click the Save button on the Standard Toolbar. The following step saves the publication again.

1

• Click the Save button on the Standard Toolbar to overwrite the previous Photorama Flyer file on the USB flash drive.

Other Ways

1. Press CTRL+S

BTW

Resaving Files
If you have previously saved a publication, when you click the Save button again, Publisher overwrites the file using the settings specified the first time you saved. To save the file with a different file name or on different media, display the Save As dialog box by clicking Save As on the File menu. Then, fill in the Save As dialog box.

Printing a Publication

After you create a publication, you often want to print it. A printed version of the publication is called a **hard copy** or **printout**.

Printed copies of your publication can be useful for the following reasons:

• Many people prefer proofreading a hard copy of the publication rather than viewing it on the screen to check for errors and readability.

• Hard copies can serve as reference material if your storage medium is lost or becomes corrupted and you need to re-create the publication.

It is a good practice to save a publication before printing it, in the event you experience difficulties with the printer.

To Print a Publication

With the completed publication saved, you may want to print it. The following step prints the contents of the saved Photorama Flyer project by clicking the Print button on the Standard toolbar (Figure 1–55 on the previous page).

1

• Ready the printer according to the printer instructions. Click the Print button on the Standard toolbar.

• When the printer stops, retrieve the hard copy of the Photorama Flyer (Figure 1–56).

Q&A

How can I print multiple copies of my publication other than clicking the Print button twice?

Click File on the menu bar and then click Print on the File menu. Increase the number in the Number of copies box, and then click the OK button.

Q&A

Do I have to wait until my publication is complete to print it?

No, you can follow these steps to print a publication at any time while you are creating it.

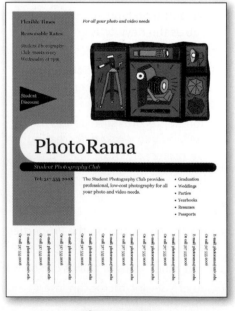

Figure 1–56

Other Ways

1. Press CTRL+P, press ENTER

Quitting Publisher

If you save a publication and then quit Publisher, the Publisher window closes. If you have made changes to a publication since the last time the file was saved, Publisher displays a dialog box asking if you want to save the changes you made to the file before it closes that window. The dialog box contains three buttons with these resulting actions:

- Yes button — Saves the changes and then quits Publisher
- No button — Quits Publisher without saving changes
- Cancel button — Closes the dialog box and redisplays the publication without saving the changes

BTW

Closing vs. quitting
Closing a publication is different from quitting Publisher. Closing a publication, by clicking Close on the File menu, leaves any other Publisher publications open and Publisher running. If no other publication is open, the Close command displays the New Publication task pane.

To Quit Publisher

You saved the publication prior to printing and did not make any changes to the project. The Photorama Flyer project now is complete, and you are ready to quit Publisher. The following steps quit Publisher.

1

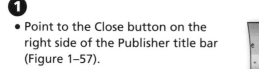

- Point to the Close button on the right side of the Publisher title bar (Figure 1–57).

2

- Click the Close button to quit Publisher.

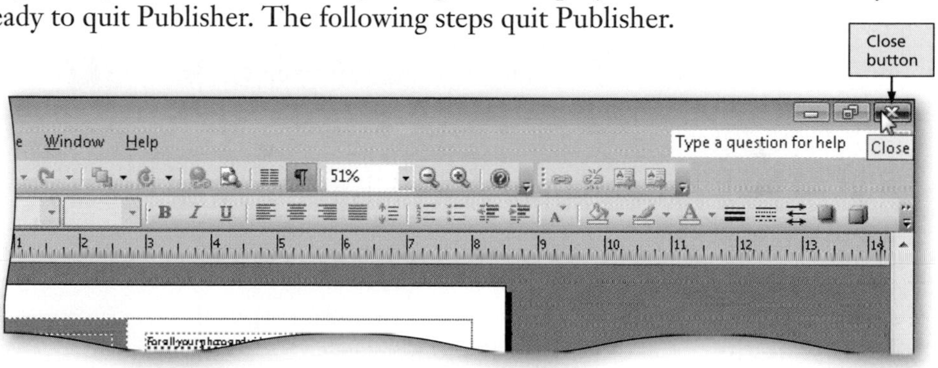

Figure 1–57

Other Ways

1. Click File on the menu bar, click Exit
2. Right-click Microsoft Publisher button on Windows taskbar, click Close on shortcut menu
3. Press ALT+F4

Starting Publisher and Opening a Publication

Once you have created and saved a publication, you may need to retrieve it from your storage medium. For example, you might want to revise the publication or reprint it. Opening a publication requires that Publisher is running on your computer.

To Start Publisher

The following steps, which assume Windows Vista is running, start Publisher.

1. Click the Start button on the Windows taskbar to display the Start menu.
2. Click All Programs on the Start menu to display the All Programs submenu.
3. Click Microsoft Office on the All Programs submenu to display the Microsoft Office submenu.
4. Click Microsoft Office Publisher 2007 on the Microsoft Office submenu to start Publisher.
5. If the Publisher window is not maximized, click the Maximize button on its title bar to maximize the window.

To Open a Publication from Publisher

Earlier in this chapter you saved your project on a USB flash drive using the file name, Photorama Flyer. The following steps open the Photorama Flyer file from the USB flash drive.

1

- With your USB flash drive connected to one of the computer's USB ports, click File on the menu bar (Figure 1–58).

Q&A

What files are shown in the Recent Publications list?

Publisher displays, by default, the five most recently opened publication file names in this list. If the file you want to open appears in the Recent Publications list, you could click it to open the file. The recent publications also are displayed at the bottom of the File menu.

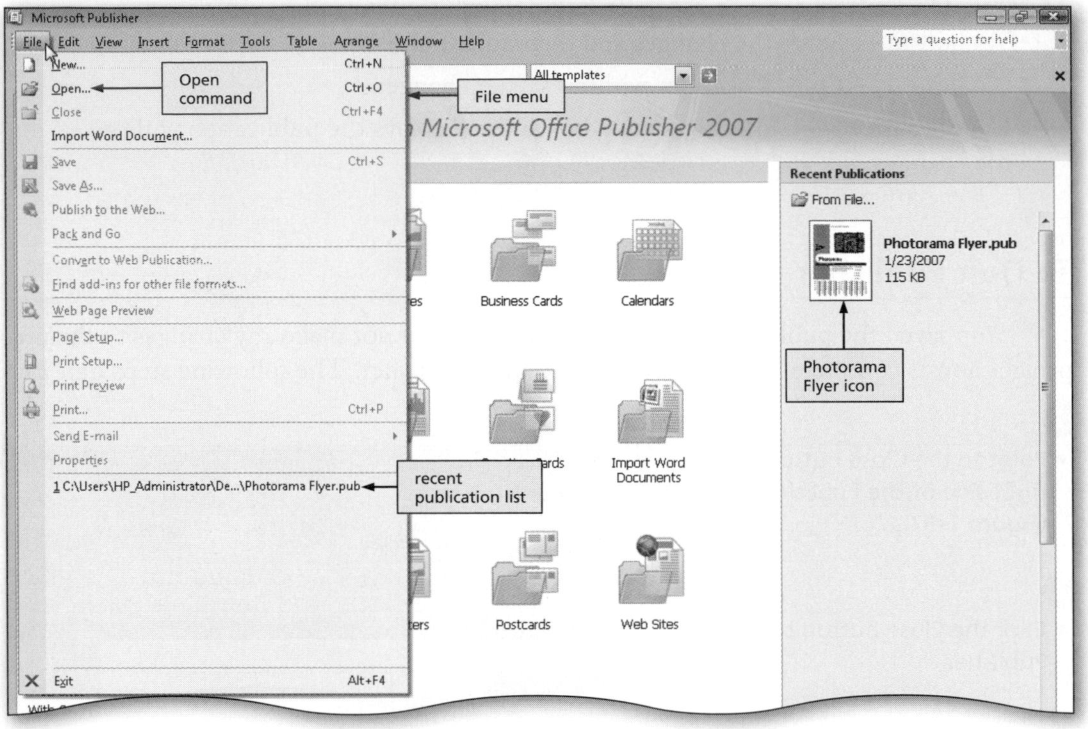

Figure 1–58

2

- Click Open on the File menu to display the Open Publication dialog box.

- If the Folders list is displayed below the Folders button, click the Folders button to remove the Folders list.

- If necessary, click Computer in the Favorite Links section and then scroll until USB (F:) appears in the list of available drives.

- Double-click to select the USB flash drive, Drive F in this case, as the new open location.

- Click Photorama Flyer to select the file name (Figure 1–59).

Q&A

How do I open the file if I am not using a USB flash drive?

Use the same process, but be certain to select your device in the Computer list.

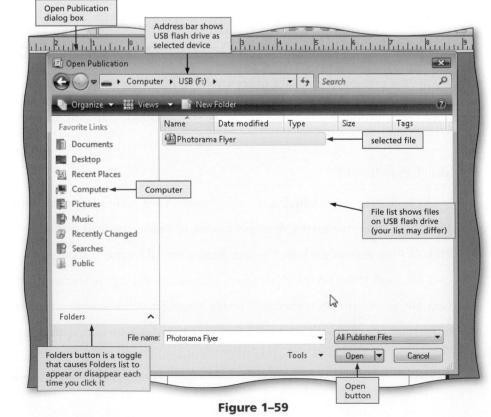

Figure 1–59

- Click the Open button to open the selected file and display the Photorama Flyer publication in the Publisher window.

- Click the Close button on the Format Publication task pane title bar (Figure 1–60).

Q&A

Why do I see the Publisher icon and publication name on the Windows taskbar?

When you open a Publisher file, a Publisher program button is displayed on the taskbar. The button in Figure 1–60 contains an ellipsis because some of its contents do not fit in the allotted button space. If you point to a program button, its entire contents appear in a ScreenTip, which in this case would be the file name followed by the program name.

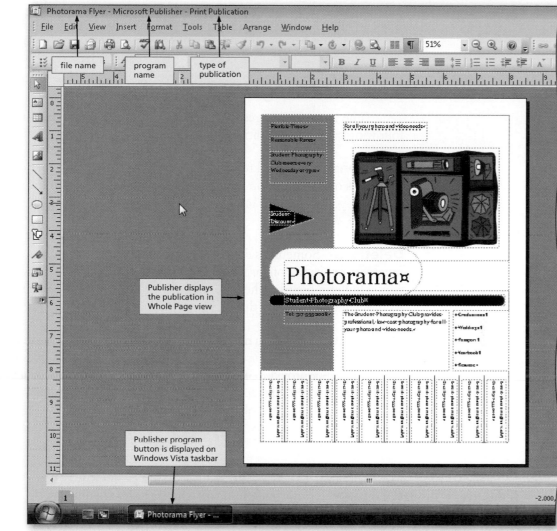

Figure 1–60

Other Ways

1. Click Open button on Standard toolbar, navigate to storage location, double-click file name
2. Press CTRL+O, navigate to storage location, select file name, press ENTER

Correcting Errors

After creating a publication, you often will find that you must make changes to it. Changes can be required because the document contains an error or because of new circumstances.

Types of Changes Made to Publications

The types of changes made to publications normally fall into one of the three following categories: additions, deletions, or modifications.

Additions Additional text, objects, or formatting may be required in the publication. Additions occur when you are required to add items to a publication. For example, in Project 1 you would like to insert a text box that will display when the flyer is published to the Web.

Deletions Sometimes deletions are necessary in a publication because objects are incorrect or are no longer needed. For example, to place this advertising flyer on the electronic bulletin board at the school, the tear-offs no longer are needed. In that case, you would delete them from the page layout.

Modifications If you make an error in a document or want to make other modifications, normal combinations of inserting, deleting, and editing techniques for text and graphics apply. Publisher provides several methods for correcting errors in a document. For each of the text error correction techniques, you first must move the insertion point to the error. For graphic modification, the object first must be selected.

To Delete the Tear-offs

If this flyer is displayed on an electronic bulletin board, the tear-offs are unnecessary and should be deleted. The following steps delete the tear-offs.

1
- Right-click any one of the tear-offs to display the shortcut menu (Figure 1–61).

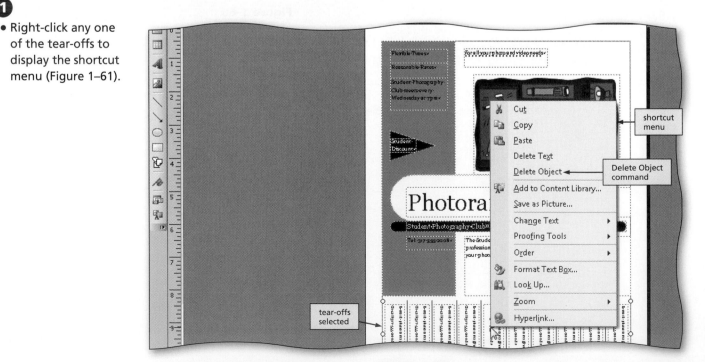

Figure 1–61

2
- Click Delete Object on the shortcut menu to delete the tear-offs (Figure 1–62).

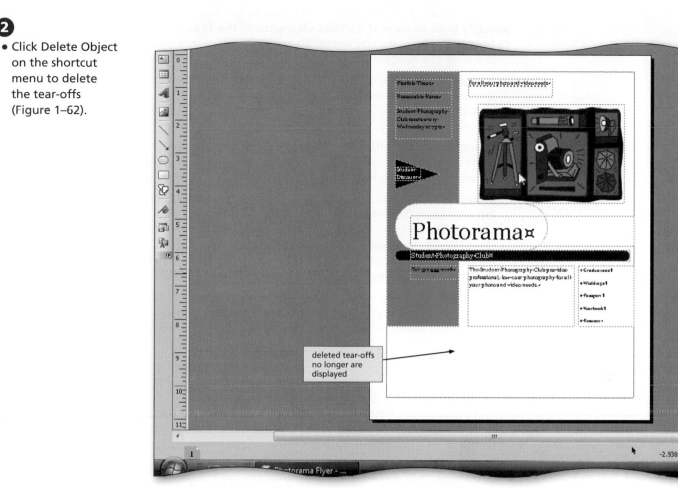

deleted tear-offs no longer are displayed

Figure 1–62

Inserting a Text Box

The next step in modifying the flyer is to create a new text box in preparation for creating a Web version of the publication. Recall that the Objects toolbar contains buttons for many different kinds of objects that you can insert into publications. In the case of a text box, you click the **Text Box button** (Figure 1-63 on the next page) and then drag in the publication to create the text box. Once it is created, you can type in the text box just as you did with those created by the template.

<table>
<tr><td>Plan
Ahead</td><td>

Identify how to format various elements of the text.

By formatting the characters and paragraphs in a publication, you can improve its overall appearance. In a flyer, consider the following formatting suggestions.

- **Increase the font size of characters.** Flyers usually are posted on a bulletin board or in a window. Thus, the font size should be as large as possible so that passersby easily can read the flyer. To give the headline more impact, its font size should be larger than the font size of the text in the body copy.

- **Change the font of characters.** Use fonts that are easy to read. The font schemes suggest using only two different fonts in a flyer, for example, one for the headline and the other for all other text. Too many fonts can make the flyer visually confusing.

- **Change the alignment and placement.** The default alignment for text in a publication is **left-aligned**, that is, flush at the left margin of the text box with uneven right edges. Consider changing the alignment of some of the text to add interest and variety to the flyer. Overall placement of objects should be done with purpose. Objects usually should be aligned with the margin or with other objects on the page. Objects similar in nature, such as organization information text boxes, should be kept in close proximity of one another.

- **Emphasize important words.** To call attention to certain words or lines, you can underline them, italicize them, or bold them. Use these formats sparingly, however, because overuse will minimize their effect and make the flyer look too busy.

</td></tr>
</table>

To Insert a Text Box in an Existing Publication

In the following step, a new text box is created in the lower portion of the flyer.

1

- Click the Text Box button on the Objects toolbar to select it and then move the mouse to the position where you want the text box to display (in this case, the lower portion of the flyer where the tear-offs were located).

- Position the mouse pointer in the upper-left corner of the empty area and then drag down and right, forming a rectangle, to create a new text box that fills the area vacated by the tear-offs (Figure 1–63).

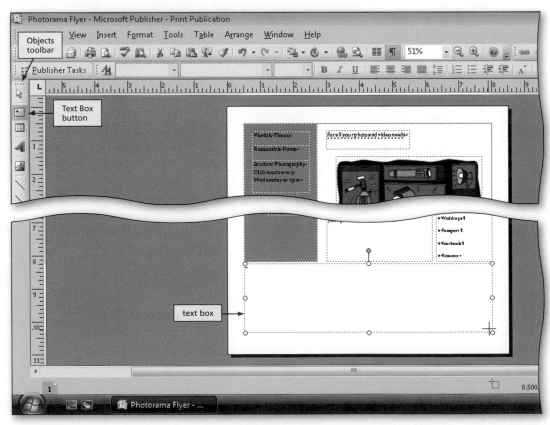

Figure 1–63

To Format Text

To make the text easier to read on an electronic bulletin board, you will change the font size and center the text as shown in the next steps. The **Font Size box** on the Formatting toolbar allows you to type in a font size for text or choose a size from a list. Font sizes are measured in points. A **point** is a measurement of the height of a typed character, approximately $1/72^{nd}$ of an inch. The **Center button** on the Formatting toolbar centers text within the text box margins.

1

- Click inside the newly created text box to position the insertion point.

- Click the Font Size box arrow on the Formatting toolbar to display the Font Size list (Figure 1–64).

Q&A

Is it better to choose the font size before I type or after?

You can do it either way, but if you have already typed the text, you must select it before choosing the new font size. Choosing the font size first eliminates that extra step.

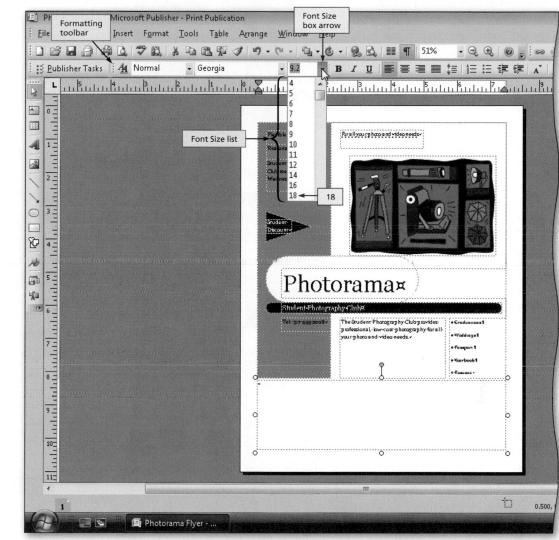

Figure 1–64

2

- Click 18 in the list to change the font size to 18 point (Figure 1–65).

Q&A

Are there other ways to increase the font size?

Yes, in later chapters you will learn how to use the Font command on the Format menu, the Increase Font Size button, and the Best Fit option to increase the font size.

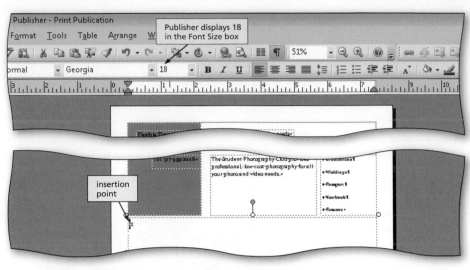

Figure 1–65

3

- Click the Center button on the Formatting toolbar to center the text (Figure 1–66).

Q&A

What are the other alignment buttons?

There are four alignment buttons on the Formatting toolbar when a text box is selected: **Align Text Left**, **Center**, **Align Text Right**, and **Justify**. The default setting for text is to align it on the left side. The Justify button causes Publisher to add extra spaces so that all the lines of a paragraph (except the last line) reach and align with both margins. You will learn about additional alignments in a later project.

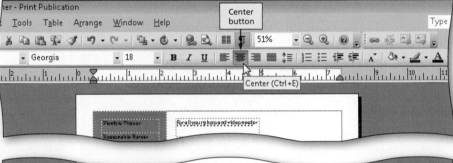

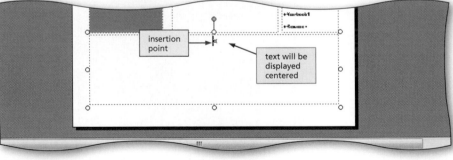

Figure 1–66

4

- Type E-mail: photorama@univ.edu to enter the text (Figure 1–67).

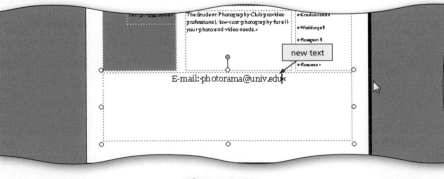

Other Ways

1. To center text, press CTRL+E

Figure 1–67

Inserting a Hyperlink

The final modification in preparation for converting this publication to a Web publication is inserting a hyperlink. A **hyperlink** is colored and underlined text or a graphic that you click to go to a file, a location in a file, a Web page, or an e-mail address. When you insert a hyperlink, you select the text or object and then click the Insert Hyperlink button on the Standard toolbar.

To Insert a Hyperlink

The **Insert Hyperlink dialog box** allows you to select options and enter Web addresses, as shown in the following steps. The TAB key is used to move from one box to another in Publisher dialog boxes.

1

- Drag through the text, photorama@univ.edu, to select it (Figure 1–68).

Q&A

Are there other ways to select the text other than dragging?

If the text were a single word, you could double-click to select it. However, because an e-mail address is actually three words separated by the at symbol (@) and a period (.), double-clicking will not select the entire e-mail address. The only other way to select the text would be to click at the beginning and SHIFT+CLICK at the end.

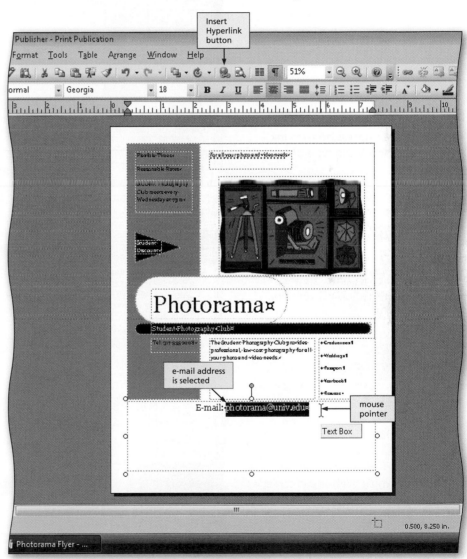

Figure 1–68

2

- Click the Insert Hyperlink button on the Standard toolbar (Figure 1–69).

🔎 **Experiment**

- When the Insert Hyperlink dialog box is displayed, one at a time, click each kind of hyperlink listed in the Link to bar. Note the different kinds of information requested.

3

- Click E-mail Address on the Link to bar to specify the type of hyperlink.

- Type photorama@univ.edu in the E-mail address text box.

- Press the TAB key to move to the next box.

- Type Photorama Web Flyer Inquiry in the Subject text box (Figure 1–70).

Q&A

What kinds of text should you enter in the Subject text box?

Because this text will become the subject line of the e-mail message when someone clicks the hyperlink on your Web site, you want to include text that identifies the message as coming from your Web flyer, as well as text that identifies from which Web site it came, should you have more than one.

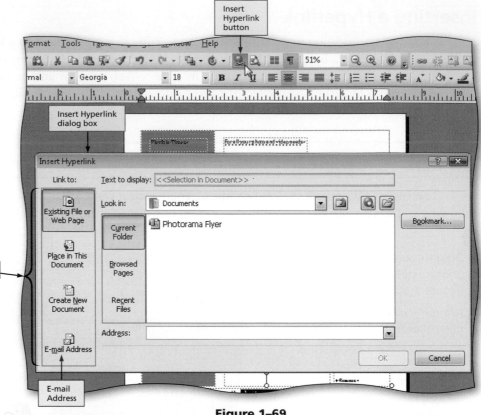

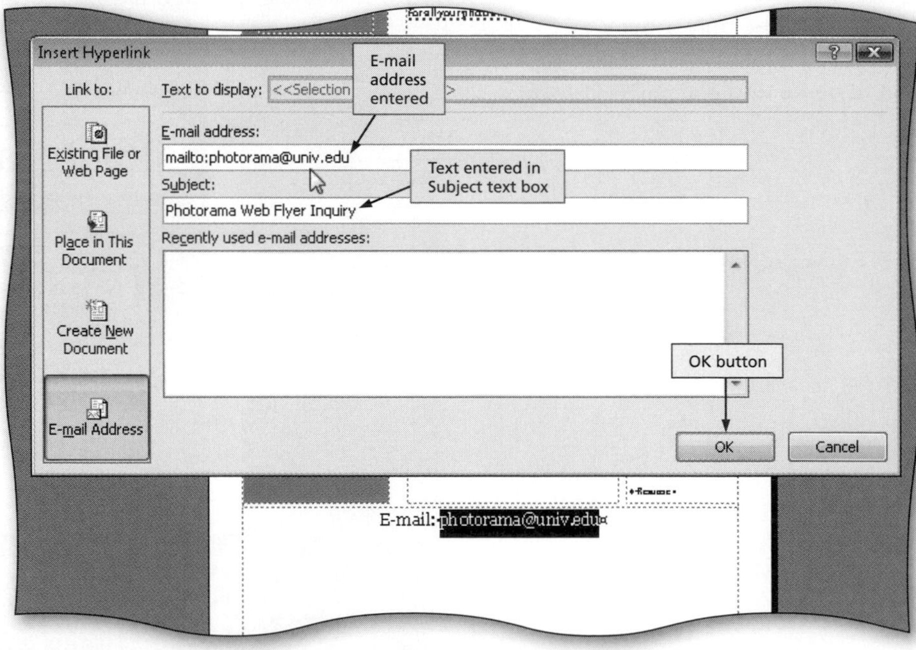

Figure 1–69

Figure 1–70

4

- Click the OK button.

Other Ways
1. Select text, click Hyperlink on the Insert menu, enter hyperlink information, click OK
2. Select text, press CTRL+K, enter hyperlink information, click OK

Creating a Web Page from a Publication

Publisher can create a Web page from your publication. It is a three-step process. First, Publisher uses a **Design Checker** to look for potential problems if the publication were transferred to the Web. Next, after saving the publication with a new file name, it will be converted to a Web publication, using the Convert to Web Publication command on the File menu. Finally, Publisher allows you to publish the Web page.

Plan Ahead

Determine whether the flyer will be more effective as a print publication, Web publication, or both.

- **Print publications** – When creating a print publication, you must consider the kind of paper you are going to use, the color options, the number of copies, and the plan for publishing. Ask yourself if the publication has to be in print to reach the target audience. How will readers find the printed publication? The included objects in the layout should be designed keeping the limitations of print and reading in mind.

- **Web publications** – Will the publication be accessible and reasonable on the Web? Is the target audience a common Web user? If so, determine whether an e-mail, Web page, or Web site would be the most efficient means of communication. How will readers find the Web page? When converting to a Web publication, determine which objects will work effectively on the Web and which ones will not. Modify the publication as necessary.

To Run the Design Checker

If your publication contains a layout that may not be appropriate, such as one with overlapping text boxes, or one with objects that extend beyond the margin, the Design Checker will alert you. If you use links or hot spots to other Web pages within your publication, Design Checker will verify the addresses if you are connected to the Web. The following steps run the Design Checker.

1
- Click Tools on the menu bar to display the Tools menu (Figure 1–71).

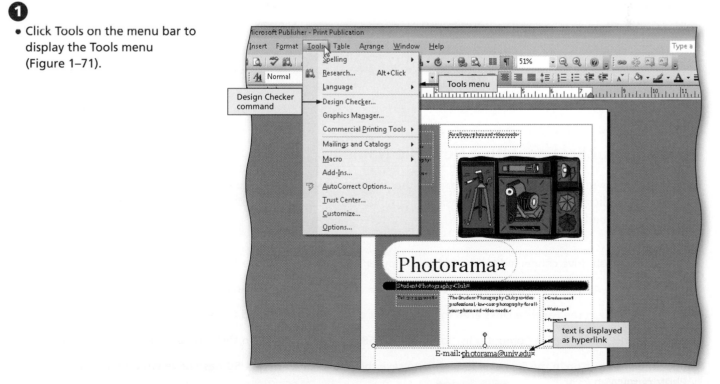

Figure 1–71

2

- Click the Design Checker command to display the Design Checker task pane. Publisher displays a message, indicating there are no problems in the publication (Figure 1–72).

Q&A

What happens if I have some design errors?

If your publication has a problem or contains a design error, the problem is displayed in the 'Select an item to fix' text box. You can click the problem's box arrow to display options to go to the error, ignore, continue, or obtain more information about the problem.

3

- Click the Close button on the Design Checker task pane title bar to close the task pane.

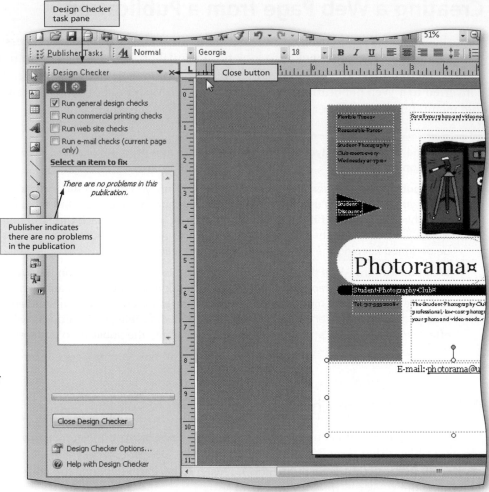

Figure 1–72

Other Ways

1. On View menu, click Task Pane, click Other Task Panes button, click Design Checker
2. Press CTRL+F1, click Other Task Panes button, click Design Checker

To Save a Publication with a New File Name

The following step illustrates how to save the publication with a new file name in preparation for converting it to a Web publication. It is important to save the publication before converting it to a Web publication so you can make changes at a later time, if necessary.

1

- With a USB flash drive connected to one of the computer's USB ports, click Save As on the File menu.

- When the Save As dialog box is displayed, type `Photorama Web Flyer` in the File name text box. Do not press the ENTER key.

- Click Computer in the Favorite Links area to display a list of available drives and folders.

- Double-click USB (F:) in the Computer list to open the USB flash drive, Drive F in this case, as the new save location.

- Click the Save button in the Save As dialog box to save the publication on the USB flash drive with the file name, Photorama Web Flyer.

Converting a Print Publication to a Web Publication

BTW

Design Checker
The Design Checker looks for appropriate layouts. If text overlaps an object, the Design Checker offers to convert the text box to a graphic so it will display properly. The Design Checker looks at all graphics and may display suggestions on those that load slowly. More about the Design Checker and information on types of graphics will be covered in future projects.

You can create two types of publications with Microsoft Publisher: print publications and Web publications. A **Web publication** is one suitable for publishing to the Web with certain objects, formatting options, hyperlinks, and other features specific to Web pages.

A command on Publisher's File menu converts publications from one type to another. Up to now, you have worked on a print publication, as noted on the title bar (Figure 1–60 on page PUB 43). Once you convert the file, you work in **Web mode**. The options available to you in Web mode are tailored specifically to Web publications so that you can create a publication that is optimized for display in a Web browser. A **browser** is a piece of software that interprets and formats files into Web pages and displays them. A Web browser, such as Microsoft Internet Explorer, can follow hyperlinks, transfer files, and play sound or video files that are embedded in Web pages. You always can determine which publication mode you are in by looking at the title bar of your open publication, which will display either Print Publication or Web Publication, depending on the publication type.

When you convert a publication from one type to the other, Publisher copies the text and graphics from your original publication into the new publication type. Because certain print features are not available in Web mode, and certain Web features are not available in Print mode, your publication may undergo formatting changes when you convert it from one publication type to the other.

To Convert a Print Publication to a Web Publication

The following steps convert a print publication to a Web publication. Two dialog boxes help you through the conversion process. Each dialog box lists the purpose of the step at the top, and then lists questions to help you make choices, and formats the publication based on your responses.

1

- Click Convert to Web Publication on the File menu to begin the process of converting a print publication to a Web publication.

- When Publisher displays the 'Save Your Current Print Publication' step, click the 'No, do not save my print publication before converting it to a Web publication' button to select it (Figure 1–73).

Q&A Why didn't I choose to save it?

Because you previously saved the file with a new name, you do not have to save the file again.

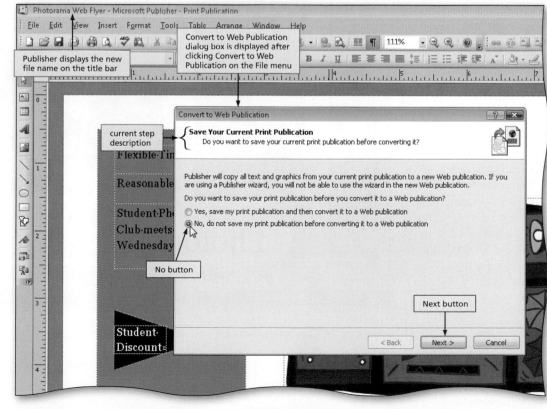

Figure 1–73

2

- Click the Next button to proceed to the second step of the conversion process.

- When the 'Add a Navigation Bar' step is displayed, click the 'No, do not add a navigation bar' button (Figure 1–74).

Q&A

Why didn't I choose to add a navigation bar?

It is a single Web page rather than a Web site, so navigation is not needed. Additionally, there are no links to other Web pages in your publication.

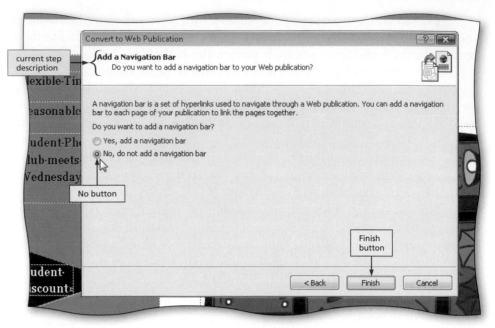

Figure 1–74

3

- Click the Finish Button to complete the process (Figure 1–75).

- Click the Close button in the Format Publication task pane.

Q&A

Why did my title bar change?

Your publication is now a Web publication, so the words, Print Publication, change to the words, Web Publication. The Web publication has not been saved in its current format, so a temporary name has been applied, labeled as Publication2 in this case.

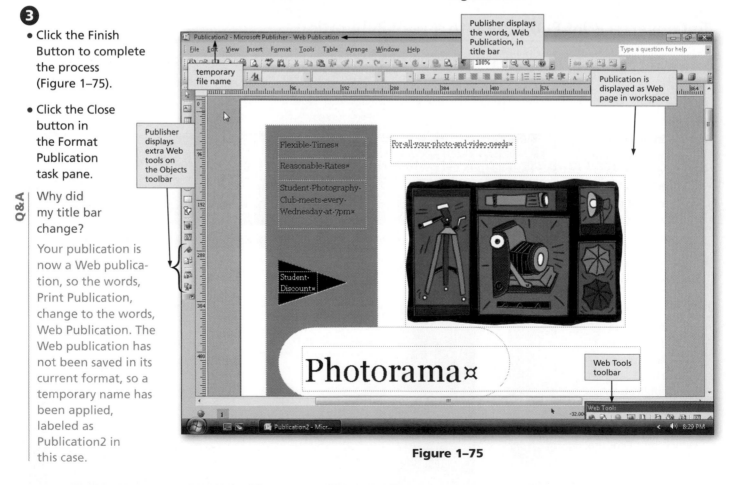

Figure 1–75

Publishing to the Web

The final step in preparing the Web flyer is to publish it to the Web. **Publishing to the Web** is the process of making Web pages available to others, for example, on the World Wide Web or on a company's intranet. Files intended for use on the Web, however, need a different format. A **Hypertext Markup Language (HTML)** file is a file capable of being stored and transferred electronically on a file server in order to display on the Web. When you publish, Publisher saves your file in a **filtered HTML format** that is smaller than regular HTML files. It can be published to and downloaded from the Internet quickly.

In Publisher, you can publish to the Web using a wizard accessed through the File menu, which creates a filtered HTML file, or you can save a publication as a Web page to a Web folder, which creates a traditional HTML file. Either way, Publisher creates an accompanying folder for each separate publication intended for the Web. A **folder** is a logical portion of a disk created to group and store similar documents. Inside this folder, Publisher will include copies of the associated graphics. Once created and uploaded, your publication can be viewed by a Web browser, such as Microsoft Internet Explorer.

BTW

Web folders
The concept of a Web folder facilitates integration of Publisher with other members of the Microsoft Office 2007 Suite and Windows Vista. With Windows Vista, you can choose to use Web style folders on your desktop, which means that the desktop is interactive, and all your folders look like Web pages. Publisher also will take care of uploading, or transferring, your files to the Web, if you are connected to an Internet service provider or host. See Appendix D for more information on Web folders.

To Publish to the Web

The following steps use the Publish to the Web command on the File menu to create a Web site from your publication. Because not all systems are connected to the Internet, and not all users subscribe to a Web hosting service, the following steps store the resulting Web files on a USB flash drive.

1

- Click Publish to the Web on the File menu.

- If a Microsoft Publisher dialog box is displayed, reminding you about Web hosting services, click its OK button.

- When the Publish to the Web dialog box is displayed, navigate if necessary, to the USB flash drive or other location on your computer (Figure 1–76).

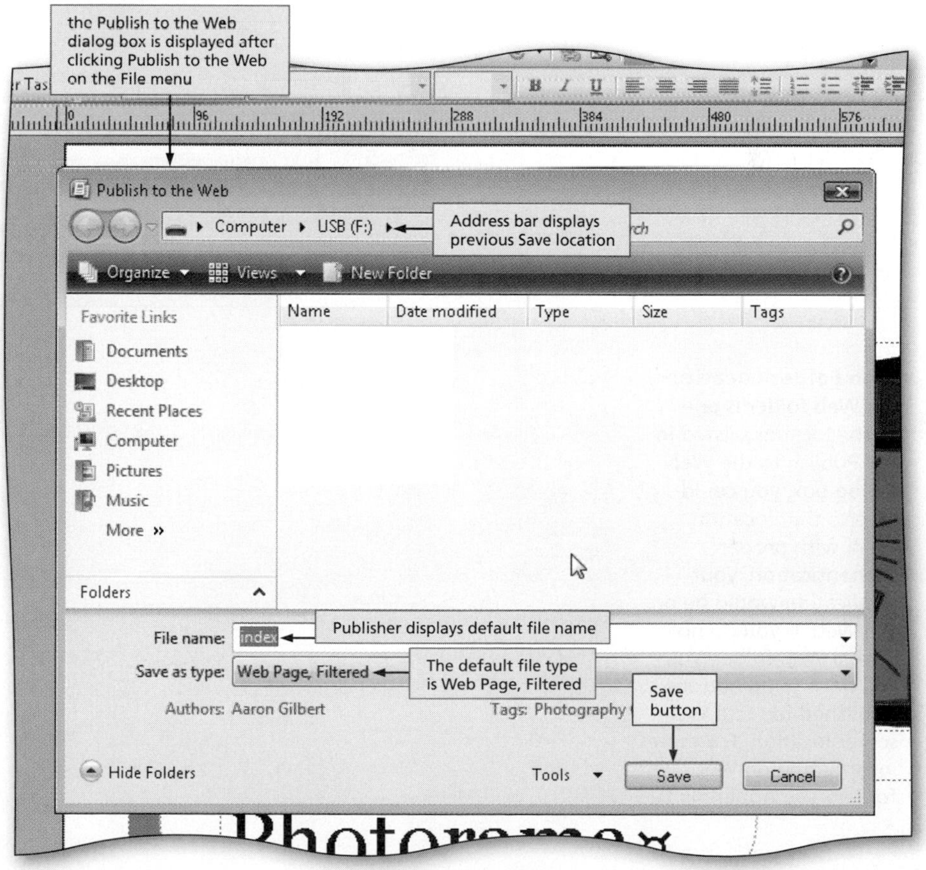

Figure 1–76

2

- Click the Save button in the Publish to the Web dialog box, to save the Web publication.

- When Publisher displays a Microsoft Office Publisher dialog box describing filtered HTML files, read the description and then click the OK button to close the dialog box (Figure 1–77).

Q&A Why did Publisher supply the name, index?

A single- file Web page or the first page in a multipage Web site is commonly called index. Browsers will display a page named index automatically when users navigate to the site.

Q&A Is my Web publication now on the Web?

No, the Web publication file is stored on your flash drive or the location to which you saved the print publication. See your instructor for ways to upload your files.

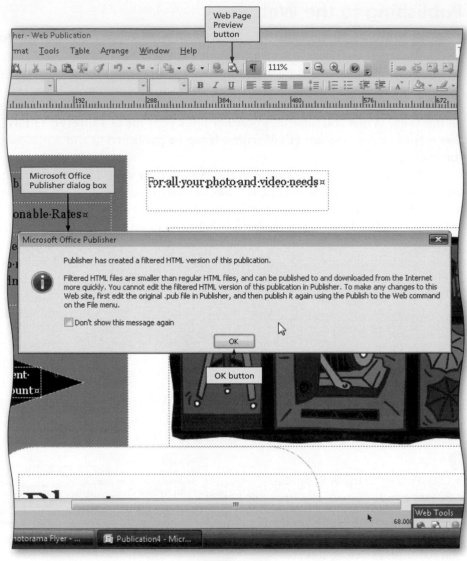

Figure 1–77

BTW

Web Folder Locations
If a Web folder is one of the locations listed in the Publish to the Web dialog box, you could save to that location; then, with proper authentication, your publication would be on the Web. If you do not have a Web folder, you will have to upload the published file to a Web server location. For more information on Web folders, see Appendix D.

To Preview the Web Publication in a Browser

To preview what the Web publication will look like on the Web, click the **Web Page Preview button** on the Standard toolbar, as shown in the following steps.

1

- Click the Web Page Preview button on the Standard tool-bar, to preview the Web publication.

- When the browser window opens, if necessary, maximize the window (Figure 1–78).

Q&A Why does my display look different?

Each brand and version of Web browser software displays infor-mation in a slightly different manner. Additionally, your browser settings, such as Text Size and Zoom level, may differ.

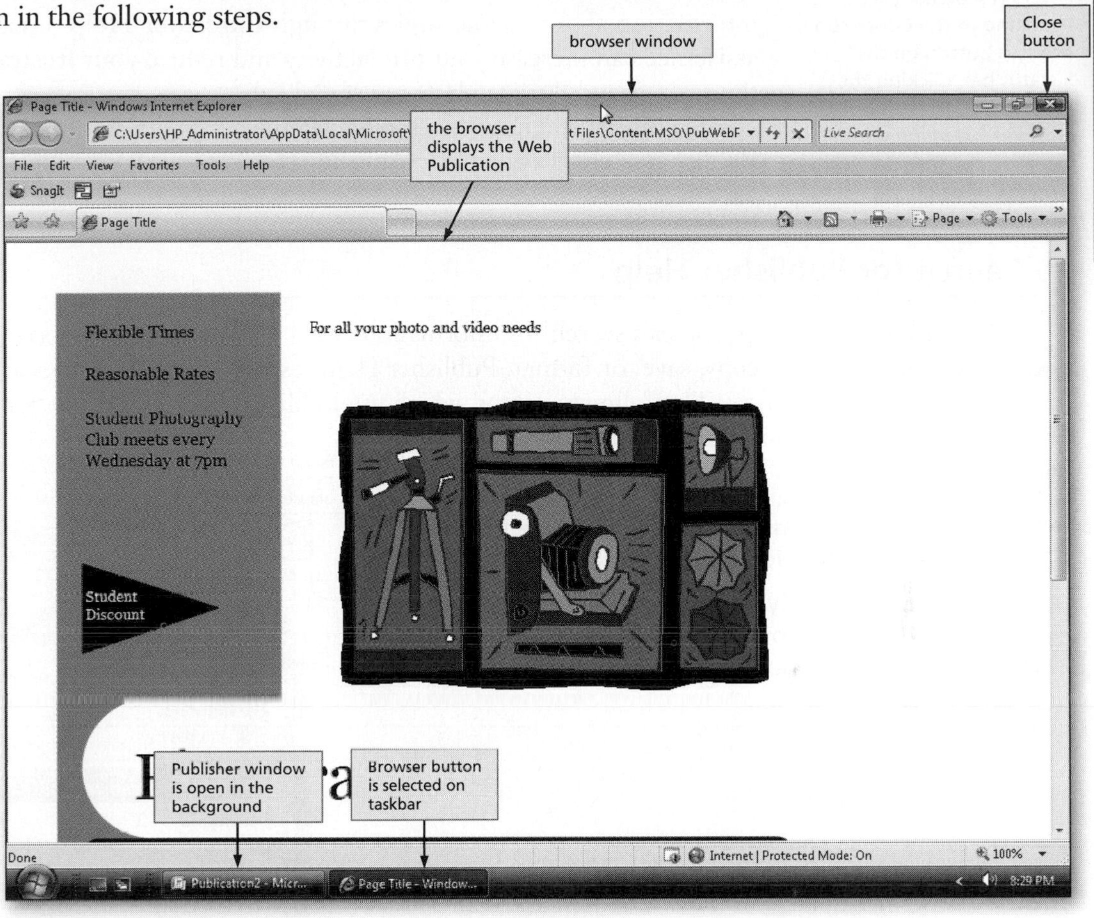

Figure 1–78

2

- Click the Close button on the browser window title bar.

Closing the Entire Publication

Sometimes, everything goes wrong. If this happens, you may want to close the publication entirely and start over with a new publication. You also may want to close a publication when you are finished with it so you can begin your next publication. If you wanted to close a publication, you would use the following steps.

To Close the Entire Publication

1 Click Close on the File menu.

2 If Publisher displays a dialog box, click the No button to ignore the changes since the last time you saved the publication.

BTW

Online Versus Offline Searches
You can determine where Help is searching by looking at the Connection Status button on the status bar. Clicking the Connection Status button provides a menu with commands for selecting online or offline searches .

Publisher Help

At any time while using Publisher, you can find answers to questions and display information about various topics through **Publisher Help**. Used properly, this form of assistance can increase your productivity and reduce your frustrations by minimizing the time you spend learning how to use Publisher.

This section introduces you to Publisher Help. Additional information about using Publisher Help is available in Appendix C.

To Search for Publisher Help

Using Publisher Help, you can search for information based on phrases, such as save a publication or format text, or key terms, such as copy, save, or format. Publisher Help responds with a list of search results displayed as links to a variety of resources. The following steps, which use Publisher Help to search for information about text boxes, assume you are connected to the Internet.

1

- Press the F1 key to access Publisher Help. In the Publisher Help toolbar, click the Home key.

- Type text box in the 'Type words to search for' text box at the top of the Publisher Help window to enter the search term (Figure 1–79).

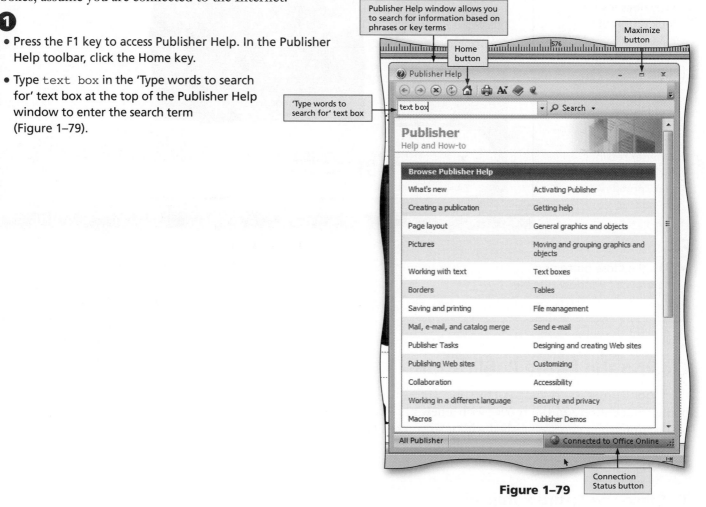

Figure 1–79

2

- Press the ENTER key to display the search results.

- Maximize the Publisher Help window (Figure 1–80).

Q&A Where is the Publisher window with the Photorama flyer publication?

Publisher is open in the background, but the Publisher Help window is overlaid on top of the Microsoft Publisher window. When the Publisher Help window is closed, the publication will reappear.

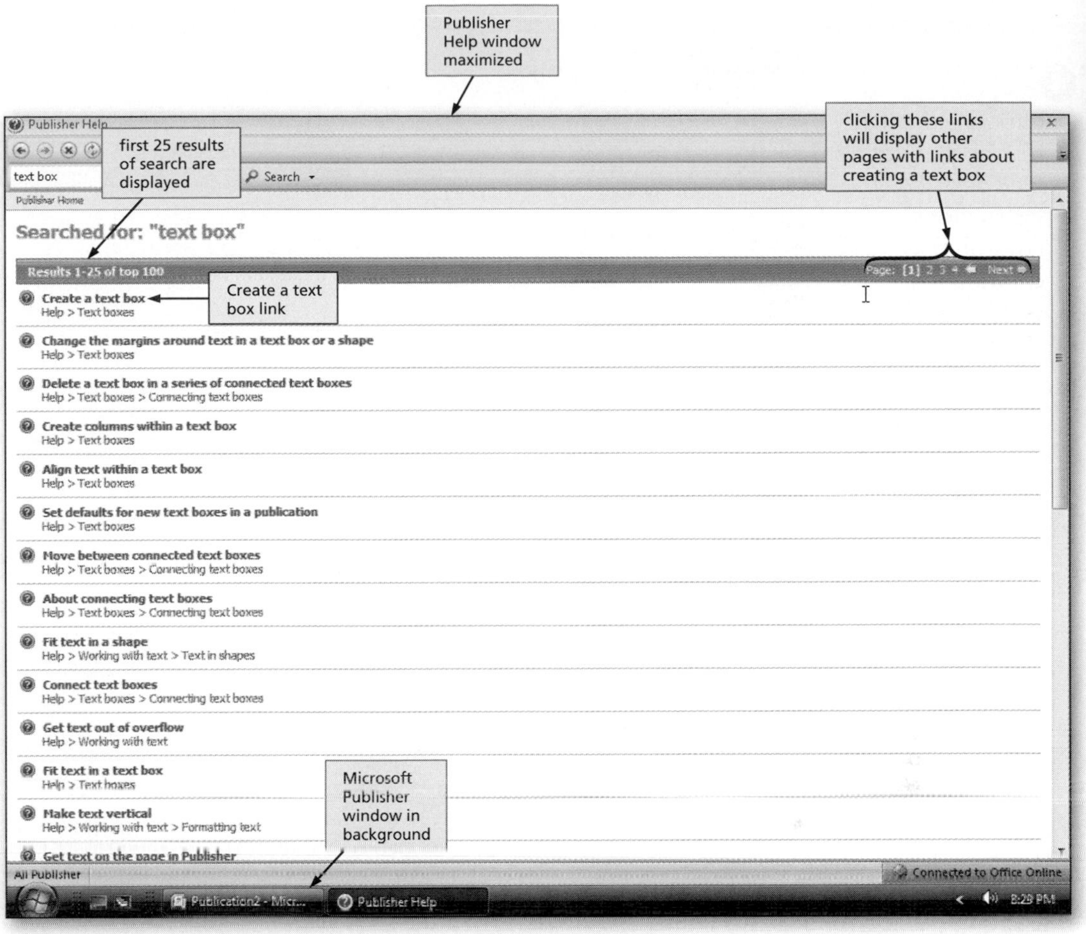

Publisher Help window maximized

clicking these links will display other pages with links about creating a text box

first 25 results of search are displayed

Searched for: "text box"

Results 1-25 of top 100

Page: [1] 2 3 4 ◀ Next ➡

Create a text box link

Create a text box
Help > Text boxes

Change the margins around text in a text box or a shape
Help > Text boxes

Delete a text box in a series of connected text boxes
Help > Text boxes > Connecting text boxes

Create columns within a text box
Help > Text boxes

Align text within a text box
Help > Text boxes

Set defaults for new text boxes in a publication
Help > Text boxes

Move between connected text boxes
Help > Text boxes > Connecting text boxes

About connecting text boxes
Help > Text boxes > Connecting text boxes

Fit text in a shape
Help > Working with text > Text in shapes

Connect text boxes
Help > Text boxes > Connecting text boxes

Get text out of overflow
Help > Working with text

Fit text in a text box
Help > Text boxes

Make text vertical
Help > Working with text > Formatting text

Get text on the page in Publisher

Microsoft Publisher window in background

All Publisher

Connected to Office Online

Publication2 - Micr...   Publisher Help   8:29 PM

Figure 1–80

3

- Click the Create a text box link to display information regarding creating text boxes (Figure 1–81).

Q&A What is the purpose of the buttons at the top of the Publisher Help window?

Use the buttons in the upper-left corner of the Publisher Help window to navigate through the Help system, change the display, show the Publisher Help table of contents, and print the contents of the window.

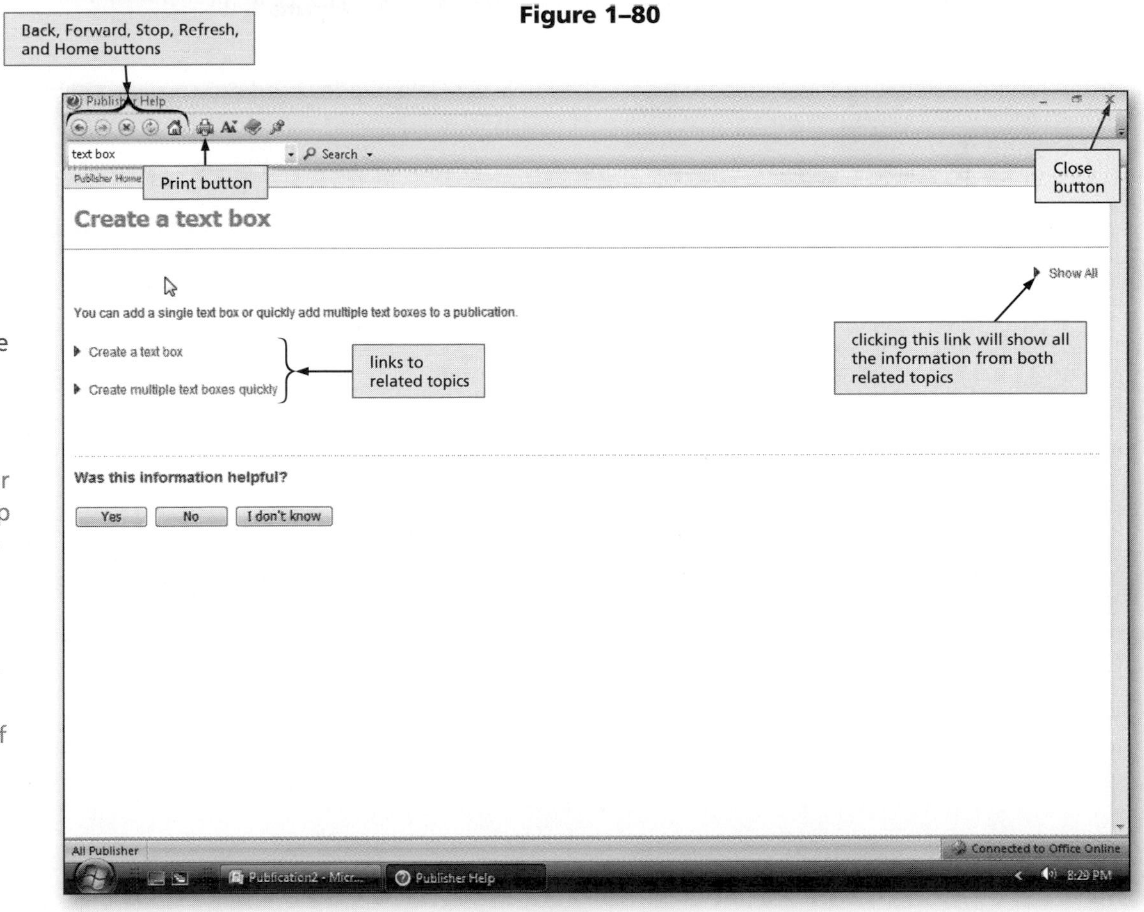

Back, Forward, Stop, Refresh, and Home buttons

Print button

Publisher Home

Close button

Create a text box

Show All

You can add a single text box or quickly add multiple text boxes to a publication.

▶ Create a text box

▶ Create multiple text boxes quickly

links to related topics

clicking this link will show all the information from both related topics

Was this information helpful?

Yes   No   I don't know

All Publisher

Connected to Office Online

Publication2 - Micr...   Publisher Help   8:29 PM

Figure 1–81

4

- Click the Create a text box link to display detailed instructions regarding creating text boxes (Figure 1–82).

Experiment

- In the upper-left portion of the Publisher Help window, click the Back button and choose another topic related to text boxes, such as Align text within a text box, or Fit text within a text box. Feel free to scroll through the list of topics and click and read any topics of interest to you.

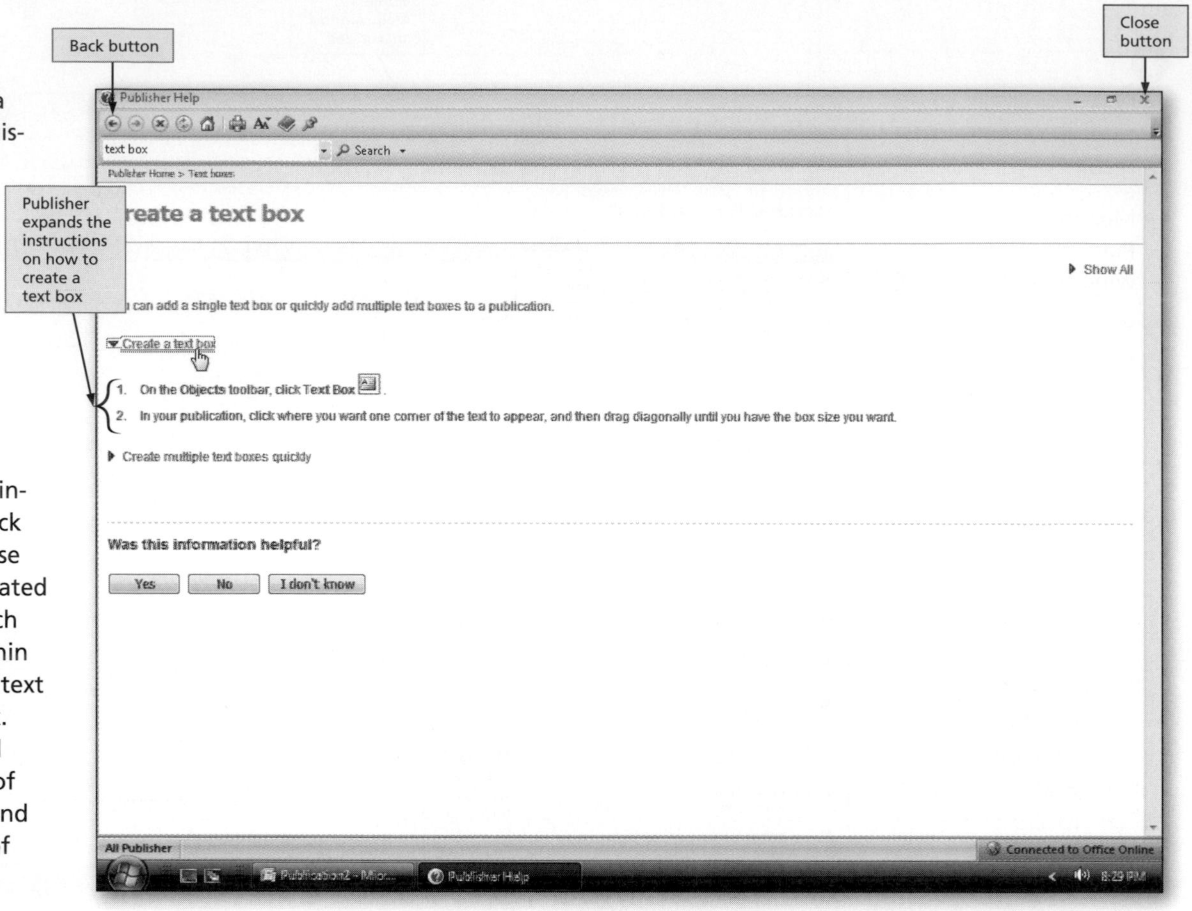

Back button

Close button

Publisher expands the instructions on how to create a text box

Publisher Help

text box ▾ 🔎 Search ▾

Publisher Home > Text boxes

reate a text box

▶ Show All

u can add a single text box or quickly add multiple text boxes to a publication.

▼ Create a text box

1. On the Objects toolbar, click Text Box ⌷.

2. In your publication, click where you want one corner of the text to appear, and then drag diagonally until you have the box size you want.

▶ Create multiple text boxes quickly

Was this information helpful?

Yes   No   I don't know

All Publisher

Connected to Office Online

Publication2 - Micr...   Publisher Help   8:29 PM

Figure 1–82

5

- Click the Close button on the Publisher Help window title bar to close the Publisher Help window and redisplay the Publisher window.

Other Ways

1. On Help menu, click Microsoft Office Publisher Help

To Quit Publisher

The following steps quit Publisher.

1 Click the Close button on the right side of the title bar to quit Publisher.

2 If necessary, click the No button in the Microsoft Office Publisher dialog box so that any changes you have made are not saved.

Chapter Summary

In this chapter you have learned how to choose a publication template, set font and color schemes, enter text in a publication, delete objects in a publication, replace a graphic, print a publication, and convert a print publication to a Web publication. The items listed below include all the new Publisher skills you have learned in this chapter.

1. Start Publisher (PUB 5)
2. Select a Template (PUB 7)
3. Set Publication Options (PUB 9)
4. Close the Task Pane (PUB 17)
5. Enter Text (PUB 19)
6. Zoom and Enter Text (PUB 21)
7. Display Formatting Marks (PUB 24)
8. Wordwrap Text as You Type (PUB 25)
9. Enter Bulleted Items (PUB 26)
10. Enter Tear-off Text (PUB 27)
11 Delete an Object (PUB 28)
12. Check Spelling as You Type (PUB 30)
13. Save a Publication (PUB 31)
14. Replace a Graphic Using the Clip Art Task Pane (PUB 34)
15. Change Publication Properties (PUB 38)
16. Save an Existing Publication with the Same File Name (PUB 40)
17. Print a Publication (PUB 40)
18. Quit Publisher (PUB 41)
19. Open a Publication from Publisher (PUB 42)
20. Delete the Tear-offs (PUB 44)
21. Insert a Text Box in an Existing Publication (PUB 46)
22. Format Text (PUB 47)
23. Insert a Hyperlink (PUB 49)
24. Run the Design Checker (PUB 51)
25. Save a Publication with a New File Name (PUB 52)
26. Convert a Print Publication to a Web Publication (PUB 53)
27. Publish to the Web (PUB 55)
28. Preview the Web Publication in a Browser (PUB 57)
29. Close the Entire Publication (PUB 57)
30. Search for Publisher Help (PUB 58)

Learn It Online

Test your knowledge of chapter content and key terms.

Instructions: To complete the Learn It Online exercises, start your browser, click the Address bar, and then enter the Web address scsite.com/pub2007/learn. When the Office 2007 Learn It Online page is displayed, click the link for the exercise you want to complete and then read the instructions.

Chapter Reinforcement TF, MC, and SA
A series of true/false, multiple choice, and short answer questions that test your knowledge of the chapter content.

Flash Cards
An interactive learning environment where you identify chapter key terms associated with displayed definitions.

Practice Test
A series of multiple choice questions that test your knowledge of chapter content and key terms.

Who Wants To Be a Computer Genius?
An interactive game that challenges your knowledge of chapter content in the style of a television quiz show.

Wheel of Terms
An interactive game that challenges your knowledge of chapter key terms in the style of the television show *Wheel of Fortune*.

Crossword Puzzle Challenge
A crossword puzzle that challenges your knowledge of key terms presented in the chapter.

Apply Your Knowledge

Reinforce the skills and apply the concepts you learned in this chapter.

Modifying Text and Formatting a Publication
Instructions: Start Publisher. Open the publication, Apply 1-1 University Bookstore Flyer, from the Data Files for Students. See the inside back cover of this book for instructions on downloading the Data Files for Students, or contact your instructor for more information about accessing the required files.

The publication you open is a flyer in which you modify the color and font schemes, replace text, delete objects, and convert the publication from print to the Web so that it looks like Figure 1–83.

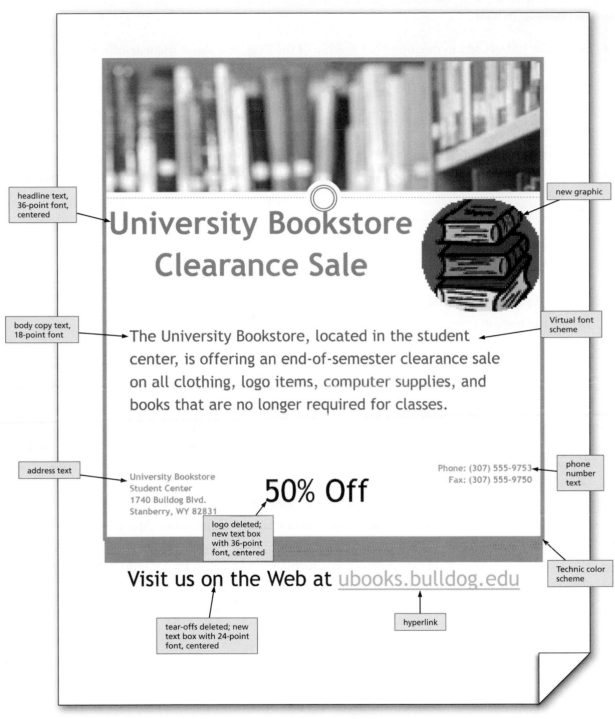

Figure 1–83

Perform the following tasks:

1. Change the color scheme to Technic.

2. Change the font scheme to Virtual.

3. Select the headline text and center it.

4. Change the font size of the headline to 36.

5. Select the body copy text and replace it with the text shown in Figure 1–83. Change the font size of the body copy to 18 point.

Continued >

Apply Your Knowledge *continued*

6. Select the address text in the lower-left portion of the flyer, just above the tear-offs. Replace the text with:

   University Bookstore

   Student Center

   1740 Bulldog Blvd.

   Stanberry, WY 82831

7. Select the text in the phone number text box in the lower-right portion of the flyer. Replace the text with:

   Phone: (307) 555-9753

   Fax: (307) 555-9750

8. Delete the logo centered above the tear-offs.

9. Insert a text box in the area vacated by the logo. Set the font size to 36 point. Set the alignment to center. Type 50% Off in the text box.

10. Delete the tear-offs.

11. Insert a text box in the area vacated by the tear-offs. Set the font size to 24 point. Set the alignment to center. Type Visit us on the Web at ubooks.bulldog.edu in the text box.

12. Select the Web address and then click the Insert Hyperlink button. Type ubooks.bulldog.edu in the Address box and then click OK in the Insert Hyperlink dialog box.

13. Double-click the book graphic to display the Clip Art task pane. Type book to replace any text in the Search for box. Click the Results should be box arrow and ensure that Movies is the only choice that displays a check mark. Click the Go button. Select a graphic similar to the one shown in Figure 1–83 on the previous page.

14. Change the publication properties, as specified by your instructor.

15. Click Save As on the File menu. Save the publication using the file name, Apply 1-1 University Bookstore Web Flyer Formatted.

16. Click Convert to Web Publication on the File menu. Choose No in response to each step in the conversion process.

17. Click Publish to the Web. When asked for a file name, type Apply 1-1 University Bookstore Web Flyer Index to replace the default text.

18. Preview the Web publication using the Web Preview button.

19. Submit the revised publications, as specified by your instructor.

Extend Your Knowledge

Extend the skills you learned in this chapter and experiment with new skills. You may need to use Help to complete the assignment.

Modifying Text and Graphics Formats

Instructions: Start Publisher. Open the publication, Extend 1-1 Strawberry Jam Flyer, from the Data Files for Students. See the inside back cover of this book for instructions on downloading the Data Files for Students, or contact your instructor for more information about accessing the required files.

You will enhance the look of the flyer shown in Figure 1–84.

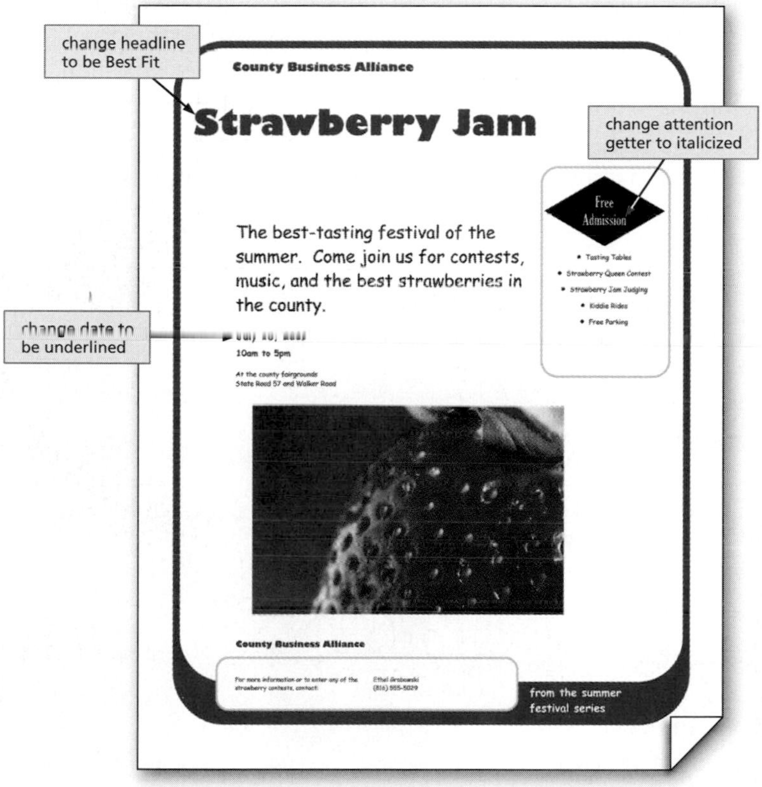

Figure 1–84

Perform the following tasks:

1.   Use Help to learn about copyfitting text, and the use of bold, underline, and italic formatting.

2.   Select inside the headline text box. Click Format on the menu bar, point to AutoFit Text, and then click Best Fit.

3.   Change several other text boxes to Best Fit.

4.   Select the words, Free Admission, in the attention getter and then click the Italic button on the Formatting toolbar.

5.   Select the words, best-tasting, in the body copy and then click the Bold button on the Formatting toolbar.

6.   Select the date and then click the Underline button on the Formatting toolbar.

7.   Change the publication properties, as specified by your instructor. Save the revised publication and then submit it in the format specified by your instructor.

Make It Right

Analyze a publication and correct all errors and/or improve the design.

Correcting Replacement Text and Spelling Errors

Instructions: Start Publisher. Open the publication, Make It Right 1-1 Violin Recital Flyer, from the Data Files for Students. See the inside back cover of this book for instructions on downloading the Data Files for Students, or contact your instructor for more information about accessing the required files.

The publication is a flyer that contains text boxes that have yet to be replaced and spelling errors, as shown in Figure 1–85. You are to replace the placeholder text in the Business Name text box by selecting it and then typing the new text, Senior Music Majors. Then, when Publisher displays the red wavy underlines, you are to correct each spelling error by right-clicking the flagged text and then clicking the appropriate correction on the shortcut menu. If your screen does not display the wavy underlines, click Tools on the menu bar and then point to Spelling to display the spelling submenu. Click Spelling Options. In the Spelling Options dialog box, click to remove the check mark in the Hide spelling errors check box.

Change the publication properties, as specified by your instructor. Save the revised publication and then submit it in the format specified by your instructor.

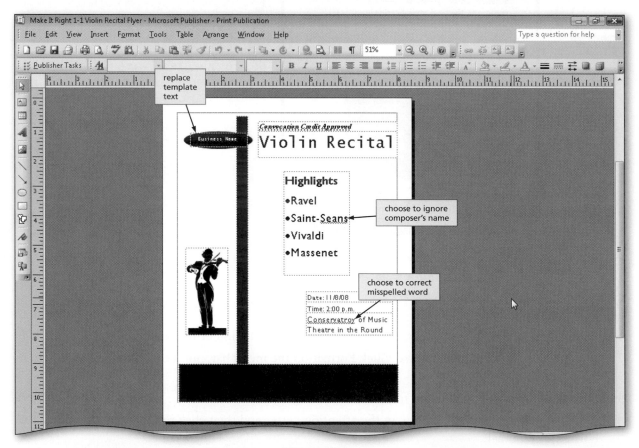

Figure 1–85

In the Lab

Design and/or create a publication using the guidelines, concepts, and skills presented in this chapter. Labs are listed in order of increasing difficulty.

Lab 1: Creating a Flyer with a Picture

Problem: You work part-time for the Alumni Association at the local college. Your supervisor has asked you to prepare a flyer that advertises a travel package for away football games. You prepare the flyer shown in Figure 1–86, using the instructions on the next page.

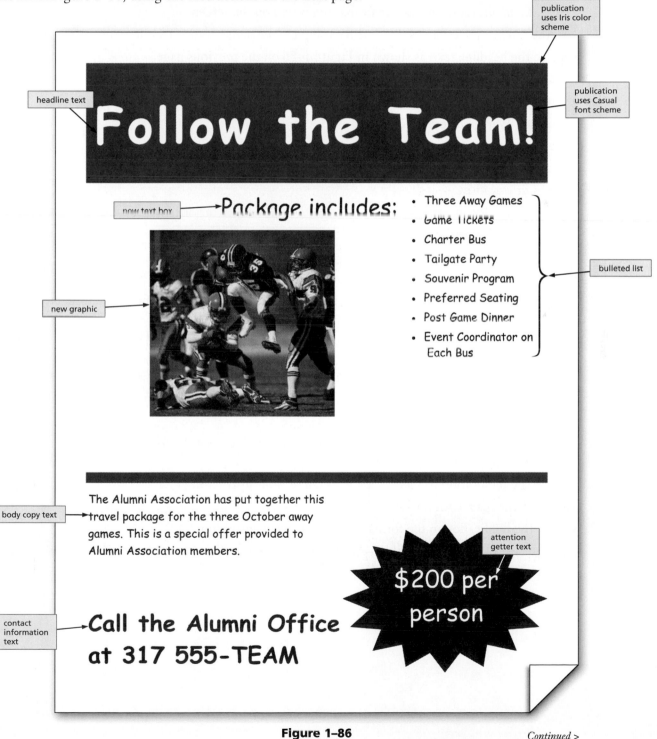

Figure 1–86

Continued >

In the Lab *continued*

Instructions: Perform the following tasks:

1. Start Publisher.
2. Choose Flyers in the catalog and then scroll down to Announcements flyers.
3. Choose the Lost Pet/Item flyer template.
4. Choose the Iris color scheme.
5. Choose the Casual font scheme.
6. Do not include tear-offs.
7. Create the publication and display formatting marks on the screen.
8. Save the publication on a USB flash drive using the file name, Lab 1-1 Follow the Team Flyer.
9. Replace the headline text, as shown in Figure 1–86 on the previous page.
10. Change the graphic to a football photograph from your system's clip art.
11. Change the template text in the bulleted list to include:
    - Three Away Games
    - Game Tickets
    - Charter Bus
    - Tailgate Party
    - Souvenir Program
    - Preferred Seating
    - Post Game Dinner
    - Event Coordinator on Each Bus
12. Zoom as necessary to edit the body copy text under the blue line. Select the text and then type: The Alumni Association has put together this travel package for the three October away games. This is a special offer provided to Alumni Association members.
13. Change the template text in the contact information text box to match Figure 1–86.
14. Change the template text in the attention getter to $200 per person.
15. Zoom to Whole Page view.
16. Insert a new text box above the graphic, near the bulleted list. Set the font size to 26 point. Type Package includes: as the text.
17. Change the publication properties, as specified by your instructor.
18. Save the flyer again with the same file name.
19. Submit the publication in the format specified by your instructor.

In the Lab

Lab 2: Creating an Award Certificate

Problem: Your boss is in charge of the Marion County IT Fair, a showcase event that displays student IT projects. She has asked you to create an award certificate for each of the participants. You decide to explore some of Publisher's other single-page templates besides flyers. You prepare the certificate shown in Figure 1–87.

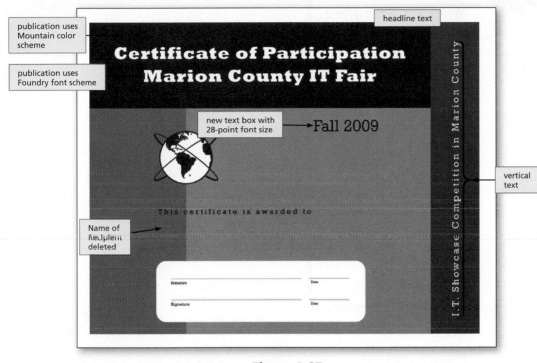

Figure 1–87

Instructions: Perform the following tasks:

1. Start Publisher. When the catalog is displayed, click the Award Certificates button in the Publication Types area.

2. In the catalog, choose the Appreciate 8 template.

3. Choose the Mountain Color scheme.

4. Choose the Foundry font scheme.

5. Click the headline text and type `Certificate of Participation`. Press the ENTER key and then type `Marion County IT Fair`.

6. Change the vertical text to read, `I.T. Showcase Competition in Marion County`.

7. Select the text, Name of Recipient text box and delete it.

8. Insert a text box below the headline. Set the font size to 28 point. Enter the text, `Fall 2009` in the new text box as shown in Figure 1–87.

9. Correct any spelling errors.

10. Run the Design Checker and correct any problems that it finds.

11. Change the document properties as specified by your instructor.

12. Save the flyer with the name, Lab 1-2 Participation Certificate.

13. Submit the publication, shown in Figure 1–87, in the format specified by your instructor.

In the Lab

Lab 3: Creating a Newspaper Advertisement

Problem: Your sorority has asked you to prepare an advertisement that promotes the spring break ski trip. The advertisement will run in the school newspaper, which prints in black and white. You prepare the advertisement as shown in Figure 1–88.

Figure 1–88

Instructions: Start Publisher. Select Advertisements from the list of Publication Types, and then choose The Works template. Accept the default customization options. Replace all the text boxes, using the text shown in Figure 1–88. Delete the logo. Use the Clip Art task pane to search for a clip art related to skiing. Chose a black-and-white graphic. Change the publication properties, as specified by your instructor. Save the publication on a USB flash drive, using the file name, Lab 1-3 Spring Break Trip Advertisement. Submit the publication, shown in Figure 1–88, in the format specified by your instructor.

Cases and Places

Apply your creative thinking and problem-solving skills to design and implement a solution.

● Easier   ●● More Difficult

● 1: Design and Create a Play Annoucement Flyer

You are in charge of creating a flyer for a local dramatic production, presented by The Oak Leaf Troupe. Use the Play Flyer template in the Announcement group, with a Burgundy color scheme and the Breve font scheme. Do not include any tear-offs. Use the techniques in Chapter 1 to edit the text boxes. The name of the play is *The Taming of the Shrew*. The author is William Shakespeare. The dates are November 9, 10, and 11. The time is 7:30 p.m. at the Performing Arts Center. The phone number at the center is 555-1217. The ticket price is $11.50. The production is sponsored by the Knights of Columbus, the Junior Business Association, and the Fine Arts Council. Choose an appropriate graphic, using the Clip Art task pane, with the search term, drama. You may delete the sponsor logos or edit them as desired. Use the concepts and techniques presented in this chapter to create and format this flyer. Be sure to check spelling and then run the Design Checker.

● 2: Design and Create an Advertising Flyer with Tear-Offs

You decide to make some spare money typing term papers and research reports for other students. Prepare a flyer with tear-offs advertising your services. Using the Perforation flyer template in the Special Offer group, choose the Ocean color scheme, Foundry font scheme, and Contact Information tear-offs. The headline should read: Professional Desktop Publishing. The tag line should read: Fast Accurate Solutions! The body copy should read as follows: Need something typed? I offer a wide variety of professional desktop publishing services using Microsoft Office Publisher 2007. Overnight service is available on most projects. Samples and references upon request. Press the ENTER key after the first sentence and before the last sentence to create three paragraphs. The bulleted list should include the following items: Letters, Memos, Reports, Term Papers, Flyers, and Brochures. The tear-offs should read: Contact Sheila at 555-8059 or sheila@college.net. The location description text box should read: Services are located close to campus. Select the graphic within its frame and then double-click it to access the Clip Art task pane. Use the search term, printer, to locate a colorful printer that matches the color scheme. Delete the Business Name text box, the organization logo, the Date of Sale text box, and the Time of Sale text box.

●●3: Design and Create a Flyer for the Sale of a Business

After 30 years, your Uncle J.R. has decided to sell his bait shop. He wants you to help him create a sales flyer. The shop is in a choice location on Smithville Lake and has an established customer base. He wants to sell the store and all its contents, including the equipment, counter, tanks, and refrigeration unit. The 900-square-foot shop recently was appraised at $200,000, and your uncle is willing to sell for cash or on contract. Use the concepts and techniques presented in this chapter to create and format a sales flyer using a template. Include a headline, descriptive body copy, a tear-off, an appropriate photograph or clip art image, and bulleted list. Be sure to check spelling in the flyer. Then, delete the tear-offs and create a text box with your uncle's e-mail address. Run the Design Checker, convert the flyer to a Web publication, and then use the Publish to the Web command to generate the Web page.

Cases and Places *continued*

••4: Design and Create a Flyer for Your Community

Make It Personal

Many communities offer free Web page hosting for religious organizations. Using a flyer template, create a Web page for a local house of worship. Include the name, address, telephone, worship and education hours, as well as the name of a contact person. If possible, include a photo or line drawing of the building. If specific colors or fonts are associated with the organization, try to find a close match among the Publisher schemes. Use the Design Checker, the Convert to Web publication command, and the Publish to the Web command to prepare your publication.

••5: Redesign and Enhance a Poorly Designed Flyer

Working Together

Public locations, such as stores, schools, and libraries, have bulletin boards or windows for people to post flyers. Often, these bulletin boards or windows have so many flyers that some go unnoticed. Locate a posted flyer on a bulletin board or window that you think might be overlooked. Copy the text from the flyer and distribute it to each team member. Each member then independently should use this text, together with the techniques presented in this chapter, to create a flyer that would be more likely to catch the attention of passersby. Be sure to check the spelling. As a group, critique each flyer and have team members redesign their flyer based on the group's recommendations. Hand in each team member's original and final flyers.

2 | Designing a Newsletter

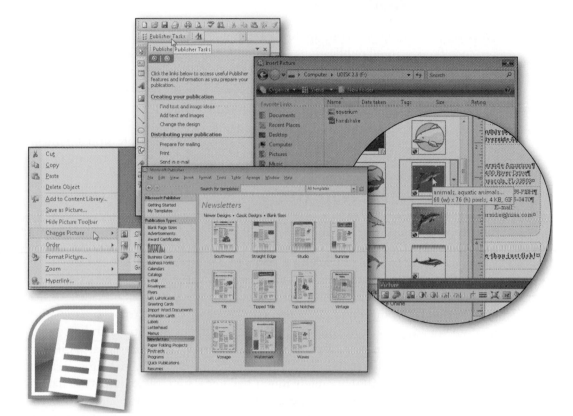

Objectives

You will have mastered the material in this chapter when you can:

- Describe the advantages of using a newsletter medium and identify the steps in its design process

- Edit a newsletter template

- Insert, delete, and navigate pages in a newsletter

- Edit a masthead

- Import text files and graphics, and continue stories across pages

- Use color scheme colors

- Insert page numbers in headers and footers

- Resize objects

- Edit captions, sidebars, and pull quotes

- Employ correct cut, copy, and paste techniques

- Check a newsletter for spelling and design errors

- Print a two-sided page

2 | Designing a Newsletter

Introduction

Desktop publishing is becoming the most popular way for businesses of all sizes to produce their printed publications. The desktop aspects of design and production make it easy and inexpensive to produce high-quality publications in a short time. **Desktop Publishing** implies doing everything from a desk, including the planning, designing, writing, and layout, as well as printing, collating, and distributing. With a personal computer and a software program, such as Publisher, you can create a professional publication from your computer without the cost and time of sending it to a professional publisher.

Project — Newsletter

Newsletters are a popular way for offices, businesses, schools, and other organizations to distribute information to their clientele. A **newsletter** usually is a double-sided multipage publication with newspaper features, such as columns and a masthead, and the added eye appeal of sidebars, pictures, and other graphics.

Newsletters have several advantages over other publication media. Typically, they are cheaper to produce than brochures. Brochures, designed to be in circulation longer as a type of advertising, usually are published in greater quantities and on more expensive paper than newsletters and are, therefore, more costly. Newsletters also differ from brochures in that newsletters commonly have a shorter shelf life, making newsletters a perfect forum for information that rapidly might become dated. Newsletters are narrower and more focused in scope than newspapers; their eye appeal is more distinctive. Many companies commonly distribute newsletters to interested audiences; however, newsletters also are becoming an integral part of many marketing plans to wider audiences because they offer a legitimate medium by which to communicate services, successes, and issues.

The project in this chapter uses a Publisher newsletter template to produce Communiquarium, the newsletter shown in Figures 2–1a and 2–1b. This monthly publication informs the community about events sponsored by the Riverside Aquarium. The institution's two-page newsletter contains a masthead, headings, articles, sidebars, pull quotes, and graphics.

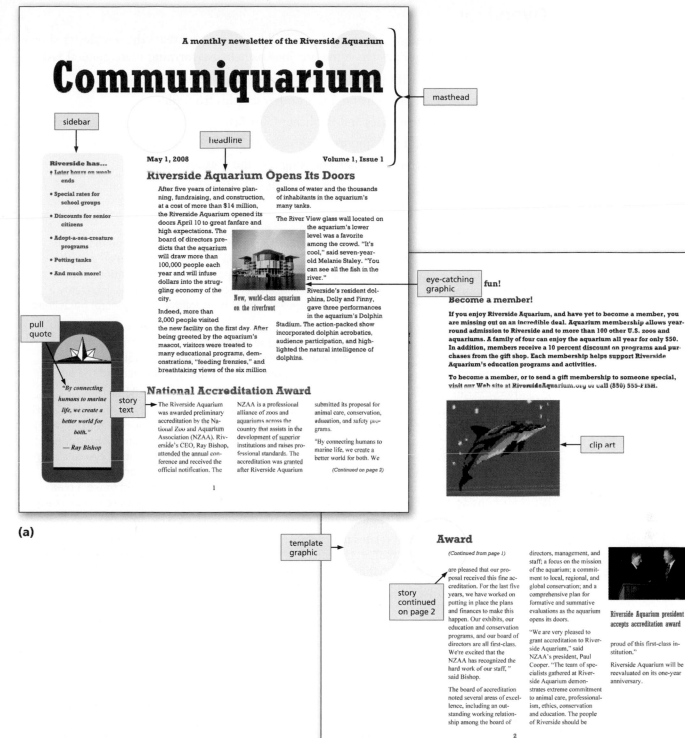

Figure 2–1

Overview

As you read through this chapter, you will learn how to create the newsletter shown in Figure 2–1a and Figure 2–1b on the previous page by performing these general tasks:

- Select a template with font and color schemes, and specify the page layout.
- Type articles from scratch and import other articles from files.
- Import graphics from files and Publisher Clip Art.
- Create sidebars and pull quotes.
- Proof the newsletter, with spell checking and the Design Checker.
- Save the newsletter and print it using duplex printing.

Plan Ahead

General Project Guidelines

When creating a Publisher newsletter, the actions you perform and decisions you make will affect the appearance and characteristics of the finished publication. Designing an effective newsletter involves a great deal of planning. A good newsletter, or any publication, must deliver a message in the clearest, most attractive, and effective way possible. As you create a newsletter, such as the project shown in Figure 2–1, you should follow these general guidelines:

1. **Decide on the purpose and audience.** Spend time brainstorming ideas for the newsletter. Think about why you want to create one. Decide on one purpose and adjust your plans to match that purpose. Decide if the audience is composed of local, interested clientele, patrons, employees, prospective customers, or family members. Keep in mind the age of your readers and their backgrounds, including both present and future readers.

2. **Plan for the layout and printing.** Decide how many pages your newsletter should be and how often you are going to produce it. Base your decisions on regular content that will continue into future newsletters. Choose the paper size and how columns, a masthead, and graphics will affect your layout. A consistent look and feel with simple, eye-catching graphics normally is the best choice for the design set. Plan to include one other graphic with each story. Usually mass-produced, collated, and stapled, you should make a plan for printing and decide if you are going to publish your newsletter in-house or externally. Choose a paper that is going to last until the next newsletter.

3. **Research the topic as it relates to your purpose and gather data.** Gather credible, relevant information in the form of articles, pictures, dates, figures, tables, and discussion threads. Plan far enough ahead so that you have time to take pictures or gather graphics for each story — even if you do not end up using them. Stay organized. Keep folders of information. Store pictures and stories together.

4. **Create the first draft.** Create a layout and masthead and receive approval if necessary. Follow any guidelines or required publication style. Reference all sources of information. Import stories and graphics as necessary. Determine the best layout for eye appeal and reliable dissemination of content.

5. **Proofread and revise the newsletter.** If possible, proofread the paper with a fresh set of eyes, that is, at least one to two days after completing the first draft. Proofreading involves reading the newsletter with the intent of identifying errors (spelling, grammar, continued notices, etc.) and looking for ways to improve it (purposeful graphics, catchy headlines, sidebars, pull quotes, etc.). Try reading the newsletter out loud, which helps to identify unclear or awkward wording. Ask someone else to proofread the paper and give you suggestions for improvements. Revise as necessary and then use the spelling and design checking features of the software.

When necessary, more specific details concerning the above guidelines are presented at appropriate points in the chapter. The chapter also will identify the actions performed and decisions made regarding these guidelines during the creation of the newsletter shown in Figure 2–1a and Figure 2–1b.

Benefits and Advantages of Newsletters

Table 2–1 lists some benefits and advantages of using the newsletter medium.

Table 2–1 Benefits and Advantages of Using a Newsletter Medium

Purpose	Benefits and Advantages
Exposure	An easily distributed publication — office mail, bulk mail, electronically A pass-along publication for other interested parties A coffee table reading item in reception areas
Education	An opportunity to inform in a nonrestrictive environment A directed education forum for clientele An increased, focused feedback — unavailable in most advertising
Contacts	A form of legitimized contact A source of free information to build credibility An easier way to expand a contact database than other marketing tools
Communication	An effective medium to highlight the inner workings of a company A way to create a discussion forum A method to disseminate more information than a brochure
Cost	An easily designed medium using desktop publishing software An inexpensive method of mass production A reusable design

Using a Newsletter Template

The Publisher newsletter templates include a four-page layout with stories, graphics, sidebars, and other elements typical of newsletters using a rich collection of intuitive design, layout, typography, and graphics tools. Because Publisher takes care of many of the design issues, using a template to begin a newsletter gives you the advantage of proven layouts with fewer chances of publication errors.

Plan Ahead

Decide on the purpose and audience.
As you consult with all parties involved in the decision to create a newsletter, make sure you have a clear purpose. Remember that newsletters both communicate and educate. Ask yourself why you want to create a newsletter in the first place.

- **Decide on the audience.** As you decide on your audience, ask yourself these questions:
  - Who will be reading the articles?
  - What are the demographics of the population? That is, what are the characteristics such as gender, age, educational background, and heritage?
  - Why do you want those people to read your newsletter?
- **Finally choose your general topic.** As you make final decisions on the topic, ask yourself these questions:
  - Will the newsletter be about the company or only about one aspect of the company?
  - Will the newsletter cover a narrow topic or be more of a general information newsletter?
  - Use the phrase, "I want to tell *<audience>* about *<topic>* because *<purpose>*."

After starting Publisher, the following pages choose a template and select font and color schemes.

To Start Publisher

If you are using a computer to step through the project in this chapter, and you want your screens to match the figures in this book, you should change your computer's resolution to 1024 × 768. For information about how to change a computer's resolution, read Appendix D.

The following steps, which assume Windows is running, start Publisher based on a typical installation. You may need to ask your instructor how to start Publisher for your computer.

Note: If you are using Windows XP, see Appendix F for alternate To Start Publisher steps.

1 Click the Start button on the Windows Vista taskbar to display the Start menu, and then click All Programs at the bottom of the left pane on the Start menu to display the All Programs list.

2 Click Microsoft Office in the All Programs list to display the Microsoft Office list, and then click Microsoft Office Publisher 2007 to start Publisher and display the Getting Started with Microsoft Office Publisher 2007 catalog.

3 If the Publisher window is not maximized, click the Maximize button next to the Close button on its title bar to maximize the window.

Newsletter Design Choices

Many design planning features are built into Publisher, including 65 different newsletter templates from which you may choose, each with its own set of design, color, font, and layout schemes.

Plan Ahead

| **Plan for the layout and printing.** |
| Choosing a layout and printing options before you even write the articles is a daunting but extremely important task. The kind of printing process and paper you will be using will affect the cost and, therefore, the length of the newsletter. Based on what you can afford to produce and distribute, the layout may need more or fewer articles, graphics, columns, and sidebars. Decide on a consistent theme with repeated elements on each page. Make conscious decisions about the kind of alignment you plan to use with the masthead, graphics, and text. Decide what kinds of features in the newsletter should be close to other features. |

To Choose a Newsletter Template and Change Options

The following steps choose a newsletter template and make design choices. The Watermark template goes along with the theme of the aquarium, as does the Tropics color scheme.

1

• Click the Newsletters button in the list of publication types to display the catalog of newsletter templates.

• Scroll to display the Watermark preview and then click the Watermark preview to select it (Figure 2–2).

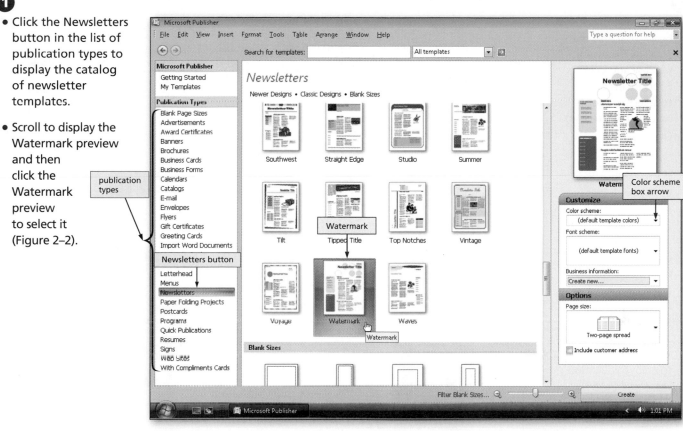

Figure 2–2

2

• In the Customize area, click the Color scheme box arrow to display the list of color schemes.

Experiment

• Scroll in the list of color schemes and click various schemes to see the preview change in the right portion of the window.

• Click Tropics in the list to change the color scheme for the publication (Figure 2–3).

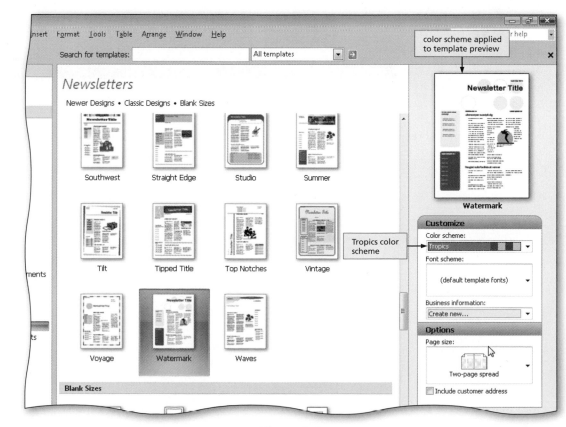

Figure 2–3

3

- Click the Font scheme box arrow and then scroll as necessary to view and click Foundry in the list to select the font scheme (Figure 2–4).

Q&A

How do the newsletter templates differ?

Each newsletter template produces four pages of stories, graphics, and other objects in the same way. The difference is the location and style of the shapes and graphics, as well as the specific kind of decorations unique to each publication set. A **publication set** is a predefined group of shapes, designed in patterns to create a template style. A publication set is constant across publication types; for example, the Watermark newsletter template has the same shapes and style of objects as does the Watermark brochure template. A publication set helps in branding a company across publication types.

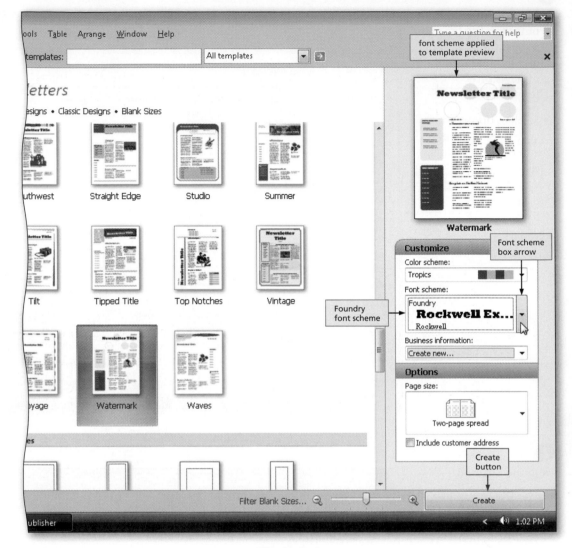

Figure 2–4

4

• Click the Create button in the lower-right corner of the window to create the publication based on the template settings (Figure 2–5).

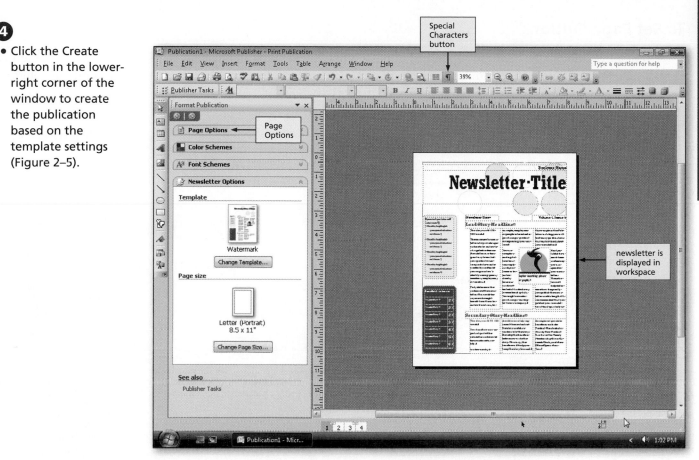

Figure 2–5

To Display Formatting Marks

As discussed in Chapter 1, it is helpful to display formatting marks, which indicate where in the publication you pressed the ENTER key, SPACEBAR, and other keys. The following step displays formatting marks.

1 If the Special Characters button on the Standard toolbar is not selected already, click it to display formatting marks on the screen.

To Set Page Options

The next steps set one final page option. Publisher newsletters typically display story text in 1, 2, or 3 columns or in a mixed format. The aquarium newsletter will use the mixed format. The choice to mix the number of columns complements the variety of articles that will be presented each month in the newsletter.

1

- Click Page Options in the Format Publication task pane to display the various options.

Experiment

- Click 1, 2, and 3 in the Columns area to view the effect on the newsletter template.

- Click Mixed in the Columns area to choose a mixed number of columns for the various stories in the newsletter (Figure 2–6).

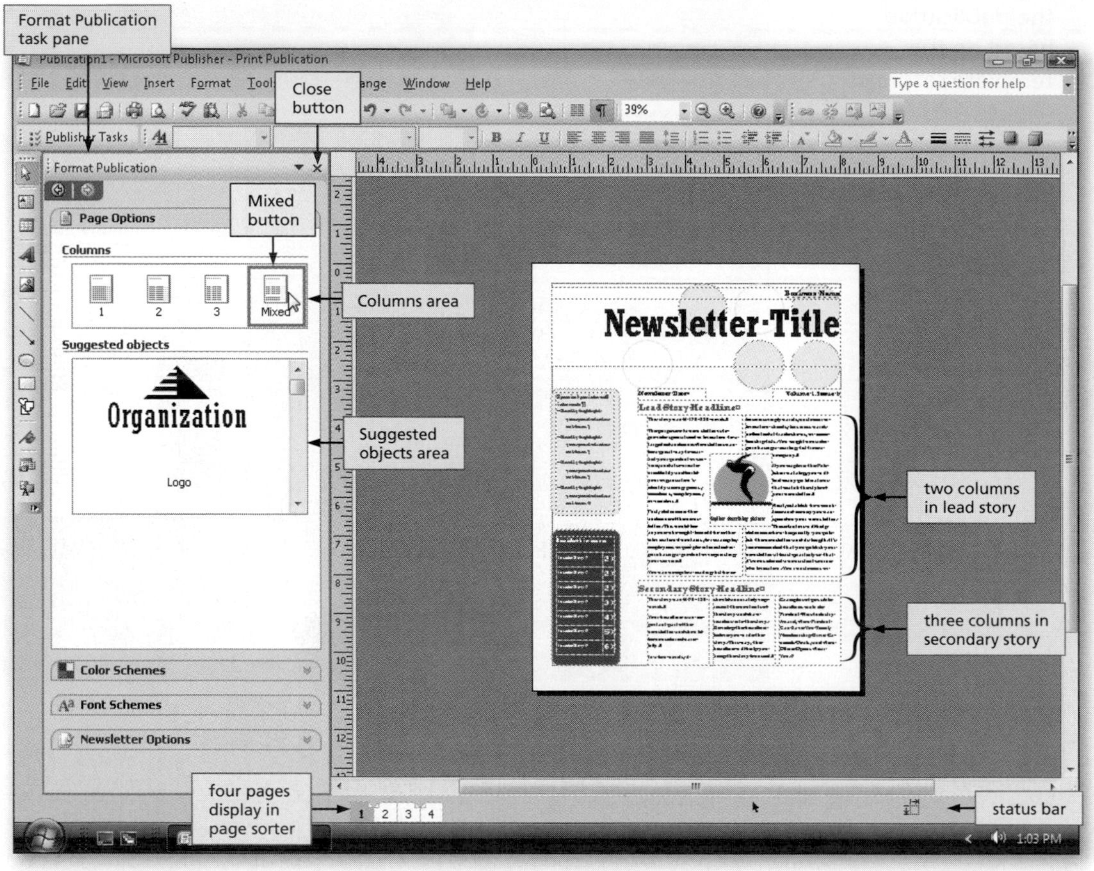

Q&A

What is the Suggested objects area?

The Suggested objects area is a list of graphical objects, including logos, table of contents, sidebars, and pull quotes typically used in newsletters.

Figure 2–6

2

- To close the task pane, click the Close button in the Format Publication task pane.

Editing the Newsletter Template

The purpose of a newsletter is to communicate and educate its readers. Publisher places the lead story in a prominent position on the page and uses a discussion of purpose and audience as the default text.

The following pages discuss how to edit various articles and objects in the newsletter.

Pagination

Each Publisher newsletter template creates four pages of text and graphics. This template is appropriate for some applications, but the aquarium staff wants to print a single-sheet, two-sided newsletter. Page 4 of the newsletter template contains objects typically used on the back page, so you will delete pages 2 and 3 to create a two-page newsletter.

Recall that the page sorter is located on the status bar. Its paged-shaped controls represent each page of the publication and can be used to go to, rearrange, or work with publication pages. You can click the page sorter to move to new pages or right-click it to display a shortcut menu.

To Change and Delete Pages in a Newsletter

The following steps change and delete pages.

1

- Click the Page 2 icon on the page sorter to display page 2 (Figure 2–7).

Q&A How do I know what page is being displayed?

The page sorter displays the selected page or pages in orange.

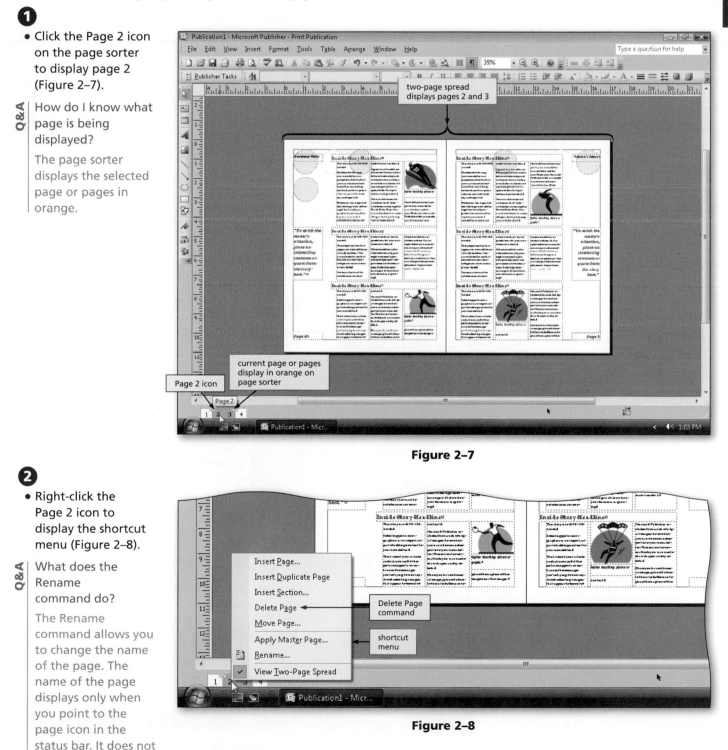

Figure 2–7

2

- Right-click the Page 2 icon to display the shortcut menu (Figure 2–8).

Q&A What does the Rename command do?

The Rename command allows you to change the name of the page. The name of the page displays only when you point to the page icon in the status bar. It does not print or display in the page layout.

Figure 2–8

3

- Click Delete Page to display the Delete Page dialog box.

- If necessary, click the Both pages option button to select it (Figure 2–9).

Q&A

What would happen if I delete only one of the two pages?

If you delete only one of the two pages, your newsletter will have an odd number of pages, which might cause problems when you print or cause a blank page to print at the end of your newsletter.

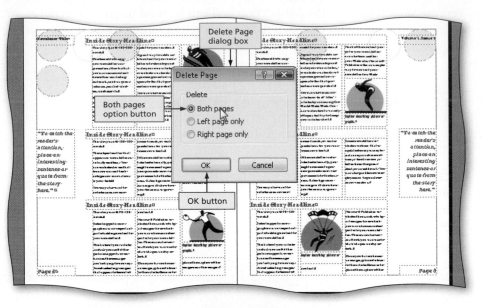

Figure 2–9

4

- Click the OK button in the Delete Page dialog box.

- If a Microsoft Publisher dialog box is displayed to confirm the deletion, click the OK button to delete the pages (Figure 2–10).

Q&A

What if I delete a page by accident?

Simply click the Undo button on the Standard toolbar.

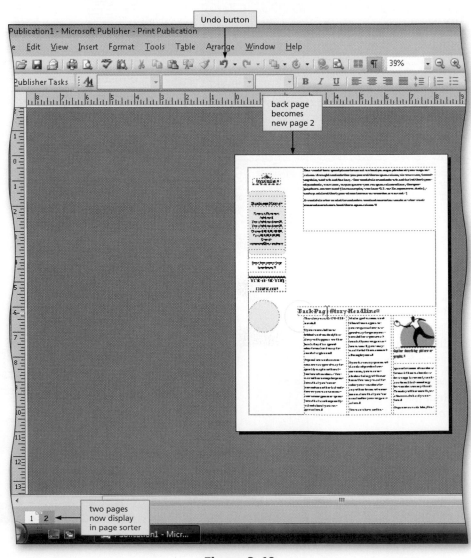

Other Ways

1. To change pages, on Edit menu, click Go to Page

2. To change pages, press CTRL+G

3. To change pages, press F5

4. To delete page, on Edit menu, click Delete Page

Figure 2–10

Editing the Masthead

Most newsletters and brochures contain a masthead similar to those used in newspapers. A **masthead** is a box or section printed in each issue that lists information, such as the name, publisher, location, volume, and date. The Publisher-designed masthead, included in the Watermark newsletter design set, contains several text boxes and color-filled shapes that create an attractive, eye-catching graphic that complements the set. You need to edit the text boxes, however, to convey appropriate messages.

Publisher incorporates four text boxes in the Watermark newsletter masthead (Figure 2–11). The newsletter title is displayed in a text box layered on top of the template graphics. A text box above the title displays the default text, Business Name. Two text boxes display in the lower portion of the masthead for the date and volume/issue.

BTW

Inserting Pages
Inserting pages in a newsletter is just as easy as deleting them. The Page command on the Insert menu provides the option of inserting a left- or right-hand page, as well as choices in the types of objects to display on the page. When you choose to insert or delete when working on the first or last page, Publisher will warn you of pagination problems and will offer you a confirmation button.

Editing Techniques

Recall that Publisher uses text-editing techniques similar to most word processing programs. To insert text, position the insertion point and type the new text. Publisher always inserts the text to the left of the insertion point. The text to the right of the insertion point moves to the right and downward to accommodate the new text.

The BACKSPACE key deletes text to the left of the insertion point. To delete or change more than a few characters, however, you first should select the text. Publisher handles selecting text in a slightly different manner from word processing programs. In Publisher, you select unedited default text, such as placeholder titles and articles in the newsletters, with a single click. To select large amounts of text, click the text and then press CTRL+A, or drag through the text. To select individual words, double-click the word, as you would in word processing.

To Edit the Masthead

The following steps edit text in the masthead.

1

- Click the Page 1 icon on the page sorter to change the display to page 1.

- Click the text, Newsletter Title, to select it.

- Press the F9 key to view the masthead at actual size (Figure 2–11).

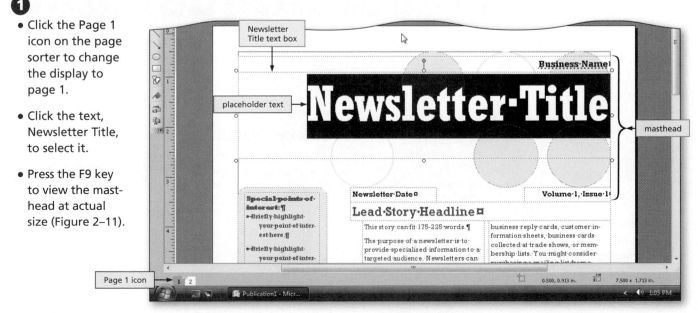

Figure 2–11

2
- Type
Communiquarium
to replace the text
(Figure 2–12).

Q&A Why does my
font look
different?

Publisher
replaces the selected
text using the font
from the design set.
Because fonts some-
times are printer-
dependent, your
font may differ from
the one shown.

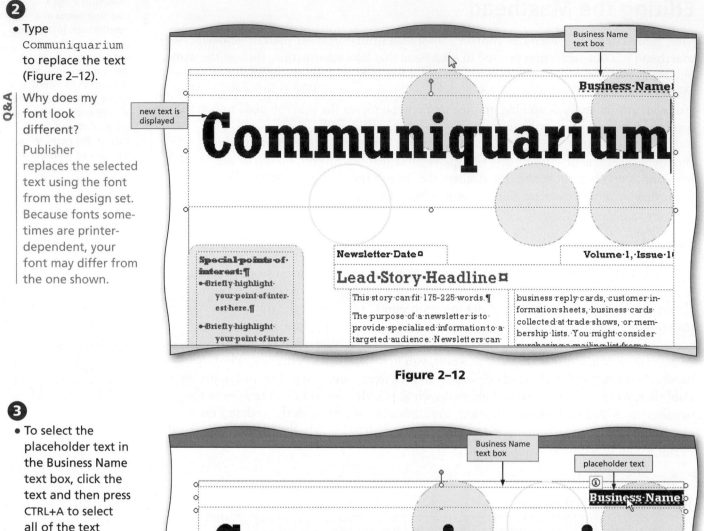

Figure 2–12

3
- To select the
placeholder text in
the Business Name
text box, click the
text and then press
CTRL+A to select
all of the text
(Figure 2–13).

Q&A Why does my
Business Name text
box have different
words?

The Business Name
text sometimes
is taken from the
Publisher installation
process. The name of
your school or busi-
ness may be displayed
in the text box.

Q&A Should I fix the red
wavy line below the
word Communiquarium?

No, you will fix it later in the chapter.

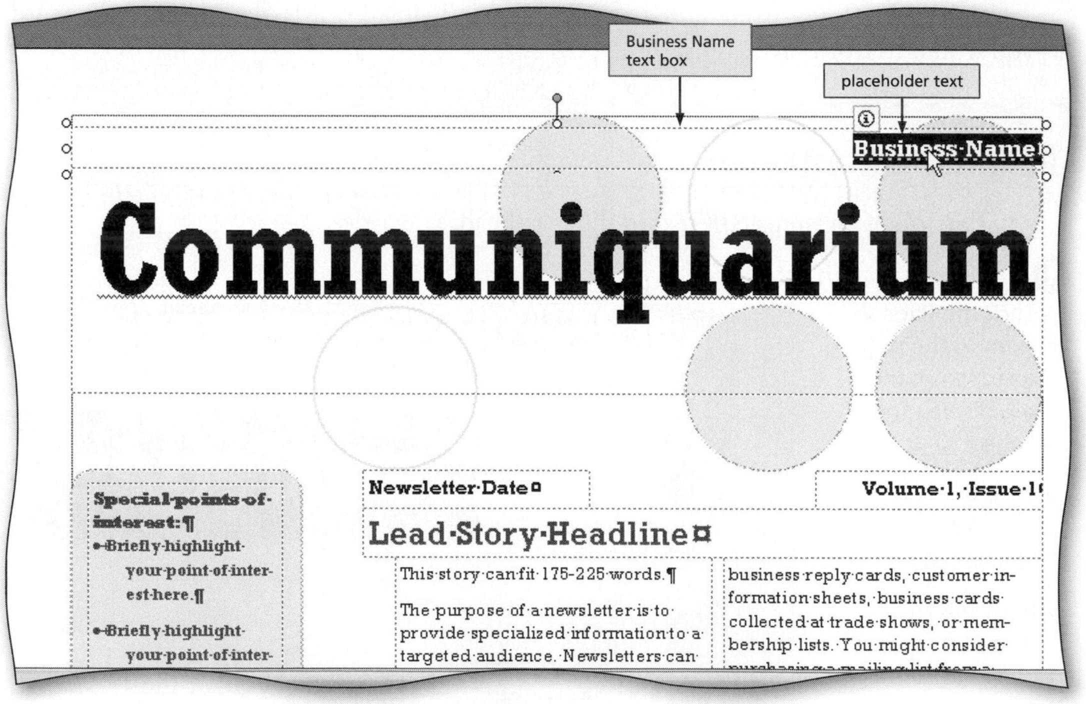

Figure 2–13

4

• Type A monthly newsletter of the Riverside Aquarium to replace the text (Figure 2–14).

Q&A

What do the blue dots mean below the text?

The blue dots are a smart tag notation. Recall that certain template text boxes are designed to hold business information, tag lines, and address data. Each of these special text boxes will display this kind of smart tag notation under the text. The dots will not print.

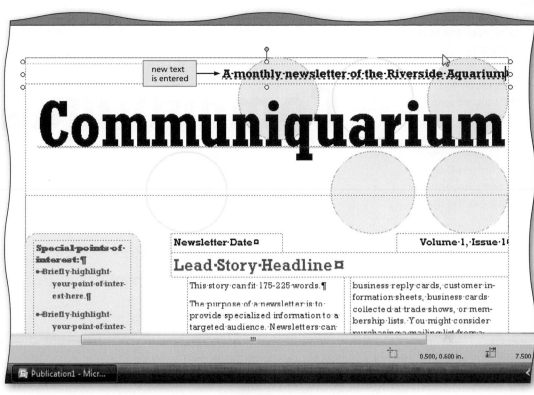

Figure 2–14

 5

• Click the text in the Newsletter Date text box (Figure 2–15).

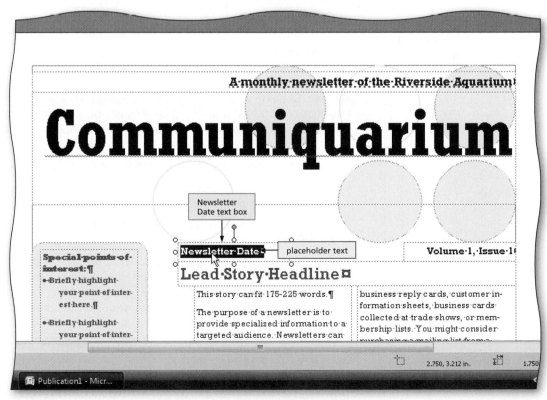

Figure 2–15

6

- **Type** May 1, 2008 to replace the text (Figure 2–16).

Q&A

Should I enter new information in the volume and issue box?

This is the first issue of the aquarium's newsletter. Only subsequent issues would require a change in that box.

Figure 2–16

Newsletter Text

You will import some stories for the newsletter; others you will type yourself.

Plan Ahead

> **Research the topic as it relates to your purpose and gather data.**
>
> - **Researching the topic.** If you have to write a story from scratch, gather your data, do your research, and have an informed reader go over your content. The same principles of audience, purpose, and topic apply to individual stories, just as they did for the newsletter as a whole. Evaluate your sources for authority, currency, and accuracy. Be especially wary of information obtained from the Web. Any person, company, or organization can publish a Web page on the Internet. Ask yourself these questions about the source:
>   - Authority: Does a reputable institution or group support the source? Is the information presented without bias? Are the author's credentials listed and verifiable?
>   - Currency: Is the information up to date? Are dates of sources listed? What is the last date revised or updated?
>   - Accuracy: Is the information free of errors? Is it verifiable? Are the sources clearly identified?
> - **Gather the data.** Identify the sources for your text and graphics. Notify all writers of important dates and allow time for gathering the data. Make a list of each story; include the author's name, the approximate length of the story, the electronic format, and associated graphics. Ask the author for suggestions for headlines. Consult with colleagues about other graphics, features, sidebars, and the masthead.
> - **Acknowledge all sources of information; do not plagiarize.** Not only is plagiarism unethical, but it also is considered an academic crime that can have severe punishments, such as failing a course or being expelled from school.
>
>   When you summarize, paraphrase (rewrite information in your own words), present facts, give statistics, quote exact words, or show a map, chart, or other graphical image, you must acknowledge the source. Information that commonly is known or accessible to the audience constitutes common knowledge and does not need to be acknowledged. If, however, you question whether certain information is common knowledge, you should document it — just to be safe.

Publisher allows users to import text and graphics from many sources, from a variety of different programs, and in many different file formats. Publisher uses the term **importing** to describe inserting text or objects from any other source into the Publisher workspace. The stories for the newsletter are included in the Data Files for Students. See the inside back cover of this book for instructions on downloading the Data Files for Students, or contact your instructor for more information about accessing the required files.

Publisher uses the term, **story**, to mean text that is contained within a single text box or a chain of linked text boxes. Each newsletter template provides **linked text boxes**, or text boxes whose text flows from one to another. In the templates, two or three text boxes may be linked automatically; however, if a story is too long to fit in the linked text boxes, Publisher will offer to link even more text boxes for easy reading.

BTW

Zooming
Recall that the F9 key toggles between the current page view and 100% magnification, or actual size. **Toggle** means the same key will alternate views, or turn a feature on and off. Editing text is easier if you view the text at 100% magnification or even larger. Page editing techniques, such as moving graphics, inserting new objects, and aligning objects, are performed more easily in Whole Page view. Toggling back and forth with the F9 key works well. You also may choose different magnifications and views in the Zoom list on the Standard toolbar.

Replacing Placeholder Text Using an Imported File

Publisher suggests that 175 to 225 words will fit in the space allocated for the lead story. The story displays in a two-column text box format that **connects,** or wraps, the running text from one linked text box to the next.

This edition of Communiquarium has three stories, two of which have been typed previously and stored using Microsoft Word. The stories, stored on the Data Disk that accompanies this text, are ready to be used in the newsletter. The third story you will type yourself. Each story will include a headline, which is a short phrase printed at the top of a story, usually in a bigger font than the story. A headline summarizes the story that follows it.

To Edit a Headline and Import a Text File

The following steps first edit the Lead Story Headline placeholder text and then import a text file to replace the Publisher-supplied default text. The text file is included in the Data Files for Students. See the inside back cover of this book for instructions on downloading the Data Files for Students, or contact your instructor for more information about accessing the required files.

1

- Click the text, Lead Story Headline, to select it.

- If necessary, zoom to 100% by clicking the Zoom In button on the Standard toolbar.

- Type `Riverside Aquarium Opens Its Doors` to replace the text (Figure 2–17).

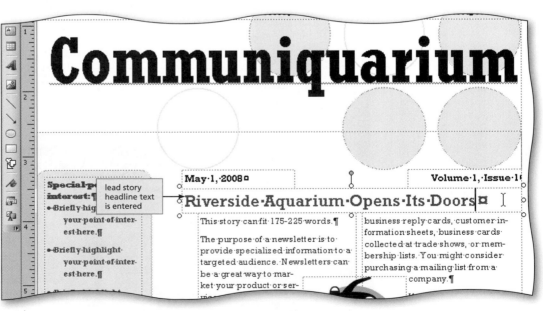

Figure 2–17

2

• Click the story below the headline (Figure 2–18).

Experiment

• Scroll as necessary to read the story to learn about design suggestions related to newsletter publications.

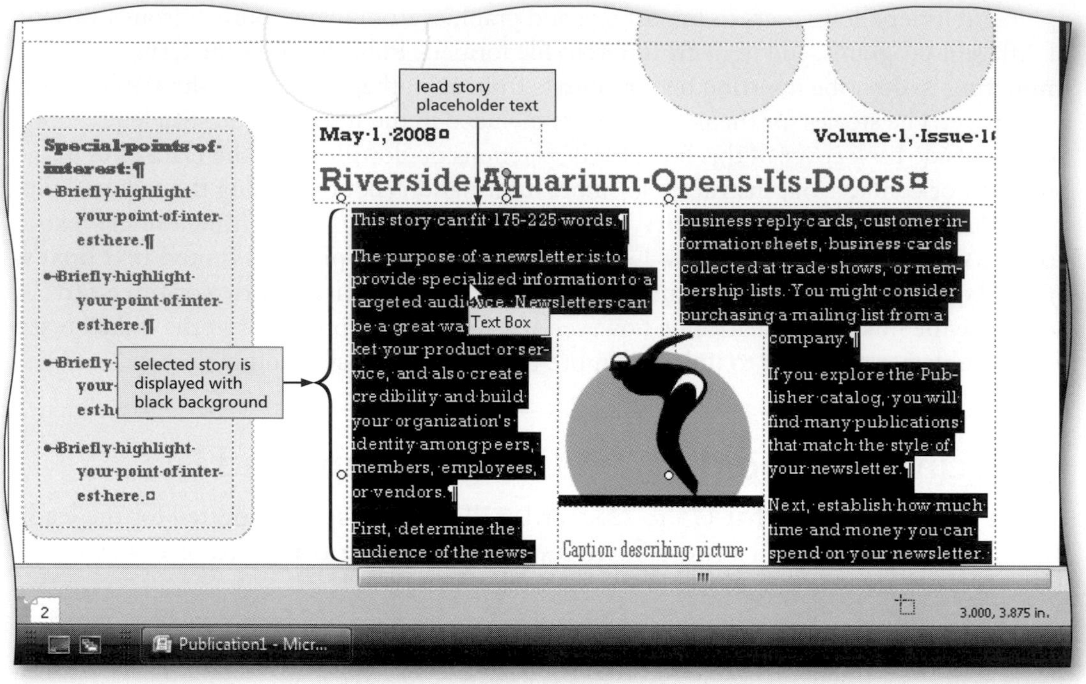

lead story placeholder text

selected story is displayed with black background

Figure 2–18

3

• Click Insert on the menu bar to display the Insert menu (Figure 2–19).

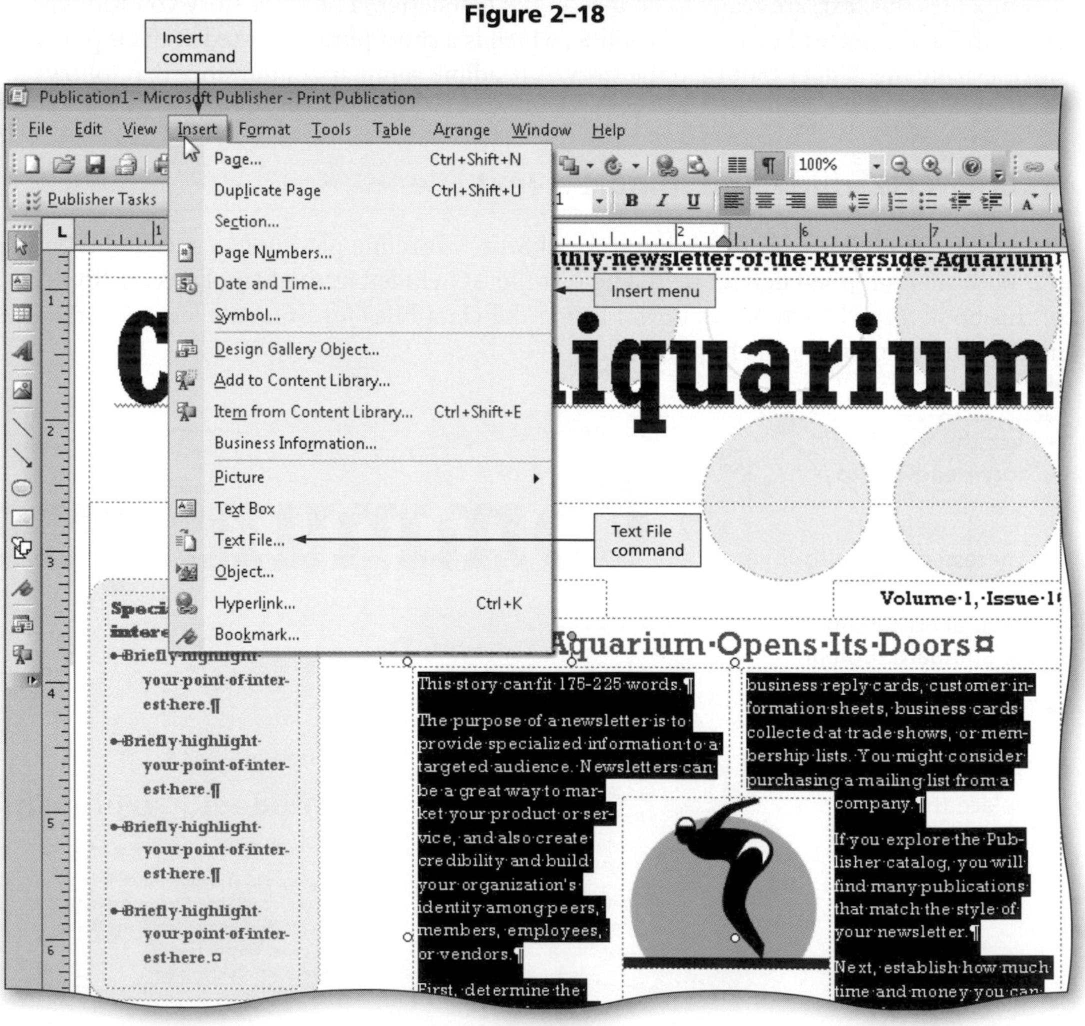

Insert command

Insert menu

Text File command

Figure 2–19

4

- Click Text File to display the Insert Text dialog box.

- If Computer is not displayed in the Favorite Links section, drag the top or bottom edge of the Insert Text dialog box until Computer is displayed.

- Click Computer in the Favorite Links section to display a list of available drives.

- If necessary, scroll until UDISK 2.0 (F:) appears in the list of available drives.

- Double-click UDISK 2.0 (F:) in the Computer list to open the USB flash drive (Figure 2–20).

Q&A

I do not have UDISK 2.0 (F:) drive. What do I do?

The name of your USB flash drive may differ. If you did not download the Data Files, see the inside back cover of this book for instructions on downloading the Data Files for Students, or contact your instructor for more information about accessing the required files.

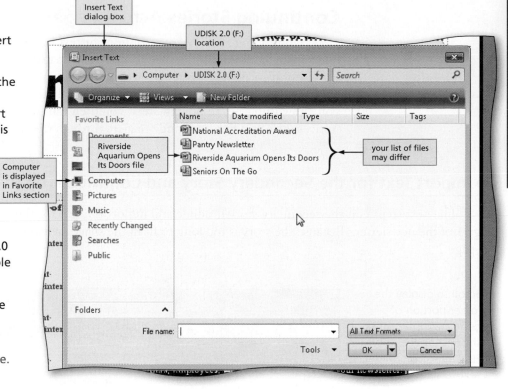

Figure 2–20

5

- Double-click the file, Riverside Aquarium Opens Its Doors, to insert the text into the newsletter (Figure 2–21).

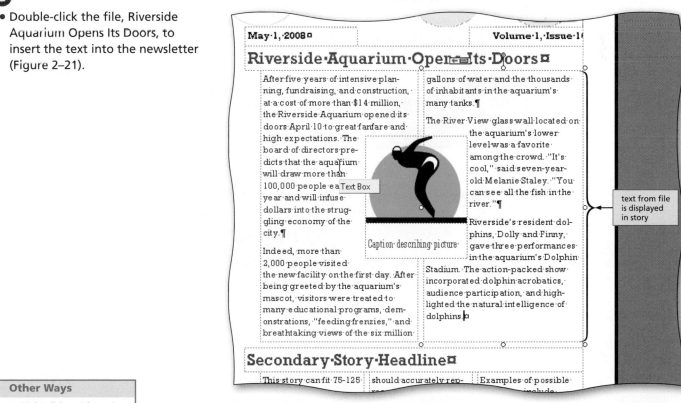

Figure 2–21

Continuing Stories Across Pages

Continuing a story across columns or text boxes is one of the features that Publisher helps you to perform. If the story contains more text than will fit in the default text box, Publisher displays a message to warn you. You then have the option to allow Publisher to connect or **autoflow** the text to another available text box, or to flow the text yourself. If you allow Publisher to flow the text, you then can format the text boxes with continued notices, or **jump lines**, to guide readers through the story.

To Import Text for the Secondary Story and Continue It on Page 2

The next steps edit the secondary story headline and import the text for the article in the lower portion of page 1 of the newsletter. Because the story is too long to fit in the space provided, you will continue the story on page 2.

1

- Scroll to display the lower portion of page 1 and then click the Secondary Story Headline placeholder text to select it.

- Type National Accreditation Award to replace the selected headline (Figure 2–22).

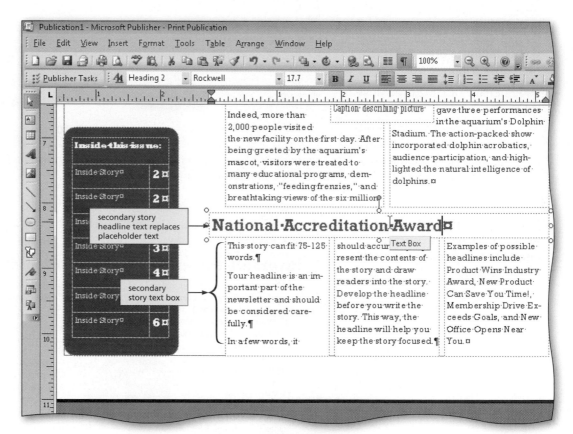

Figure 2–22

2

- Click the text in the secondary story text box to select it.

- Click Insert on the menu bar and then click Text File to open the Insert Text dialog box.

- Navigate to the UDISK 2.0 (F:) drive, if necessary (Figure 2–23).

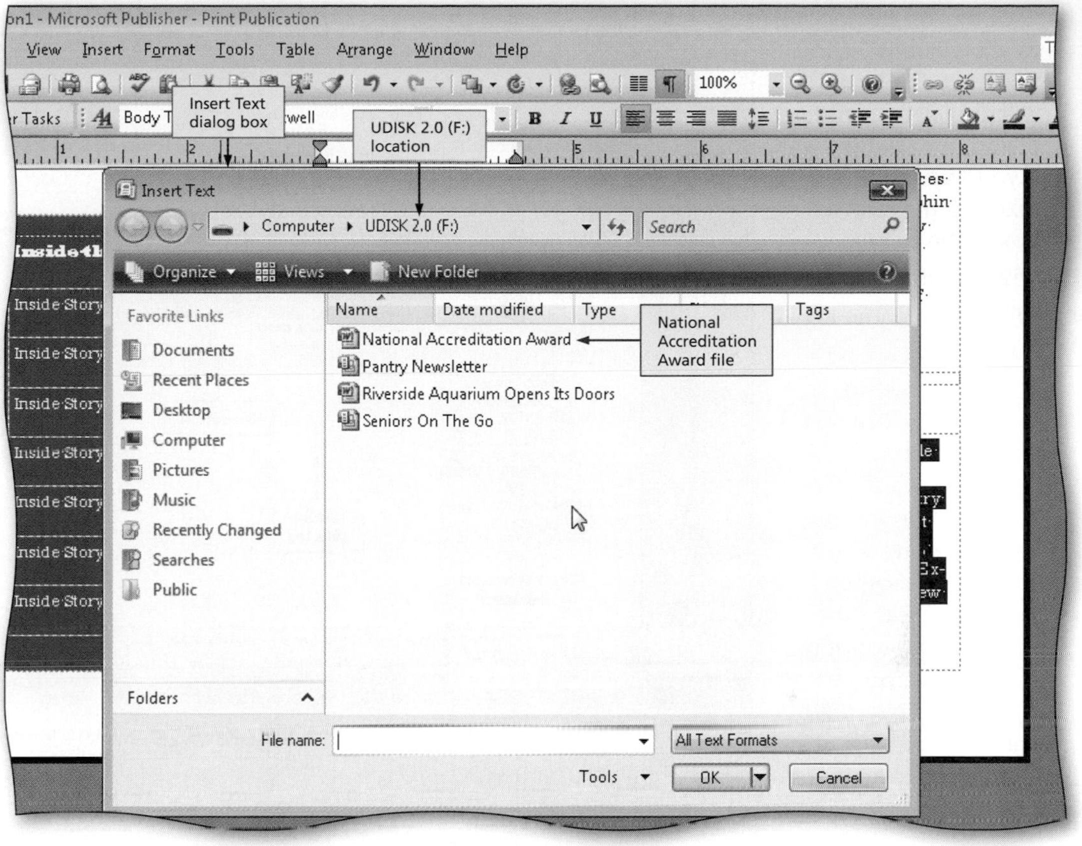

Figure 2–23

3

- Double-click the file, National Accreditation Award, to insert it in the publication. Publisher will display a dialog box asking if you want to use autoflow (Figure 2–24).

Q&A Where is the rest of the story?

As much text as possible was added to the secondary story text boxes. Because the story did not fit, a dialog box helps you make decisions about the rest of the story.

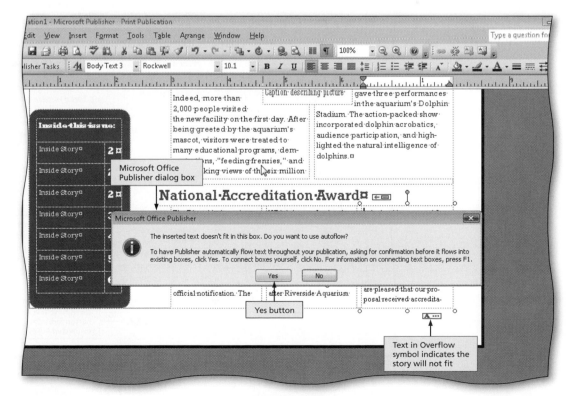

Figure 2–24

4

- Click the Yes button to allow Publisher to flow text. Publisher will display a second dialog box asking if you want to flow text into the selected box at the top of page 2. (Figure 2–25).

Q&A

What if I click the No button?

If you click the No button, the extra text is stored in an overflow area, waiting for you to resolve the issue by connecting the text to another box yourself, cutting the story, or reducing the font size. Stories with **text in overflow** will cause a Design Checker error.

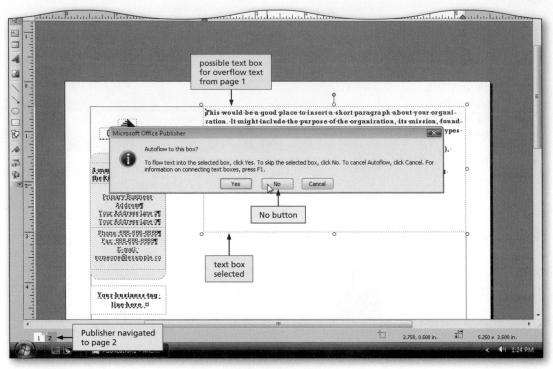

Figure 2–25

5

- Click the No button to cause Publisher to move to the back page story and display another dialog box about autoflowing. (Figure 2–26).

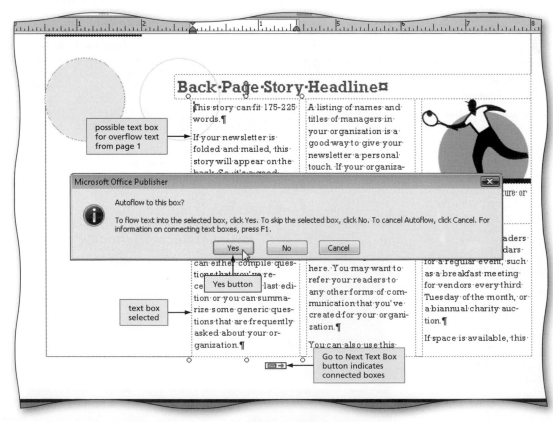

Figure 2–26

6

- Click the Yes button to autoflow into the back page story (Figure 2–27).

Q&A

What if I have no spare text boxes to flow into?

Publisher will ask if you want new text boxes created. If you answer yes, Publisher will automatically create text boxes on a new page.

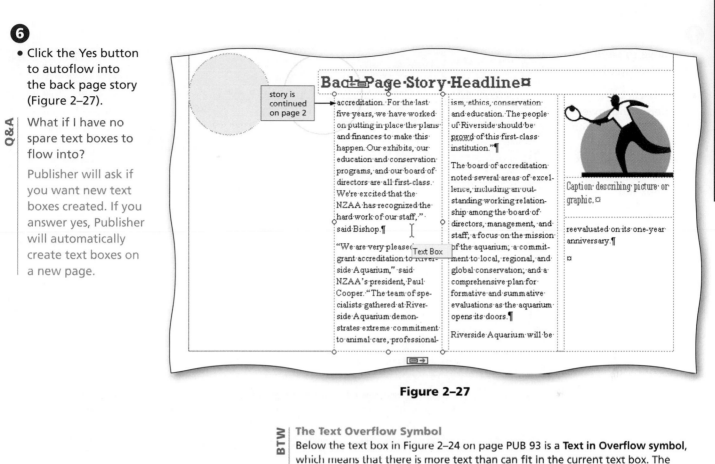

Figure 2–27

story is continued on page 2

BTW

The Text Overflow Symbol
Below the text box in Figure 2–24 on page PUB 93 is a **Text in Overflow symbol**, which means that there is more text than can fit in the current text box. The **overflow area** is an invisible storage location within your publication to hold extra text — similar to a clipboard, but saved with the publication. The overflow area is not electricity-dependent, like the system or Office clipboard. It is saved with the document. You can move your text out of overflow and back into your publication by one of several means: flowing text into a new text box, autofitting text, enlarging the text box, changing the text size, changing the margins within the text box, or deleting some of the text in the text box.

To Format with Continued Notices

In the story that flows from page 1 to page 2, the steps on the next page format the last box on page 1 with a **continued on notice**. Then, on page 2, the first text box is formatted with a **continued from notice**. To access the formatting options for text boxes, double-click the border of the text box. The Text Box tab in the Format dialog box displays options to flow stories from one page to another. The placement of the notices and the page numbering is automatic.

1

- To move to page 1, click the Page 1 icon.

- Double-click the border of the lower-right text box. When Publisher displays the Format Text Box dialog box, click the Text Box tab.

- Click to display a check mark in the Include "Continued on page ..." check box (Figure 2–28).

Q&A

What do I do if my dialog box is covering up the text box?

The setting changes will take place when you click the OK button. If you want to see both the dialog box and the text box, you can drag the title bar of the dialog box to the left, as shown in Figure 2–28.

Figure 2–28

2

- Click the OK button.

- To move to page 2, click the Page 2 icon.

- Double-click the border of the lower-left text box. When Publisher displays the Format Text Box dialog box, click the Text Box tab.

- Click to display a check mark in the Include "Continued from page ..." check box (Figure 2–29).

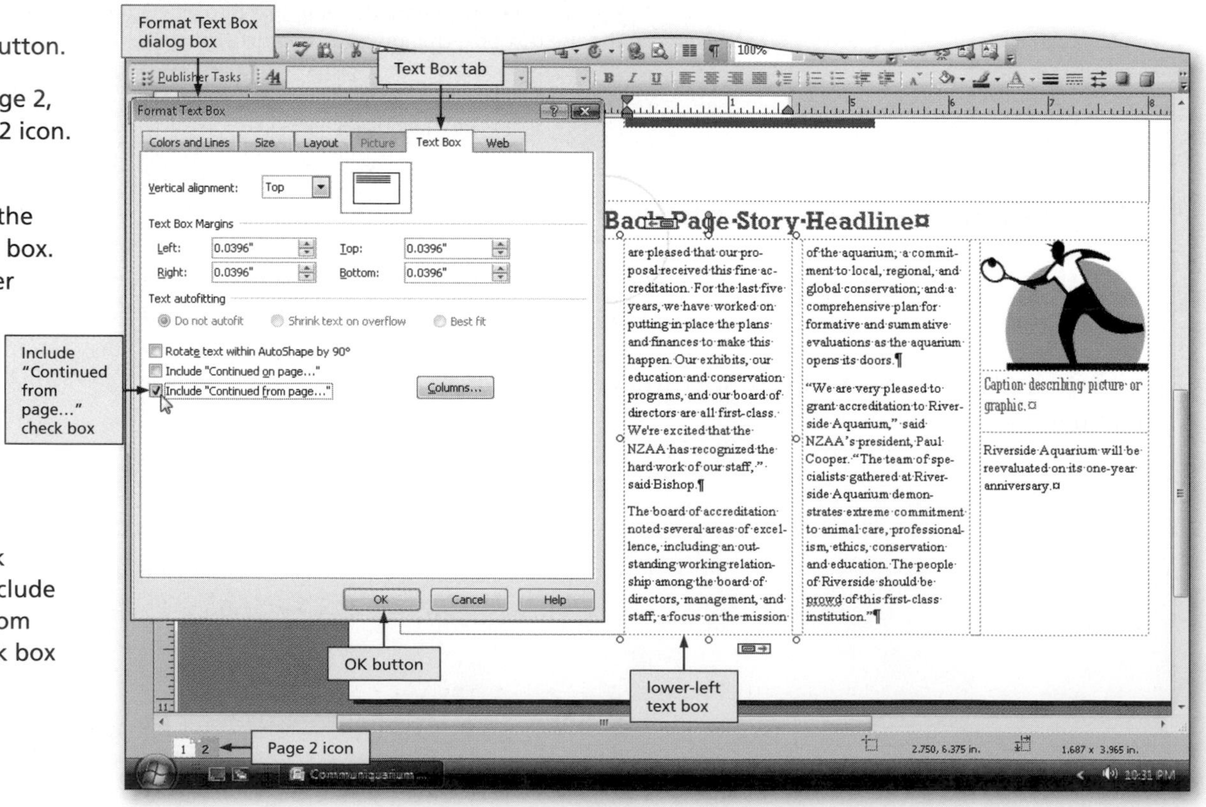

Figure 2–29

3

- Click the OK button (Figure 2–30).

🔍 **Experiment**

- Move between pages 1 and 2 and look at the jump lines with the supplied page numbers.

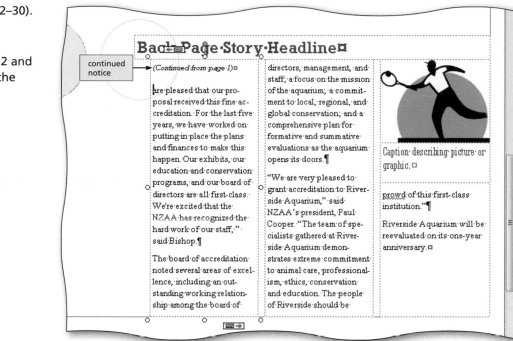

Figure 2–30

continued notice

Back Page Story Headline¤

(Continued from page 1)¤

are pleased that our pro-posal received this fine ac-creditation. For the last five years, we have worked on putting in place the plans and finances to make this happen. Our exhibits, our education and conservation programs, and our board of directors are all first-class. We're excited that the NZAA has recognized the hard work of our staff," said Bishop.¶

The board of accreditation noted several areas of excel-lence, including an out-standing working relation-ship among the board of

directors, management, and staff, a focus on the mission of the aquarium; a commit-ment to local, regional, and global conservation; and a comprehensive plan for formative and summative evaluations as the aquarium opens its doors.¶

"We are very pleased to grant accreditation to River-side Aquarium," said NZAA's president, Paul Cooper. "The team of spe-cialists gathered at River-side Aquarium demon-strates extreme commitment to animal care, professional-ism, ethics, conservation and education. The people of Riverside should be

Caption describing picture or graphic.¤

proud of this first-class institution."¶

Riverside Aquarium will be reevaluated on its one-year anniversary.¤

Other Ways

1. Select text box, click Format on menu bar, click Text Box, click Text Box tab, click continued notice check box
2. Right-click selected text box, click Format Text Box, click Text Box tab, click continued notice check box

To Replace the Back Page Story Headline

The following steps replace the Back Page Story Headline.

1 Select the text, Back Page Story Headline.

2 Type Award to replace the text (Figure 2–31).

BTW

Importing Text
Importing the articles instead of typing them saves time and adds the convenience of using word processing. Publisher accepts most file formats from popular word processing programs and text editors.

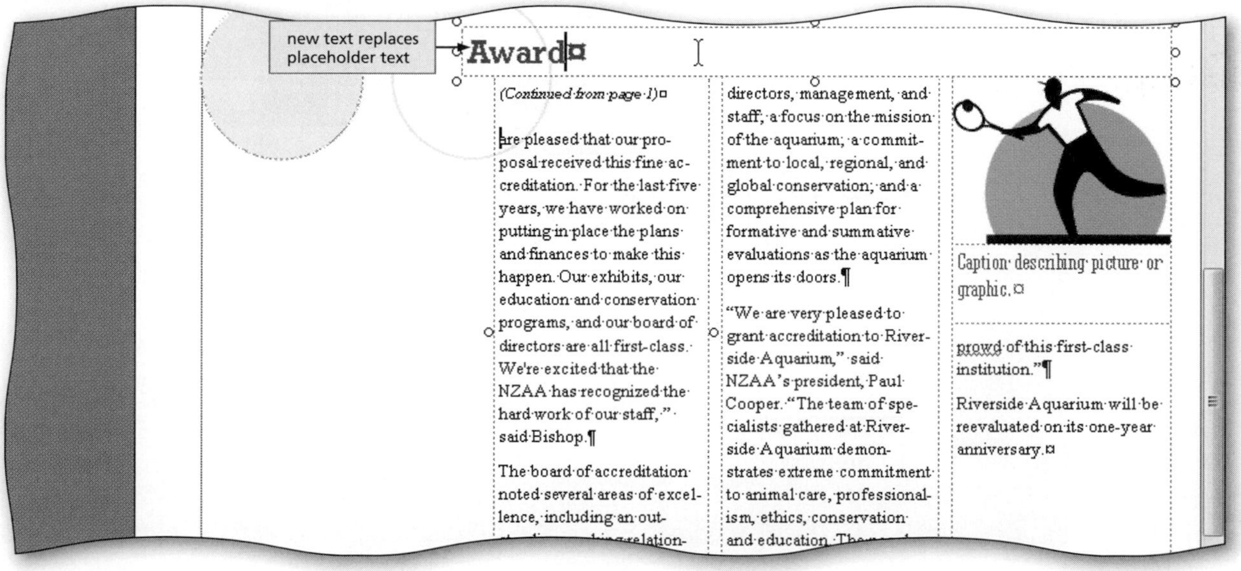

new text replaces placeholder text

Award¤

(Continued from page 1)¤

are pleased that our pro-posal received this fine ac-creditation. For the last five years, we have worked on putting in place the plans and finances to make this happen. Our exhibits, our education and conservation programs, and our board of directors are all first-class. We're excited that the NZAA has recognized the hard work of our staff," said Bishop.¶

The board of accreditation noted several areas of excel-lence, including an out-standing working relation-

directors, management, and staff, a focus on the mission of the aquarium; a commit-ment to local, regional, and global conservation; and a comprehensive plan for formative and summative evaluations as the aquarium opens its doors.¶

"We are very pleased to grant accreditation to River-side Aquarium," said NZAA's president, Paul Cooper. "The team of spe-cialists gathered at River-side Aquarium demon-strates extreme commitment to animal care, professional-ism, ethics, conservation and education. The people

Caption describing picture or graphic.¤

proud of this first-class institution."¶

Riverside Aquarium will be reevaluated on its one-year anniversary.¤

Figure 2–31

Editing Stories in Microsoft Word

You have seen that you can edit text directly in Microsoft Publisher or import text from a previously stored file. A third way to edit text is to use Microsoft Word as your editor. Publisher provides an easy link between the two applications.

If you need to edit only a few words, it is faster to stay in Publisher. If you need to edit a longer story that appears on different pages in a publication or one that has not been previously stored, it might be easier to edit the story in Word. Many users are accustomed to working in Word and want to take advantage of available Word features, such as grammar checking and revision tracking. It sometimes is easier to drag and drop paragraphs in a Word window rather than performing the same task in a Publisher window, especially when it involves moving across pages in a larger Publisher publication.

Occasionally, if you have many applications running, such as virus protection and other memory-taxing programs, Publisher may warn you that you are low on computer memory. In that case, close the other applications and try editing the story in Word again.

While you are working on a story in Word, you cannot edit the corresponding text box in Publisher. Editing your stories in Word allows you to manipulate the text using the full capabilities of a word processing program.

To Edit a Story Using Word

In the Communiquarium newsletter, the back page contains a text box to display more information or articles about the organization. The aquarium's informational text has not been previously stored in a file for importing, so it must be typed. The following steps use Microsoft Word in conjunction with Publisher to create the text. Microsoft Word version 6.0 or later must be installed on your computer for this procedure to work.

1

- Scroll to display the text box in the upper-right portion of page 2.

- Select the placeholder text.

- Click Edit on the menu bar to display the Edit menu (Figure 2–32).

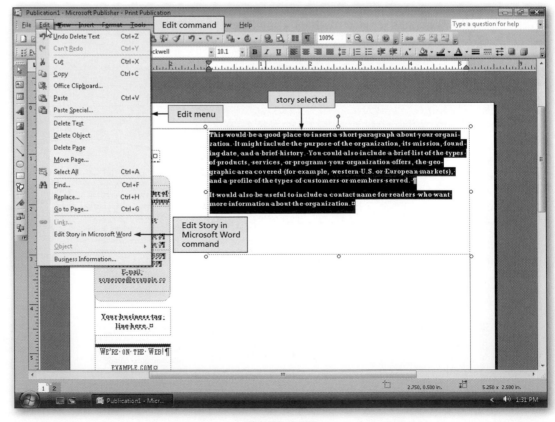

Figure 2–32

2

- Click the Edit Story in Microsoft Word command to launch the application.

- When Microsoft Word starts in a new window, maximize the window if necessary, by double-clicking the title bar.

- Press CTRL+A to select all of the text (Figure 2–33).

Q&A

Why are my fonts different?

Usually, the text displays the same formatting as the previous text in Publisher. Your display may differ depending on available fonts.

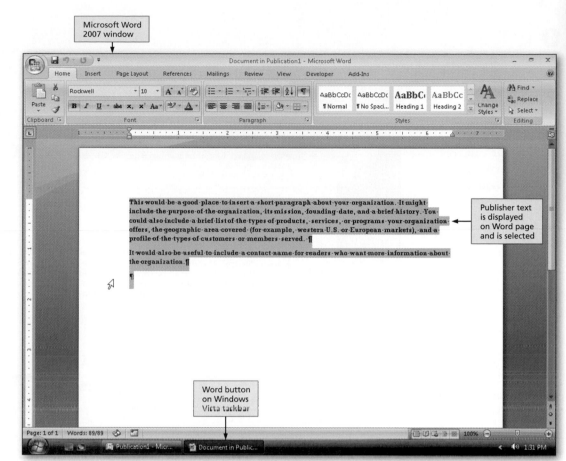

Figure 2–33

3

- Type Join the fun! and then press the ENTER key.

- Type Become a member! and then press the ENTER key (Figure 2–34).

Q&A

Why are my formatting marks not showing in Microsoft Word?

It is possible that someone has turned off formatting marks. Click the Show/Hide ¶ button to turn them on and off.

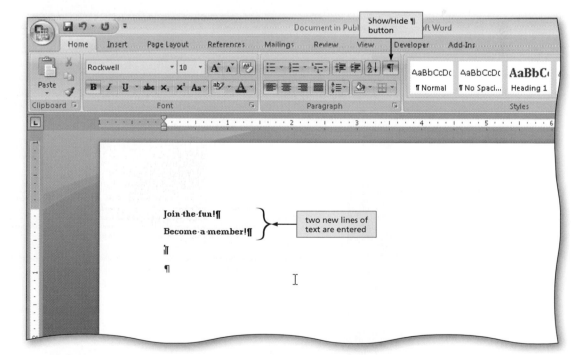

Figure 2–34

4

- Type If you enjoy Riverside Aquarium, and have yet to become a member, you are missing out on an incredible deal. Aquarium membership allows year-round admission to Riverside and to more than 100 other U.S. zoos and aquariums. A family of four can enjoy the aquarium all year for only $50. In addition, members receive a

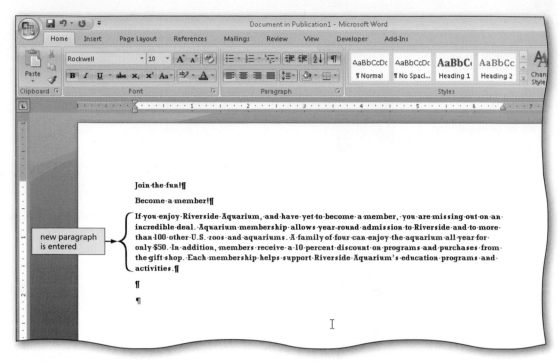

10 percent discount on programs and purchases from the gift shop. Each membership helps support Riverside Aquarium's education programs and activities. and then press the ENTER key (Figure 2–35).

Figure 2–35

5

- Type To become a member, or to send a gift membership to someone special, visit our Web site at RiversideAquarium. org or call (850) 555-FISH. to finish the text (Figure 2–36).

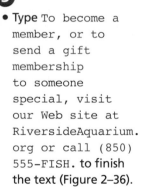

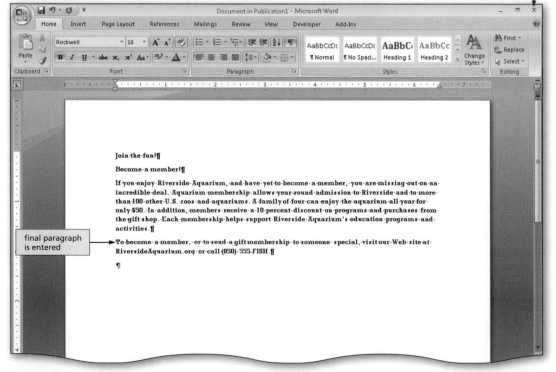

Figure 2–36

6

- Click the Close button on the title bar of the Document in Publication1 – Microsoft Word window to close it (Figure 2–37).

Q&A Why do I see only gray lines instead of the text?

Launching Microsoft Word from within Microsoft Publisher is a drain on your system's memory and on the refresh rate of your screen. Try going to page 1 and then back to page 2 to refresh the screen.

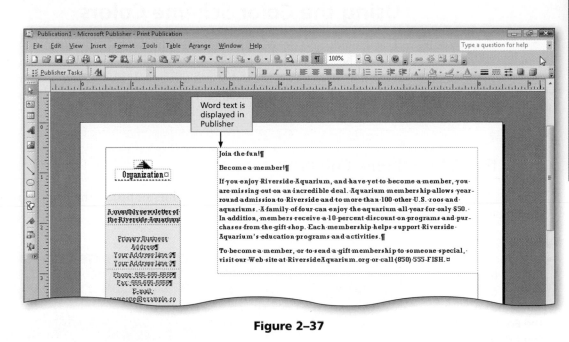

Figure 2–37

Other Ways

1. Right-click article, point to Change Text, click Edit Story in Microsoft Word

To Change the Font Size

The following steps change the font size of the first two paragraphs of the newly imported story.

1 Drag to select the first two paragraphs of text.

2 On the Formatting toolbar, click the text in the Font Size box to select it.

3 Type 14 and then press the ENTER key. Do not deselect the first two paragraphs of text (Figure 2–38).

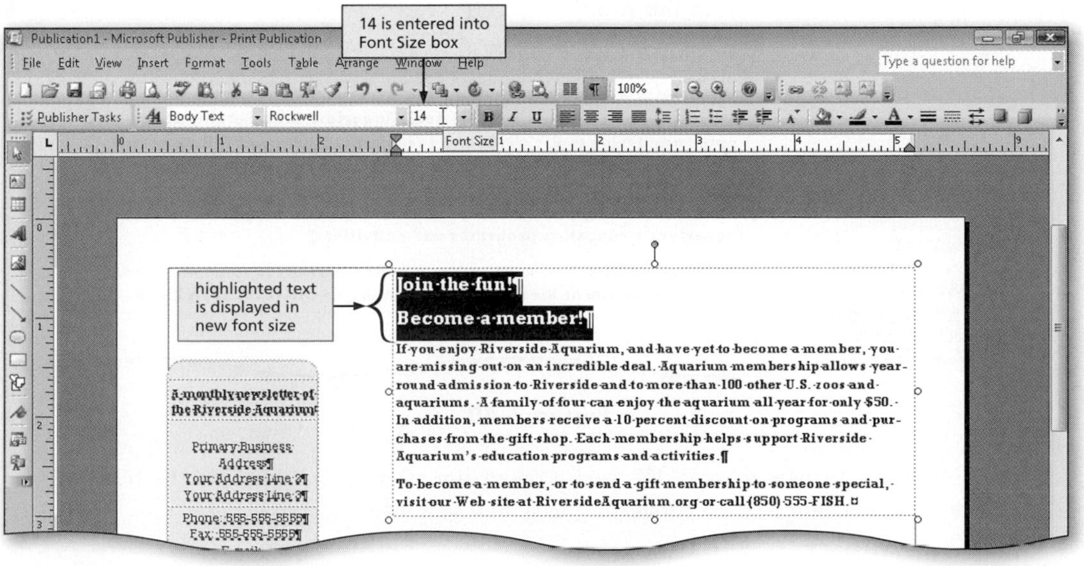

Figure 2–38

Using the Color Scheme Colors

The Tropics color scheme chosen earlier in this chapter contains complementary colors that can be used for text, graphics, or backgrounds. Publisher automatically displays the color scheme colors at the top of each dialog box and button menu that has to do with color, allowing you to choose the correct tint or shade that matches the other colors in your publication.

To Use the Color Scheme Colors

The following steps change the font color of the first two lines of text in the story to match the color in the color scheme.

1

- With the first two lines of the story at the top of page 2 still selected, click the Font Color button arrow on the Formatting toolbar to display the button menu (Figure 2–39).

Q&A How many colors are in the color scheme?

Publisher provides a main color, which is usually black for standard text; five accent colors, the first of which is used for headlines in newsletters, for example; a hyperlink color; and a color for hyperlinks that have been previously clicked.

Figure 2–39

2

- Click the Accent 3 (Red) color to change the font color of the selected text.

- Click outside the text box to deselect the text (Figure 2–40).

Q&A What if I change my mind about the color scheme?

Any text or object color chosen from the color scheme or top row of the Font Color button menu automatically will convert when you choose the new scheme. If you choose a color scheme that is not in the five basic colors of the color scheme, the color will not change when converting to a new scheme.

Figure 2–40

To Delete the Logo and Edit Other Text Boxes on Page 2

The following steps delete the logo and edit other text boxes on page 2.

1 In the upper-left portion of page 2, right-click the logo, and then click Delete Object on the shortcut menu.

2 Click the text in the Primary Business Address text box. Press CTRL+A to select all of the text. Type `Riverside Aquarium` and press the ENTER key.

3 Type `1400 River Drive` and then press the ENTER key.

4 Type `Pensacola, FL 32503` to finish the address.

5 Click the text in the Phone text box. Press CTRL+A to select all of the text. Type `Phone: (850) 555-FISH` and press the ENTER key.

6 Type `Fax: (850) 555-3470` and then press the ENTER key.

7 Type `E-mail: riverside@nzaa.com` to finish the phone and e-mail information.

8 Click the text in the business tag line text box. Press CTRL+A to select all of the text. Type `More than just fish!` to replace the default tag line text.

9 Right-click the text in the 'We're on the Web' attention getter text box and then click Delete Object on the shortcut menu to delete the text box (Figure 2–41).

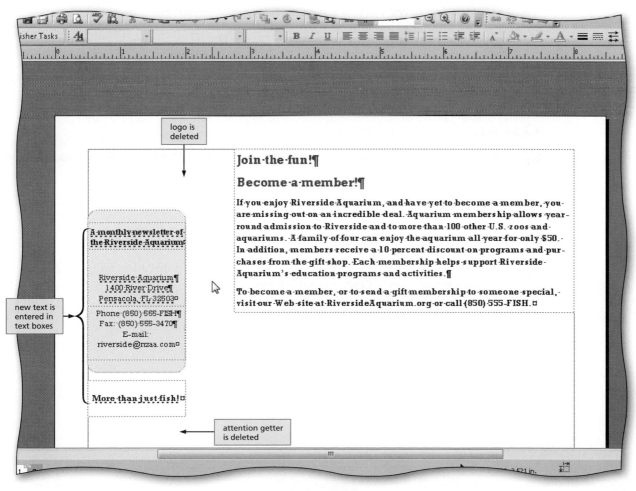

Figure 2–41

Selecting Text and Objects

In the previous steps and throughout Chapters 1 and 2, you have selected text and graphics. Table 2–2 lists some editing techniques used to select various items using the mouse.

Table 2–2 Techniques for Selecting Text and Objects with the Mouse	
Item to Select	**Mouse Action**
Block of text or sentence	Click at beginning of selection, scroll to end of selection, position mouse pointer at end of selection, hold down SHIFT key, and then click; or drag through the text
Character(s)	Drag through character(s)
Graphic	Click the graphic
Picture with caption	Click the picture, and then click the picture again
Line	Move mouse to left of line until mouse pointer changes to a right-pointing block arrow and then click
Lines	Move mouse to left of text until mouse pointer changes to a right-pointing block arrow, and then drag up or down; or triple-click
Paragraph	Triple-click paragraph
Word	Double-click the word
Words	Drag through the words

To Save an Intermediate Copy of the Newsletter

A good practice is to save intermediate copies of your work. That way, if your computer loses power or you make a serious mistake, you always can retrieve the latest copy from disk. With the masthead and story headlines edited, and the text files imported, it now is a good time to save the entire newsletter before continuing. For a detailed example of the procedure summarized below, refer to pages PUB 31 through PUB 33 in Chapter 1.

1 With a USB flash drive connected to one of the computer's USB ports, click the Save button on the Standard toolbar.

2 Type Communiquarium Newsletter in the File name text box to change the file name. Do not press the ENTER key.

3 Navigate to your USB flash drive (Figure 2–42).

4 Click the Save button in the Save As dialog box to save the publication on the USB flash drive with the file name, Communiquarium Newsletter.

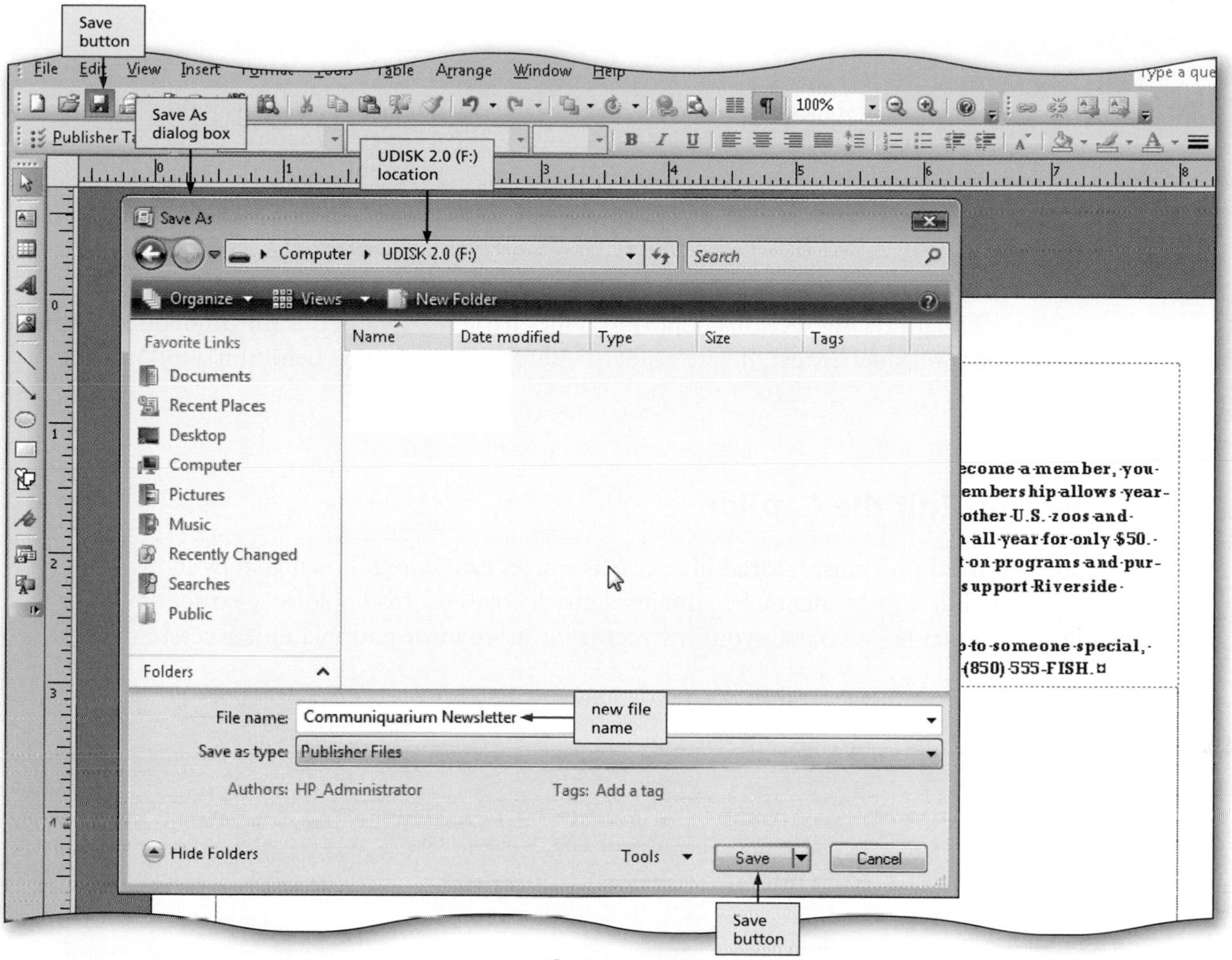

Figure 2–42

Using Graphics in a Newsletter

Most graphic designers employ an easy technique for deciding how many graphics are too many. They hold the publication at arm's length and glance at it. Then, closing their eyes, they count the number of things they remember. Remembering more than five graphics indicates too many; two or fewer indicates too few. Without question, graphics can make or break a publication. The world has come to expect them. Used correctly, graphics enhance the text, attract the eye, and brighten the look of the publication.

You can use Publisher's clip art images in any publication you create, including newsletters. Publisher also accepts graphics and pictures created by other programs, as well as scanned photographs and digital photos. You can import and replace graphics into publications in the same way that you imported stories and replaced template text. Once inserted, graphics can be resized and moved to appropriate locations. In newsletters, you should use photographs as true-to-life representations, such as pictures of employees and products. Drawings, on the other hand, can explain, instruct, entertain, or represent images for which you have no picture. The careful use of graphics can add flair and distinction to your publication.

Graphics do not have to be images and pictures. They also can include tables, charts, shapes, lines, boxes, borders, pull quotes, and sidebars. A **sidebar** is a small piece of text, set off with a box or graphic, and placed beside an article. It contains text that is not vital to understanding the main text, but usually adds interest or additional information. Tables of contents, art boxes, and bulleted points of interest are examples of sidebars. A **pull quote** is an excerpt from the main article to highlight the ideas or to attract readers. As with other graphics, it adds interest to the page. Pull quotes, like sidebars, can be set off with a box or graphic.

BTW

Saving
Click the Save button on the Standard toolbar often. When you do, the stored copy on your system is updated with the current changes. The file name remains the same. You then can retrieve the publication later, if the unexpected happens.

Plan
Ahead

> **Create the first draft.**
> As you insert graphics and arrange stories, follow any guidelines from the authors or from
> the company for which you are creating the newsletter. Together, determine the best layout
> for eye appeal and reliable dissemination of content. Make any required changes. Print a
> copy and mark the places where sidebars and pull quotes would make sense. Verify that all
> photographs have captions.

The following sections import graphics from the Data Files for Students, edit the
captions and sidebar text, delete a sidebar (but not the graphic behind it), and insert a
pull quote.

To Replace a Graphic and Edit the Caption

Graphics can be imported from previously stored files, just as stories can. The following steps show how
to import graphics from the Data Files for Students. See the inside back cover of this book for instructions on
downloading the Data Files for Students, or contact your instructor for more information about accessing the
required files.

1

- To display the first page of
the newsletter, click the
Page 1 icon on the page
sorter.

- Right-click the workspace,
which is the gray area behind
the newsletter, and point to
Zoom (Figure 2–43).

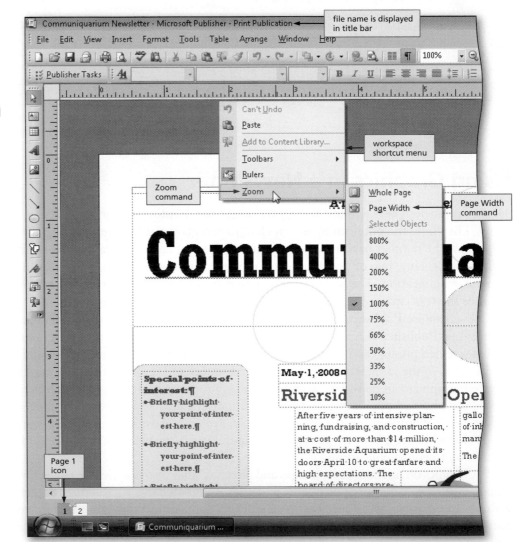

Figure 2–43

2

- Click Page Width to zoom to page width.

- Click the graphic in the lead story to select the grouped graphic and caption object.

- Click the graphic again to select only the picture.

- Right-click the graphic to display the shortcut menu.

- Point to Change Picture to display its submenu (Figure 2–44).

What is the toolbar that appeared on the screen?

When a picture is selected, Publisher offers you its Picture toolbar in case you want to make changes to the picture.

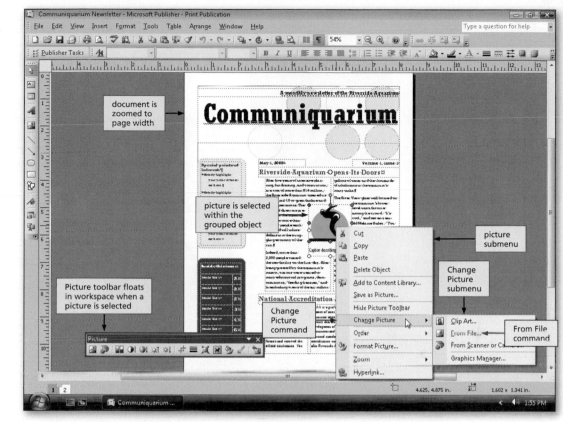

Figure 2–44

3

- Click the From File command to open the Insert Picture dialog box.

- Navigate to the UDISK 2.0 (F:) drive (Figure 2–45).

What do the other choices on the Change Picture submenu do?

The **Clip Art command** opens the Clip Art task pane to allow you to search for an appropriate graphic. The **From Scanner or Camera command** allows you to import directly from a digital camera or flatbed scanner

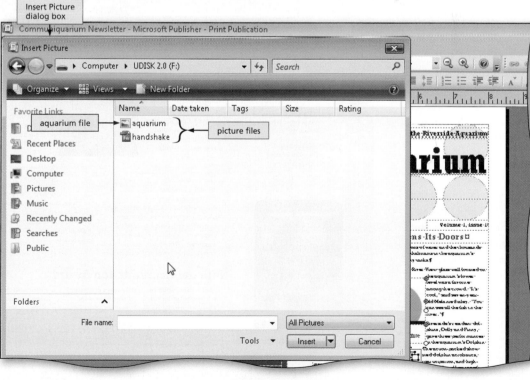

Figure 2–45

without intermediary software. The **Graphics Manager command** opens the Graphics Manager task pane to allow you to choose from among graphics already used in the publication.

4

- To insert the picture, double-click the file, aquarium (Figure 2–46).

Q&A

What if I choose a bigger or smaller picture?

If necessary, imported graphics may be resized to better complement the stories. Publisher automatically wraps the text around the graphic regardless of its size.

Figure 2–46

5

- Select the text in the caption.

- Zoom to 100%.

- Type New, world-class aquarium on the riverfront to replace the selected placeholder text (Figure 2–47).

Q&A

What if I do not want a caption?

If you do not want a caption, you can ungroup the object by clicking the **Ungroup Objects button** and then deleting the text box. Deleting the text only, will cause an error when running the Design Checker because it will leave an empty box in the publication.

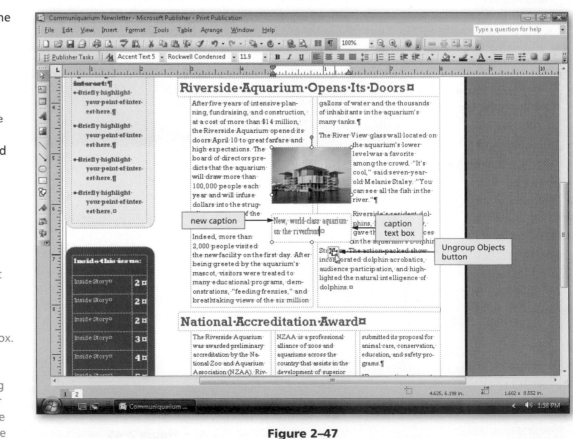

Figure 2–47

To Replace a Graphic on Page 2 and Edit the Caption

1 Go to page 2 of the newsletter.

2 Select only the picture in the Award story to prepare to replace it.

3 Right-click the picture to display the shortcut menu. Point to Change Picture and then click From File on the Change Picture submenu to display the Insert Picture dialog box.

4 If necessary, navigate to the USB flash drive to view the pictures stored there.

5 Double-click the picture, handshake, to place it in the publication.

6 Select the text in the Caption text box. Type `Riverside Aquarium president accepts accreditation award` to replace the placeholder text (Figure 2–48).

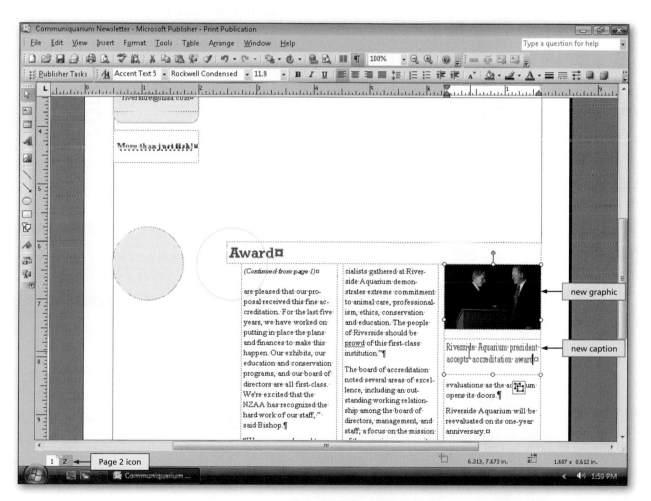

Figure 2–48

To Insert a New Picture from Clip Art

Recall that you have used the Clip Art task pane to replace template graphics. You also have replaced template graphics with imported files. The final graphic in the newsletter will not replace a previous graphic. The next steps insert a new picture from Clip Art, using the menu.

1

- Click the workspace to deselect the picture.

- Scroll as necessary to display the upper half of page 2 in the newsletter.

- Click Insert on the menu bar and then point to Picture (Figure 2–49).

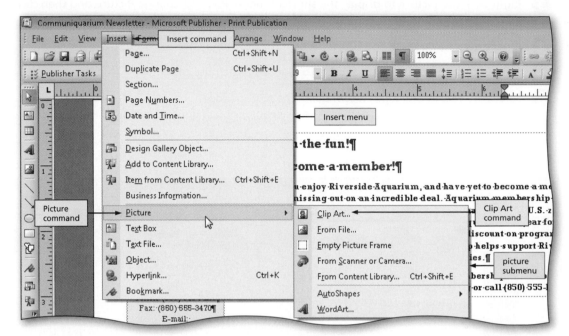

Figure 2–49

2

- Click Clip Art to display the Clip Art task pane.

- Type `dolphin` in the Search for box.

- If necessary, click the Search in box arrow and then click Everywhere in the list.

- If Necessary, click the Results should be box arrow and then click All media types in the list.

- Click the Go button to search for clip art related to the term, dolphin (Figure 2–50).

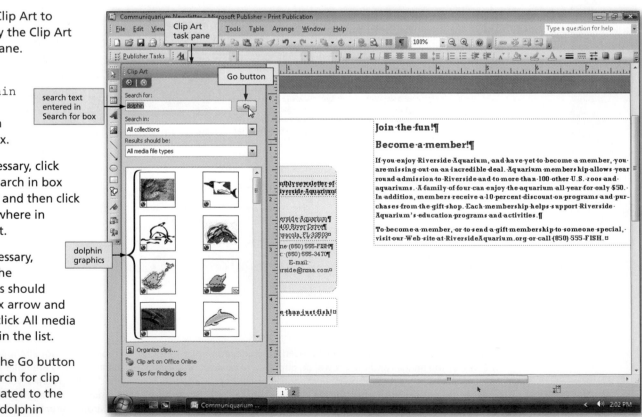

Figure 2–50

3

- Scroll to find a picture of a dolphin similar to the one shown in Figure 2–51.

- To insert the picture into the newsletter, click the picture.

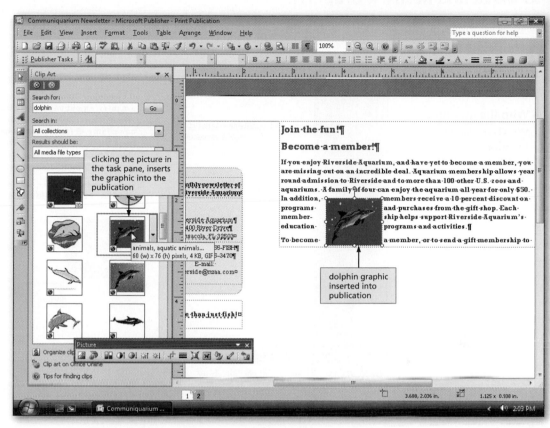

Figure 2–51

Moving and Resizing Objects

Sometimes objects are not in the right place. In those cases you have to select the object and then move the object by dragging its gray, dotted-line border.

Sometimes pictures and graphics are not the right size. In that case you need to resize the object. To resize any object in Publisher, select the object, and then drag a handle. A handle is one of several small shapes displayed around an object when the object is selected. To resize by dragging, position the mouse pointer over one of the handles and then drag the mouse. Pressing the CTRL key while dragging keeps the center of the graphic in the same place while resizing. Pressing the SHIFT key while dragging maintains the graphic's proportions while resizing. Finally, pressing the CTRL+SHIFT keys while dragging maintains the proportions and keeps the center in the same place. You will learn about more ways to resize and position graphics in a later chapter.

To Move and Resize a Graphic

The following steps move the dolphin graphic and resize it.

- If necessary, close the Clip Art task pane.

- With the graphic still selected, drag it to a location below the text box, as shown in Figure 2–52.

- Point to the lower-right handle.

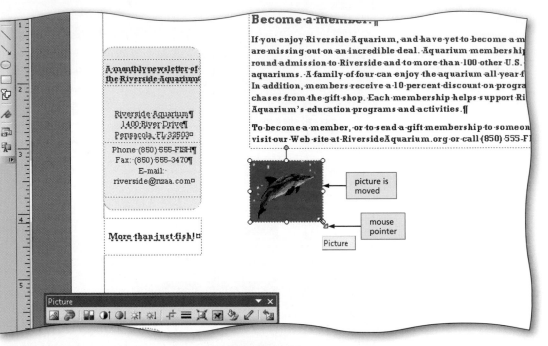

Figure 2–52

2

- SHIFT+drag the handle until the graphic is approximately 2.5 inches wide, as measured by the horizontal ruler (Figure 2–53).

Q&A

How can I tell if it is 2.5 inches wide?

The size does not have to be exact in this newsletter. Zooming until the graphic is closer to the rulers is one way to measure more precisely. You also can see the size change on the right side of the status bar as you drag.

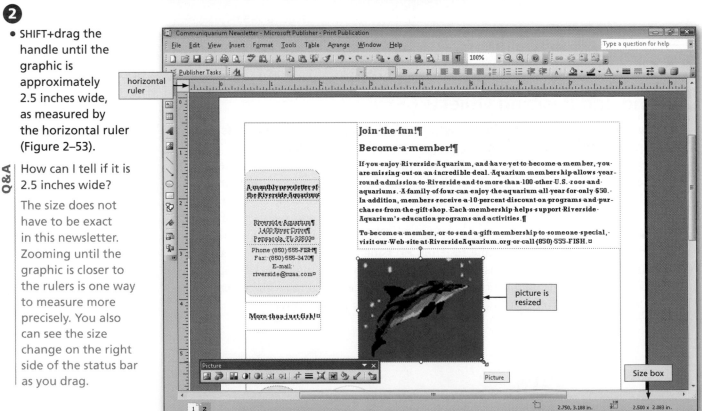

Figure 2–53

To Edit a Sidebar

The Watermark newsletter template includes two sidebars on page 1. The first is a bulleted list of special points of interest. The following steps edit that bulleted list.

1

- Go to page 1 of the newsletter.

- Right-click the gray, dotted border of the Special points of interest sidebar in the upper-left part of page 1.

- Point to Zoom on the shortcut menu to display its submenu (Figure 2–54).

Figure 2–54

2

- Click the Selected Objects command to center the sidebar and display it at the largest possible magnification that still fits in the workspace.

- Select the text, Special points of interest:.

- Type Riverside has... to replace the text (Figure 2–55).

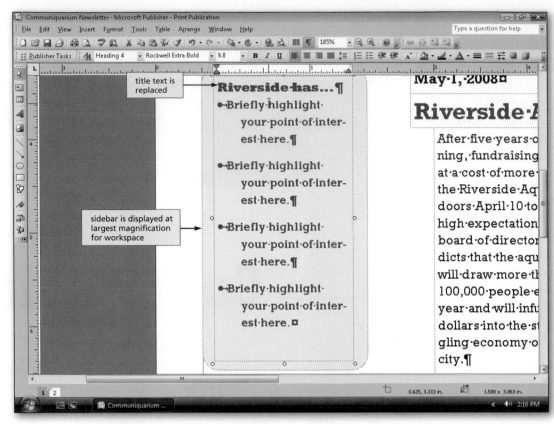

Figure 2–55

3

- Select the bulleted list.

- Type·Later hours on weekends and then press the ENTER key.

- Type·Special rates for school groups and then press the ENTER key.

- Type·Discounts for senior citizens and then press the ENTER key.

- Type·Adopt-a-sea-creature programs and then press the ENTER key.

- Type·Petting tanks and then press the ENTER key.

- Type·And much more! to complete the list (Figure 2–56).

Q&A

How do I turn off or change the bullets?

Recall that you can turn off bullets by clicking the Bullets button on the Formatting toolbar. You also can change the format of bullets by clicking Bullets and Numbering on the Format menu.

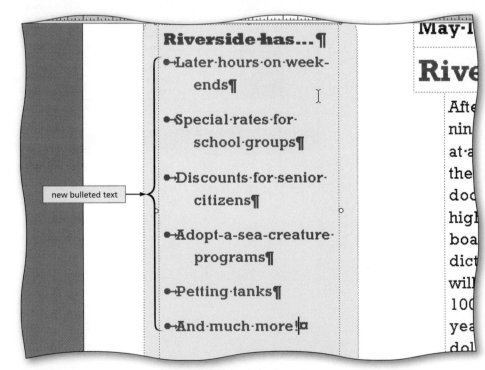

Figure 2–56

To Delete the Sidebar

The other sidebar in the Watermark newsletter template is a table of contents. Because the newsletter now has only two pages, a table of contents is not necessary. The following steps delete the sidebar.

1 Press the F9 key to return to 100% magnification.

2 Scroll to display the Inside this issue sidebar.

3 Right-click the text in the sidebar, and then click Delete Object on the shortcut menu (Figure 2–57).

BTW

A sidebar table many times is used as an index to locate articles in longer newsletters. Many newsletters have a table of contents, not only to reference and locate, but also to break up a long text page and attract readers to inside pages. Tables can be used for purposes other than displaying contents and page numbers. You will learn more about tables in a later project.

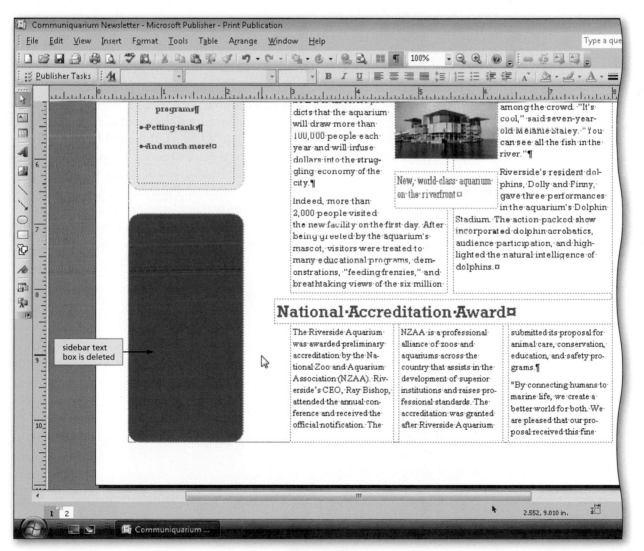

Figure 2–57

Inserting a Pull Quote

People often make reading decisions based on the size of the story. Using a pull quote brings a small portion of the text to their attention and invites readership. Pull quotes especially are useful for breaking the monotony of long columns of text. Desktop publishers also use pull quotes to add visual interest. Finally, pull quotes and sidebars are good multiple entry devices, offering readers many ways to digest information. Layout specialists say article titles and pull quotes should summarize the intended message.

The final step to complete page 1 of the newsletter is to create a pull quote using Publisher's Design Gallery. The **Design Gallery** is a group of objects that you can place in your publications, including sidebars, pull quotes, mastheads, and other individual objects. To access the Design Gallery, you click the **Design Gallery Object button** on the Objects toolbar.

The pull quote in this newsletter will contain a quote from the National Accreditation Award story and should be placed appropriately on the page to grab the reader's attention. Publisher has many ways for you to copy, cut, and paste text. You can use the buttons on the Standard toolbar, you can use the commands on the Edit menu, or you can use the commands on the short-cut menu, which display when you right click selections. **Copying** involves placing a copy of the selected item on the Clipboard. **Cutting** involves removing the selected item from the publication and then placing it on the Clipboard. **Pasting** is the process of copying an item from the Clipboard into the document at the location of the insertion point. When you cut or copy, Publisher transfers the text or objects to the system Clipboard. The **system Clipboard** maintains a copy of the most current copy or cut. On the other hand, the **Office Clipboard task pane**, accessed via a command on the Edit menu, maintains up to 24 previous copies and cuts.

When you cut and paste text for the pull quote, Publisher will display a Paste Options button. When the **Paste Options button** is clicked, Publisher will display the choice of keeping the source formatting of the copied text or changing the text to match the new formatting. The Paste Options button gives you greater control and flexibility in choosing the format for a pasted item. The button appears just below pasted text.

To Insert a Pull Quote

The following steps insert a pull quote from the Design Gallery and use the Standard toolbar and Paste Options button as text is copied and pasted.

1

• With the lower-left portion of page 1 still displayed, click the Design Gallery Object button on the Objects toolbar.

Experiment

• When the Design Gallery window is displayed, one at a time click the buttons down the left side of the window and take note of the various kinds of available objects.

• Click the Pull Quotes button in the list (Figure 2–58).

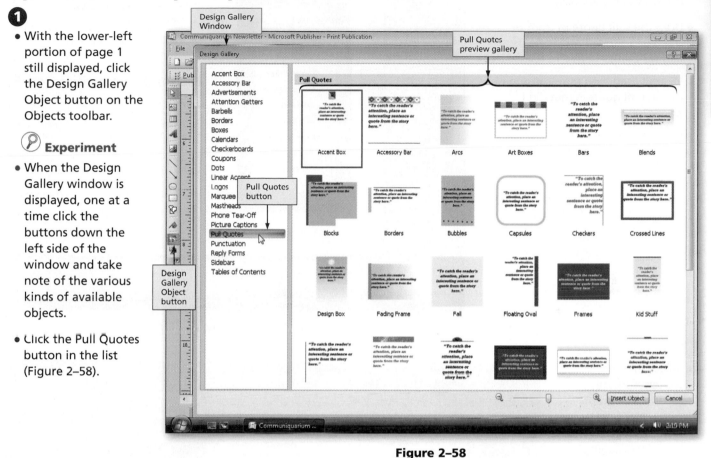

Figure 2–58

2

• Scroll to and then click the Voyage preview shown in Figure 2–59.

Q&A

How do I know which one to choose?

The previews display in alphabetical order in the Pull Quotes pane. Some of them match a specific design set, while others are merely decorative. You should choose one that complements your publication and makes the quote stand out.

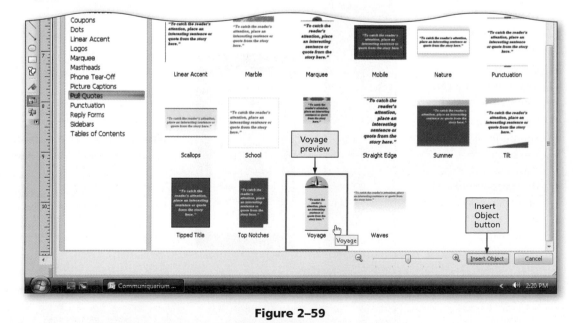

Figure 2–59

❸

- Click the Insert Object button to insert the pull quote and close the Design Gallery window.

- Drag the pull quote in front of the blue rounded rectangle (Figure 2–60).

When I drag, text moves instead of the pull quote. What did I do wrong?

When you want to move an object, you must drag it by its border — the gray dotted line surrounding the object. If your text moved, you dragged the text rather than the entire object.

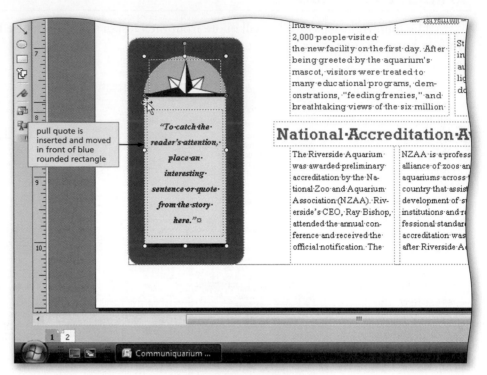

pull quote is inserted and moved in front of blue rounded rectangle

Figure 2–60

❹

- Select the first sentence in the second paragraph of the National Accreditation Award story by dragging. Do not include the quotation mark at the beginning of the sentence (Figure 2–61).

Other than dragging, how can I select the sentence?

You can click at the beginning of the sentence — in this case, after the quotation mark — and then SHIFT+click at the end of the sentence.

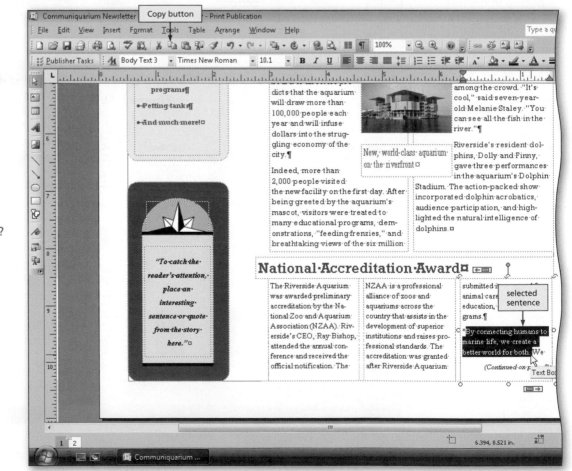

Copy button

selected sentence

Figure 2–61

5

- Click the Copy button on the Standard toolbar to copy the selected text.

- Click the placeholder text in the pull quote to select it (Figure 2–62).

Q&A Can I use shortcut keys to copy and paste?

Yes, you can use CTRL+C to copy and then CTRL+V to paste. See the Quick Reference at the end of the book for more ways to do these tasks.

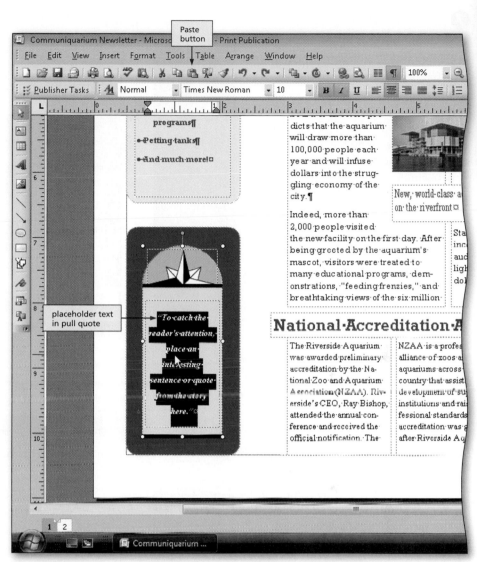

Figure 2–62

6

- Click the Paste button on the Standard toolbar to paste the text from the clipboard (Figure 2–63).

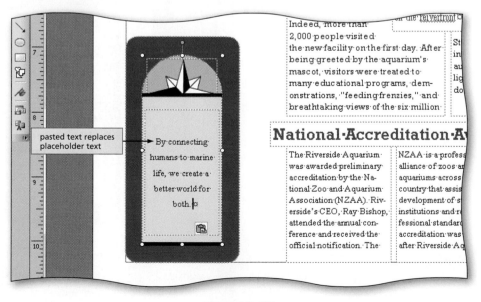

Figure 2–63

7

- Click the Paste Options button to display its menu (Figure 2–64).

Q&A

What if I do not want to display the Paste Options button?

You can choose not to display the Paste Options button by clicking Tools on the menu bar, clicking Options, and then clicking the Edit tab. Finally, clear the Show Paste Options button check box.

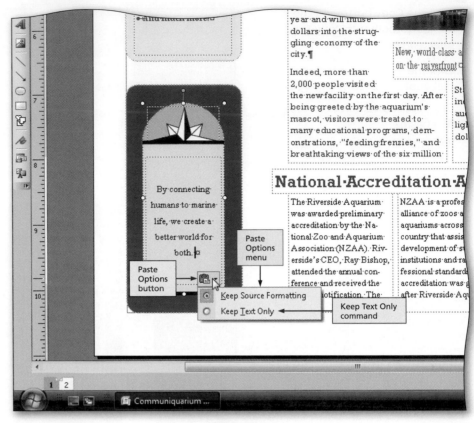

Figure 2–64

8

- Click the Keep Text Only command to maintain the pull quote's formatting (Figure 2–65).

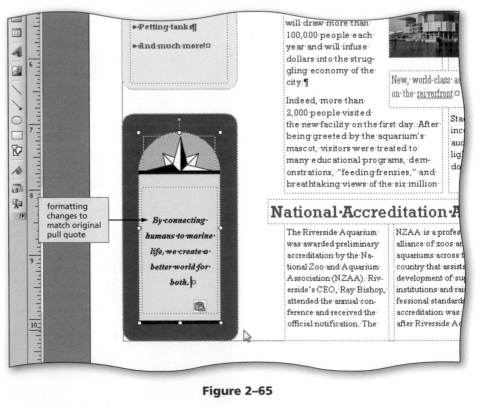

Figure 2–65

Other Ways

1. On Insert menu, click Design Gallery Object

To Finish Formatting the Pull Quote

1 Click at the beginning of the quotation and then type a quotation mark to begin the quote.

2 Click at the end of the quotation. Press the backspace key to remove the space after the period, if necessary. Type a quotation mark to end the quotation.

3 Press the ENTER key to move to the next line.

4 Type -- Ray Bishop to finish the pull quote (Figure 2–66).

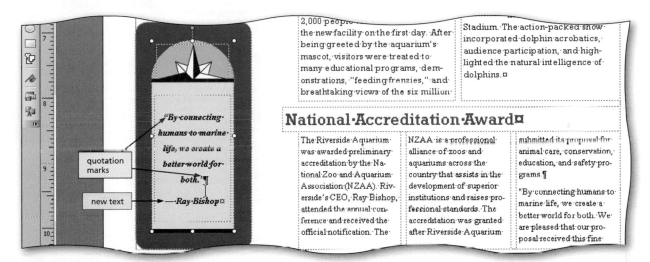

Figure 2–66

Moving Text

To move text, such as words, characters, sentences, or paragraphs, you first select the text to be moved and then use drag-and-drop editing or the cut-and-paste technique to move the selected text. With **drag-and-drop editing**, you drag the selected item to the new location and then insert, or *drop*, it there. Moving text in this manner does not transfer data to either clipboard; neither does it cause Publisher to display the Paste Options button. Any format changes to the text must be made manually.

When moving text between pages, use the cut-and-paste method. When moving text a long distance or between application programs, use the Office Clipboard task pane to cut and paste. When moving text a short distance, the drag-and-drop technique is more efficient. Thus, the steps on the following pages demonstrate drag-and-drop editing.

To Move Text

The editor of the newsletter has decided that two paragraphs should be inverted so the story will read better. The following steps select and move a paragraph on page 2 in the Award story. You will triple-click to select the paragraph and then drag-and-drop it to its new location. You should be sure that drag-and-drop editing is enabled by clicking Options on the Tools menu. On the Edit Tab, make sure the Drag-and-drop text editing check box displays a check mark.

1

- Go to page 2 of the newsletter.

- If necessary, scroll to display the story in the lower portion of the page (Figure 2–67).

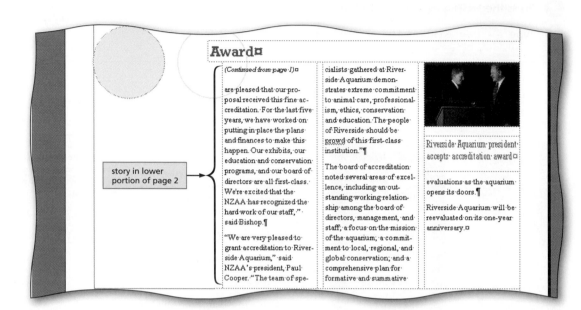

Figure 2–67

2

- Triple-click the paragraph that begins with the words, The board of accreditation noted, to select the paragraph (Figure 2–68).

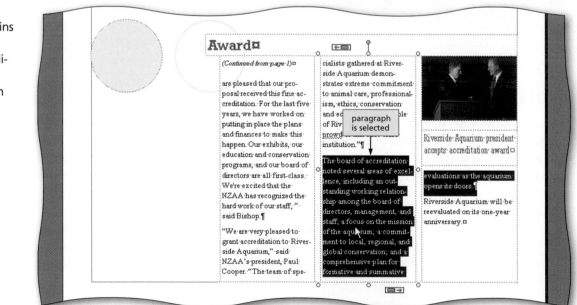

Figure 2–68

3

- Drag the selection to the destination location — before the previous paragraph — as shown in Figure 2–69. Do not release the mouse button.

Q&A What if I accidentally drag text to the wrong location?

Click the Undo button on the Standard Toolbar and try again.

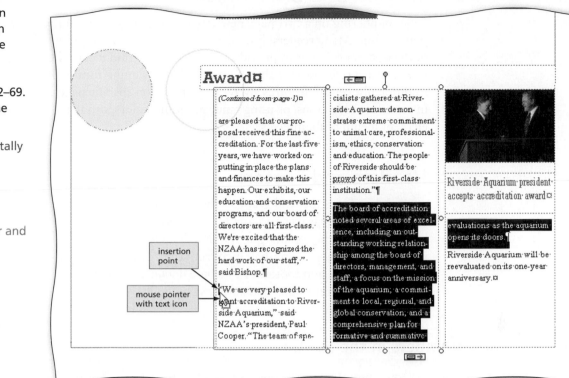

Figure 2–69

4

- Release the mouse button to move the selected text to the location of the mouse pointer.

- To deselect the text, click the workspace (Figure 2–70).

Q&A Can I use drag-and-drop editing to move any selected item?

Yes, you can select words, sentences, phrases, and graphics and then use drag-and-drop editing to move them.

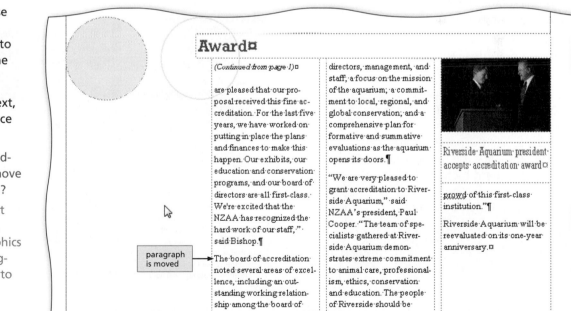

Figure 2–70

Other Ways

1. Select item, click Cut button on Standard toolbar, click where text is to be pasted, click Paste button on Standard toolbar

2. Right-click selected item, click Cut on shortcut menu, right-click where text is to be pasted, click Paste on shortcut menu

3. Select item, press CTRL+X, position insertion point where text is to be pasted, press CTRL+V

Inserting Page Numbers

Page numbering on a two-page newsletter probably is not as important as it is for longer publications. Many readers, however, reference articles and points by page numbers. Part of the design process is to provide a consistent look and feel to the layout, so page numbers can furnish a reference for the organization in designing future, perhaps longer, newsletters. Additionally, certain features always may appear on specific pages. Placing page numbers in prominent locations, or using fancy fonts and colors, can make page numbers a design element in and of themselves.

Headers and Footers

A **header** is text and graphics that print at the top of each page in a document. Similarly, a **footer** is text and graphics that print at the bottom of every page. In Publisher, headers print in the top margin, one-half inch from the top of every page, and footers print in the bottom margin, one-half inch from the bottom of every page. In addition to text and graphics, headers and footers can include document information, such as the page number, current date, current time, and author's name.

To Insert Page Numbers in the Footer

The following steps insert an automatic page number so it will be displayed in the footer on all pages.

1

- Click Insert on the menu bar and then click Page Numbers to access the Page Numbers dialog box (Figure 2–71).

Q&A

I do not see a Page Numbers dialog box. What did I do wrong?

It is possible that your cursor was positioned inside another text box on the page, so Publisher may have inserted the page number at that point. Click the Undo button on the Standard toolbar, click the workspace so that no text box is selected, and then try again.

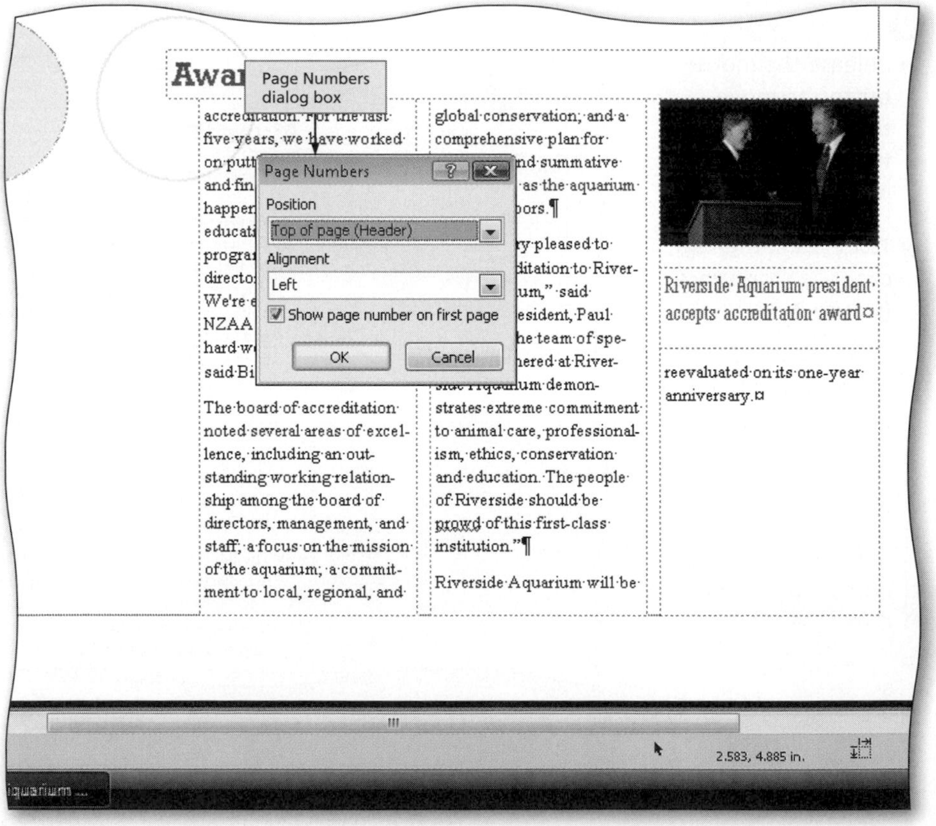

Figure 2–71

2

- Click the Position box arrow and then click Bottom of page (Footer) to position the page number in the footer.

- Click the Alignment box arrow and then click Center to select the alignment within the footer (Figure 2–72).

Q&A

Are the headers and footers similar to the ones in Microsoft Word?

They are similar, but not exactly the same. In Word 2007, the headers and footers are chosen from a gallery and then edited. In Publisher 2007, you can access the headers and footers by inserting a page number, or from the View menu.

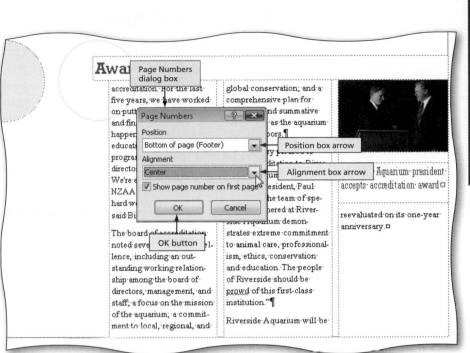

Figure 2–72

3

- Click the OK button to close the Page Numbers dialog box.

Experiment

- Use the page sorter to move between page 1 and 2 and look at the change in page number.

- Go to page 1 of the newsletter (Figure 2–73).

Q&A

How do I place other text or graphics in a header or footer?

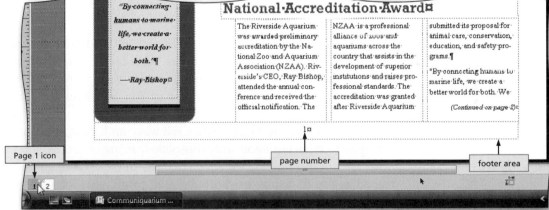

Figure 2–73

You can double-click the header or footer to place the cursor in the header or footer text box. You then can type as you would in any text box, or enter specific pieces of text, such as business information, dates, or times. Options on the Insert menu allow you to insert graphics, as well as dates and times derived from the operating system that update automatically when the publication is edited or printed.

Other Ways

1. Click Insert Page Number button on Header and Footer toolbar

BTW

Accessing Headers and Footers

You can access the header and footer areas by clicking Header and Footer on the View menu. Publisher opens a special layout with a text box at the top and bottom that you can use to add additional information. A Header and Footer toolbar helps you insert the page number, date, and time, and it helps you move between the header and footer boxes as well.

Checking a Newsletter for Errors

As discussed in Chapter 1, once you complete a publication, you might find it necessary to make changes to it. Before submitting a newsletter to a customer or printing service, you should proofread it. While **proofreading**, you look for grammatical errors and spelling errors. You want to be sure the layout, graphics, and stories make sense. If you find errors, you must correct, make changes, or edit the newsletter.

Plan Ahead

> **Proofread and revise the newsletter.**
> As you proofread the newsletter, look for ways to improve it. Check all grammar, spelling, and punctuation. Be sure the text is logical and transitions are smooth. Where necessary, add text, delete text, reword text, and move text to different locations. Ask yourself these questions:
>
> • Does the title suggest the topic?
>
> • Is the first line of the story enticing the reader to continue?
>
> • Is the purpose of the newsletter clear?
>
> • Are all sources acknowledged?

The final phase of the design process, therefore, is a synthesis involving proofreading, editing, and publishing. Publisher offers several methods to check for errors in your newsletter. None of these methods is a replacement for careful reading and proofreading.

Spelling Errors

Similar to the spell checking programs in word processing applications, Publisher looks for misspelled words in text boxes. As you type text in a text box, Publisher checks your typing for possible spelling errors. Recall that if a typed word is not in the dictionary, a red wavy underline is displayed below it. You can check the entire newsletter for spelling errors at once or as you are typing.

When a word is flagged with a red wavy underline, it is not in Publisher's dictionary. A flagged word is not necessarily misspelled, as many names, abbreviations, and specialized terms are not in Publisher's main dictionary. In these cases, instruct Publisher to ignore the flagged word. To display a list of suggested corrections for a flagged word, right-click it, and then click a replacement word on the shortcut menu.

When using imported text, as in the newsletter, it may be easier to check all the spelling at once. Publisher's check spelling feature looks through the selected text box for errors. Once errors are found, Publisher offers suggestions and provides the choice of correcting or ignoring the flagged word. If you are creating this project on a personal computer, your text boxes may contain different misspelled words, depending on the accuracy of your typing.

To Check the Newsletter for Spelling Errors

The Spelling command is accessed through the Tools menu. The following steps illustrate how to check your newsletter for spelling errors. You may encounter spelling mistakes you have made while typing. Choose to correct those errors as necessary. The following steps check the newsletter for spelling errors.

1

- With page 1 of the Communiquarium Newsletter still displayed, scroll up, and then click the masthead text box.

- Click the Spelling button on the Standard toolbar to start the spell checking process (Figure 2–74).

Q&A

What if my newsletter did not find the same word as the figure?

If Publisher is flagging a different word, it may be that you already removed the flag on the word Communiquarium by right-clicking the red wavy flag earlier. Or you may not have started in the masthead text box.

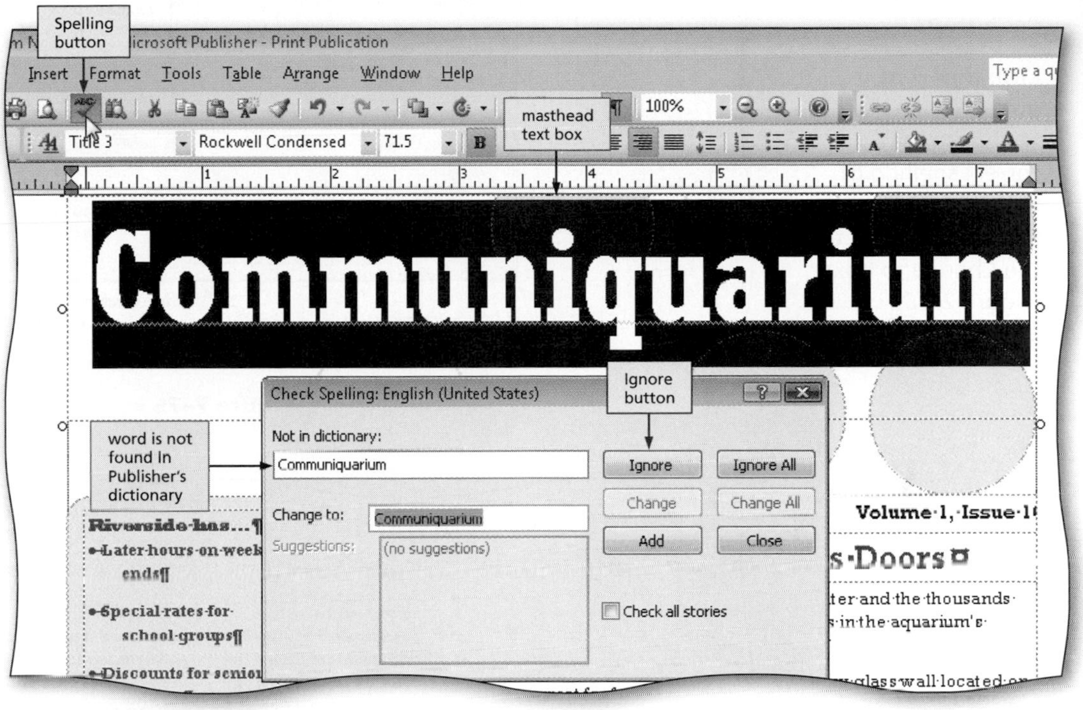

Figure 2–74

2

- Click the Ignore button to ignore the name of the newsletter that is not in Publisher's dictionary (Figure 2–75).

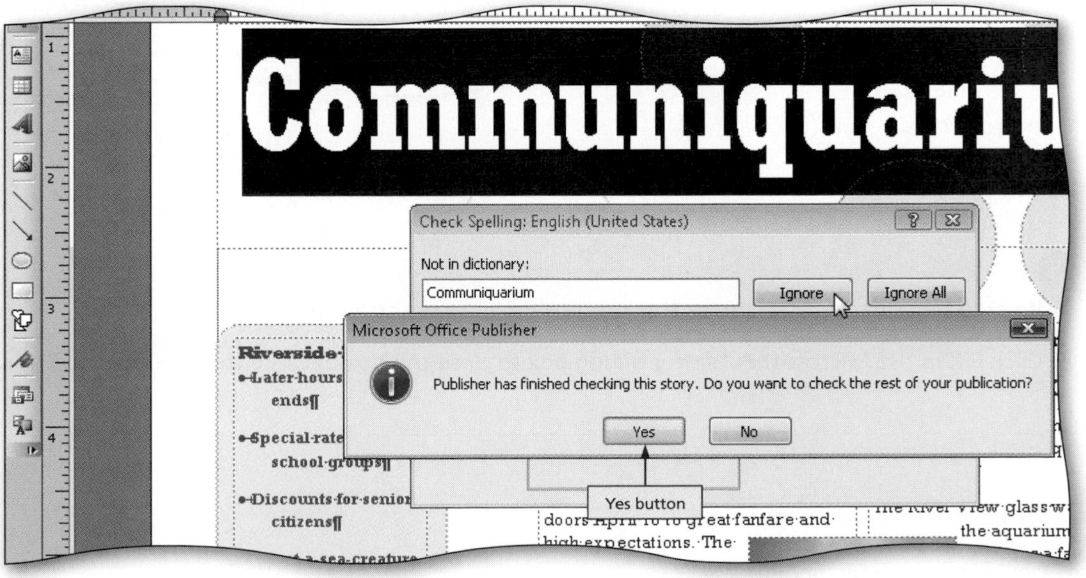

Figure 2–75

3

- If Publisher displays a dialog box asking if you want to check the rest of the publication, click the Yes button.

- Click the word, proud, in the list to choose the correct spelling of the flagged word and to transfer it to the Change to box (Figure 2–76).

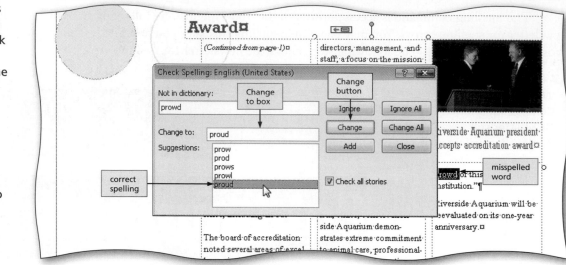

Figure 2–76

4

- Click the Change button to change the word, prowd, to proud (Figure 2–77).

Q&A

When should I click the Add button?

Only click the Add button when you are absolutely sure that you want to add the flagged word to Publisher's dictionary, and only on your own computer system. Acceptable additions might be your name, the name of a company you deal with, or foreign words, if you are completely sure of the spelling. Do not click the Add button in a lab setting or on someone else's computer.

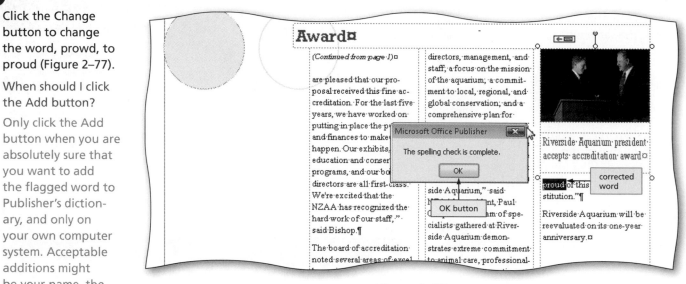

Figure 2–77

5

- If you have other errors, choose the appropriate measure to fix or ignore them.

- Click OK in the Microsoft Publisher dialog box to close the box because the spelling check is complete.

Other Ways

1. On Tools menu, point to Spelling, click Spelling on Spelling submenu

2. Press F7

BTW

Even if text is checked for spelling before it is imported, Publisher flags words, phrases, and punctuation not found in its dictionary. The process is worth the time it takes, but again, there is no substitute for proofreading the text yourself.

Checking the Newsletter for Design Errors

You now are ready to check the newsletter for design errors as you did in Chapter 1. The Design Checker can check single pages or entire publications for a specific type of error or all types of errors. The Design Checker looks for errors related to design issues and object interaction, providing comments and correction choices. Design errors are the most common type of problem when submitting a publication to a professional printer. In a later project, you will learn that, in addition to the interactive Design Checker, Publisher's Pack and Go Wizard checks for errors related to embedded fonts and graphics. Some of the errors flagged by the Design Checker include:

- Empty frames
- Covered objects
- Text in overflow area
- Objects in nonprinting region
- Disproportional pictures
- Spacing between sentences
- Low resolution graphics

To Check the Newsletter for Design Errors

In the following steps, Publisher checks for all kinds of design errors throughout the newsletter.

1 Click Tools on the menu bar and then click Design Checker to start the process.

2 If the Design Checker finds errors, choose to fix or ignore them as necessary. When the Design Checker terminates, close the Design Checker task pane.

To Save an Existing Publication with the Same File Name

The publication now is complete. You should save the newsletter again. The following step saves the publication again.

1 Click the Save button on the Standard toolbar to overwrite the previous Communiquarium Newsletter file on the USB flash drive.

Creating a Template

Newsletters typically retain their masthead, color scheme, font scheme, and other graphics from issue to issue. In a first issue, you must make design choices and implement them to make the newsletter display correctly, which takes time and review. You do not have to do all of that for subsequent issues. Once the decisions have been made, and the publication distributed, you can reuse the same publication as a template. Additionally, Publisher can add it to the templates on your system.

The **Publisher Tasks task pane** offers shortcuts and links to access some of the more powerful Publisher features and information as you design and distribute publications, including the ability to create a template from a newsletter.

To Access the Publisher Tasks Task Pane

The following step accesses the Publisher Tasks task pane.

1

- Click the Publisher Tasks button on the toolbar to open the Publisher Tasks task pane (Figure 2–78).

Q&A

How does the Publisher Tasks task pane assist me?

The task pane offers links and information about creating and distributing publications and tracking a publication's effectiveness in the market. Some of the links open dialog boxes. Others present a list of options or open a Help window. Still, others open a browser and transfer you to a Web page with information.

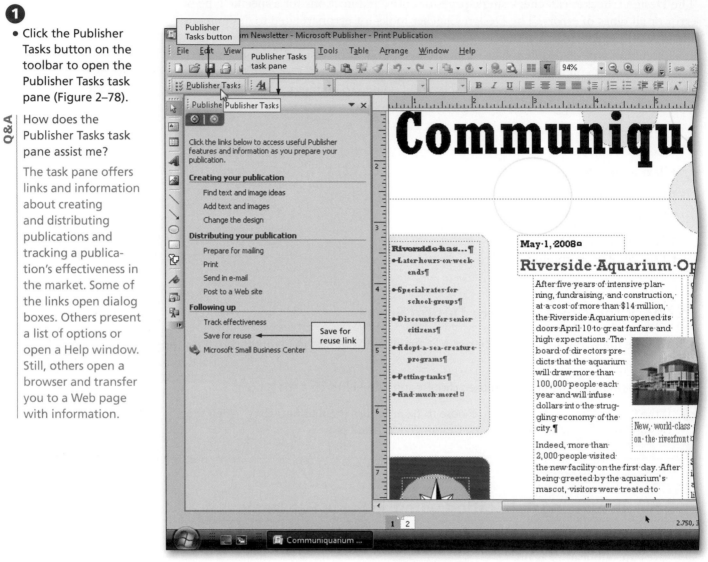

Figure 2–78

Other Ways
1. With any task pane visible, click Other Task Panes button, click Publisher Tasks   2. Press CTRL+F1, click Other Task Panes button, click Publisher Tasks

Setting File Properties at the Time of Creation

Recall that in Chapter 1, you set file properties using the Properties command from the File menu. Two specific properties can be set at the time you create a publication or template. The author and tag properties can be entered into any of the Save As dialog boxes, which can save you several steps. A tag is a custom file property used to help find and organize files. Although there are many properties associated with files, tags are often the most useful because you can add tags to your files that contain words or phrases that make the files easier to find. Adding or changing properties to a file when you create and save it eliminates the need to find the file and apply properties afterwards. Later, to find a file containing a tag, you can type tag words into the Search box of any Windows Vista folder.

To Create a Template with Property Changes

With the Publisher Tasks task pane still open, the following steps create a template. The template will be stored on a USB flash drive. It is not recommended to save templates on lab computers or computers belonging to other people.

1

- With a USB flash drive connected to one of the computer's USB ports, click the link, Save for reuse, to view the Save for reuse tasks (Figure 2–79).

Figure 2–79

2

- Click the link, Save as a template, to open the Save As Template dialog box (Figure 2–80).

🔎 **Experiment**

- Click the Save as type box arrow to view the many types of file formats available for publications.

- If necessary, click the Save as type box arrow, and then click Publisher Template to select the file format.

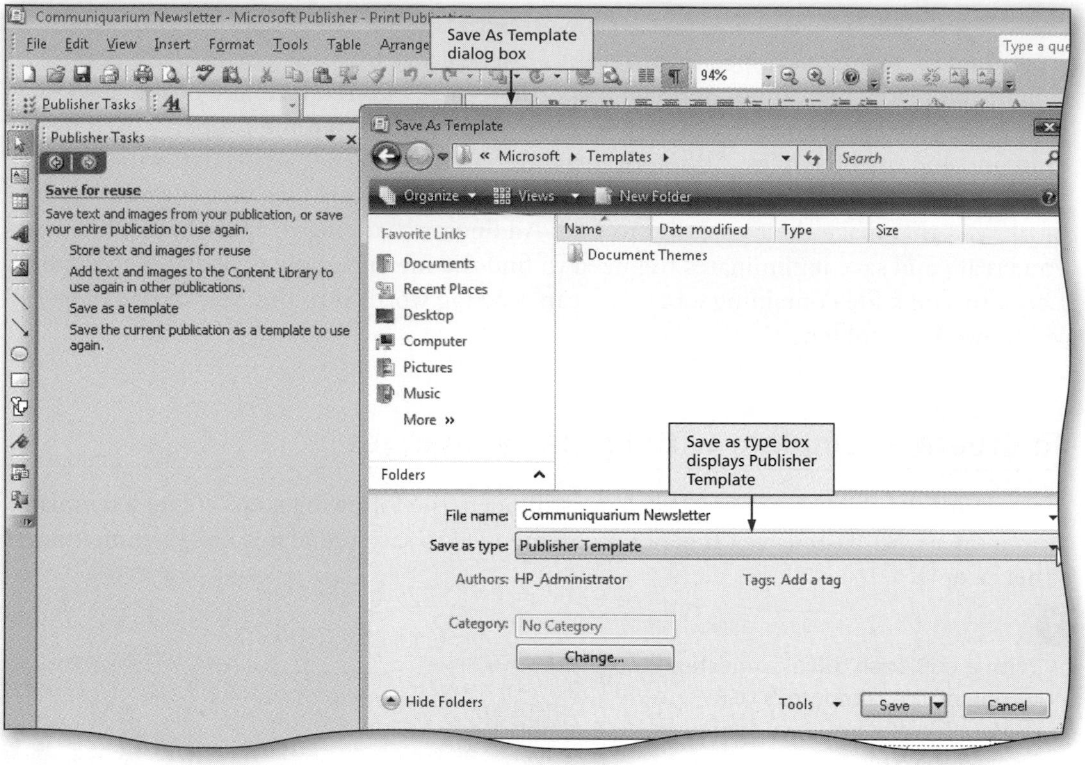

Figure 2–80

3

- If necessary, click the text in the File name text box to select it.

- Type Communiquarium Newsletter Template to name the template. Do not press the ENTER key (Figure 2–81).

- Navigate to your USB flash drive.

Q&A

What does the Change button do?

If you plan on creating many templates, you can organize them into categories. Clicking the Change button opens a dialog box that allows you to create or navigate to categories of templates.

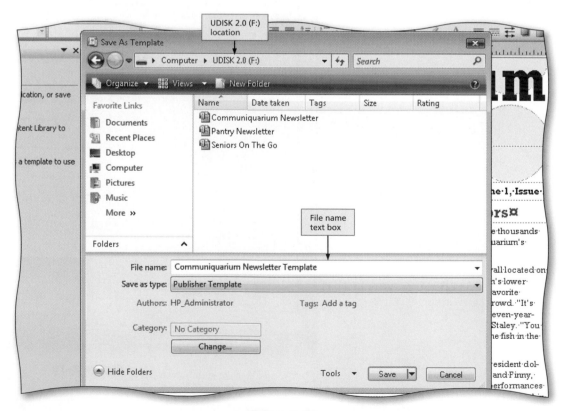

Figure 2–81

4

- If your name does not display next to the word, Authors, in the lower portion of the dialog box, double-click the text and then type your name to replace the text.
- Click the Tags text box and then type `monthly newsletter volume 1` to add the tag words (Figure 2–82). The current text in the Tags text box will disappear as you start to type.

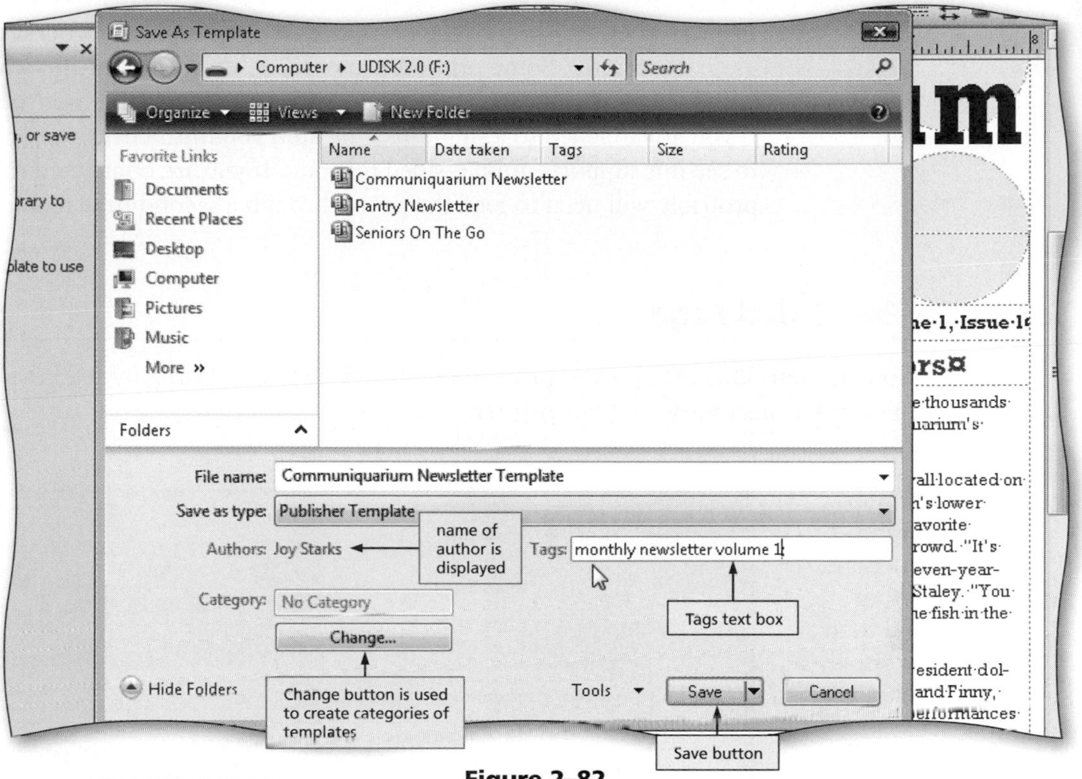

Figure 2–82

5

- Click the Save button to save the template.
- Close the task pane (Figure 2–83).

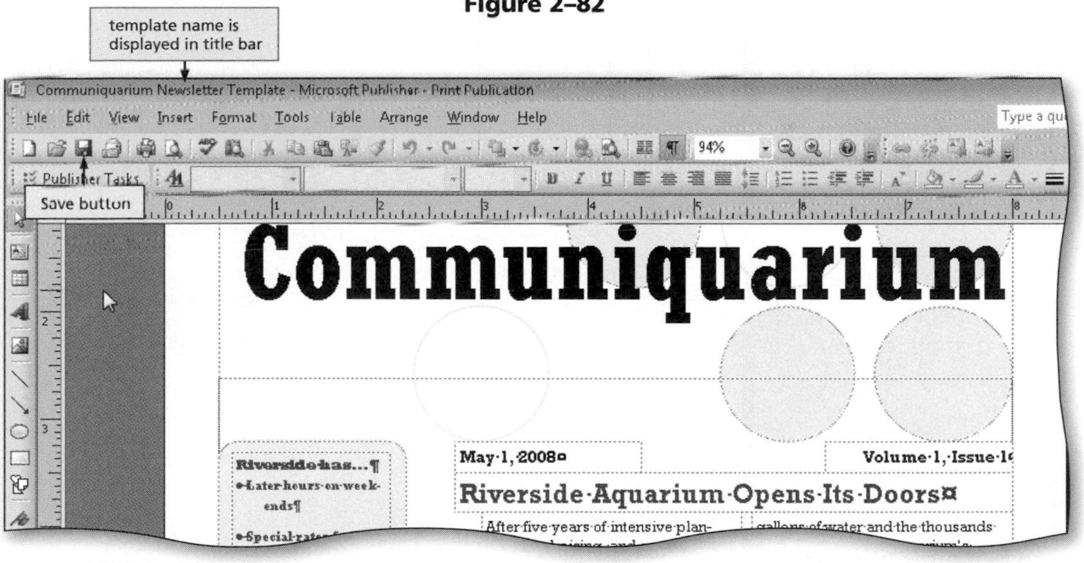

Figure 2–83

Q&A Where should a company store its templates?

On a business computer, for an organization that routinely uses templates, you should save templates in the default location. Publisher stores templates within the application data in a folder named, Templates. Templates stored in the default location display in the catalog when you click the My Templates button. However, templates can be stored anywhere, on a personal system, on a Web server, or on a common drive for use among employees or students.

BTW Tags are one of many properties available to attach to files to help you find and organize the files. In addition to tags, other properties include the Date Modified, Author, and Subject. Tags are not a part of the actual contents of a file. They become the keywords in the Properties dialog box. Unlike some properties, which are predefined, tags can be anything you choose, such as "Brochures," "Vacation," or "My Stuff."

Printing a Two-Sided Page

Printing the two pages of the newsletter back to back is a process that is highly dependent upon the printer. Some printers can perform **duplex printing**, which prints both sides before ejecting the paper, while other printers require the user to reload the paper manually. If you are attached to a single-user printer, you must check the printer's documentation to see if it supports double-sided printing. If you are connected to a network printer, you probably will need to feed the paper through a second time manually.

To Print a Two-Sided Page

The following steps illustrate how to print the first page and then manually feed the page through a second time. Adjust the steps as necessary for your printer.

1

- Ready the printer according to the printer instructions. Click File on the menu bar and then click Print to display the Print dialog box.

- Click Current page in the Print range area to print only the current page (Figure 2–84).

Q&A What if my dialog box is different?

Look for a check box that says current page. If you do not have one, look for a box that allows you to specify a certain page and enter the number 1.

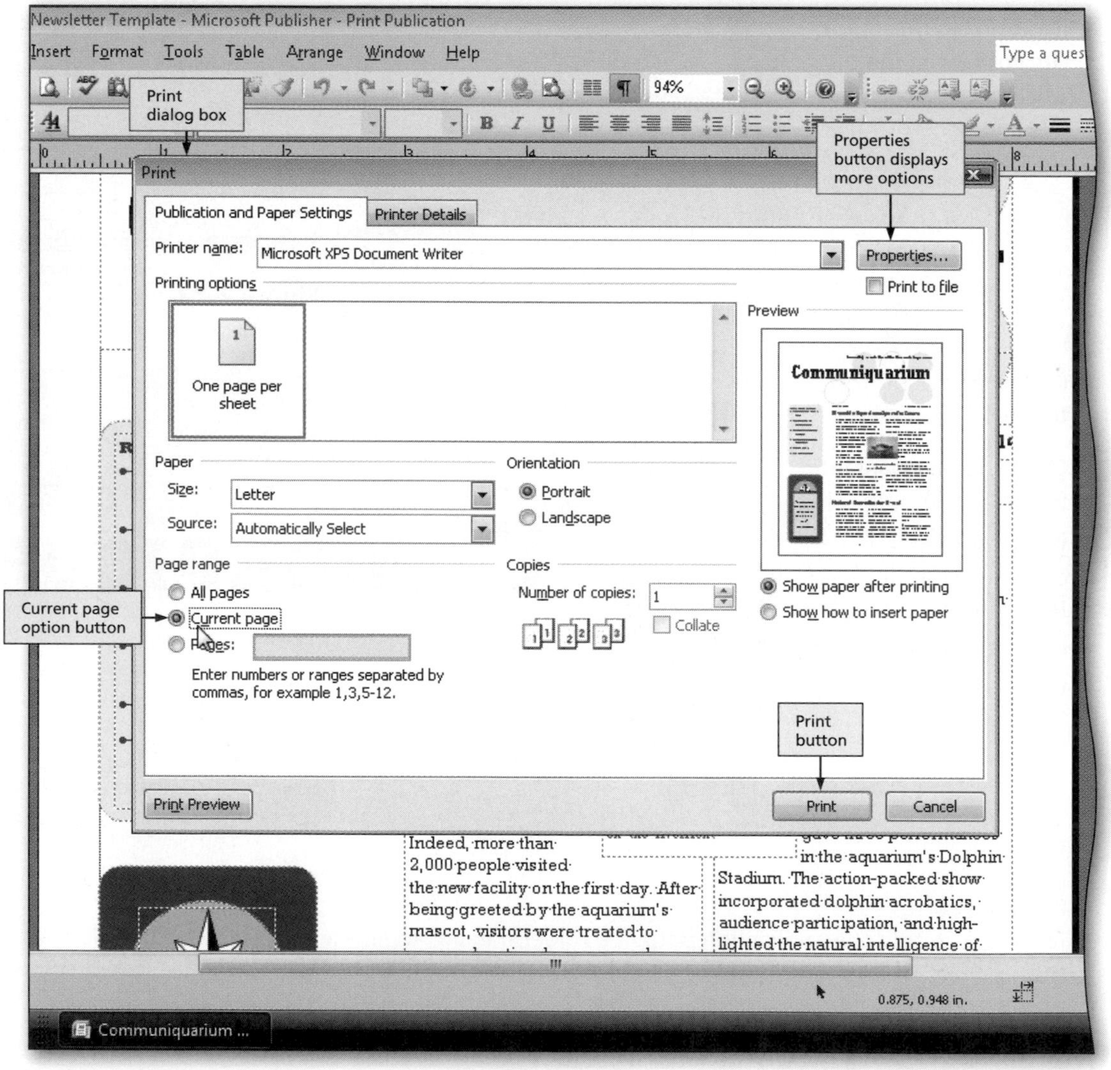

2

- Click the Print button to begin the printing process.

- When printing is complete, retrieve the printout.

Q&A Why is it taking so long to print?

Publications with lots of text and graphics take longer to print. As long as progress is being made, your print process is fine. If after several minutes it has not even started to print, consult your instructor or lab technician.

Figure 2–84

3

- After retrieving the printout, wait a few seconds for it to dry. Reinsert the printout in the manual tray of the printer, usually blank side down, top first.

- Navigate to page 2.

- To print the current page, click Print on the File menu, and then choose to print the current page.

Other Ways
1. Press CTRL+P

BTW

If you have an Options button, a Properties button, or an Advanced Print Settings button in your Print dialog box (Figure 2–84), you may be able to duplex print. Check your printer documentation, or click the button for more information. If you are unsure how to load the paper, you can run a test page through the printer. Mark an X in the upper-right corner of a blank sheet and then insert the sheet into the printer, noting where the X is. If your printer has a Manual Feed button or Paper Source list, be sure to click Manual. Print the first page. Note where the X is in relation to the printed page and turn the paper over to print the other side accordingly. In a later project, you will learn more about types of paper best suited for printing on both sides, as well as how to prepare a publication for a printing service.

To Quit Publisher

This project is complete. The following steps quit Publisher.

1 To quit Publisher, click the Close button on the right side of the title bar.

2 If a Microsoft Office Publisher dialog box is displayed, click the No button so that any changes you have made are not saved.

Chapter Summary

In this chapter you have learned how to select template options for a newsletter, edit the masthead and sidebar, import stories and graphics, create original stories using the Edit in Microsoft Word command, insert a pull quote from the Design Gallery, insert a page number in a footer, cut and paste, drag and drop, check the spelling, and use the design checker. The items listed below include all the new Publisher skills you have learned in this chapter.

1. Choose a Newsletter Template and Change Options (PUB 78)
2. Display Formatting Marks (PUB 81)
3. Change and Delete Pages in a Newsletter (PUB 83)
4. Edit the Masthead (PUB 85)
5. Edit a Headline and Import a Text File (PUB 89)
6. Import Text for the Secondary Story and Continue It on Page 2 (PUB 92)
7. Format with Continued Notices (PUB 95)
8. Replace the Back Page Story Headline (PUB 97)
9. Edit a Story Using Word (PUB 98)
10. Change the Font Size (PUB 101)
11. Use the Color Scheme Colors (PUB 102)
12. Delete the Logo and Edit Other Text Boxes on Page 2 (PUB 103)
13. Replace a Graphic and Edit the Caption (PUB 106)
14. Replace a Graphic on Page 2 and Edit the Caption (PUB 109)
15. Insert a New Picture from Clip art (PUB 110)
16. Move and Resize a Graphic (PUB 112)
17. Edit a Sidebar (PUB 113)
18. Delete the Sidebar (PUB 115)
19. Insert a Pull Quote (PUB 117)
20. Finish Formatting the Pull Quote (PUB 121)
21. Move Text (PUB 122)
22. Insert Page Numbers in the Footer (PUB 124)
23. Check the Newsletter for Spelling Errors (PUB 127)
24. Access the Publisher Tasks Task Pane (PUB 130)
25. Create a Template with Property Changes (PUB 131)
26. Print a Two-Sided Page (PUB 134)

Learn It Online

Test your knowledge of chapter content and key terms.

Instructions: To complete the Learn It Online exercises, start your browser, click the Address bar, and then enter the Web address scsite.com/pub2007/learn. When the Office 2007 Learn It Online page is displayed, click the link for the exercise you want to complete and then read the instructions.

Chapter Reinforcement TF, MC, and SA

A series of true/false, multiple choice, and short answer questions that test your knowledge of the chapter content.

Flash Cards

An interactive learning environment where you identify chapter key terms associated with displayed definitions.

Practice Test

A series of multiple choice questions that test your knowledge of chapter content and key terms.

Who Wants To Be a Computer Genius?

An interactive game that challenges your knowledge of chapter content in the style of a television quiz show.

Wheel of Terms

An interactive game that challenges your knowledge of chapter key terms in the style of the television show *Wheel of Fortune*.

Crossword Puzzle Challenge

A crossword puzzle that challenges your knowledge of key terms presented in the chapter.

Apply Your Knowledge

Reinforce the skills and apply the concepts you learned in this chapter.

Revising Text and Paragraphs in a Publication

Instructions: Start Publisher. Open the publication, Apply 2-1 Pantry Shelf Newsletter Draft, from the Data Files for Students. See the inside back cover of this book for instructions on downloading the Data Files for Students, or contact your instructor for more information about accessing the required files.

The publication you open is a four-page newsletter. You are to revise the publication as follows: enter the date in the masthead, move a paragraph, delete pages, enter a caption, insert a pull quote with text, insert page numbers, resize a graphic, and check the publication for errors. The revised publication is shown in Figure 2–85.

Perform the following tasks:

1. Enter the current date in the empty text box below the volume in the masthead.

2. Select the second paragraph in the lead story. Use drag-and-drop editing to move this paragraph so that it is the next to the last paragraph in the publication.

3. Below the graphic in the lead story, enter the following caption in the text box: Guardian Angel Award. Center the caption text.

4. Use the Design gallery to select the Tilt pull quote. Move the pull quote to a position above the Dates to Remember sidebar.

5. From the first paragraph in the lead story, select the words on the plaque, beginning with the text, 2008 Guardian Award. Copy the selection. Paste the selection, replacing the text in the pull quote.

6. Select the graphic of the line on the right side of page 1. Use the Line Color box arrow on the Formatting toolbar to change the color to the Accent 3 (Blue) color of the Wildflower color scheme.

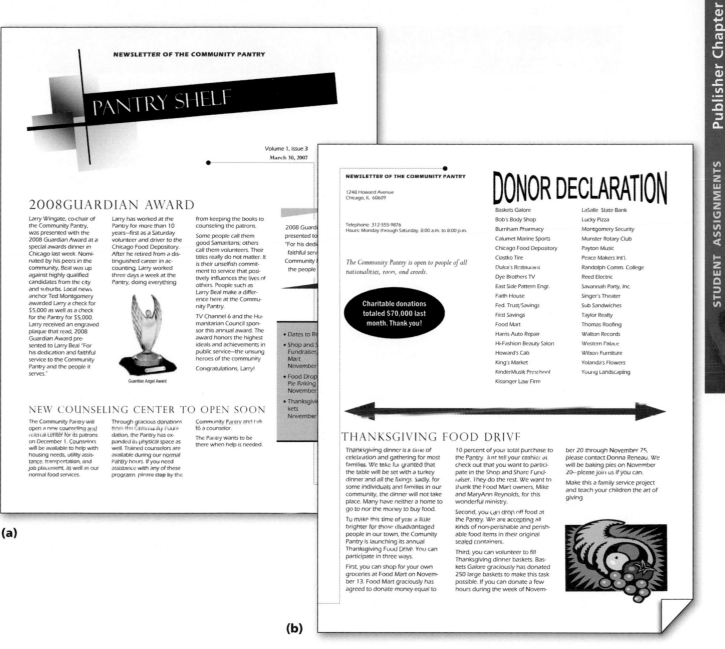

(a)

(b)

Figure 2–85

7. Delete pages 2 and 3 of the publication.

8. Insert page numbers in the lower-right corner of the footer on both of the remaining pages.

9. Repeat Step 6 for the graphic of the line on the left side of page 2.

10. On page 2, resize the cornucopia graphic to fill the space below the last line of the article.

11. Use Publisher's thesaurus to change the Publisher, incorporated, to the Publisher, integrated, in the first sentence of the second paragraph.

12. Run the publication through the Design Checker and check the spelling. Fix any errors you find. Choose to ignore names of people and businesses.

13. Change the publication properties, as specified by your instructor.

14. Save the publication using the file name, Apply 2-1 Pantry Shelf Newsletter Modified.

15. Print the publication using duplex printing.

Extend Your Knowledge

Extend the skills you learned in this chapter and experiment with new skills. You may need to use Help to complete the assignment.

Working with Text in Overflow and the Design Gallery

Instructions: Start Publisher. Open the publication, Extend 2-1 Evergreen Newsletter Draft, from the Data Files for Students. See the inside back cover of this book for instructions on downloading the Data Files for Students, or contact your instructor for more information about accessing the required files.

You will link a text box from page 1 that has text in overflow with an empty box on page 2, format both with continued notices, insert a headline and picture with a caption for the new text box, insert and format page numbers in the header, and fix any spelling and design errors.

Perform the following tasks:

1. In the second story on page 1, click the third text box. Notice that the Text in Overflow symbol is displayed.

2. Edit the story in Microsoft Word. Insert a blank line before the last paragraph, which begins a second internship listing in the story.

3. Return to Publisher. Select the third text box in the secondary story.

4. Use the Create Text Box Link button in the Connect Text Boxes toolbar to begin the process of making the story flow to page 2. Notice the mouse pointer change after clicking the button.

5. Move to page 2 of the publication and click the large, empty text box to indicate the location to which the story should flow.

6. Add continued notices on page 1 and page 2.

7. Create an appropriate headline for the second part of the story on page 2.

8. Insert a page number only on page 2, in the header, centered.

9. Make other appropriate changes to the publication, such as inserting a graphic with a caption from the design gallery and then searching for an appropriate clip art using the task pane.

10. Use the spelling and design checking features of Publisher.

11. Save the newsletter with a new name and print the newsletter using duplex printing (Figure 2–86).

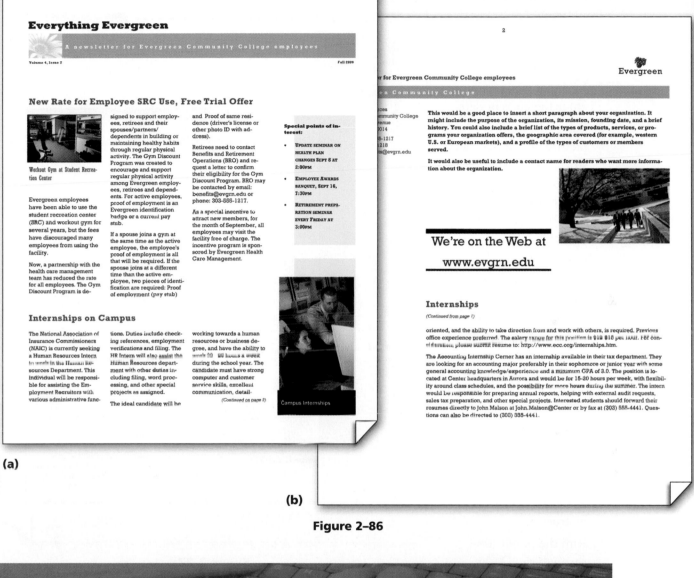

(a)

(b)

Figure 2–86

Make It Right

Analyze a publication and correct all errors and/or improve the design.

Inserting Missing Continued Notices and Masthead Elements

Instructions: Start Publisher. Open the publication, Make It Right 2-1 History Newsletter Draft, from the Data Files for Students. See the inside back cover of this book for instructions on downloading the Data Files for Students, or contact your instructor for more information about accessing the required files.

The publication is a newsletter that is missing several elements, as shown in Figure 2–87 on the next page. You are to insert these missing elements: masthead volume number, issue number and date, a graphic for the lead story, a footer with a page number, and continued notices.

Continued >

Make It Right *continued*

Perform the following steps:

1. In the first empty text box below the newsletter title, enter Volume 7 Issue 4.

2. In the second text box, enter the current date.

3. Select the empty picture box in the lead story. Use the clip art task pane to find a picture of a building. Do not use a clip art drawing.

4. Create a footer for each page with the page number centered.

5. Find the story with text that flows from page 1 to page 2. Format the appropriate boxes with continued notices. Insert an appropriate title on page 2.

6. Change the publication properties, as specified by your instructor.

7. Run the publication through the Design Checker and check the spelling. Fix any errors you find. Choose to ignore names of people and businesses.

8. Save the revised publication and then submit it in the format specified by your instructor.

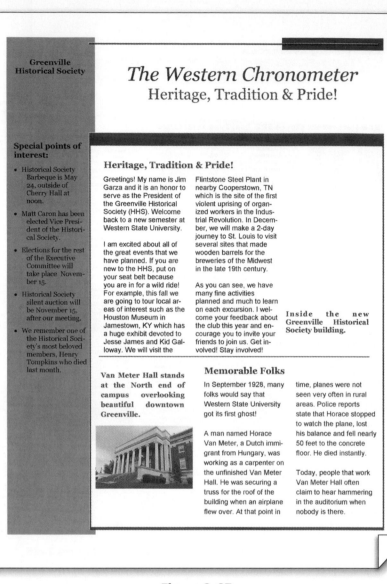

Figure 2–87

In the Lab

Design and/or create a publication using the guidelines, concepts, and skills presented in this chapter. Labs are listed in order of increasing difficulty.

Lab 1: Creating a Blank Newsletter Template with a Masthead

Problem: As a student working in the English department, you have been asked to create a template for the College of Liberal Arts monthly alumni newsletter. The College wants a four-page newsletter in black and white, with space for many articles (including one where they highlight a member of the COLA alumni), a masthead, pictures with captions, and an attention getter. Each month a faculty member from the English department will work with the template, replacing default text. You prepare a newsletter template similar to the one whose first page is shown below (Figure 2–88).

Perform the following tasks:

1. Start Publisher. Select the Refined newsletter template with a two-column format. Choose the Black and White color scheme and the Literary font scheme.

2. The title of the newsletter is `The COLA Alumnus`. The Business Name text will be `A Newsletter from the College of Liberal Arts`. Use Volume X and Issue X as the text in the template boxes, which will be replaced each month. Use the Insert menu's Date and Time command to enter a template date. (*Hint*: Click the Update Automatically check box.)

3. On pages 2 and 3, replace the quotation text boxes with the Marquee pull quote from the Design Gallery.

4. On page 2, delete the graphic and insert an attention getter from the Design Gallery. Replace the default text of the attention getter with the words, `Attention Getter`, so template users will understand the purpose.

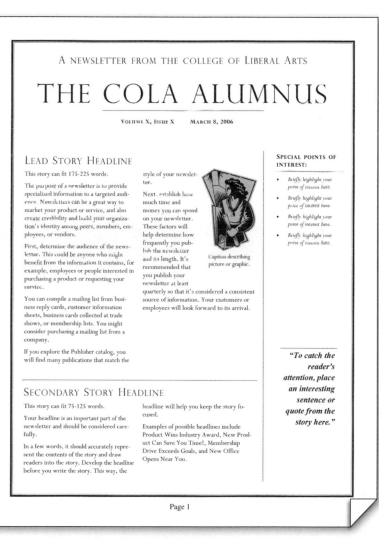

Figure 2–88

5. On page 3, change one of the headlines to `Alumni of the Month`.

6. Insert page numbers at the bottom of pages 1 and 4, centered.

7. Save the publication on a USB flash drive, using Lab 2-1 COLA Newsletter Template as the file name. E-mail the newsletter as an attachment to your instructor.

In the Lab

Lab 2: Newsletter Analysis

Problem: Obtain a copy of a newsletter that you regularly receive or one from a friend, company, or school. Using the principles in this chapter, analyze the newsletter.

Instructions: Start Publisher. Open the publication, In the Lab 2-2 Newsletter Analysis Table, from the Data Files for Students. See the inside back cover of this book for instructions on downloading the Data Files for Students, or contact your instructor for more information about accessing the required files. Use a word processing program to fill in each empty cell in the table as it applies to your selected newsletter. The table is displayed below:

Newsletter Name:	Your Name:
Purpose:	
Audience:	
Paper:	
Distribution:	
Font & Color Scheme:	
Consistency:	
Alignment:	
Repeated Elements:	
Jump Lines, Sidebars, Pull Quotes, etc.:	

Print the table and attach a copy of the newsletter. Turn in both to your instructor.

In the Lab

Lab 3: Researching Computer-Related Jobs

Problem: You are a college student currently enrolled in an introductory business class. Your assignment is to prepare a short newsletter about computer-related jobs. Research three computer-related jobs, using journals, interviews, or the Web, and prepare a two-page newsletter.

Instructions: Perform the following tasks:

1. Gather your data and prepare electronic versions of your research.
2. Start Publisher. Choose a template, column style, font style, and color style.
3. Delete pages 2 and 3.
4. Replace the masthead text boxes with appropriate data. Name your newsletter.
5. Choose your favorite computer-related job as the lead story.
6. Choose the longest of your three articles for the secondary story and have Publisher flow the text into one of the text boxes on page 2.
7. Import the third story into a vacant text box on page 2.
8. Delete any text boxes that have to do with a company name, address, or phone. Delete a logo if it is displayed.
9. Use the design gallery to insert an attention getter. Replace the attention getter text with your name.
10. Check the spelling and design of the newsletter.
11. Save the publication on a USB flash drive, using Lab 2-3 Computer Jobs Newsletter as the file name.
12. Print the newsletter using duplex printing and turn it in to your instructor.

Cases and Places

Apply your creative thinking and problem-solving skills to design and implement a solution.

• EASIER   •• MORE DIFFICULT

• 1: Create a Vacation Club Newsletter

Use the Voyage Newsletter template to create a two-page newsletter for the Seniors Abroad Club. This local club of senior citizens gets together to take group trips. For the newsletter title, use Seniors On The Go, and place today's date in the masthead. Include an article heading for the lead story, which concerns the club's most recent trip to London (you may use the default text in the story itself), and a secondary article heading that tells how to pack lightly for trips overseas. Add a list of dates for the upcoming trips to Paris, the Caribbean, and Tokyo in the Special points of interest sidebar. Replace the graphics with suitable pictures using the Clip Art task pane.

• 2: Create a Band Booster Quarterly Newsletter

The two-page newsletter will be sent to band students, parents, and other interested parties. Use the Rhythm template, the Concourse color scheme, and the Literary font scheme. The name of the newsletter is High Notes. Use the name of your school as the business name. The newsletter should feature the most recent performance as the lead story. You may write a story about a recent musical performance at your school. The secondary story should be about a "Band Member of the Month." You may use yourself as the band member or a friend who plays an instrument. If either story flows onto the back page, create jump lines. If necessary, create a story related to an individual band in the school system to include on the back page. Include a sidebar with upcoming competitions and events. Use another sidebar for a future trip payment schedule. Incorporate clip art or photographs. Make sure that any graphics downloaded from the Web have no copyright restrictions. Save the newsletter as a template for the band boosters to use next quarter. For extra credit on this assignment, create a list of instructions for template users.

•• 3: Create a Restaurant Review Newsletter

You are a member of a restaurant and food review club. Because you have a background in desktop publishing, you prepare the monthly two-page newsletter for club members. Your assignment is to design the newsletter and develop the next issue. The newsletter should have a feature article and some announcements for club members. Your feature article could discuss/review a restaurant, a deli, an online or in town grocery store, a recipe, or any other aspect of food or food service. Use the Internet, visit a restaurant, interview restaurant or grocery store patrons, prepare a dish using a new recipe, and so on, to obtain information for the articles. The feature article should be continued on page 2. Enhance the newsletter with color and font schemes, graphics, sidebars, and pull quotes.

•• 4: Create a Newsletter about the Month You Were Born

Make It Personal

Did you ever wonder what world events took place during the month you were born (besides your birth)? For example, what happened with respect to politics, world affairs, and the economy? What made headline news? Were there any scientific breakthroughs? What was on television and at the box office? Were any famous people born? Did anyone famous die? What songs topped the charts? What was happening in the world of sports? Research the newsworthy events that took place during the month and year you were born (i.e., July 1985) by looking through newspapers, magazines, searching the Web, and/or interviewing family and friends. Create a two-page newsletter with articles about that month. Include the date in the masthead. Use appropriate graphics, a sidebar, a pull quote, WordArt, and other newsletter objects.

Continued >

Cases and Places *continued*

•• 5: Create a Newsletter about Spring Break Vacation Destinations

Working Together

Your school newspaper is planning a four-page insert to review spring break destinations. Your team is to design and write that insert, using a Publisher newsletter template. The newsletter should have a lead story that reviews the most popular destination. Other articles could review locations, transportation, group rates, new passport or travel regulations, security at the airport, etc. As a group, decide on the name of the newsletter and design the masthead. Each team member independently is to write at least three paragraphs for a story. Then, the team should meet as a group to combine all of the documents so you can place them into the newsletter on appropriate pages. If articles are too long to fit in a template box, decide where to continue the stories. Use jump lines. On the first page, include a sidebar, listing the top five destinations. Use appropriate graphics, sidebars, and pull quotes. Make sure that any graphics downloaded from the Web have no copyright restrictions. Run the publication through the Design Checker and check the spelling. Fix any errors you find. Choose to ignore names of people and businesses.

3 | Publishing a Tri-Fold Brochure

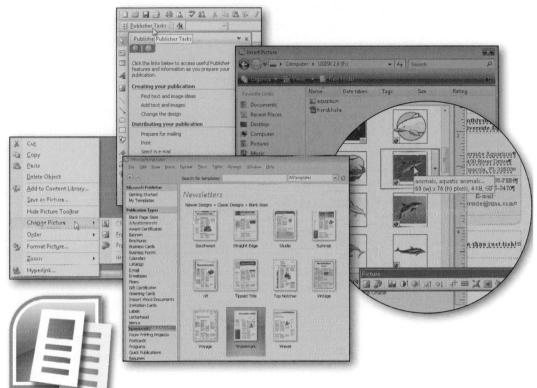

Objectives

You will have mastered the material in this project when you can:

- Discuss advantages of the brochure medium
- Choose brochure options
- Create a custom color scheme
- Edit brochure template text boxes
- Use AutoCorrect options and the Format Painter
- Create a font style and format paragraphs
- Edit a Sign-up form
- Describe the use of graphic formats
- Wrap text around a graphic
- Create a logo from scratch using AutoShapes

- Format AutoShapes in the scratch area
- Duplicate, resize, and reposition objects
- Create a composite object in the scratch area
- Create a WordArt object
- Create a watermark on the Master Page
- Choose appropriate printing services, paper, and color libraries
- Prepare a publication for outside printing
- Use the Pack and Go Wizard

3 | Publishing a Tri-Fold Brochure

Introduction

Whether you want to advertise a service, event, or product, or merely want to inform the public about a current topic of interest, brochures are a popular type of promotional publication. A **brochure**, or pamphlet, usually is a high-quality document with lots of color and graphics, created for advertising purposes. Businesses that may not be able to reach potential clientele effectively through traditional advertising, such as newspapers and radio, can create a long-lasting advertisement with a well-designed brochure.

Brochures come in all shapes and sizes. Colleges and universities produce brochures about their programs. The travel industry uses brochures to entice tourists. In addition, service industries and manufacturers display their products using this visual, hands-on medium.

Project — Brochure

The project in this chapter shows you how to build the two-page, tri-fold brochure shown in Figure 3–1. The brochure informs secondary school teachers about a Tech Camp summer program, held at the local college. Each side of the brochure has three panels. Page 1 (Figure 3–1a) contains the front and back panels, as well as the inside fold. Page 2 (Figure 3–1b) contains a three-panel display that, when opened completely, provides the reader with more details about the event and a sign-up form.

On page 1, the front panel contains shapes, text boxes, and a graphic designed to draw the reader's attention and inform the reader of the intent of the brochure. The back panel, which displays in the middle of page 1, contains the name of the school, the address, telephone numbers, and the organization logo. The inside fold, on the left, contains an article about the details of the program.

The three inside panels on page 2 contain more information about the camp, a list of topics or tracks, and a form the reader may use to register.

Overview

As you read through this chapter, you will learn how to create the newsletter shown in Figure 3–1 by performing these general tasks:

- Select a brochure template and specify the layout options.
- Create a new color scheme and style for the brochure.
- Copy formatting, using styles and the Format Painter button.
- Create a logo from an AutoShape and format it.
- Use WordArt to create a watermark on page 2 of the brochure.
- Proof the brochure with spell checking and the design checker.
- Prepare the brochure for commercial printing.

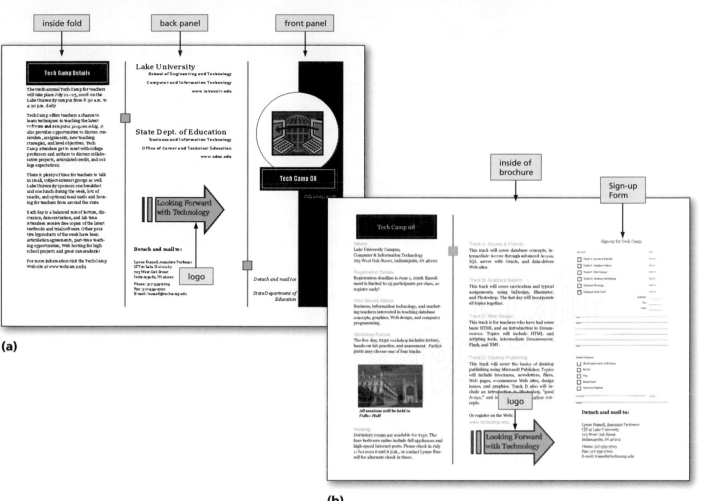

Figure 3–1

General Project Guidelines

When creating a Publisher brochure, the actions you perform and decisions you make will affect the appearance and characteristics of the finished publication. As you create a brochure, such as the project shown in Figure 3–1, you should follow these general guidelines:

1. **Decide on the purpose, shelf life, and layout.** Spend time brainstorming ideas for the brochure. Think about why you want to create one. Decide on the purpose of the brochure. Is it to inform, sell, attract, or advertise an event? Adjust your template, fonts, colors, and graphics to match that purpose. Brochures commonly have a wider audience than newsletters and flyers. They need to last longer. Carefully consider whether to add dated material or prices. Create a timeline of effectiveness and plan to have the brochure ready far in advance. Decide how many panels your brochure should be, and how often you are going to produce it. If you are working for someone, draw a storyboard and get it approved before you begin. Think about alignment of objects, proximity of similar data, contrast, and repetition.

2. **Create the brochure.** Gather all the information, such as stories, graphics, logos, colors, shapes, style information, and watermarks. Use a template until you are very experienced in designing brochures. Save copies or versions along the way. If you have to create objects from scratch, have someone else evaluate your work and give you constructive feedback. If you are using forms in your brochure, verify the manner in which the viewer will return the form. Check and double-check all prices, addresses, and phone numbers.

(continued)

(continued)

3. **Proofread, revise, and add the final touches.** If possible, proofread the brochure with a fresh set of eyes, that is, at least one to two days after completing the first draft. Insert repeated elements and special objects, such as watermarks and logos, which need to be placed around or in back of other objects. Look at text wrapping on every graphic. Ask someone else to proofread the brochure and give you suggestions for improvements. Revise as necessary and then use the spelling and design checking features of the software.

4. **Plan for printing.** Consult with commercial printers ahead of time. Brochures are more effective on heavier paper, with strong colors and glossy feels. Choose a paper that is going to last. Discuss commercial printing color modes and fonts. Check to make sure the commercial printer can accept Microsoft Publisher 2007 files. Designing an effective brochure involves a great deal of planning. A good brochure, or any publication, must deliver a message in the clearest, most attractive, and effective way possible.

When necessary, more specific details concerning the above guidelines are presented at appropriate points in the chapter. The chapter also will identify the actions performed and decisions made regarding these guidelines during the creation of the brochure shown in Figure 3–1 on the previous page.

The Brochure Medium

Brochures are professionally printed on special paper to provide long-lasting documents and to enhance the graphics. The brochure medium intentionally is tactile. Brochures are meant to be touched, carried home, passed along, and looked at, again and again. Newspapers and fliers usually are produced for short-term readership on paper that soon will be thrown away or recycled. Brochures frequently use a heavier stock of paper so that they can stand better in a display rack.

The content of a brochure needs to last longer, too. On occasion, the intent of a brochure is to educate, such as a brochure on health issues in a doctor's office. More commonly, though, the intent is to market a product or sell a service. Prices and dated materials that are subject to frequent change affect the usable life of a brochure.

Typically, brochures use a great deal of color, and they include actual photographs instead of drawings or graphic images. Photographs give a sense of realism to a publication and should be used to show people, places, or objects that are real, whereas images or drawings more appropriately are used to convey concepts or ideas.

Many brochures incorporate newspaper features, such as columns and a masthead, and the added eye appeal of logos, sidebars, shapes, and graphics. Small brochures are separated into panels and folded. Larger brochures resemble small magazines, with multiple pages and a stapled binding.

Brochures, designed to be in circulation for longer periods as a type of advertising, ordinarily are published in greater quantities and on more expensive paper than newsletters and are, therefore, more costly. The cost, however, is less prohibitive when produced **in-house** using desktop publishing rather than hiring an outside service. The cost per copy sometimes is less than a newsletter because brochures are produced in mass quantities.

Table 3–1 lists some benefits and advantages of using the brochure medium.

Table 3–1 Benefits and Advantages of Using the Brochure Medium	
Aspect	**Benefits and Advantages**
Exposure	An attention getter in displays
	A take-along document encouraging second looks
	A long-lasting publication due to paper and content
	An easily distributed publication — mass mailings, advertising sites
Information	An in-depth look at a product or service
	An opportunity to inform in a nonrestrictive environment
	An opportunity for focused feedback using tear-offs and forms
Audience	Interested clientele and retailers
Communication	An effective medium to highlight products and services
	A source of free information to build credibility
	An easier method to disseminate information than a magazine

Besides the intent and content of the brochure, you must consider the shape and size of the page when designing this type of publication. Publisher can incorporate a variety of paper sizes, from the standard $8\frac{1}{2} \times 11$-inch to the $8\frac{1}{2} \times 24$-inch. You also can design smaller brochures, such as those used as liner notes for CD jewel cases or inserts for videotapes. In addition, you need to think about how the brochure or pamphlet will be folded. Publisher's brochure templates can create three or four panels. Using the page setup options, you can even create special folds, such as book or card folds.

Plan Ahead

Decide on the purpose, shelf life, and layout.
The first impression of a company sometimes is through its brochure. Thus, it is important that your brochure appropriately reflects the essence of the business, item, or event. Determine the shelf life of your brochure and its purpose.

Choose your template, font, colors, panels, and forms. Choose a template that matches the feeling of your topics. Use colors and fonts already in use In graphics from the company, school, or event organizers.

After starting Publisher, the following pages choose a template and select font and color schemes.

To Start Publisher

If you are using a computer to step through the project in this chapter, and you want your screens to match the figures in this book, you should change your computer's resolution to 1024×768. For information about how to change a computer's resolution, read Appendix D.

The following steps, which assume Windows is running, start Publisher based on a typical installation. You may need to ask your instructor how to start Publisher for your computer.

Note: If you are using Windows XP, please see Appendix F for alternate steps.

1 Click the Start button on the Windows Vista taskbar to display the Start menu, and then click All Programs at the bottom of the left pane on the Start menu to display the All Programs list.

2 Click Microsoft Office in the All Programs list to display the Microsoft Office list, and then click Microsoft Office Publisher 2007 to start Publisher and display the Getting Started with Microsoft Office Publisher 2007 catalog.

3 If the Publisher window is not maximized, click the Maximize button next to the Close button on its title bar to maximize the window.

Plan Ahead	**Create the brochure.**
	Gather all the information and objects. Once you make a few changes, save a copy as the rough draft version. As you add new objects, verify the accuracy of all your information. Get a second opinion on anything created from scratch.

Creating a Tri-Fold Brochure

Publisher-supplied templates use proven design strategies and combinations of objects, which are placed to attract attention and disseminate information effectively. The options for brochures differ from other publications in that they allow you to choose from page sizes, special kinds of forms, and panel/page layout options.

Making Choices about Brochure Options

For the Tech Camp brochure, you will use an informational brochure template, named Spotlight, making changes to its page size, customer address, sign-up form, color scheme, and font scheme. **Page size** refers to the number of panels in the brochure. The **Customer address** selection offers choices about whether to include the customer's address in the brochure. **Form options**, which display on page 2 of the brochure, include None, Order form, Response form, and Sign-up form. The **Order form** displays fields for the description of items ordered as well as types of payment information, including blank fields for entering items, quantities, and prices. The **Response form** displays check box choices and fields for comments, and blanks for up to four multiple-choice questions and a comment section. The **Sign-up form** displays check box choices, fields for time and price, as well as payment information.

All three forms are meant to be detached and mailed in as turnaround documents. Each form contains blanks for the name and address of prospective customers or clients. The company not only verifies the marketing power of its brochure but also is able to create a customer database with the information.

To Choose Brochure Options

The following steps choose a brochure template and make design choices. In the Customize area, the Spotlight template and the Impact font scheme are used to highlight the topic of the brochure. The color scheme will be created later in the project. In the Options area, a 3-panel format is used, and a sign-up form is inserted.

BTW

How Brochures Differ
Each brochure template produces two pages of graphics, business information text boxes, and story boxes. The difference is in the look and feel of the front panel, the location and style of the shapes and graphics, the design of any panel dividers, and the specific kind of decorations unique to each publication set.

1

- Click Brochures in the list of publication types to display the catalog of brochure templates.

- At the top of the catalog, click Classic Designs. Scroll to display the informational brochure previews. Click the Spotlight preview to select it (Figure 3–2).

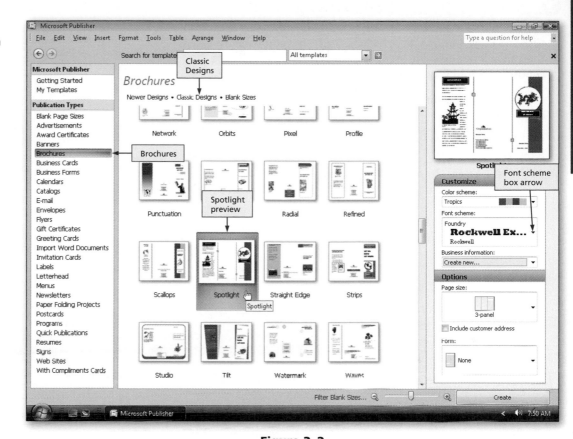

Figure 3–2

2

- In the Customize area, click the Font scheme box arrow to display the list of font schemes.

🔍 **Experiment**

- Scroll in the list of font schemes and click various schemes to see the previews change.

- Click Impact in the list to change the font scheme for the publication (Figure 3–3).

Q&A Why does my customize area look different?

The customize area displays the most recently used color and font schemes.

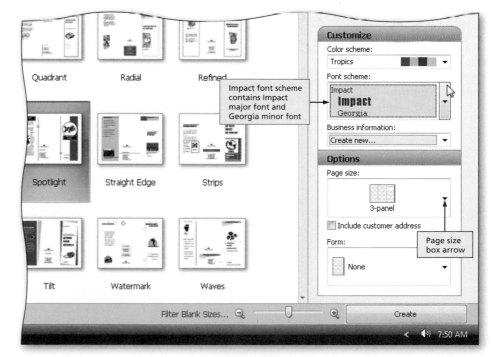

Figure 3–3

3

• In the Options area, if necessary, click the Page size box arrow and then click 3-panel in the list to choose a tri-fold brochure.

• Click the Form box arrow (Figure 3–4).

Q&A

Do I need to change the color scheme?

Publisher by default chooses the color scheme from the previous editing session on your system. Because you will create a custom color scheme later in the project, it does not make any difference which color scheme displays at this point.

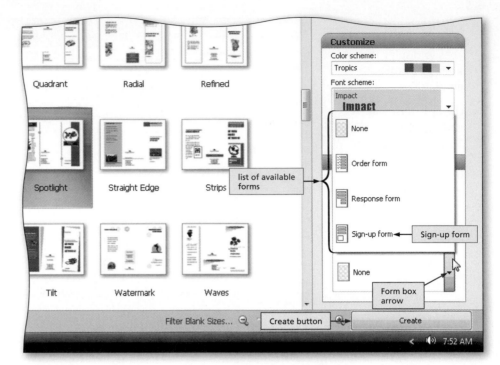

Figure 3–4

4

• Click Sign-up form in the list to choose the Sign-up form option.

• Click the Create button in the lower-right corner of the window to create the publication based on the template settings (Figure 3–5).

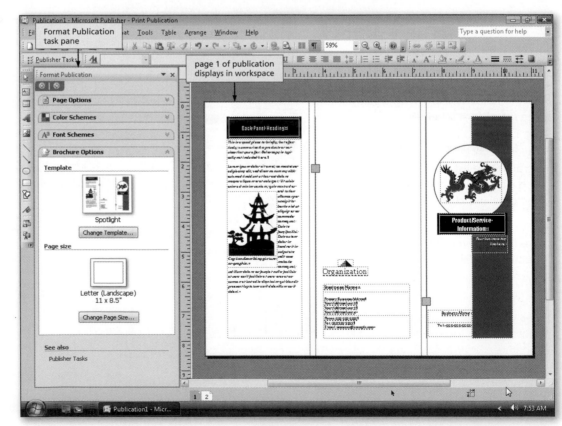

Figure 3–5

Custom Color Schemes

Recall that a color scheme is a predefined set of harmonized colors that you can apply to text and objects. Text and objects with an applied color scheme will change automatically when you switch to a new color scheme or modify the current color scheme. Publisher provides an option for users to create their own color schemes rather than using one of the predefined sets. Creating a **custom color scheme** means choosing your own colors to use in a publication. You may choose one main color, five accent colors, a hyperlink color, and a followed hyperlink color. The **main color** commonly is used for text in major eye-catching areas of the publication. The first accent color is used for graphical lines, boxes, and separators. The second accent color typically is used as fill color in prominent publication shapes. Subsequent accent colors may be used in several ways, including shading, text effects, and alternate font color. The hyperlink color is used as the font color for hyperlink text. After a hyperlink is clicked, the color changes to show users which path, or trail, they have clicked previously.

Custom color schemes can be given a name that will appear in the Apply a color scheme list. The chosen colors also appear on the Fill Color, Line Color, and Font Color button menus.

The Tech Camp brochure will use accent colors of blue and gold, which are the school colors, other accent colors of light blue and tan, as well as a basic black main color for text. Publisher displays an option to create a custom color scheme on the task pane. Publisher then allows users to choose the various colors and name the scheme.

To Open the Create New Color Dialog Box

The following steps create a custom color scheme.

1
- If the Special Characters button on the Standard toolbar is not selected already, click it to display formatting marks on the screen.

- With the Format Publication task pane still displayed, click Color Schemes to access the color scheme options (Figure 3–6).

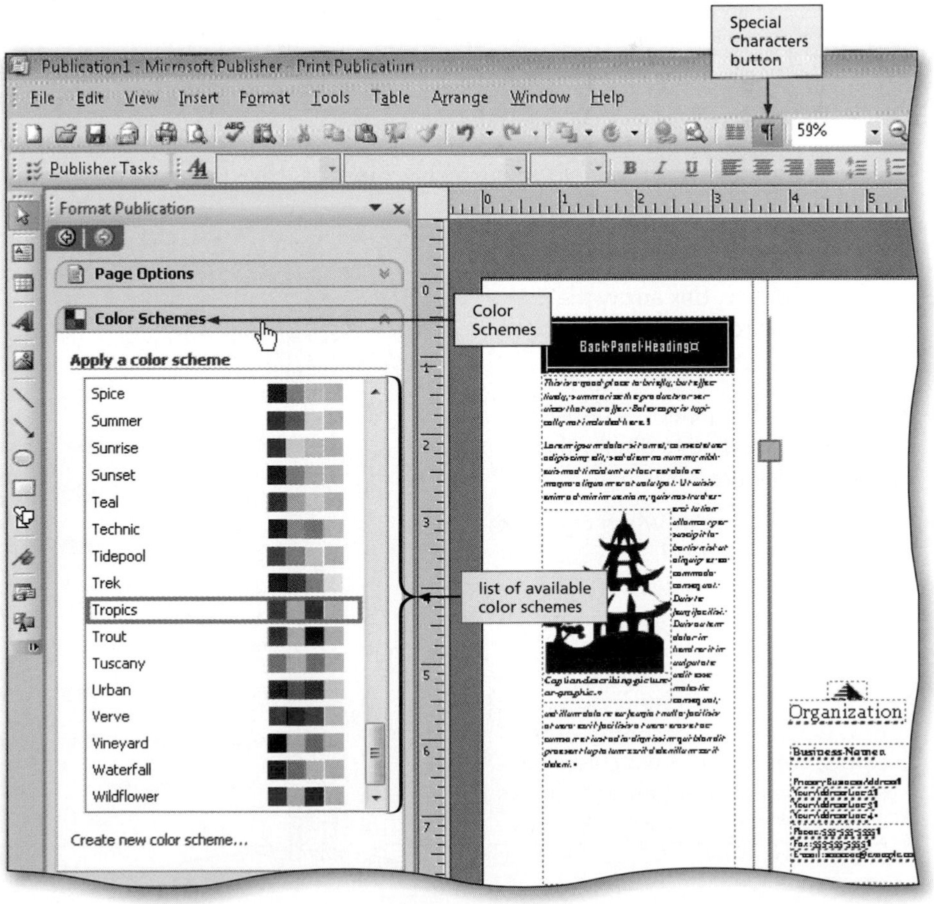

Figure 3–6

2

- Click the Create new color scheme link to open the Create New Color Scheme dialog box (Figure 3–7).

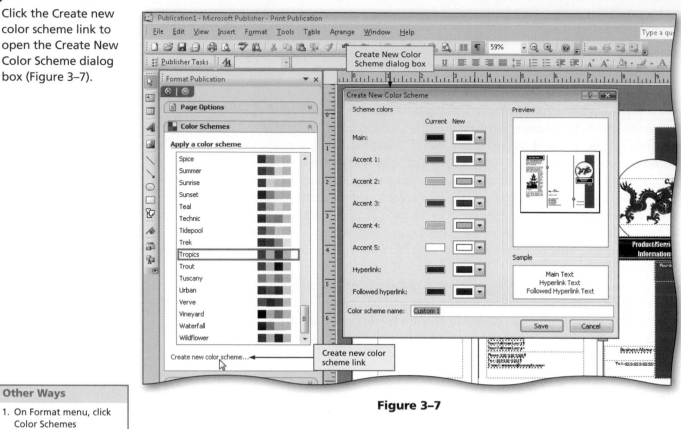

Figure 3–7

To Change an Accent Color

The following steps select an accent color for the custom color scheme.

1

- In the Scheme colors area, click the second New box arrow that corresponds to the Accent 1 color to display a palette of color choices.

- When the color palette is displayed, point to Dark Blue to display the screentip (Figure 3–8).

Q&A

What colors display when you click the New box arrow?

Publisher presents 40 of the common printing colors for desktop printers in a small palette. You can click the More Colors button to display the Colors dialog box, where you can choose other colors, create your own colors by entering color numbers, or choose a publishing color system, such as **Pantone**, a popular color system for professional printing.

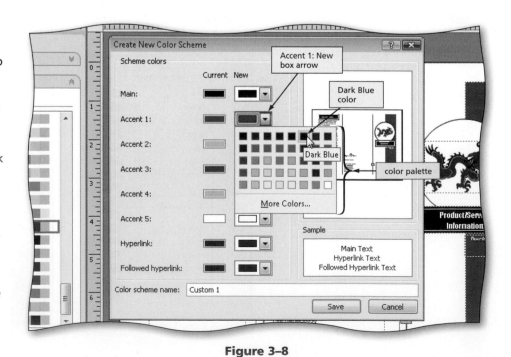

Figure 3–8

2

• Click Dark Blue to select the Accent 1 color (Figure 3–9).

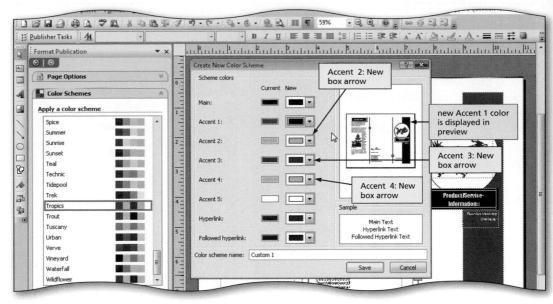

Figure 3–9

To Select More Accent Colors

The following steps select more accent colors.

1 Click the Accent 2, New box arrow. Click Gold.

2 Click the Accent 3, New box arrow. Click Pale Blue.

3 Click the Accent 4, New box arrow. Click Tan (Figure 3–10).

BTW

Color Palette
The More Colors link (Figure 3–8) on each color palette opens a Color dialog box where you can select a standard color from the more than 140 colors in the color spectrum. Another tab in the Color dialog box allows you to customize a color by entering the red, green, and blue (RGB) color values. A final tab allows you to select a processed, or prepackaged color, such as Pantone.

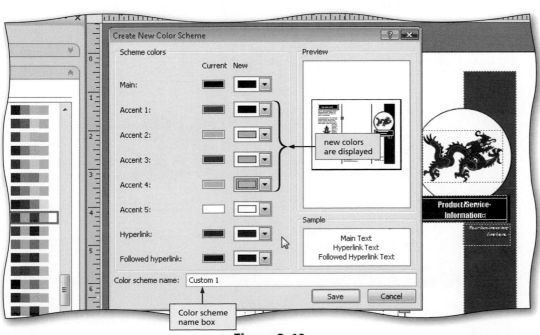

Figure 3–10

To Save a New Color Scheme

The following steps save the new color scheme for the Tech Camp brochure.

1

- In the Create New Color Scheme dialog box, select the text in the Color scheme name text box and then type `School Colors` to replace the text (Figure 3–11).

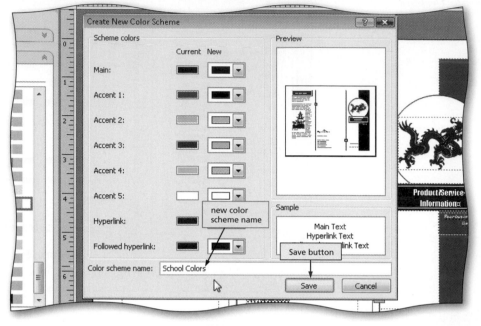

Figure 3–11

2

- Click the Save button to save the color scheme (Figure 3–12).

3

- Close the Format Publication task pane by clicking the Close button.

Color Changes
The scheme colors automatically apply to the standard publication objects in the brochure. Any objects, such as the default logo, that are filled with nonscheme colors remain the same when you change the color scheme.

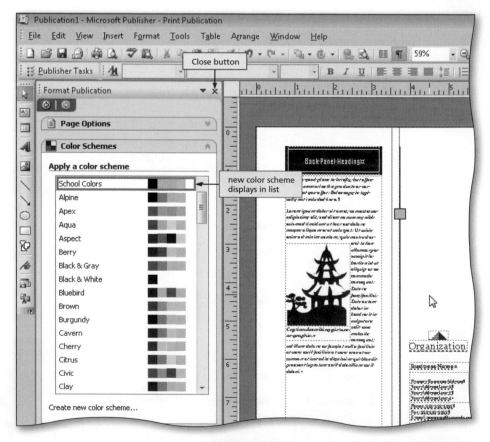

Figure 3–12

To Save the Publication

Now that several important options have been chosen, it is a good practice to save the publication. The following steps save the publication with the file name, Tech Camp Brochure. For a detailed example of the procedure summarized below, refer to pages PUB 31 through PUB 33 in Chapter 1.

 With a USB flash drive connected to one of the computer's USB ports, click the Save button on the Standard toolbar.

 Type Tech Camp Brochure in the File name text box to change the file name. Do not press the ENTER key.

3 Navigate to your USB flash drive.

4 Click the Save button in the Save As dialog box to save the publication on the USB flash drive with the file name, Tech Camp Brochure.

BTW

Automatic Saving
Publisher can save your publication at regular intervals for you. On the Tools menu, click Options, and then click the Save tab. Select the Save AutoRecover info every check box. In the minutes box, specify how often you want Publisher to save files. Do not use AutoRecover as a substitute for regularly saving your work.

Deleting Objects on Page 1

In the Tech Camp brochure, you will not use a graphic in the left panel on page 1, so it can be deleted. You also will create a new logo for the brochure, so the logo in the middle panel of page 1 can be deleted.

To Delete Objects

The following steps delete objects on page 1.

 In the left panel of page 1, right-click the grouped picture and caption. On the shortcut menu, click Delete Object.

 In the middle panel, right-click the organization logo. On the shortcut menu, click Delete Object.

Replacing Text

Recall that editing text in the brochure involves selecting the current text and replacing it with new, appropriate text in one of two ways: editing text directly in Publisher or using Word to facilitate editing. If you need to edit only a few words, it is faster to use a Publisher text box with the accompanying Publisher tools. If you need to edit a long story, however, perhaps one that appears on different pages in a publication, it might be easier to edit the story in Word.

Publisher inserts placeholder text on page 1 of its supplied templates. This placeholder text may be selected by a single click. Alternately, personal information components, designed to be changed or personalized for a company, are best selected by dragging through the text. When you change a personal information component, all matching components in the publication change due to the synchronization that is built into those special text boxes.

Table 3–2 displays the text that needs to be replaced on page 1 of the brochure.

Table 3–2 Page 1 Text

Location	Publisher-Supplied Text and Text Boxes	New Text
Right Panel	Public/Service Information	Tech Camp 08
	Your business tag line here.	July 21–25, 2008
	Business Name	Co-sponsored by: Lake University
	Tel: 555 555 5555	State Department of Education
Middle Panel	Business Name	For more information contact:
	Address	Lynne Russell, Associate Professor CIT at Lake University 723 West Oak Street Indianapolis, IN 46202
	Phone/Fax/E-mail	Phone: 317-555-9705 Fax: 317-555-9702 E-mail: lrussell@techcamp.edu
Left Panel	Back Panel Heading	Tech Camp Details
	Back Panel Story	The tenth annual Tech Camp for teachers will take place July 21 – 25, 2008, on the Lake University campus from 8:30 a.m. to 4:30 p.m. daily. Tech Camp offers teachers a chance to learn techniques in teaching the latest software and computer programming. It also provides opportunities to discuss curriculum, assignments, new teaching strategies, and level objectives. Tech Camp attendees get to meet with college professors and authors to discuss collaborative projects, articulated credit, and college expectations. There is plenty of time for teachers to talk in small, subject-interest groups as well. Lake University sponsors one breakfast and one lunch during the week, lots of snacks, and optional housing and meal cards for teachers from around the state. Each day is a balanced mix of lecture, discussion, demonstration, and lab time. Attendees receive free copies of the latest textbooks and trial software. Other positive byproducts of the week have been articulation agreements, part-time teaching opportunities, Web hosting for high school projects, and great camaraderie! For more information, visit the Tech Camp Web site at www.techcamp.edu

To Edit Text in the Brochure

The following steps edit both placeholder and personal information text on page 1 of the brochure.

1
- Click the Product/Service Information text box in the right panel on page 1. Press the F9 key to zoom the placeholder text box (Figure 3–13).

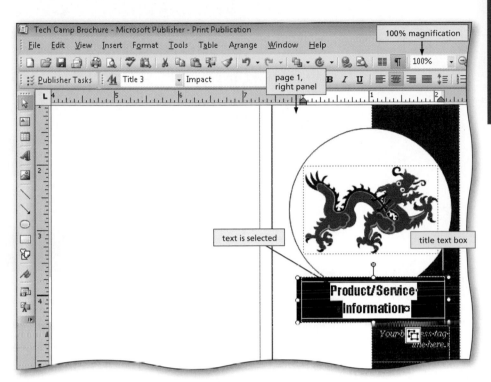

Figure 3–13

2
- Type Tech Camp 08 to replace the title text.
- Drag through the text in the tag line text box to select it (Figure 3–14).

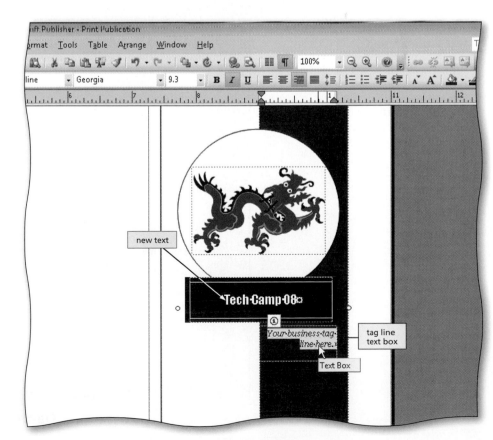

Figure 3–14

3

- Type `July 21-25, 2008` to replace the text (Figure 3–15).

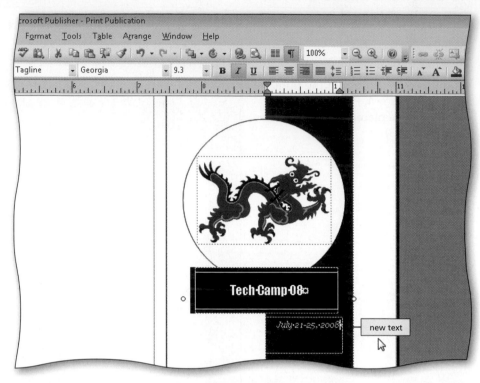

Figure 3–15

4

- Scroll down in the right panel to display the business name text box.

- To select the text, click inside the text box and then press CTRL+A.

- Type `Co-sponsored by: Lake University` to replace the text.

- Do not click outside of the text box (Figure 3–16).

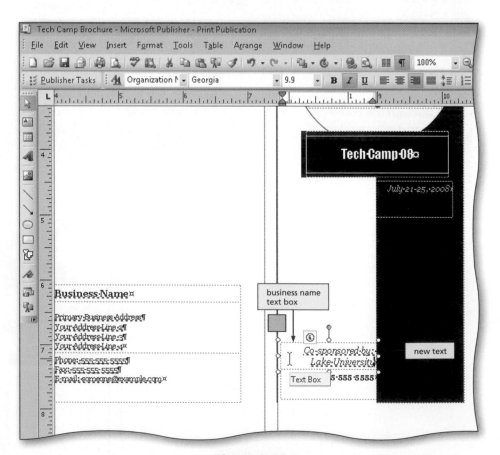

Figure 3–16

To Undo Synchronization

Recall that the business name text box is a synchronized object, which means that all business name text boxes change when you edit any one of them. Other synchronized objects include the personal information boxes, such as the address and telephone text boxes, as well as tear-offs, which you synchronized in Chapter 1. Because you want to edit each business name text box individually, the following steps use the Undo button on the Standard toolbar to undo synchronization.

1 Click outside of the business name text box.

2 Click the Undo Update Fields button on the Standard toolbar.

3 Zoom to Whole Page (Figure 3–17).

BTW

The Undo Button
The Undo button takes on a new name depending upon the previous task. If you have just changed the font scheme, the screentip will say Undo Font Schemes. In Figure 3–17, the synchronization was an example of updating a field, so the button is called the Undo Field Update button. The same is true for the Redo button.

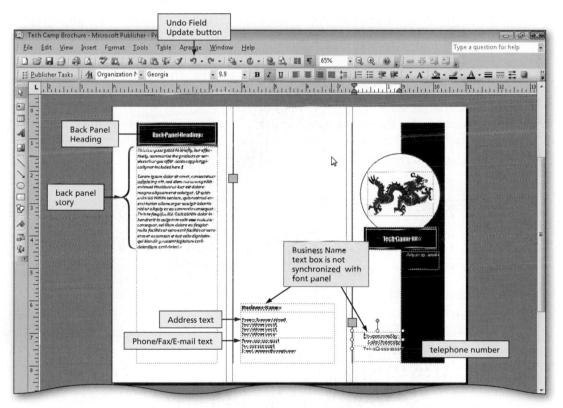

Figure 3–17

To Replace the Other Text Boxes on Page 1

The following step replaces the rest of the placeholder text on page 1. Alternately, you can import the text for the back panel story from the Data Disk associated with this book. The name of the file is Tech Camp Details. For a detailed example of the import procedure, refer to pages PUB 89 through PUB 91 in Chapter 2.

1 Zoom, scroll, and select as necessary to replace the other text boxes on page 1 with the new text from Table 3–2 on page PUB 158. After you edit the business name text box in the middle panel, do not forget to click the Undo button to cancel the synchronization. You may keep the synchronization of the address and telephone text boxes.

Font Styles

Each of the font schemes contains numerous styles. In Publisher, a **style** is a combination of formatting characteristics, such as font size, colors, effects, and formatting, which are named and stored for each font scheme. When you select a font scheme, Publisher creates styles for titles, headings, accent text, body text, list bullets, normal text, and personal information components, using the fonts from the font scheme. For example, in the Impact font scheme, Heading 2 uses the Georgia font, black and bolded, with a font size of 16 and a line spacing of 1.14 spaces.

Applying a Style

When you apply a style, all of the formatting instructions in that style are applied at one time. To apply a style to new text, select the style from the Style list on the Formatting toolbar and then type the text. Alternately, you can select the text first and then select the style. In a later chapter, you will learn that Publisher also has a Styles task pane to help you edit and import styles.

To Insert a Text Box and Apply a Font Scheme Style

The following steps create a new text box for the middle panel of page 1, apply styles, and then insert text. In the Impact font scheme, the Heading 2 style is used for the first line of text, which is bold with a font size of 16. The other lines use Heading 4, which is bold, aligned right, with a font size of 8.3.

1

- With page 1 of the brochure still displayed, scroll to the upper portion of the middle panel. If necessary, type 100% in the Zoom box to increase the magnification.

- Click the Text Box button on the Objects toolbar and then drag a text box approximately 3 inches × 1.5 inches, as shown in Figure 3–18.

Q&A

How do I know how big the text box is?

As you drag to create the text box, you can watch the Object Size area of the status bar. Your text box measurements do not have to be exact.

Later, you will learn to use the Measurements toolbar, or the Format Text Box dialog box to set exact measurements.

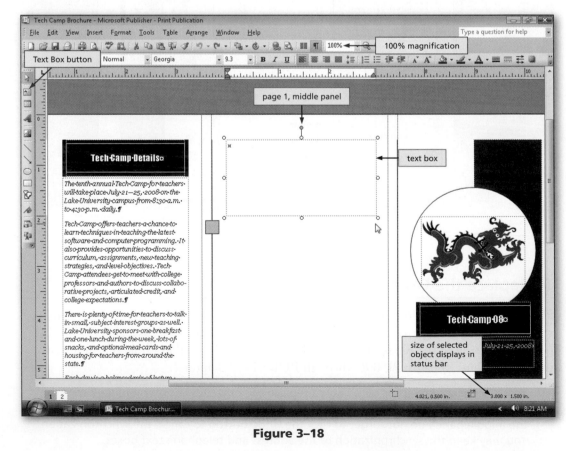

Figure 3–18

2
- Click the Style box arrow on the Formatting toolbar to display the styles.

🔍 **Experiment**

- Scroll in the list of styles to view the various font sizes, alignments, and formatting.

- Scroll, if necessary, and then point to Heading 2 in the list (Figure 3–19).

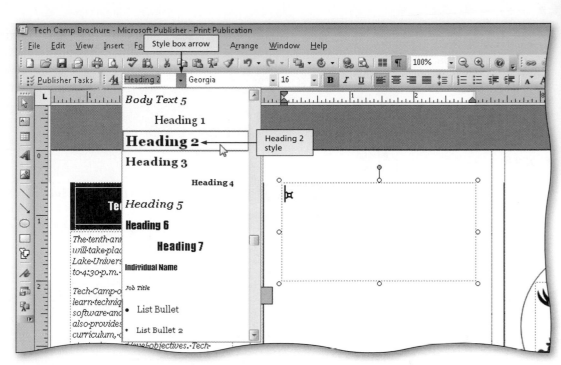

Figure 3–19

3
- Click Heading 2 to select the style.

- Type Lake University and then press the ENTER key (Figure 3–20).

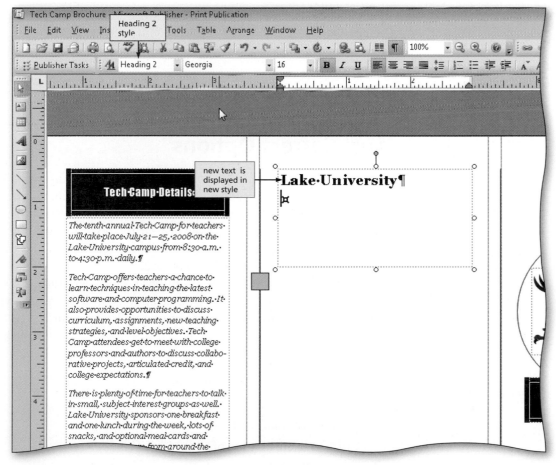

Figure 3–20

4

- Click the Style box arrow on the Formatting toolbar to display the styles.

- Scroll and then click Heading 4 to select the style.

- Type School of Engineering and Technology and then press the ENTER key.

- Type Computer and Information Technology and then press the ENTER key.

- Type www. lakeuniv.edu to complete the text (Figure 3–21).

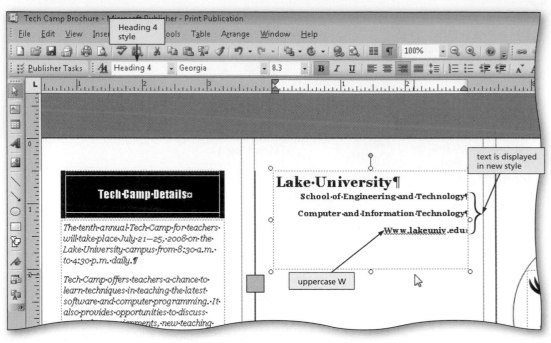

Figure 3–21

Q&A

Why did the first letter of the Web page address capitalize itself?

Publisher tries to help you by capitalizing the beginning of sentences and paragraphs for you. As you will learn in the next series of steps, this autocorrect feature can be reversed for individual occurrences or turned off for all occurrences.

AutoCorrect Options

Publisher assists you by correcting certain kinds of common errors. While these **AutoCorrect options** can be turned on or off from the Tools menu, individual occurrences can be edited with the **AutoCorrect Options button**, one of the smart tags in Publisher. Recall that a smart tag displays just below or near the text to which it applies. The AutoCorrect Options smart tag first displays as a small blue rectangle under the correction. When you point to the smart tag, it displays a button.

The following AutoCorrect options typically are turned on in an initial installation of Publisher. You can create specific exceptions or define your own automatic replacement text by clicking AutoCorrect Options on the Tools menu.

- Show AutoCorrect Options button
- Correct TWo INtial CApitals
- Capitalize first letter of sentences
- Capitalize first letter of table cells
- Capitalize names of days
- Correct accidental use of cAPS LOCK key
- Replace text as you type
- Automatically use suggestions from the spelling checker

To Use the AutoCorrect Options Button

The next steps turn off autocorrection for capitalization of the first letter in the URL. **URL** is an acronym for Uniform Resource Locator that refers to a Web address. Web addresses typically begin with the letters www.

1

- Move the mouse pointer near the capital W in the URL to display the smart tag (Figure 3–22).

Q&A

My Web page address does not have a capital W. What should I do?

If your Web page address does not have a capital W, it is possible that someone already has turned that feature off on your system. You can skip to the next section or turn the feature back on by clicking AutoCorrect Options on the Tools menu. Make sure the Capitalize first letter of sentences check box displays a check mark.

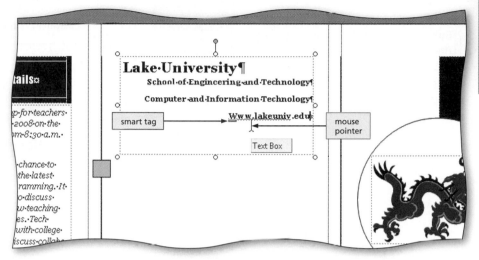

Figure 3–22

2

- Point to the smart tag to display the AutoCorrect Options button (Figure 3–23).

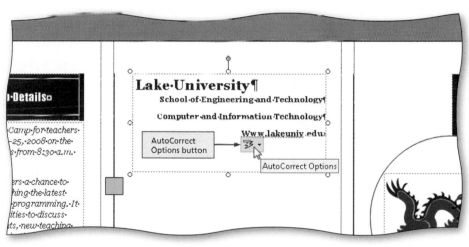

Figure 3–23

3

- Click the AutoCorrect Options button to display its menu (Figure 3–24).

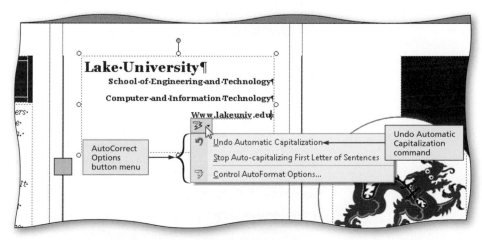

Figure 3–24

4

- Click Undo Automatic Capitalization to cancel the capital first letter (Figure 3–25).

Q&A

Why did the red wavy line disappear?

By default, Publisher does not flag text that begins with the lowercase letters, www, because it is normally a URL. When it was uppercase, Publisher warned you that it might be the beginning of a sentence with a misspelled word.

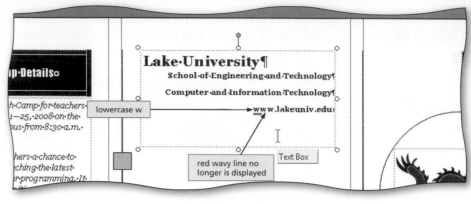

Figure 3–25

To Create Another Text Box

A second text box with styles is created in the following steps.

1 To create another text box, click the Text Box button on the Objects toolbar and then drag a second text box below the first, approximately the same size.

2 Select the style, Heading 2. Type `State Dept. of Education` and then press the ENTER key.

3 Select the style, Heading 4. Type `Business and Information Technology` and press the ENTER key.

4 Type `Office of Career and Technical Education` and then press the ENTER key.

5 Type `www.sdoe.edu` to complete the text.

6 Point to the smart tag button to display the AutoCorrect Options button. Click the AutoCorrect Options button and then click Undo Automatic Capitalization to cancel the capital first letter (Figure 3–26).

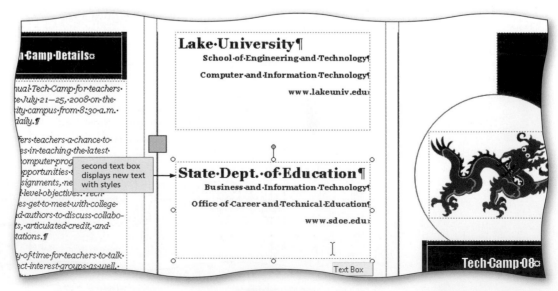

Figure 3–26

To Apply a Style to Existing Text

In the previous steps, you chose a style and then typed the text. Now you will apply a style to existing text. You first select the text, and then select the style.

1 Select the text in the left panel story.

2 Zoom to Whole Page using the F9 key.

3 Select the Body Text 3 style (Figure 3–27).

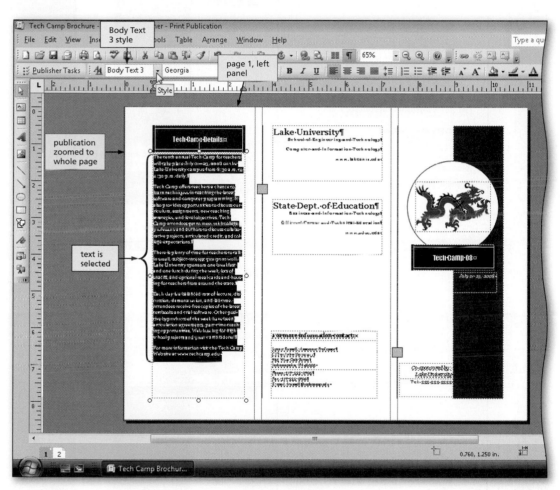

Figure 3–27

The Format Painter

Another way to apply specific formatting other than using a style is to copy the formatting from existing text or objects with the Format Painter button on the Standard toolbar. When using the Format Painter with text, click the Format Painter button, click anywhere in the source text, click the Format Painter button, and then click the destination text. The Format Painter changes all of the text in the destination paragraph. To format smaller or larger portions of, drag the destination text. To apply formatting to multiple locations, double-click the Format Painter button so that it stays on. In those cases, when you finish, click the Format Painter to turn it off.

To Use the Format Painter

The following steps copy the formatting from one text box to another, in the lower part of the right panel on page 1.

1

- With page 1 of the brochure still displayed, scroll to the lower portion of the right panel and zoom to 100%.

- Click the text in the co-sponsored by text box (Figure 3–28).

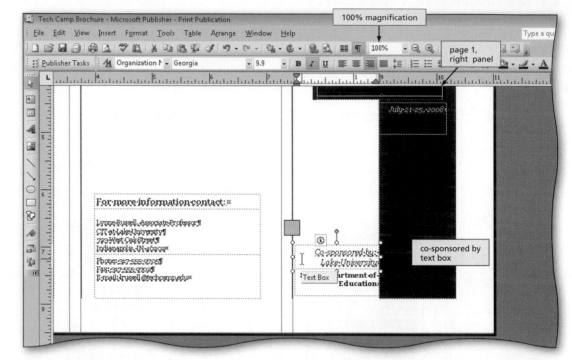

Figure 3–28

2

- Click the Format Painter button on the standard toolbar to copy the formatting.

- Position the mouse pointer inside the state department text box (Figure 3–29).

Q&A Why does the mouse pointer display a paintbrush?

The mouse pointer changes when a format has been copied. Once you apply the format by clicking somewhere else, the paintbrush will disappear.

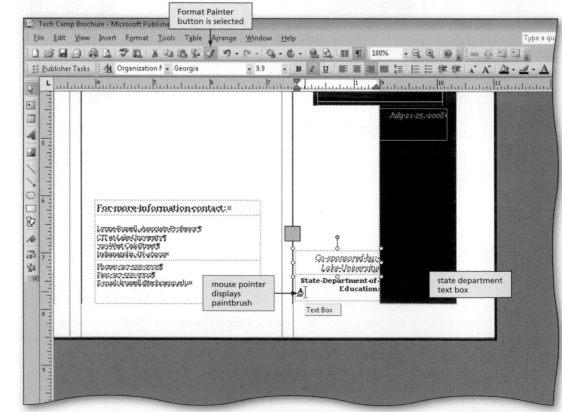

Figure 3–29

3

- Click the text in the state department text box to copy the formatting.

- If necessary, click the Align Text Right button on the Standard toolbar to align the text on the right side (Figure 3–30).

Q&A

Can I use the format painter on objects other than text?

Yes. You can copy applied formatting of a graphic, WordArt, shapes, fills, or any object from the Design Gallery. If you can change the style or set formatting options, you can copy them from one object to another.

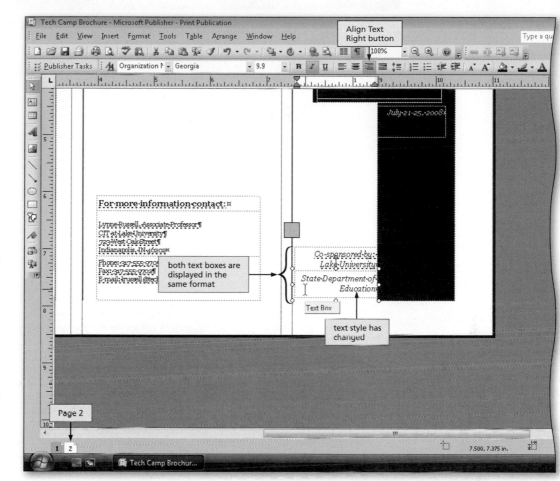

Figure 3–30

To Switch to Page 2

1 Click Page 2 on the page sorter.

2 Zoom to Whole Page.

Creating a New Style

Publisher allows you to create a new style from scratch or based on a current style or text selection. Creating a new style is a good idea when you have multiple text passages that have to be formatted identically, and the desired attributes are not saved as a current style.

In the Tech Camp brochure, first you will enter the text shown in Table 3–3 on the next page. Then, you will create a style for the inside, secondary headings. The text in italics will be formatted as headings later in this project.

BTW

Font Scheme Options
The Font scheme options link in the lower portion of the Font Schemes task pane includes options to update custom text styles in order to match one of the fonts used in the current font scheme. It also allows you to override applied text formatting, which changes only the font; it does not affect any other text formatting. A third option allows users to adjust font sizes to maintain the same area covered by the original block of text. This option may cause the font size to increase or decrease from the size set in the style, but it will prevent the text from reflowing.

Table 3–3 Text for Page 2, Left and Middle Panels		
Location	**Publisher-Supplied Text and Text Boxes**	**New Text**
Left Panel	Main Inside Heading	Tech Camp 08
	Main Inside Story	*Where* Lake University Campus, 723 West Oak St., Indianapolis, IN 46202 *Registration Details* Registration deadline is June 1, 2008. Enrollment is limited to 25 participants per class, so register early! *Who Should Attend* Business, information technology, and marketing teachers interested in teaching database concepts, graphics, Web design, and computer programming. *Workshop Format* The five-day, $250 workshop includes lecture, hands-on lab practice, and assessment. Participants may choose one of four tracks. *Housing* Dormitory rooms are available for $150. The four-bedroom suites include full appliances and high-speed Internet ports. Please check in July 17 between 6 and 8 p.m., or contact Lynne Russell for alternate check in times.
	Caption	All sessions will be held in Fuller Hall.
Middle Panel	Secondary Story	*Track A: Access & Friends* This track will cover database concepts, intermediate Access through advanced Access, SQL server with Oracle, and data-driven Web sites. *Track B: Graphics Galore!* This track will cover curriculum and typical assignments, using InDesign, Illustrator, and Photoshop. The last day will incorporate all topics together. *Track C: Web Design* This track is for teachers who have had some basic HTML and an introduction to Dreamweaver. Topics will include HTML and scripting tools, intermediate Dreamweaver, Flash, and XML. *Track D: Desktop Publishing* This track will cover the basics of desktop publishing, using Microsoft Publisher. Topics will include brochures, newsletters, fliers, Web pages, e-commerce Web sites, design issues, and graphics. Track D also will include an introduction to Photoshop, "good design," and technical communication concepts. Complete and mail the attached form, or register on the Web at www.techcamp.edu.

To Enter Text on Page 2

The following steps enter text with styles for page 2 of the brochure. The new text displays in Table 3–3. Do not try to create the italics in your publication. You will format the headings later in the chapter. Zoom and select text as necessary.

1 In the left pane, click the Main Inside Heading text and then type `Tech Camp 08` to replace the text.

2 Select the story below the heading.

3 To select a style, click the Style box arrow, and then if necessary, click Body Text 3.

4 Replace the text by typing the main inside story text from Table 3–3.

5 Select the text in the caption below the picture in the left panel. Type the new caption text from Table 3–3 to replace the text.

6 Select all of the text in the middle panel text box using CTRL+A.

7 To select a style, click the Style box arrow and then click Accent Text 6.

8 Replace the text by typing the main inside story text from Table 3–3. Use the AutoCorrect Options button as necessary.

9 Zoom to Whole Page (Figure 3–31).

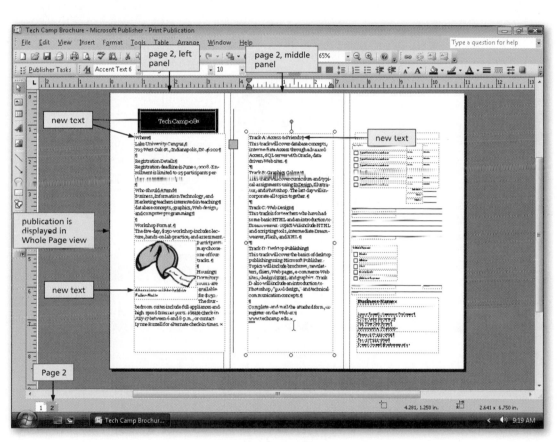

Figure 3–31

To Open the Styles Task Pane

Now that text has been entered, the step on the next page opens the Styles task pane, in preparation for formatting the headings with a new style.

1

- Click the Styles button on the Formatting toolbar to display the Styles task pane (Figure 3–32).

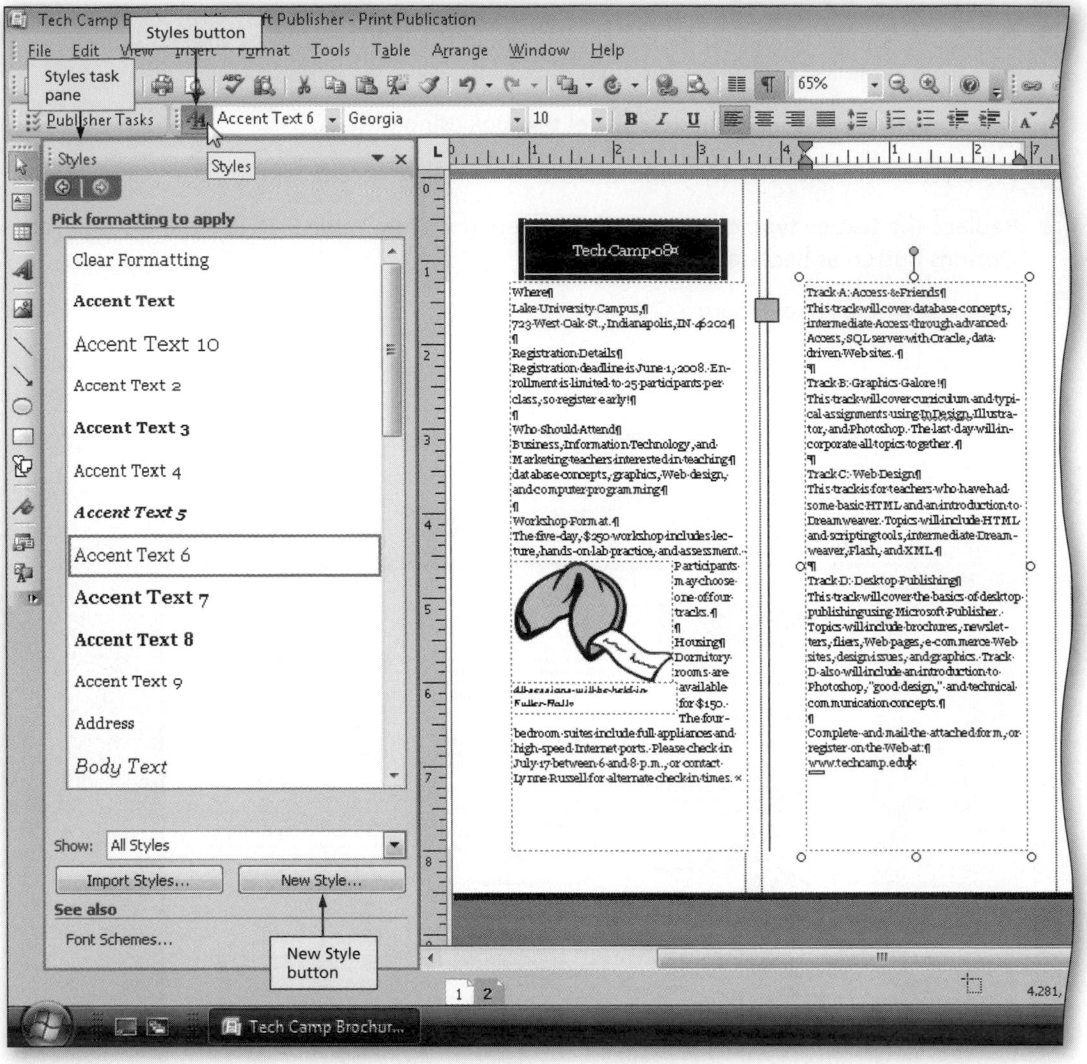

Figure 3–32

Other Ways

1. On Format menu, click Styles
2. From any other task pane, click Other Task Panes button, click Styles

To Create a New Style

The following steps create a new Style named Tech Camp, setting the font to Arial Rounded MT Bold, the font style to Regular, the font size to 10, and the font color to Light Orange.

1

- In the Styles task pane, click the New Style button to display the New Style dialog box.

- In the Enter new style name box, type Tech Camp to name the style (Figure 3–33).

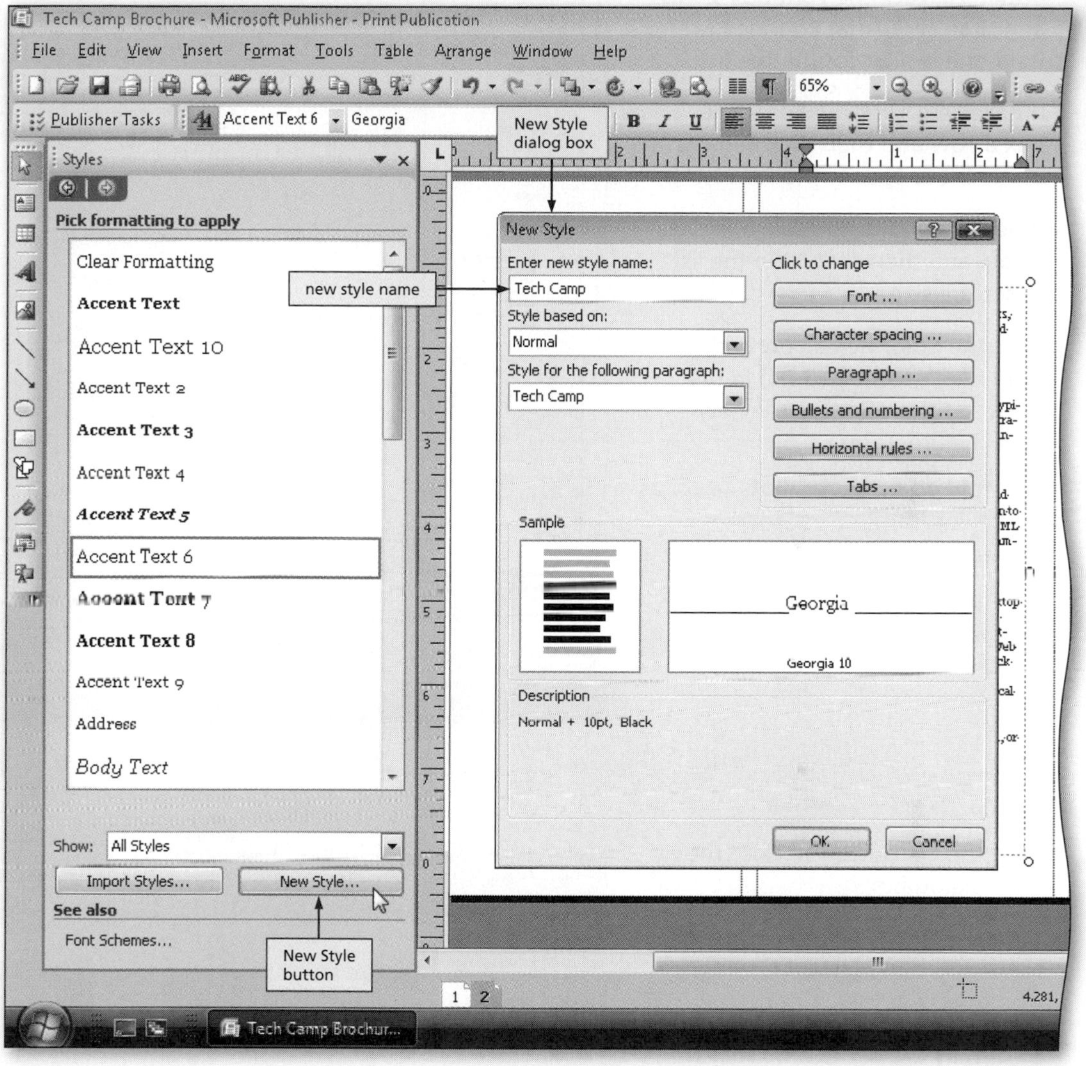

Figure 3–33

2

- Click the Font button to display the Font Dialog box.

- When the Font dialog box is displayed, click the Font box arrow and then click Arial Rounded MT Bold or a similar font in the list.

- If necessary, click the Font style box arrow and then click Regular in the list to specify the font style.

- If necessary, click the Size box arrow and then click 10 in the list to set the size.

- Click the Color box arrow and then click Accent 2 (Gold) in the list to set the color for the new style (Figure 3–34).

Q&A What if I do not have that particular font?

You can use any font that is bold and contrasts the text in the stories.

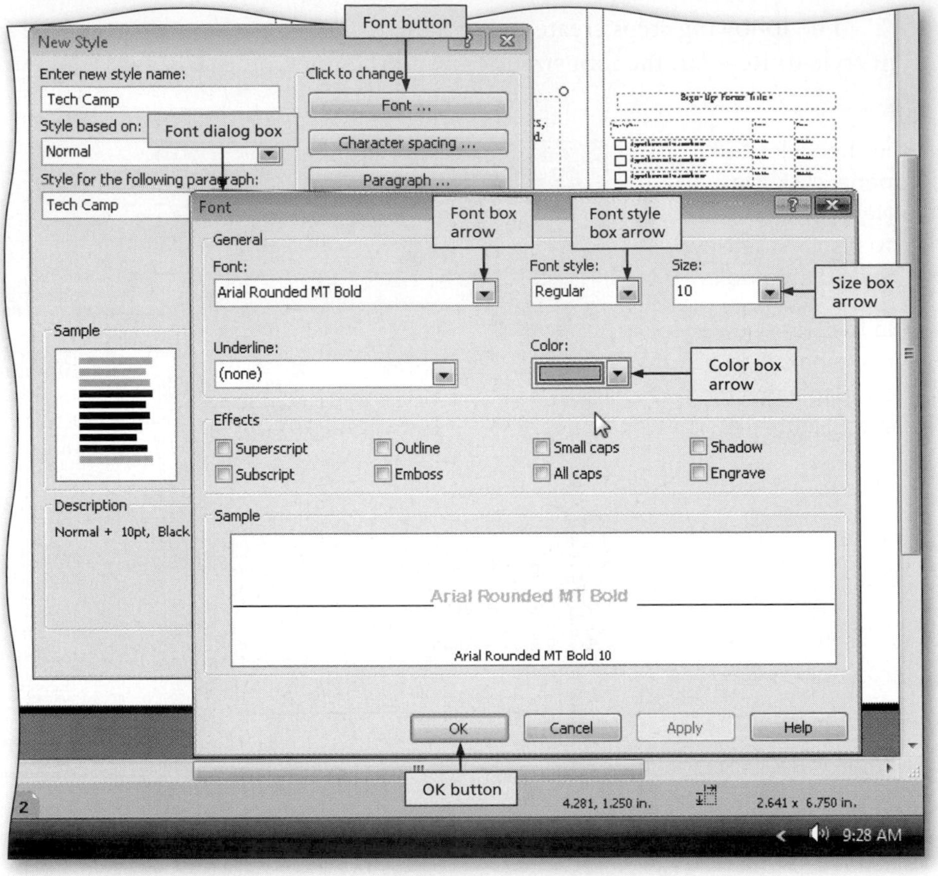

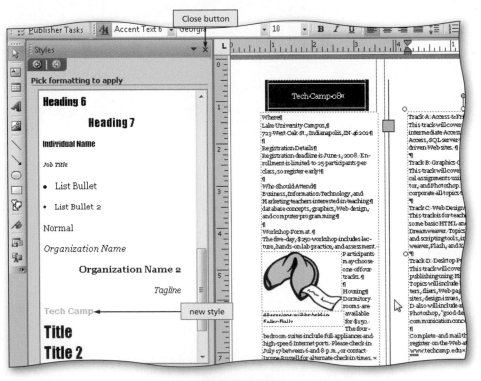

Figure 3–34

3

- Click the OK button to close the Font dialog box.

- Click the OK button to close the New Style dialog box.

- Scroll in the Styles task pane to display the Tech Camp style (Figure 3–35).

Q&A Will the new style appear in the drop-down list in the Formatting toolbar?

Yes, Publisher will add the new style and display its name in the Styles list, both in the Styles task pane and when clicking the Style box arrow.

4

- Close the Styles task pane.

Figure 3–35

To Apply the New Style

1

- Select the first heading text in the main inside story. Headings are identified by italics in Table 3–3 on page PUB 170.

- Zoom to 100%.

- Click the Style box arrow. Scroll as necessary and click Tech Camp in the list to apply the new style.

- Click outside the selection to view the new formatting (Figure 3–36).

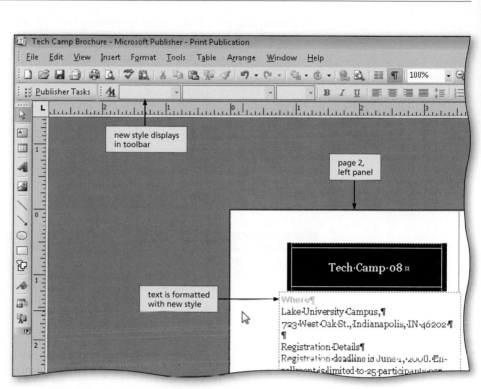

Figure 3–36

2

- Repeat step 1 for each of the headings italicized in Table 3–3 (Figure 3–37).

Q&A

Could I use the Format Painter to copy the formatting attributes to all of the other headings?

Yes, you can edit the formatting either way, or you could use the Styles task pane.

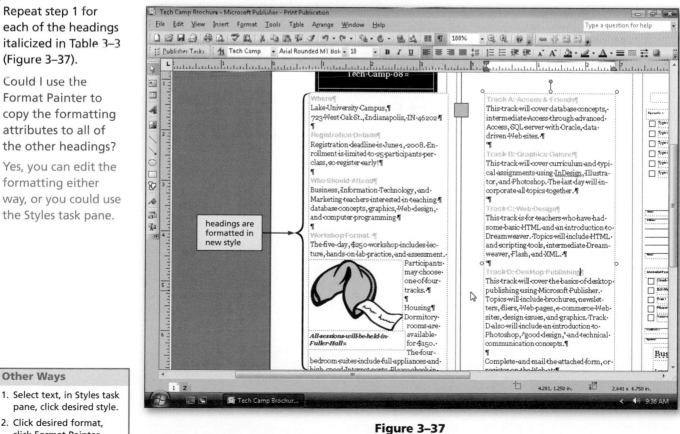

Other Ways

1. Select text, in Styles task pane, click desired style.

2. Click desired format, click Format Painter button, click new text.

Figure 3–37

Formatting Fonts

Publisher provides many ways to format fonts. Font schemes assist with major and minor fonts. Styles further specify sizes and formatting. Publisher also provides several font effects and line spacing options using menu options and toolbar buttons.

Font Effects

You have learned about font schemes, fonts, font sizes, formatting, and styles. Another way to format fonts is to use an effect. An **effect** is a special font option to add distinction to your text, including such ornamentation as outlining, embossing, and shadows.

Table 3–4 lists the font effects available in Publisher. The specific appearances of the font effects are printer- and screen-dependent.

Table 3–4 Font Effects	
Font Effect	**Description**
All caps	Formats lowercase letters as capitals. All caps formatting does not affect numbers, punctuation, nonalphabetic characters, or uppercase letters.
Emboss	The selected text appears to be raised off the page in relief.
Engrave	The selected text appears to be imprinted or pressed into the page.
Outline	Displays the inner and outer borders of each character.
Shadow	Adds a shadow beneath and to the right of the selected text.
Small caps	Formats selected lowercase text as capital letters and reduces their size. Small caps formatting does not affect numbers, punctuation, nonalphabetic characters, or uppercase letters.
Subscript	Lowers the selected text below the baseline.
Superscript	Raises the selected text above the baseline.

BTW

Superscripts and Subscripts
Two special font effects are superscript and subscript. A superscript is a character that appears slightly higher than other text on a line, such as that used in footnotes (reference[1]). A subscript describes text that is slightly lower than other text on a line, such as that used in scientific formulas (H_2O).

Using a Font Effect

The following steps apply an Outline font effect as new text is entered for the Sign-Up Form Title in the right panel of page 2.

To Apply a Font Effect

1

- In the right panel on page 2, right-click the text, Sign-Up Form Title, to display the shortcut menu.

- Point to Change Text to display the submenu (Figure 3–38).

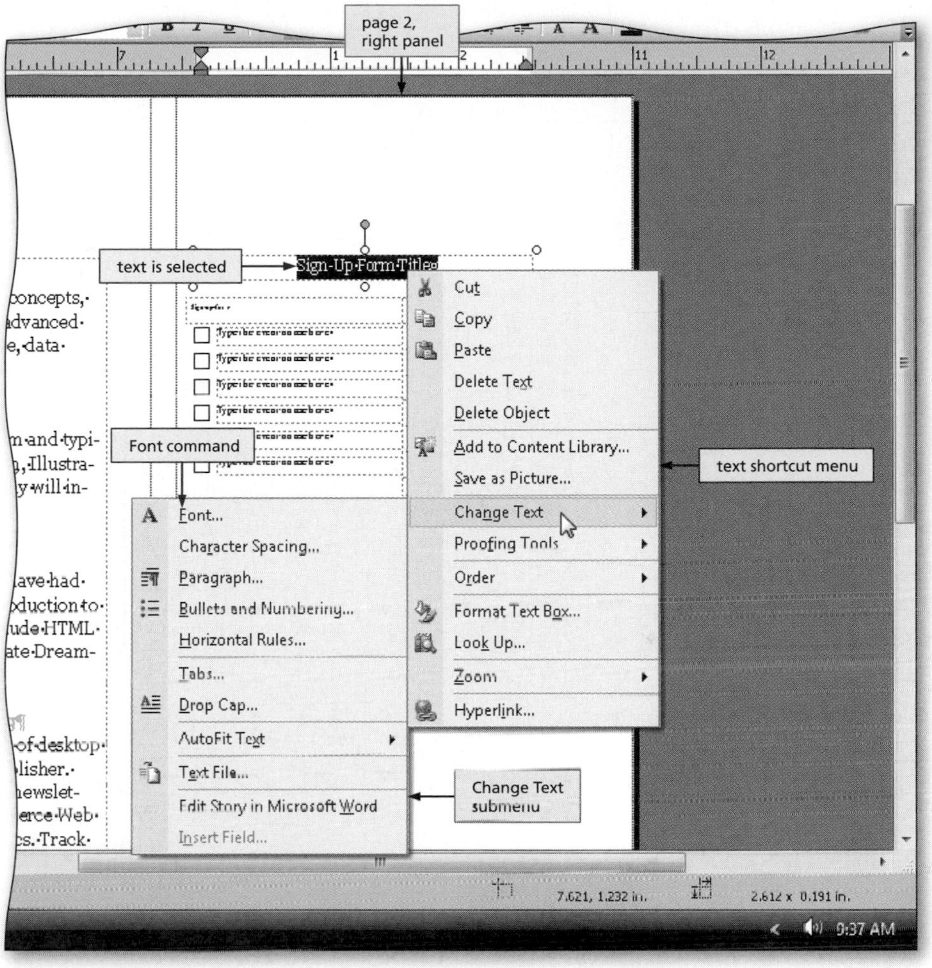

Figure 3–38

2

- Click Font on the Change Text submenu to display the Font dialog box.

- Click Outline in the Effects area (Figure 3–39).

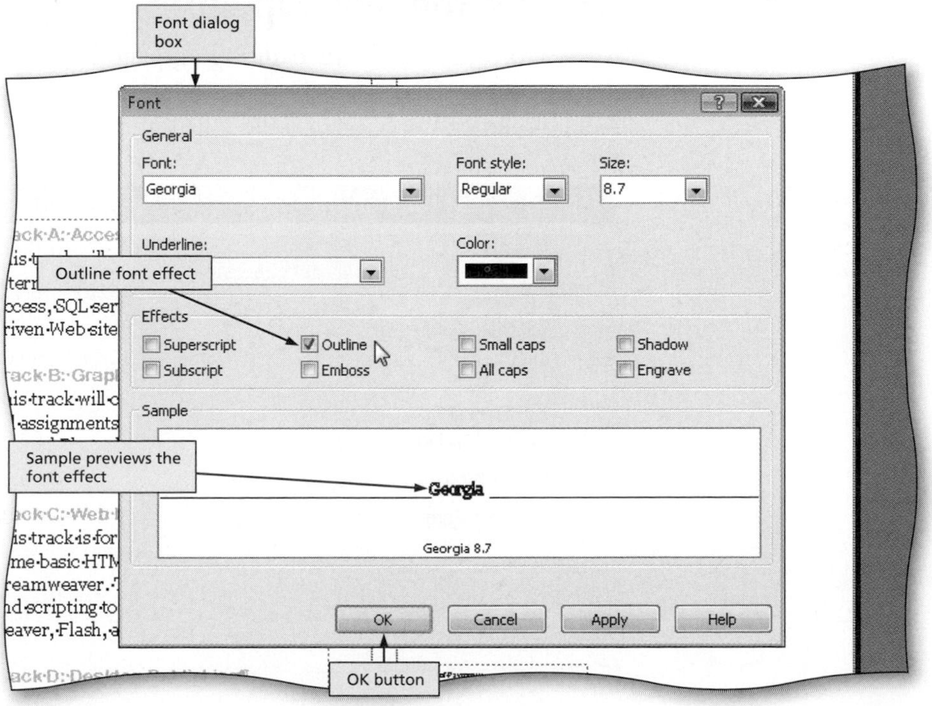

Figure 3–39

3

- Click the OK button.
- Type `Sign-up for Tech Camp` to replace the text.
- Zoom to 200% (Figure 3–40).

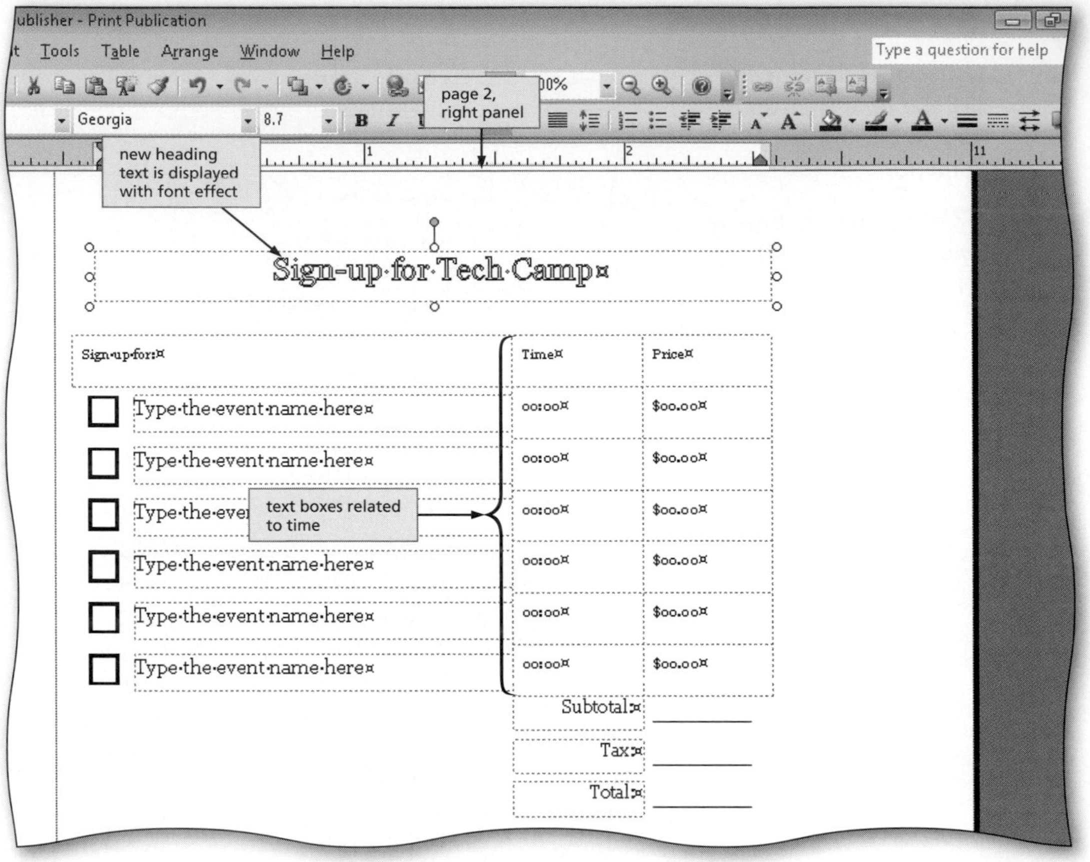

Figure 3–40

Other Ways
1. On Format menu, click Font, click desired effect

Editing the Sign-Up Form

To complete the text editing on page 2, the following steps describe how to edit the Sign-up form. Table 3–5 displays the text for event titles and prices. In the form, you will delete the text in the boxes related to time.

Table 3–5 Text for Sign-up Form

Item Description	Price
Track A: Access & Friends	$250.00
Track B: Graphics Galore	$250.00
Track C: Web Design	$250.00
Track D: Desktop Publishing	$250.00
Optional Housing	$150.00
Optional Meal Card	$150.00

To Edit the Sign-Up Form

1

- One at a time, select the text in each of the center text boxes related to time. Press the DELETE key to delete the text.

- One at a time, click each event and price text box and then enter the new text from Table 3–5 (Figure 3–41).

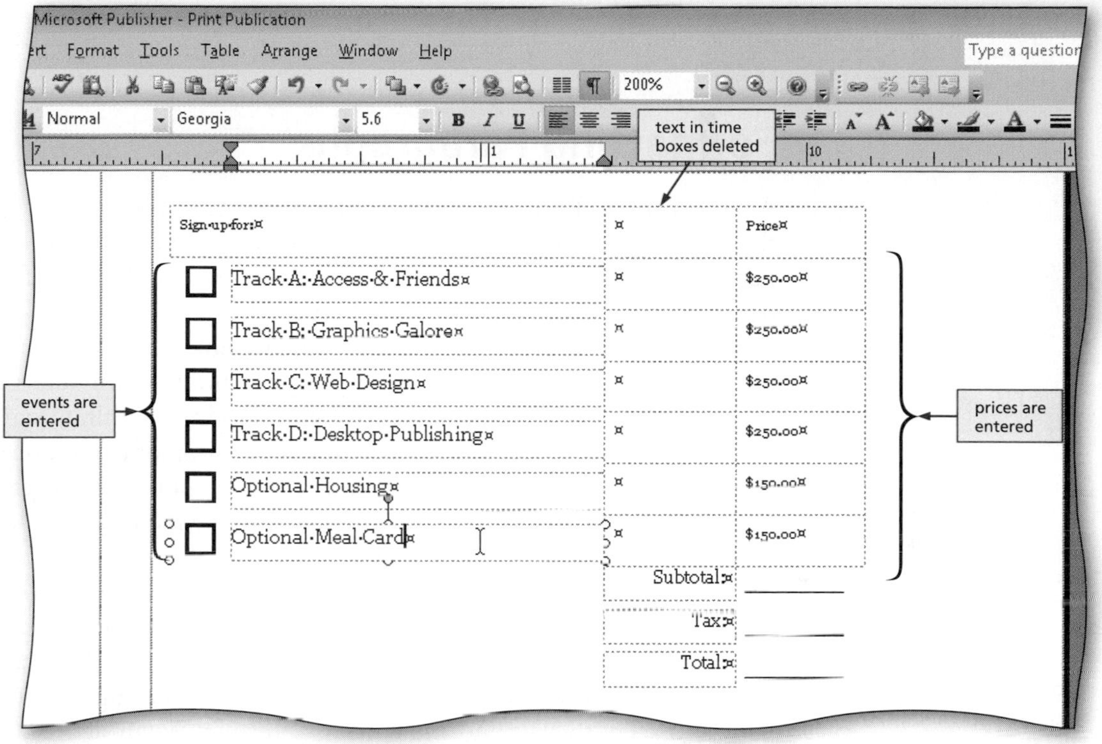

Figure 3–41

2

- Scroll down and select the text, Check, in the Method of Payment area.

- Type Check made out to Tech Camp to replace the text (Figure 3–42).

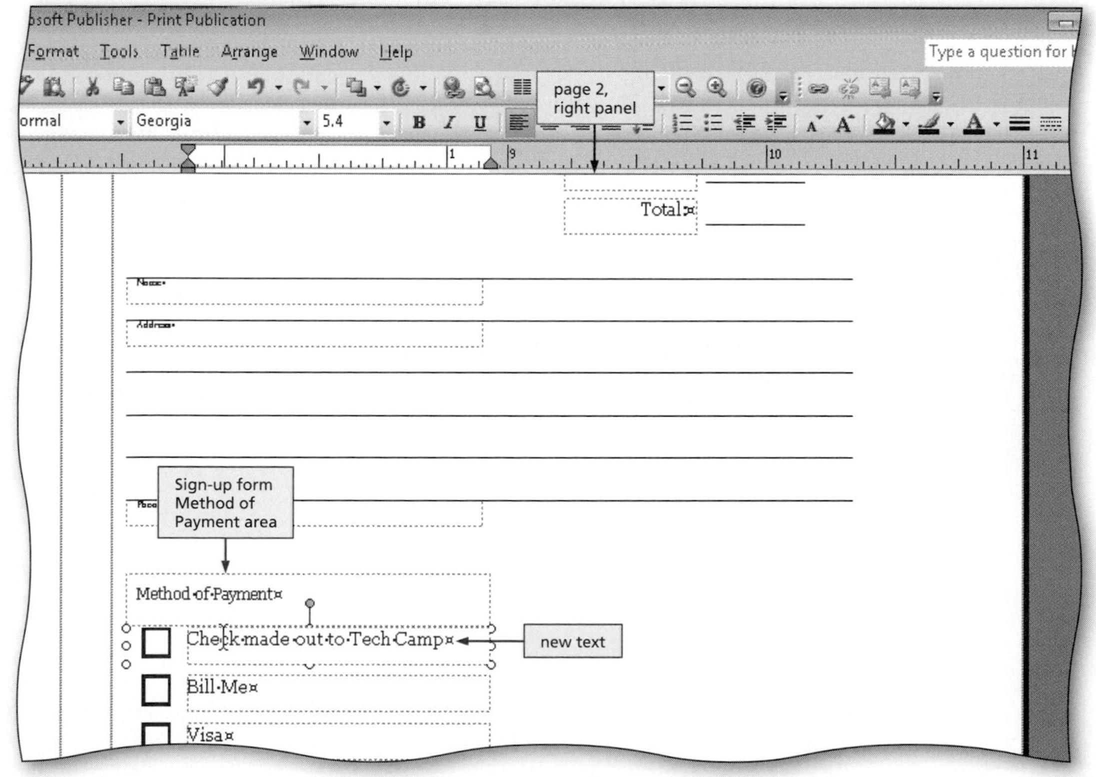

Figure 3–42

To Finish Text Replacement on Page 2

1 On page 2, in the right panel, select the text in the business name text box.

2 Type Detach and mail to: to replace the text.

Formatting Paragraphs

A **paragraph** in Publisher, as well as in most word processing programs, consists of the text you type until you press the ENTER key. Pressing the ENTER key creates a **hard return**, or paragraph, in a text box. Recall that certain kinds of formatting are paragraph-dependent, such as bullets and numbering.

Publisher allows users to change the indentation, alignment, line spacing, baseline guides, and paragraph spacing of paragraphs. **Indentation** determines the distance of the paragraph from either the left or right margins. Within margins, you can increase or decrease the indentation of a paragraph or group of paragraphs. You also can create a negative indent (also known as an exdent), which pulls the paragraph out toward the left margin. You also can create a hanging indent, in which the first line of the paragraph is not indented, but subsequent lines are.

Alignment refers to horizontal appearance and orientation of the edges of the paragraph: left-aligned, right-aligned, centered, or justified. For example, in a left-aligned paragraph (the most common alignment), the left edge of the paragraph is flush with the left margin. **Justified alignment** adjusts the horizontal spacing of text within text boxes, so that all lines, except the last line of the paragraph, align evenly along both the left and right margins. Justifying text creates a smooth edge on both sides. Publisher also allows users to create a rarely used **Distribute** alignment, which justifies even the last line of the paragraph.

Line spacing is the amount of space from the bottom of one line of text to the bottom of the next line. Publisher adjusts the line spacing to accommodate the largest font or the tallest graphic in that line.

You can use **baseline guides** to align text lines precisely across multiple columns. Publisher also allows you to set when and how lines and paragraphs break across text boxes. For example, you may want to specify that if one line of a paragraph moves to a new column, text box, or page, the entire paragraph should move.

Paragraph spacing determines the amount of space above or below a paragraph.

Changing the Paragraph Spacing

The following steps illustrate how to adjust the line spacing of the paragraphs to 1.5 inches.

To Change the Paragraph Spacing

1

- Zoom and scroll as necessary to select all of the text in the middle panel text box.

- Right-click the selection and then point to Change Text (Figure 3–43).

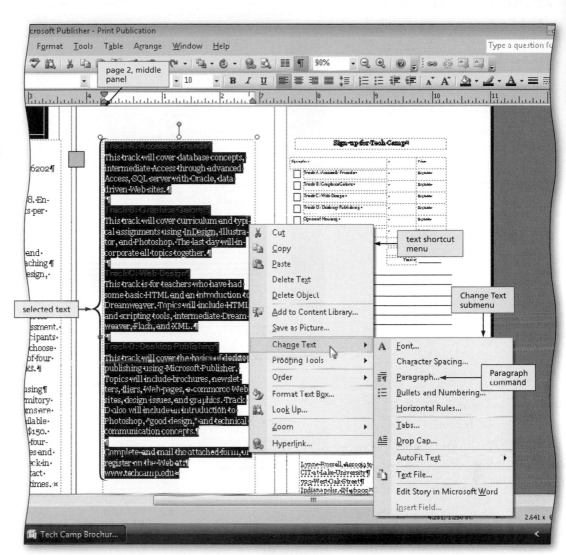

Figure 3–43

2

• On the Change Text submenu, click Paragraph to display the Paragraph dialog box.

• In the Line spacing area, select the text in the After paragraphs box, if any, and then type 1.5 to enter the new value (Figure 3–44).

Q&A

Why does the Between lines box say 1.14sp?

The template text was set to 1.14 spaces between lines for easier reading. When you typed in the new text, you did not change the line spacing.

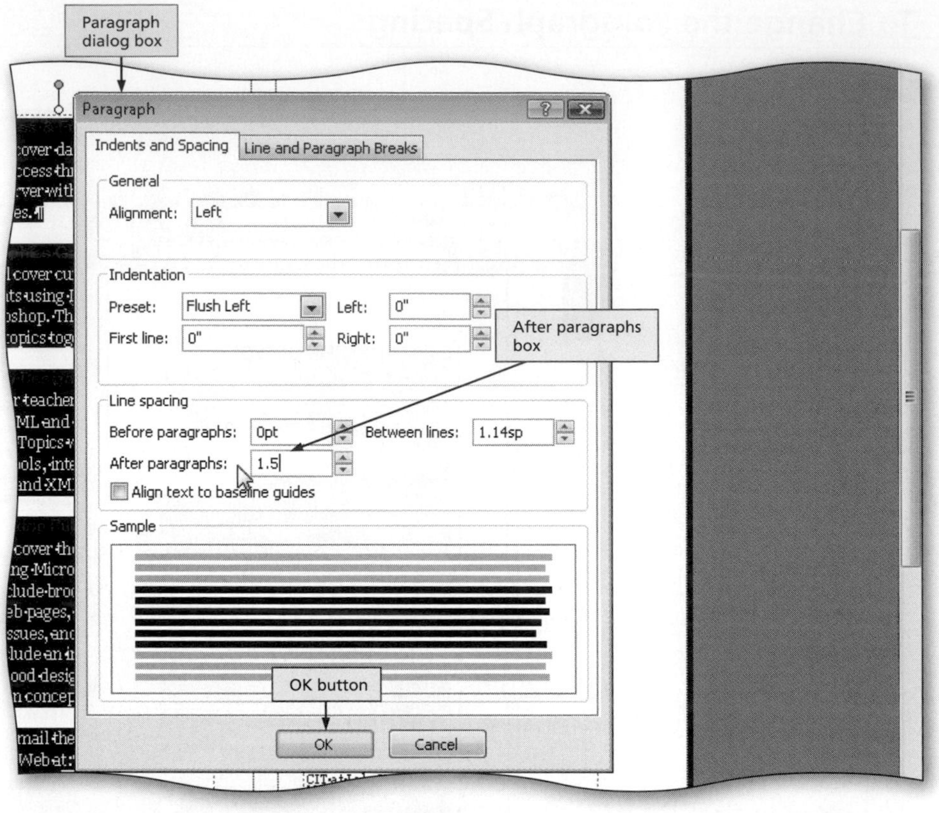

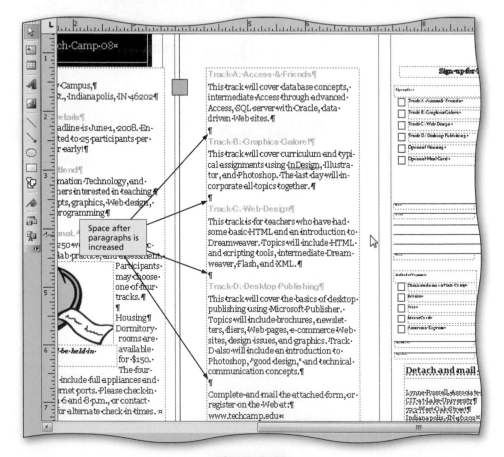

Figure 3–44

3

• Click the OK button to close the dialog box.

• Click outside the text box to remove the highlighting (Figure 3–45).

Figure 3–45

Other Ways

1. On Format menu, click Paragraph

Using Photographs in a Brochure

The advent of inexpensive photo CDs, along with Web access, has increased exponentially the possibilities for photographic reproduction in publications. Regular cameras using popular types of film now can take pictures that are ultimately digitized, a process that previously required digital cameras. **Digitizing** means converting colors and lines into digital impulses capable of being read by a computer. Digitized photos and downloaded graphics from the Web, combined with high-resolution production from scanners, create endless possibilities. Small businesses now can afford to include photographs in their brochures and other types of publications.

Publisher can accept photographs and images from a variety of input sources. Each graphic you import has a file name, followed by a dot or period, followed by a three-letter extension. Publisher uses **extensions** to recognize individual file formats.

You can choose from a number of common graphics file formats, including the **bitmap** format (which creates a picture made from a series of small dots), scanned pictures, and photographs. Publisher supports all the major file formats. However, each year, new graphic formats are introduced, and older graphic formats are retired. Depending on your installation of Publisher, you may need to install a filter for some formats. A **filter** is a set of instructions that the operating system and Publisher use to import and display graphics. Not all filters are installed in order to save disk space. Table 3–6 displays a list of supported file formats.

Table 3–6 Supported Graphic Formats	
Graphic Formats	**Filter May Be Needed**
Compressed Macintosh PICT (.pcz)	X
Computer Graphics Metafile (.cgm)	X
CorelDraw (.cdr)	X
Encapsulated PostScript (.eps)	X
Graphics Interchange Format, CompuServe format (.gif or .gfa)	
JPEG File Interchange Format (.jpeg, .jpg, .jfif, or .jpe)	
Macintosh PICT (.pct or .pict)	X
Microsoft Windows Bitmap (.bmp)	
Portable Network Graphics (.png)	
TIFF, Tagged Image File Format (.tif or .tiff)	
Windows Enhanced Metafile (.emf)	
Windows Metafile (.wmf)	
WordPerfect Graphics (.wpg)	X

BTW

Widows and Orphans
The Paragraph dialog box contains a Line and Paragraph Breaks tab where you can set widow and orphan control. A **widow** is the last line of a paragraph printed by itself at the top of a connected text box. An **orphan** is the first line of a paragraph printed by itself at the bottom of a connected text box. Choices include keeping the lines together and starting the paragraph in a new text box.

BTW

More Graphics
Microsoft supplies many free graphics and add-ins for your Microsoft Office products, which you may download from the Microsoft Web site. To do this, click Help on the menu bar and then click Microsoft Office Online. When your browser displays the Web page, follow the links to Products and then click Check for free updates.

Inserting a Photograph from a File

Publisher can insert a photograph into a publication by accessing the Clip Art task pane, by externally importing from a file, by directly importing an image from a scanner or camera, or by creating a new drawing.

Recall that when a Publisher template has grouped a picture with its caption, clicking either will select both. To further select only the picture or only the caption text box, a second click is required.

To Insert a Photograph

1 Click the picture/caption grouped object in the left panel of page 2.

2 Double-click the picture to display the Clip Art task pane.

3 Type university in the Search for box. If necessary, click the Search in box arrow and then click Everywhere in the list. To search for only pictures, click the Results should be box arrow and then make sure Photographs is the only box with a check mark.

4 Click the Go button to search for clip art related to the term, university.

5 When the clips are displayed, scroll to find a picture of a building similar to the one shown in Figure 3–46. To insert the picture into the brochure, click the picture.

6 Close the Clip Art task pane.

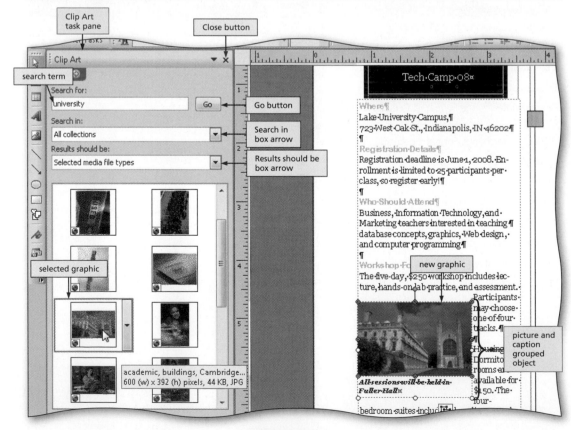

Figure 3–46

Wrapping Text around Pictures

The way that text wraps, or adjusts itself around objects, is called **text wrapping**. Text wrapping applies to text boxes, graphics, and all other kinds of shapes that are close to, or overlapping, other Publisher objects. You can choose how you want the text to wrap around an object using one of the following **wrapping styles**. **Square** wraps text around all sides of the selected object. **Tight** wraps text as closely as possible to the object. **Through** wraps text around the perimeter and inside any open portions of the object. **Top and bottom** wraps text above and below the object, but not on either side. The **None** option removes all text wrapping formatting so that text does not wrap around the object. If the object is transparent, the text behind it will show through. Otherwise, the text will be hidden behind the object.

BTW

Text Wrapping
Publisher text boxes automatically wrap around other objects on the page. The Format dialog box associated with most objects also contains text wrapping options on the Layout sheet. If text wrapping appears to be unavailable, one of the objects may be transparent. In that case, press CTRL+T.

To Text Wrap

1

- If necessary, select the object you wish to text wrap, in this case the picture and caption grouped object.

- Click the Text Wrapping button on the Picture toolbar to display its options (Figure 3–47).

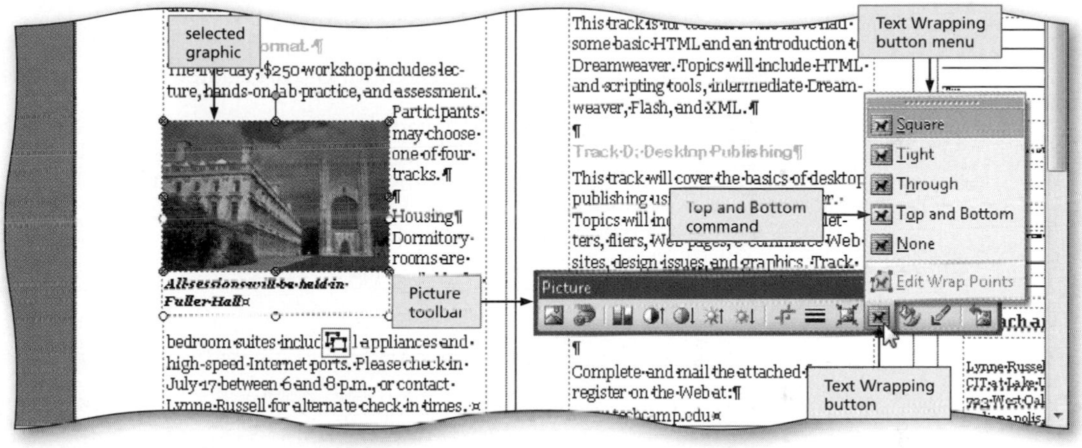

Figure 3–47

2

- Click Top and Bottom to select the text wrapping style.

- Drag to reposition the picture and caption to a location between paragraphs, as shown in Figure 3–48.

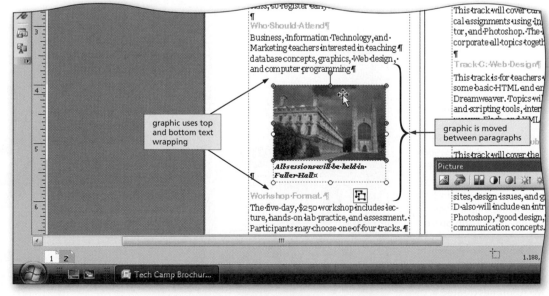

Figure 3–48

Replacing Graphics on Page 1

The following steps describe how to use the Clip Art task pane to replace the graphics on page 1.

To Replace the Graphics in the Left Panel of Page 1

1 Click Page 1 on the page sorter.

2 Zoom and scroll as necessary to display the right panel.

3 Click the grouped graphic in the right panel, and then double-click the picture to display the Clip Art task pane.

4 Type technology in the Search for box.

5 If necessary, click the Search in box arrow and then click Everywhere in the list.

6 Click the Results should be box arrow and click All media types.

7 Click the Go button to search for clip art related to the term, technology.

8 When the clips are displayed, scroll to find a graphic similar to the one shown in Figure 3–49.

9 To insert the picture into the brochure, click the picture (Figure 3–49).

10 Close the Clip Art task pane.

BTW

Clip Art Sources
In addition to the clip art images included in the previews, other sources for clip art include retailers specializing in computer software, the Internet, bulletin board systems, and online information systems. A **bulletin board system** is a computer system that allows users to communicate with each other and share files. Microsoft has created a special page on its Web site where you can add new clips to the Clip Organizer.

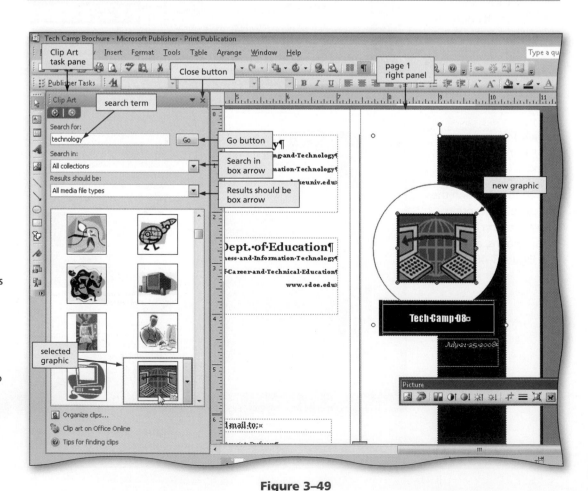

Figure 3–49

Creating a Logo from Scratch

Many types of publications use logos to identify and distinguish the page. A **logo** is a recognizable symbol that identifies a person, business, or organization. A logo may be composed of a name, a picture, or a combination of symbols and graphics. In a later project, you will learn how to add a permanent logo to an information set for a company.

Creating a Shape for the Logo

The logo in the Tech Camp brochure is a shape with colors and text. Created individually in the workspace, the logo easily is positioned and sized to the proper places in the brochure. The logo appears both on the back of the brochure (middle panel of page 1) and on the inside of the brochure (middle panel of page 2).

The background of the logo is from the AutoShapes menu. Accessed through the Objects toolbar, the AutoShapes menu displays seven categories of shapes you may use as graphics in a publication. These shapes include lines, connectors, basic shapes, block arrows, stars, and banners, among others. **AutoShapes** differ from WordArt in that they do not contain text; rather, they are graphic designs with a variety of formatting options, such as color, border, size, and shadow.

The workspace, also called the **scratch area**, can serve as a kind of drawing board to create new objects. Without disturbing any object already on the publications page, you can manipulate and edit objects in the workspace and then move them to the desired location. The rulers and status bar display the exact size of the new object. Moving objects off the page and into the workspace sometimes is advantageous as well. Small objects that are difficult to revise on the publication can be moved into the workspace, magnified and edited, and then moved back. As you place new objects in the workspace, more workspace room is allocated.

The steps on the next page illustrate creating the logo in Publisher's workspace to the right of the brochure.

BTW

Logos
A logo is a recognizable symbol that identifies you or your business. If you do not want to create one from scratch, the Design Gallery contains many logo styles from which you may choose. Although Publisher's logo styles are generic, commercial logos typically are copyrighted. Consult with a legal representative before you commercially use materials bearing clip art, logos, designs, words, or other symbols that could violate third-party rights, including trademarks.

BTW

Formatting Options
You can set the fill color, line weight, and line color for new AutoShapes or drawing objects, such as curves, lines, and WordArt, in the current publication, using the Format dialog box. Right-click an AutoShape or drawing object that has the attributes, such as line fill or text color, that you want to use as the default. Then, on the shortcut menu, click the Format option. In the dialog box, click the Colors and Lines tab. Finally, select the Apply settings to new AutoShapes check box.

To Create a Shape for the Logo

1

- On page 1, zoom to Whole Page.

- Drag the horizontal scroll box to the right, to view more of the workspace (Figure 3–50).

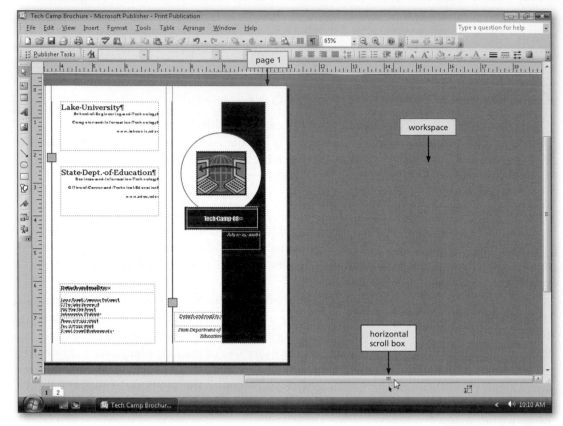

Figure 3–50

2

- Click the AutoShapes button on the Objects toolbar to display the available groups of shapes.

- Point to Block Arrows on the AutoShapes menu to display the submenu.

- Point to the Striped Right Arrow shape (Figure 3–51).

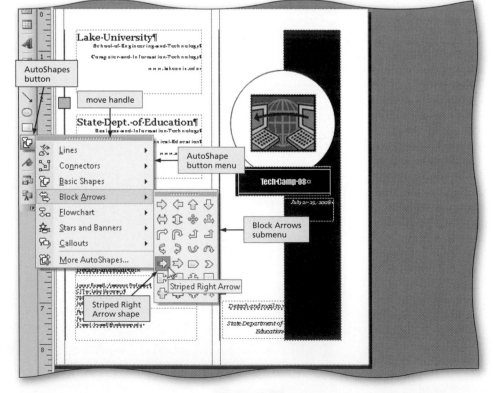

Figure 3–51

3

- Click the Striped Right Arrow shape and then move the mouse pointer to the workspace to the right of the brochure.

- Drag down and to the right until the shape is approximately 2.5 × 1.5 inches. Release the mouse button.

- To quickly zoom to 100%, press the F9 key (Figure 3–52).

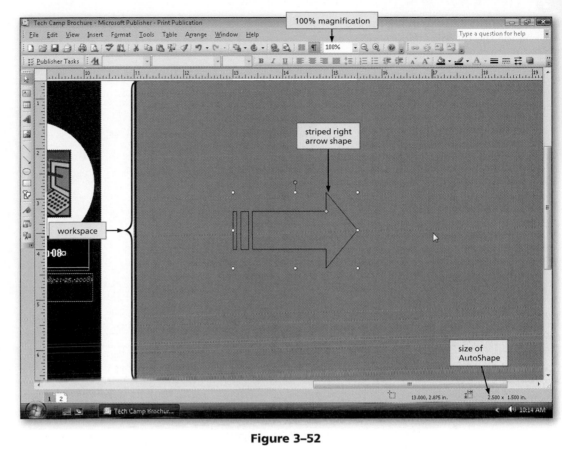

Figure 3–52

To Fill a Shape with Color

The following steps fill the AutoShape with the gold color from the color scheme.

1

- With the AutoShape still selected, click the Fill Color button arrow on the Formatting toolbar to display the scheme colors (Figure 3–53).

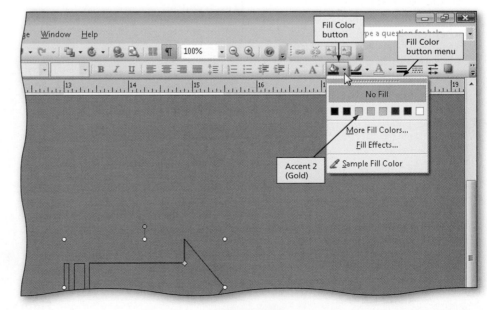

Figure 3–53

2

• Click Accent 2 (Gold) in the list to change the fill color (Figure 3–54).

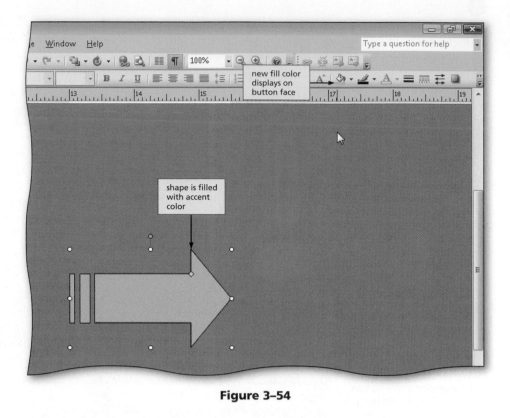

Figure 3–54

To Edit AutoShape Lines

The following steps edit both the color and style of the lines around the AutoShape.

1

• With the AutoShape still selected, click the Line Color button arrow on the Formatting toolbar to display the colors in the color scheme (Figure 3–55).

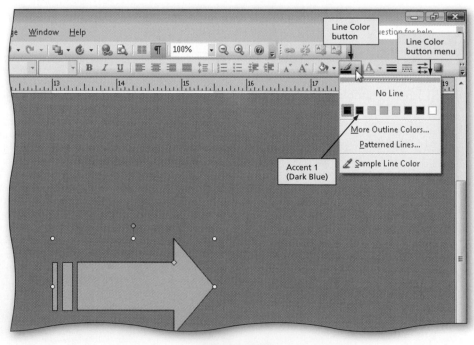

Figure 3–55

2

• Click Accent 1 (Dark Blue) in the list to change the line color (Figure 3–56).

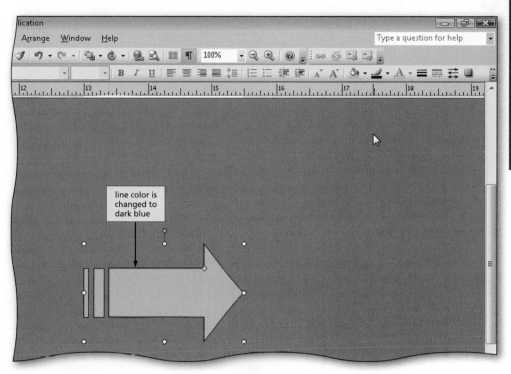

Figure 3–56

3

• With the AutoShape still selected, click the Line/Border Style button on the Formatting toolbar to display the list (Figure 3–57).

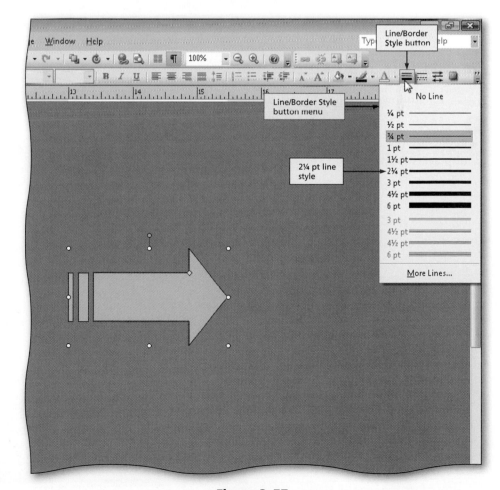

Figure 3–57

• Click 2 ¼ pt in the list to choose a style for the line (Figure 3–58).

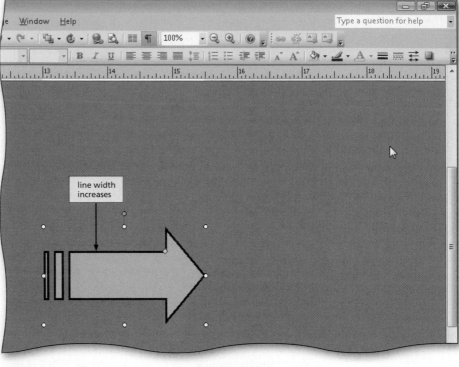

Figure 3–58

To Add Text to an AutoShape

The following steps add text to the AutoShape using the Accent 1 (Dark Blue) color.

❶

• Right-click the AutoShape to display its shortcut menu (Figure 3–59).

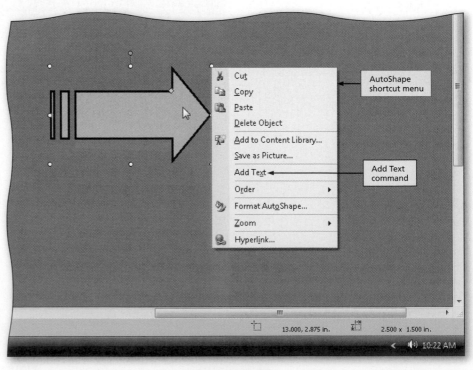

Figure 3–59

2

- Click Add Text to position the cursor inside the AutoShape.

- Click the Font color button arrow and then click Accent 1 (Dark Blue) in the list to select the font color.

- Type `Looking Forward with Technology` to enter the text (Figure 3–60).

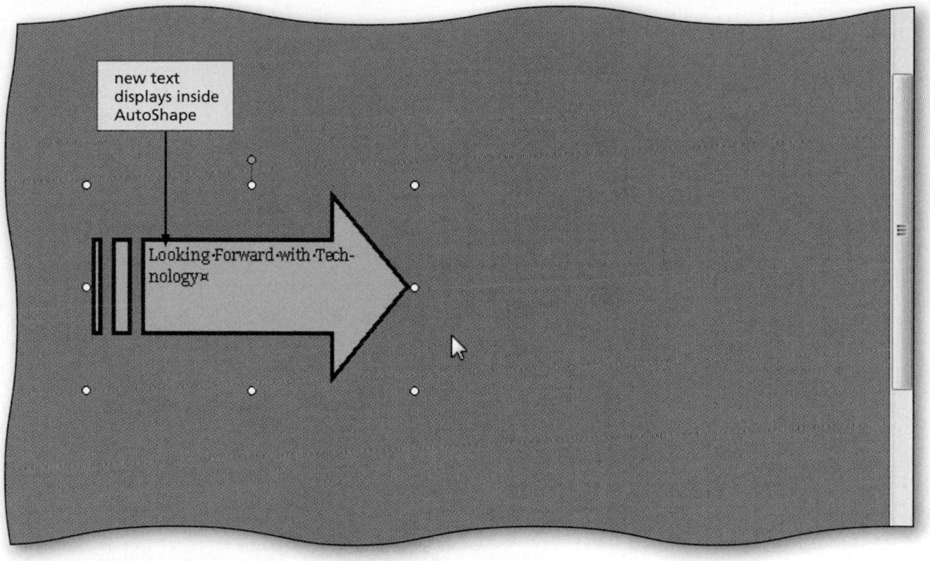

new text displays inside AutoShape

Looking·Forward·with·Technology¤

Figure 3–60

To Fit Text

Publisher has three **AutoFit Text** options to adjust the size of text in text boxes or shapes. The default value is **Do Not AutoFit**, where text is displayed in the exact font size selected in the Formatting toolbar. A second way is to use the **Best Fit** option in which Publisher adjusts the size of the text to as big a size as possible to fit the box or shape. The third way, **Shrink Text On Overflow**, allows Publisher to adjust the size of your text only when it is necessary to keep text from overflowing.

1

- Right-click the AutoShape to display its shortcut menu.

- Point to Change Text to display the Change Text submenu.

- Point to AutoFit Text to display the AutoFit Text submenu (Figure 3–61).

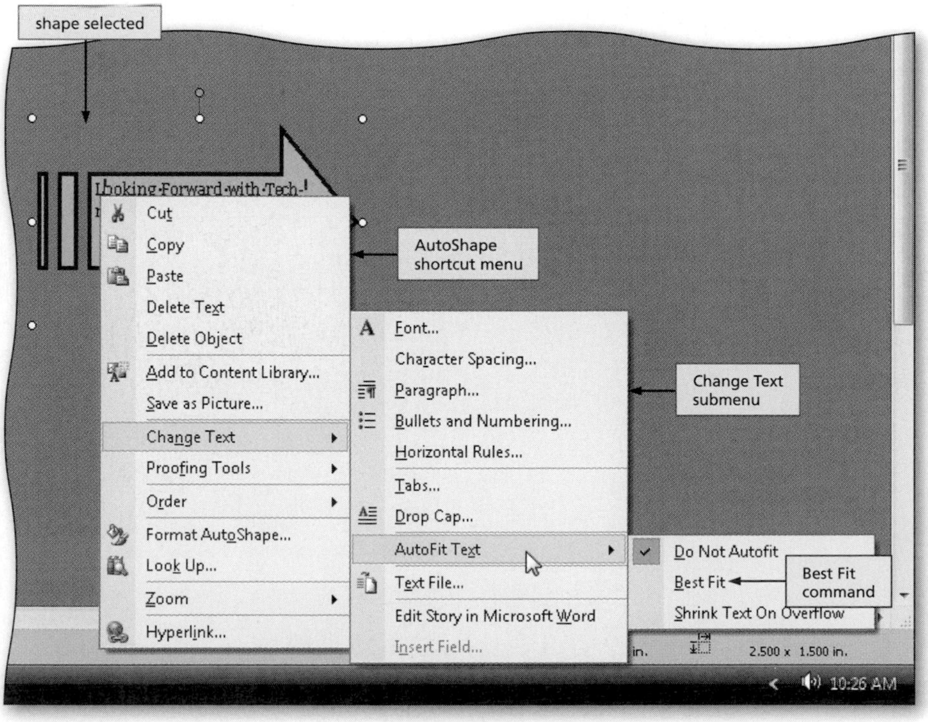

shape selected

Looking·Forward·with·Tech·!

✄	Cut
▣	Copy
▣	Paste
	Delete Text
	Delete Object
▤	Add to Content Library...
	Save as Picture...
	Change Text ▶
	Proofing Tools ▶
	Order ▶
▨	Format AutoShape...
▨	Look Up...
	Zoom ▶
▨	Hyperlink...

AutoShape shortcut menu

A	Font...
	Character Spacing...
▤	Paragraph...
▤	Bullets and Numbering...
	Horizontal Rules...
	Tabs...
▤	Drop Cap...
	AutoFit Text ▶
▤	Text File...
	Edit Story in Microsoft Word
	Insert Field...

Change Text submenu

✔ Do Not Autofit
Best Fit ◀
Shrink Text On Overflow

Best Fit command

2.500 x 1.500 in.

10:26 AM

Figure 3–61

2

- Click Best Fit to adjust the size of the text (Figure 3–62).

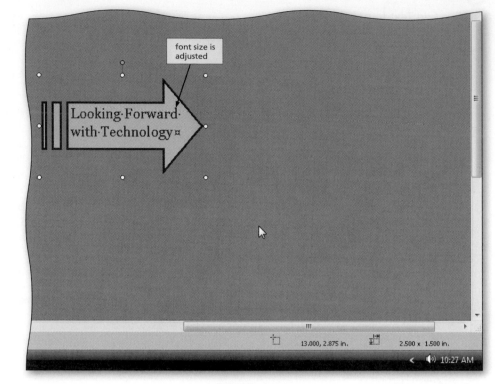

Figure 3–62

To Copy the Logo

The next step makes a copy of the logo by pressing the CTRL key while dragging.

1

- Point to the logo. When the mouse pointer changes to a double two-headed arrow, CTRL+DRAG to an empty location in the workspace (Figure 3–63).

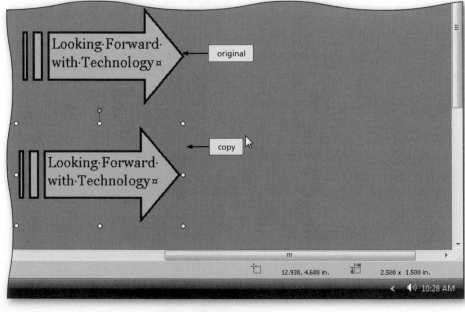

Figure 3–63

To Reposition and Resize the Logos

1

• Click the Zoom Out button on the Standard toolbar several times until the entire page layout and workspace area are visible.

• Point to one of the logos. When the mouse pointer changes to a double two-headed arrow, drag the logo to a position above the contact information in the middle panel of page 1.

• If necessary, to resize the logo and make it fit in the empty space, SHIFT+DRAG a corner. Drag to reposition, if necessary, and position the logo as shown in Figure 3–64.

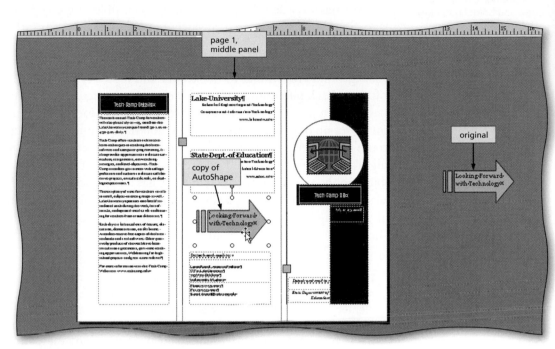

Figure 3–64

2

• Click Page 2 on the page sorter.

• Point to the logo in the workspace. When the mouse pointer changes to a double two-headed arrow, drag the logo to a position below the URL in the middle panel of page 2.

• To resize the logo and make it fit in the empty space, SHIFT+DRAG a corner. Drag to reposition, if necessary, and position the logo as shown in Figure 3–65.

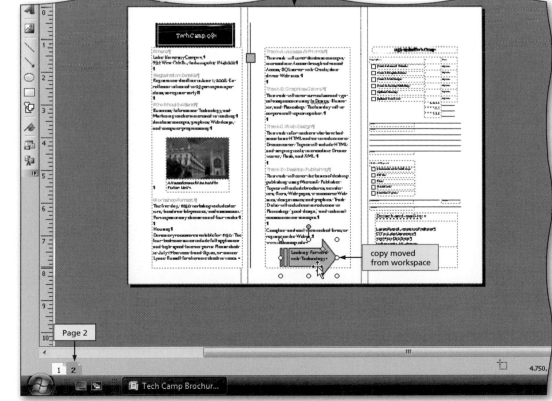

Figure 3–65

BTW

Nudging
You can drag objects to new positions, or you can press and hold the ALT key while pressing the arrow keys to **nudge** objects to new positions. If you increase the magnification of the screen, you can resize and reposition objects precisely. For instance, at 400% magnification, you can move an object .003 inch by pressing and holding the ALT key and then pressing an arrow key. The Arrange menu also contains options for nudging and aligning. The Measurements toolbar allows you to enter exact horizontal and vertical positions, as well.

Creating a Watermark with WordArt

A **watermark** is a semi-transparent graphic, visible in the background on the printed page. Some watermarks are translucent; others can be seen on the paper when held up to the light. Other times the paper itself has a watermark when it is manufactured. In Publisher, watermarks are created by placing text or graphics on a **master page**, which is a background area similar to the header and footer area in traditional word processing software. Each publication starts with one master page. A master page can contain anything that you can put on a publication page, as well as headers, footers, and layout guides that can be set up only on a master page. If you have a multipage document, you can choose to use two different master pages for cases such as facing pages in a book, in which you might want different graphics in the backgrounds. If you want to display master page objects only on certain pages, Publisher has an **Ignore Master Page command** that causes the master page not to display. This is useful for cases such as background images on every page except the title page in a longer document, or a watermark on the inside of a brochure but not on the front.

Plan Ahead

> **Proofread, revise, and add the final touches.**
> Add logos, watermarks, headers, footers, and other objects on the master page or repeated elements on the publication itself. Double-check that each repeated element is exactly alike.
>
> Proofread the brochure several times before using the Pack and Go Wizard to take your publication to the printer. Proofreading involves reading the brochure with the intent of identifying errors and looking for ways to improve it. Ask someone else to proofread the paper and give you suggestions for improvements. Revise as necessary and then use the spelling and design checking features of the software.

To Access the Master Page

In the Tech Camp brochure, you will create two master pages. The master page for page 1 will contain no objects. The master page for page 2 will contain a watermark. The following steps access the master page.

1

- Click Page 1 on the page sorter.

- Click View on the menu bar to display the View menu (Figure 3–66).

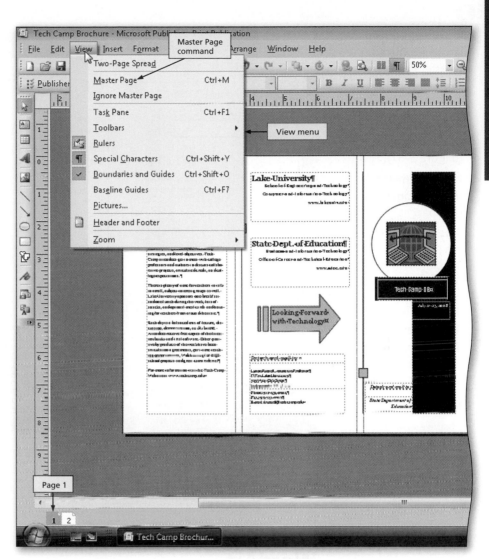

Figure 3–66

2

- Click Master Page to access the Edit Master Pages task pane.

- Zoom and scroll as necessary to display the entire page (Figure 3–67).

Q&A

What is the Edit Master Pages toolbar?

The Edit Master Pages toolbar displays when viewing a master page. The toolbar contains buttons to insert, delete, duplicate, and change master pages, as well as options to display the layout guides, display two facing master pages, and close the master page view entirely.

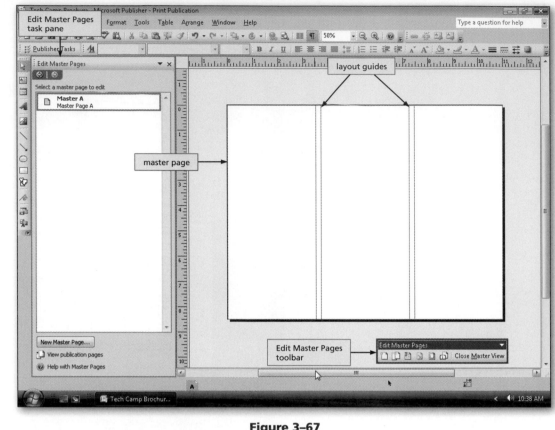

Figure 3–67

WordArt

WordArt is a gallery of text styles that works with Publisher to create fancy text effects. A WordArt object actually is a graphic and not text. Publication designers typically use WordArt to create eye-catching headlines and banners or watermark images. WordArt uses its own toolbar to add effects to the graphic.

Inserting a WordArt Object

The Tech Camp brochure will use a WordArt object, with the text, Tech Camp, as a watermark on page 2. A text box with font effects could be formatted to create a similar effect, but using WordArt increases the number of special effect possibilities and options.

To Insert a WordArt Object

The following steps explain how to add a WordArt object as the watermark on the master page of the brochure.

1

- Click the Insert WordArt button on the Objects toolbar.

- When the WordArt Gallery dialog box is displayed, click the first WordArt style in the top row, if necessary (Figure 3–68).

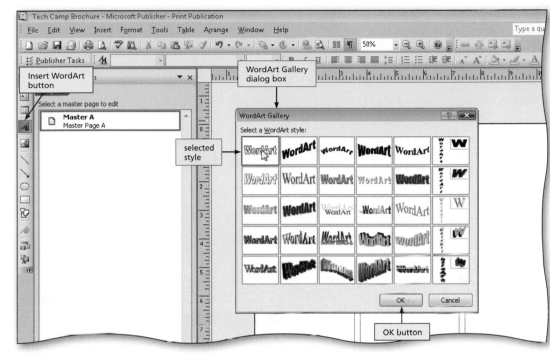

Figure 3–68

2

- Click the OK button.

- When Publisher displays the Edit WordArt Text dialog box, type Tech Camp as the new text (Figure 3–69).

- Click the OK button.

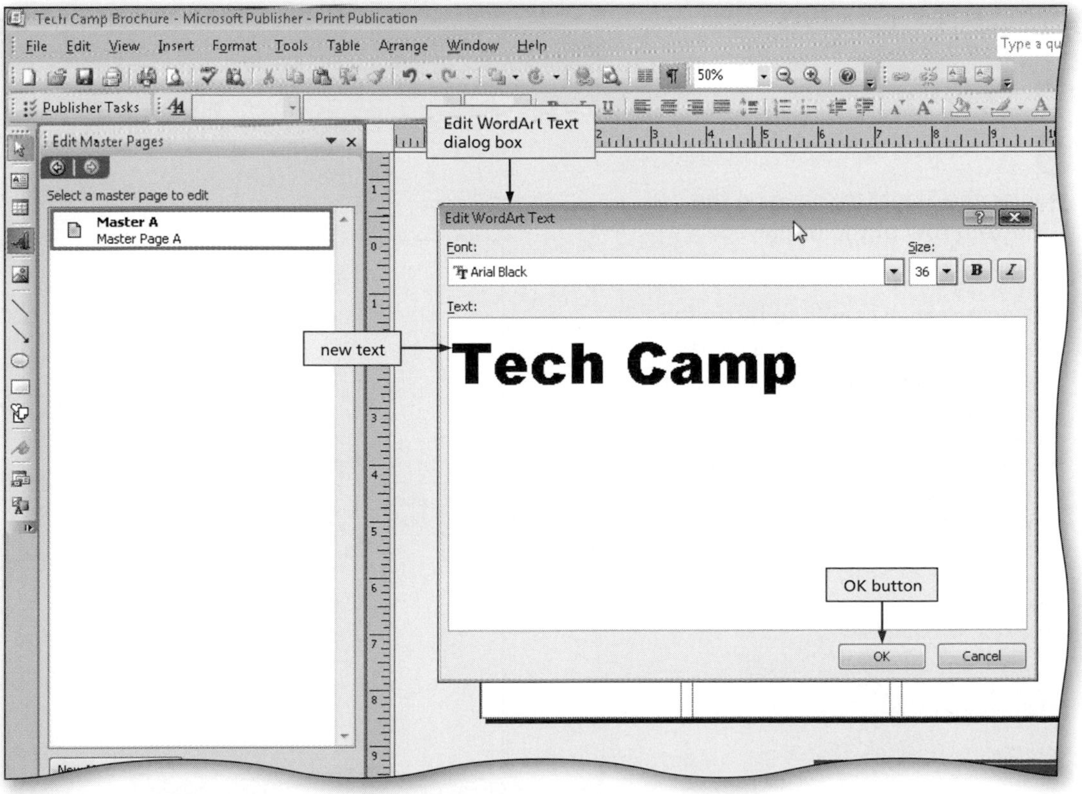

BTW

WordArt Spelling
Keep in mind that WordArt objects are drawing objects; they are not treated as Publisher text. Thus, if you misspell the contents of a WordArt object and then check the publication, Publisher will not flag the misspelled word(s) in the WordArt text.

Figure 3–69

To Format WordArt

The WordArt toolbar contains several buttons to help you format WordArt objects. The following steps use the WordArt Shape button to change the general shape of the WordArt object.

❶

- With the WordArt object selected, click the WordArt Shape button on the WordArt toolbar (Figure 3–70).

Q&A

Where is my WordArt toolbar?

The WordArt toolbar usually displays when a WordArt object is selected. If your toolbar does not display, you may have closed it by accident. To redisplay the WordArt toolbar, point to Toolbars on the View menu, and then click WordArt on the Toolbars submenu.

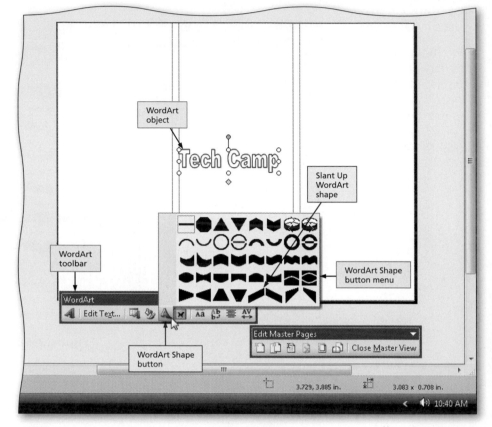

Figure 3–70

❷

- Click the Slant Up shape on the bottom row of the displayed shapes.

- Drag a corner handle to resize the object to approximately 6 inches wide and 6 inches tall, as noted on the status bar.

- Drag the WordArt object to the upper-center part of the page (Figure 3–71).

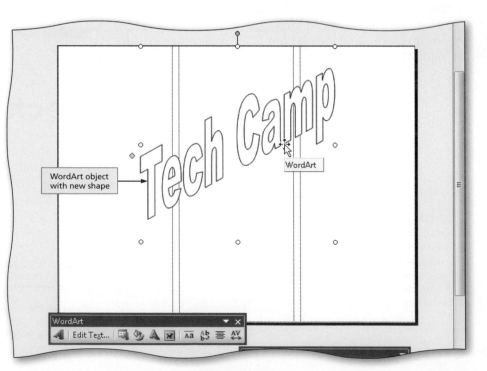

Figure 3–71

3

- Click the Format WordArt button on the WordArt toolbar to display the Format WordArt dialog box.

- In the Line area, click the Color box arrow and then click Accent 3 (Pale Blue) in the list.

- Click the Dashed box arrow (Figure 3–72).

Q&A

What do the other buttons on the WordArt toolbar do?

Each button displays its name in a screen tip when you point to it. The buttons toward the left create a new WordArt object and change the basic text, style, format, and shape. The buttons toward the right change how the text and characters are displayed, with features such as text wrapping, letter heights, vertical text, alignment, and character spacing.

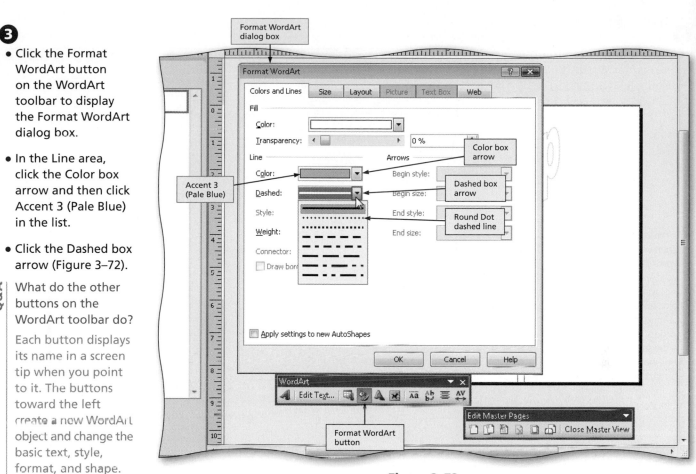

Figure 3–72

4

- Click the Round Dot dashed line (Figure 3–73).

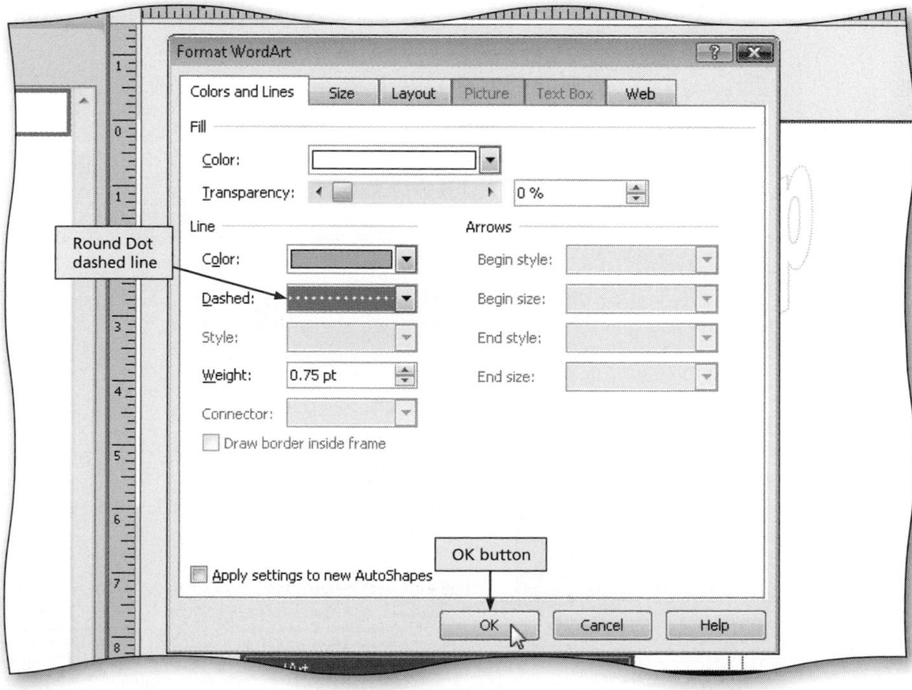

Figure 3–73

5

- Click the OK button to close the Format WordArt dialog box (Figure 3–74).

Formatting WordArt
When you click the Format WordArt button on the WordArt toolbar, Publisher displays options for fill color, lines, size, spacing, rotating, shadows, and borders, as well as many of the same features Publisher provides on its Formatting toolbar, such as text wrapping, alignment, bold, italics, underline, and fonts.

Other Ways

1. Click Insert WordArt button on the WordArt toolbar

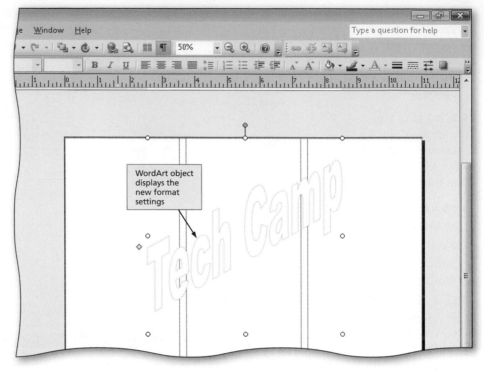

Figure 3–74

To Close the Master Page

1 On the Edit Master Pages toolbar, click the Close Master View button to return to the document.

2 Close the task pane, if necessary, and then zoom to Whole Page (Figure 3–75).

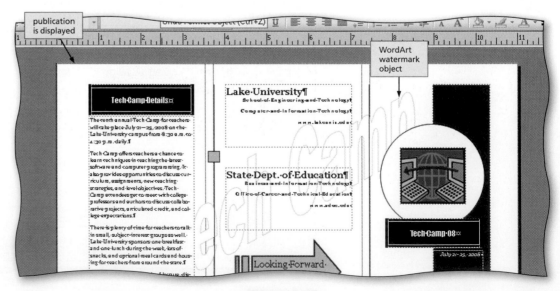

Figure 3–75

Completing the Watermark

The final step in creating the watermark is to change the transparency of the text boxes on page 2 and then choose to ignore the master page so that it does not display on page 1. Text box transparency refers to whether the area around the text is a solid color, such as white, or clear. To make a text box transparent, you can press CTRL+T. Pressing CTRL+T a second time toggles back to a solid background.

To Remove the Watermark from Page 1

The next step removes the watermark from page 1 by choosing to ignore the master page.

1

- With page 1 displayed, click View on the menu bar and then click the Ignore Master Page command (Figure 3–76).

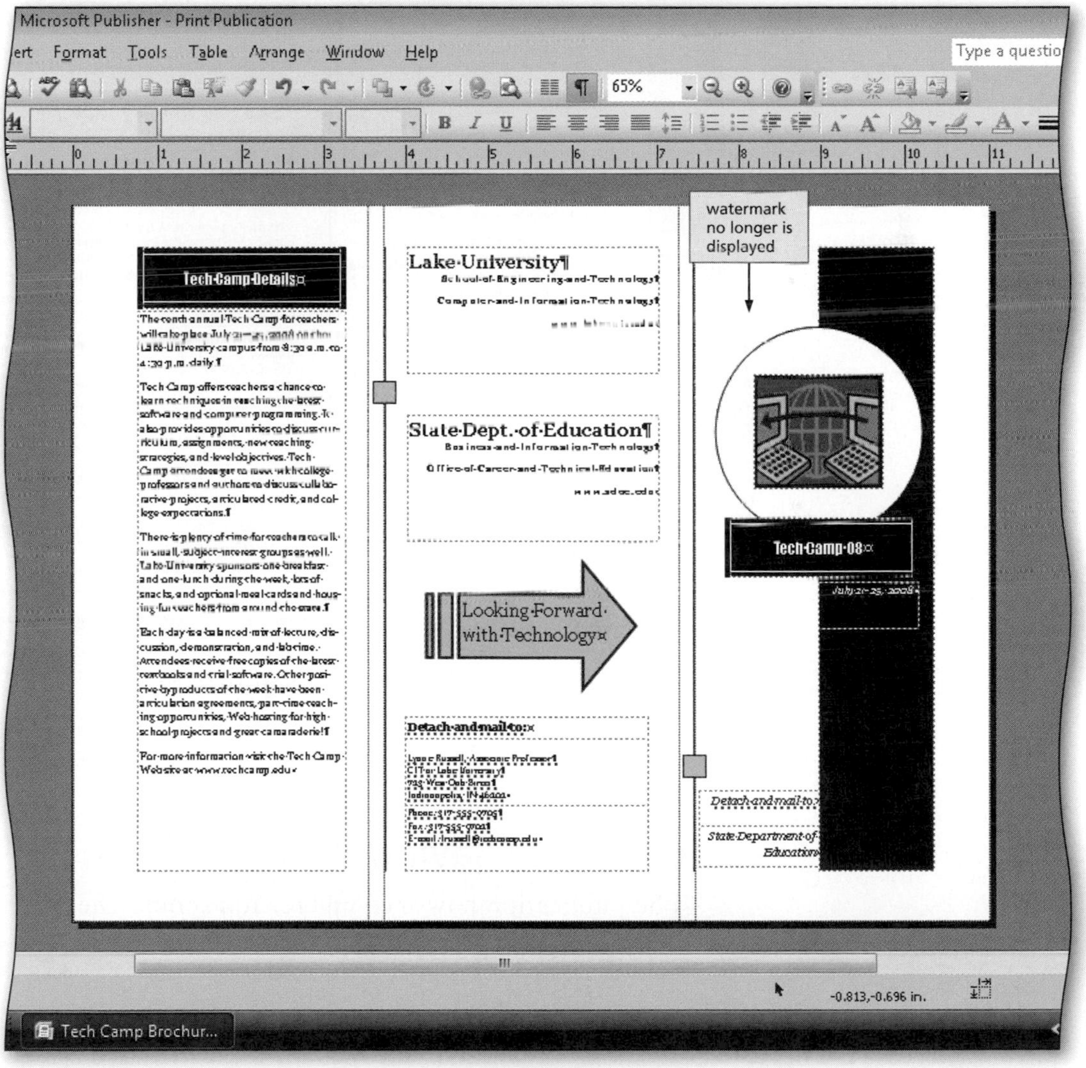

Figure 3–76

To Make Text Boxes Transparent

The next steps change the transparency of the two text boxes in the left and middle panel of page 2.

- Click Page 2 on the page sorter and then zoom to Whole Page.

- Select the text box in the left panel and then press CTRL+T to make it transparent.

- Select the text box in the middle panel and then press CTRL+T to make it transparent (Figure 3–77).

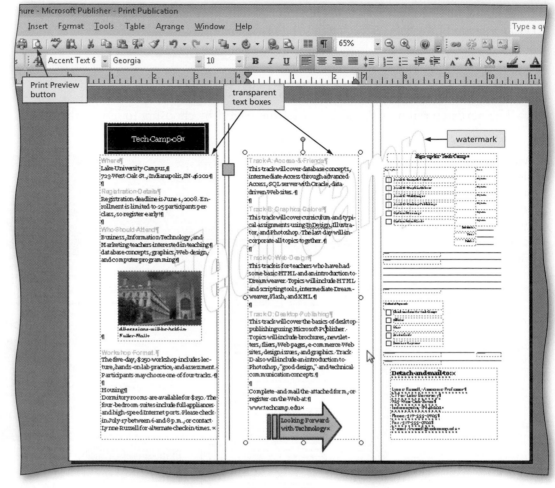

Figure 3–77

Checking and Saving the Publication

The publication now is complete. You should check for spelling errors in the publication, run the Design Checker, and then save the publication again.

To Check the Publication and Save Again

1 Click the Spelling button on the Standard toolbar. If Publisher flags any words, fix or ignore them as appropriate.

2 When Publisher asks to check the entire document, click the Yes button.

3 Click Tools on the menu bar and then click Design Checker. Ignore any messages about extra space, empty text boxes, or picture resolution.

4 If the Design Checker identifies any other errors, fix them as necessary.

5 Close the Design Checker task pane.

6 Click the Save button on the Standard toolbar.

Outside Printing

When they need mass quantities of publications, businesses generally **outsource**, or submit their publications to an outside printer, for duplicating. You must make special considerations when preparing a document for outside printing.

Previewing the Brochure before Printing

The first step in getting the publication ready for outside printing is to examine what the printed copy will look like from your desktop. The following steps preview the brochure before printing.

To Preview the Brochure before Printing

1 Click the Print Preview button on the Standard toolbar (Figure 3–78).

2 Click the Page Up button in the toolbar to view page 1.

3 Click the Close button on the Print Preview toolbar.

BTW

Two-Page View
You also can view two pages of the brochure at once by clicking the Multiple Pages button on the Print Preview toolbar. While viewing two full pages with intensive graphics and text may give you a good overview of the publication, it provides few checking capabilities.

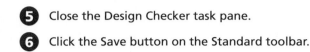

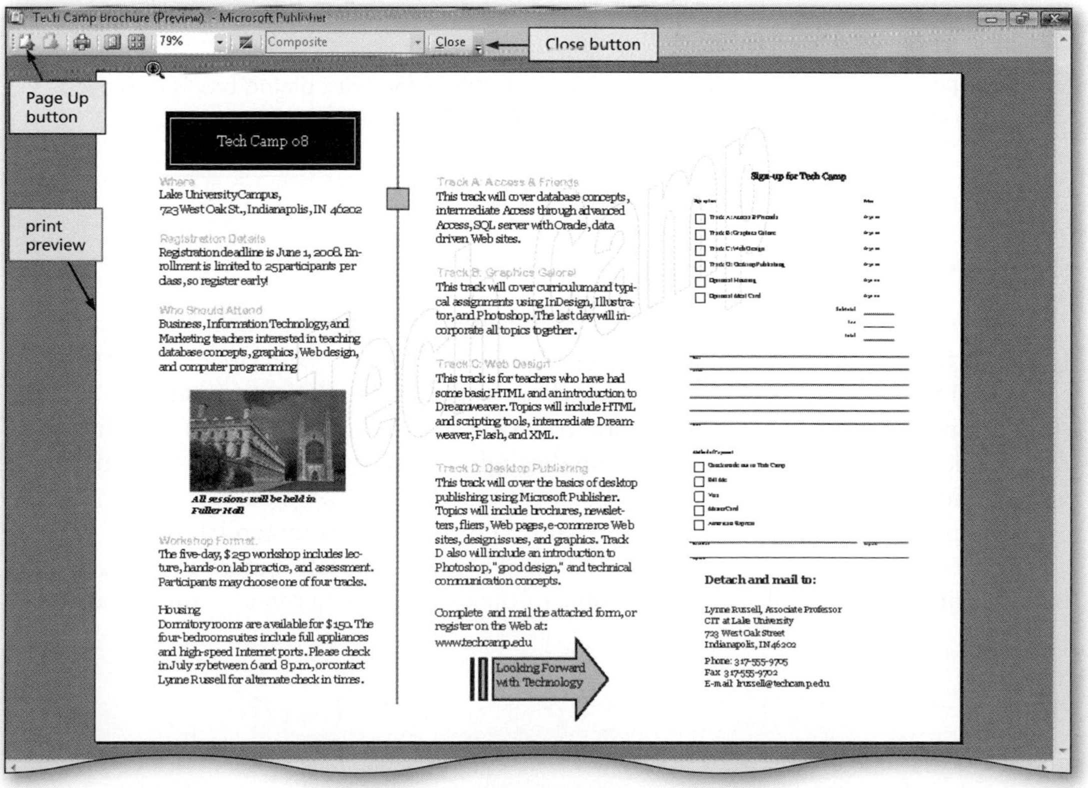

Figure 3–78

Printing the Brochure

The next sequence of steps recommends publishing this brochure on a high grade of paper to obtain a professional look. A heavier stock paper helps the brochure to stand up better in display racks, although any paper will suffice. If you do use a special paper, be sure to click the Properties or Advanced Settings button in the Print dialog box for your printer and then specify the paper you are using. Following your printer's specifications, print one side of the paper, turn it over, and then print the reverse side. The completed brochure prints as shown in Figure 3–1 on page PUB 147. You then can fold the brochure to display the title panel on the front.

Plan Ahead

> **Plan for printing.**
> Make a firm decision that quality matters and consult with several commercial printers ahead of time. Get prices, color modes, copies, paper, and folding options in writing before you finish your brochure. Brochures are more effective on heavier paper, with strong colors and glossy feels. Together with the commercial printer, select a paper that is going to last. Check to make sure the commercial printer can accept Microsoft Publisher 2007 files.

To Print the Brochure

BTW

Printer Memory
Some printers do not have enough memory to print a wide variety of images and color. In these cases, the printer prints up to a certain point on a page and then chokes — resulting in only the top portion of the publication printing. Check with your instructor to see if your printer has enough memory to work with colors.

1 Ready the printer according to the printer instructions, and insert paper.

2 With page 1 displaying in the workspace, click File on the menu bar and then click Print. When the Print dialog box is displayed, click Current page. If necessary, click the Properties button to choose a special paper. Click the OK button.

3 When page 1 finishes printing, turn the page over and reinsert it top first (or as your printer requires) into the paper feed mechanism on your printer.

4 Click Page 2 on the page sorter.

5 Click File on the menu bar and then click Print. When the Print dialog box is displayed, again click Current page and then click the OK button.

Printing Considerations

If you start a publication from scratch, it is best to **set up** the publication for the type of printing you want before you place objects on the page. Otherwise, you may be forced to make design changes at the last minute. You also may set up an existing publication for a printing service. In order to provide you with experience in setting up a publication for outside printing, this project takes you through the preparation steps — even if you are submitting this publication only to your instructor.

Printing options, such as whether to use a copy shop or commercial printer, have advantages and limitations. You may have to make some trade-offs before deciding on the best printing option. Table 3–7 shows some of the questions you can ask yourself about printing.

Table 3–7 Picking a Printing Option

Consideration	Questions to Ask	Desktop Option	Professional Options
Color	Is the quality of photographs and color a high priority?	Low- to medium-quality	High quality
Convenience	Do I want the easy way?	Very convenient and familiar	Time needed to explore different methods, unfamiliarity
Cost	How much do I want to pay?	Printer supplies and personal time	High-resolution color/high quality is expensive; the more you print, the less expensive the per copy price
Quality	How formal is the purpose of my publication?	Local event; narrow, personal audience	Business, marketing, professional services
Quantity	How many copies do I need?	1 to 10 copies	10 to 500 copies: use a copy shop; 500+ copies: use a commercial printer
Turnaround	How soon do I need it?	Immediate	Rush outside printing is probably an extra cost

Paper Considerations

Professional brochures are printed on a high grade of paper to enhance the graphics and provide a longer lasting document. Grades of paper are based on weight. Desktop printers commonly use **20 lb. bond paper**, which means they use a lightweight paper intended for writing and printing. A commercial printer might use 60 lb. glossy or linen paper.

The finishing options and their costs are important considerations that may take additional time to explore. **Glossy paper** is a coated paper, produced using a heat process with clay and titanium. **Linen paper**, with its mild texture or grain, can support high-quality graphics without the shine and slick feel of glossy paper. Users sometimes pick a special stock of paper, such as cover stock, card stock, or text stock. This textbook is printed on 45 lb., blade-coated paper. **Blade-coated paper** is coated and then skimmed and smoothed to create the pages you see here.

These paper and finishing options may sound burdensome, but they are becoming conveniently available to desktop publishers. Local office supply stores have shelf after shelf of special computer paper specifically designed for laser and ink-jet printers. Some of the paper you can purchase has been prescored for special folding.

Color Considerations

When printing colors, desktop printers commonly use a color scheme called **RGB**. RGB stands for the three colors — red, green, and blue — that are used to print the combined colors of your publication. Professional printers, on the other hand, can print your publication using color scheme processes, or **libraries**. These processes include black and white, spot color, and process color.

Spot Colors

If you choose black plus one spot color in a publication, Publisher converts all colors except for black to tints of the selected spot color. If you choose black plus two spot colors, Publisher changes only exact matches of the second spot color to 100 percent of the second spot color. All other colors in the publication, other than black, are changed to tints of the first spot color. You then can apply tints of the second spot color to objects in the publication manually.

Offset Printing

Your printing service may use the initials SWOP, which stand for Standard for Web Offset Printing — a widely accepted set of color standards used in Web offset printing. Web offset printing has nothing to do with the World Wide Web. It is merely the name for an offset printing designed to print thousands of pieces in a single run from a giant roll of paper.

T-Shirts

You can use Publisher to create T-shirt designs with pictures, logos, words, or any of the Publisher objects. You need thermal T-shirt transfer paper that is widely available for most printers. Then create your design in Publisher. On the File menu, click Page Setup. On the Printer & Paper sheet, select Letter. If your design is a picture, clip art, or WordArt, flip it horizontally. If your design includes text, cut it from the text box, and insert it into a WordArt object; then flip it horizontally.

In **black-and-white printing**, the printer uses only one color of ink (usually black, but you can choose a different color if you want). You can add accent colors to your publication by using different shades of gray or by printing on colored paper. Your publication can have the same range of subtleties as a black-and-white photograph.

A **spot color** is used to accent a black-and-white publication. Newspapers, for example, may print their masthead in a bright, eye-catching color on page 1 but print the rest of the publication in black and white. In Publisher, you may apply up to two spot colors with a color matching system called **Pantone**. **Spot-color printing** uses semi-transparent, premixed inks typically chosen from standard color-matching guides, such as Pantone. Choosing colors from a **color-matching library** helps ensure high-quality results, because printing professionals who license the libraries agree to maintain the specifications, control, and quality.

In a spot-color publication, each spot color is **separated** to its own plate and printed on an offset printing press. The use of spot colors has become more creative in the last few years. Printing services use spot colors of metallic or florescent inks, as well as screen tints, to get color variations without increasing the number of color separations and cost. If your publication includes a logo with one or two colors, or if you want to use color to emphasize line art or text, then consider using spot-color printing.

Process-color printing means your publication can include color photographs and any color or combination of colors. One of the process-color libraries, called **CMYK**, or **four-color printing**, is named for the four semi-transparent process inks — cyan, magenta, yellow, and black. CMYK process-color printing can reproduce a full range of colors on a printed page. The CMYK color model defines color as it is absorbed and reflected on a printed page rather than in its liquid state.

Process-color printing is the most expensive proposition; black-and-white printing is the cheapest. Using color increases the cost and time it takes to process the publication. When using either the spot-color or process-color method, the printer first must output the publication to film on an **image setter**, which recreates the publication on film or photographic paper. The film then is used to create color **printing plates**. Each printing plate transfers one of the colors in the publication onto paper in an offset process. Publisher can print a preview of these individual sheets showing how the colors will separate before you take your publication to the printer.

A new printing technology called **digital printing** uses toner instead of ink to reproduce a full range of colors. Digital printing does not require separate printing plates. Although not yet widely available, digital printing promises to become cheaper than offset printing without sacrificing any quality.

Publisher supports all three kinds of printing and provides the tools commercial printing services need to print the publication. You should ask your printing service which color-matching system it uses.

Choosing a Commercial Printing Tool

After making the decisions about printing services, paper, and color, you must prepare the brochure for outside printing. The first task is to assign a color library from the commercial printing tools, as illustrated in the following steps.

To Choose a Commercial Printing Tool

1

- Click Tools on the menu bar.
- Point to Commercial Printing Tools (Figure 3–79).

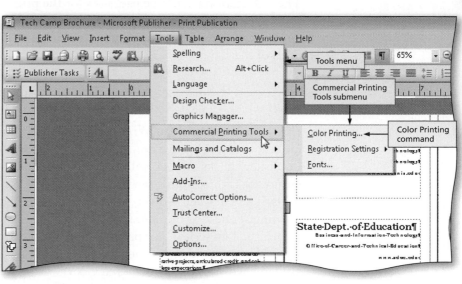

Figure 3–79

2

- Click Color Printing on the Commercial Printing Tools submenu.
- When the Color Printing dialog box is displayed, click Process colors (CMYK) (Figure 3–80).

3

- Click the OK button in the information dialog box.
- Click the OK button in the Color Printing dialog box.

CMYK Colors
When Process Colors are selected, Publisher converts all colors in text, graphics, and other objects to CMYK values and then creates four plates, regardless of the color scheme originally used to create the publication. Some RGB colors, including some of Publisher's standard colors, cannot be matched exactly to a CMYK color. After setting up for process-color printing, be sure to evaluate the publication for color changes. If a color does not match the color you want, you will have to include the new color library when you pack the publication.

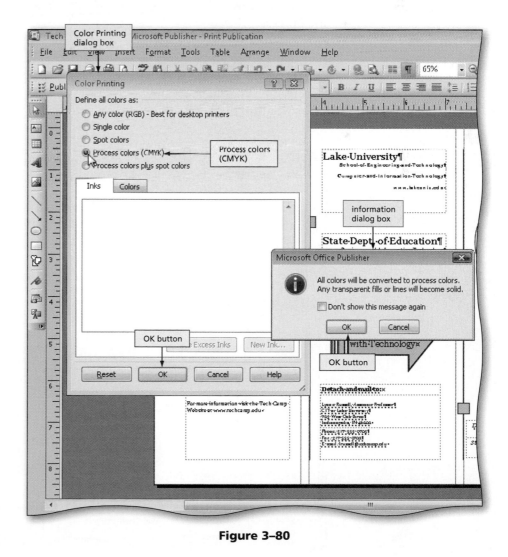

Figure 3–80

Packaging the Publication for the Printing Service

The publication file can be packaged for the printing service in two ways. The first way is to give the printing service the Publisher file in Publisher format using the Pack and Go Wizard. The second way is to save the file in a format called Encapsulated PostScript. Both of these methods are discussed in the following sections.

Using the Pack and Go Wizard

The **Pack and Go Wizard** guides you through the steps to collect and pack all the files the printing service needs and then compress the files to fit on one or more disks. Publisher checks for and embeds the TrueType fonts used in the publication. **Embedding** ensures that the printing service can display and print the publication with the correct fonts. The Pack and Go Wizard compresses all necessary files and fonts to take to the printing service. At the end of Publisher's packing sequence, you are given the option of printing a composite color printout or color separation printout on your desktop printer.

You need either sufficient space on a floppy disk or another formatted disk readily available when using the Pack and Go Wizard. Graphic files and fonts require a great deal of disk space. In the next series of steps, if you use a storage device other than the one on which you previously saved the brochure, save it again on the new disk before beginning the process.

To Use the Pack and Go Wizard

The following steps illustrate using the Pack and Go Wizard to ready the publication for submission to a commercial printing service. As you progress through the wizard, read each screen for more information.

①

- With a USB flash drive connected to one of the computer's USB ports, click File on the menu bar.

- Point to Pack and Go to display its submenu (Figure 3–81).

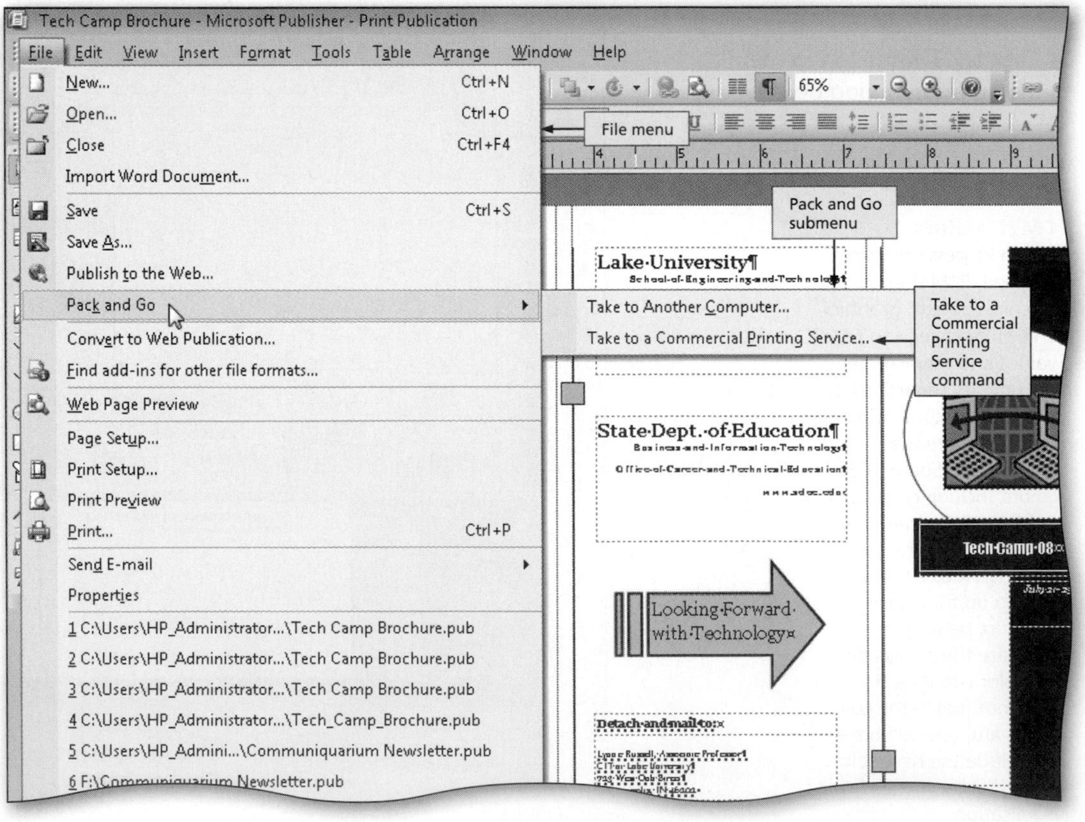

Figure 3–81

2

- Click Take to a Commercial Printing Service on the Pack and Go submenu to begin the process (Figure 3–82).

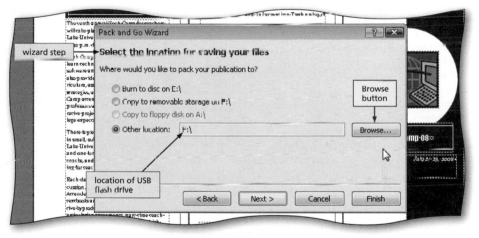

Figure 3–82

3

- Click the Next button to display the second dialog box in the wizard.

- Click the Browse button, navigate to your USB flash drive, and then click the OK button (Figure 3–83).

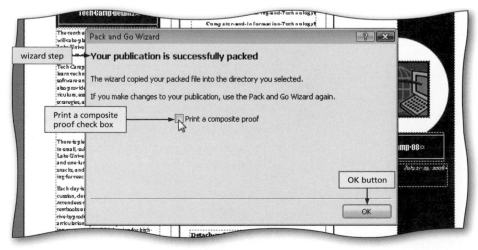

Figure 3–83

4

- Click the Next button to display the Include fonts and graphics dialog box.

- Click the Next button to display the Pack my publication dialog box.

- Click the Finish button.

- When the final dialog box is displayed, remove the check mark in the 'Print a composite proof' box, if necessary (Figure 3–84).

- Click the OK button.

Figure 3–84

The files are saved in a compressed format on the USB flash drive, with the same name as your Publisher file. If you make changes to the publication after packing the files, be sure to run the Pack and Go Wizard again so that the changes are part of the packed publication.

Using PostScript Files

If your printing service does not accept Publisher files, you can hand off, or submit, your files in PostScript format. **PostScript** is a page definition language that describes the document to be printed in language that the printer can understand. The PostScript printer driver includes a page definition language translator to interpret the instructions and print the document on a printer or a PostScript output device, such as an image setter. Because you cannot open or make changes directly to a PostScript file, everything in the publication must be complete before saving it.

Nearly all printing services can work with some type of PostScript file, either regular PostScript files, known as **PostScript dumps**, or **Encapsulated PostScript** (**EPS**) files, which are graphic pictures of each page. If you hand off a PostScript file, you are responsible for updating graphics, including the necessary fonts, and ensuring that you have all the files your printing service needs. Publisher includes several **PostScript printer drivers** (**PPD**) and their description files to facilitate printing at the publisher. You must install a PPD before saving in PostScript form. Because the most common installation of Publisher is for a single user in a desktop environment, this project will not take you through the steps involved to install a PostScript printer driver. That process would necessitate using original operating system disks and a more thorough knowledge of PostScript printers. Ask your printing service representative for the correct printer driver, and see your Windows documentation for installing it. Then use the Save As command on the File menu to save the publication in PostScript format.

Another question to ask your printing service is whether it performs the **prepress tasks** or a **preflight check**. You may be responsible for making color corrections, separations, setting the printing options, and other printing tasks.

BTW

PostScript Files
If you decide to hand off a PostScript dump, or file, to an outside printer or service bureau, include a copy of the original document as well — for backup purposes. Many shops slowly are changing over from Macintosh-based to cross-platform based operations. If something happens, the printer technician can correct the error from the original without another trip by you to the print shop.

Quitting Publisher

The following steps quit Publisher.

To Quit Publisher

1 Click the Close button on the Publisher title bar.

2 If a dialog box displays reminding you to save the document, click the No button.

Chapter Summary

In this chapter you were introduced to the brochure medium. You learned how to create custom color schemes, apply font effects, and change paragraph formatting. You learned about the use of photographs versus images, and how to insert a photograph from a file. After entering new text and deleting unwanted objects, you created a logo using a formatted shape and autofitted text. You used WordArt to create a watermark on the master page. You also learned about design and printing considerations, such as overlapping, separations, color libraries, paper types, and costs. In anticipation of taking the brochure to a professional publisher, you previewed and printed your publication and then used the Pack and Go Wizard to create the necessary files. The items listed below include all the new Publisher skills you have learned in this chapter.

1. Choose Brochure Options (PUB 150)
2. Open the Create New Color Dialog Box (PUB 153)
3. Change an Accent Color (PUB 154)
4. Save a New Color Scheme (PUB 156)
5. Edit Text in the Brochure (PUB 159)
6. Insert a Text Box and Apply a Font Scheme Style (PUB 162)
7. Use the Auto Correct Options Button (PUB 165)
8. Use the Format Painter (PUB 168)
9. Open the Styles Task Pane (PUB 171)
10. Create a New Style (PUB 173)
11. Apply the New Style (PUB 175)
12. Apply a Font Effect (PUB 177)
13. Edit the Sign-Up Form (PUB 179)
14. Change the Paragraph Spacing (PUB 181)
15. Text Wrap (PUB 185)
16. Create a Shape for the Logo (PUB 188)
17. Fill a Shape with Color (PUB 189)
18. Edit AutoShape Lines (PUB 190)
19. Add Text to an AutoShape (PUB 192)
20. Fit Text (PUB 193)
21. Copy the Logo (PUB 194)
22. Reposition and Resize the Logos (PUB 195)
23. Access the Master Page (PUB 196)
24. Insert a WordArt Object (PUB 199)
25. Format WordArt (PUB 200)
26. Remove the Watermark from Page 1 (PUB 203)
27. Make Text Boxes Transparent (PUB 204)
28. Choose a Commercial Printing Tool (PUB 209)
29. Use the Pack and Go Wizard (PUB 210)

Learn It Online

Test your knowledge of chapter content and key terms.

Instructions: To complete the Learn It Online exercises, start your browser, click the Address bar, and then enter the Web address `scsite.com/pub2007/learn`. When the Office 2007 Learn It Online page is displayed, click the link for the exercise you want to complete and then read the instructions.

Chapter Reinforcement TF, MC, and SA
A series of true/false, multiple choice, and short answer questions that test your knowledge of the chapter content.

Flash Cards
An interactive learning environment where you identify chapter key terms associated with displayed definitions.

Practice Test
A series of multiple choice questions that test your knowledge of chapter content and key terms.

Who Wants To Be a Computer Genius?
An interactive game that challenges your knowledge of chapter content in the style of a television quiz show.

Wheel of Terms
An interactive game that challenges your knowledge of chapter key terms in the style of the television show *Wheel of Fortune*.

Crossword Puzzle Challenge
A crossword puzzle that challenges your knowledge of key terms presented in the chapter.

Apply Your Knowledge

Reinforce the skills and apply the concepts you learned in this chapter.

Revising Text and Paragraphs in a Publication
Instructions: Start Publisher. Open the publication, Apply 3-1 Fall Concert Series Brochure Draft, from the Data Files for Students. See the inside back cover of this book for instructions on downloading the Data Files for Students, or contact your instructor for more information about accessing the required files.

You are to revise the publication as follows: enter new text and text boxes, replace some graphics, create a logo, delete objects, create a fancy heading, and check the publication for errors. Finally, you will pack the publication for a commercial printing service. The revised publication is shown in Figure 3–85.

Perform the following tasks:

1. On page 1, make the following text changes, zooming as necessary:

   a. Click the text, Seminar or Event Title. Type `Music Among the Maples` to replace the text.

   b. Drag through the text, Business Name. Type `The Performing Arts Center` to replace the text.

   c. In the lower portion of the right panel of page 1, insert a text box below Performing Arts Center. Click the Font Color button arrow on the Formatting toolbar and then click white on the color palette. Press CTRL+E to center the text. Press F9 to increase the magnification. Type `In conjunction with the Kansas City Symphonic Orchestra` and then press the enter key. Type `2009 Fall Concert Series` to complete the entry.

   d. Use the Format Painter button to copy the formatting from the Performing Arts Center text box to the new text box.

   e. Delete the organization logo in the middle panel.

2. In the left panel, double-click each of the three graphics, one at a time. Use the keywords, violin, conductor, and entertainment, respectively, to search for pictures similar to Figure 3–85a.

(a)

(b)

Figure 3–85

3. Click Page 2 on the page sorter. Delete the text box in the middle panel by right-clicking the text box and then clicking Delete Object on the shortcut menu. Delete the picture of the graduate and its caption. Drag the instruments picture upward to the center of the panel.

4. Select the entire story in the left panel on page 2. Change the line spacing to 1.5 and the alignment to justified.

5. Create a 5-point Star AutoShape button in the workspace. Use the Accent 1 scheme color to fill the star. Create a centered text box using the Best Fit option and a white font color. Insert the letters KCSO, the abbreviation for the Kansas City Symphonic Orchestra. Autofit the text for best fit. Drag the object to an empty location in the middle panel.

6. In the right panel, select the Sign-up Form Heading. Type the text, `Order Fall Concert Series Tickets`. Apply an emboss font effect.

7. Check spelling and run the Design Checker. Correct errors if necessary.

8. Click File on the menu bar and then click Save As. Use the file name, Apply 3-1 Fall Concert Series Brochure Modified.

9. Click Tools on the menu bar, point to Commercial Printing Tools, and then click Color Printing. When the Color Printing dialog box is displayed, click Process colors (**CMYK**). When Publisher displays an information dialog box, click the OK button; then, click the OK button in the Color Printing dialog box.

10. Click File on the menu bar. Point to Pack and Go and then click Take to a Commercial Printing Service on the Pack and Go submenu. Click the Next button in each progressive dialog box. Store the resulting compressed file on your flash drive. When the final dialog box is displayed, click the Finish button.

11. When the wizard completes the packing process, if necessary, click the Print a composite proof check box to display its check mark. The composite will print on two pages.

Extend Your Knowledge

Extend the skills you learned in this chapter and experiment with new skills. You may need to use Help to complete the assignment.

Working with Objects in Brochures

Instructions: Start Publisher. Open the publication, Extend 3-1 Hayes Menu Draft, from the Data Files for Students. See the inside back cover of this book for instructions on downloading the Data Files for Students, or contact your instructor for more information about accessing the required files.

You will make the following changes to the tri-fold, two-sided menu: edit the text boxes, change the pictures, create a WordArt, autofit several text boxes, replace the map, and enter menu items on page 2.

Perform the following tasks:

1. On page 1 of the menu, change the graphic in the left and right panels to a photograph of a hamburger. You may use clip art graphics, or one of your own. If you use a picture you did not take, make sure you have permission to use the graphic.

2. Create a new color scheme with black as the Main color, red as the Accent 1 color, an Accent 2 color based on the dominant color in your hamburger photograph, and a lighter version of that color for Accent 3.

3. Create a WordArt with the text, Hayes, using a style of your choice. Place a copy of the WordArt above the business name text box in the right panel and above the hours text box in the middle panel. Resize the WordArt as necessary.

4. Enter Hayes Hamburgers as the title of the menu. Use the phrase, where every burger is cooked to order, in the business name text box above the title.

5. Enter appropriate hours, address, and phone numbers in the text boxes in the middle and right panels.

6. Use the text in Table 3–8 for the story in the left panel. Autofit all text boxes on page 1.

Table 3–8 Text for Page 1	
Location	**Text**
Left Panel Heading Story	For over 25 years, Camden's has been the most popular hamburger restaurant. Located "Four Blocks from the Beach," we are within walking distance from all downtown hotels as well as the Gardner Convention Center. A local landmark, Camden's is well-known in the Tri-state area for its cooked-to-order burgers and homemade pies.
Left Panel Lower Text Box	We accept most credit cards, including Visa, Mastercard, Discover, and American Express.

7. Click the large background graphic that appears as a watermark on page 1. Move it to the master page.

8. Go to page 2 and replace the fields with your favorite foods and local prices. Move the large background graphic that appears as a watermark to a second master page. Use Help if necessary to create the second master page.

9. Open a Web browser and go to a mapping Web site, such as mapquest.com or maps.google.com. Enter your address, or an address you know of, into the appropriate text boxes of the Web page. When the map displays, choose a printer-friendly version. Press the Print Screen key on your keyboard. Paste the resulting graphic into your Publisher document. Use the crop tool on the Picture toolbar to crop the graphic so it displays only the map. Resize the graphic to fit in the space on page 1, middle pane.

10. Save a copy of the publication with the file name, Extend 3-1 Hayes Menu Revised. Print a copy using duplex printing.

Make It Right

Analyze a publication and correct all errors and/or improve the design.

Correcting Transparency Errors, Illegible Text, and Format Inconsistencies

Instructions: Start Publisher. Open the publication, Make It Right 3-1 Health Plan Brochure Draft, from the Data Files for Students. See the inside back cover of this book for instructions on downloading the Data Files for Students, or contact your instructor for more information about accessing the required files.

The publication is a brochure that has transparency errors, illegible text, and format inconsistencies, as shown in Figure 3–86. You are to correct the errors.

Figure 3–86

Perform the following steps:

1. The official color for Healthy Iowa is a medium purple. Change the color scheme to match more closely the industry color and help brand the brochure.
2. Change all of the graphics to appropriate health care graphics so the brochure is more effective.
3. Wrap the text around all of the graphics so there is no overlap.
4. On page 1 in the shape text, change the font color so that the text is more legible. Autofit the text.
5. CTRL+Drag the upper graphic on page 1 to a location in the workspace. Go to page 2 and drag the copy to a position in the lower part of the left panel.
6. On page 2, copy the formatting from the left panel heading to the other headings on the back page.
7. Right-justify all the prices in the right panel.
8. Correct all spelling and design errors.
9. Save the brochure with the name, Make It Right 3-1 Health Plan Brochure Revised.

In the Lab

Lab 1: Creating a Brochure Layout with One Spot Color

Problem: A large company in the paper industry is planning a seminar for their salespeople. They would like you to create a sample brochure, advertising the event. The theme is "Reach Your Goal." They would like a tri-fold brochure with a graphic related to the paper industry and a large blue logo with white slanted lettering, spelling the word, GOAL. On the inside of the brochure, the manager would like a response form to gain some knowledge of the participants' backgrounds. Note that your finished product is only a design sample; if the recipients like the sample, they will submit text for the other text boxes.

Instructions: Start Publisher and perform the following tasks to create the design sample shown in Figures 3–87a and 3–87b.

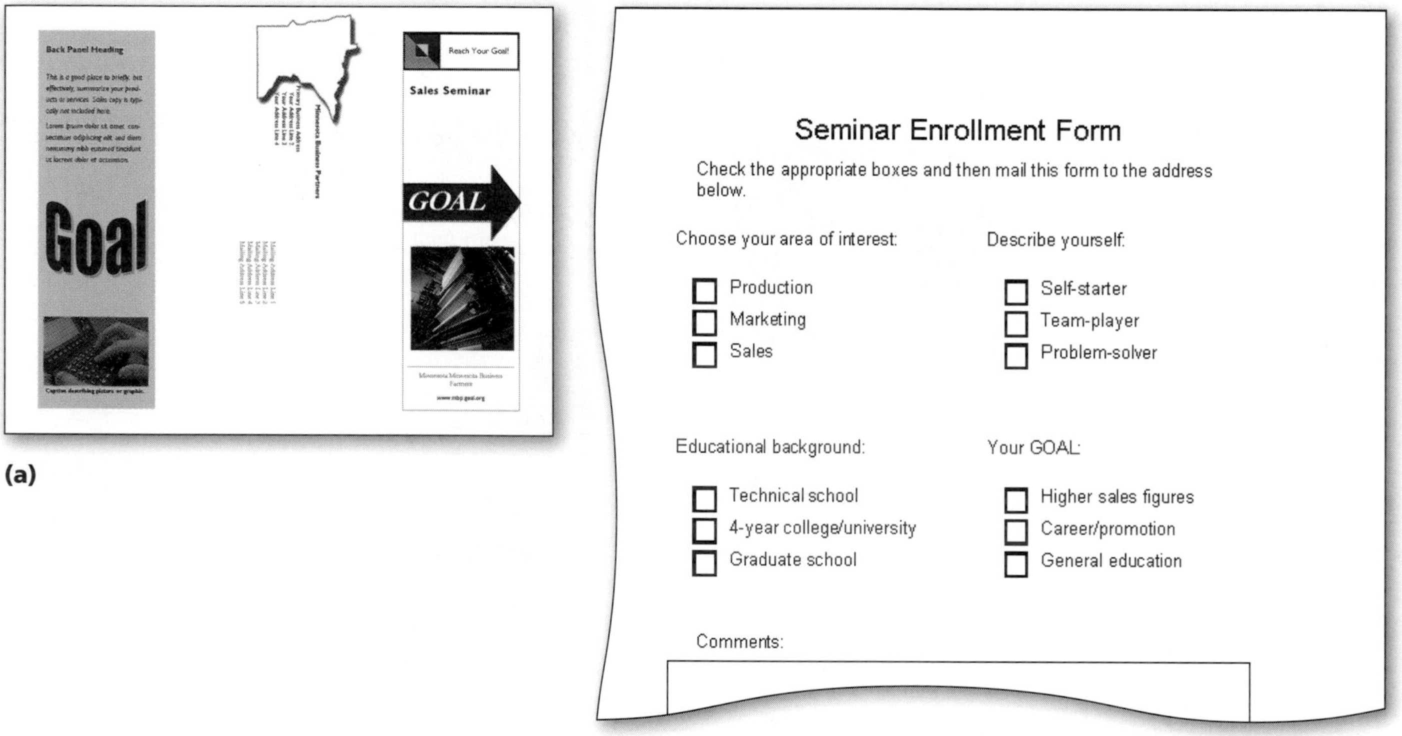

(a)

(b)

Figure 3–87

1. From the catalog, choose the Accent Box Informational Brochure. Choose to display the customer address and a response form.

2. Edit the text frames in the right panel as shown in Figure 3–87a. Delete the logo in the middle panel.

3. Double-click the graphic in the front panel. Insert a clip using the keywords, paper mills.

4. Click the AutoShapes button on the Objects toolbar. Point to Block Arrows and then click the Right Arrow shape. In the workspace, shift-drag to create an arrow approximately two inches square. Use the Fill Color button to choose Accent 1.

5. Add the text GOAL, in a white font color, and autofit it. Choose an appropriate style and font effect.

6. Drag the logo to the empty space above the picture.

7. Create a WordArt for the left panel, as shown in Figure 3–87a. Use the Can Down WordArt shape.

8. Go to the master page. On the Insert menu, point to Picture, and then click From File. Insert the file named, Minnesota, from the data disk. Rotate the image by dragging the green rotation handle 90°to the right. Drag the image to the upper-right corner of the center panel.

9. Navigate to page 2. Use the Ignore Master Page command to remove the graphic of the state from page 2.

10. In the Response Form in the right panel of page 2, make the text changes as indicated in Figure 3–87b.

11. Save the publication using the file name, Lab 3-1 GOAL Brochure. Print a copy for your instructor.

In the Lab

Lab 2: Creating a CD Liner

Problem: Your friend has recorded a new CD of his original guitar music. Knowing of your interest in desktop publishing, he has asked you to create the CD liner. You decide to create a publication with two panels, front and back, using Publisher's CD liner template.

Instructions: Perform the following tasks to create the two-panel, two-sided CD liner, as shown in Figures 3–88a and 3–88b on the next page.

1. Start Publisher.

2. In the catalog, click Labels, and then click the CD/DVD Labels link. When Publisher displays the previews, click the CD/DVD Booklet preview.

3. Choose the Glacier color scheme and the Modern font scheme.

4. Edit the text in both panels, as shown in Figure 3–88a.

5. Select the large rectangle border in the right panel. Press CTRL+T to make the rectangle transparent, in preparation for the watermark.

6. Replace the picture in the right panel using the Clip Art task pane. Search using the keyword, guitar.

7. Copy the graphic using the Copy button on the Standard toolbar.

8. On the Insert menu, click Page to insert a new blank page to follow page 1. Click Page 2 on the status bar, if necessary.

9. Paste the picture from page 1. Drag it to the left panel and shift-drag a corner handle, resizing so it fills the entire panel.

10. Create a large text frame in the left panel. Make it transparent so the picture shows through. Use a white font color. Type the text as shown in Figure 3–88b.

11. Go to the master page. Use the Clip Art task pane to search for an appropriate line drawing graphic, similar to the one in Figure 3–88b, for a watermark effect using the keyword, music.

12. Drag the music graphic to the right panel and shift-drag a corner handle, resizing so it fills the entire panel. Close the master page. (*Hint*: Do not forget to use the Ignore Master Page on page 1.)

13. On page 2, using the Design Gallery Object button, insert a Voyage style table of contents. Make it transparent. Edit the table of contents, as shown in Figure 3–88b.

14. Check the spelling and design of the publication. Save the publication on a floppy disk, using the file name, Lab 3-2 Guitar CD Liner.

15. Print a copy of the CD liner, using duplex printing. The default settings will print the liner in the middle of an 8½ × 11-inch piece of glossy paper if possible. Use your printer dialog box to choose to display crop marks. Trim the printout.

Continued >

In the Lab *continued*

(a)

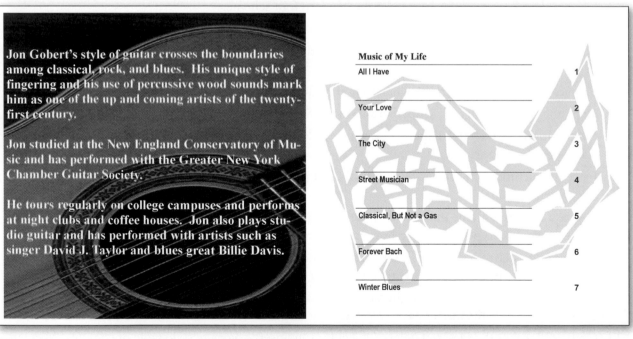

(b)

Figure 3–88

In the Lab

Lab 3: Creating a Travel Brochure

Problem: Alpha Zeta Mu fraternity is planning a ski trip to Sunset Mountain, Colorado, during spring break. They have asked you to design a brochure that advertises the trip. They would like a full-color tri-fold brochure on glossy paper that includes pictures of Sunset Mountain, a sign-up form, and the Alpha Zeta Mu logo. The fraternity plans to use mailing labels when it distributes the brochures.

Instructions: Perform the following tasks to create the brochure, as shown in Figures 3–89a and 3–89b.

(a)

(b)

Figure 3–89

1. From the catalog, choose the Straight Edge Informational Brochure. Choose a 3-panel display, choose to include the customer address, and select the Sign-up form.

2. Choose the Clay Color scheme and the Textbook font scheme.

3. On Page 1, in the right panel, edit the brochure title, Spring Break Ski Trip, as shown in Figure 3–89a. Delete the tag line and telephone number text boxes in the lower portion of the right panel. Delete the address text box in the center of the middle panel.

4. Table 3–9 on the next page displays the text for the left panel. Enter the text. Press CTRL+A to select all of the text. On the Format menu, click Paragraph. Choose left alignment, and then type 2.5 in the between lines text box. Close the Paragraph dialog box. With the text still selected, click the Font Color button and select White in the color palette. Using Table 3–9 on the next page, edit the text for the middle and right panels. Your fonts may display differently.

Continued >

In the Lab continued

Table 3–9 Text for Page 1

Location	Text
Left Panel Heading	Sunset Mountain
Left Panel	Located in the beautiful Colorado Rockies, Sunset Mountain's extreme elevation allows it to boast the latest ski season in Colorado and one of the longest ski runs at more than a mile! Sunset Mountain is off the beaten path, so lifts are not crowded. Four double chairlifts accommodate 1,000 people per hour, so you never have a long wait to begin your skiing adventure. Whether you are into bunny slopes or telemark skiing, you will love Sunset Mountain.
Left Panel Caption	Sunset Mountaintop
Middle Panel	University Spring Break Alpha Zeta Mu 1050 Greek Row P.O. Box 1050-3211 Kansas City, MO 64118
Right Panel	University Spring Break March 7–10, 2009

5. Click Page 2 on the page sorter.
6. Table 3–10 displays the text for the three stories on Page 2. Enter the text and headings, as shown in Figure 3–89b on the previous page. Use the Format Painter button to ensure that the headings use the same style.

Table 3–10 Text for Page 2

Location	Text
Winter Sports: Skiing and Beyond	Sunset Mountain offers a wide variety of winter sports, including downhill and cross-country skiing, as well as snowboarding, tubing, and bobsledding. Downhill slopes for beginner, intermediate, and advanced skiers are groomed daily. Experienced ski instructors conduct small group lessons. If skiing isn't your "thing," think variety! Sunset Mountain is offering an advanced tubing course this season, with banked turns and jumps to make your trip down the mountain more exciting.
Left Panel Caption	Ski rental available
Alpha Zeta Mu Ski Trip	Alpha Zeta Mu Fraternity is sponsoring a 4-day, 3-night ski trip to Colorado. Fraternity members and their guests will fly from Kansas City International to Denver on JLM Airlines and then board a free shuttle to Sunset Mountain. All package option prices are based on Alpha Zeta Mu's ability to book at least 20 people, two to a room, with a maximum of 40. You may mix and match any of the options. You will receive a confirmation postcard in the mail.
Lodging	Sunset Mountain Lodge is the only bed and breakfast among the seven lodging experiences on Sunset Mountain. Nestled among the tall lodge pole pines, the lodge offers modern rooms with full baths. An optional dinner package is available at a modest cost. Other amenities include a game room, hot tub, meeting room, and of course, the grand hearth — where the fireplace always is lit, and the hot cinnamon cocoa always is ready!
Middle Panel Caption	Visit the lodge at: www.skicolorado.com
Order Form Detail	Alpha Zeta Mu Ski Trip March 7–10 Round trip MCI/Denver/MCI $300.00 4 days, 3 nights w/breakfast $325.00 3 days ski rental and lift tickets $125.00 2-hour ski lesson $50.00 3-dinner option $50.00 Single-day lift ticket $40.00

7. Replace each of the template graphics. Using the Clip Art task pane, search for graphics, similar to the ones shown in Figure 3–89 on page PUB 221, that are related to lodge, mountain, fireplace, and skiing. Replace the placeholder graphics in the brochure.

8. Click the AutoShapes button on the Objects toolbar, point to Stars and Banners, and then click the Wave shape. Drag a wave shape in the scratch area, approximately 1.6×1.2 inches in size. Use the Fill Color button to fill the shape with Accent 1 (Dark Red).

9. Add the text, AZM, to the AutoShape, using a white font. Autofit the text.

10. Create a second copy of the shape.

11. With the copy of the grouped shape selected, click Arrange on the menu bar and then click Rotate Right. Drag a corner handle to resize the shape to approximately $1 \times .75$ inches. Drag the shape to the middle panel, as shown in Figure 3–89a.

12. Check the publication for spelling. Run the Design Checker. Fix any errors.

13. Click Tools on the menu bar and then point to Commercial Printing Tools. Click Color Printing. When the Color Printing dialog box is displayed, click Process colors (CMYK).

14. Check the spelling and design of the publication. Save the publication using the file name, Lab 3-3 Ski Trip Brochure.

15. Print the publication two sided. Fold the brochure and submit it to your instructor.

Cases and Places

Apply your creative thinking and problem solving skills to design and implement a solution.

• EASIER   •• MORE DIFFICULT

• 1: Youth Baseball League Brochure

Use the Ascent Event brochure template to create a brochure announcing the Youth Baseball League. Pick an appropriate color and font scheme. Type Preseason Sign-Up as the brochure title. Type Youth Baseball League as the Organization name. Type your address and telephone number in the appropriate text boxes. Delete the logo. Replace all graphics with sports-related clip art. Edit the captions to match. The league commissioner will send you content for the stories at a later date. Include a sign-up form on page 2. Edit the sign-up form event boxes as displayed in Table 3–11.

Table 3–11 Sign-Up Form Check Box Content		
Event Name	**Time**	**Price**
Preschool T-Ball: ages 4 and 5	10:00 a.m.	$35.00
Pee-Wee T-Ball: ages 6 and 7	11:00 a.m.	$35.00
Coach Pitched: ages 8 and 9	1:00 p.m.	$50.00
Intermediate: ages 10 and 11	2:30 p.m.	$50.00
Advanced: ages 12 and 13	4:00 p.m.	$50.00
City Team: audition only	6:00 p.m.	TBA

On a separate piece of paper, make a table similar to Table 3–1 on page PUB 149, listing the type of exposure, kinds of information, audience, and purpose of communication. Turn in the table with your printout.

Continued >

Cases and Places *continued*

• 2: Creating a Menu

Bob Bert of Bert's Beanery has hired you to "spice up" and modernize the look of the restaurant's menu. You decide to use a menu template to create a full-color menu for publication at a local copy shop. Bob wants special attention paid to his famous "Atomic Chili®," which is free if a customer can eat five spoonfuls without reaching for water. You will find the registered trademark symbol in the Symbol dialog box. Bob serves salads, soups, and sandwiches a la carte. He has several family specials, as well as combo meals and a variety of drinks and side dishes.

•• 3: Recreating a Logo

Using the Blank Print Publications link in the catalog, re-create as closely as possible your school or company logo on a full-page publication. Use the AutoShapes button, fill and font colors, text boxes, and symbols to match the elements in your logo. You also may use WordArt. Ask your instructor or employer for clip art files, if necessary. Use the workspace scratch area to design portions of the logo and then layer and group them before dragging them onto the publication.

•• 4: Creating a new Color Scheme

Make It Personal

Create a new color scheme named, My Favorite Colors. Use the Color Scheme task pane to access the Color Schemes dialog box. Choose colors that complement one another. Using the Publisher catalog, create a blank publication. Insert six different AutoShapes and fill each with a color from your color scheme. Create text box captions for each of the AutoShapes, identifying the name of the shape and the color. Print the publication.

•• 5: Exploring Commercial Printing

Working Together

Individually, visit or call several local copy shops or commercial printers in your area. Ask them the following questions: What kind of paper stock do your customers choose for brochures? What is the most commonly used finish? Do you support all three color processes? Will you accept files saved with Microsoft Publisher Pack and Go, or EPS files? What prepress tasks do you perform? Come back together as a group and create a blank Publisher publication to record your answers. Create a table with the Insert Table button on the Objects toolbar. Insert the questions down the left side. Insert the names of the print shops across the top. Fill in the grid with the answers they provide.

E-Mail Feature

Creating an E-Mail Letter Using Publisher

Objectives

You will have mastered the material in this project when you can:

- Select and format an e-mail letter template
- Insert an e-mail hyperlink
- Choose a logo design and add a background
- Preview and send an e-mail message using Publisher

Introduction

E-mail, short for electronic mail, is a popular form of communication to transmit messages and files via a computer network. For businesses, e-mail can be an efficient and cost-effective way to keep in touch with customers. E-mail is used in ways similar to traditional mail. With it, you can send correspondence, business communications, greeting cards, letters, brochures, newsletters, and other types of publications.

Project — E-Mail Message

The project in this feature illustrates how to create and send an e-mail message using Publisher 2007. An **e-mail message** or **e-mail letter** displays traditional correspondence-related text and graphics, as well as hyperlinks, similar to a Web page. All of the objects in an e-mail message are displayed in the body of the message rather than as a separate publication attached to the e-mail.

When you send an e-mail message, recipients can read the message using HTML-enabled e-mail programs, such as GMail, AOL, Yahoo!, or the current versions of Microsoft Outlook and Outlook Express. **HTML-enabled e-mail** allows the sender to include formatted text and other visuals to improve the readability and aesthetics of the message. The majority of Internet users can access HTML-enabled mail. With e-mail messages, recipients do not need to have Publisher installed to view e-mail messages because the page you send will be displayed as the body of the e-mail message. Sending a one-page publication by e-mail to a group of customers or friends is an efficient and inexpensive way to deliver a message.

Publisher provides several ways to create an e-mail message. You can use a template, create an e-mail message from scratch, or convert a single page of another publication into an e-mail message, expanding the use of your existing content. Publisher's e-mail message templates are preformatted to the correct page size. The templates use placeholder text and graphics that download quickly and are suitable for the body of an e-mail message.

A second way to create an e-mail message is to send a single page of another publication type as an e-mail message, although some adjustments may need to be made to the width of your publication in order for it to fit in an e-mail message.

When you send an entire publication as an **e-mail attachment**, the recipient must have Microsoft Publisher 2002 or a later version installed to view it. When the recipient opens the attached file, Publisher automatically opens and displays the publication. Unless you convert it, a multipage publication must be sent as an e-mail attachment.

An **e-mail merge** can be created when you want to send a large number of messages that are mostly identical, but you also want to include some unique or personalized information in each message. An e-mail merge creates content that is personalized for each recipient on a mailing list. You will learn about several kinds of merged publications in Chapter 5.

The type of e-mail publication you choose depends on the content and the needs of the recipients. Table 1 describes specific audiences and the appropriate kinds of e-mail publications.

Table 1 Publisher E-Mail Types

Audience Characteristic	E-Mail Message	E-Mail Merge	E-Mail Attachment
Recipients definitely have Publisher			X
Recipients may not have Publisher	X	X	
Recipients need to read and print the content in its original format			X
Recipients may not have HTML-enabled e-mail	X	X	
Recipients need personalized messages		X	

Figure 1 displays an e-mail message sent to a list of participants or members of a health care plan. The e-mail message includes a colorful heading, a logo, a graphic, and directions for obtaining more information about a fitness initiative sponsored by the health care provider.

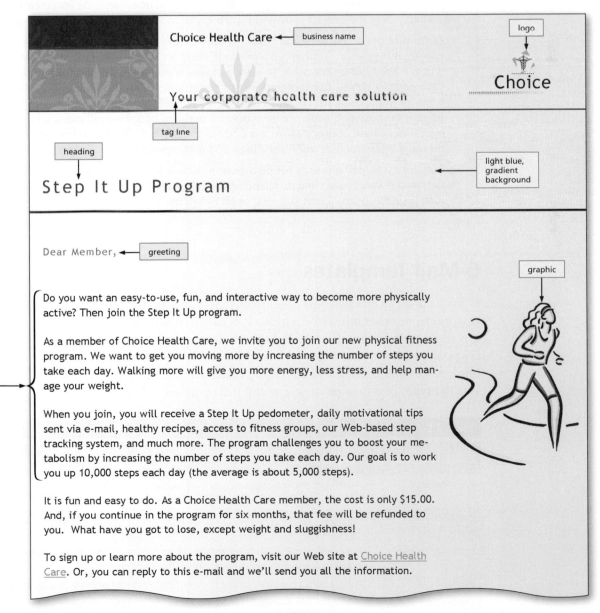

Figure 1

This E-Mail Feature is for instructional purposes only. You do not have to be connected to the Internet or have an e-mail program on your system in order to create the e-mail message. You can create and save the e-mail message on a flash drive rather than send it via e-mail.

Overview

As you read through this feature, you will learn how to create the e-mail message shown in Figure 1 on the previous page by performing these general tasks:

- Edit an e-mail message template.
- Save an e-mail message.
- Preview and send an e-mail message.

Plan Ahead

> **General Project Guidelines**
>
> When creating a Publisher publication, the actions you perform and decisions you make will affect the appearance and characteristics of the finished document. As you create an e-mail message, such as the project shown in Figure 1, you should follow these general guidelines:
>
> 1. **Customize the e-mail message.** Your e-mail message should present, at a minimum, your contact information, a greeting, a message body, a salutation, a link to your Web site, and the ability to unsubscribe. The body of your message should present honestly all your positive points. Ask someone else to proofread your message and give you suggestions for improvements. Choose a color scheme, font scheme, page size, and graphic that fit your purpose and audience. Improve the usability of the e-mail message by creating hyperlinks where appropriate in the body of the message. Enhance the look of the e-mail message by creating or inserting a logo and a background.
>
> 2. **Prepare the e-mail message for distribution.** Check for spelling errors and run Publisher's design checker. Correct any problems. Preview the publication in a browser and then send it to yourself to see how it will look as an e-mail message.

E-Mail Templates

E-mail can be an efficient and cost-effective way to keep in touch with friends, customers, coworkers, or other interested parties. It is easy to design and send professional-looking e-mail using Publisher. Each of Publisher's design sets features several e-mail publication types, so you can create and send e-mail that is consistent in design with the rest of the business communication and marketing materials that you create using Publisher. Table 2 lists the types of e-mail publications and their purpose.

Table 2 E-Mail Template Publications	
E-Mail Template	**Purpose**
Event/Activity	A notice of a specific upcoming activity or event containing a combination of pictures, dates, times, maps, agenda, and the ability to sign up
Event/Speaker	A notice of a specific upcoming event that includes a speaker and usually contains pictures, dates, times, and a map
Featured Product	A publication that provides information about a company and a specific product or service, including graphics and Web page links for more information
Letter	A more personalized document to correspond with one or more people, including specific information on a single topic

Table 2 E-Mail Template Publications *(continued)*	
E-Mail Template	**Purpose**
Newsletter	A publication that informs interested clientele about an organization or business with stories, dates, contact information, and upcoming events
Product List	A sales-oriented publication to display products, prices, and special promotions, including Web page links for more information

Creating an E-Mail Message

The following steps open an e-mail message template.

To Open an E-Mail Template

1

• Start Publisher, as described in the steps on page PUB 4 through PUB 5.

• In the catalog, click E-mail.

• In the Newer Designs area, scroll down to the Letter previews and then click the Brocade preview.

• In the Customize area, select the Origin color scheme and the Opulent font scheme (Figure 2).

2

• Click the Create button.

• If necessary, click the Special Characters button on the Standard toolbar to display paragraph marks.

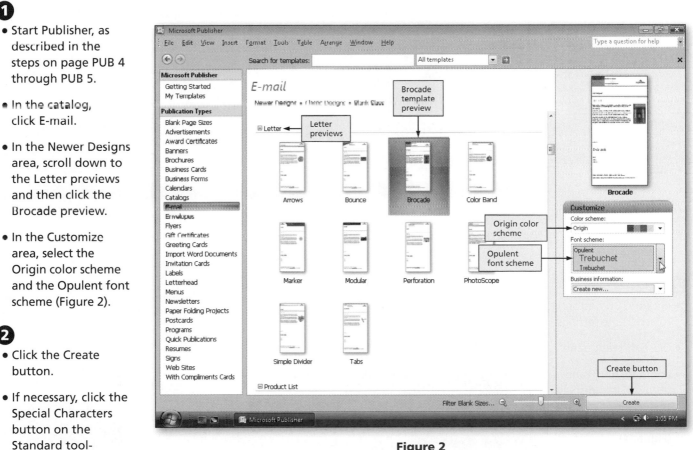

Figure 2

What if I want to send an e-mail to someone who does not have Publisher?

E-mail messages display in the body of the e-mail and do not require Publisher. If you are sending an attachment and are worried that your recipients may not have Publisher installed on their system, you can send your publication in a different format. Publisher can create PDF files or XPS files, which have free or inexpensive viewers. The files then can be attached to an e-mail message.

To Customize the E-Mail Page Size

The following steps change the page size of the e-mail message.

1

- In the Format Publication task pane, click the Change Page Size button to display the Page Setup dialog box.

- In the E-mail area, click the Short button to choose a short page format (Figure 3).

Q&A

What are the other settings in the Page Setup dialog box?

As you will learn in a future chapter, you can set the margins and choose various paper sizes and layouts in the Page Setup dialog box. The e-mail sizes include the standard width of 5.818 inches, a long e-mail (up to 66 inches), a short e-mail (up to 11 inches), or a custom size.

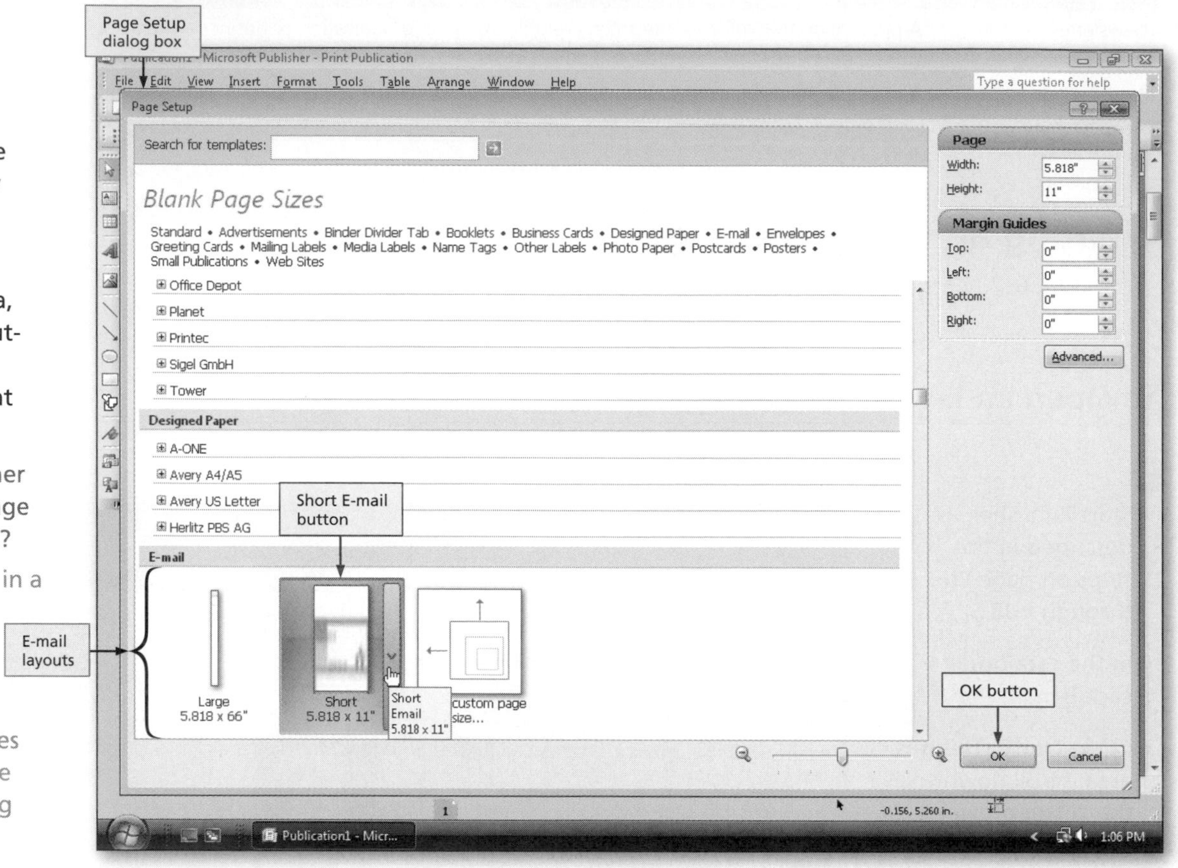

Figure 3

2

- Click the OK button to accept the settings.

- Close the task pane.

- Zoom to 100% and then scroll to display the upper portion of the page layout (Figure 4).

Figure 4

Editing Text

The text boxes in an e-mail letter template include the business name, the tag line, the heading, the salutation, the body of the letter, the closing, the signature block, and the contact text box at the bottom of the e-mail letter.

To Edit the Headings and Greeting

BTW

E-Mail Templates
E-mail letter templates contain text boxes, logos, hyperlinks, and graphics. To customize the e-mail letter, you replace the placeholder text and graphics with your own content, just as you would in any other template publication.

The following steps edit the placeholder text in the upper portion of the e-mail letter. Your placeholder text may differ from that shown in the figures.

1 Select the placeholder text in the business name text box. Type `Choice Health Care` to replace the text. Select the placeholder text in the tag line text box. Type `Your corporate health care solution` to replace the text.

2 Select the text, Letter, in the heading text box. Type `Step It Up Program` to replace the text. Select the text, Dear Customer, in the salutation text box. Type `Dear Member,` to replace the text (Figure 5).

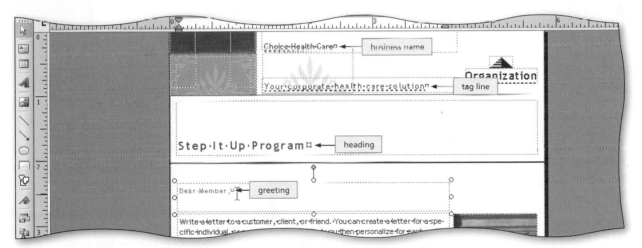

Figure 5

Editing the Body of the E-Mail Letter

Table 3 displays the text for the body of the e-mail letter.

Table 3 Text for Body of E-Mail Letter

Text
Do you want an easy-to-use, fun, and interactive way to become more physically active? Then join the Step It Up program.
As a member of Choice Health Care, we invite you to join our new physical fitness program. We want to get you moving more by increasing the number of steps you take each day. Walking more will give you more energy, less stress, and help manage your weight.
When you join, you will receive a Step It Up pedometer, daily motivational tips sent via e-mail, healthy recipes, access to fitness groups, our Web-based step tracking system, and much more. The program challenges you to boost your metabolism by increasing the number of steps you take each day. Our goal is to work you up 10,000 steps each day (the average is about 5,000 steps).
It is fun and easy to do. As a Choice Health Care member, the cost is only $15.00. And, if you continue in the program for six months, that fee will be refunded to you. What have you got to lose, except weight and sluggishness!
To sign up or learn more about the program, visit our Web site at Choice Health Care. Or, you can reply to this e-mail, and we'll send you all the information.

To Edit the Body of the E-Mail Letter

The following steps replace the text in the body of the e-mail letter.

1 Select the text in the body of the e-mail letter.

2 Enter the text from Table 3 on the previous page, pressing the ENTER key after each paragraph (Figure 6).

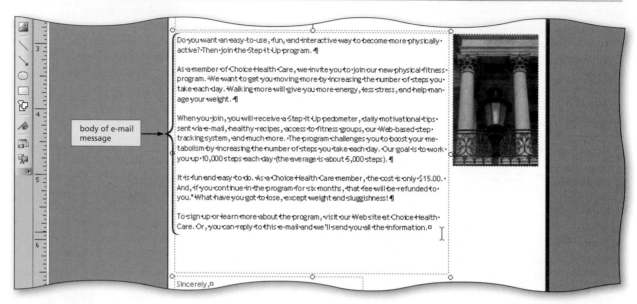

Figure 6

To Edit the Closing Text Boxes

To complete the text box editing in the e-mail letter, the next steps edit the signature block and contact information.

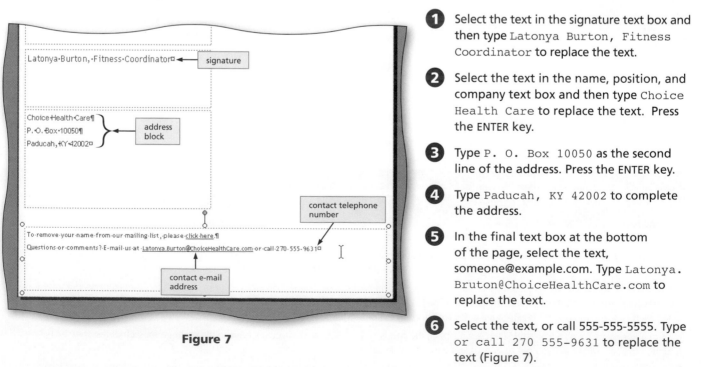

Figure 7

1 Select the text in the signature text box and then type `Latonya Burton, Fitness Coordinator` to replace the text.

2 Select the text in the name, position, and company text box and then type `Choice Health Care` to replace the text. Press the ENTER key.

3 Type `P. O. Box 10050` as the second line of the address. Press the ENTER key.

4 Type `Paducah, KY 42002` to complete the address.

5 In the final text box at the bottom of the page, select the text, someone@example.com. Type `Latonya. Bruton@ChoiceHealthCare.com` to replace the text.

6 Select the text, or call 555-555-5555. Type `or call 270 555-9631` to replace the text (Figure 7).

Creating a Hyperlink

E-mail messages can contain hyperlinks, just as Web pages do. Recall that a hyperlink is a colored and underlined text or a graphic that you click to go to a file, a location in a file, a Web page, or an e-mail address. When you insert a hyperlink, you select the text or object and then click the Insert Hyperlink button on the Standard toolbar. When clicked, hyperlinks can take the viewer to an existing file or Web page, another place in the publication, a new document, or open an e-mail program and create a new message. For a more detailed description of how to insert hyperlinks, see pages PUB 49 through PUB 50 in Chapter 1.

Editing the Hyperlink

In the body of the e-mail letter template, the words, Choice Health Care, should display as a hyperlink to open the company's Web page. In the final text box at the bottom of the page, the words, click here, should display as a hyperlink that opens the user's e-mail program and creates a new message. For a more detailed description of how to insert hyperlinks, see pages PUB 49 through PUB 50 in Chapter 1.

To Edit the Hyperlinks

1 In the body of the e-mail letter template, select the words, Choice Health Care, in the last paragraph.

2 Click the Insert Hyperlink button on the Standard toolbar to display the Insert Hyperlink dialog box.

3 In the Address text box, type www.choicehealthcare.com in the Address text box.

4 Click the OK button.

5 Select the text, click here, in the contact information text box at the bottom of the page.

6 Click the Insert Hyperlink button on the Standard toolbar.

7 When the Insert Hyperlink dialog box is displayed, click E-mail Address in the Link to bar on the left.

8 In the E-mail address text box, type unsubscribe@ChoiceHealthCare.com as the entry.

9 Click the OK button.

E-Mail Logos and Graphics

Most of the e-mail templates contain both logos and graphics that you can edit to suit your publication. In the upper-right corner of the Brocade e-mail letter template, Publisher displays one of the predesigned logos from the Design Gallery. A **logo** is a recognizable symbol that identifies a person, business, or organization. A logo may be composed of text, a picture, or a combination of symbols. Most Publisher-supplied logos display in templates as a grouped object, combining a graphic and text.

Farther down in the e-mail letter, Publisher displays a graphic that you can change to reflect the purpose of your publication. You edit e-mail graphics in the same way as you edit graphics in other publications. You can select a clip art clip, insert a graphic from a file, or import a graphic from a scanner or digital camera.

To Edit the Logo

The following step edits the graphic and text in the logo of the e-mail letter. Because the purpose of the letter is to inform members of a health care plan about a new fitness program, a graphic representing medicine is appropriate. Not all graphics are appropriate for logos. You need to choose a graphic that will display well in a very small area. Your graphic should not have a lot of fine details. Some large clip art is too big to fit within a small logo and might need to be resized before being used.

1

- Click the logo to select it. Zoom to 200%. Double-click the graphic within the logo to display the Clip Art task pane.

- When the Clip Art task pane is displayed, search for clip art related to the word, medicine.

- Choose a graphic similar to the one shown in Figure 8.

- Double-click the text, Organization, to select it. Type Choice to replace the text.

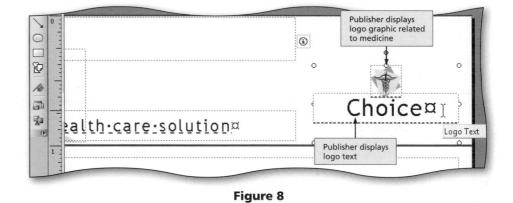

Figure 8

To Edit the Graphic

The next steps edit the graphic that displays next to the body of the letter.

1 Scroll as necessary and then double-click the graphic that displays next to the body of the letter.

2 When the Clip Art task pane is displayed, search for clip art related to the word, fitness.

3 Choose a graphic similar to the one shown in Figure 9.

Figure 9

Backgrounds

You can add a **background** to an e-mail or Web publication by applying a color, gradient, picture, texture, or pattern. A background should not be detailed or busy because it displays behind the text and graphics. Simple backgrounds will not add significantly to the download time. If you select a custom picture file for your background texture, make sure it is 20 kilobytes (KB) or smaller. Large picture files will require people who are viewing your Web site to wait a long time for the graphic to download. If you select a picture for a background, the picture is repeated (or tiled) to create the background texture for your Web pages. A background is not the same as a master page. When you add a background, the publication's master page does not change. Avoid changing the background on master pages in e-mail and Web publications. Special effects applied to master pages do not display correctly when they are viewed in some Web browsers.

To Add a Background

The following step adds a background to the e-mail publication.

1

- Click Format on the menu bar and then click Background to open the Background task pane.

- In the Apply a background area, click the 30% tint of Accent 2 button, and then click the Gradient fill (vertical) preview that displays white on the left and light blue on the right (Figure 10).

Figure 10

To Check for Spelling and Design Errors

BTW

E-Mail Hyphenation
If your e-mail
publication contains text
with hyphenation, some
e-mail programs may
insert gaps in the e-mail
message, and it may not
appear as you intended.
To fix the problem, on
the Tools menu, point
to Language, and then
click Hyphenation. In the
Hyphenation dialog box,
clear the Automatically
hyphenate this story
check box. Delete any
hyphens that remain in
your text.

The publication now is complete. Before you send the e-mail message, you should use the Design Checker to check the message for potential issues, such as fonts that do not display well online and text that may be exported as an image — which increases the file size of the e-mail message. The following steps describe how to check the publication for spelling and design errors.

1 Click the Spelling button on the Standard toolbar. Correct any errors. Click the Yes button when Publisher asks you to check the rest of the document.

2 On the Tools menu, click Design Checker. Click the Run e-mail checks (current page only) check box so that it displays a check mark.

3 If you have objects that are positioned slightly off the page, ignore the error message. Correct any other problems and then close the Design Checker task pane.

To Save the E-Mail Letter

The following steps save the e-mail letter. For a detailed example of the procedure summarized below, refer to pages PUB 31 through PUB 33 in Chapter 1.

1 With a USB flash drive connected to one of the computer's USB ports, click the Save button on the Standard toolbar.

2 Type `Choice Health Care E-mail Letter` in the File name text box to change the file name. Do not press the ENTER key.

3 Navigate to your USB flash drive.

4 Click the Save button in the Save As dialog box to save the publication on the USB flash drive with the file name, Choice Health Care E-mail Letter.

Sending an E-Mail Letter

E-mail letters can be sent to one or more people. Many organizations create a **listserv**, which is a list of interested people with e-mail addresses who want to receive news and information e-mails about the organization. A listserv e-mail is one e-mail sent to every-one on the list. Listserv e-mails always should contain a link to allow recipients to remove their name from the list to prevent receiving future e-mails.

Using the Send E-Mail Command

The steps on the next page describe how to preview and then send an e-mail using Publisher's Send E-mail command. You do not have to send the e-mail, nor do you have to be connected to the Internet to perform the steps.

To Preview and Send a Publication via E-Mail

1

- With the publication displayed, click File on the menu bar and then point to Send E-mail (Figure 11).

Q&A

Do most people prefer to receive a publication as an e-mail attachment?

Whether or not to use an attachment depends on the purpose and the size of the attachment. For immediate viewing, such as an announcement, letter, or card, it is better to send a single page in the body of an e-mail. With an attachment, the person receiving your e-mail will need to have Publisher installed to open and view the publication. Additionally, with a large attachment, you may run the risk of the e-mail being blocked by firewalls and filters at the receiving end.

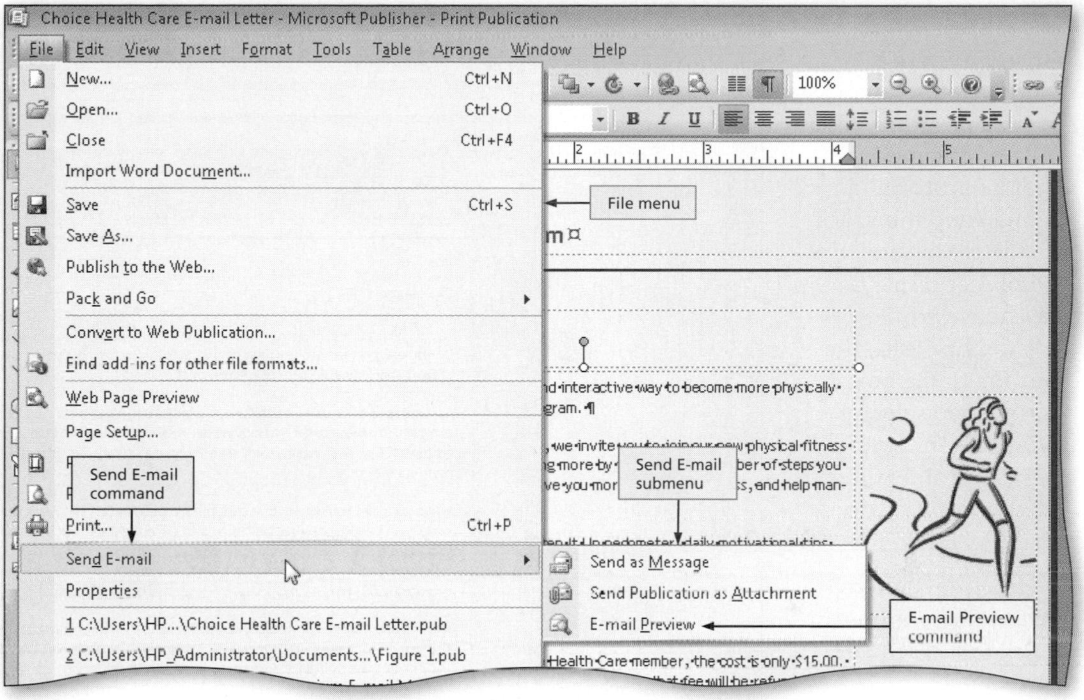

Figure 11

2

- Click the E-mail Preview command on the Send E-mail submenu (Figure 12).

Experiment

- Scroll through the e-mail letter and try clicking the hyperlinks. The Choice Health Care Web site is fictional and will not open, but the click here hyperlink will display an e-mail dialog box if your system is configured with an e-mail program, such as Microsoft Outlook.

- Click the Close button on any open e-mail window without sending or saving the e-mail.

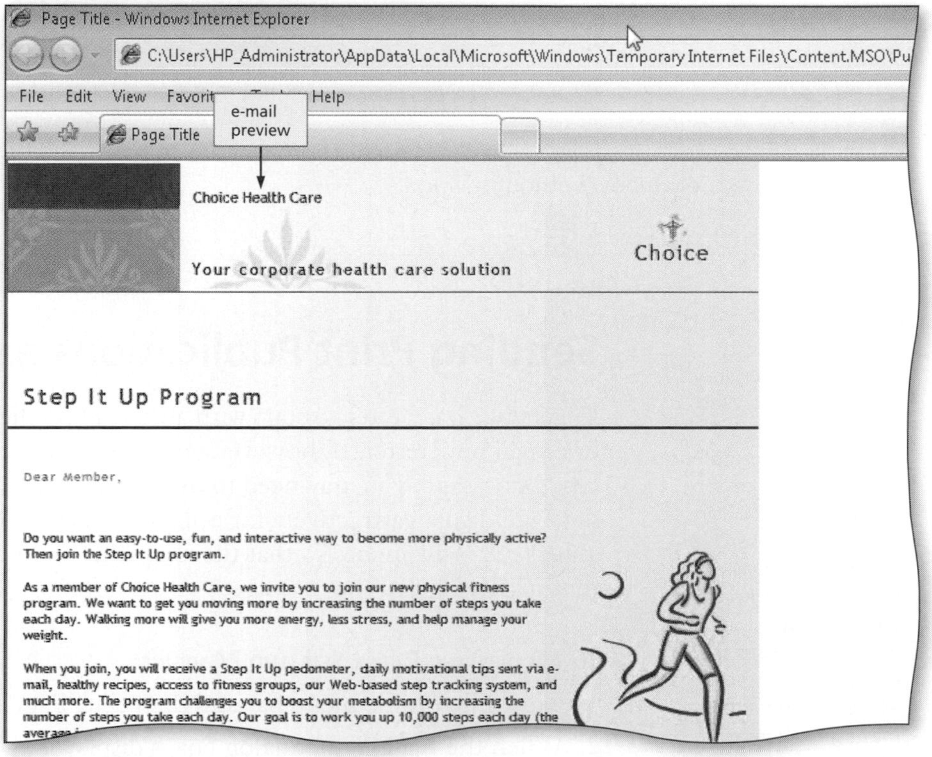

Figure 12

3

- Click the Close button on the e-mail preview.

- If your system is connected to an e-mail program, click File on the menu bar, point to Send E-Mail and then click Send as Message. If Publisher displays a Choose Profile dialog box, click the Profile Name box arrow and select your system's e-mail profile; then click the OK button (Figure 13).

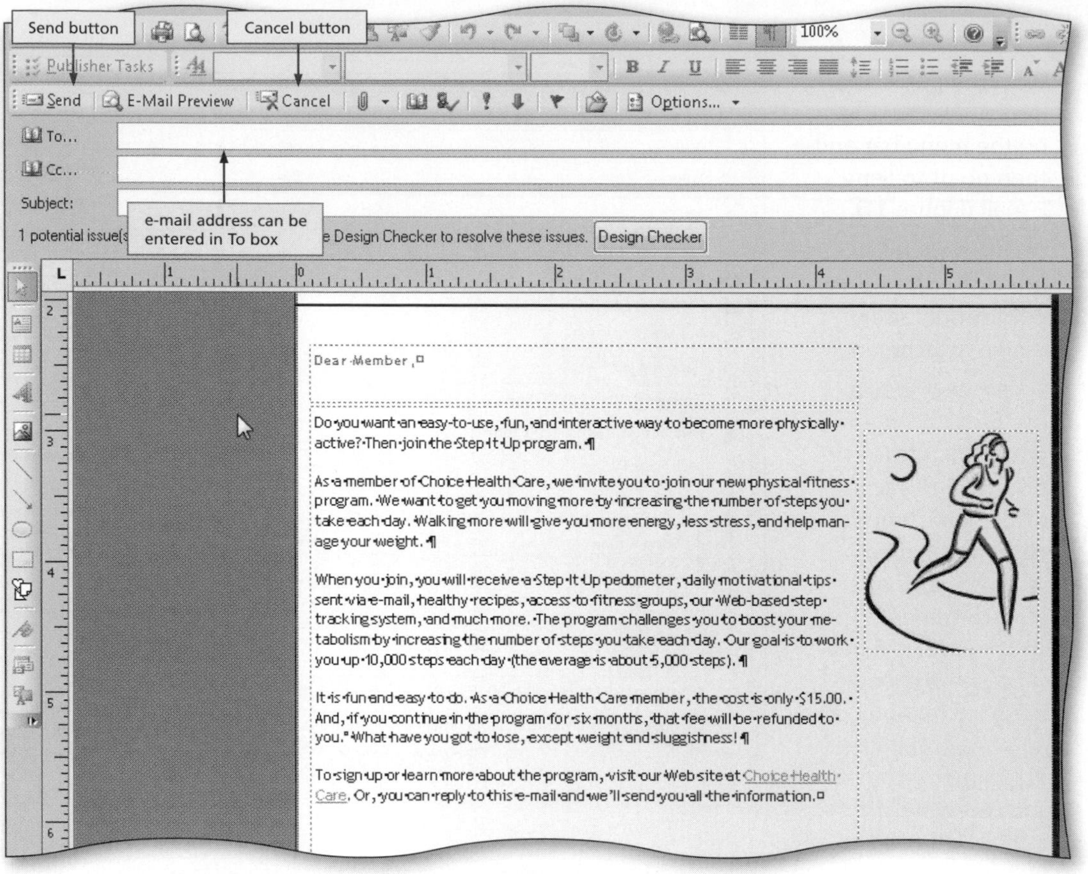

Q&A

What if my system wants to configure Outlook to send an e-mail?

If you are not sure how to configure your system for e-mail, or you do not want to check your e-mail via an e-mail program, click the Cancel button. Configuring your system with an e-mail program is not complicated, however. Windows Vista asks for your name, your e-mail address, and your password. It then determines the kind of e-mail program and connection you need.

Figure 13

4

- If you want to send the e-mail, type your e-mail address in the To box and then click the Send button. To cancel the request, close the window without saving.

BTW

Web Mail

Many e-mail service providers use a Web browser interface, so setting up an e-mail program is not necessary. Corporate and business communications commonly use the Microsoft Outlook e-mail program, which allows access to e-mail addresses for everyone in the company as well as tools to manage other forms of communication and scheduling.

Sending Print Publications as E-Mail Messages

In general, it is better to start with an e-mail publication template such as the e-mail letter or e-mail newsletter. If, however, you want to send a page of another publication as an e-mail message, you may need to modify the width and margins to ensure that the message will display attractively for e-mail recipients. The typical page size of an e-mail message is 5.8×11 inches so that the recipients will not need to scroll horizontally to view the entire width of the message.

To Modify the Paper Size and Margins

1. Click File on the menu bar and then click Page Setup.
2. When the Page Setup dialog box is displayed, if necessary, scroll to the e-mail layouts.

3. Click the Create custom page size preview and then enter the new width and height entries in the Width and Height boxes.

4. Click the OK button.

It is a good idea to send the publication to yourself first to see how it will look before sending it to other recipients.

If you have already created specific print publications that you would like to send electronically, you can convert the publication to a single-page e-mail message. For example, if you create a newsletter for customers, you can send it to your e-mail list as well as distributing it on paper. When you convert your publication, Publisher gives you the options to send the current page or all pages. If you choose to send all pages, Publisher combines the contents of all pages onto one e-mail page.

To Send a Multiple Page Publication as an E-mail Message

1. Open the publication that contains the page or pages that you want to send as an e-mail message.

2. On the File menu, point to Send E-mail, and then click Send as Message.

3. In the Send as Message dialog box, click Send all pages and then click the OK button.

4. Follow the steps.

You can preview this page and rearrange text and graphics. If Publisher cannot determine where to fit some objects, the **Extra Content** task pane will display the objects for you to manually place.

Occasionally, you may encounter unexpected formatting results when sending a page of a publication as an e-mail message. Some of these problems have easy solutions, while others involve the unavoidable loss of formatting. You can take measures to prevent formatting problems as you add and manipulate text and graphics in your publication.

To Quit Publisher

The final step quits Publisher.

1 Click the Close button on the Publisher title bar. If Publisher displays a dialog box, click its No button.

Feature Summary

This feature introduced you to creating an e-mail message by illustrating how to select and format an e-mail template. The feature then showed how to edit both the text boxes and graphics. Next, you learned how to choose a logo design, insert a background, and create an e-mail hyperlink. Finally, the project showed how to preview and send a publication as an e-mail message. The items listed below include all the new Publisher skills you have learned in this chapter.

1. Open an E-Mail Letter Template (PUB 229)
2. Customize the E-Mail Page Size (PUB 230)
3. Edit the Logo (PUB 234)

4. Add a Background (PUB 235)
5. Preview and Send a Publication via E-Mail (PUB 237)

In the Lab

Design and/or create a publication using the guidelines, concepts, and skills presented in this chapter. Labs are listed in order of increasing difficulty.

Lab 1: Creating an E-Mail Featured Product List

Problem: You work for a company that sells music on the Web. Your boss wants you to send an e-mail out to all previous customers advertising the newest songs. You decide to use a Publisher E-mail Featured Product template to design the e-mail message.

Instructions:

1. Start Publisher and choose the e-mail template named Watermark in the Featured Product templates. Select the Aspect color scheme and the Foundry font scheme. Select a short page size.

2. Add a background to your e-mail by using the Background command on the Format menu.

3. Think of a name for your music company and replace it in the heading. Use the phrase, Our Web songs are safe and spyware-free!, as the tag line text.

4. Replace the logo graphic with a piece of clip art. Use the keyword, media, in your search. Replace the logo text with the words, Web Songs.

5. Replace the larger graphic with one picturing an MP3 player. Describe your favorite artist or song in the lower text boxes.

6. Edit the hyperlink at the bottom to reflect your e-mail address.

7. Check the publication for spelling and design errors.

8. Save the publication with the file name, Lab EF-1 Web Songs E-Mail. Preview the e-mail.

In the Lab

Lab 2: Sending a Newsletter as an E-Mail Message

Problem: You created the newsletter shown in Figure 2-1 on page PUB 75. You decide to send the first page of the newsletter as an e-mail publication.

Instructions:

1. Open the file you created in Project 2. (If you did not create the publication in Project 2, see your instructor for a copy.)

2. On the File menu, point to Send E-mail, and then click Send as Message.

3. When Publisher asks if you want to save the publication, click the No option.

4. When Publisher asks if you want to send one page or multiple pages, select one page.

5. Scroll through and identify articles, lists, and graphics from the original newsletter. Delete any objects that you feel are not needed in the e-mail message.

6. In the Format Publication task pane, locate the Extra Content area. Insert two appropriate objects back into the publication.

7. Add a background of your choice.

8. Check the publication for spelling and design errors. If Publisher displays the error that text is not Web-ready, choose to use it in the e-mail message as an image.

9. Save the publication as Lab EF-2 Communiquarium E-Mail. Preview the e-mail and send it to your instructor.

4 | Using Business Information Sets

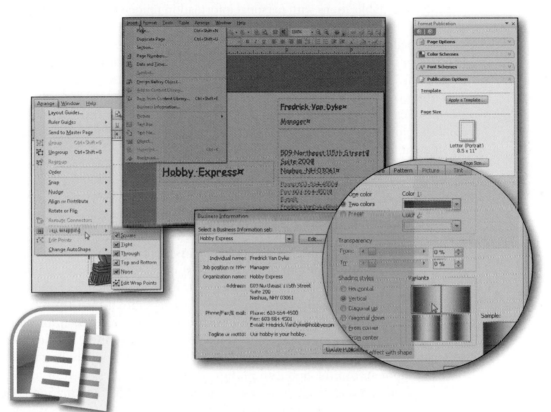

Objectives

You will have mastered the material in this chapter when you can:

- Create a blank publication and edit the margin and ruler guides

- Create, use, and delete a business information set

- Use letterhead production techniques to create a letterhead from scratch

- Use the Arrange menu to snap, align, distribute, order, rotate, and flip objects

- Crop a graphic and edit wrap points

- Save an edited graphic as a picture file

- Fill an AutoShape with a picture and add a border and shadow

- Create a gradient fill with tints, shades, patterns, and textures

- Use the Content Library

- Insert a date that updates automatically

- Create, edit, and format a table

- Use the Measurement toolbar

- Create a business card

- Select multiple objects

- Close publications without quitting

4 | Using Business Information Sets

Introduction

Customizing publications with personal information unique to the business, organization, or individual user expands the possibilities for using Publisher as a complete application product for small businesses. Whether you are creating publications from scratch or using a template, pieces of business information can be inserted automatically and consistently across documents. Publisher fills many needs. People create large text boxes and use Publisher like a word processor. Others create a table and perform mathematical and statistical operations or embed charts as they would with a spreadsheet. Still others create a database and use Publisher for mass mailings, billings, and customer accounts. Publisher's capabilities make it an efficient tool in small business offices — without the cost and learning curve of some of the high-end, dedicated application software.

Project — Business Information Sets

Storing permanent information about a business facilitates the customization of publications. Publisher automatically can insert data from its business information set. A **business information set** is a group of customized information components about an individual or an organization that can be used to generate information text boxes across publications. Many of the templates automatically create business information text boxes to incorporate the data from the business information set. Publications created from scratch also can integrate a business information set by including one or more of the components in the publication. For example, you can save your name, address, and telephone number in the business information set. The information is displayed automatically when inserted by you or by a template.

To illustrate some of the business information features of Microsoft Publisher, this project presents a series of steps to create a business information set. The business information set will be used in a letterhead created from scratch and a business card. The letterhead includes a specialized graphic saved to the Content Library and a gradient shape. A letter typed on the letterhead will include a table. The project creates publications for a hobby store named Hobby Express, as shown in Figure 4–1.

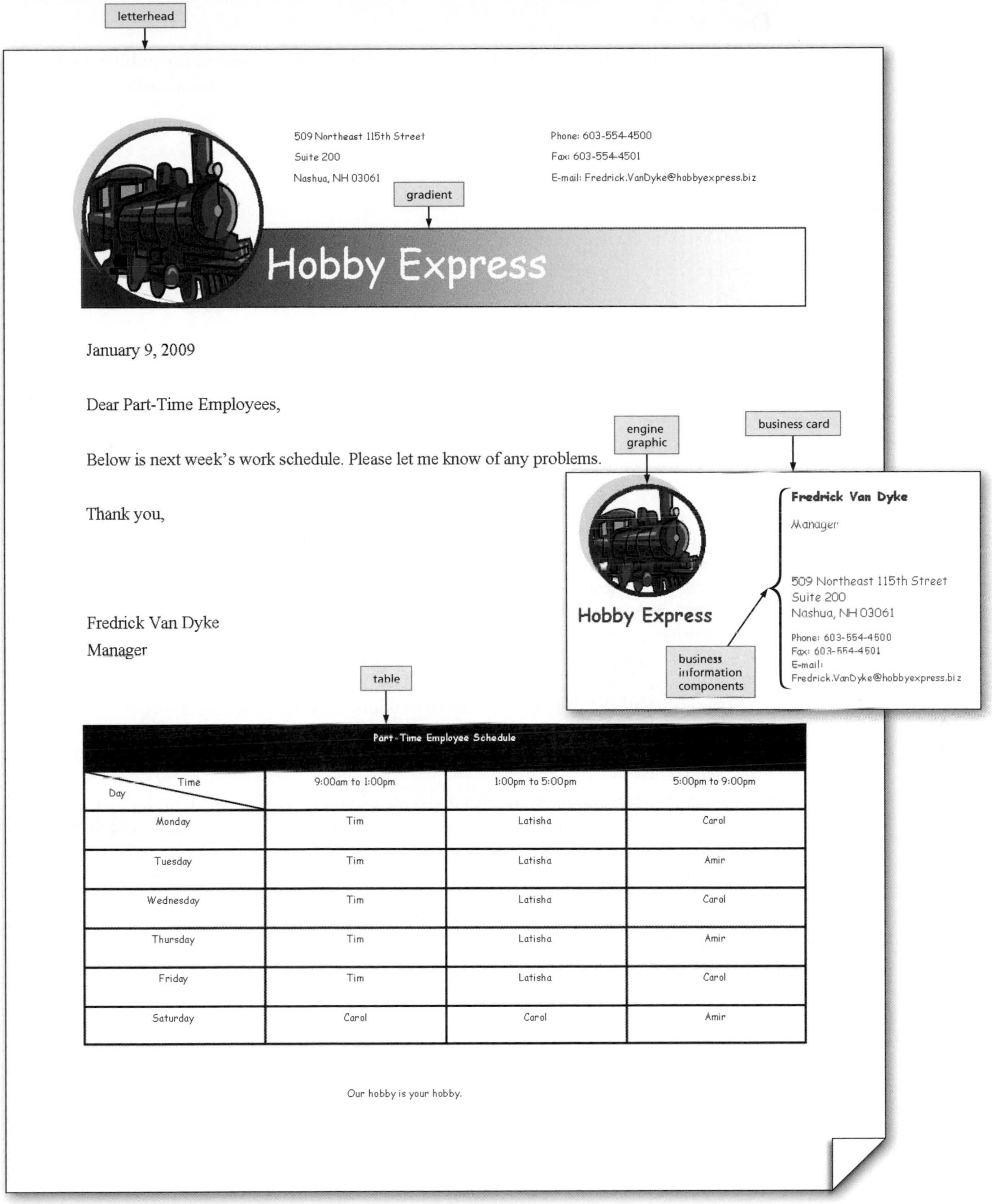

letterhead

509 Northeast 115th Street
Suite 200
Nashua, NH 03061

Phone: 603-554-4500
Fax: 603-554-4501
E-mail: Fredrick.VanDyke@hobbyexpress.biz

gradient

Hobby Express

January 9, 2009

Dear Part-Time Employees,

Below is next week's work schedule. Please let me know of any problems.

Thank you,

engine graphic

business card

Fredrick Van Dyke
Manager

Fredrick Van Dyke

Manager

509 Northeast 115th Street
Suite 200
Nashua, NH 03061

Phone: 603-554-4500
Fax: 603-554-4501
E-mail:
Fredrick.VanDyke@hobbyexpress.biz

Hobby Express

business information components

table

Part-Time Employee Schedule			
Day \ Time	9:00am to 1:00pm	1:00pm to 5:00pm	5:00pm to 9:00pm
Monday	Tim	Latisha	Carol
Tuesday	Tim	Latisha	Amir
Wednesday	Tim	Latisha	Carol
Thursday	Tim	Latisha	Amir
Friday	Tim	Latisha	Carol
Saturday	Carol	Carol	Amir

Our hobby is your hobby.

Figure 4–1

Overview

As you read through this chapter, you will learn how to create the publications shown in Figure 4–1 on the previous page by performing these general tasks:

- Select a blank publication and specify the page layout
- Use business information sets in publications
- Create a letterhead from scratch
- Edit a graphic image
- Insert and format AutoShapes using fill effects
- Use the features of the Arrange menu
- Use the Content Library
- Create a business card

Plan Ahead

General Project Guidelines

When creating a Publisher publication from scratch, the actions you perform and decisions you make will affect the appearance and characteristics of the finished publication. As you create publications, such as the project shown in Figure 4–1 on the previous page, you should follow these general guidelines:

1. **Decide on the purpose, schemes, and paper size.** Define the purpose of the publication. Does it fill a need for the customer? Decide if perhaps a template is a better choice than starting from scratch. Choose the color and font schemes that are suitable for the customer. Research publications that are similar to the one you have decided to create from scratch. Choose a paper size that is compatible with others used in the industry.

2. **Choose a layout and elements.** Carefully consider the necessary elements and their placement. Choose margins and ruler guides that will help standardize the publication. Decide whether to add dated material or prices. Decide on the kind of paper and your plan for printing. If you are working for someone, draw a storyboard and get it approved before you begin. Think about alignment of elements, proximity of similar data, contrast, and repetition.

3. **Create the publication.** Gather all the necessary components, such as information about the business, graphics, logos, and watermarks. Use the software to create nonprinting lines for visual alignment of elements. Use exact measurements where possible. If you need to create objects from scratch, have someone else evaluate your work and give you constructive feedback. If you are using tables in your publication, verify the number of rows and columns needed and table formatting. Check and double-check all business information data. Proofread, revise, and add the final touches. Look at text wrapping on every graphic. Revise as necessary and then use the spelling and design checking features of the software.

To Start Publisher

If you are using a computer to step through the project in this chapter, and you want your screens to match the figures in this book, you should change your computer's resolution to 1024×768. For information about how to change a computer's resolution, read Appendix D.

The following steps, which assume Windows is running, start Publisher based on a typical installation. You may need to ask your instructor how to start Publisher for your computer.

Note: If you are using Windows XP, see Appendix F for alternate steps.

1 Click the Start button on the Windows Vista taskbar to display the Start menu, and then click All Programs at the bottom of the left pane on the Start menu to display the All Programs list.

2 Click Microsoft Office in the All Programs list to display the Microsoft Office list, and then click Microsoft Office Publisher 2007 to start Publisher and display the Getting Started with Microsoft Office Publisher 2007 catalog.

3 If the Publisher window is not maximized, click the Maximize button next to the Close button on its title bar to maximize the window.

BTW

Using Publisher
The advances in desktop publishing, combined with the convenience and quality of desktop printers, have created a surge in the popularity of programs such as Microsoft Publisher 2007. Businesses that used programs such as Adobe Illustrator and QuarkXpress are switching to Publisher because of the Windows intuitive commands, the more than 2,000 templates and wizards, the easy learning curve, and the integration with other Office applications.

Creating a Company Letterhead

In many businesses, **letterhead** is preprinted stationery with important facts about the company and blank space to display the text of the correspondence. Letterhead, typically used for official business communication, is an easy way to convey company information to the reader and quickly establish a formal and legitimate mode of correspondence. The company information is displayed in a variety of places — across the top, down the side, or split between the top and bottom. Although most business letterhead is 8½-by-11 inches, other sizes are becoming more popular, especially with small agencies and not-for-profit organizations.

Generally, it is cost effective for companies to outsource the printing of their letterhead. Designing the letterhead in-house and then sending the file to a commercial printer saves design consultation time, customization, and money. Black-and-white or spot-color letterhead is more common and less expensive than composite or process color.

Sometimes preprinted letterhead may not be purchased because of its expense, color, or limited quantity. In these cases, companies can design their own letterhead and save it in a file. Employees open the letterhead file, create the rest of their document, and then save the finished product with a new name — thus preserving the original letterhead file. Alternately, businesses can print multiple copies of their blank letterhead and then, using other application software, prepare documents to print on the letterhead paper. All of these types of letterhead production can be used in any combination to produce professional publications.

For the Hobby Express company, the letterhead will consist of business information components, a picture, and a decorative rectangle, as shown in Figure 4–1 on page PUB 227.

<table>
<tr>
<td>Plan
Ahead</td>
<td>

Decide on the purpose, schemes, and paper size.
Define the purpose of the publication. Choose a font scheme and color scheme to match the customer's logo or company colors. If it is a letterhead or business card, define which pieces of business information you plan to use. Does the proposed publication fulfill the need? If you are working from scratch, look at similar publication templates. Choose a paper size that is compatible with others used in the industry.

</td>
</tr>
</table>

Creating a Blank Publication

When you first start Publisher, the catalog displays a list of templates and recent publications. Most users select a publication template and then begin editing. It is not always the case, however, that a template will fit every situation. Sometimes you want to think through a publication while manipulating objects on a blank page, trying different shapes, colors, pictures, and effects. Other times you may have specific goals for a publication that do not match any of the templates. For these cases, Publisher makes available **blank publications** with no preset objects or design, allowing you to start from scratch.

To Select a Blank Publication

The following steps describe how to select a blank print publication from the catalog.

1

- Click Blank Page Sizes in the list of publication types to display the catalog of blank page sizes.

Experiment

- Scroll through the catalog to see the available blank page sizes and types of blank publications.

- Scroll in the catalog to display the Letter (Portrait) 8.5 × 11" preview in the Standard area.

- Click the preview to select it (Figure 4–2).

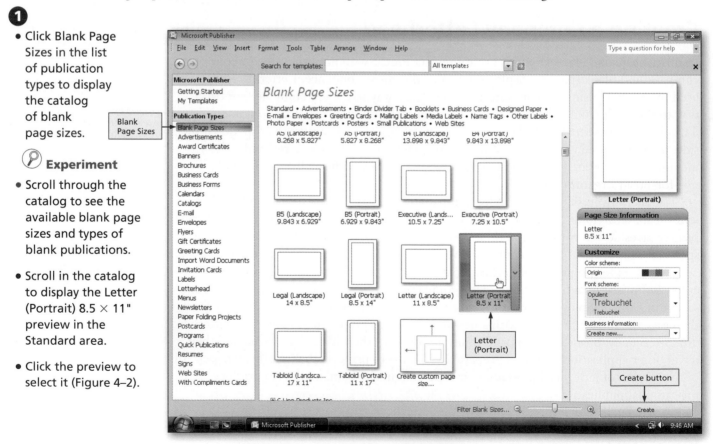

Figure 4–2

2

- Click the Create button to display the publication layout.

- If necessary, zoom to Whole Page.

- If the Special Characters button on the Standard tool-bar is not selected already, click it to display formatting marks on the screen (Figure 4–3).

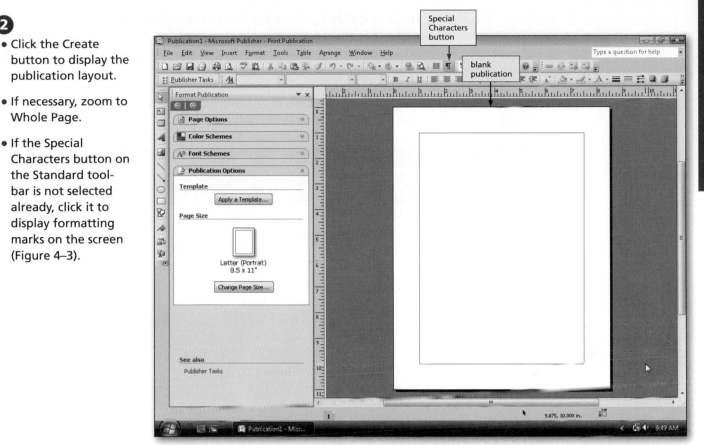

Figure 4–3

Other Ways

1. In open publication, click New button on Standard toolbar

Creating a Business Information Set

Business information sets save data about a company in a file. This data then is used in publications whenever you need it, or when a Publisher template incorporates it. For example, rather than typing the name of the company multiple times, you can insert the data from a component in the business information set. A **component** is a specific field in the set, such as an individual's name, job position or title, organization name, address, phone and fax numbers, e-mail address, tagline, or logo. When inserting a component, Publisher places a text box in your publication and supplies the text.

Creating and Editing the Business Information Set

Publisher allows you to create and save as many different business information sets as you want using the Business Information command on the Edit menu. If you have more than one set saved, you can choose the set you need from a list. The sets are stored with the Publisher application files on your system. When you create a new publication, the business information set used most recently populates the new publication. When Publisher first is installed, the business information is generic, with words such as Your Title and Business Name. In a lab situation, the business information set may be populated with information provided when Microsoft Office 2007 was installed.

BTW

Starting with a Blank Publication
If you want Publisher to start with a blank pub-lication, rather than the catalog, each time you start the program do the following: click Tools on the menu bar and then click Options. In the Options dialog box, click the General tab. Remove the check mark in the Show Publication Types when starting Publisher check box.

If you edit a text box within a publication that contains data from the business information set, you change the set for that publication only, unless you choose to update the set. To affect changes for all future publications, you edit the business information set through the Edit menu. You can edit the stored business information set at any time — before, during, or after performing other publication tasks.

Table 4–1 displays the data for each of the components in the business information set that you will create for the hobby store in this project.

Table 4–1 Data for Business Information Components	
Components	**Data**
Individual name	Fredrick Van Dyke
Job or position or title	Manager
Organization name	Hobby Express
Address	509 Northeast 115th Street Suite 200 Nashua, NH 03061
Phone, fax, and e-mail	Phone: 603-554-4500 Fax: 603-554-4501 E-mail: Fredrick.VanDyke@hobbyexpress.biz
Tagline or motto	Our hobby is your hobby.
Business Information set name	Hobby Express

To Create a Business Information Set

The following steps create a business information set for Hobby Express. You will enter data for each component. The logo will be added later in the project.

1
- Click Edit on the menu bar to display the Edit menu (Figure 4–4).

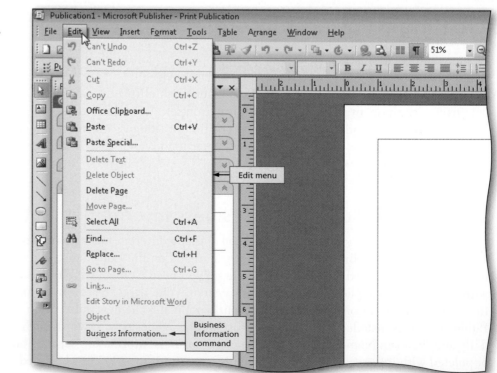

Figure 4–4

2

- Click Business Information to open the Create New Business Information Set dialog box (Figure 4–5). If Publisher displays the Business Information dialog box, click the New button.

Q&A Why does my screen look different?

If you have saved sets on your system, Publisher will display the Business Information dialog box first, to allow you to select a set. Clicking the New button opens a Create New Business Information Set dialog box.

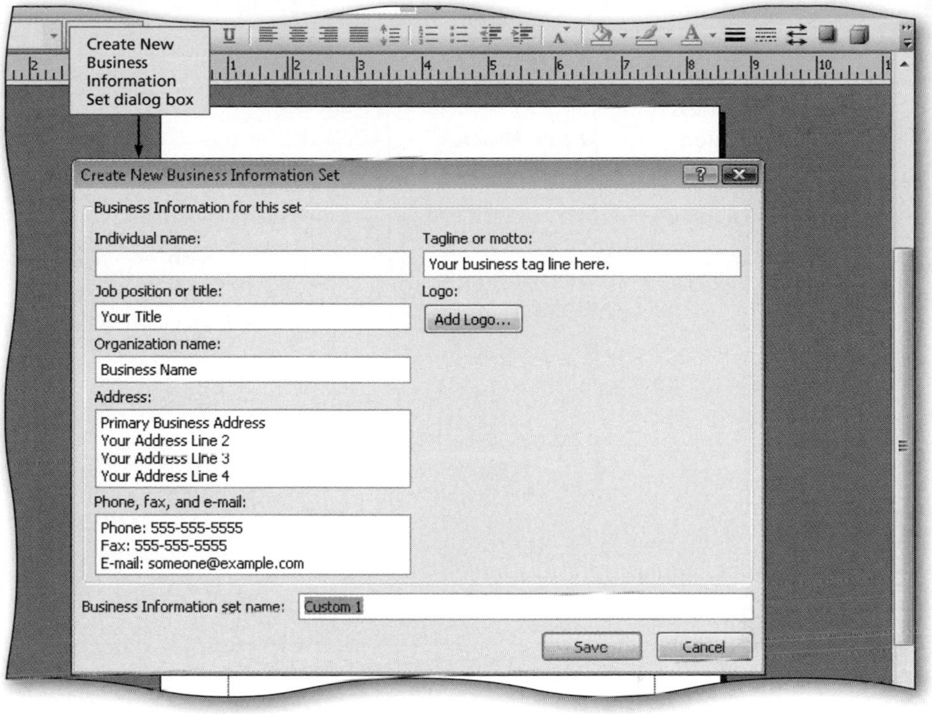

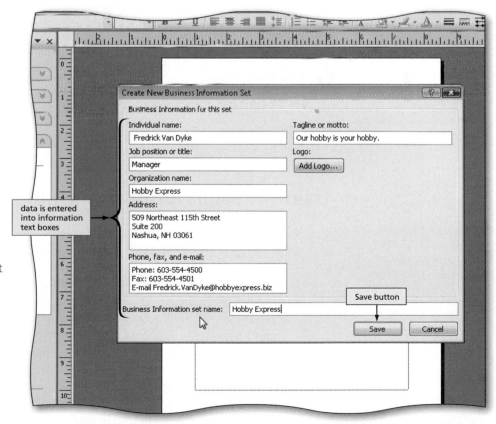

Figure 4–5

3

- Enter the data from Table 4–1, pressing the TAB key to move from one text box to the next (Figure 4–6).

Q&A How do I delete data once it is inserted in a component?

To delete text from a text box in the Create New Business Information Set dialog box, press the DELETE key. To delete a business information component in the publication, delete its text box; however, this does not delete it permanently form the set. You will learn how to delete an entire business information set later in this project.

Figure 4–6

4

- Click the Save button to save the business information set and display the Business Information dialog box (Figure 4-7).

Q&A

Does saving the business information set also save the publication?

No, you are saving a separate, internal data file that contains only the data in the components.

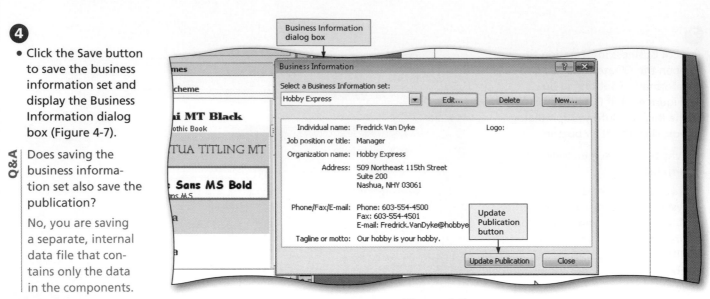

Figure 4–7

5

- Click the Update Publication button.

Other Ways

1. In publication, click smart tag button, click Edit Business Information, enter data, click Update Publication

To Set the Color and Font Schemes

The following steps set the color and font schemes.

1 In the Format Publication task pane, click Color Schemes. Click the Color Schemes box arrow. Scroll, if necessary, and then click Parrot in the list.

2 Click Font Schemes. Click the Font Schemes box arrow. Scroll to and then click Casual in the list.

3 Close the Format Publication task pane.

Using Margin and Ruler Guides

BTW

Multiple Business Information Sets
Using different business information sets allows you to maintain alternate information about your business; a second or related business, such as a major supplier or home business; an outside organization for which you maintain information, such as scouting or sports; and your personal home/family information.

Recall that Publisher uses various types of guides to help with object placement and alignment, including margin guides, grid guides, baseline guides, ruler guides, and object boundaries. Margin guides are displayed as nonprinting blue, dotted lines on each page of a publication. The margin guides reside in the background and repeat on each page of a publication, serving as a template for uniformity in multipage publications. When more than one person works on a publication, margin guides ensure that the final product has consistent margins. By default, the margin guides are placed one inch from the edge of the paper. You can position objects closer to the edge of the paper if your printer is capable of printing close to the edge. The size of the **printing area**, or printable region, varies among printers and depends on paper size. Most printers leave a small area around the edge of the paper unprinted. On a desktop printer, the printable area can include the space up to three-tenths of an inch from the edge; others can require five-tenths to seven-tenths of an inch. If you know your printer's nonprintable area, you can ensure that the elements on the page do not go beyond the printing area. If your publication is destined for a commercial printer, you should consult the print professional about printable areas. The size of the paper and the purpose of the publication also make a difference in the printable area. Labels, envelopes, and business cards display a variety of different margins in Publisher depending on the number of elements per sheet and the size of the publication. Web pages, designed for electronic publication rather than print, display layout guides at the edge of the publication page.

Choose a layout and elements.

Look at samples of similar publications and note the elements used. Choose placement and layout for a reason. Decide which objects should align with each other. Keep similar data together. If you are including business information components, keep the address and phone text boxes in the same part of the publication. Find ways to repeat color and the name of the customer or company. Decide how you will add contrast and interest to the publication by including a graphic or placing a component in a different location on the page.

Plan Ahead

Changing the Margins

To change the margins, you can use the Page Setup dialog box as shown in the next series of steps. Setting margins through the Page Setup dialog box is new to Publisher 2007 — a feature that now aligns more closely with the other Office applications. Previously in Publisher, margins were changed via the Layout Guides command on the Arrange menu. With Publisher 2007, you now can use either method to change the margins.

To Edit the Margin Guides

The following steps change the margins to .75 inches by editing the margin guides using the Page Setup dialog box.

1

- If the margin guides are not displayed, click View on the menu bar and then click Boundaries and Guides to display them.

- Click File on the menu bar, and then click Page Setup to display the Page Setup dialog box (Figure 4–8).

Q&A

Why does my Page Setup dialog box look different?

Someone may have resized the dialog box previously. You can drag the edge of the dialog box to resize it, or double-click the title bar to maximize it. Changes also might have been made to the magnification of the Blank Page Sizes catalog area. The slider and buttons in the lower-left corner affect how many templates are displayed in the catalog.

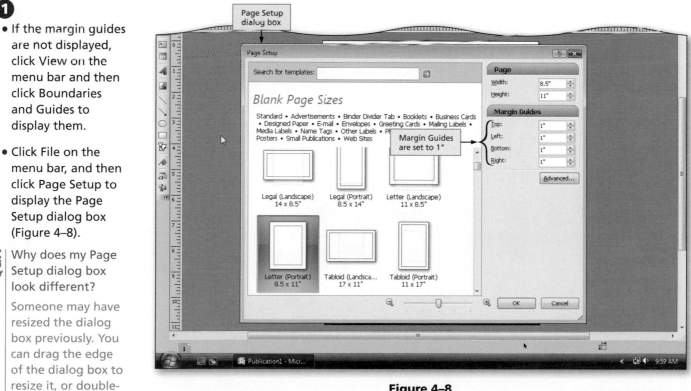

Figure 4–8

2

- Drag to select the text in the Top box and then type .75 to replace it.

- Press the TAB key to move to the Left box.

- Repeat the process, typing .75 in each of the other three boxes in the Margin Guides area to change all of the margins to .75 inches (Figure 4–9).

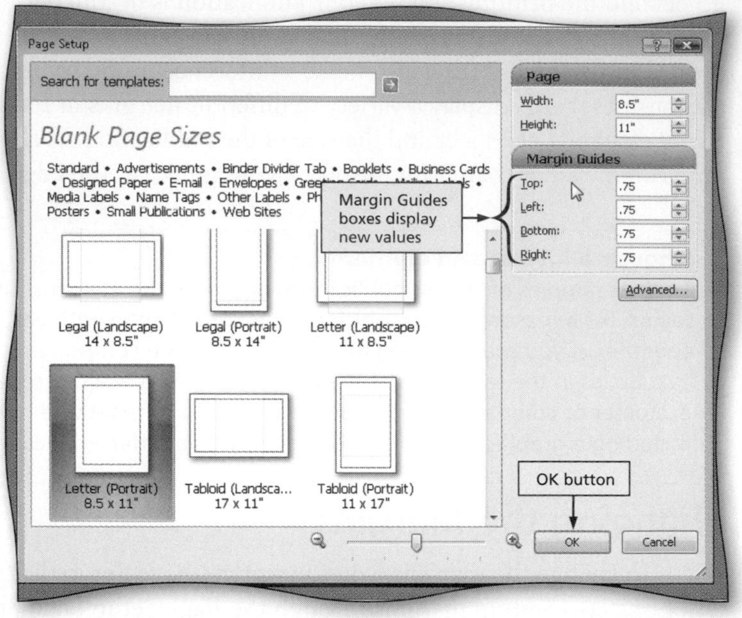

Figure 4–9

3

- Click the OK button in the Page Setup dialog box.

- Close the Format Publication task pane (Figure 4–10).

Q&A

Can I use something other than inches for the margin settings?

Yes, you can use centimeters, picas, points, or pixels. To edit the unit of measurement, on the Tools menu, click Options. On the General tab, click the Measurement units box arrow and then select a unit of measurement.

Figure 4–10

Other Ways

1. On Arrange menu, click Layout Guides, enter new margin settings, click OK

2. On View menu, click Master Page, drag margin guide

Using Rulers and Ruler Guides

To measure and place objects on the page layout, in addition to using the margin guides, you can use Publisher's rulers. Recall that vertical and horizontal rulers are displayed at the left and top of the workspace. These rulers can be moved to any place in the workspace to help measure and align objects and other guides by pressing the SHIFT key and dragging. Publisher allows users to move both rulers at once by SHIFT-dragging the gray box at the intersection of the two rulers.

You also can drag a **ruler guide** from the ruler, which results in a green dotted line displayed across the page. Added to individual pages on an as-needed basis, ruler guides help align objects. Ruler guides that are created on a master page are visible on every page of the publication to which that master page is applied.

BTW

Object Margins
In addition to the page margins, each object on the page has its own individual boundary margins. For instance, text boxes are preset with a 0.04-inch margin, which means that text on all four sides begins 0.04 inches from the edge of the frame, and thus away from any other object snapped to the text box.

To Move a Ruler

The following step moves a ruler.

1

- If the rulers are not displayed, click View on the menu bar and then click Rulers. SHIFT+drag the vertical ruler to the left edge of the page layout (Figure 4–11).

Q&A

Why did my mouse pointer change?

The mouse pointer changes to a two-headed arrow as you SHIFT+drag the ruler.

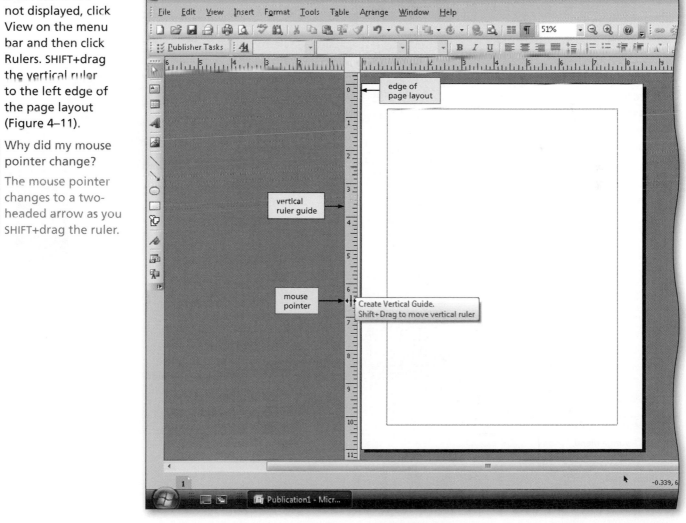

Figure 4–11

To Create a Ruler Guide

The following steps drag from the horizontal ruler to create two ruler guides.

1

• Point to the horizontal ruler at the top of the workspace. When the mouse pointer changes to a two-headed horizontal arrow, drag a ruler guide down to the 1.75-inch mark on the vertical ruler (Figure 4–12).

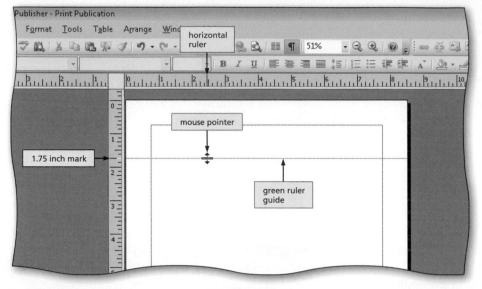

Figure 4–12

2

• Drag another ruler guide from the horizontal ruler to the 2.5-inch mark on the vertical ruler (Figure 4–13).

3

• SHIFT+drag the vertical ruler back to the left edge of the workspace.

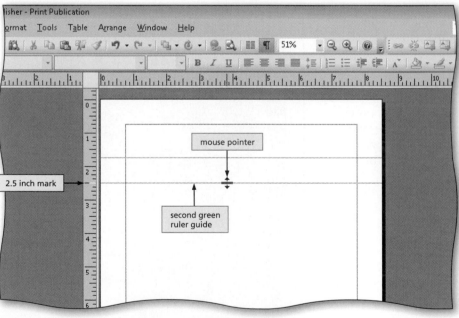

Figure 4–13

Using Business Information

The letterhead will contain three components from the business information set: the Address; the Phone, fax, and e-mail; and the Tagline or motto. When you insert a specific component, Publisher places a text box with the information in the center of the screen with a preset font and font size. You then may move the text box and format the text as necessary. Applied formatting affects the current publication only.

The desktop publishing goals of placing objects in proximity of one another, aligning objects, repeating patterns, and providing contrast all involve placing objects on the page in a planned, purposeful manner. **Snapping** facilitates that objective. When you move an object such as a business information text box close to a ruler or guide, Publisher will **snap** to the boundary, which means its edge will line up with the other object's boundary. Snapping aligns objects perfectly without any overlap. The Snap command is on the Arrange menu and allows you to snap to a guide, a ruler mark, or another object's boundary. Snapping to rulers and guides is turned on by default in an initial installation of Publisher. Objects will still snap to guides even when guides are hidden.

Another way to position objects is to align or distribute them. On the Arrange menu, the **Align or Distribute command** offers you choices to align or distribute groups of objects relative to one another, or to position single objects relative to the margins. The alignment options include left, right, center, top, middle, and bottom; the distribute options include horizontally and vertically.

The following step verifies that snapping is turned on.

BTW

Hiding Toolbars
If you find the toolbars on your screen distracting, or if you merely want to increase the size of the workspace, you can hide the toolbars. On the View menu, point to Toolbars, and then click each toolbar name on the Toolbars submenu to turn it on or off. You also can hide the rulers using the View menu, thus increasing the size of the workspace.

To Turn On Snapping

1

- Click Arrange on the menu bar, and then point to Snap to display the Snap submenu.

- On the Snap submenu, if To Ruler Marks does not display a check mark, click To Ruler Marks. If To Guides does not display a check mark, click To Guides (Figure 4–14).

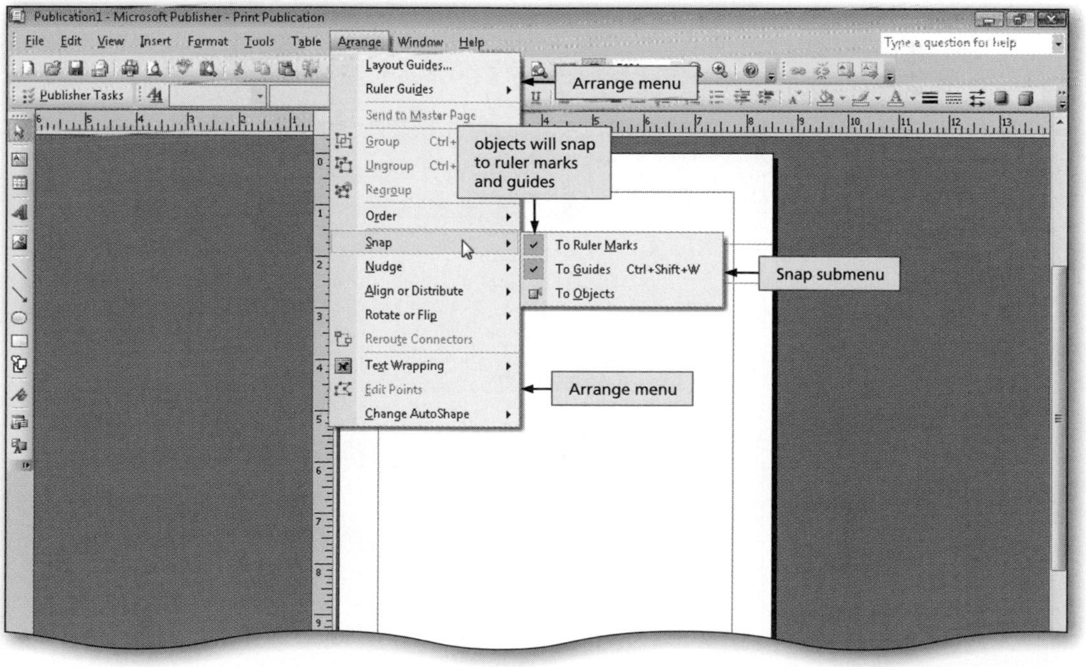

Figure 4–14

Other Ways

1. To snap to guides, press CTRL+SHIFT+W

Plan Ahead	**Create the publication.**
	Add information from the business set to the required locations in the publication. Then add graphics. Order and layer objects appropriately. If you have to create objects from scratch, have someone else evaluate your work and give you constructive feedback. Use appropriate and legible formatting for any tables and shapes.

To Insert and Position Business Information Set Components

The following steps insert and position business information text boxes.

1

- Zoom to Page Width.

- To display the Insert menu, click Insert on the menu bar (Figure 4–15).

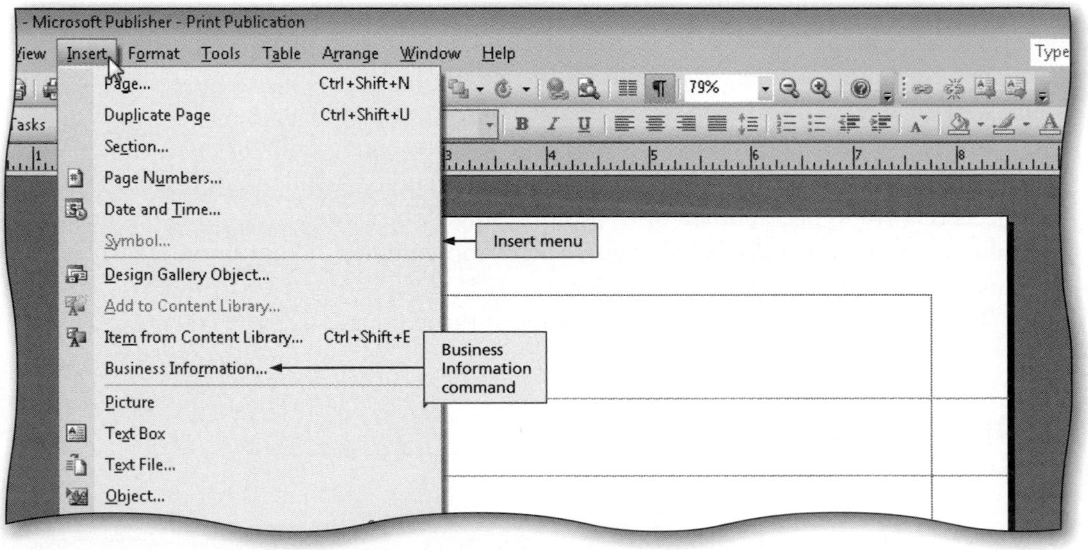

Figure 4–15

2

- Click Business Information to display the Business Information task pane.

- In the task pane, double-click the Phone/Fax/E-mail component to insert it into the publication (Figure 4–16).

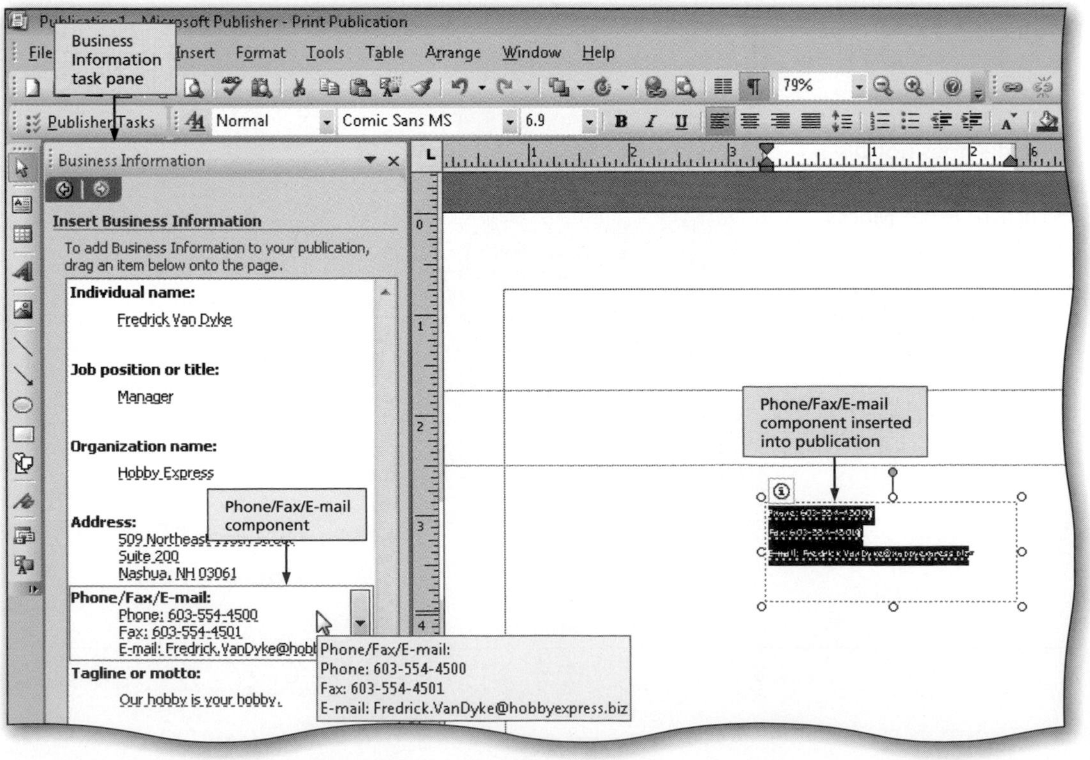

Figure 4–16

3

- Drag the new text box to a position in the upper-right corner of the publication until it snaps to the margin and ruler guide, as shown in Figure 4–17.

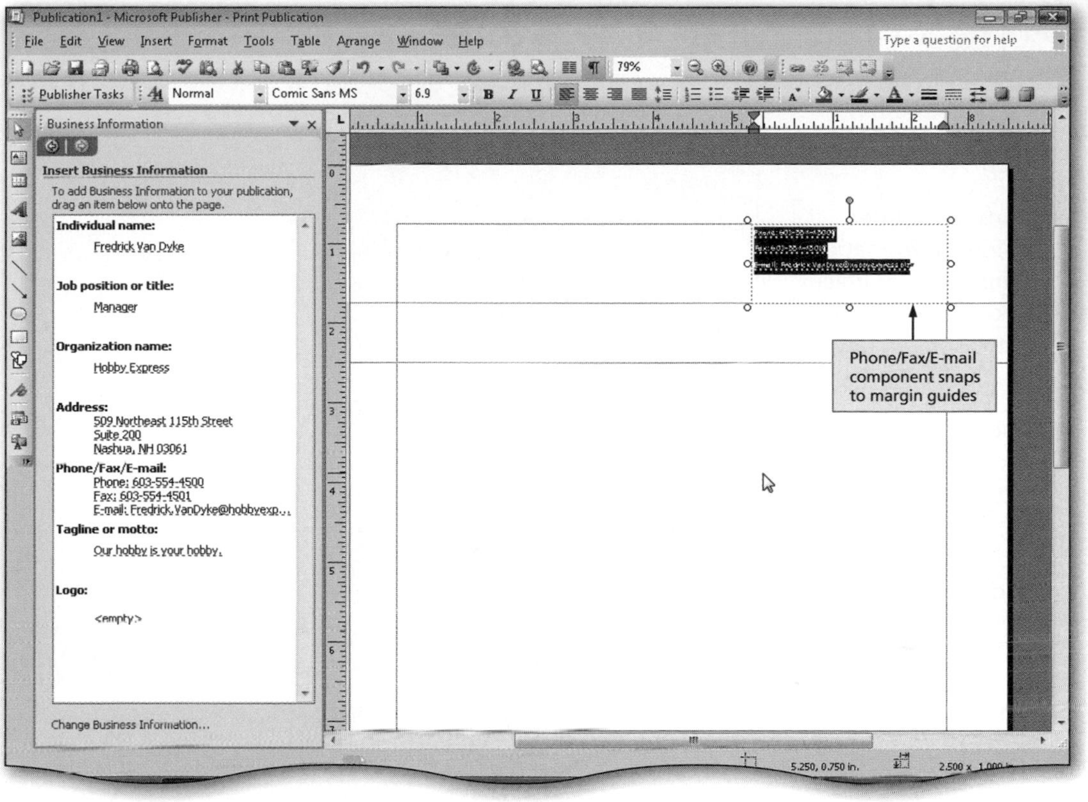

Figure 4–17

4

- Click outside of the text box to deselect it.

- In the task pane, double-click the Address component to insert it into the publication.

- Drag the new text box to a position in the upper-center of the publication until it snaps to the margin and ruler guide, left of the Phone/Fax/E-mail text box, as shown in Figure 4–18.

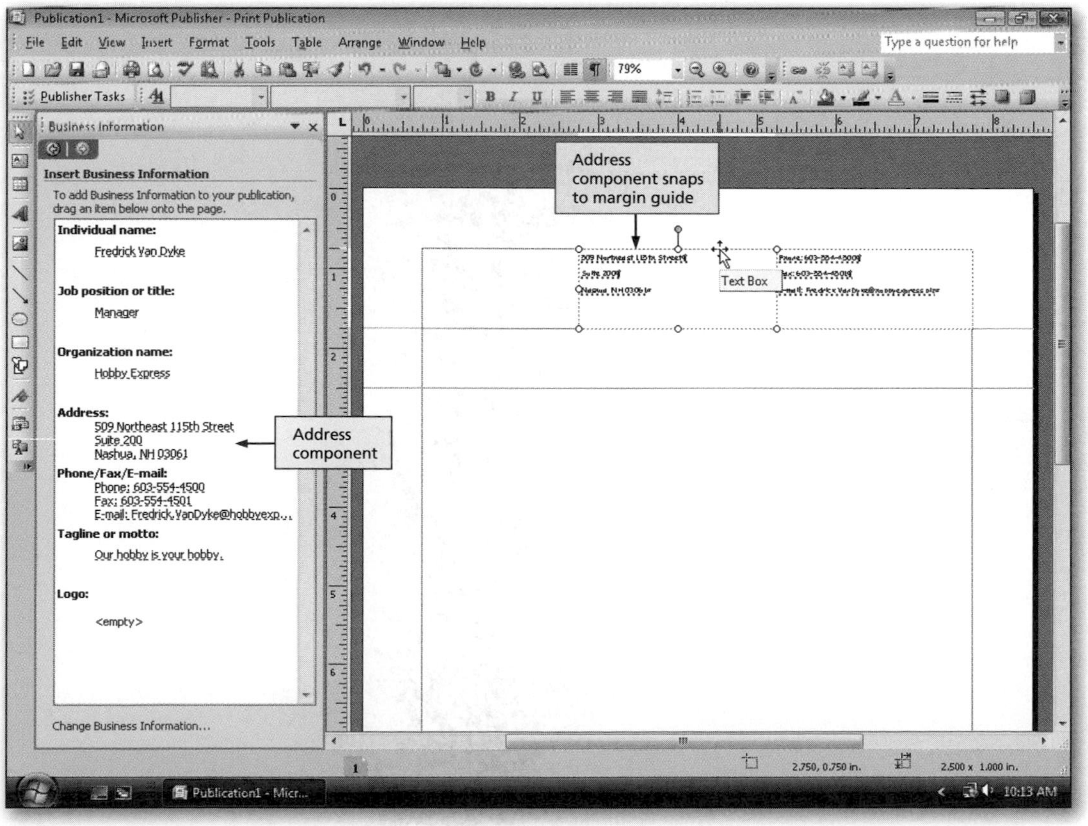

Figure 4–18

5

- Deselect the text box.

- Scroll to the lower half of the page layout.

- To insert another business information component, double-click the Tagline or motto component in the task pane.

- Drag the new text box to the lower portion of the page so it snaps to the margin guide, as shown in Figure 4–19.

6

- Close the task pane.

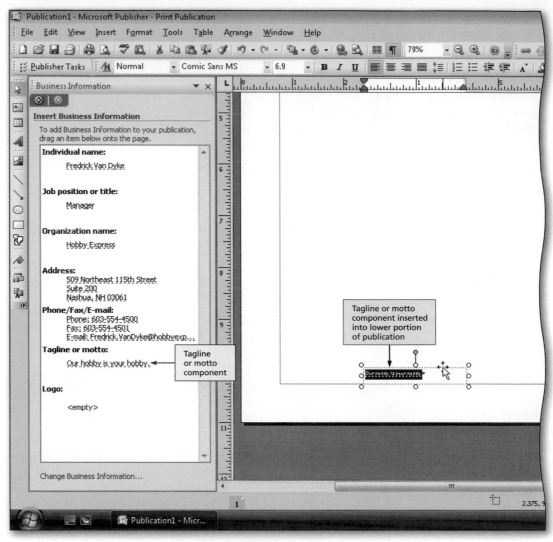

Figure 4–19

To Center a Text Box Relative to the Margins

The next steps center the text box containing the tag line relative to the margins.

1

- With the text box selected, click Arrange on the menu bar and then point to Align or Distribute to display the Align or Distribute submenu.

- If the align and distribute commands are not available, click Relative to Margin Guides. Click Arrange on the menu bar again, and then point to Align or Distribute (Figure 4–20).

Q&A How do I know if the commands are available or not?

If Publisher displays a menu command in gray and it cannot be clicked, it is not available.

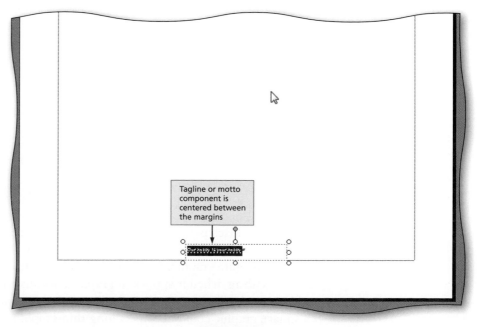

Figure 4–20

2

- Click Align Center to align the text box centered between the margins (Figure 4–21).

Q&A Will the align and distribute commands align my text within the text box?

No, the align and distribute commands work on objects, not text. If you want to center the text within the text box, click the Center button on the Formatting toolbar.

Figure 4–21

Editing Graphics

Recall that you have inserted graphics or pictures into publications by choosing them from the Clip Art task pane, or by importing them from a file. You also created a graphic shape to use as a logo. Graphics add value and visual flair to publications, however to create a unique publication for a business, it is good to enhance and customize the graphic through editing. Many times customers are bored by stock graphics and clip art because of their overuse. A well-edited graphic not only contributes to the uniqueness of the publication, but also adds a personal touch. Publications with edited graphics do not look rigid or computer-generated.

Publisher offers many ways to edit graphics other than size and position. Many graphic manipulations can be performed using the Picture toolbar. Table 4–2 lists the buttons on the Picture toolbar and their functions.

Table 4–2 Picture Toolbar Buttons

Name	Function
Insert Picture	Opens the Insert Picture dialog box to browse for pictures on your system
Insert Picture from Scanner or Camera	Automatically retrieves picture scanned or digitized from the installed hardware on your system
Color	Allows users to select one of the color effects for the picture, including automatic, grayscale, black and white, and washout
More Contrast	Percentage of black in all colors increases
Less Contrast	Percentage of white in all colors increases
More Brightness	All colors become lighter
Less Brightness	All colors become darker
Crop	Trims the vertical or horizontal edges of an object
Line/Border Style	Presents a variety of lines and borders to display at the edges of the picture
Compress Pictures	Presents options for compressing the size of the graphic depending upon its ultimate use
Text Wrapping	Changes the way text will be displayed around the edges of the picture — choices include Square, Tight, Through, Top and Bottom, None, and Edit Wrap Points
Format Picture	Opens the Format Picture dialog box to make more changes to the picture, such as exact size, position, or alternative text
Set Transparent Color	Allows you to click a picture color, which then changes to transparent
Reset Picture	Resets all changes to the picture so it is displayed in its original size, format, and color

When you **recolor** a graphic you make a large-scale color change to the entire graphic. When chosen, the color applies to all parts of the graphic, with the option of leaving the black parts black. It is an easy way to convert a color graphic to a black and white line drawing in order to print more clearly. The reverse also is true; if you have a black and white graphic, you can convert it to a tint or shade of any one color.

Scaling, when it applies to graphics, means changing the vertical or horizontal size of the graphic by a percentage. Scaling can create interesting graphic effects. For example, a square graphic could become a long thin graphic suitable for use as a single border if the scale height were increased to 200% and the scale width were reduced to 50%. Caricature drawings and intentionally distorted photographs routinely use scaling. When used for resizing, scaling is appropriate to make a graphic fit in tight places.

Using other Picture toolbar buttons, you can increase the contrast or brightness of a graphic. **Contrast** is the saturation or intensity of the color; the higher the contrast percentage, the more intense the color. **Brightness** is the amount of black or white added to the color. The higher the brightness percentage, the more white is added.

For the Hobby Express letterhead, you will create two graphics: an edited clip of a train engine and a rectangle with a gradient fill and text.

Creating the Clip Art Graphic

The graphic for Hobby Express is a picture of an engine. First, the graphic will be created by choosing a clip, cropping it, flipping the image, and then saving it to a storage device. Then the graphic will be edited by placing it inside a circular shape, adding a border of the same color, and creating a shadow. The following steps insert a clip using the Clip Art task pane.

To Insert Clip Art

1 Scroll to display the upper half of the publication. Click Insert on the menu bar, point to Picture, and then click Clip Art on the Picture submenu to view the Clip Art task pane.

2 Type engine in the Search for box.

3 If necessary, click the Search in box arrow and then click Everywhere in the list.

4 To search for only pictures, click the Results should be box arrow and then click All media types in the list.

5 Click the Go button to search for clip art related to the term, engine.

6 When the clips are displayed, scroll to find a clip art of a train engine similar to the one shown in Figure 4–22.

7 Click the preview to insert the picture into the publication (Figure 4–22).

BTW

EPS Format
Most pictures imported into Publisher can be recolored. This procedure does not apply to pictures that are in Encapsulated PostScript (EPS) format, however. EPS is a graphic file format that is created using the PostScript page description language. EPS graphics are designed to be printed to PostScript compatible printers and cannot be recolored.

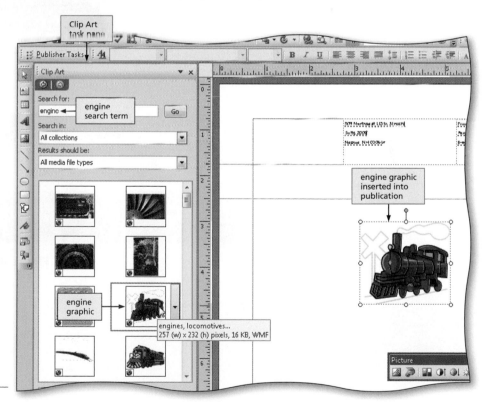

Figure 4–22

Cropping a Graphic

The engine graphic has light blue smoke, a crossing sign, and tracks that are not needed in the final display. If a picture is too large to fit in the space you designated for it, or if you want to display only a portion of a picture, Publisher allows you to **crop**, or trim, the vertical or horizontal edges of an object. Pictures often are cropped to focus attention on a particular area.

To Crop a Graphic

The following steps use the Crop tool to remove portions of the edge of the graphic from the display.

1

- Close the Clip Art task pane and zoom to 100%.

- Click the graphic to select it, if necessary.

Where is the picture toolbar?

If the Picture toolbar does not display, right-click the graphic and then click Show Picture Toolbar.

- On the Picture toolbar, click the Crop button to select the Crop tool (Figure 4–23).

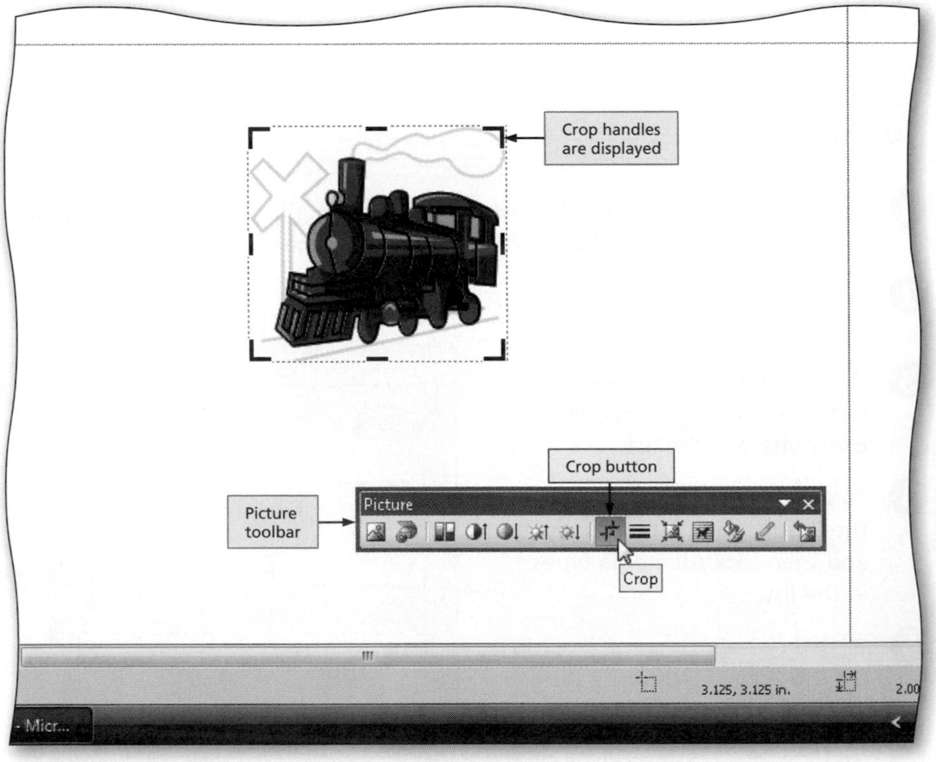

Figure 4–23

2

- Point to the center crop handle on the top of the graphic. When the mouse pointer changes to a push pin, drag down to the edge of the engine to crop the top edge of the graphic (Figure 4–24).

Q&A Can I crop from a corner?

Yes, you can crop from a corner by dragging a corner cropping handle. The resulting crop removes part of the picture from both sides. Cropping from the corner is especially useful for cropping large areas.

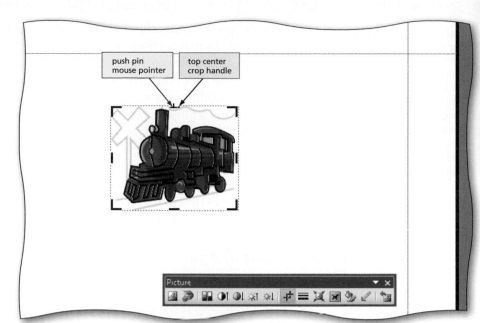

Figure 4–24

3

🔎 **Experiment**

- Push the side and corner crop handles back and forth at different magnifications to see how much Publisher crops from the graphic.

- Point to the center crop handle on the left. When the mouse pointer changes to a push pin, drag right to the edge of the engine to crop the left edge of the graphic (Figure 4–25).

4

- Crop the other two edges, as necessary, by dragging one of the cropping handles.

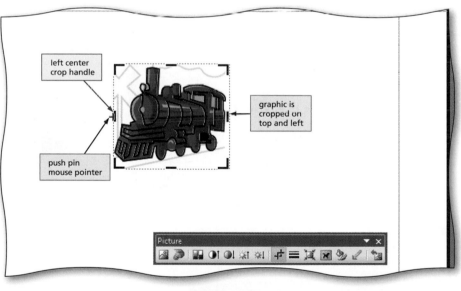

Figure 4–25

Other Ways	
1. On Format menu, click Picture, click Picture tab, enter Crop from measurements	2. Right-click picture, click Format Picture, click Picture tab, enter Crop from measurements

BTW

Cropping and Resizing

Cropping is different from resizing. Both techniques change the overall size of the graphic display; however, with cropping you eliminate part of the graphic from the display while maintaining the size of the objects in the picture. With resizing, the entire graphic is displayed at a different size. For additional editing possibilities, you can also resize a cropped graphic or crop a resized graphic. If you want to undo a cropping effect, you can click the Reset Picture button on the Picture toolbar.

Cropping GIF files
Although Publisher has basic photo editing capabilities, it is not a complete photo editing solution. You cannot crop an AutoShape, WordArt object, or an animated graphic or movie. To crop an animated GIF, use an animated GIF editing program, and then insert the file again.

Cropping to a Nonrectangular Shape

The following steps crop the engine graphic even further to fine tune the edges. To remove small portions of a graphic in Publisher, you adjust its outline. Every picture has an adjustable **outline** around it. An outline is made up of wrapping points and lines around the edge of the graphic. These wrapping points are displayed as small black rectangles. The outline is nonrectangular as opposed to the boundary that you cropped earlier; editing the wrapping points creates a nonrectangular graphic. Outlines also are edited when customized text wrapping is desired. The text will wrap around the wrapping points rather than the boundary of the graphic. Neither cropping nor editing the wrapping points are permanent changes; you can drag outward to display more of the graphic. If you want to make the edits permanent, you can compress the picture by clicking the Compress Pictures button on the Picture toolbar.

To Crop to a Nonrectangular Shape

1
- Click Arrange on the menu bar and then point to Text Wrapping to display the Text Wrapping submenu (Figure 4–26).

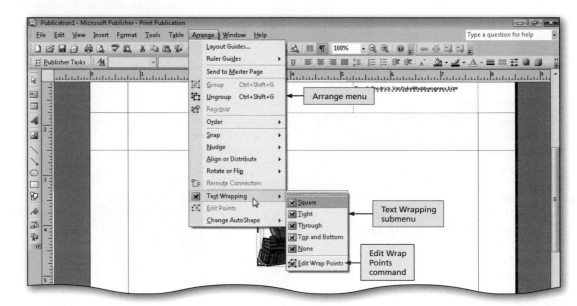

Figure 4–26

2
- Click Edit Wrap Points to display the outline of the graphic (Figure 4–27).

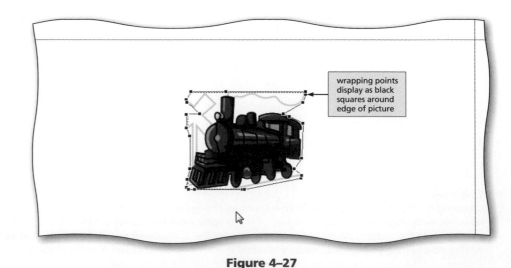

Figure 4–27

❸

- One at a time, drag the wrapping points to the edge of the engine. You do not have to be exact (Figure 4–28).

Q&A

What if I make a mistake?

If you drag too far or to an incorrect position, you can fix it by dragging the wrapping point to a new location — even farther away from the graphic, if you like. To delete a wrapping point, press CTRL+click. To add a new wrapping point, ATL+drag the outline.

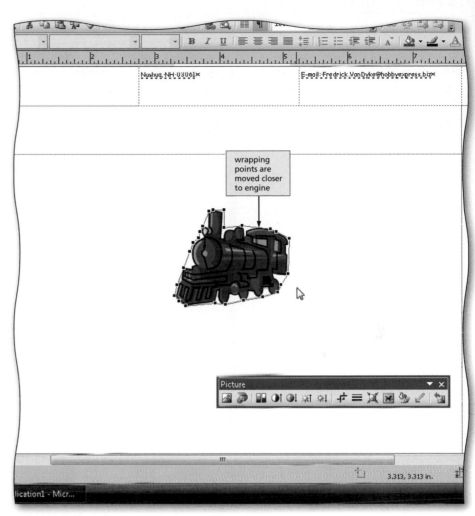

Figure 4–28

Rotating and Flipping Objects

When you **rotate** an object in Publisher, you turn it so that the top of the object faces a different direction. For example, a picture of a person could be rotated to look like that person was standing on his or her head. Each selected object in Publisher displays a green rotation handle that can be used to freely rotate the object. To rotate in 5-degree increments, hold down the SHIFT key while dragging the rotation handle. To rotate an object on its base, hold down the CTRL key and drag the green rotation handle — the object will rotate in a circle by pivoting around the handle. Other rotation percentages can be entered in the Format dialog box for the given object.

Publisher also allows you to **flip** objects, or turn them over. For example, a picture of a person facing left could be flipped horizontally so it would appear that the person is facing right. Publisher provides four options to flip an object. You can flip horizontally, flip vertically, flip right 90°, or flip left 90°.

BTW

Ungrouping Clip Art
If you want to edit a graphic further, many clip art graphics can be broken down into parts or ungrouped. Then you can delete the parts you do not want. First select the graphic, then, on the Arrange menu, click Ungroup. If Publisher displays a message about converting an imported picture, click the Yes button. Each part of the graphic becomes a separate piece that can be edited or deleted.

To Flip an Object

The following steps flip the engine graphic horizontally.

1

- With the graphic selected, click Arrange on the menu bar, and then point to Rotate or Flip to display the Rotate or Flip submenu (Figure 4–29).

Q&A What does Free Rotate mean?

The Free Rotate command places green rotation handles on each of the four corners of a selected object. As you drag a rotation handle, the graphic rotates while keeping the center of the graphic in the same place on the page. Pressing the CTRL key while you rotate a corner handle keeps the opposite corner in the same place on the page and rotates around it.

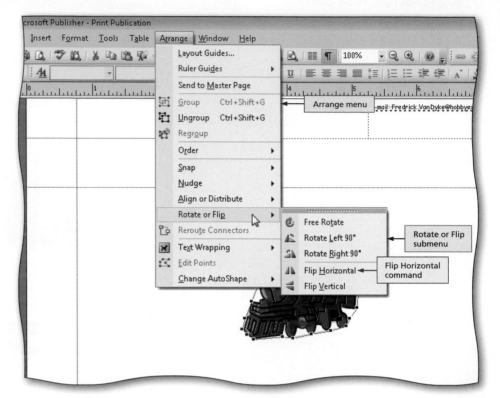

Figure 4–29

2

- Click Flip Horizontal to make the graphic face the opposite direction.

- Deselect the graphic (Figure 4–30).

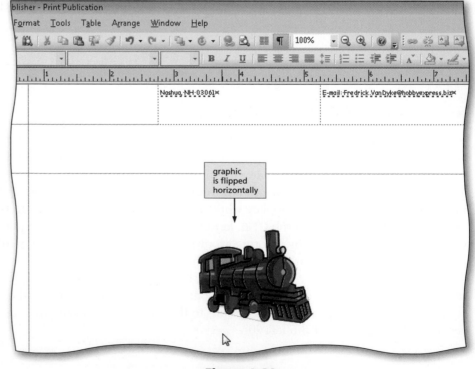

graphic is flipped horizontally

Figure 4–30

Saving Edited Graphics

Because a graphic that you edit in Publisher is stored only in the publication in which you use it, it is a good idea to save the graphic independently. That way you can use it in other publications and in other formatting and editing situations. The following steps save the graphic with the file name, Hobby Express Engine.

To Save Clip Art as a Picture

1

- With a USB flash drive connected to one of the computer's USB ports, right-click the graphic to display the shortcut menu (Figure 4–31).

2

- Click Save as Picture to open the Save As dialog box.

- Type Hobby Express Engine in the File name text box to change the file name. Do not press the ENTER key.

- Navigate to your USB flash drive (Figure 4–32).

What is the PNG Portable Network Graphics Format?

PNG is the default format for saving graphics from within Publisher publications. **PNG** is a graphic file format that is supported by some World Wide Web browsers. PNG files are compressed bitmap files that support variable transparency of images and brightness on different computers. You can save the graphic in other formats by clicking the Save as type box arrow and then choosing a format in the list.

3

- Click the Save button in the Save As dialog box to save the graphic on the USB flash drive with the file name, Hobby Express Engine.

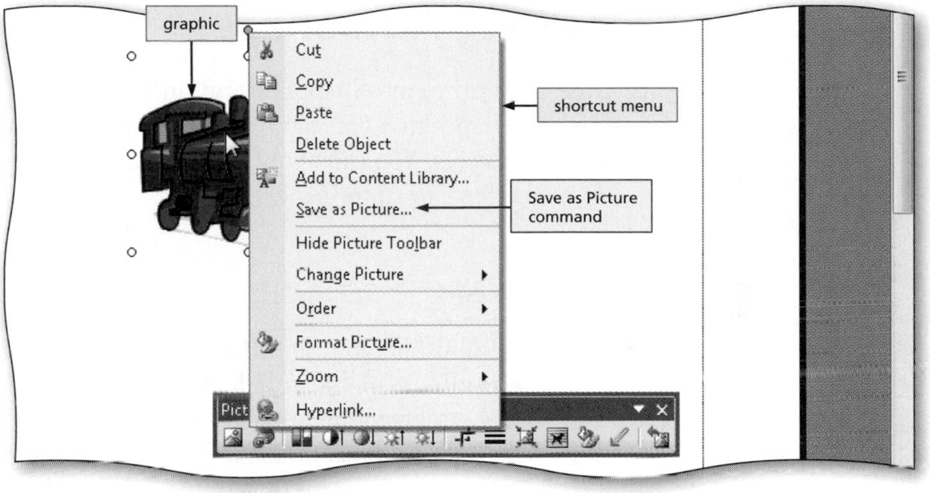

Figure 4–31

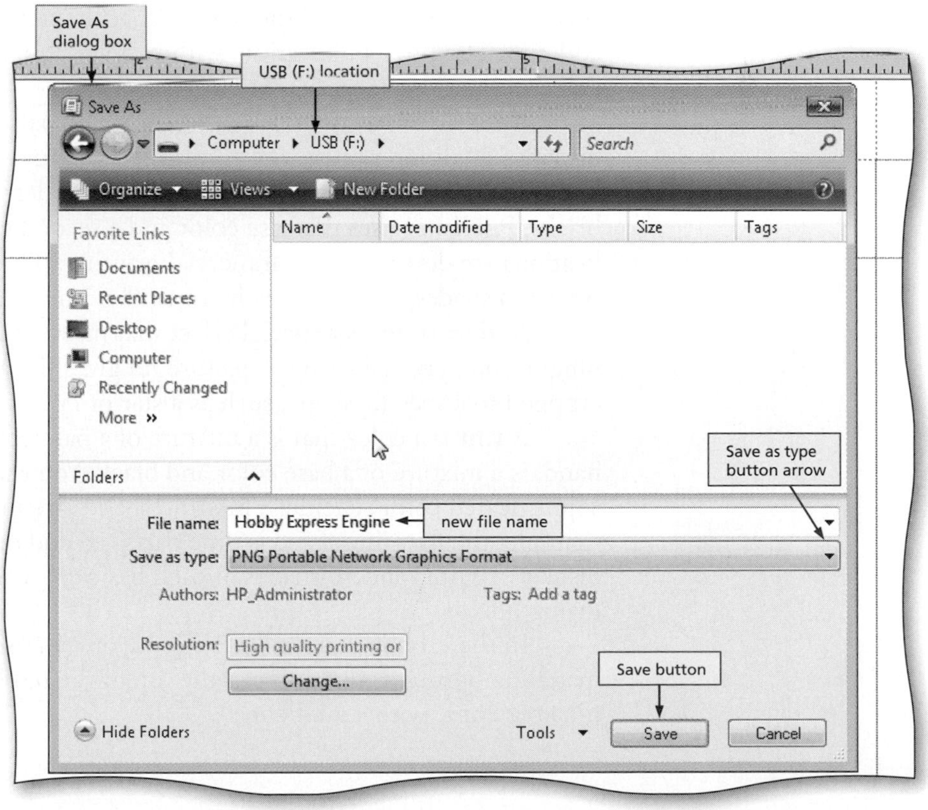

Figure 4–32

To Delete the Graphic

Now that you have saved the graphic, and because you will use the graphic in a different way later in the project, the following step deletes the graphic from the publication layout for the time being.

1 Select the graphic if necessary.

2 Press the DELETE key.

Editing AutoShapes

Recall that the AutoShapes button on the Objects toolbar displays many different kinds of AutoShapes that you can use to create logos, graphics, banners, shapes, and other ornamental objects. You can apply fill effects, line/border styles, shadows, 3-D styles, and other special effects to AutoShapes.

Fill Effects

In Publisher, you can **fill**, or paint, the inside of any object with a color or with an effect. **Fill effects** include gradient colors, textures, patterns, pictures, and tints/shades. Fill effects can be applied to text boxes, shapes, and even WordArt objects in Publisher. Fill effects add subtle contrast and create an illusion of texture and depth.

Using a gradient fill draws attention and heightens interest. A **gradient** is a gradual progression of colors and shades, usually from one color to another color, or from one shade to another shade of the same color. Gradient fills create a sense of movement and add dimension to a publication, with patterns ranging from stars and swirls to arrows and three-dimensional abstractions.

A **texture** is a combination of color and patterns without gradual shading. Publisher provides 24 different textures from which you may choose.

Patterns include variations of repeating designs such as lines, stripes, checks, and bricks. Publisher uses the base color and a second color to create the pattern. When publications are destined for commercial printing, patterns usually are more expensive than tints and shades, because they increase the time it takes to image the file to film.

A **picture fill** is a special effect that inserts clip art or your own graphic to create a unique and personal shape. A picture fill gives the appearance of a picture that has been cropped to a specific shape, such as a star or circle.

A **tint** is a color that is a mixture of a base color and white. A **shade**, on the other hand, is a mixture of a base color and black. You use tints and shades to create a more sophisticated color scheme. Tints and shades are incremented in 10-percent intervals. For example, the first tint of red is nine parts red and one part white. Therefore, Publisher displays 10 tints and 10 shades of each basic color on the Tints sheet in the Fill Effects dialog box.

In the Hobby Express letterhead, you will use a circular shape with a picture fill, matching border, and shadow at the top of the publication. Later in the project you will fill a rectangle with a gradient.

To Insert and Position an AutoShape

The following steps insert and position an oval AutoShape in the publication. To create a circle, you press and hold the SHIFT key while dragging the oval.

1 On the Objects toolbar, click the AutoShapes button, point to Basic Shapes, and then click Oval in the list.

2 Move the mouse pointer into the publication, and then SHIFT+drag to create a circle approximately 1.75 inches by 1.75 inches, as shown in the status bar.

3 Drag the circle to a location in the upper-left corner of the publication. The circle will snap to the margin and ruler guides (Figure 4–33).

BTW

Choosing Shapes
Determining what shape to use with pictures is an important decision. If your picture is square, you can insert it into a circle, but you may lose the edges, or your picture may display distorted. If your picture is rectangular, however, an oval shape may be interesting and aesthetically pleasing. If you want to focus on the center, a star shape may help direct the viewer's attention.

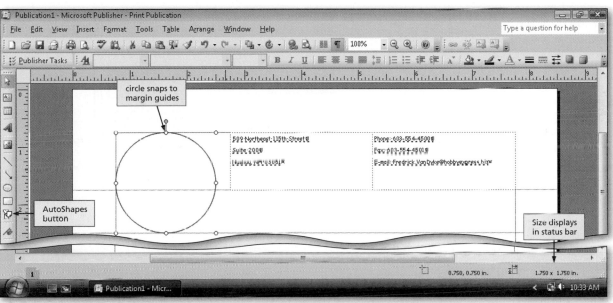

Figure 4–33

To Fill an AutoShape with a Picture

The following steps fill the circle with the previously saved picture.

1

• With the AutoShape still selected, click the Fill Color button arrow on the Standard toolbar to display its palette (Figure 4–34).

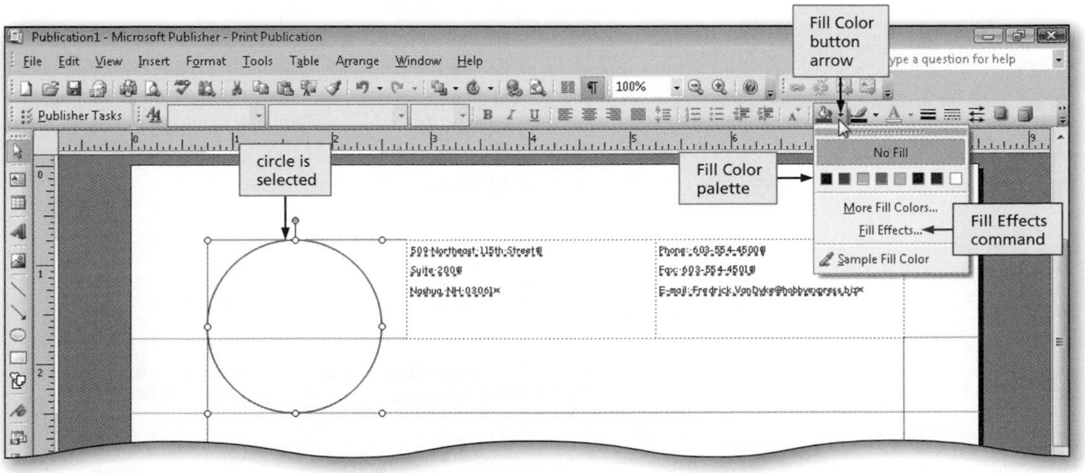

Figure 4–34

2

- Click Fill Effects to open the Fill Effects dialog box.

- Click the Picture tab to display the options for filling the shape with a picture (Figure 4-35).

Q&A

In addition to selecting a picture, what are the other available settings?

To maintain proportions and prevent distortion of a picture when it is inserted into a shape, makes sure the **'Lock picture aspect ratio' check box** displays a check mark. If you want the entire picture, regardless of any possible distortion, remove the check mark. The **'Rotate fill effect with shape' check box** commonly applies to nonsymmetrical shapes such as arrows or banners. For example, if the check box does not display a check mark, and you rotate the banner, a picture fill stays upright no matter how much the banner is rotated.

3

- With a USB flash drive connected to one of the computer's USB ports, click the Select Picture button to display the Select Picture dialog box.

- Navigate to the USB flash drive and select the Hobby Express Engine file (Figure 4–36).

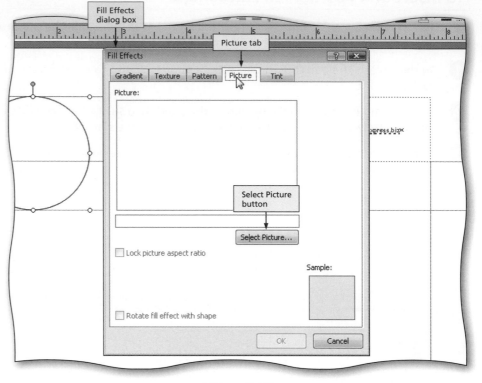

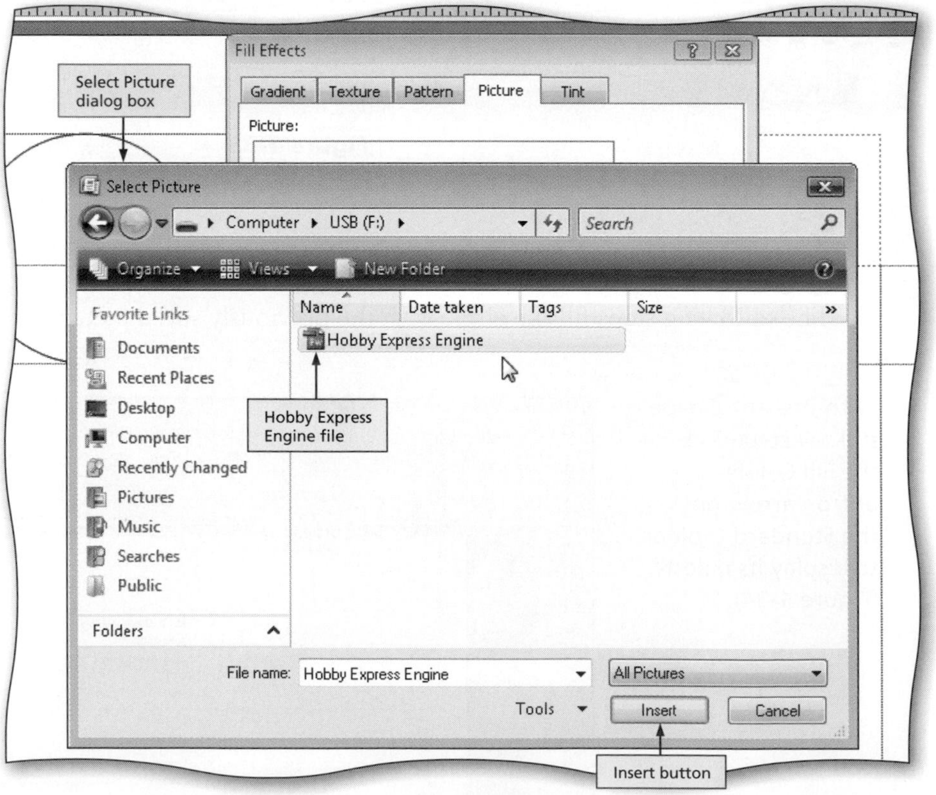

Figure 4–35

Figure 4–36

4

- Click the Insert button in the Select Picture dialog box to select the picture.

- Click the OK button in the Fill Effects dialog box to close it and insert the picture (Figure 4–37).

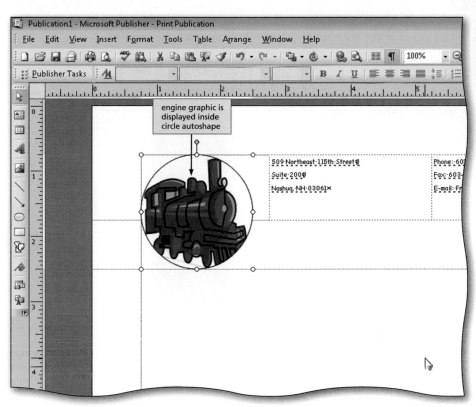

Figure 4–37

To Select a Line Color

The following steps choose a color for the border of the graphic. Publisher adds **line colors** to the edges of each shape. Black is the default color. The color can be changed or removed entirely. In the graphic, the line color will match the dark blue color in the engine graphic. A new feature of Publisher 2007 is the capability of selecting a color from anywhere in the page layout and adding it to the color scheme. You then can apply the new color to a font, line, or fill.

1

- With the graphic still selected, click the Line Color button arrow on the Formatting toolbar to display its palette (Figure 4–38).

Q&A

How can I remove a border?

Select the object, click the Line Color button and then click No Line.

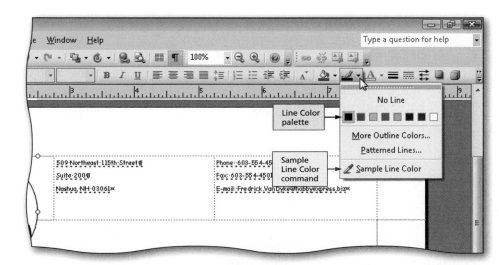

Figure 4–38

2

- Click the Sample Line Color command in the palette to select it.

- Move the mouse pointer to a location inside the graphic, and click the dark blue color in the graphic (Figure 4–39).

Q&A Why did my mouse pointer change to an eyedropper shape?

When a Publisher command samples a color, the mouse pointer displays an eyedropper as if it were picking up or suctioning the color from the display.

Other Ways

1. On Format menu, click AutoShape, click Colors and Lines tab, in Line area, click Color box arrow, click color

2. Right-click shape, click Format AutoShape on shortcut menu, click Colors and Lines tab, in Line area, click Color box arrow, click color

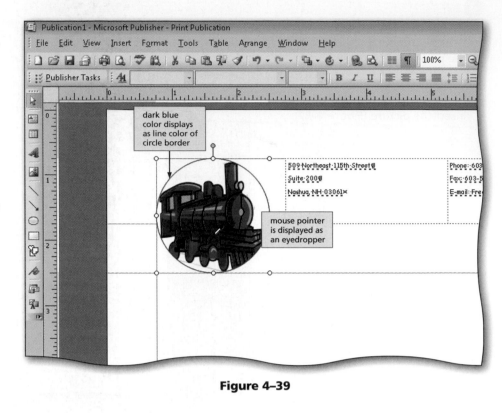

Figure 4–39

Line/Border Styles

The following steps choose a line/border style for the graphic. Line borders for graphics are measured in quarter- and half-inch increments. You also can choose no line, double-lines, and other styles using the **Line/Border button** on the Standard toolbar. For more variety, the **Dash Style button** offers borders such as dashed and dotted lines. If you are adding a border to a rectangle, text box, or the entire page, the **BorderArt button** in the Format AutoShape dialog box offers graphical borders, such as hearts, Christmas trees, or decorative squares and triangles.

To Select a Line/Border Style

In the following steps, you will edit the AutoShape to add a solid line from the Line/Border button list, with a weight of 3 points. Recall that a point is a physical measurement that is approximately equal to 1/72nd of an inch. A point is not always the same as a pixel. A **pixel**, short for picture element, is a single resolution unit on the display. Only if your monitor's resolution is set to 72 pixels per inch is a point the same as a pixel.

1

- With the graphic still selected, click the Line/Border Style button on the Formatting toolbar to display its palette (Figure 4–40).

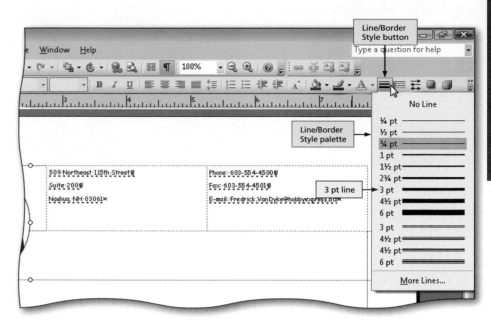

Figure 4–40

2

- Click 3 pt in the list to select a border style (Figure 4–41).

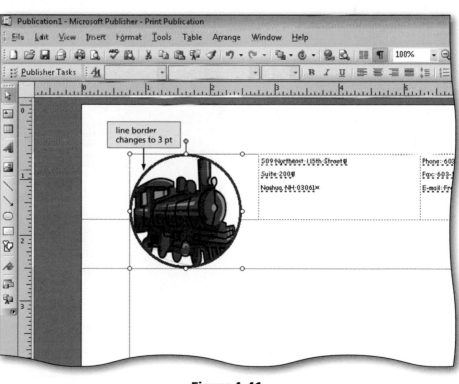

Figure 4–41

Other Ways
1. On Picture toolbar click Line/Border Style button

Shadows

A **shadow** is a light-colored extension of an object's border, on one or more sides, to simulate a direction of light at various angles. Shadows can be applied to shapes, text boxes, and even text. You can add or remove a shadow, change the direction of a shadow, change the distance of the shadow from the object, or change the color of the shadow.

To Add a Shadow

The following steps add a shadow on the upper-left corner of the Hobby Express graphic.

1

• With the graphic still selected, click the Shadow Style button on the Formatting toolbar to display its list (Figure 4–42).

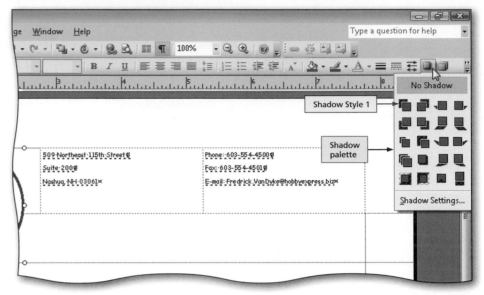

Figure 4–42

2

• Click Shadow Style 1 to select the style (Figure 4–43).

Q&A

Why is the shadow blue?

Publisher uses Accent 4 from the color scheme as the default color for shadows. You can change the shadow to a different color by clicking the Shadow button again and then clicking Shadow Settings in the list. The resulting Shadow Settings toolbar displays a Shadow Color button.

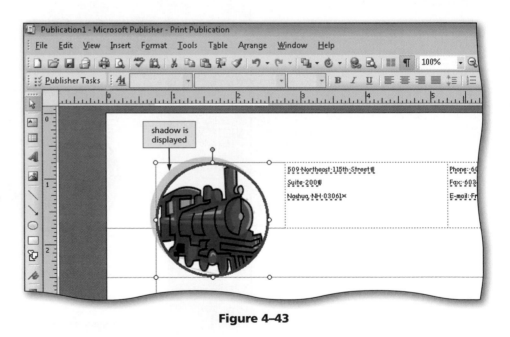

Figure 4–43

Creating the Rectangle Graphic

A second AutoShape in the Hobby Express Newsletter is a rectangle with a gradient fill and text.

To Create a Gradient Fill Effect

The following steps show how to draw a rectangle and fill it with a gradient fill effect.

1

- Click the AutoShapes button on the Objects toolbar, point to Basic Shapes, and then click the Rectangle shape.

- In the publication, drag a rectangle that fills the area between the two ruler guides from the left to the right margin. The rectangle will cover part of the graphic (Figure 4–44).

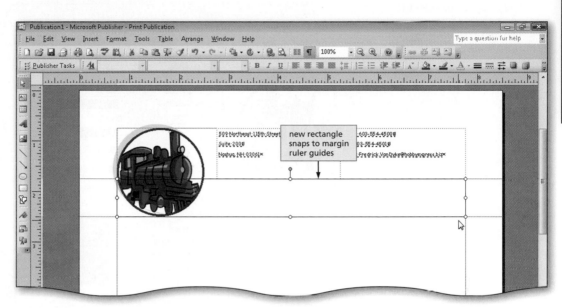

Figure 4–44

2

- With the rectangle still selected, click the Fill Color button arrow on the Formatting toolbar, and then click Fill Effects to display the Fill Effects dialog box.

- If necessary, click the Gradient tab.

Experiment

- In the Colors area, click One color to view the previews of single-color gradients from dark to light of the same color. Click Preset and then click the Preset colors box arrow, choosing different predefined gradients, such as Horizon, Calm Water, and Rainbow.

- In the Colors area, click Two colors.

- Click the Color 1 box arrow to display its list (Figure 4–45).

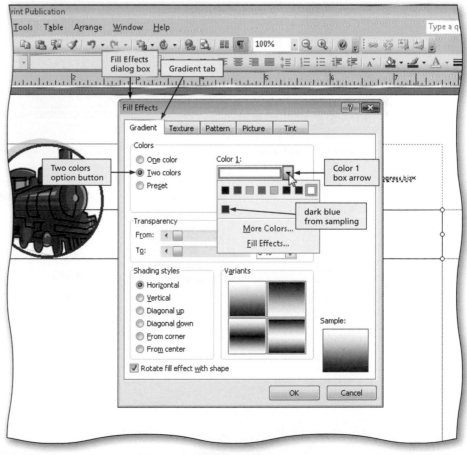

Figure 4–45

3

- Click the dark blue color that was added to the color scheme earlier in the chapter to select it.

- Click the Color 2 box arrow (Figure 4–46).

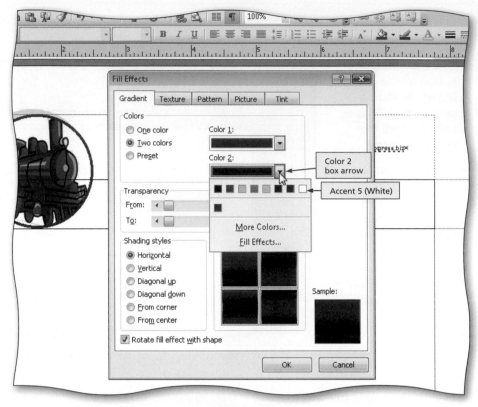

Figure 4–46

4

- Click Accent 5 (White).

🔍 **Experiment**

- In the Shading styles area, click each of the style option buttons one at a time. Look at the variant previews.

- In the Shading styles area, click Vertical to select a vertical gradient.

- In the Variants area, click the upper-left variant to select a gradient going from left to right, blue to white (Figure 4–47).

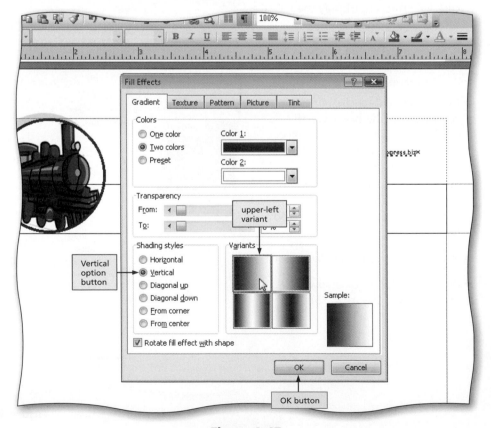

Figure 4–47

5
• Click the OK button
(Figure 4–48).

Q&A

What other elements can I fill with effects?

You can fill text boxes, master pages, Web page backgrounds, tables, pictures, and WordArt with gradients, texture, patterns, pictures, or tints.

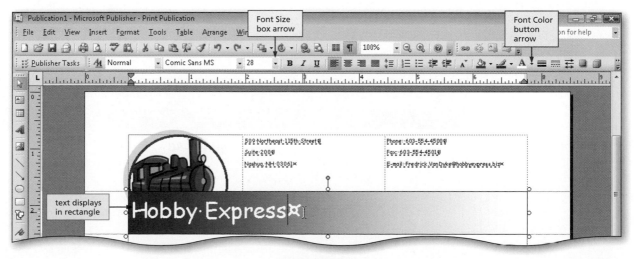

Figure 4–48

Other Ways		
1. Double-click rectangle, click Colors and Lines tab, choose settings	2. On Format menu, click AutoShape, click Colors and Lines tab, choose settings	3. Right-click rectangle, click Format AutoShape, click Colors and Lines tab, choose settings

To Add Text to an AutoShape

The following steps add text to the AutoShape using the Accent 5 (White) color.

1 Right-click the rectangle AutoShape to display its shortcut menu.

2 Click Add Text to position the cursor inside the AutoShape.

3 Click the Font Size box arrow, and then click 28 in the list.

4 Click the Font Color button arrow, and then click Accent 5 (White) in the list to select the font color.

5 Type Hobby Express to enter the text (Figure 4–49).

BTW

Color Palettes
If your color palette contains fewer colors than shown in this book, your system may be using a different color palette setting. The figures in this book were created using Highest Color (32 bit). To check your color palette setting, return to the Windows Vista desktop, right-click the desktop, click Personalize on the shortcut menu, click the Display Settings link, and locate the Colors box.

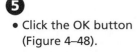

Figure 4–49

Changing the Order

The **Order command** will be used to display the rectangle behind the first graphic. In Publisher, **ordering**, or **layering**, means to make purposeful decisions on how objects layer on top of each other. The layer order, or z-order, of the stack is determined by the order in which the objects were created. Objects that can be reordered include AutoShapes, tables, text boxes, and clip art.

To change the order of layering, you must select the object and then choose to bring it either forward, backward, to the front, or to the back.

To Change the Order

The following steps move the rectangle to the back.

1

- Right-click the rectangle to display its shortcut menu.

- Point to Order to display the Order submenu (Figure 4–50).

Q&A

What if I need to reorder an object that is completely hidden and I cannot select it?

If the object is hidden, select any object and then press the TAB key or SHIFT+TAB repeatedly until the object that you want is selected.

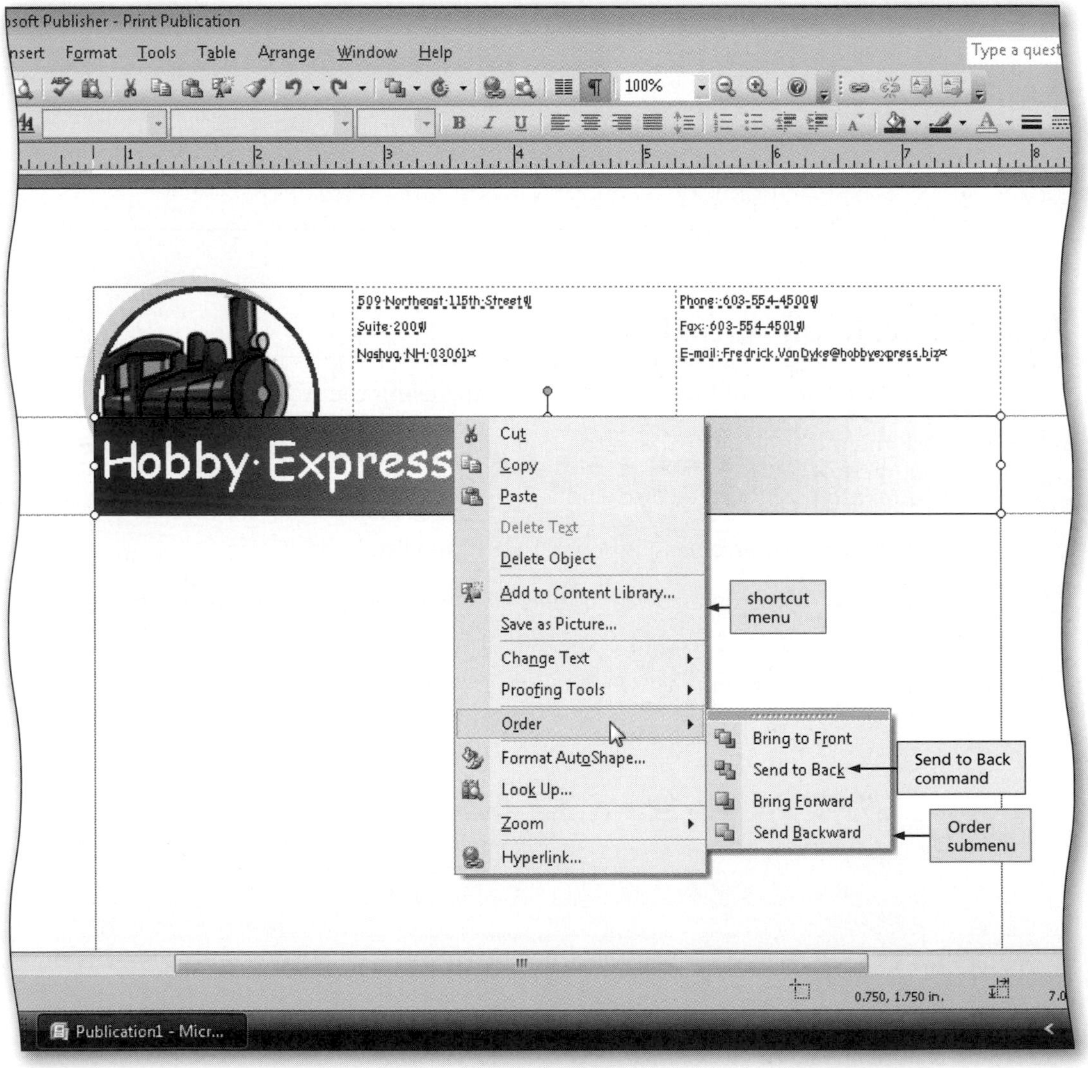

Figure 4–50

❷

🔍 **Experiment**

- Try clicking each of the ordering options and then look in the page layout to see what happens.

- On the Order submenu, click Send to Back to move the object behind other objects, in this case the graphic of the engine (Figure 4–51).

Q&A

Why did the text move over?

By default the picture wrapping style is square, so even text within another shape, such as the rectangle, wrapped around the train engine graphic.

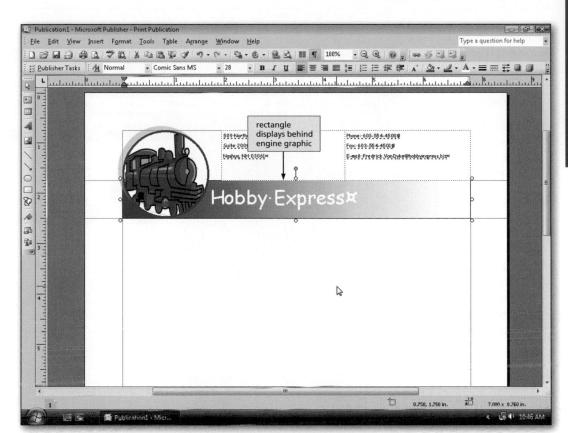

Figure 4–51

Using an Automatic Date

Publisher and other Microsoft Office applications can access your system's stored date and time. You then can retrieve the current date and/or time and display it in a variety of formats. Additionally, you can choose either to update the date and time automatically each time the file is accessed or keep a static date and time.

Inserting a Date in the Letterhead

To make the letterhead more functional for the company, you will insert a large text box in which users can type their text. The date appears at the top of most letters. Using the Date and Time dialog box, the steps on the next page show how to insert a date that will be current whenever the user opens the letterhead to prepare a new letter.

To Insert an Automatic Date

①

- Zoom to Whole Page and deselect the rectangle AutoShape.

- Click the Text Box button on the Objects toolbar to select the tool.

- Drag a rectangle that begins at the left margin, just below the second ruler guide, and continues to the right margin and down to the tag line text box to create a large text box in the letterhead (Figure 4–52).

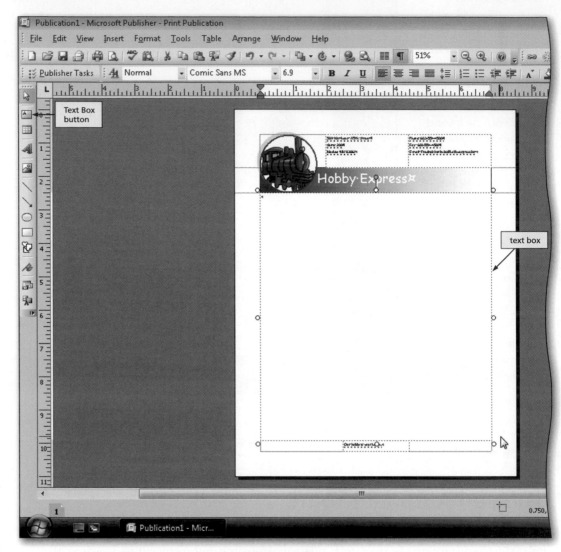

Figure 4–52

②

- Press the F9 key to zoom the text box to 100%.

- Click the Font box arrow, and click Times New Roman in the Font list.

- Click the Font Size box arrow, and click 12 in the Font Size list.

- Press the ENTER key to create a blank line.

- Click Insert on the menu bar to display the Insert menu (Figure 4–53).

Q&A

Why am I setting the font before I type?

If you set the font before typing in a text box, the font will apply to all future text in the box. It is easier to set it before than to select all of the text later and then set the font.

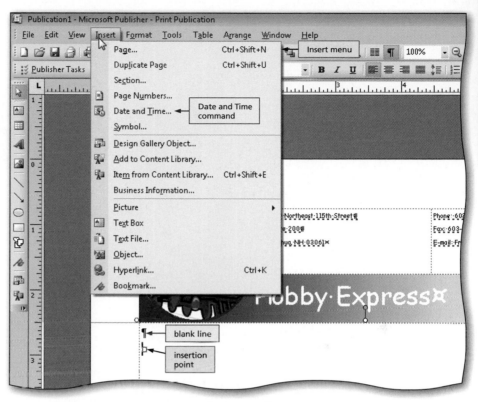

Figure 4–53

③

- Click Date and Time to display the Date and Time dialog box.

Experiment

- Scroll in the list of Available formats to view the various ways that Publisher can insert the date or time.

- Click the third format in the Available formats list to select it.

- Click the Update automatically check box so that it displays a check mark (Figure 4–54).

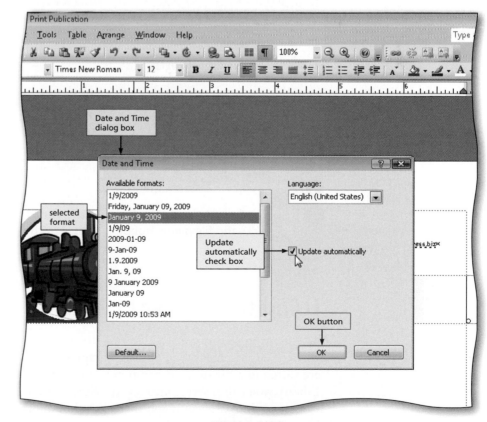

Figure 4–54

4

- Click the OK button to close the dialog box.

- Press the ENTER key twice to create a blank line after the date (Figure 4–55).

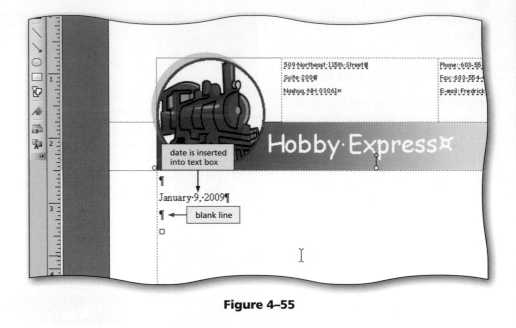

Figure 4–55

Saving the Letterhead

The Hobby Express letterhead is complete. The following steps save the letterhead.

Note: If you are using Windows XP, see Appendix F for alternate steps.

To Save the Letterhead

1 With a USB flash drive connected to one of the computer's USB ports, click the Save button on the Standard toolbar.

2 Type Hobby Express Letterhead in the File name text box to change the file name. Do not press the ENTER key.

3 Navigate to your USB flash drive.

4 Click the Save button in the Save As dialog box to save the publication on the USB flash drive with the file name, Hobby Express Letterhead.

Using the Content Library

The **Content Library** is a single location where you can store Publisher objects that you wish to reuse, such as logos, stories, graphics, shapes, or other kinds of media. The objects are stored in a file on your computer system. Once an object is added to the Content Library, you can insert it into any publication on that system. To add an object to the Content Library, select it and then click the Add to Content Library command on the Insert menu. You then can give your object a name, specify the object type, and store it within a category. The Content Library task pane allows you to create and manage up to 64 categories of content, select objects by date, and preview, delete, and reorder objects.

To Add to the Content Library

The following steps add the engine graphic to the Content Library. Later in the chapter you will insert the engine graphic into another publication.

1
- Right-click the engine graphic to display the shortcut menu (Figure 4–56).

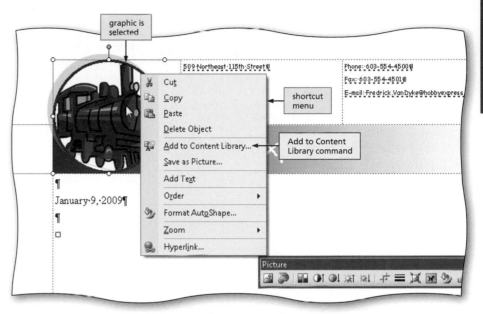

Figure 4–56

2
- Click Add to Content Library to display the Add Item to Content Library dialog box.

- Click the Title box and then press CTRL+A to select the current title. Type Hobby Express Graphic to replace the text.

- In the Categories area, click Business (Figure 4–57).

Q&A What does the Edit Categories button do?

The Edit Categories button displays a dialog box where you can name and create more categories, delete categories, and change the order in which the categories display.

Figure 4–57

3
- Click the OK button to close the Add Item to Content Library dialog box.

- Close the Content Library task pane.

Other Ways

1. On Insert menu, click Add to Content Library
2. In Content Library task pane, click Add selected items to Content Library

To Close a Publication Without Quitting Publisher

The following step closes the letterhead file without quitting Publisher to again display the catalog.

1

- Click File on the menu bar, and then click Close to close the publication without quitting Publisher. If Publisher asks you to save the publication again, click the No button (Figure 4–58).

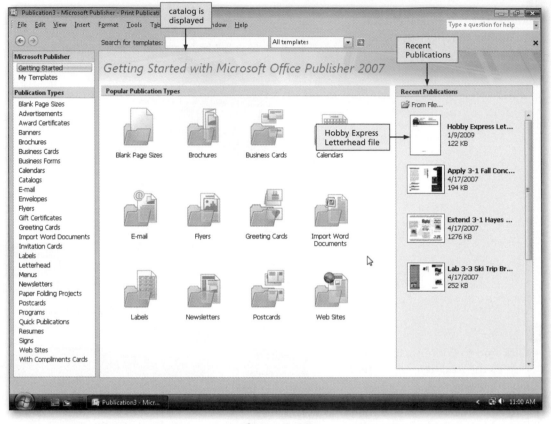

Figure 4–58

Other Ways

1. Press CTRL+F4

Read-Only Files

Once a generic letterhead is created, it is a good idea to change the file's attribute to read-only. That way, users will be forced to save the publication with a new file name when they open the file, keeping the original letterhead intact for the next user. If you wanted to assign the read-only attribute to a file, you would close the file and then perform the following steps.

TO SET A FILE TO READ-ONLY

1. In any Windows Explorer window, right-click the file icon. On the shortcut menu, click Properties to display the Properties dialog box.

2. If necessary, click the General tab. Place a check mark in the Read-only check box.

3. Click the OK button.

To Open a Recent Publication

The following steps open the letterhead file from the Recent Publications list in the Publisher catalog.

1 With the Publisher Catalog displayed (Figure 4–58), click the Hobby Express Letterhead file in the list of Recent Publications to open the file.

2 If the task pane is displayed, click the Close button in the task pane title bar.

To Use the Letterhead

The following steps enter text in the letterhead.

1 Click below the date in the large text box to position the cursor. Zoom to 100%.

2 Type Dear Part-Time Employees, to begin the letter.

3 Press the ENTER key twice to create a blank line in the letter.

4 Type Below is next week's work schedule. Please let me know of any problems. and then press the ENTER key twice.

5 Type Thank you, and then press the ENTER key four times.

6 Type Fredrick Van Dyke and then press the ENTER key.

7 Type Manager to complete the letter (Figure 4–59).

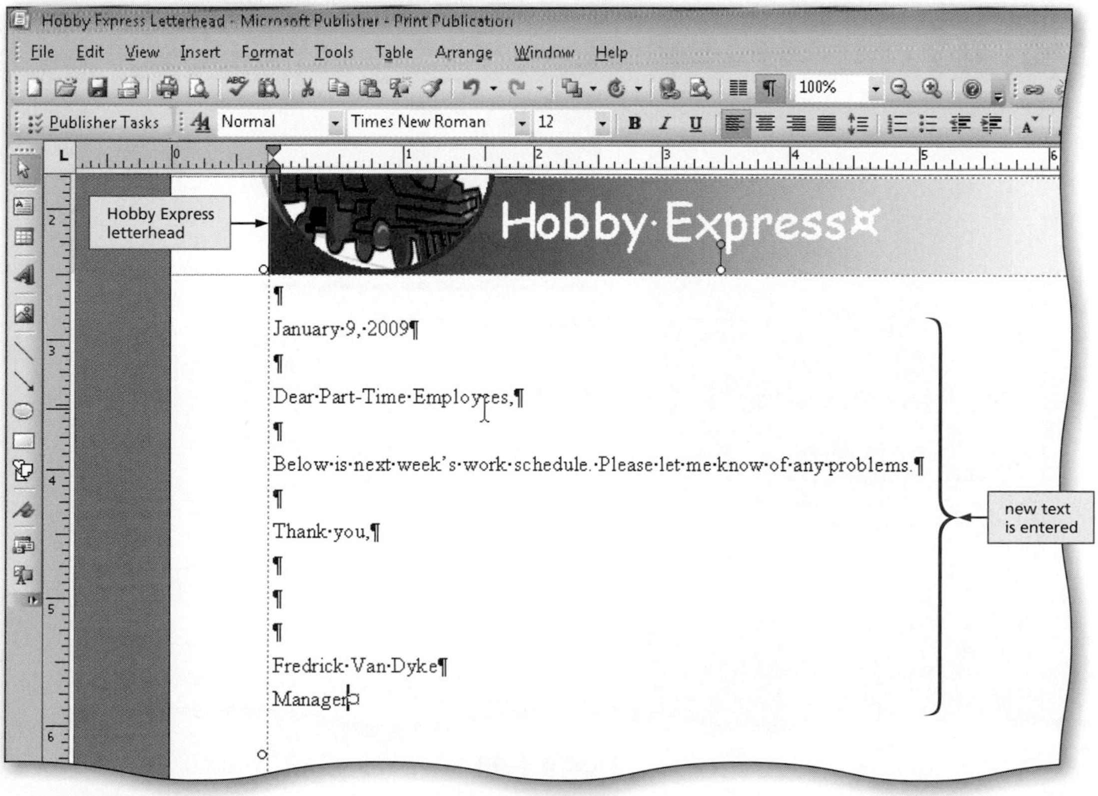

Figure 4–59

Using Tables

A Publisher **table** is a collection of rows and columns. The intersection of a row and column is called a **cell**. Cells can be filled with text or graphical data. Within a table, you easily can rearrange rows and columns, change column widths and row heights, and insert diagonal lines. You can format the cells to give the table a professional appearance. You also can edit the inner grid lines and outer border of a table. For these reasons, many Publisher users create tables rather than using large text boxes with tabbed columns. Tables allow you to input data in columns as you would for a schedule, price list, resume, or table of contents.

Creating Tables

The Hobby Express store will use a table in a letter to part-time employees. You will format it using the Create Table dialog box. The first step is to draw an empty table in a publication, using the **Insert Table button** on the Objects toolbar and then choosing the number of rows and columns and a table style.

BTW

Using the Workspace
Placing objects in the workspace is an easy way to move them from one page to the next. Simply drag the object into the blank scratch area of the workspace, click the new page icon in the Page Navigation control, and then drag the object onto the new page. Publisher allows you to save a publication with objects still in the scratch area of the workspace. Be sure to remove them, however, to avoid confusion before submitting a file to a commercial printer.

To Create a Table

The following steps create a table.

- If necessary, zoom to Whole Page and deselect the text box.

- Click the Insert Table button on the Objects toolbar to select it.

- Move the mouse pointer into the publication below the closing of the letter, and then drag to create a rectangle approximately 6 inches by 3 inches. Do not release the mouse button (Figure 4–60).

Q&A

Why do I have to hold the mouse button down?

Holding the mouse button down allows you to see the table and adjust the size if necessary before formatting it. As soon as you release the mouse button, the Create Table dialog box is displayed.

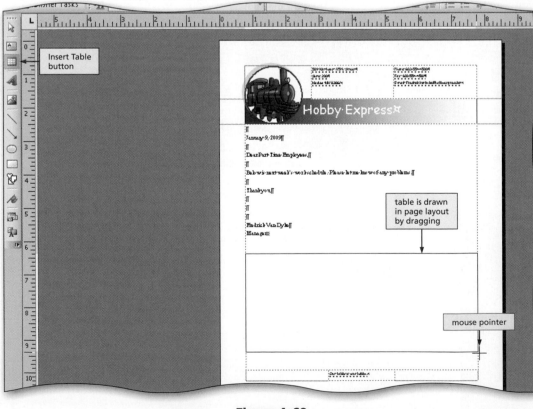

Figure 4–60

2

- Release the mouse button to display the Create Table dialog box.

- Type 8 in the Number of rows box. Press the TAB key.

- Type 4 in the Number of columns box.

🔍 **Experiment**

- Click on several of the formats in the Table format list, looking at the resulting sample and reading about the suggested purpose.

- Scroll as necessary in the Table format list, and then click List with Title 3 to select the format (Figure 4–61).

3

- Click the OK button. If Publisher displays a dialog box asking if you want to resize the table, click the Yes button.

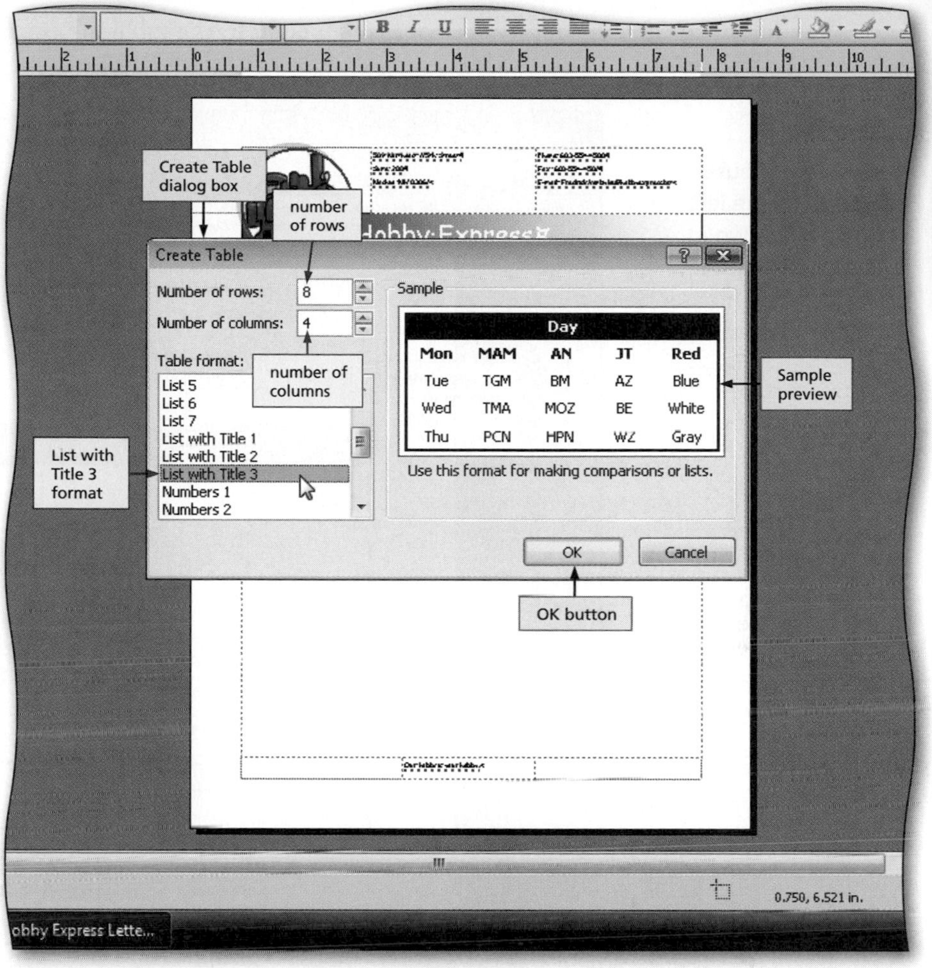

Figure 4–61

Other Ways

1. On Table menu, point to Insert, click Table

Selecting Within Tables

To customize a table, or data within a table, first you must select the cell(s) and then apply the appropriate formats. Table 4–3 describes techniques to select items in a table.

Table 4–3 Selecting Items in a Table	
Items To Select	**Action**
Cell	Triple-click the cell or drag through the text.
Column	Point to the top of the column. When the mouse pointer becomes a downward pointing arrow, click.
Contiguous cells, rows, or columns	Drag through the cells, rows, or columns.
Deselect	Click outside of the table.
Entire table	On the Table menu, click Select, and then click Table.
Row	Point to the left of the row. When the mouse pointer becomes a right block arrow, click.
Text in next cell	Press the TAB key.
Text in previous cell	Press the SHIFT+TAB keys.

To Select Portions of a Table

The following steps select rows two through eight in the table in preparation for further formatting.

1

- Zoom to 100%.
- Move the mouse pointer to the left side of row two in the table to display the selection mouse pointer (Figure 4–62).

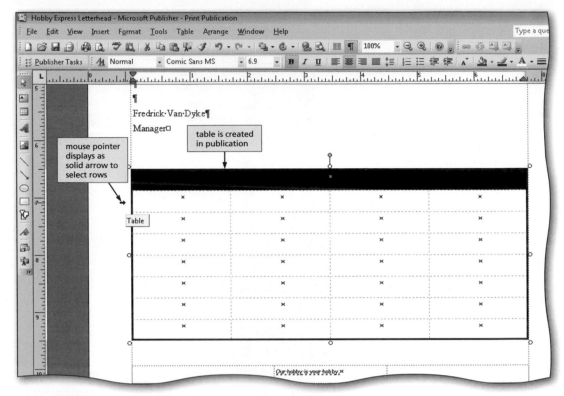

Figure 4–62

2

- Drag down the left side of the table to select rows two through eight (Figure 4–63).

Figure 4–63

Other Ways
1. On Table menu, point to Select, click Row

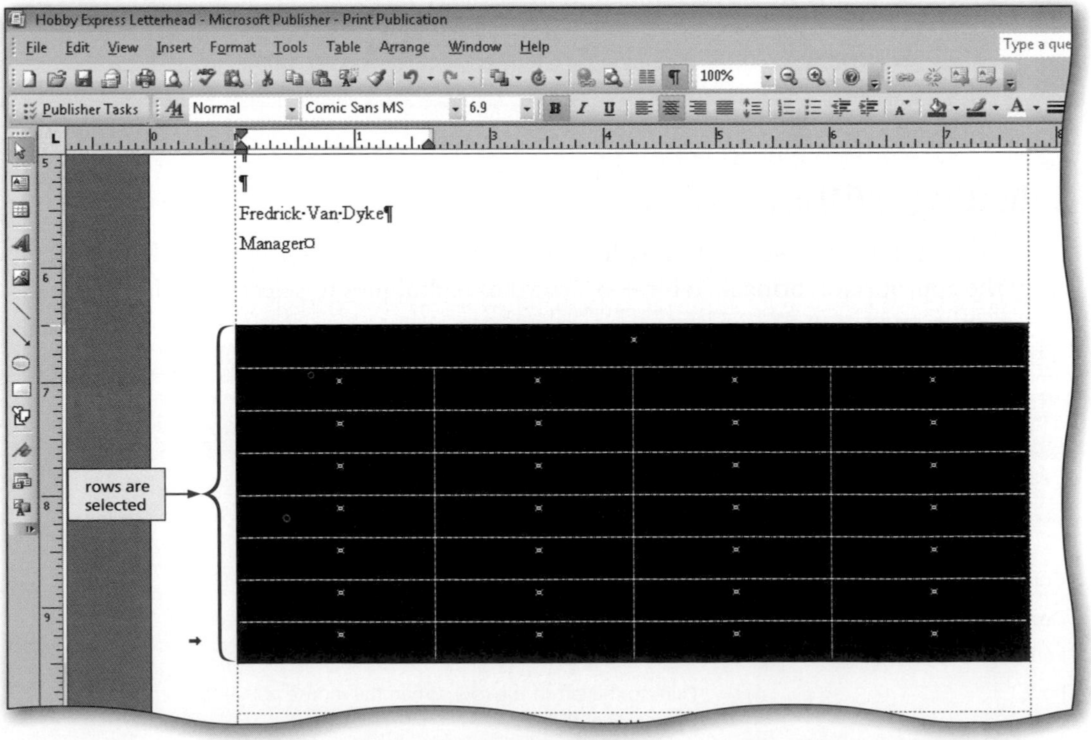

Formatting Tables

Some of the formats in the Table Formats list include tables that display gray gridlines on the screen, but not on the hard copy or printed page. If you want gridlines to display on the printed copy, you must format the table.

To Format the Table

The following steps add printable gridlines to rows two through eight in the table.

1

- Right-click the selected cells to display the shortcut menu (Figure 4–64).

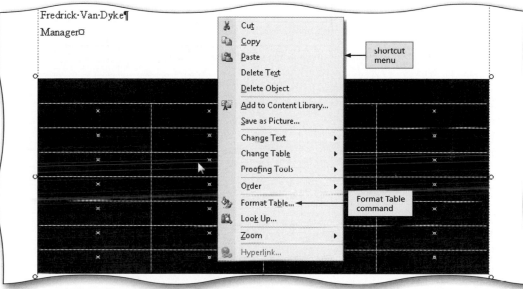

Figure 4–64

2

- Click Format Table to display the Format Table dialog box. If necessary, click the Colors and Lines tab.

🔍 **Experiment**

- Click the different preset buttons and look to see how the preview changes. Notice that buttons currently applied to the preview turn blue.

- In the Presets area, click the third preset button to display all borders (Figure 4–65).

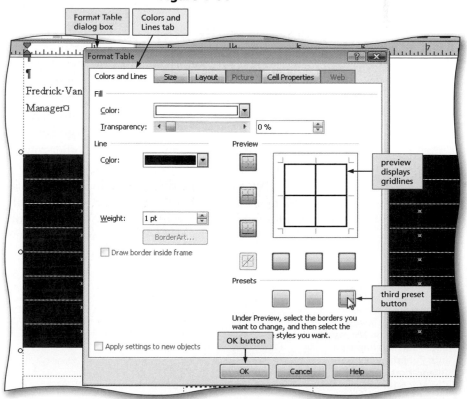

Figure 4–65

③

- Click the OK button.

- Deselect the table to view the darkened grid lines (Figure 4–66).

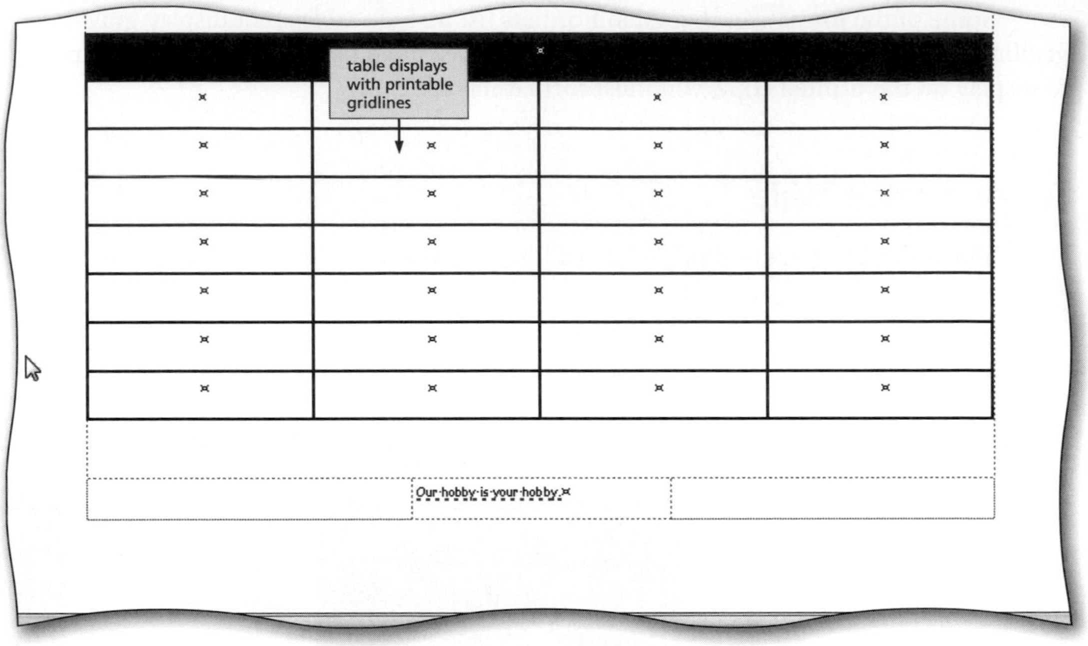

Q&A

What other formatting can I do to tables?

As you have seen in other formatting dialog boxes, you can change the fill and line color of most objects. This applies to tables as well. You also can change the weight of the lines that form the grid and borders of the table. On other tab sheets in the Format Table dialog box, you can adjust the size, location, text wrapping, alignment, and margins.

Figure 4–66

Other Ways

1. On Format menu, click Table, edit selections, click OK button

2. On Formatting toolbar, click Line/Border Style button, click More Lines, edit selections, click OK button

Merge Cells and Cell Diagonals

When you insert a table, Publisher creates evenly spaced columns in the table, with some simple formatting for table, row, and column headings in some cases. The List with Title 3 format applies a black background with white text to the first row. The first row is an example of a merged cell, which means that cells have been merged to form one, larger text box to hold data. To manually **merge cells**, select contiguous cells and then click Merge Cells on the Table menu. The other rows are formatted with a white background and black text.

Another formatting change that you can make to a cell is to add a cell diagonal. A **cell diagonal** is a line that splits the cell diagonally, creating two triangular text boxes. Commonly used for split headings or multiple entries per cell, the cell diagonal can be slanted from either corner.

BTW

Integrating Excel
If you already have a table created in Microsoft Excel, you can import it into Publisher. See the Integration Feature after Chapter 6 for details about embedding and linking Excel worksheets.

To Create a Cell Diagonal

The following steps create a cell diagonal for a split heading in the table.

1

- Click the first cell in the second row to position the cursor.

- Click Table on the menu bar to display the Table menu (Figure 4–67).

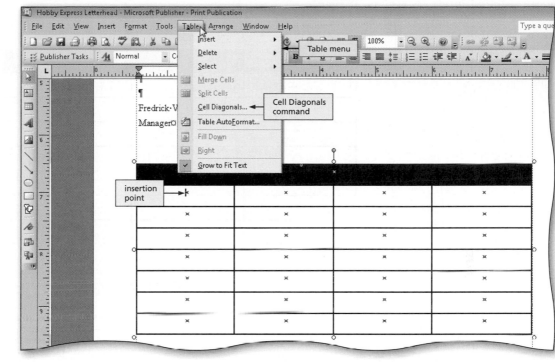

Figure 4–67

2

- Click Cell Diagonals to display the Cell Diagonals dialog box.

- Click Divide down (Figure 4–68).

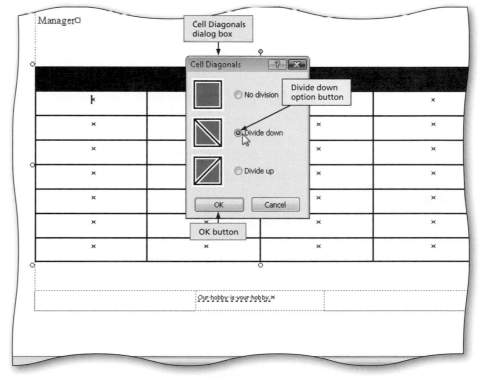

Figure 4–68

3

- Click the OK button to close the Cell Diagonals dialog box.

- Deselect the cell (Figure 4–69).

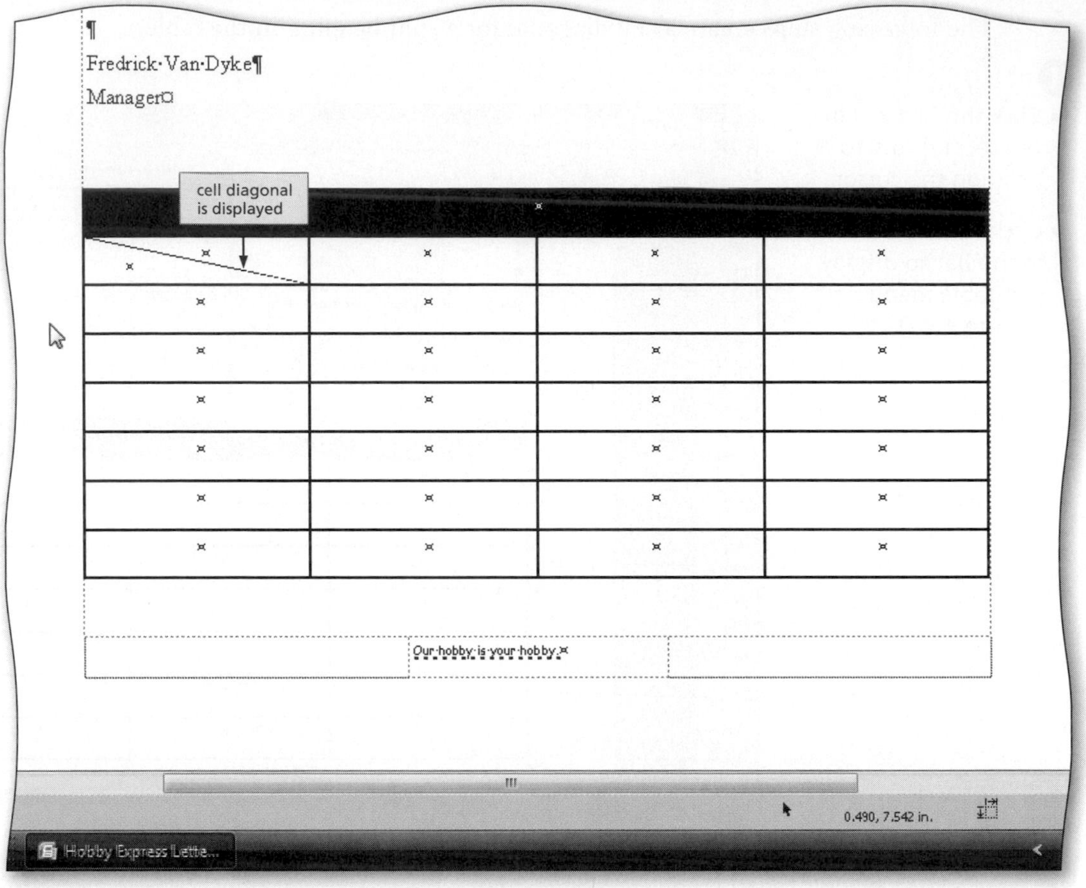

Figure 4–69

BTW

Resizing Tables
You can resize tables, rows, and columns in Publisher. To resize the entire table, drag a corner sizing handle. To resize a row or column, point to a **gridline**, or cell border, and then SHIFT+drag. Dragging a cell border without using the SHIFT key resizes the single row or column, but moves all other rows and columns, as well.

Entering Data

Typing data into a table is similar to typing in any text box; however, efficiently navigating cells is an important skill when entering data into a table. To advance from one cell to the next, press the TAB key or the RIGHT ARROW key. To move to the previous cell, press SHIFT+TAB or the LEFT ARROW key. To advance from one row to the next, press the DOWN ARROW key; do not press the ENTER key. The ENTER key is used to begin new paragraphs within a cell. To advance from one row to the next, press the DOWN ARROW key.

To Enter Data into a Table

The following steps enter the data into the table.

1

- Zoom to 125%.

- Click the cell in the top row of the table to position the cursor in the cell.

- Type `Part-Time Employee Schedule` and then press the ENTER key.

- Type `January 12-17, 2009` to complete the cell.

- Press the TAB key to move to the next cell (Figure 4–70).

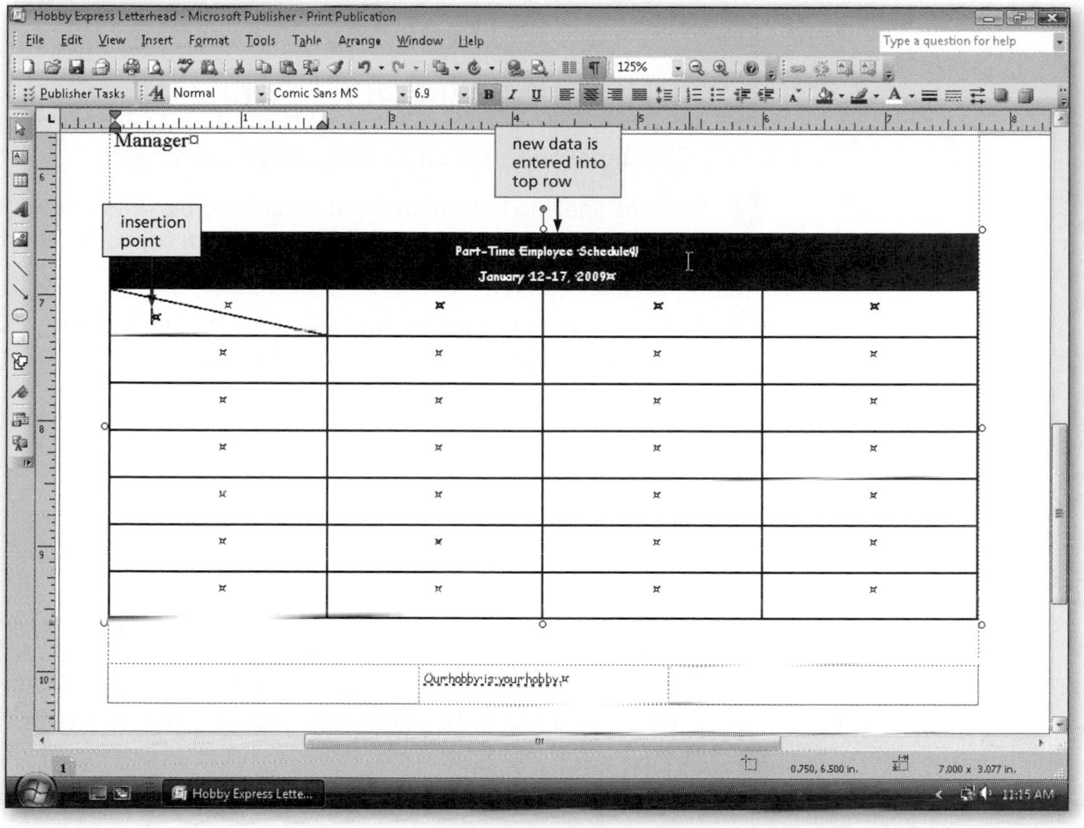

Figure 4–70

2

- Type `Day` and then press the TAB key. Type `Time` to complete the cell with the cell diagonal.

- Continue to press the TAB key and enter the data shown in Figure 4–71.

- If necessary, select the second row in the table and then click the Bold button to remove the bold formatting.

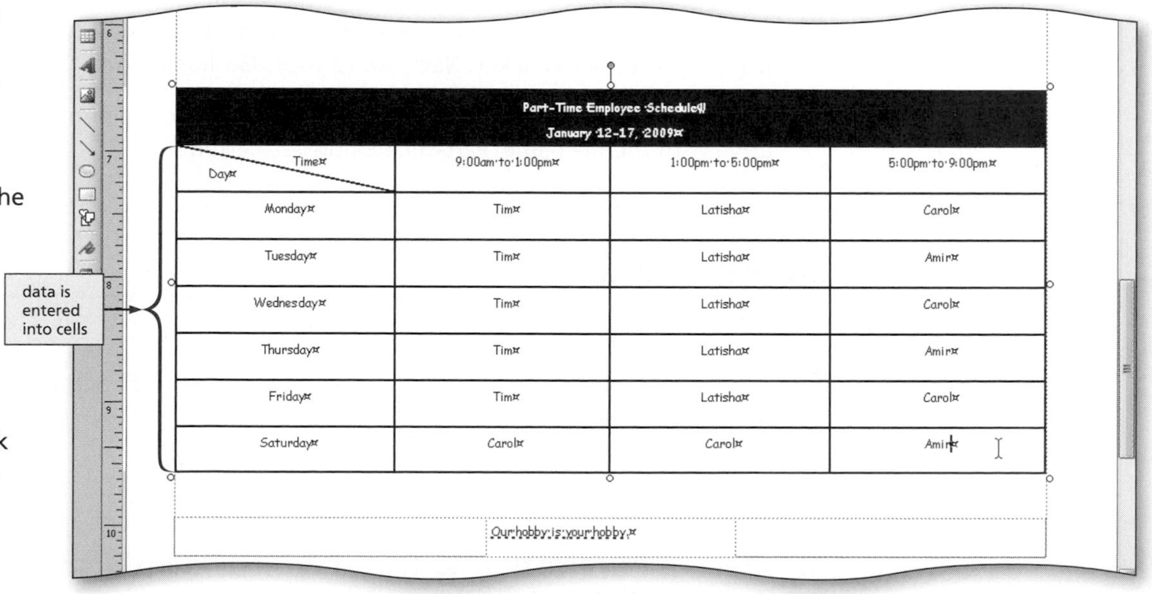

Figure 4–71

Checking the Publication for Errors

Even if you only have used business information components in your publication, you should run the spell checking feature and design checker before saving the publication. And if you have created a letter or table in the publication, the spell checking feature will help confirm that you have typed everything correctly.

To Check the Publication for Errors

The following steps check the publication for errors.

1 Click the Spelling button on the Standard toolbar. If Publisher flags any words, fix or ignore them as appropriate. If Publisher asks to check the entire document, click the Yes button.

2 Click Tools on the menu bar, and then click Design Checker. Ignore any messages about extra space, empty text boxes, or picture resolution. If the Design Checker identifies any other errors, fix them as necessary.

3 Close the Design Checker task pane.

Saving the Letter

The letter to the part-time employees is complete. You will use the Save As command in order to avoid overwriting the reusable letterhead file. The following steps save the letterhead with the name Part-Time Employee Letter.

To Save the Letter

1 With a USB flash drive connected to one of the computer's USB ports, click the Save As on the File menu.

2 Type `Part-Time Employee Letter` in the File name text box to change the file name. Do not press the ENTER key. Navigate to your USB flash drive.

3 Click the Save button in the Save As dialog box to save the publication on the USB flash drive with the file name, Part-Time Employee Letter.

To Print the Letter

The following steps print the letter file.

1 Ready the printer according to the printer instructions, and insert paper. With the publication displaying in the workspace, click File on the menu bar and then click Print. Click the Print button.

To Close a Publication without Quitting Publisher

The following step closes the letter file without quitting Publisher, to again display the catalog.

 Click File on the menu bar and then click Close.

Business Cards

Another way companies are saving money on publishing costs is by designing their own business cards. A **business card** is a small publication, 3½ by 2 inches, printed on heavy stock paper. It usually contains the name, title, business, and address information for an employee as well as a logo, distinguishing graphic, or color to draw attention to the card. Many employees want their telephone, pager, and fax numbers on their business cards in addition to their e-mail and Web page addresses, so that colleagues and customers can reach them quickly.

Business cards can be saved as files to send to commercial printers or printed by desktop color printers on special perforated paper.

The Business Card Template

Because the business information set contains information about the Hobby Express company, using a business card template is the quickest way to create a business card. Not only does the template set the size and shape of a typical business card, it also presets page and printing options for the easiest production.

The next sequence of steps uses the New Publication task pane to produce a business card for the owner at the Hobby Express company. The created template automatically uses information from the business information set edited earlier in this project. You will insert the engine graphic from the Content Library.

To Create a Business Card

1 With the catalog still displayed, click Business Cards in the list.

2 Scroll down to Classic Designs, and then click the Offset preview.

3 Select the Parrot color scheme and the Casual font scheme.

4 Click the Create button.

5 Close the task pane (Figure 4–72).

6 Right-click the phone, fax, and e-mail text box. Point to Change Text, point to AutoFit Text, and then click Best Fit.

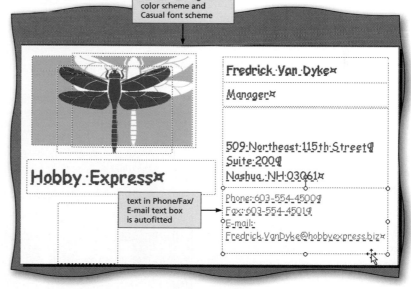

Figure 4–72

Editing the Business Card

The Offset template uses information from the primary business information set, placing typical business card components in appropriate places in the publication. Choosing a different business information set and editing the layout further customizes the business card. The term **layout** refers to both the process and the result of planning and arranging objects in a publication. Sending objects behind other objects, layering, and aligning objects are part of editing the layout.

The step sequence on the next page selects the Hobby Express information set, if it is not already selected.

To Select a Different Business Information Set

1 Click Edit on the menu bar, and then click Business Information.

2 When the Business Information dialog box is displayed, click the 'Select a Business Information set' box arrow, and then click Hobby Express in the list.

3 Click the Update Publication button.

Using the Select Objects Button

The **Select Objects button** is the default button in the Objects toolbar and is used to select, move, and group objects in the workspace. With the Select Objects button, to select an object you click its boundary. To move an object, you drag its boundary. To select multiple objects, you can SHIFT+click each object. Or, if the objects are close together with no object in between, you simply can drag around them.

If you want to keep the selected objects grouped together, you can group them by clicking the Group Objects button. Publisher displays the **Group Objects button** automatically, when multiple objects are selected. By clicking the button, the objects become a group that stays together for purposes such as cutting, pasting, moving, and formatting. A grouped object displays an Ungroup Objects button to remove, if necessary, the grouping feature.

In the Hobby Express business card, you will select the graphic objects by dragging around them, and then delete them in preparation for inserting the engine graphic.

To Select Multiple Objects

The following step selects multiple objects.

1

• With the Select Objects button selected in the Objects toolbar, drag around the colored shapes and graphic in the upper-left corner of the business card to select them (Figure 4–73).

Q&A How do I know where to drag?

Start dragging outside the business card, in the work space. As you drag, a rectangular boundary line will display. Drag down and to the right until the boundary displays clearly around all of the objects that you want to include in the group. When you release the mouse, the objects are displayed with selection boundaries.

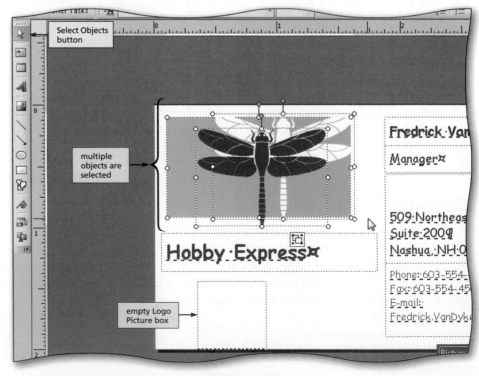

Figure 4–73

To Delete Multiple Objects

The following steps delete multiple objects.

1 With the multiple objects selected, press the DELETE key to delete the objects.

2 Select the empty Logo Picture box, and then press the DELETE key to delete the object.

To Insert from the Content Library

The following steps insert the engine graphic from the Content Library into the business card.

1

- Click Insert on the menu to display the Insert menu (Figure 4–74).

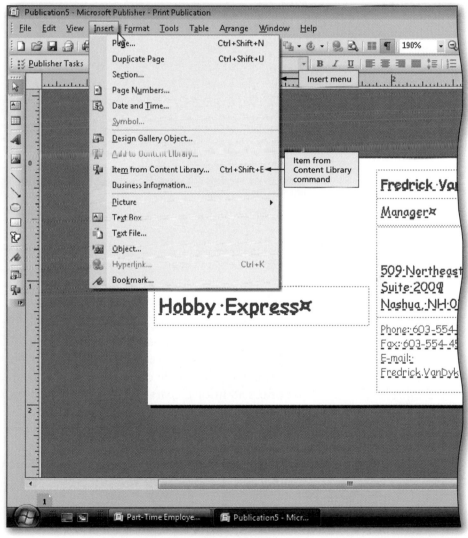

Figure 4–74

2

- Click Item from Content Library to display the Content Library task pane.

🔍 **Experiment**

- Click the Category box arrow to view the current categories of content. Click the Type box arrow and scroll to view the available types of objects.

- Double-click the engine graphic in the list to insert a copy into the publication (Figure 4–75).

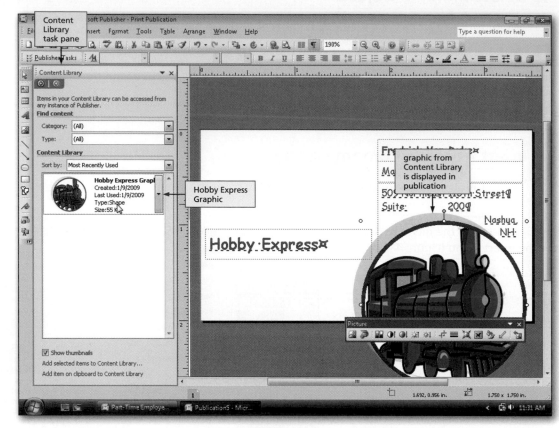

Figure 4–75

Other Ways

1. Press CTRL+SHIFT+E
2. On Objects toolbar, click Item from Content Library button

Using the Measurement Toolbar

To place objects precisely, rather than estimate by dragging and resizing, you use the Measurement toolbar to enter the exact values for width, height, left edge, and top of the object. The **Measurement toolbar** not only sets the location and size of an object, but sets the angle of rotation as well. If the object is text, the Measurement toolbar offers additional character spacing or typesetting options. The Measurement toolbar is a floating toolbar with nine text boxes. It can be accessed by clicking Toolbars on the View menu or by double-clicking one of the Object boxes on the status bar. Entries can be typed in each box or chosen by clicking the appropriate arrows. Table 4–4 lists the first five boxes on the Measurement toolbar, which edit the position, size, and rotation of an object.

Table 4–4 Position, Size, and Rotation Boxes on the Measurement Toolbar		
Box Name	**Specifies**	**Preset Unit Of Measurement**
Horizontal Position	Horizontal distance from the upper-left corner of the page to the upper-left corner of the object	Inches
Vertical Position	Vertical distance from the upper-left corner of the page to the upper-left corner of the object	Inches
Width	Width of object	Inches
Height	Height of object	Inches
Rotation	Rotate the object counterclockwise from the original orientation	Degrees

The following step demonstrates how to position the rectangle precisely using the Measurement toolbar.

To Position Objects Using the Measurement Toolbar

1

- With the engine graphic still selected, double-click the Object Size box on the status bar to display the Measurement toolbar.

- Type .19 in the x box and then press the TAB key.

- Type .1 in the y box and then press the TAB key.

- Type 1 in the Width box and then press the TAB key.

- Type .95 in the Height box and then press the ENTER key (Figure 4–76).

- Click the Close button on the Measurement toolbar to close it. If necessary, click the Close button on the Picture toolbar to close it.

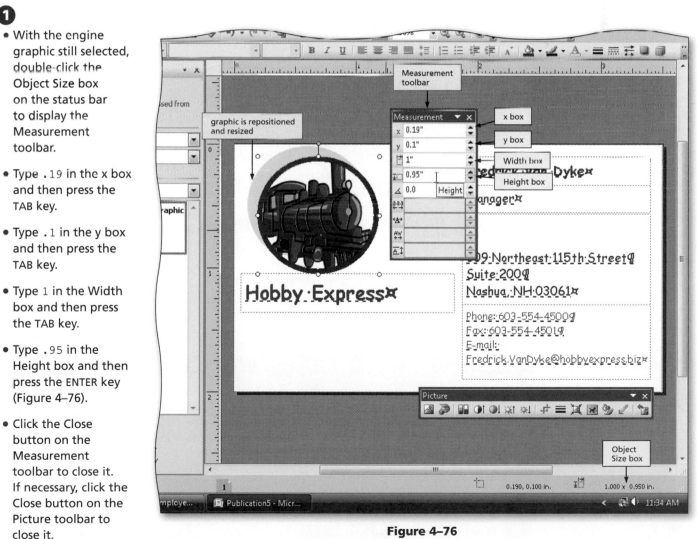

Figure 4–76

Saving and Printing the Business Card

The business card is complete, and you are ready to save and print it. If you have perforated paper available, the Print dialog box contains buttons to customize the number of cards per sheet.

Follow these steps to save and print the business card publication.

To Save and Print the Business Card

1 With a USB flash drive connected to one of the computer's USB ports, click the Save button on the Standard toolbar.

2 Type `Hobby Express Business Card` in the File name text box to change the file name. Do not press the ENTER key.

3 Navigate to your USB flash drive. Click the Save button in the Save As dialog box to save the publication on the USB flash drive with the file name, Hobby Express Business Card.

4 Click the Print button on the Standard toolbar and retrieve the printout, as shown in Figure 4–1 on page PUB 227.

Deleting Content

In lab situations, where many students work on the same machines throughout the day, it is a good idea to delete content you have created that is stored on the computer system.

To Delete Content from the Content Library

The following steps delete the engine graphic from the Content Library. Deleting from the Content Library does not delete the graphic from saved publications.

1

- In the Content Library task pane, click the graphic button arrow to display its menu (Figure 4–77).

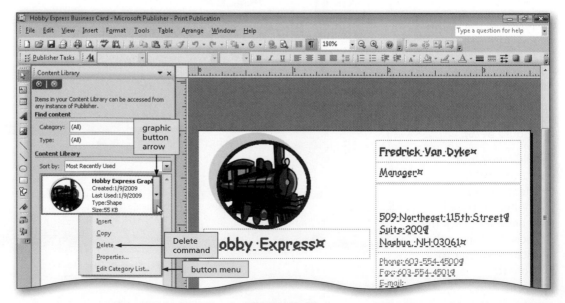

Figure 4–77

2

- Click Delete on the button menu to remove the content (Figure 4–78).

3

- When Publisher asks if you want to permanently remove the content, click the OK button.

- Close the Content Library task pane.

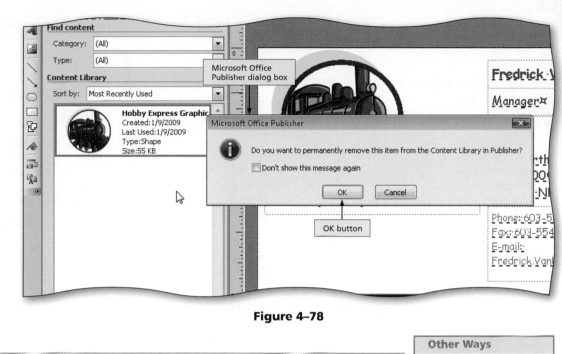

Figure 4–78

To Delete the Business Information Set

The following steps delete the Hobby Express business information set. Deleting the business information set does not delete the information from saved publications.

1

- Click Edit on the menu bar, and then click Business Information to display the Business Information dialog box (Figure 4–79).

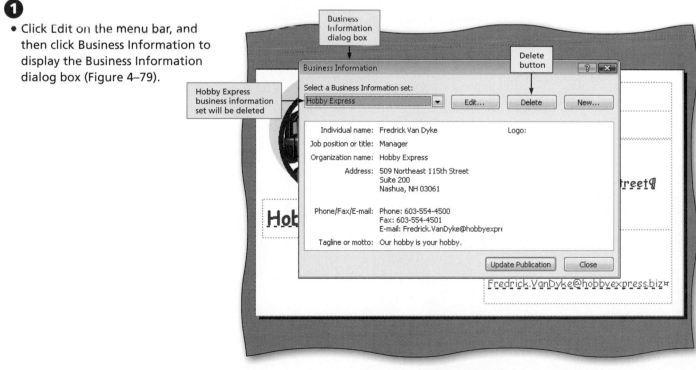

Figure 4–79

2

- With Hobby Express selected, click the Delete button to delete the business information set (Figure 4–80).

3

- When Publisher asks to confirm the deletion, click the Yes button (Figure 4-80).

- Click the Close button in the Business Information dialog box.

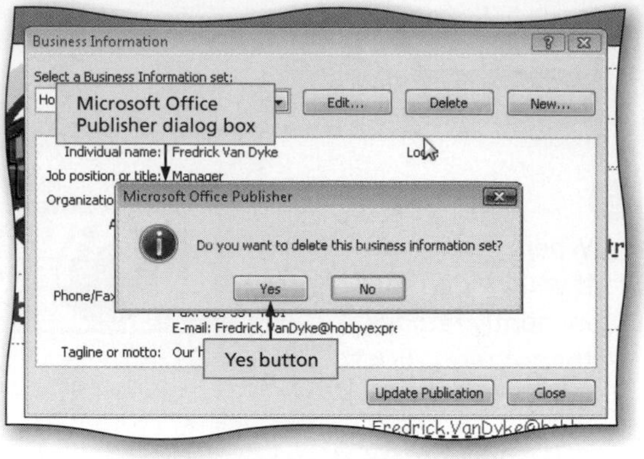

Figure 4–80

Quitting Publisher

The following steps quit Publisher.

To Quit Publisher

1 Click the Close button on the Publisher title bar.

2 If a dialog box is displayed reminding you to save the document, click the No button.

Chapter Summary

In this chapter you have learned how to personalize and customize publications. First, you created the business information set with its many components, then you used the information to create a letterhead from scratch. You created an original graphic by cropping, editing wrapping points, flipping, adding a border and shadow, and inserting it in an AutoShape. Next, you added the graphic to the Content Library and used the same business information set to create a business card. The items listed below include all the new Publisher skills you have learned in this chapter.

1. Start Publisher with a Blank Publication (PUB 245)
2. Select a Blank Publication (PUB 246)
3. Create a Business Information Set (PUB 248)
4. Edit the Margin Guides (PUB 251)
5. Move a Ruler (PUB 253)
6. Create a Ruler Guide (PUB 254)
7. Turn on Snapping (PUB 255)
8. Insert and Position Business Information Text Boxes (PUB 256)
9. Center a Text Box Relative to the Margins (PUB 259)
10. Crop a Graphic (PUB 262)
11. Crop to a Nonrectangular Shape (PUB 264)
12. Flip an Object (PUB 266)
13. Save Clip Art as a Picture (PUB 267)
14. Select a Line Color (PUB 271)
15. Select a Line/Border Style (PUB 272)
16. Add a Shadow (PUB 274)
17. Create a Gradient Fill Effect (PUB 275)
18. Add Text to an AutoShape (PUB 277)
19. Change the Order (PUB 278)
20. Insert an Automatic Date (PUB 280)
21. Add to the Content Library (PUB 283)
22. Create a Table (PUB 286)
23. Select Portions of a Table (PUB 288)
24. Format the Table (PUB 289)
25. Create a Cell Diagonal (PUB 291)
26. Select Multiple Objects (PUB 296)
27. Insert from the Content Library (PUB 297)
28. Position Objects Using the Measurement Toolbar (PUB 299)
29. Delete Content from the Content Library (PUB 300)
30. Delete the Business Information Set (PUB 301)

Learn It Online

Test your knowledge of chapter content and key terms.

Instructions: To complete the Learn It Online exercises, start your browser, click the Address bar, and then enter the Web address scsite.com/pub2007/learn. When the Office 2007 Learn It Online page is displayed, click the link for the exercise you want to complete and then read the instructions.

Chapter Reinforcement TF, MC, and SA
A series of true/false, multiple choice, and short answer questions that test your knowledge of the chapter content.

Flash Cards
An interactive learning environment where you identify chapter key terms associated with displayed definitions.

Practice Test
A series of multiple choice questions that test your knowledge of chapter content and key terms.

Who Wants To Be a Computer Genius?
An interactive game that challenges your knowledge of chapter content in the style of a television quiz show.

Wheel of Terms
An interactive game that challenges your knowledge of chapter key terms in the style of the television show *Wheel of Fortune*.

Crossword Puzzle Challenge
A crossword puzzle that challenges your knowledge of key terms presented in the chapter.

Apply Your Knowledge

Reinforce the skills and apply the concepts you learned in this chapter.

Editing Tables

Instructions: Start Publisher. Open the publication, Apply 4-1 Stock Table, from the Data Files for Students. See the inside back cover of this book for instructions on downloading the Data Files for Students, or contact your instructor for more information about accessing the required files.

The publication you open is an unformatted table in which you modify the fill color, remove borders, merge cells, and create diagonals. The resulting publication is shown in Figure 4–81.

Blue Chip Stocks									
Investment Analysis									
Stock	Symbol	Date Acquired	Shares	Initial Price Per Share	Initial Cost	Current Price Per Share	Current Value	Gain/Loss	Percent Gain/Loss
3M	MMM	06/12/00	394	$ 79.750	$ 31,421.50	$ 120.250	$ 47,378.50	$ 15,957.00	50.78%
Caterpillar	CAT	03/15/00	750	34.250	25,687.50	44.500	33,375.00	7,687.50	29.93%
Coca-Cola	KO	08/01/00	975	58.750	57,281.25	44.125	43,021.88	(14,259.38)	▮▮▮
DuPont	DD	09/12/01	850	33.125	28,156.25	42.250	35,912.50	7,756.25	27.55%
General Electric	GE	12/08/99	525	29.500	15,487.50	26.625	13,978.13	(1,509.38)	▮▮▮
General Motors	GM	10/05/99	810	37.375	30,273.75	40.000	32,400.00	2,126.25	7.02%
Intel	INTC	10/03/02	875	13.000	11,375.00	18.750	16,406.25	5,031.25	44.23%
Microsoft	MSFT	01/15/02	250	64.350	16,087.50	56.375	14,093.75	(1,993.75)	▮▮▮
Wal-Mart	WMT	07/09/99	925	32.625	30,178.13	45.250	41,856.25	11,678.13	38.70%
Total					$ 245,948.38		$ 278,422.25	$ 32,473.88	13.20%

Figure 4–81

Perform the following tasks:

1. To insert a new row above the current rows of the table, select the first row of the table. On the Table menu, point to Insert, and then click Rows Above. Repeat the process to insert a second row above the current rows.

2. In row 1, column 1, type Blue Chip Stock. Drag across the cells in the first row, and then click Merge Cells on the Table menu. Press CTRL+A to select all of the text. Change the font size to 28.

3. In row 2, column 1, type Investment Analysis. Drag across the cells in the first row, and then click Merge Cells on the Table menu. Change the font size to 18.

4. Use the Fill Color button to fill the first two rows with a light blue fill color.

5. Select the cells in row 3, columns 1 and 2. Merge the cells. In the new row 3, column 1, create a cell diagonal, dividing down. On the left side of the diagonal, type the word Stock; on the right side of the diagonal, type the word Symbol.

6. Bold the text in the first three rows.

7. Select the first three rows. Bold the text.

8. In the last column, select any cell with a negative number. Format the fill color to be red.

9. Select the entire table. Right-click the selection, and then click Format Table on the shortcut menu. On the Colors and Lines tab, select the first preset to remove the borders.

10. Select the first two rows. Right-click the selection, and then click Format Table on the shortcut menu. On the Colors and Lines tab, select the second preset to display borders around the edges only.

11. Change the publication properties, as specified by your instructor.

12. Click Save As on the File menu. Save the publication using the file name, Apply 4-1 Stock Table Formatted.

13. Submit the revised publication, as specified by your instructor.

Extend Your Knowledge

Extend the skills you learned in this chapter and experiment with new skills. You may need to use Help to complete the assignment.

Editing Graphics

Instructions: Start Publisher. Open the publication, Extend 4-1 Tiger Graphic, from the Data Files for Students. See the inside back cover of this book for instructions on downloading the Data Files for Students, or contact your instructor for more information about accessing the required files.

You will edit the graphic so it displays as shown in Figure 4–82.

Perform the following tasks:

1. Use Help to learn more about recoloring graphics and changing shadow settings.

2. Recolor the graphic to a dark orange, leaving the black parts black.

3. Crop the tiger to display only the head.

4. Use the Measurement toolbar to resize the graphic to 2 inches by 1.75 inches.

5. Edit wrapping points as necessary to remove the background. Keep as much of the whiskers as possible.

6. Flip the tiger so it faces the other way.

Figure 4–82

7. Use the Save as Picture command to save the tiger as a PNG graphic on your USB drive.

8. Delete the tiger graphic from the publication.

9. Create a Hexagon autoshape, approximately 4 inches by 4 inches.

10. Access the Fill Effects dialog box and the Picture tab. Insert the picture of the tiger into the hexagon.

11. Add a border that is 6 pt, multiline in style, based on a sample of the darkest color in the picture.

12. Add a shadow that displays up and to the right of the graphic. Recolor the shadow to the dark orange sampled in the previous step. Adjust the thickness of the shadow, using the Shadow Settings toolbar.

13. Change the publication properties, as specified by your instructor. Save the revised publication, and then submit it in the format specified by your instructor.

Make It Right

Analyze a publication and correct all errors and/or improve the design.

Correcting Replacement Text and Spelling Errors

Instructions: Start Publisher. Open the publication, Make It Right 4-1 Insurance Company Letterhead, from the Data Files for Students. See the inside back cover of this book for instructions on downloading the Data Files for Students, or contact your instructor for more information about accessing the required files.

The publication shown in Figure 4–83 is a letterhead containing graphics that are ordered and layered incorrectly. The date is in a format that will not update automatically. The graphic is cropped incorrectly. You are to fix these errors in a way that displays the graphics correctly and formats the date to update automatically.

Perform the following tasks:

1. Remove the border of the orange shape.

2. Select the light green rectangle and send it to the back.

3. Click the text and then bring it to the front.

4. Select the picture in the upper right corner of the publication and drag it into the workspace to the right of the page layout for easier editing.

5. Crop the picture so it displays the face and shoulders of the man.

6. Display the wrapping points close to the man's head and shoulders. If necessary, to add more wrapping points, CTRL+click the boundary of the graphic. Edit the wrapping points to remove most of the background.

7. Drag the picture back into the page layout. Resize the picture to fill the area within the ruler guides. Bring the picture to the front, if necessary.

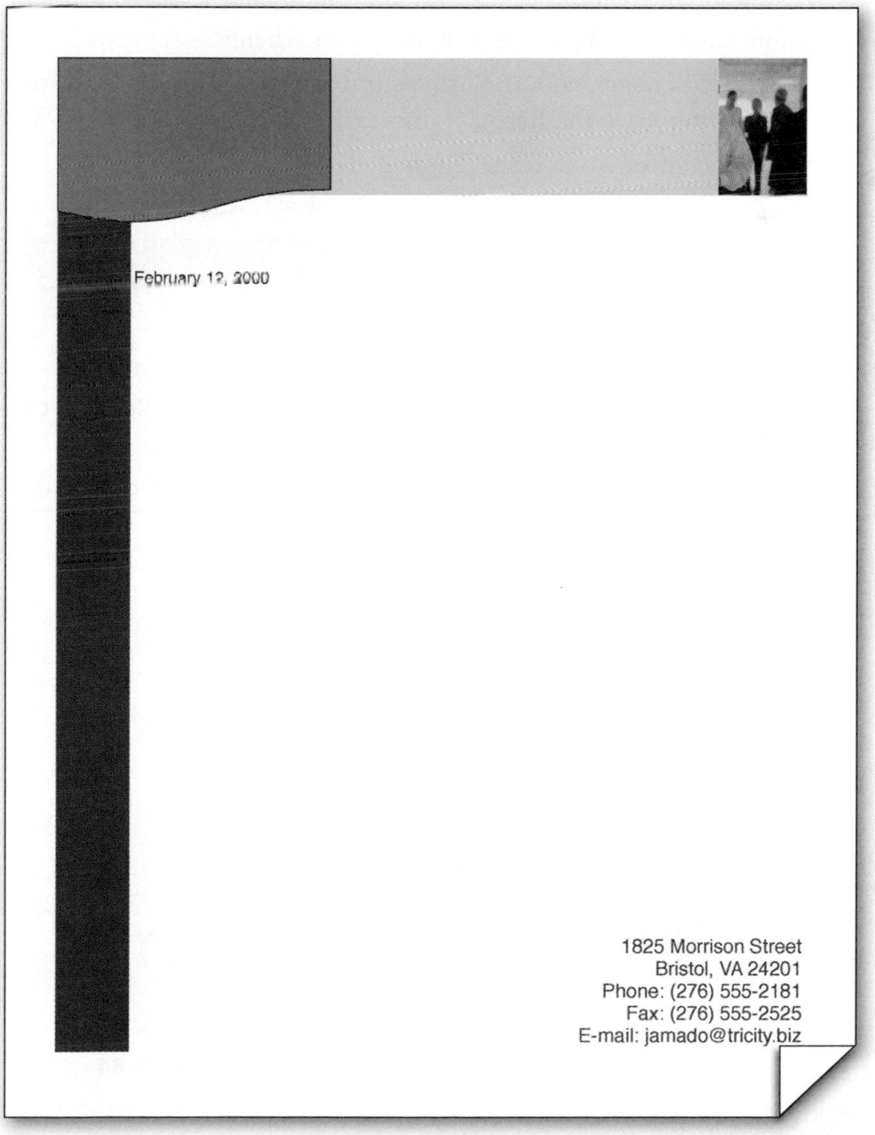

February 12, 2000

1825 Morrison Street
Bristol, VA 24201
Phone: (276) 555-2181
Fax: (276) 555-2525
E-mail: jamado@tricity.biz

Figure 4–83

8. Change the publication properties, as specified by your instructor. Save the revised publication, and then submit it in the format specified by your instructor.

In the Lab

Design and/or create a publication using the guidelines, concepts, and skills presented in this chapter. Labs are listed in order of increasing difficulty.

Lab 1: Creating a Business Information Set

Problem: You work part-time for the state music teachers' association. You have to prepare several publications related to the upcoming marching band season and the field band competitions. You decide that keeping a business information set with all the pertinent information would save you a lot of time.

Instructions: Perform the following tasks:
1. Start Publisher.
2. Choose Blank Page sizes in the catalog, and then click Letter (Landscape) 11" × 8.5". Create the publication with the default font and color scheme.
3. On the Edit menu, choose Business Information. If Publisher displays a previous business information set in the Business Information dialog box, click the New button.
4. Enter the information from Figure 4–84.

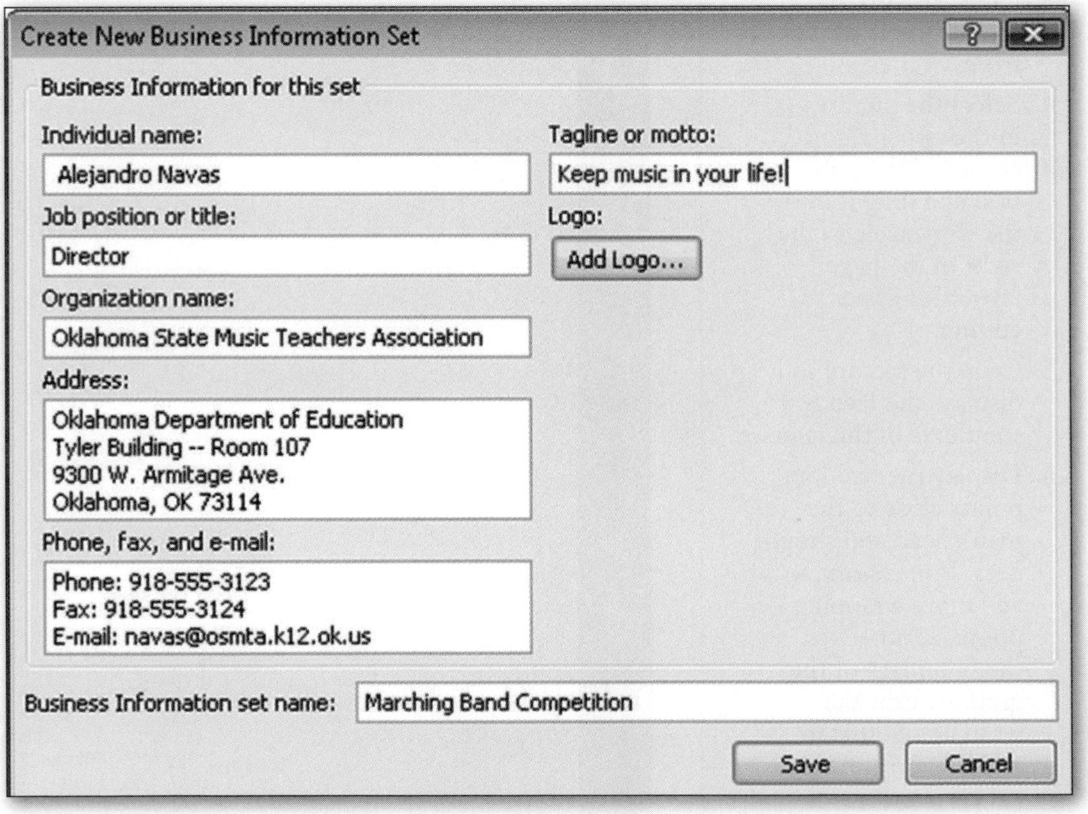

Figure 4–84

5. Press the PRINT SCREEN key to capture a picture of the screen. Click the Save button and then click the Update Publication button.
6. On the Edit menu, click Paste. When the screen shot is displayed in the publication, use the Crop tool to crop the edges of the graphic close to the dialog box.

7. With the graphic still selected, click Arrange on the menu bar, point to Text Wrapping, and then click Edit Wrap Points. Move the wrapping points closer to the dialog box to remove any remaining edges. Try to wrap to the rounded corners at the top of the dialog box.

8. Right-click the graphic, and then click Save as Picture.

9. Save the graphic as a PNG file on a USB flash drive using the file name, Lab 4-1 Graphic.

10. Quit Publisher without saving the publication.

11. Submit the graphic in the format specified by your instructor.

In the Lab

Lab 2: Creating a Letterhead and Business Card

Problem: Your friend is the volunteer commissioner for the local children's soccer league. Because he is responsible for organizing the teams, ordering equipment, and scheduling games, fields, and officials, he has asked you to create some stationery for his correspondences. You prepare the letterhead and business card shown in Figure 4–85.

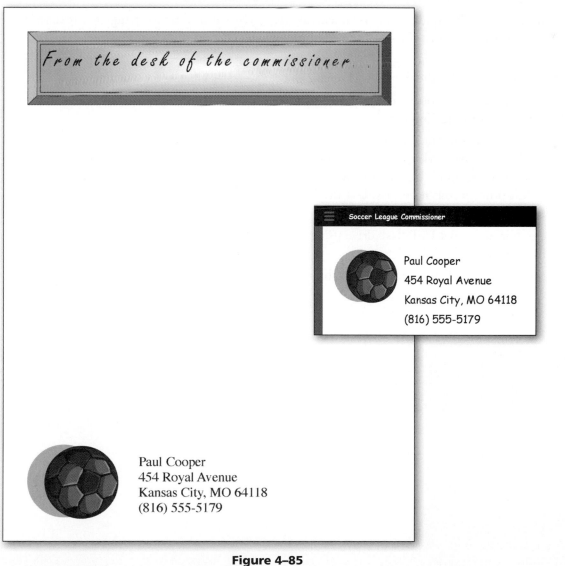

Figure 4–85

Continued >

Instructions: Perform the following tasks with a computer:

1. Start Publisher with a blank publication. On the Arrange menu, click Layout Guides and then set the margins to .5 inches.

2. At the bottom of the page, insert a graphic relating to soccer. Resize and crop it as necessary. Insert a text box next to the graphic. Change the font size to 20, and then type the name and address as shown in Figure 4–85.

3. Click the AutoShapes button on the Objects toolbar. Point to Basic Shapes, and then click Bevel. Draw a bevel shape at the top of the page. Use the Measurement toolbar to adjust the size of the bevel as follows: 7.5 inches wide, 1.5 inches tall, and .5 inch margins.

4. Click the Fill Color button arrow on the Formatting toolbar, and then click Fill Effects. Click the Gradient tab. Click the One color option button. Choose a color that complements the graphic. Drag the Dark to Light scroll box all the way to the right.

5. Click the Line Color button on the Formatting toolbar. On the color palette, choose a red color.

6. In front of the bevel, insert a text box for the heading. Use a script font that resembles handwriting and a font size of at least 24. Type From the desk of the commissioner ... in the text box. Click the Line Color button to make the text box line color red.

7. Select all the text in the heading, and then use the Measurement toolbar to change the text scaling to 150%. If necessary, adjust the size and position of the text box as shown in Figure 4–85. Choose Best Fit.

8. Save the publication with the file name, Lab 4-2 Soccer Letterhead, and then print a copy.

9. Select the graphic at the bottom of the page and add it to the Content Library. Select the address text box and add it to the Content Library.

10. Click New on the file menu. Choose a business card template from the catalog. When the business card is displayed in the workspace, select multiple objects that comprise a business card graphic, if necessary, and delete them. Use the Content Library task pane to insert the graphic and address text box. Edit other text as necessary. Use the Measurement toolbar and the Best Fit option to reposition objects.

11. Save the publication on a USB flash drive using the file name, Lab 4-2 Soccer Business Card, and then print a copy.

12. Delete the two objects from the Content Library, before quitting Publisher.

In the Lab

Lab 3: Experimenting with Fills

Problem: You have decided to investigate the different gradient fills among the tints, shades, patterns, and textures available in Publisher 2007. You create a blank publication sampler for future reference.

Instructions: Perform the following tasks with a computer:

1. Start Publisher.

2. Create a blank publication, 8.5-by-11 inches, portrait orientation.

3. On the Arrange menu, click Layout Guides. Change the margin guides to 1 inch on all four sides, if necessary.

4. Click the Grid Guides tab. Set the columns to 3 and the rows to 5. Close the Layout Guides dialog box.

5. Draw a rectangle that fills the first cell outlined by the grid guides. Copy the rectangle and then deselect it. Paste a new rectangle and drag it to the second cell, so that it snaps in place. Paste 13 more times to create a total of 15 rectangles.

6. One at a time, select each rectangle. Use the Fill Color button on the Formatting toolbar to fill each rectangle as follows:

   - Fill one rectangle with a solid color, no border.
   - Fill one rectangle with a different solid color and a 3 pt black border.
   - Fill one rectangle with a one-color gradient, using a From center shading style.
   - Fill one rectangle with a two-color gradient, using a Diagonal down shading style.
   - Fill one rectangle with a texture from the list, using a dashed border style.
   - Fill one rectangle with a dark texture from the list, using a contrasting border color.
   - Fill one rectangle with a black and white striped pattern.
   - Fill one rectangle with a different pattern, using colors other than black and white.
   - Fill one rectangle with a picture and no border.
   - Fill one rectangle with a picture and flip it vertically.
   - Fill one rectangle with a tint of 20% (do not use black or white).
   - Fill one rectangle with a shade of 60% (do not use black or white).
   - Fill one rectangle with a filling of your choice, and add a shadow.
   - Fill one rectangle with a filling of your choice, and add a 3-D Style.
   - Fill one rectangle with a solid color and Border Art.

7. Change the publication properties, as specified by your instructor.

8. Save the publication on a USB flash drive, using the file name, Lab 4-3 Fill Sampler. Submit the publication in the format specified by your instructor.

Cases and Places

Apply your creative thinking and problem-solving skills to design and implement a solution.

● EASIER ●● MORE DIFFICULT

● 1: Dairy Barn Letterhead

The Dairy Barn, a local farmer's market, has asked you to create a new letterhead. They would like a wave shape with a gradient fill to serve as a background for the words, Drink Milk! Use a blank page publication and insert a wave shape using the AutoShapes button on the Objects toolbar and the Stars and Banners list. Position the arrow in the upper-left corner of the page. Use a text box for the company name. Insert a text box at the bottom of the page and type the address and telephone number: 1350 Ridgeway Avenue, Mesa, AZ 85211, (480) 554-3770. Insert a graphic of dairy products or fresh produce in the upper corner opposite the shape.

● 2: Personal Business Cards

Start Publisher and choose a Business Card template from the list. Edit the business information set with your personal data. Use your own name and the title, Student Extraordinaire. Enter the name and address of your school or workplace as the organization. Choose a color scheme. In the Business Information dialog box, click Update Publication. Print the business card with the business information components. Delete your business information set if you used a lab computer.

●● 3: Creating an Information Set for your School

Create a business information set for your school. With permission, use your instructor's name and title. Choose four different letterhead templates, and insert the business information. Print each letterhead on a color printer, if possible. Write a paragraph about your favorite of the four templates. Describe the graphics, placement of components, and page layout.

●● 4: Employee Time Card

A+ Auto Repair needs a time card. The owner has just hired two extra mechanics and an office manager because business is booming. Using a blank landscape publication, create a time card table. Create text boxes for the employees to enter their name, employee number, and date. Create a table using an appropriate auto format. The table should have eight columns — one for headings and one for each day of the week. The table should have seven rows — one for headings and two sets of alternating In: and Out: rows and totals. Print multiple copies for the A+ Auto Repair's employees.

●● 5: Service Learning Opportunities

Working Together

As a group, find a local not-for-profit agency that needs documents such as letterhead and business cards. Discuss with the agency manager the needs of the agency and the skills of your group. As a group, decide on consistent fonts, colors, logos, and styles. Individually, create different business publications for the agency. Bring the publications to the group, discuss each one, and make recommendations for change. Edit the publications and submit them to your instructor. Submit final copies to the agency.

5 | Merging Publications and Data

Objectives

You will have mastered the material in this project when you can:

- Use a letterhead template
- Create and format a drop cap
- Explain character spacing techniques
- Track and kern characters
- Use the Measurement toolbar to edit spacing
- Do a mail merge
- Create and customize a Publisher address list
- Produce a form letter
- Connect an address list with a main publication

- Filter data and insert field codes
- Use tabs and markers
- Differentiate among tab styles and indents
- Create and print merged labels
- Do a catalog merge
- Insert picture fields into the catalog merge area
- Insert a calendar
- Find and replace text

5 | Publisher Merge Features

Introduction

Whether you want individual letters sent to everyone on a mailing list, personalized envelopes for a mass mailing, an invoice sent to all customers, or a printed set of mailing labels to apply to your brochures, you can use Publisher to maintain your data and make the task of mass mailing and merged document creation easier.

Merged publications, such as form letters, should be timely and professional looking, yet at the same time, individualized and personal. Used regularly in both business and personal correspondence, a **form letter** has the same basic content no matter to whom it is sent; however, items such as name, address, city, state, and zip code change from one form letter to the next. Thus, form letters are personalized to the addressee. An individual is more likely to open and read a personalized letter or e-mail than a standard Dear Sir or Dear Madam message. With word processing and database techniques, it is easy to generate individual, personalized documents for a large group and include features unique to desktop publishing.

Publisher extends personalized document creation to any type of publication. For instance, in Publisher, you can merge data and publications. Merging is useful particularly when applied to catalogs or product announcements with pictures. If you had to import pictures and associated data into a catalog or booklet one item at a time, it would be tedious and time consuming. Publisher's Catalog Merge feature makes it easy to create professional catalogs using an external data source. A **data source** is a file that may contain only a list of names and addresses, or it also may include paths to pictures, product part numbers, postal bar codes, customer purchase history, accounts receivable, e-mail addresses, and a variety of additional data that you want to use in a mail or catalog merge.

Project — Publisher Merge Features

The project in this chapter shows you how to create a form letter with merged fields, a catalog with data from a database, and a personalized label for each addressee from a Publisher mailing list, as shown in Figure 5–1. The letter (Figure 5–1a) informs interested people about homes for sale in their community. The catalog (Figure 5–1b) displays pictures and information about 10 houses. Both will be included in an envelope with a label (Figure 5–1c).

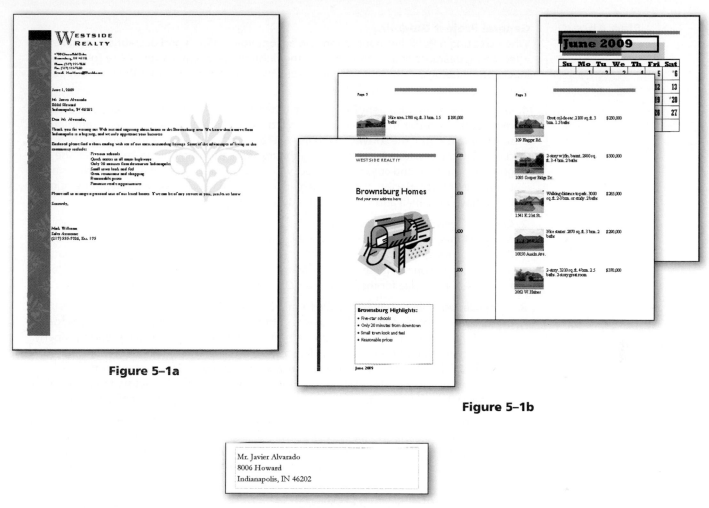

Figure 5–1a

Figure 5–1b

Figure 5–1c

The letter contains merged fields including names, addresses, and subdivision preference. The catalog displays pictures of the houses, the addresses, descriptions, and the price of each house. The label displays the mailing address.

Overview

As you read through this chapter, you will learn how to create the publications shown in Figure 5–1 by performing these general tasks:

- Select a letterhead template and specify the layout options
- Create a mailing list
- Create a form letter and merge the mailing list data
- Select a catalog template and adjust the pagination
- Merge catalog data and insert a calendar
- Select a label template and merge with the mailing list
- Print the publications

Plan Ahead

General Project Guidelines

When creating a Publisher publication, the actions you perform and decisions you make will affect the appearance and characteristics of the finished document. As you create form letters, labels, and catalogs, such as those in the project shown in Figure 5–1 on the previous page, you should follow these general guidelines:

1. **Identify the main document for the form letter.** When creating form letters, you either can create the letter from scratch or use a letterhead template. A letterhead template saves time because the software prepares a letter with graphics and formatting. Then, you customize the resulting letter by writing the text and inserting unique field codes. Use text, graphics, formats, and colors that reflect you or your business, such as drop caps. Consider unique character spacing. Include a name, postal mailing address, and telephone number. If you have an e-mail address and Web address, include those as well.

2. **Create or specify the data source.** The data source contains the variable, or changing, values for each letter. A data source can be a Publisher address list, an Access database table, an Outlook contacts list, or an Excel worksheet. If the necessary and properly organized data already exists in one of these Office programs, you can instruct Publisher to use the existing file as the data source for the mail merge. Otherwise, you can create a new data source.

3. **Compose the main document for the form letter.** A main document contains the constant, or unchanging, text, punctuation, spaces, and graphics. It also includes field codes for the parts of the document that should change, referencing the data in the data source properly. The finished publication should look like a symmetrically framed picture with evenly spaced margins, all balanced below an attractive letterhead. The content of the main document for the form letter should contain proper grammar, correct spelling, logically constructed sentences, flowing paragraphs, and sound ideas. Be sure to proofread it carefully.

4. **Merge the main document with the data source to create the form letters.** Merging is the process of combining the contents of a data source with a main document. You can print the merged letters on the printer or place them in a new publication, which you later can edit. You also have the option of merging all data in a data source, or just merging a portion of it.

5. **Generate mailing labels and envelopes.** To generate mailing labels and envelopes for the form letters, follow the same process as for the form letters. That is, determine the appropriate data source, create the label or envelope main document, and then merge the main document with the data source to generate the mailing labels and envelopes.

When necessary, more specific details concerning the above guidelines are presented at appropriate points in the chapter. The chapter also will identify the actions performed and decisions made regarding these guidelines during the creation of the form letters shown in Figure 5–1 as well as related documents.

To Start Publisher

If you are using a computer to step through the project in this chapter and you want your screens to match the figures in this book, you should change your computer's resolution to 1024 × 768. For information about how to change a computer's resolution, read Appendix D.

The following steps, which assume Windows is running, start Publisher based on a typical installation. You may need to ask your instructor how to start Publisher for your computer.

Note: If you are using Windows XP, see Appendix F for alternate steps.

 Click the Start button on the Windows Vista taskbar to display the Start menu, and then click All Programs at the bottom of the left pane on the Start menu to display the All Programs list.

② Click Microsoft Office in the All Programs list to display the Microsoft Office list, and then click Microsoft Office Publisher 2007 to start Publisher and display the Getting Started with Microsoft Office Publisher 2007 catalog.

③ If the Publisher window is not maximized, click the Maximize button next to the Close button on its title bar to maximize the window.

Identify the main document for the form letter.
Be sure the main document for the form letter includes all essential business letter elements. All business letters should contain a date line, inside address, message, and signature block. Many business letters contain additional items such as a special mailing notation(s), an attention line, a salutation, a subject line, a complimentary close, reference initials, and an enclosure notation.

**Plan
Ahead**

To Use a Letterhead Template

You will use a letterhead template for the form letter. The following steps choose a letterhead template, a font scheme, and a color scheme for the form letter.

① With the catalog displayed, click the Letterhead button in the list of Publication Types and then click the Brocade preview.

② In the Customize area, select the Aspect color scheme and the Etched font scheme. Click the Include logo check box so that it does not display a check mark.

③ Click the Create button. When the publication is displayed, close the task pane. If the Special Characters button on the Standard toolbar is not selected already, click it to display formatting marks on the screen (Figure 5–2).

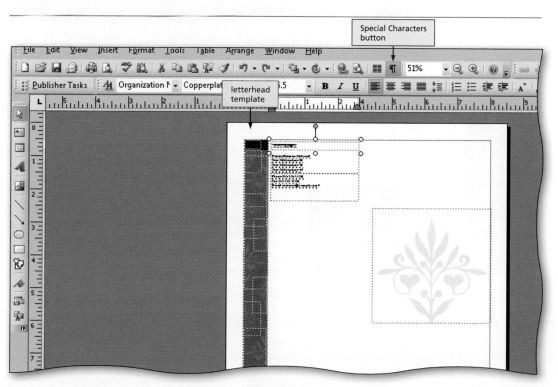

Figure 5–2

To Edit the Letterhead Text Boxes

The following steps edit the text boxes at the top of the letterhead. Each text box will display new information. In the Business Name text box, the smart tag will be removed, and the text box then will be resized. Recall that a smart tag indicates data from the business information set and displays text underlined with a blue dotted line. When you point to a smart tag, a button appears, giving access to the smart tag menu.

1

- Zoom to 200%. Scroll to the upper-left portion of the publication.

- Enter the text from Figure 5–3.

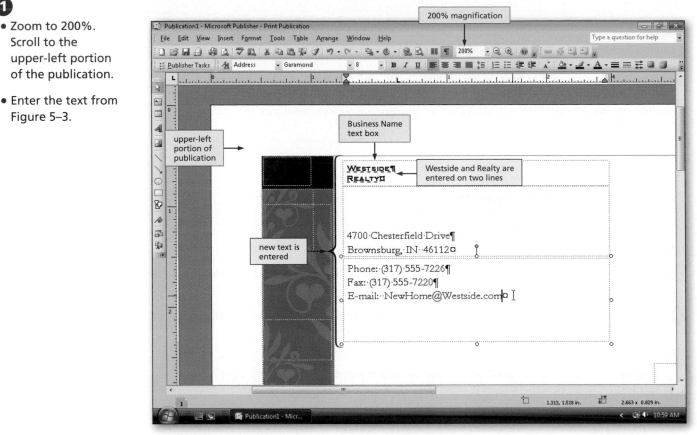

Figure 5–3

2

- Select the Business Name text box.

Q&A

Could I enter this information into the business information set rather than type it directly into the text boxes of the publication?

Yes, if you plan on using the business information multiple times, it would be a good idea to do so. For this project, however, it is just as easy to type the data into the publication itself.

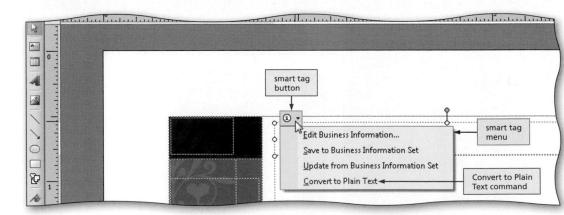

Figure 5–4

- Point to the selected text, and then, when the smart tag button is displayed, click the smart tag button to display its menu (Figure 5–4).

- Click Convert to Plain Text.

Why am I converting this to plain text?

Converting to plain text removes the blue dotted underline and no longer displays the smart tag button, providing less distraction as you format the text later in the chapter.

- Drag the lower-center sizing handle down until the text box is approximately .5 inches high (Figure 5–5).

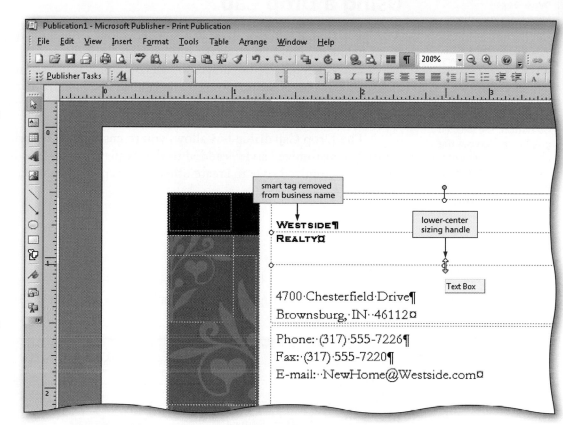

Figure 5–5

- Right-click the text in the Business Name text box to display the shortcut menu. Point to Change Text. On the Change Text submenu, point to AutoFit Text, and then click Best Fit (Figure 5–6).

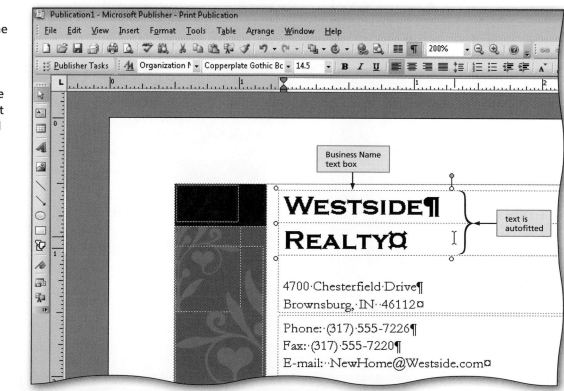

Figure 5–6

Using a Drop Cap

A dropped capital letter, or **drop cap**, is a decorative large initial capital letter extending down below the other letters in the line. A drop cap is displayed larger than the rest of the characters in the line or paragraph and commonly is used to mark the beginning of an article or text box. If the text wraps to more than one line, the paragraph typically wraps around the dropped capital letter. You can format up to 15 contiguous letters and spaces as drop caps at the beginning of each paragraph.

The Drop Cap dialog box allows you to customize the style of the drop cap. Once created, a customized style is added to the Available drop caps list so that you can use the new customized style to create other drop caps in the current publication.

To Create and Format a Drop Cap

The following steps create and format a dropped capital letter W to be placed in the Business Name text box.

1

- Click to the left of the letter W in Westside.

- Click Format on the menu bar to display its menu (Figure 5–7).

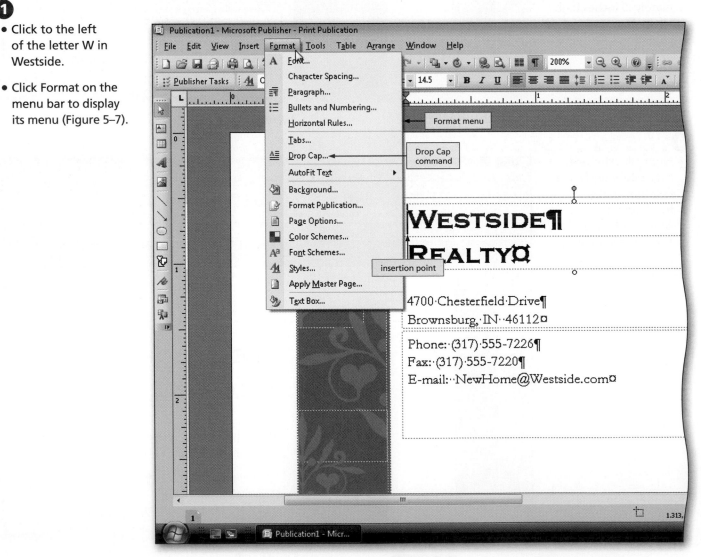

Figure 5–7

②

- Click Drop Cap to display the Drop Cap dialog box.

- If necessary, click the Drop Cap tab.

🔍 **Experiment**

- Scroll from left to right in the Available drop caps area to view the different default styles.

- In the Available drop caps area, click a preview that is similar to the one shown in Figure 5–8.

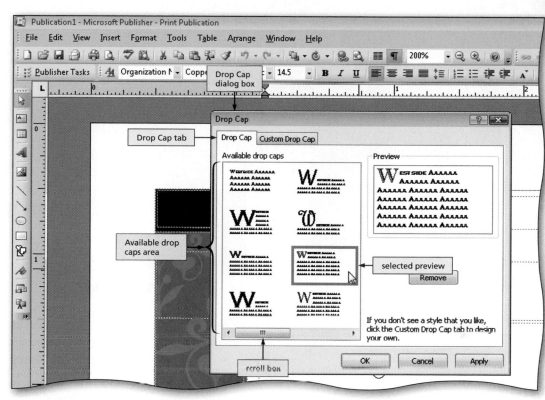

Figure 5–8

③

- Click the Custom Drop Cap tab. In the 'Select letter position and size' area, click Dropped, if necessary.

Q&A What are the other formatting options?

The **Up** setting extends the letter above the paragraph, rather than sinking it into the first few lines of the text. The **Lines** setting changes the number of lines that display to the right of the dropped cap. In addition, you can adjust the size of the letters, the number of letters, and all of the font options.

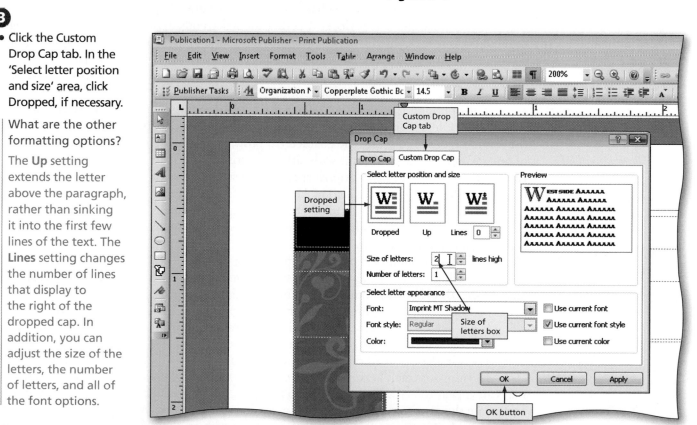

Figure 5–9

④

- If necessary, delete any number in the Size of letters box and then type 2 to enter the new size (Figure 5–9).

5
• Click the OK button (Figure 5–10).

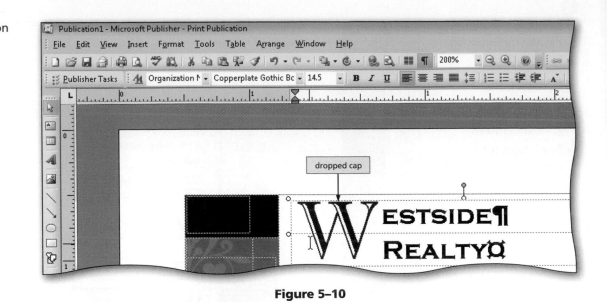

Figure 5–10

BTW

Subsetting
A file prepared for submission to a commercial printer includes all fonts from the publication. If you use only a small number of characters from a font, as in drop caps or for headlines, you can have Publisher embed only the characters you used from the font. Embedding only part of a font is called **subsetting**. The advantage of font subsetting is that it decreases the overall size of the file. The disadvantage is that it limits the ability to make corrections at the printing service. If the printing service does not have the full font installed on its computer, corrections can be made only by using the characters included in the subset.

Character Spacing

Sometimes you need to fine-tune the spacing between characters on the page. For instance, you may want to spread characters apart for better legibility. Other times, you may want to move characters closer together for space considerations, without changing the font or font size. Or, you may be using a font that employs **proportional spacing** or different widths for different characters. For example, in a proportionally spaced font, the letter i is more narrow than the letter m. This book uses a proportionally spaced font, as do most books, newspapers, and magazines.

The opposite of proportional spacing is **monospacing**, where every letter is the same width. Older printers and monitors were limited to monospaced fonts because of the dot matrix used to create the characters. Now, almost all printers, with the exception of line printers, are able to print with either proportionally spaced or monospaced fonts. Because most fonts use proportional spacing, the scaling, tracking, and kerning features in Publisher allow you many ways to make very precise character spacing adjustments.

Scaling, the process of shrinking or stretching text, changes the width of individual characters in text boxes. Recall that the WordArt toolbar has a button for scaling; however, scaling also is available for any text box by using the Measurement toolbar or by using the Character Spacing command on the Format menu.

Tracking refers to the adjustment of the general spacing between all selected characters. Tracking text compensates for the spacing irregularities caused when you make text much bigger or much smaller. For example, smaller type is easier to read when it has been tracked loosely. Tracking maintains the original height of the font and overrides adjustments made by justification of the margins. Tracking is available only if you are working on a print publication. It is not available with Web publications.

Kerning, or **track kerning**, is a special form of tracking related to pairs of characters that can appear too close together or too far apart, even with standard tracking. Kerning can create the appearance of even spacing and is used to fit text into a given space or adjust line breaks. For instance, certain uppercase letters such as T, V, W, and Y often are kerned when they are preceded or followed by a lowercase a, e, i, o, or u. With manual kerning, Publisher lets you choose from normal, expanded, and condensed kerning for special effects. Publisher applies automatic kerning to 14-point text and larger. Text in a smaller point size usually does not need to be kerned, unless the font contains many serifs. A **serif** is a short decorative stroke or fancy corner on individual letters. Fonts that are **sans serif** do not display the decoration.

The lower four boxes on the Measurement toolbar (Figure 5–11) are useful because they provide many possible combinations for spacing characters, as shown in Table 5–1.

Table 5–1 Character Spacing Tools on the Measurement Toolbar		
Box Name	**Specifies**	**Preset Unit of Measurement**
Text Scaling	Width of the text	Percent
Tracking	General space between characters	Percent
Kerning	Subtle space between paired characters	Point size
Line Spacing	Vertical spacing between lines of selected text	Space (1 for single)

Tracking Characters

In the Westside Realty form letter, you will track the characters in the business name. Creating more general space between characters will help show off the serif font used in the font scheme.

To Track Characters

The following step selects the text Westside Realty and uses the Measurement toolbar to track the text more loosely.

1

- Select the text Westside Realty.

- Double-click the status bar to display the Measurement toolbar.

- In the Tracking box, click the Up button until the tracking percentage is equal to 150% (Figure 5–11).

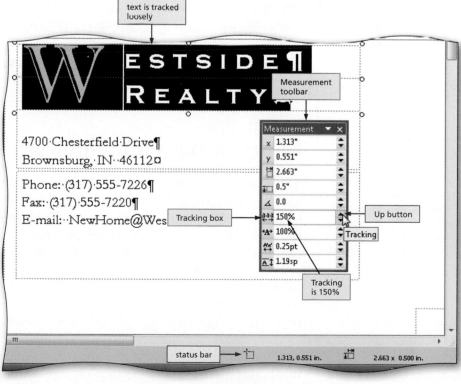

Figure 5–11

Other Ways

1. On Format menu, click Character Spacing, enter tracking settings

Kerning Character Pairs

In the Westside Realty form letter, you will kern the first two letters of Westside Realty, which will bring the small text closer to the large drop cap.

To Kern Character Pairs

The following steps select and then kern two characters using the Measurement toolbar.

1

- Select the letters W and E in Westside Realty.

- On the Measurement toolbar, in the Kerning box, click the Down button until the kerning point is -10.05 (Figure 5–12).

2

- Close the Measurement toolbar.

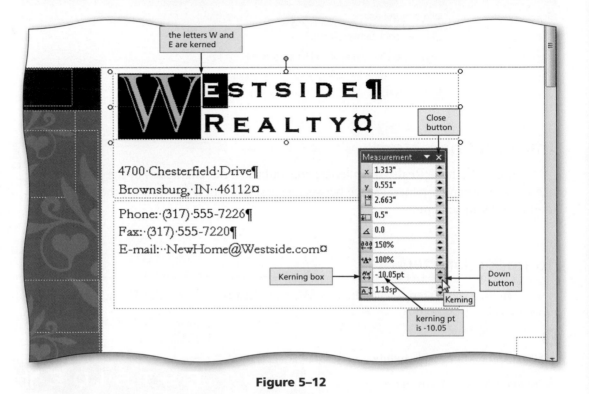

Figure 5–12

Merging Data into Publications

The process of generating an individualized publication for mass mailing involves creating a main publication and a data source. The two then are merged, or blended, into a series of publications ready for printing or saving. **Merging** is the process of combining the contents of a data source with a main publication. The **main publication** contains the constant or unchanging text, punctuation, space, and graphics, embedded with **variables** or changing values from the data source. A **data source** or database is a file where you store all addresses or other personal information for customers, friends and family, or merchants with whom you do business. The term **database** generically describes a collection of data, organized in a manner that allows easy access, retrieval, and use of that data.

Personalizing contact with your customers means increased revenue. Addressing customers by name and remembering their preferences is the kind of personal attention that builds customer loyalty. When retail establishments keep close track of customers' interests, customers usually respond by returning and spending more time and money there. When you include content in a mailing that addresses your customers' specific interests, the customers are more likely to pay attention and respond.

Publisher allows users to create data sources internally, which means using Publisher as both the creation and editing tool. Publisher creates a special database that can be edited independently by using Microsoft Access; however, you do not need to have Microsoft Access or any database program installed on your system to use a Publisher data source.

If you plan to **import**, or bring in data from another application, Publisher can accept data from a variety of other formats, as shown in Table 5–2.

Table 5–2 Data Formats		
Data-Creation Program	**Version**	**File Extension**
Any text files, such as those generated with WordPad or Notepad	Text or comma-delimited	.txt and .csv
dBase	III, IV, and V	.dbf
Microsoft Access	All versions	.mdb and .mdbx
Microsoft Excel	3.0, 4.0, 5.0, 7.0, and 8.0	.xls and .xlsx
Microsoft FoxPro	2.0, 2.5, and 2.6	.fxd
Microsoft List Builder	All versions	.bcm
Microsoft Outlook	All versions	.pst
Microsoft Word tables or merge data documents	All versions	.doc and .docx
Microsoft Works (no formulas)	All Windows versions and MS-DOS 3.0	.wdb
SQL Server	2000 or 2005	.odc
Schema	All versions	.ini

Plan
Ahead

Create the data source.

When you create a data source, you will need to determine the fields it should contain. That is, you will need to identify the data that will vary from one merged document to the next. Following are a few important points about fields:

- For each field, you may be required to create a field name. Because data sources often contain the same fields, some programs create a list of commonly used field names that you may use.

- Field names must be unique; that is, no two field names may be the same.

- Fields may be listed in any order in the data source. That is, the order of fields has no effect on the order in which they will print in the main document.

- Organize fields so that they are flexible. For example, break the name into separate fields: title, first name, and last name. This arrangement allows you to customize fields.

Creating a Publisher Address List

In Publisher, data sources are called **address lists**. Publisher allows you to create as many address lists as you like, providing a customizable interface in which to enter the data. Each address list is a table of rows and columns that hold customer information. Within the address lists, **columns** represent fields of information, such as name, address, phone, etc. The preset columns include Title, First Name, Last Name, Company Name, Address Line 1, Address Line 2, City, State, ZIP Code, Country, Home Phone, Work Phone, and E-mail Address. You can create more columns or rename columns. Each **row** becomes an entry in a Publisher address list. Similar to a record in other database applications, an **entry** represents all of the information about one person, client, or business in the address list.

Address Lists
You can maintain multiple address lists for data sources, such as employees or vendors, if you use different names. The Edit Address List command (Figure 5-13) permits you to specify the data source.

For this project, you will create a Publisher address list containing information about the prospective home buyers, gathered from the company's Web site. First, you will open the New Address List dialog box. Then you will customize the fields, renaming one of the default fields as Preferred Location, and deleting those columns you do not need. Finally, you will enter the data. You can create or edit address lists at any time, from any publication, just as you did with business information sets.

When you create an address list in Publisher, you can edit its entries without closing the current publication. If you are using a data source from another program, such as Microsoft Excel or Microsoft Word, you cannot edit the data source without closing the Publisher publication.

To Create the Address List

The following steps begin the process to create an address list by displaying the New Address List dialog box.

1

- Click Tools on the menu bar, and then point to Mailings and Catalogs to display the Mailings and Catalogs submenu (Figure 5–13).

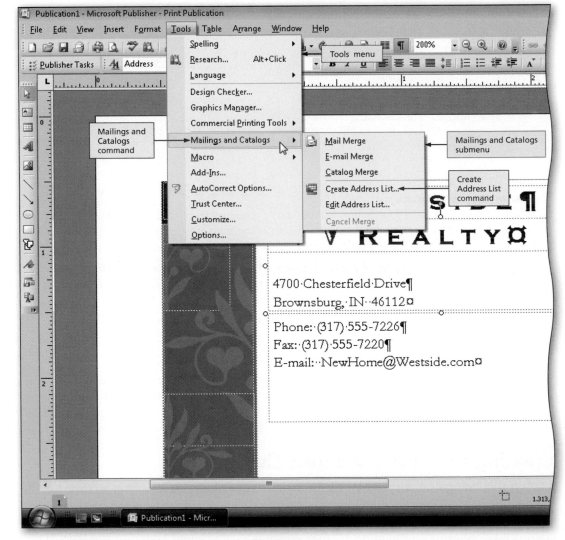

Figure 5–13

2

• Click Create Address List to display the New Address List dialog box (Figure 5–14).

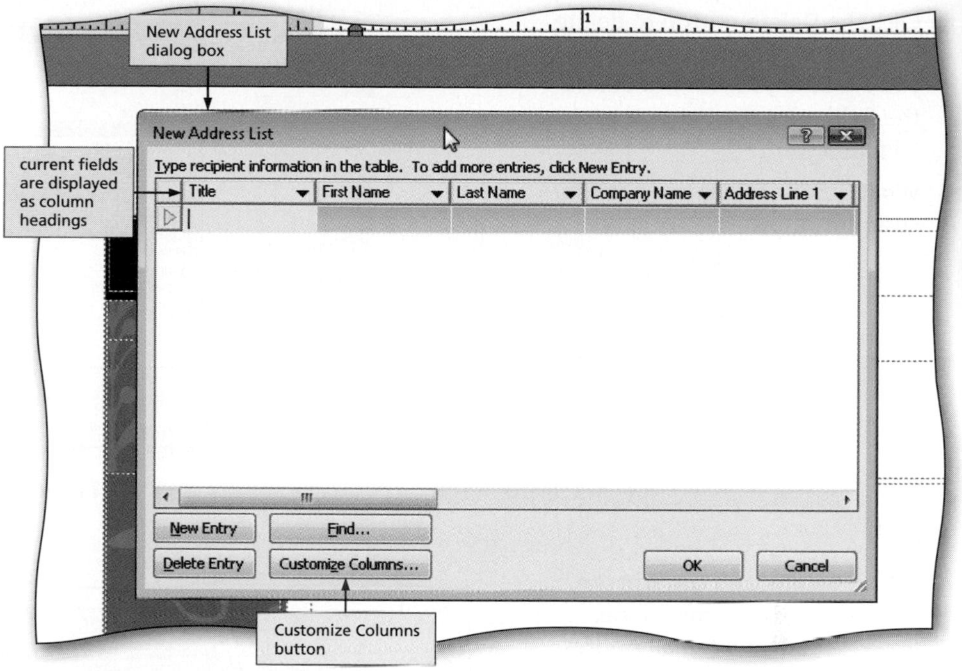

Figure 5–14

To Customize Address List Columns

To customize the fields of data, the next steps edit the columns in the New Address List dialog box.

1

• With the New Address List dialog box displayed, click the Customize Columns button to display the Customize Address List dialog box.

• Click Company Name in the Field Names list to select it (Figure 5–15).

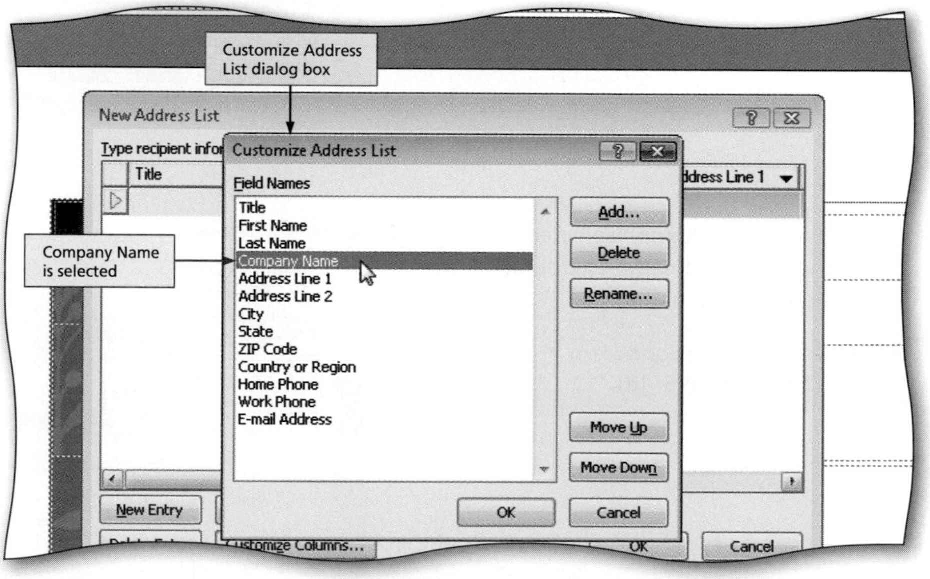

Figure 5–15

2

- Click the Delete button to delete the field. When Publisher asks if you are sure you want to delete the field, click the Yes button (Figure 5–16).

Q&A What other options do I have for customization?

You can add a new column, rename a column, or move columns up and down to place the fields in the desired order, with user-friendly names.

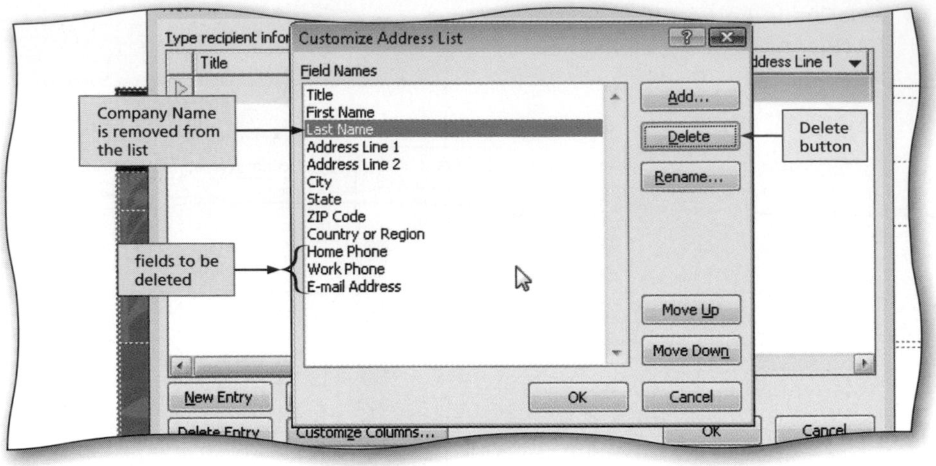

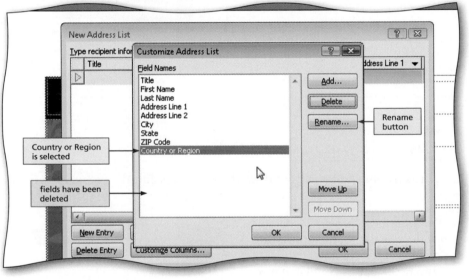

Figure 5–16

3

- Select, delete, and confirm the deletion of the Home Phone, Work Phone, and E-mail Address fields (Figure 5–17).

Q&A Can I delete multiple columns at one time?

No, you must select them and delete them individually.

Figure 5–17

4

- With Country or Region selected, click the Rename button to display the Rename Field dialog box.

- Type `Preferred Location` in the To box (Figure 5–18).

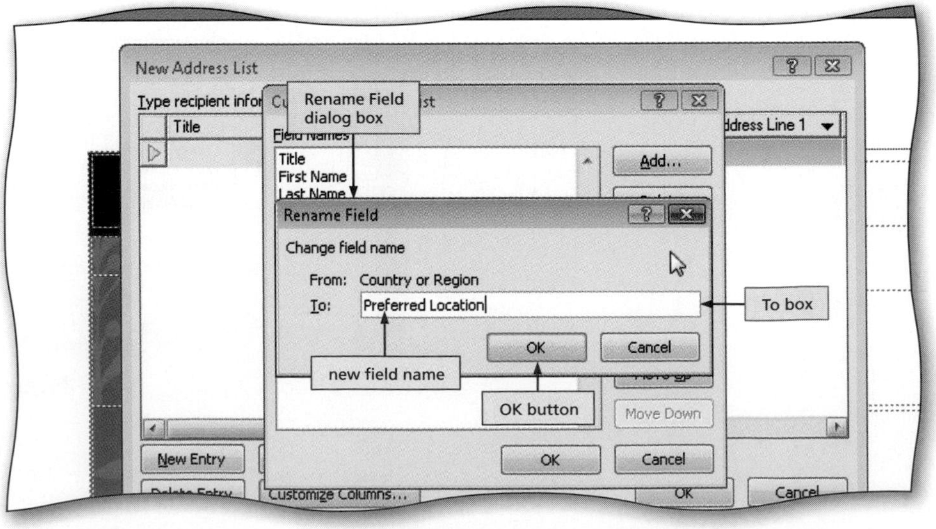

Figure 5–18

5

- Click the OK button to close the Rename Field dialog box and return to the Customize Address List dialog box.

🔍 **Experiment**

- Experiment with moving the fields to different locations by selecting individual fields, and then clicking the Move Up button or the Move Down button.

- If the fields are not in the same order as shown in Figure 5–19, select a field and then click the Move Up button or the Move Down button to correct the order.

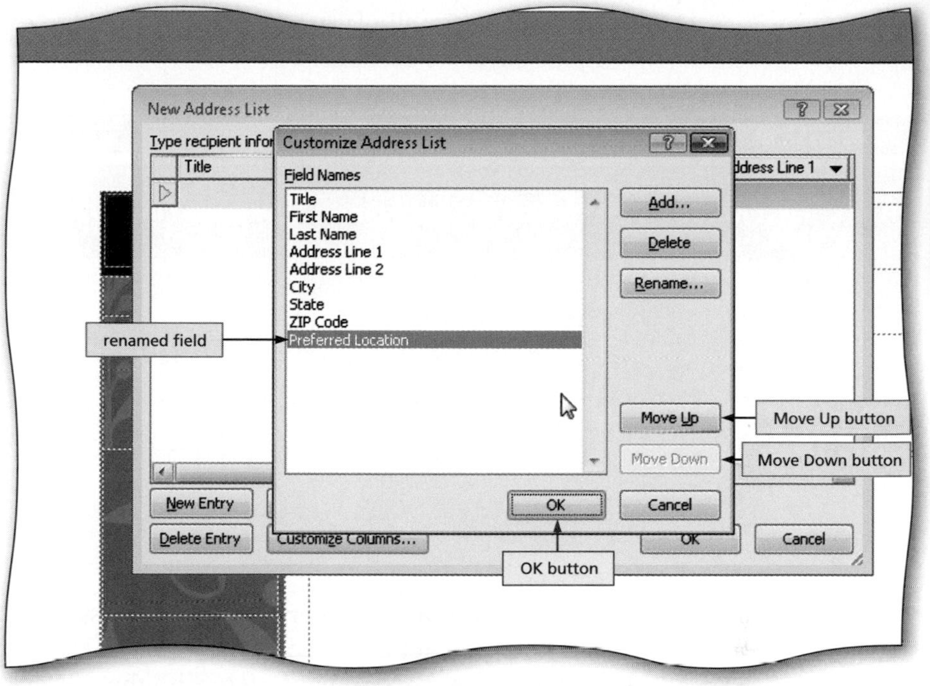

Figure 5–19

6

- Click the OK button to close the Customize Address List dialog box and return to the New Address List dialog box (Figure 5–20).

Q&A Where is the Preferred Location column?

You can use the scroll bar to view the other columns and the new field name.

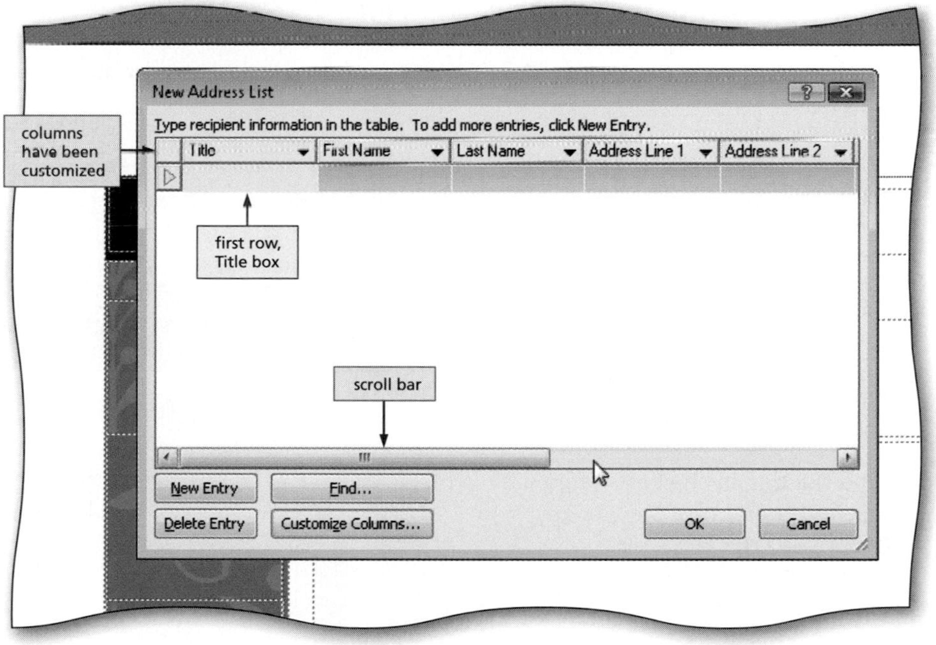

Figure 5–20

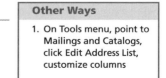

Other Ways

1. On Tools menu, point to Mailings and Catalogs, click Edit Address List, customize columns

Entering Data into the Address List

Table 5–3 displays the data that Westside Realty wants to store about their prospective home buyers or customers.

Table 5–3 Customer Address List Data

Title	First Name	Last Name	Address Line 1	Address Line 2	City	State	ZIP Code	Preferred Location
Dr.	Eric	Kantor	1400 Mall Drive	Suite B	Brownsburg	IN	46112	Carmel
Mr.	Javier	Alvarado	8006 Howard		Indianapolis	IN	46202	Brownsburg
Mr.	Ari	Javari	150 Grant Building	Office 24 East	Carmel	IN	46033	Brownsburg
Rev.	Solomon	Walter	Eastwood Church	247 Antioch Ave.	Avon	IN	46123	Brownsburg
Ms.	Teresa	Chen	942 Sealy Ave.		Brownsburg	IN	46112	Indianapolis
Mr.	Nathan	Reneau	1400 Mall Drive	Suite K	Avon	IN	46123	Brownsburg
Ms.	Marsha	Elana	1135 Calumet		Pittsboro	IN	46167	Indianapolis

Notice that some customers have no Address Line 2. You will leave that field blank. As you enter data, do not press the space bar at the end of the field. As you will see later in the chapter, extra spaces can interfere with the display of the merged fields.

To Enter Data into the Address List

The following steps enter the first record into the address list, using the information from Table 5–3.

1

- With the New Address List dialog box displayed, click the box in the first row, below the Title heading, if necessary.
- Type Dr. in the Title box and then press the TAB key.
- Type Eric in the First Name box and then press the TAB key.
- Type Kantor in the Last Name box and then press the TAB key (Figure 5–21).

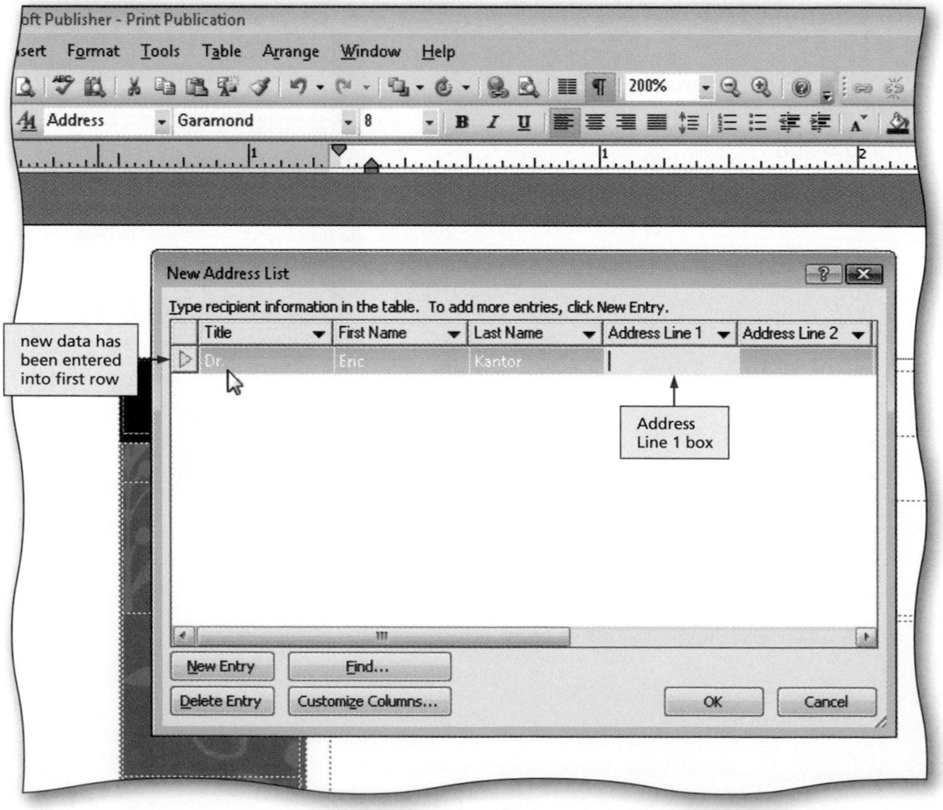

Figure 5–21

2

- Continue to enter data from the first row in Table 5–3. Press the TAB key to advance to each new text box. Do not press the TAB key at the end of the row (Figure 5–22).

Q&A

What does the Find button do?

When you click the Find button, Publisher displays the Find Entry dialog box. In this dialog box, you can look for specific pieces of data that have been typed so far in the address list. The Find Entry dialog box lets you search the entire list or specific fields.

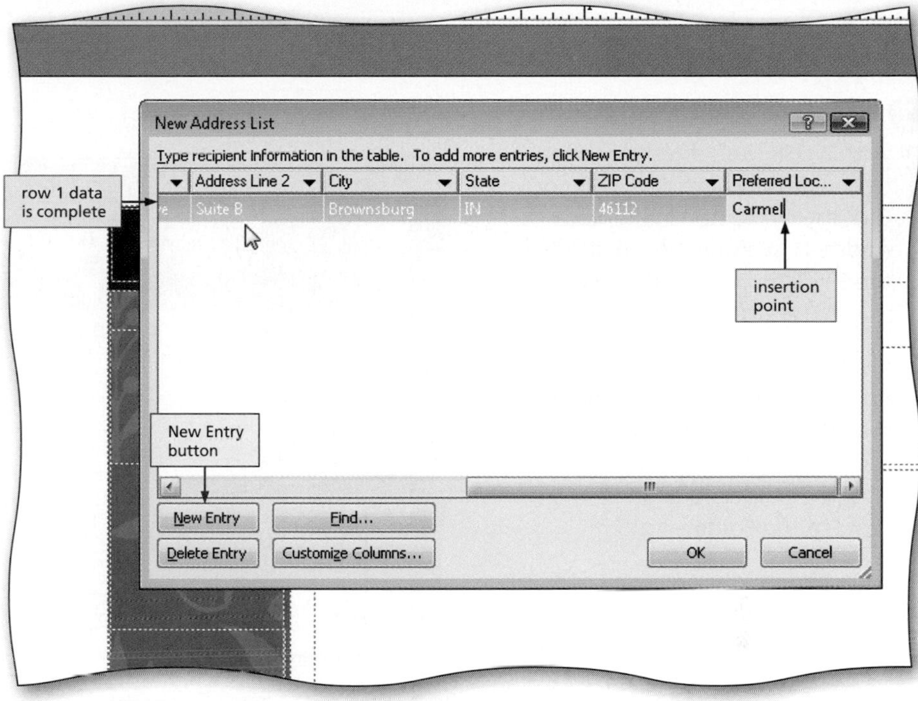

Figure 5–22

To Create New Entries in the Address List

The next step creates new entries or rows in the address list.

1

- Click the New Entry button to create a new row in the list, and then enter the data from the second row of Table 5–3.

- Continue to add data from Table 5–3, clicking the New Entry button after each row of information in the table is complete. Press the TAB key to move from column to column. Press the TAB key twice to skip an empty field.

- When you finish the last entry, do not click the New Entry button (Figure 5–23).

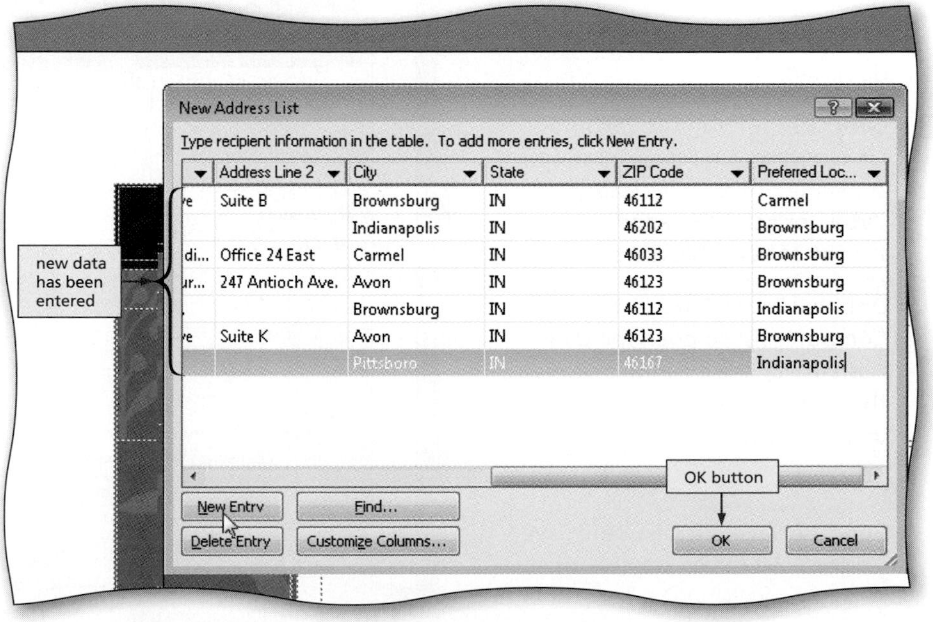

Figure 5–23

To Save the Address List

The following steps save the address list on a USB flash drive with the name Westside Realty Prospective Home Buyers.

1

- With a USB flash drive connected to one of the computer's USB ports, click the OK button in the New Address List dialog box to display the Save Address List dialog box.

- If the Navigation pane is not displayed, click the Browse Folders button to expand the dialog box. If a Folders list is displayed below the Folders button, click the Folders button to remove the Folders list.

- Type Westside Realty Prospective Home Buyers in the File name box. Do not press the ENTER key (Figure 5–24).

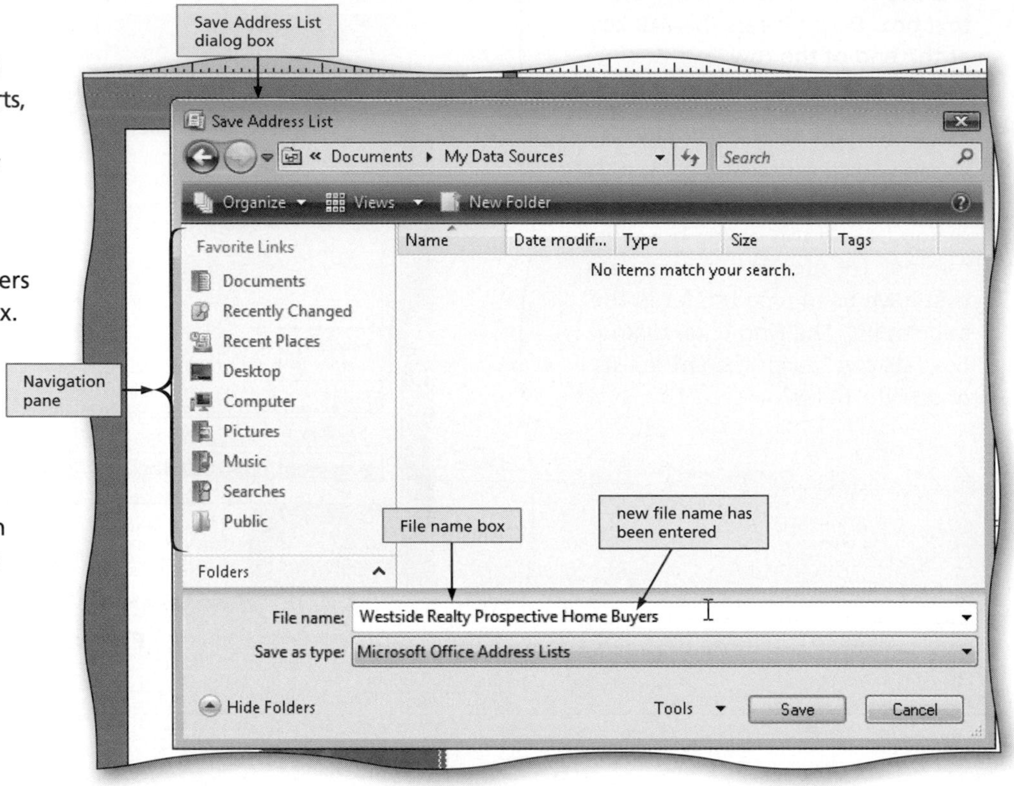

Figure 5–24

2

- If Computer is not displayed in the Favorite Links section, drag the top or bottom edge of the Save As dialog box until Computer is displayed.

- Click Computer in the Favorite Links section to display a list of available drives. If necessary, scroll until USB (F:) appears in the list of available drives.

- Double-click USB (F:) in the Computer list to open the USB flash drive, Drive F in this case, as the new save location (Figure 5–25).

3

- Click the Save button in the Save Address List dialog box.

Figure 5–25

Creating the Form Letter

With the address list complete, you now will begin the body of the main publication.

**Plan
Ahead**

> **Compose the main document for the form letter.**
> A main document contains both the constant, or unchanging, text, as well as field codes for merged fields. The content of the main document for the form letter should contain the date, inside address block, greeting, body, closing, and salutation. It should use proper grammar, correct spelling, logically constructed sentences, flowing paragraphs, and sound ideas. Be sure to proofread it carefully.

To Start the Form Letter

The following steps create a text box to start the form letter.

1

- Zoom to Whole Page.

- Click the Text Box button in the Objects toolbar.

- Drag a large, rectangular text box that begins below the phone/fax/e-mail text box and extends to the bottom margin. The rectangle should fill the space between the decorative border and the right margin, covering the watermark graphic (Figure 5–26).

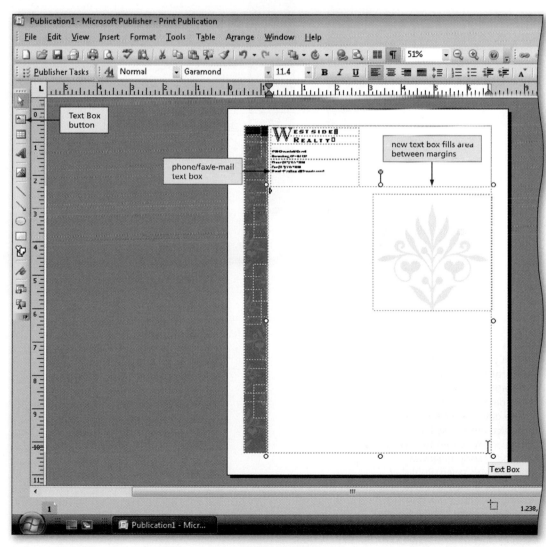

Figure 5–26

2

- Press the F9 key to zoom the text box to 100%.

- Press CTRL+1 to change to single spacing.

- Type June 1, 2009 and then press the ENTER key twice (Figure 5–27).

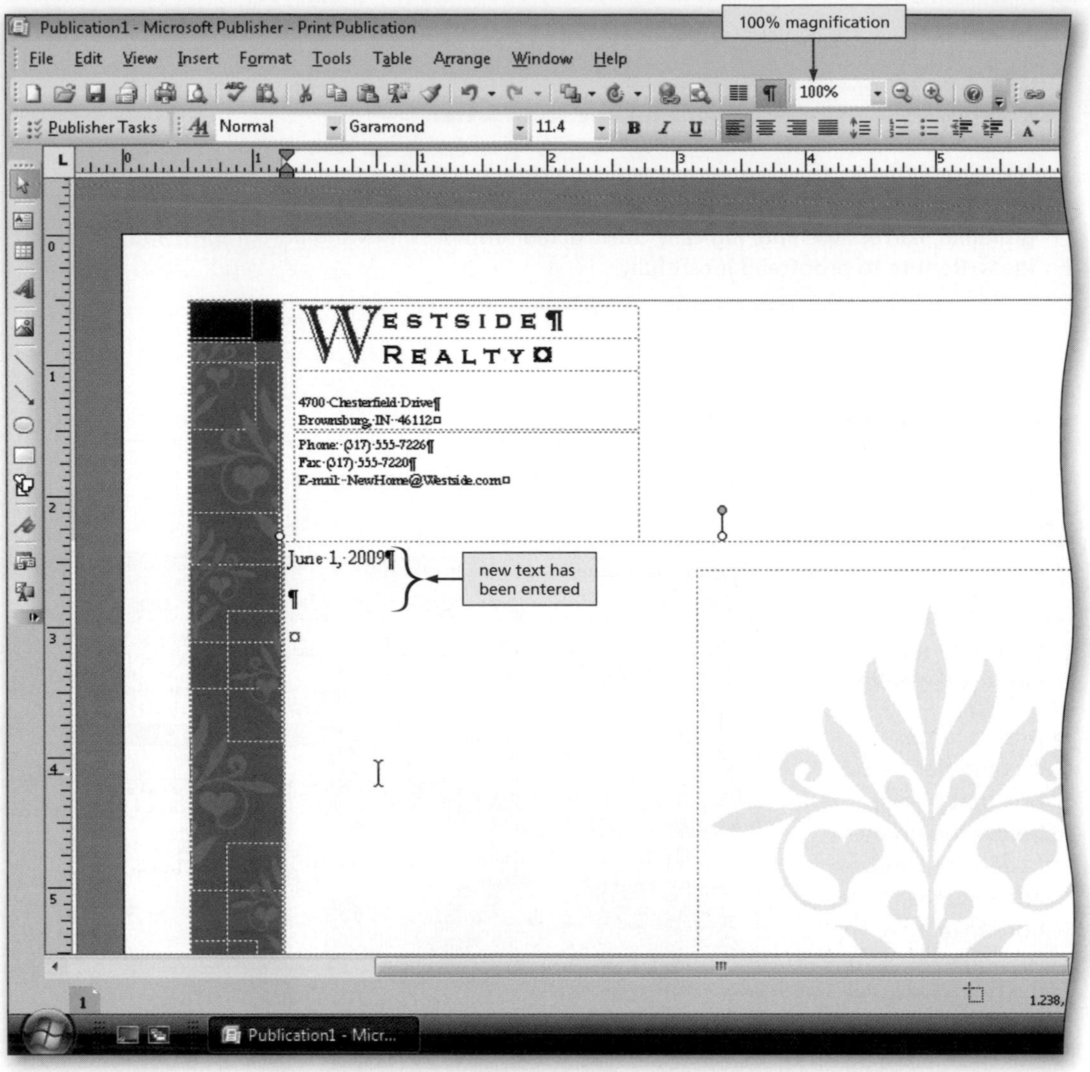

Figure 5–27

BTW

Main Publications
When you open a main publication, Publisher attempts to open the associated data source file, too. If the data source is not in exactly the same location (i.e., drive and folder) as when it originally was merged and saved, Publisher displays a dialog box indicating that it cannot find the data source. When this occurs, click the Find Data Source button to display the Open Data Source dialog box, and locate the data source file yourself.

Connecting the Address List to the Form Letter

The **Mail Merge task pane** displays several steps to help you merge a main publication with an address list. The first step explains how the mail merge works, and connects the address list to the publication.

To Connect the Address List

The following steps begin the merge process by connecting the main publication to the address list.

1

- Click Tools on the menu bar, point to Mailings and Catalogs, and then click Mail Merge to display the Mail Merge task pane.

- If necessary, click the 'Use an existing list' option button to select it in the task pane (Figure 5–28).

Q&A

Why does my Mail Merge task pane look different?

If you have already connected the current publication to a data source, the Mail Merge Task Pane displays the location and name of the currently connected data source instead of the option buttons to create or connect to a list. If you are connected to the wrong database, click Tools on the menu bar, point to Mailings and Catalogs, and then click Cancel Merge. You then can begin Step 1 again.

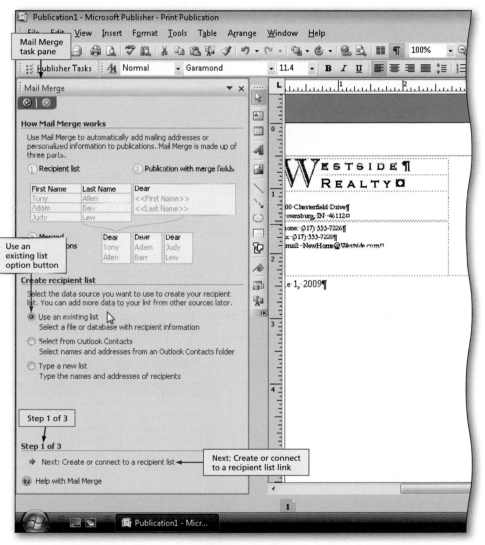

Figure 5–28

2

- With the USB drive containing your address list connected to your computer, at the bottom of the task pane, click the 'Next: Create or connect to a recipient list' link to display the Select Data Source dialog box.

- Navigate to the USB drive (Figure 5–29).

Q&A

What do the other buttons do in the Select Data Source dialog box?

The **New Source button** helps you connect to a server-based data file. It opens a Data Connection Wizard that allows you to choose the type of data source and the server location. The **All Data Sources button** presents a list of acceptable file types. When you choose a file type from the list, Publisher displays files only of that type and existing folders in the current location.

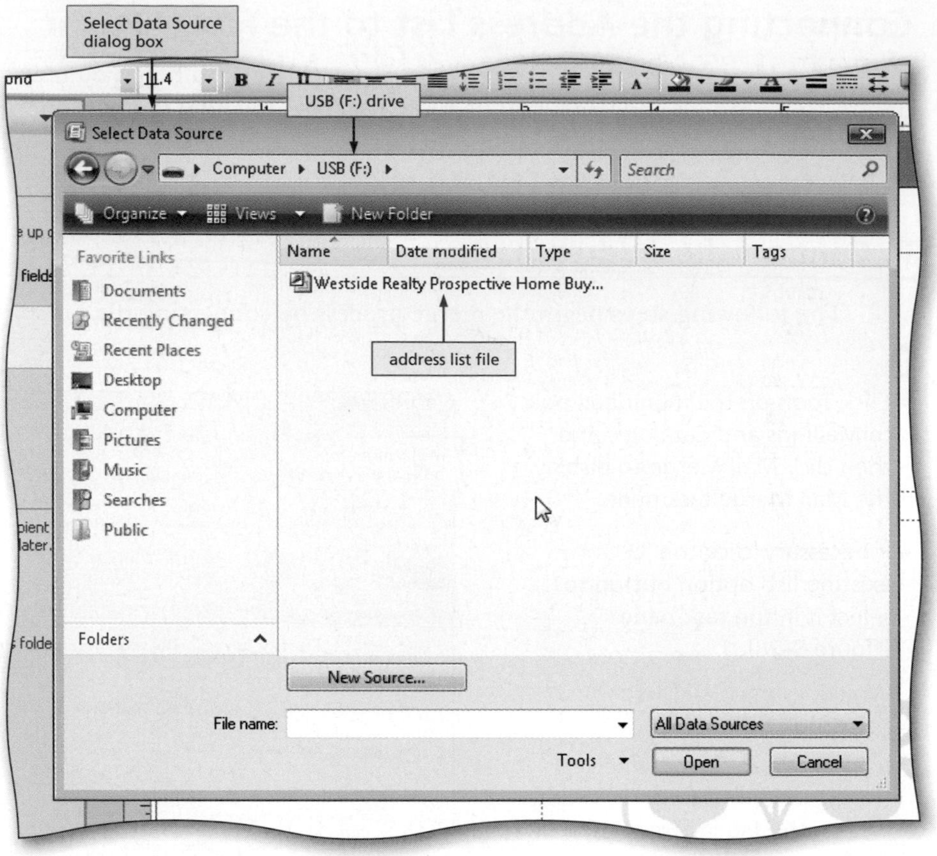

Figure 5–29

3

- Double-click the file named Westside Realty Prospective Home Buyers to display the list of mail merge recipients (Figure 5–30).

Q&A

What if I cannot find my file?

You may have a different file type selected. If the button next to the File name box does not say All Data Sources, click it and then select All Data Sources in the list. The file was created earlier in this chapter and saved on a USB drive connected to your system. If you did not create the file, see your instructor for a copy of the file.

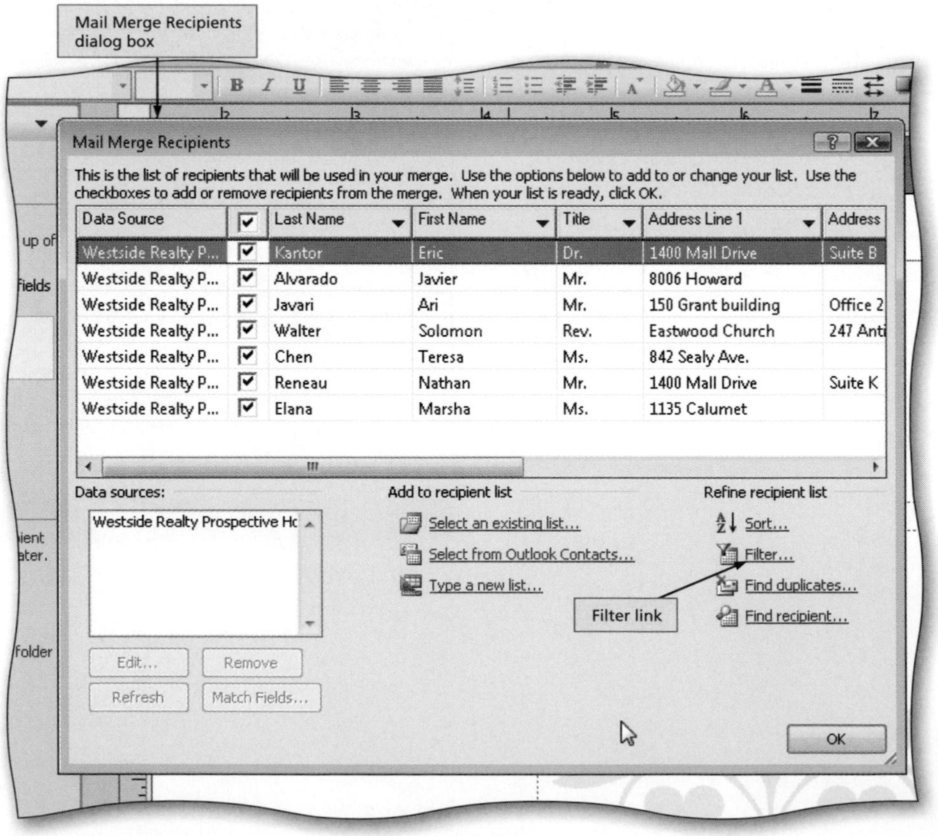

Figure 5–30

To Filter Recipients

The next steps filter the recipients list to choose only those home buyers interested in purchasing homes in the Brownsburg area.

1

• With the Mail Merge Recipients dialog box still selected, click the Filter link to display the Filter and Sort dialog box. If necessary, click the Filter Records tab.

• Click the Field box arrow, and then scroll as necessary and click Preferred Location in the list. If necessary, click the Comparison box arrow and then click Equal to in the list.

• In the Compare to box, type Brownsburg to filter the list. (Figure 5–31).

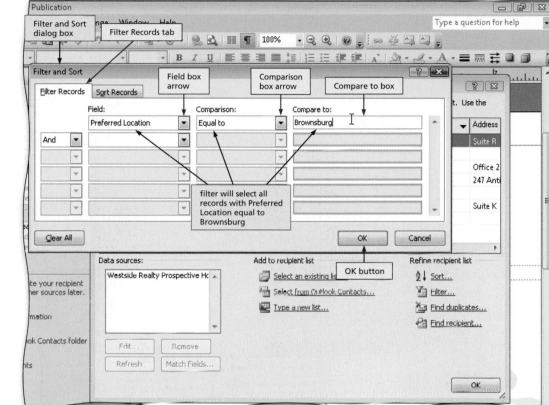

Figure 5–31

2

• Click the OK button in the Filter and Sort dialog box to accept the filter settings (Figure 5–32).

Q&A
Why did my list become shorter?

If you used the filter correctly, the recipients list is shorter because it displays only those people who were interested in purchasing homes in the Brownsburg area.

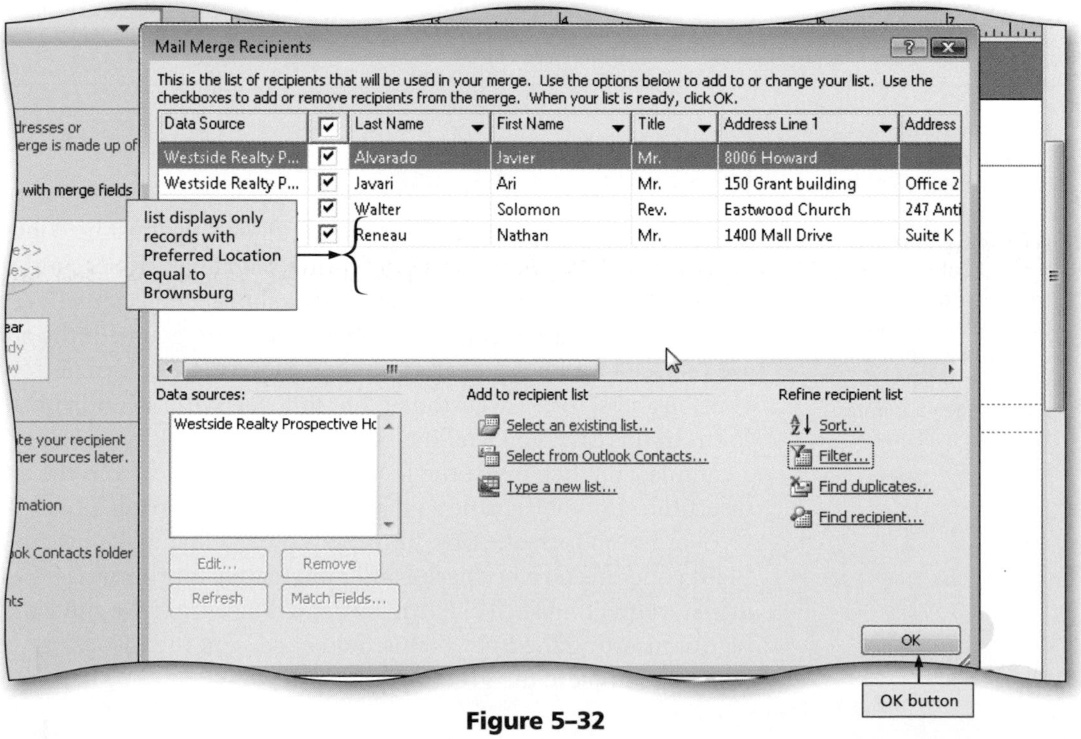

Figure 5–32

3

• Click the OK button in the Mail Merge Recipients dialog box to accept the list and continue to the second step in the Mail Merge task pane (Figure 5–33).

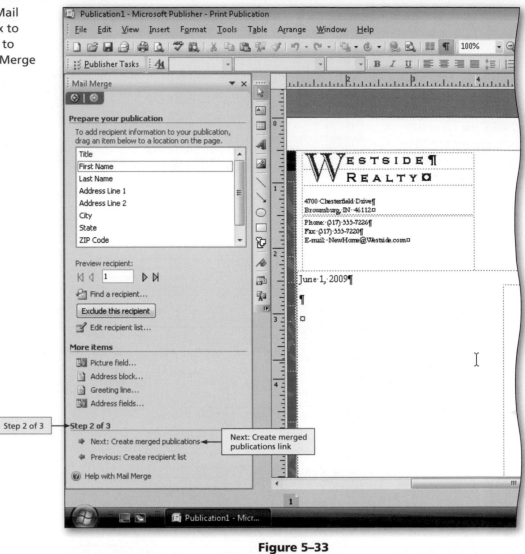

Figure 5–33

BTW

Filter and Sort
The Filter and Sort links (shown in Figure 5–32 on the previous page) allow you either to merge a subset of records from your data source or to sort your data in a particular order. The filter and sort links do not change your data source or mail merge permanently.

Inserting Field Codes

A publication designed for merging not only must be connected to its data source, but also must contain form fields, sometimes called field codes, in the publication. A **field code** is placeholder text in the publication that shows Publisher where to insert the information from the data source. Once the publication is merged with the address list, the field codes are replaced with unique information. For example, a form letter may say, Thank you for your business, to every customer, but follow it with the individual customer's name, such as John. In this case, you would type the words, `Thank you for your business`, insert a comma, and then insert the form field, First Name, from the address list. Publisher would insert the customer's name so that the letter would read, Thank you for your business, John.

You can format, copy, move, or delete a field code just as you would regular text. Field codes need to be spaced and punctuated appropriately. For instance, if you want to display a greeting such as Dear Katie, you need to type the word Dear followed by a space before inserting the First Name field code. You then would type a comma after the field code, to complete the greeting.

To insert a field code from the Mail Merge task pane, you either can position your insertion point in the publication and click the field code, or drag the field code from the task pane to the publication, dropping it at the appropriate location.

Publisher allows you to insert field codes from the address list into the main publication one field at a time or in predefined groups. For example, if you wanted to display the amount due from an address list, you would choose that one field from the task pane. To use predefined groups, you would use a **grouped field code**, which is a set of standard fields, such as typical address fields or salutation fields, preformatted and spaced with appropriate words and punctuation. For example, instead of entering the field codes for Title, First Name, Last Name, Company Name, Address Line 1, and so on, you can choose the grouped field, Address Block, that includes all the fields displayed correctly.

To Insert Grouped Field Codes

The following steps insert grouped field codes for the address block and greeting line in the form letter.

1

- With the second step of the Mail Merge task pane still displayed, ensure that the insertion point is positioned two lines below the date.

- Click the Address block link in the task pane to display the Insert Address Block dialog box (Figure 5–34).

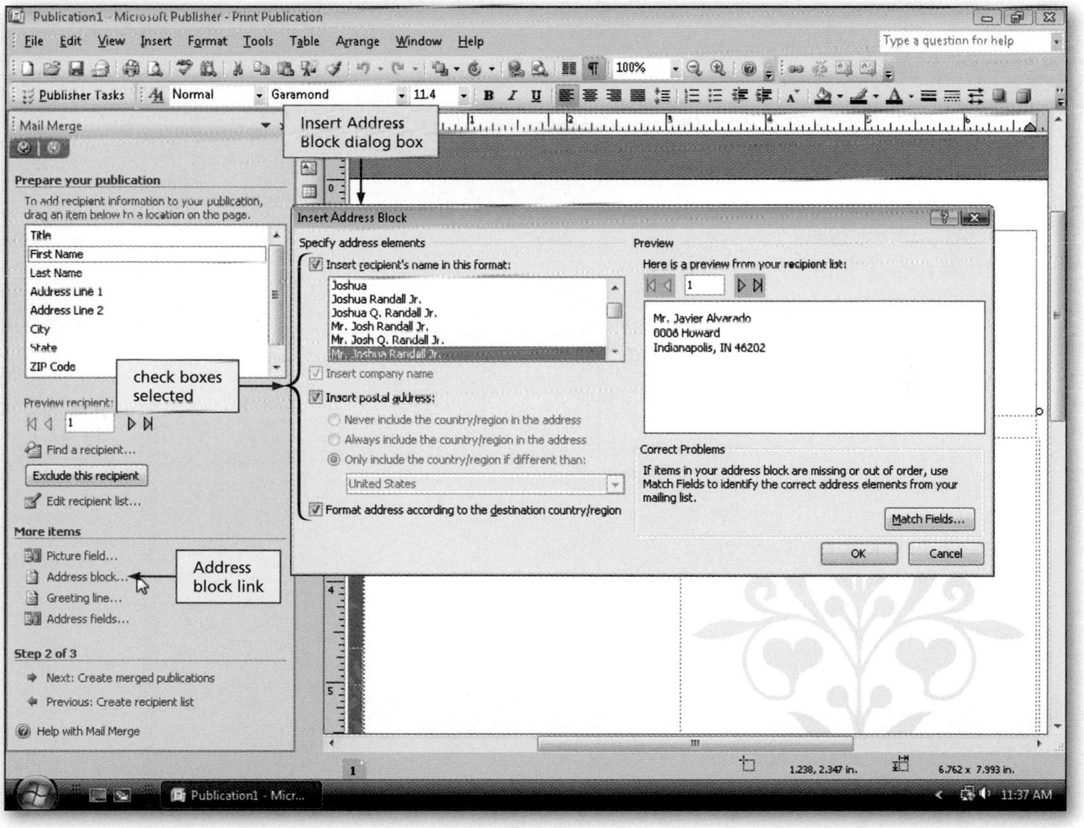

Q&A

What is the difference between an Address block and Address fields?

The Address block link will include fields in the current address list. If you choose Address fields, Publisher displays a list of typical address fields that could be matched with different data sources. That way, if you choose to send a form letter to two different address lists, Publisher will try to match the fields consistently. For example, one address source might include a middle initial or company name, while another one might not.

Figure 5–34

2

- If necessary, click each of the check boxes so that they display check marks.

🔎 **Experiment**

- One at a time, click the formats in the 'Insert recipient's name in this format' list. View the changes in the preview. Click the Next button to view other entries from the address list.

- Click the format, Mr. Joshua Randall Jr., in the 'Insert recipient's name in this format' list. In the Preview area, click the Previous button, if necessary, until the first recipient in your data source is displayed (Figure 5–35).

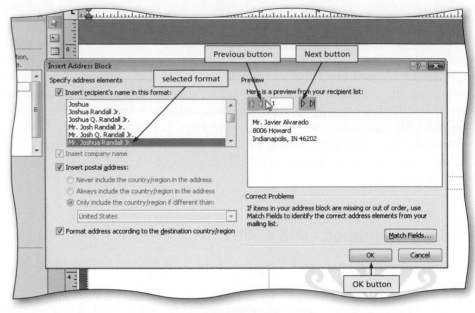

Figure 5–35

3

- Click the OK button to insert the address block into the form letter.

- If necessary, click at the end of the inserted address block to reveal the field code (Figure 5–36).

Q&A What do the chevron symbols represent?

Each field code displays chevrons to let you know that it is not actual text. When you point to a field code, Publisher also displays a smart tag named Merge Field. When you click the Merge Field button, a field code menu displays commands to help you edit or delete the field code.

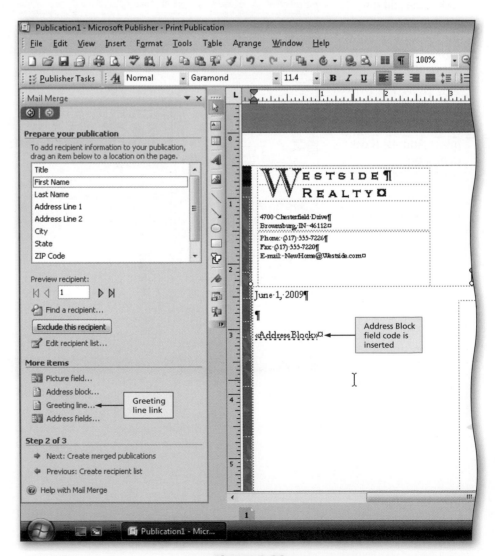

Figure 5–36

4

- Press the ENTER key twice, and then click the Greeting line link to display the Insert Greeting Line dialog box.

Experiment

- One at a time, click the box arrows to view the various kinds of greeting formats. Notice how the preview changes with each selection.

- If necessary, choose the various settings shown in Figure 5–37.

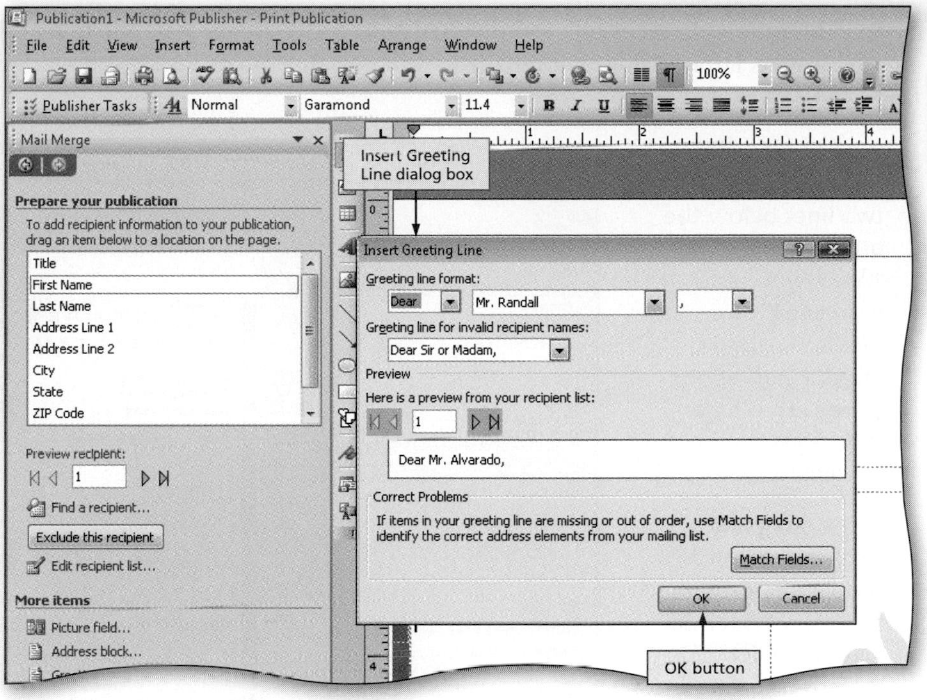

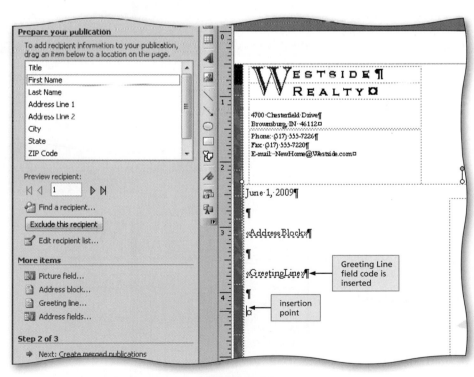

Figure 5–37

5

- Click the OK button to insert the Greeting Line field code into the publication.

- If necessary, click at the end of the inserted greeting line to reveal the field code.

- Press the ENTER key twice to move the insertion point in the publication (Figure 5–38).

Figure 5–38

To Insert Individual Field Codes

The following steps insert individual field codes as you type the body of the form letter. You will finish the merge process later in this chapter.

1

- With the insertion point positioned two lines below the greeting line, type Thank you for visiting our Web site and inquiring about homes in the and then press the spacebar key.

- In the task pane, scroll in the list of recipient information to display Preferred Location. Click Preferred Location to insert the field code into the publication.

- Press the spacebar key. Type area. and then press the spacebar key again to complete the sentence (Figure 5–39).

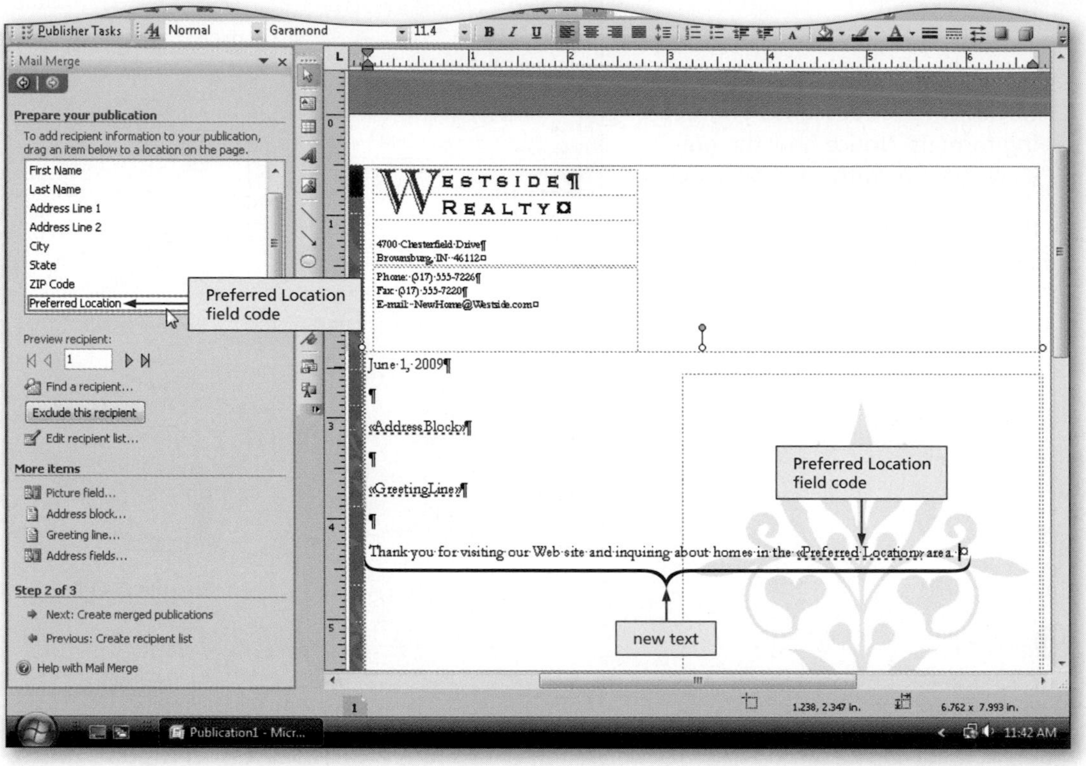

Figure 5–39

2

- Type We know that a move from and then press the spacebar key.

- In the task pane, click City to insert the field code into the publication.

- Press the spacebar key. Type is a big step, and we truly appreciate your business. to complete the sentence (Figure 5–40).

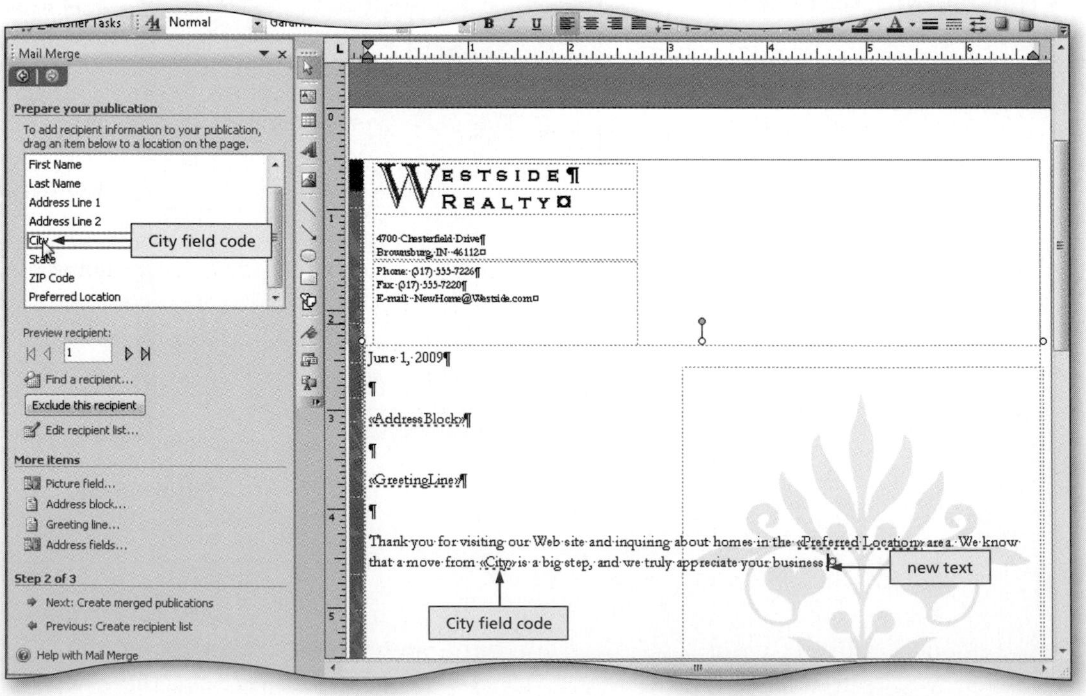

Figure 5–40

❸

- Press the ENTER key twice.

- Type Enclosed please find a short catalog with ten of our most outstanding listings. Some of the advantages of living in this community include:

- Press the ENTER key.

- Close the task pane (Figure 5–41).

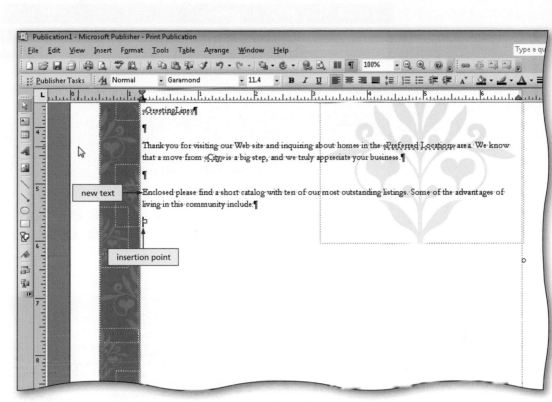

Figure 5–41

Other Ways

1. Drag field from Mail Merge task pane into publication

Working with Tabs and Markers

Publisher uses tabs and markers to help position margins and indentures within text boxes. A **tab**, or tab stop, is a horizontal location inside a text box as noted by a **tab stop marker** in the Publisher ruler. Once the tab is set, you position the insertion point at a tab stop by pressing the TAB key. The default setting is for tabs to exist at every .5 inches in a text box.

The triangles and rectangles on the ruler are called **markers**. They help you position the margins in a text box and change how paragraphs indent. An **indent** is an automatic positioning of the left margin in the first line of a paragraph, which occurs when you press the ENTER key.

Sometimes it is difficult to determine whether to use tab stops or indents. Use tab stops when you want to indent paragraphs as you go, or when you want a simple column. When the tab stop is positioned for a long passage of text, using the TAB key to indent the first line of each paragraph is inefficient, because you must press it each time you begin a new paragraph. In these cases, it is better to use an indent because it automatically carries forward when you press the ENTER key.

You can drag markers to any place on the ruler within the text box boundaries. You can click a marker to display a dotted line through the publication, to see in advance where the marker is set. Markers are paragraph-specific, which means that when you set the tabs and indents, they apply to the current paragraph. Once the tabs and indents are set, however, pressing the ENTER key carries forward the markers to the next paragraph.

The **tab selector** is located at the left end of the ruler. It displays an icon representing the alignment of the text at the tab stop — left, right, center, decimal. A **decimal tab** is a tab that aligns numbers at a decimal point. Table 5–4 on the next page lists the types of tab alignments and their common uses.

BTW

Empty Fields
If you have empty or blank fields in your data source, Publisher will omit the field when the publication is merged. For instance, if no second address line exists, Publisher will move the other fields up during the print process in order to fill the gap.

Table 5–4 Types of Tab Alignments		
Name	**Action**	**Purpose**
Left tab	Text begins at tab stop and moves to the right	Used for most tabbing
Right tab	Text begins at tab stop and moves to the left	Used for indexes, programs, and lists
Center tab	Text is centered at the tab stop as it is typed	Used to center a list within a column
Decimal tab	Aligns numbers only, around a decimal point, independent of the number of digits	Used for aligning currency amounts in a list

The tab stop alignment can be changed by clicking Tabs on the Format menu, by double-clicking an existing marker, or by clicking the tab selector until it displays the type of tab that you want (Figure 5–42).

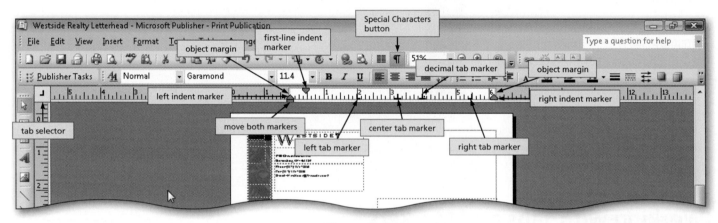

Figure 5–42

Zero Point
The tab selector is the intersection of the horizontal and vertical rulers. Recall that you can drag the rulers to new locations to assist in placing and aligning objects. You also can CTRL+click or CTRL+drag the tab selector to change the publication's zero point or ruler origin. The **zero point** is the position of 0 inches on the ruler. It is useful for measuring the width and height of objects on the page without having to add or subtract from a number other than zero. To change the ruler back, so that the zero point is at the top-left corner of the printed page, double-click the tab selector.

A **leader tab** is a special kind of right-justified tab in which the blank space to the left of the text is filled with a certain character. Customized via the Tabs dialog box, a leader repeats the character from the previous text or tab stop to fill in the tabbed gap. For example, a printed musical program might contain the name of the composition on the left and the composer on the right. If the program were created using a leader tab, that space in between would be filled by dots or periods to help the viewer's eye follow across to the matching composer. Available leader styles include None, Dot, Dash, Line, and Bullet.

Table 5–5 explains the functions of the markers and buttons on the ruler and how to modify them.

Table 5–5 Ruler Tools

Tool Name	Description	How to Change	Other Ways
First-line indent marker	The position at which paragraphs begin	Drag to desired location	On Format menu, click Tabs
Left indent marker	The left position at which text wraps	Drag to desire location	On Format menu, click Tabs
Move both markers	A small rectangle used to move both the left indent marker and the first-line indent marker at the same time	Drag to desired location	On Format menu, click Tabs
Object margins	Gray indicates the area outside the object margin; white indicates the area inside the object margin	Resize object	On Format menu, click Text Box, click Size tab
Right indent marker	The right position at which text wraps to the next line	Drag to desired location	On Format menu, click Tabs
Tab selector	Displays the current alignment setting: left, right, center, or leader	Click to toggle choice	Double-click tab stop marker
Tab stop marker	Displays the location of a tab stop	Click to create; drag to move	On Format menu, click Tabs

Recall that the Special Characters button shown in Figure 5–42 on the Standard toolbar makes visible special nonprinting characters to help you format text passages, including tab characters (→), end-of-paragraph marks (¶), and end-of-frame marks (¤).

Inserting a Tab Stop

The following step shows how to add a tab stop at 1.25 inches in the form letter text box by clicking the horizontal ruler. A tab stop will ensure that the data is aligned properly.

To Insert a Tab Stop

1

- With the insertion point located two lines below the text in the form letter, zoom to 150%.

- Click the horizontal ruler at the 1.25" mark to create a left tab stop. Move the mouse down slightly so the tab stop is visible (Figure 5–43).

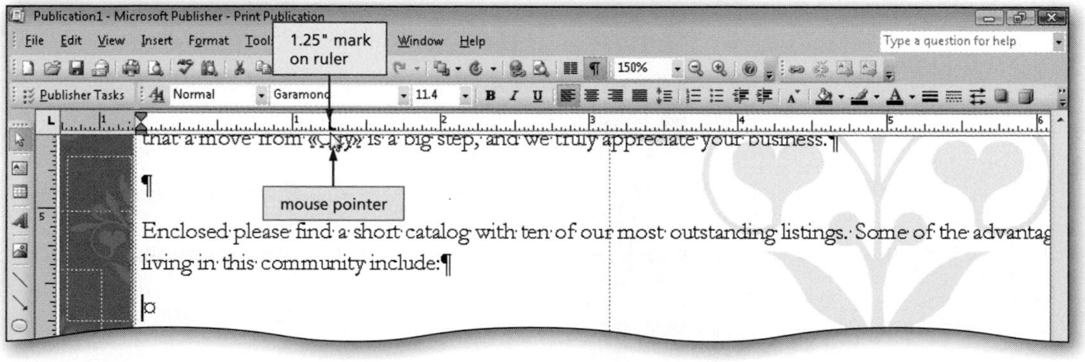

Figure 5–43

Q&A

Is the tab always a left-justified tab?

Left tab is the default setting. If you want to change the tab style, click the tab selector until you see the tab style you want and then click the ruler at the tab stop location.

To Enter Tabbed Text

The following steps enter tabbed text.

1

- Press the TAB key to move the insertion point to the tab stop.

- Type Five-star schools and then press the ENTER key (Figure 5–44).

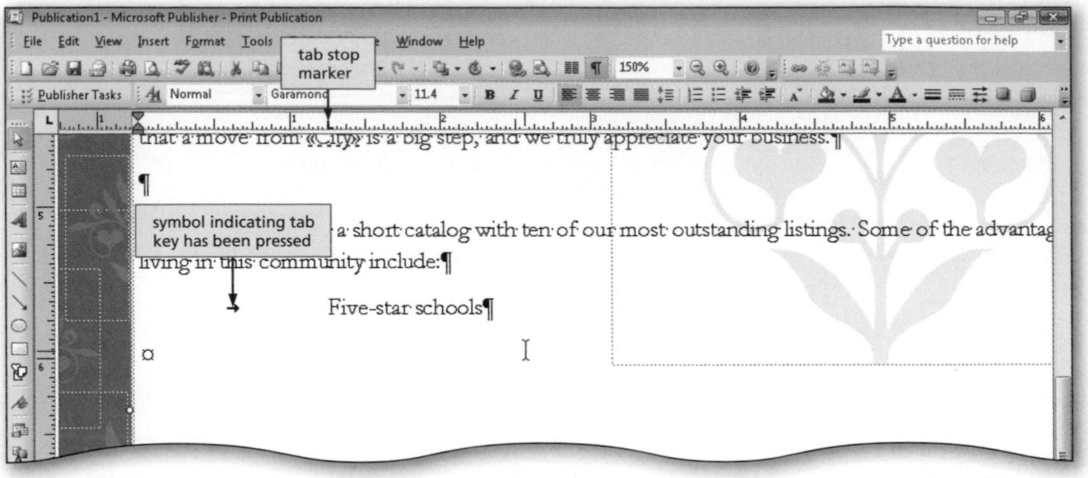

Figure 5–44

2

- Continue to enter the tabbed text shown in Figure 5–45, pressing the TAB key at the beginning of each line and the ENTER key at the end of each line (Figure 5–45).

Q&A

How do I delete a tab?

To delete a tab, drag the tab marker from its location in the ruler to the tab selector and drop it there. Or you can click Tabs on the Format menu, select the tab stop location, and then click the Clear button.

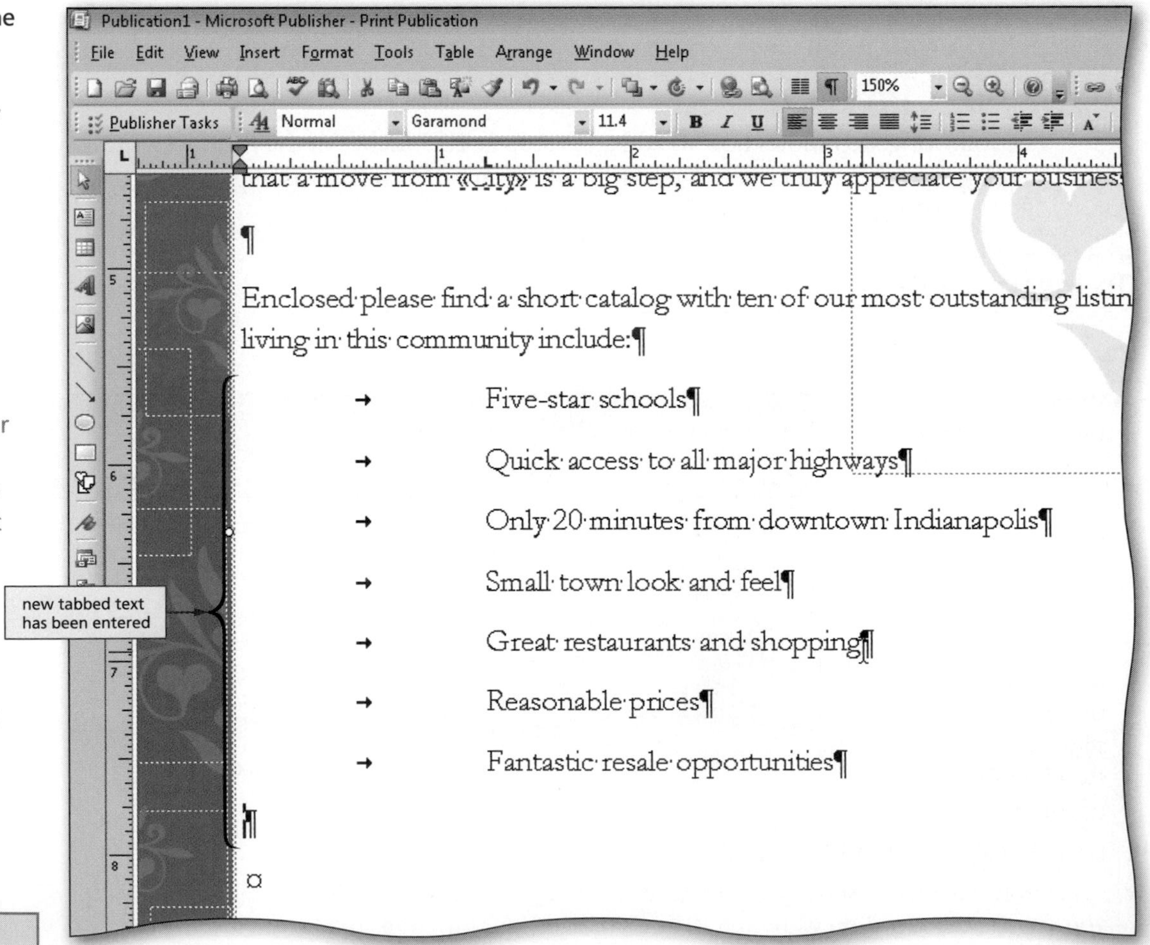

Figure 5–45

Other Ways

1. On Format menu, click Tabs, enter desired tab stop location

To Finish the Form Letter Text

The following steps enter the rest of the form letter text.

1 Type `Please call to arrange a personal tour of our listed homes. If we can be of any service to you, just let us know.` to compete the body of the letter. Press the ENTER key twice to create a blank line before the salutation.

2 Type `Sincerely,` and then press the ENTER key four times.

3 Type `Mark Williams` and then press the ENTER key.

4 Type `Sales Associate` and then press the ENTER key.

5 Type `(317) 555-7226, Ext. 175` to complete the closing (Figure 5–46).

BTW

Hanging Indents
A first-line indent placed to the left of the left margin sometimes is called a hanging indent or exdent. Exdents typically are found in bibliographies and alphabetized listings. Creating an exdent saves keystrokes and formatting time.

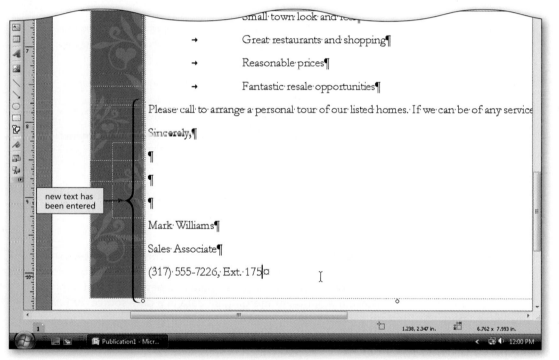

Figure 5–46

To Save the Form Letter

The following steps save the publication with the file name, Westside Realty Form Letter. For a detailed example of the procedure summarized below, refer to pages PUB 31 through PUB 33 in Chapter 1.

1 With a USB flash drive connected to one of the computer's USB ports, click the Save button on the Standard toolbar.

2 Type `Westside Realty Form Letter` in the File name text box to change the file name. Do not press the ENTER key.

3 Navigate to your USB flash drive.

4 Click the Save button in the Save As dialog box to save the publication on the USB flash drive.

Printing the Merged Document

The body of the text, including the field codes, is complete. You now must complete the merge process in order to print the documents. Normally, you do not save individual copies of the merged publications because they are all the same and take up memory on your storage device — especially if you are merging with a long list. If you needed to do so later, you could merge the main publication and the address list again to create the publications. If you decide to save the merged publication, Publisher allows you to perform various printing and saving operations, as shown in Table 5–6.

Table 5–6 Create Merged Publication Options

Option	Description
Print	Print the merged pages
Print preview	Preview each page of the merged pages
Merge to a new publication	Create a new publication with the merged pages, which you can edit further or print
Add to existing publication	Add the merged pages to the end of the existing publication
Print recipient list	Create a hard copy of the recipient list of the current merge for your records, including filters or sorts
Save a shortcut to recipient list	Create a shortcut to the address list used in the current merge
Export recipient list to new file	Create a new file based on the filtered or sorted address list used in the current merge

You will complete the merge and print the merged pages, creating hard copies of the form letter with data from the address list.

Plan Ahead

Merge the main document with the data source to create the form letters.
Merging is the process of combining the contents of a data source with a main document. You can print the merged letters on the printer or place them in a new document, which you later can edit. You also have the option of merging all data in a data source, or just merging a portion of it from a filter or sort.

To Print Merged Pages

The following steps return to the Mail Merge task pane to complete the merging process and print the resulting letters. Because you have already connected to the data source, the Mail Merge task pane will display its Prepare your publication step when you display the task pane.

1

• Click Tools on the menu bar, point to Mailings and Catalogs, and then click Mail Merge to display the Mail Merge task pane (Figure 5–47).

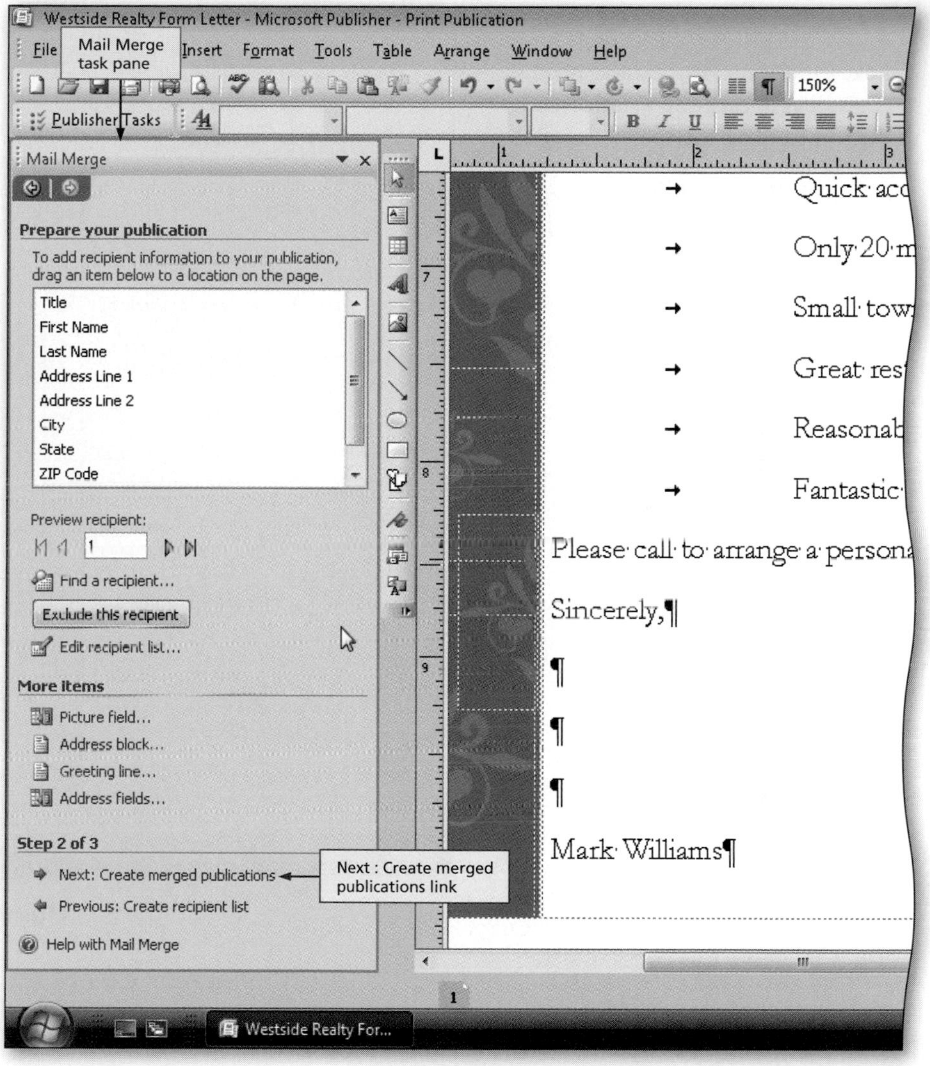

Figure 5–47

2

- Click the 'Next: Create merged publications' link to display the Create merged publications step in the task pane (Figure 5–48).

3

- Ready the printer. Click the Print link. When the Print dialog box is displayed, click the Print or OK button to print the merged pages.

- Retrieve the printouts.

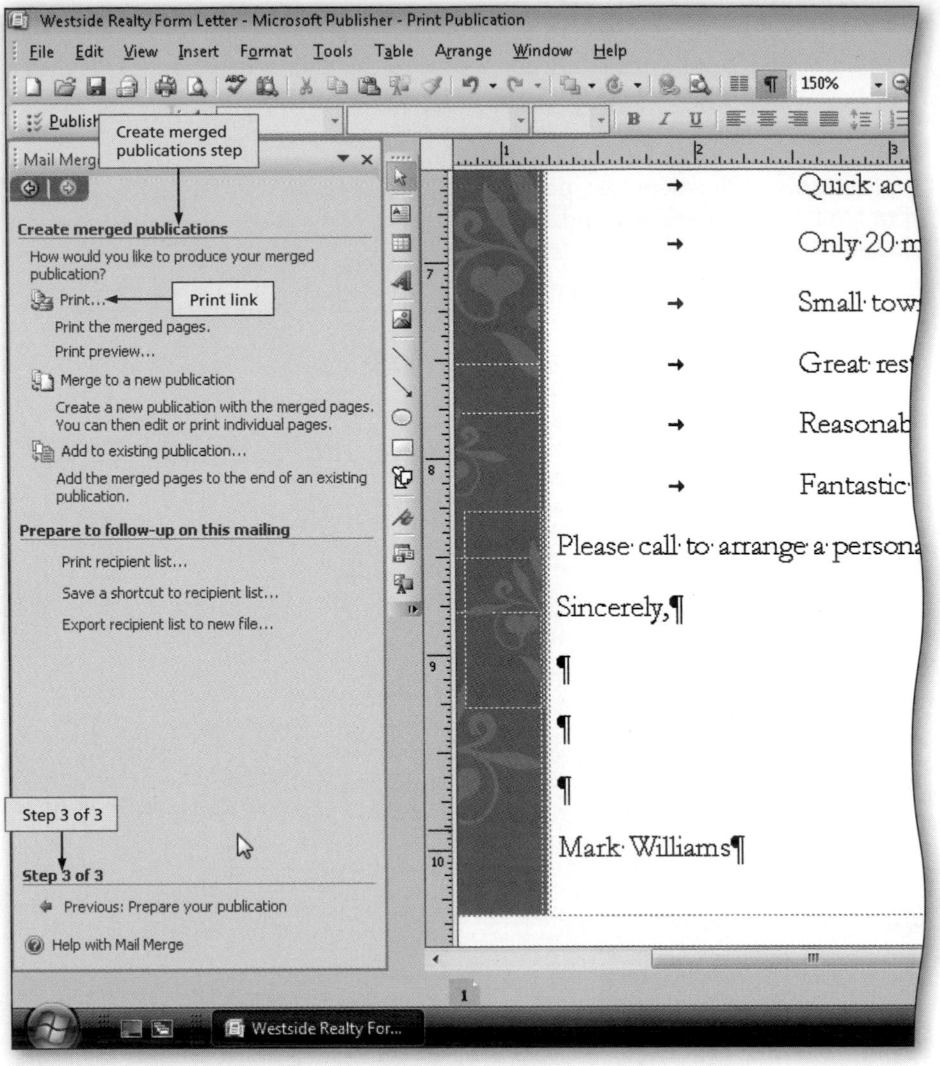

Figure 5–48

Other Ways

1. On Standard toolbar, click Print button

To Close the Publication

The next step closes the publication without quitting Publisher.

1 Click File on the menu bar and then click Close to redisplay the Publisher catalog. If Publisher asks if you want to save the changes, click the No button.

Creating Labels

Another application for merging involves the use of mailing labels. For documents that are not available electronically and for large quantities that have been mass produced, a mailing label sometimes is the most economical method of addressing correspondences. Paper supply companies produce labels for desktop printers in a variety of sizes and configurations.

Generate mailing labels and envelopes.
A label should contain the addressee's full name and address, positioned approximately in the vertical and horizontal center of the envelope. An envelope should contain the sender's full name and address in the upper-left corner of the envelope. Both label and envelope templates supply text boxes for easy insertion of merged fields.

Plan Ahead

To Use the Label Template

The following steps create a main publication using a label template to merge with the address list.

1. With the Publisher catalog still displayed, click Labels.
2. Click the Medium Mailing Address Label (Avery 5161) preview.
3. Click the Create button to display the label template (Figure 5–49).

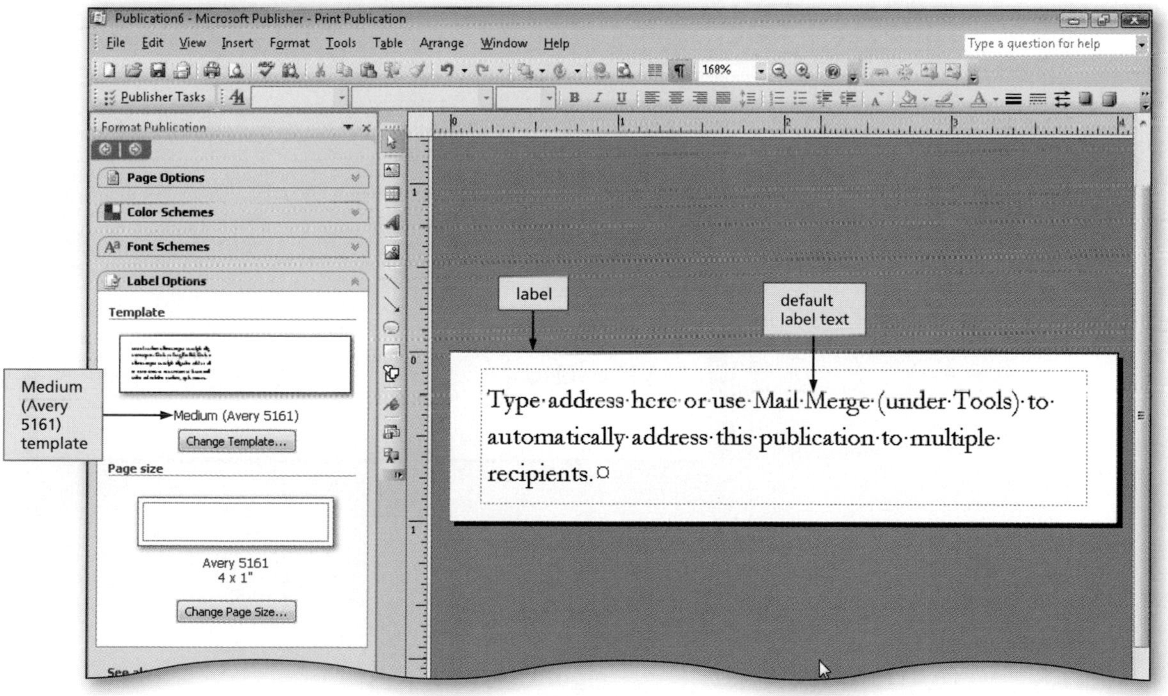

Figure 5–49

To Insert Field Codes and Merge

The following steps insert field codes, using the same mail merge techniques that you learned earlier in this chapter.

1. Click the Other Task Panes button in the title bar of the Format Publication task pane, and then click Mail Merge in the list to display the Mail Merge task pane. If necessary, click the 'Use an existing list' option button to select it.
2. In the lower portion of the task pane, click the 'Next: Create or connect to a recipient list' link to display the Select Data Source dialog box. Navigate to your USB drive. Double-click the file, Westside Realty Prospective Home Buyers, to display the Mail Merge Recipients dialog box.

3 Click the Filter link to display the Filter and Sort dialog box. Click the Field box arrow, and then click Preferred Location. If necessary, click the Comparison box arrow and then click Equal to in the list. In the Compare to box, type Brownsburg.

4 Click the OK button in the Filter and Sort dialog box. Click the OK button in the Mail Merge Recipients dialog box.

5 Click the default text in the label, and then click the Address block link in the task pane to display the Insert Address Block dialog box.

6 Accept the default settings for the address block, and click OK to return to the task pane.

7 Click the text box in the label to reveal the inserted grouped code.

8 In the task pane, click the 'Next: Create merged publications' link to proceed to the next step (Figure 5–50).

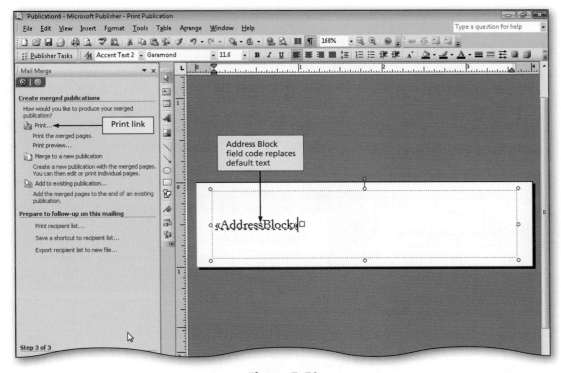

BTW

OCR Address Fonts
You can edit the fonts for field codes to affect the way they print after merging. Many businesses use the OCR A Extended font. **OCR** stands for optical character recognition, which means that the post office can scan the address easily with electronic equipment, thereby speeding up the processing.

Figure 5–50

Label Print Settings

When printing labels, you have three choices in the **Print Setup dialog box**. You can print one label per sheet, which might be appropriate for larger mailing labels or labels created for the front of folders; you can print multiple copies on the page of the same address for future mailings; or, you can print multiple, different addresses on the page, which is suitable for a one-time mass mailing.

Publisher can save the merged files as one large file on the disk. If you are planning to print labels many times, it might be beneficial to save to one large file. Note, however, that saving to one large file requires a large amount of disk space, and that the data is **static**, which means that updates to the data are not reflected. Rather than saving, you can merge the label and address list again if you need to print at a future time, and the new merge will include any updates to the address list.

To Change the Print Settings and Print Labels

The following steps change the print settings and then print the labels.

1

• Ready the printer.

• Click the Print link in the Mail Merge task pane to display the Print dialog box.

• Click the Publication and Paper Settings tab, if necessary.

🔎 **Experiment**

• In the Printing options area, click each of the options individually and view the changes in the Preview area.

• In the Printing options area, click Multiple pages per sheet, if necessary (Figure 5–51).

2

• Click the Print button.

• Retrieve the printout.

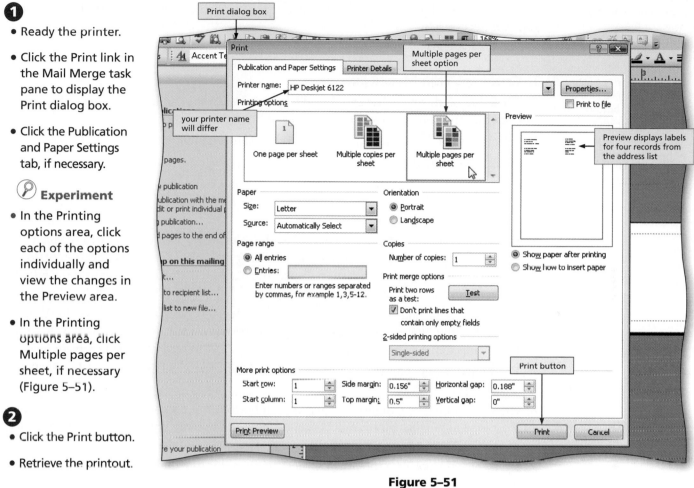

Figure 5–51

Other Ways	
1. On File menu, click Print Merge, click Multiple pages per sheet, click Print	2. On File menu, click Print Setup, click Multiple pages per sheet; on Standard toolbar, click Print button

To Close the Label Publication

The final step is to close the label publication without saving the merged file.

1 Click File on the menu bar, and then click Close. When Publisher asks if you want to save the changes, click the No button.

Envelopes

Envelopes are manufactured in a variety of sizes and shapes. The most common sizes are #6 personal envelopes that measure 3⅝ by 6½ inches and #10 business envelopes that measure 4⅛ by 9½ inches. You also can customize the page layout to instruct Publisher to print envelopes for invitations, cards, and mailers. Merging an address list with an envelope template avoids using labels at all.

Printing Multiples
If the publication page size is one-half the size of your paper or smaller, you can print multiple copies of the page on each printed sheet, even if the publication is not a label. These special sizes, chosen in the Page Setup dialog box, will create a Page Options button that displays in the Print dialog box. You can choose how many copies of the publication to print per page and specify custom margin and gap measurements. The book fold option or book fold imposition will place two pages on opposite facing pages. If your printer supports paper as large as 11-by-17 inches, you can print two standard publication pages, side by side.

Envelopes
Microsoft has many envelope templates for occasions such as holidays, weddings, parties, and graduations. On a system that is connected to the Internet, start Publisher and then type envelope in the 'Type a question for help' box. Publisher will display many templates in the Search Results task pane. Click any template to see a preview before downloading.

Although the majority of businesses outsource their preprinted envelopes, most desktop printers have an envelope-feeding mechanism that works especially well for business envelopes. Check your printer documentation for any limitations on the size and shape of envelopes. For testing purposes, you can print envelopes on 8½-by-11-inch paper, if necessary.

If you needed to print envelopes, you would perform the following steps.

To Create and Print Merged Envelopes

1. Click File on the menu bar and then click New. When the Publisher catalog is displayed, click the Envelopes button in the list of Publication Types.

2. Select an appropriate envelope template, or scroll down in the catalog to select a blank size.

3. Click the Create button.

4. Click Tools on the menu bar, point to Mailings and Catalogs, and then click Mail Merge. When the task pane is displayed, if necessary, click the 'Use an existing list' option button to select it.

5. In the lower portion of the task pane, click the 'Next: Create or connect to a recipient list' link to display the Select Data Source dialog box. Navigate to the location of your address list. Double-click the file to display the Mail Merge recipients dialog box. Filter the list, if necessary. Click the OK button in the Mail Merge Recipients dialog box.

6. Click the default address text in the label, or create a text box for the address. In the task pane, click the Address block link to display the Insert Address Block dialog box. Accept the default settings for the address block, and click OK to return to the task pane.

7. Ready the printer. Click the Print link in the Mail Merge task pane to display the Print dialog box.

8. Click the 'Show how to insert paper' option button, and then click the link to open the Envelope Setup dialog box. Select the feed method used by your printer, and then click the OK button.

9. Feed the envelope into the printer, click the Print button, and then retrieve the printed envelope.

Catalog Merge

In Publisher, a catalog is a collection of pictures and descriptive details, representing items for sale. Catalogs can be created for print or for the Web. Publisher has **catalog templates** to assist you in designing catalogs, and it has a catalog merge that populates the catalog easily. A **catalog merge** is the process of combining information from a data source with a template to create pages that display multiple records per page. You can add the merged pages to an existing publication or create a new publication.

In planning a catalog, you first must decide on the best way to market a product, and then choose a template that matches your style. Publisher has templates for both e-commerce and printed media. Many businesses try to customize catalogs and use customer profiling to target certain markets. A catalog is a significant investment due to production, printing, and distribution costs. Publishing a catalog can be the largest single marketing cost in an annual budget.

The Publisher catalog templates create eight pages of content with replaceable graphics and text boxes. You can select the page size, font scheme, and color scheme of the catalog, just as you do with other publications. Additionally, with catalogs, you can choose the content layout of specific pages, selecting the number of columns, forms, calendars, featured items, or table of contents for those specific pages.

As a marketing tool, a catalog helps you compete for preferred status with buyers. Catalogs streamline the buying cycle by providing complete descriptions and easy buying steps while cutting out inefficiencies, omissions, and lost opportunities. Planned and distributed correctly, catalogs reach a wider market than brochures and newsletters, and they cut down on redundant forms of contact, such as answering questions over the phone or rerunning newspaper ads.

Due to the graphical, full-color nature of most catalogs and the high-quality paper that commonly is used, planning is essential to keep a catalog project on schedule and on budget. You must identify resource requirements and formulate strategies that drive business growth. Typically, a business can reuse and repurpose catalog content for other forms of advertisements, such as seasonal promotion publications. Many companies store pictures and data together in database files ready to populate catalogs, brochures, and Web sites.

The data source for Publisher's catalog merge commonly is a table of data that includes product numbers or ID numbers as well as paths to pictures you want to use in the catalog. A **path** is the route Publisher must take through your computer's file system to find the picture file and the file name. For example, if a .jpg picture file named Dog is located on the USB (F:) storage device in a folder named Pictures, the path would be F:\Pictures\Dog.jpg. If the file is located in the same folder as the merged publication, the path is simply the file name; thus, in the previous example, the path would be Dog.jpg.

Generally, for classroom purposes you should keep the main publication and the data source in the same folder on the same storage device. If you are using the Data Files for Students, these data sources may be stored in a different location from your saved publications. See your instructor for directions on moving files when necessary.

Creating the Westside Realty Catalog

The Westside Realty Catalog will have four pages. The front and back pages come from a template. The two inside pages will be generated using the catalog merge feature of Publisher.

The following steps open a catalog template.

To Open a Catalog Template

1 With the Publisher catalog still displayed, click the Catalogs button in the list of publication types.

2 Click the Color Band preview.

3 In the Customize area, select the Aspect color scheme and the Etched font scheme.

4 Click the Create button (Figure 5–52 on the next page).

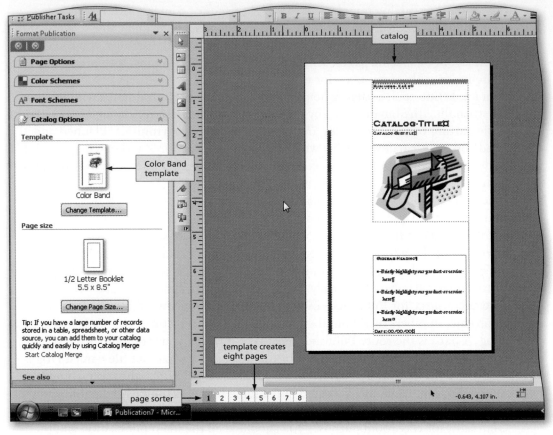

Figure 5–52

To Delete Pages

The following steps delete the inside pages of the template.

1 On the page sorter, right-click page 2. Click Delete Page on the short-cut menu. When Publisher displays a Delete Page dialog box, select Both pages, if necessary, and then click OK. If Publisher displays a message about the multipage spread, click the OK button.

2 Repeat Step 1 to delete all but the first and last page, and then navigate to page 1 (Figure 5–53).

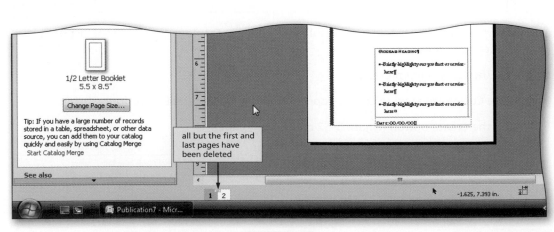

Figure 5–53

To Edit Template Text Boxes

The following steps edit the template text boxes on page 1.

1 Zoom to 100% and scroll to the top of page 1.

2 Select the text in the Business Name text box. Type Westside Realty to replace the text.

3 Click the text in the Catalog Title text box. Type Brownsburg Homes to replace the text.

4 Click the text in the Catalog Subtitle text box. Type Find your new address here to replace the text.

5 Scroll to the bottom of the page, and then click the text, Sidebar Heading. Type Brownsburg Highlights: to replace the text.

6 Click the bulleted list in the sidebar. Type Five-star schools and then press the ENTER key. Type Only 20 minutes from downtown and then press the ENTER key. Type Small town look and feel and then press the ENTER key. Type Reasonable prices to complete the bulleted list.

7 Click the text in the Date text box. Type June 2009 to replace the text.

8 Zoom to display the entire page (Figure 5–54).

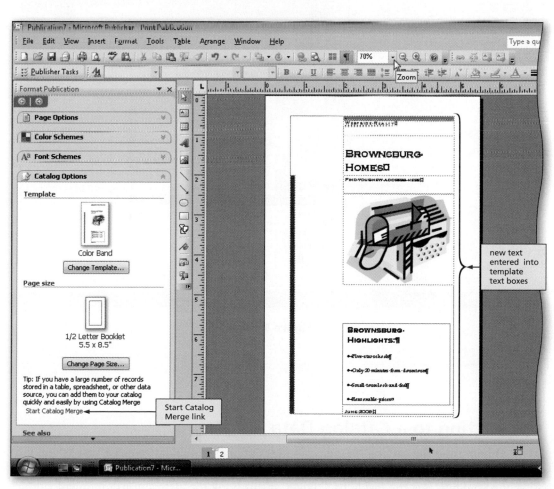

Figure 5–54

Starting the Catalog Merge

You can start the catalog merge from the Format Publication task pane associated with any of the catalog templates, or you can use the menu system as you did with the Mail Merge. When you start the catalog merge, Publisher automatically adds a page or pages to your publication and inserts a catalog merge area. The **catalog merge area**, also called the **repeatable area**, is a box in the publication into which field codes are inserted. When the merge is complete, data from the data source will populate each field, and the catalog merge area will repeat to display multiple records on each page.

To Start the Catalog Merge

The following step starts the catalog merge.

1

- With the catalog's Format Publication task pane displayed, click the Start Catalog Merge link to display the Catalog Merge task pane (Figure 5–55).

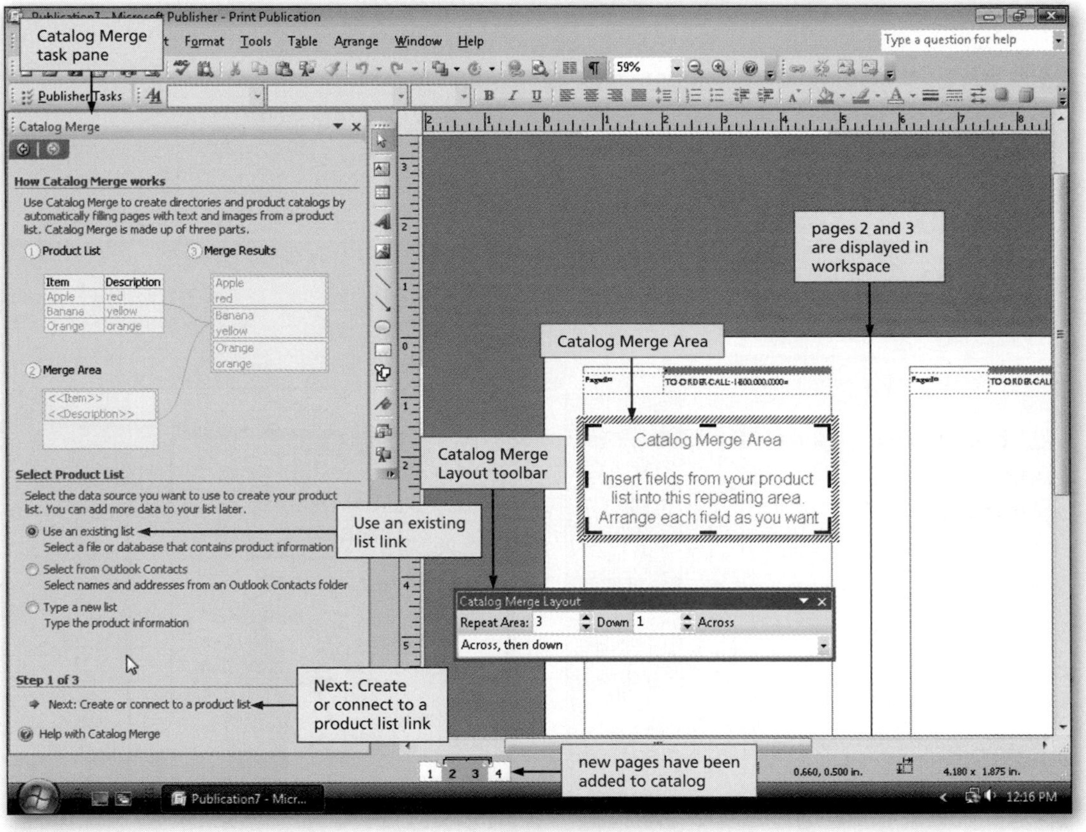

Figure 5–55

Other Ways

1. On Tools menu, point to Mailings and Catalogs, click Catalog Merge

Connecting to a Catalog Data Source

When using the catalog merge, you must connect to the data source, just as you did with mail merge. The data source for the Westside Realty catalog is included in the Data Files for Students. See the inside back cover of this book for instructions on downloading the Data Files for Students, or contact your instructor for more information about accessing the required files. The data source file contains relative paths to the pictures of the houses; therefore, the data source file must remain in the same folder as the pictures.

To Connect to a Catalog Data Source

The following steps connect to the catalog data source.

1

- In the Catalog Merge task pane, if necessary, click the 'Use an existing list' option button to select it.

- Click the 'Next: Create or connect to a product list' link to display the Select Data Source dialog box.

- Navigate to the USB drive or other location that contains the Data Files for Students. Double-click the folder named Houses (Figure 5–56).

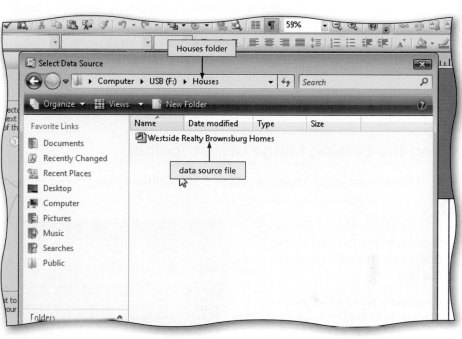

Figure 5–56

2

- Double-click the file named Westside Realty Brownsburg Homes to display the Catalog Merge Product List dialog box (Figure 5–57).

3

- Because you will use all 10 records in this database, click the OK button to return to step 2 of the Catalog Merge task pane.

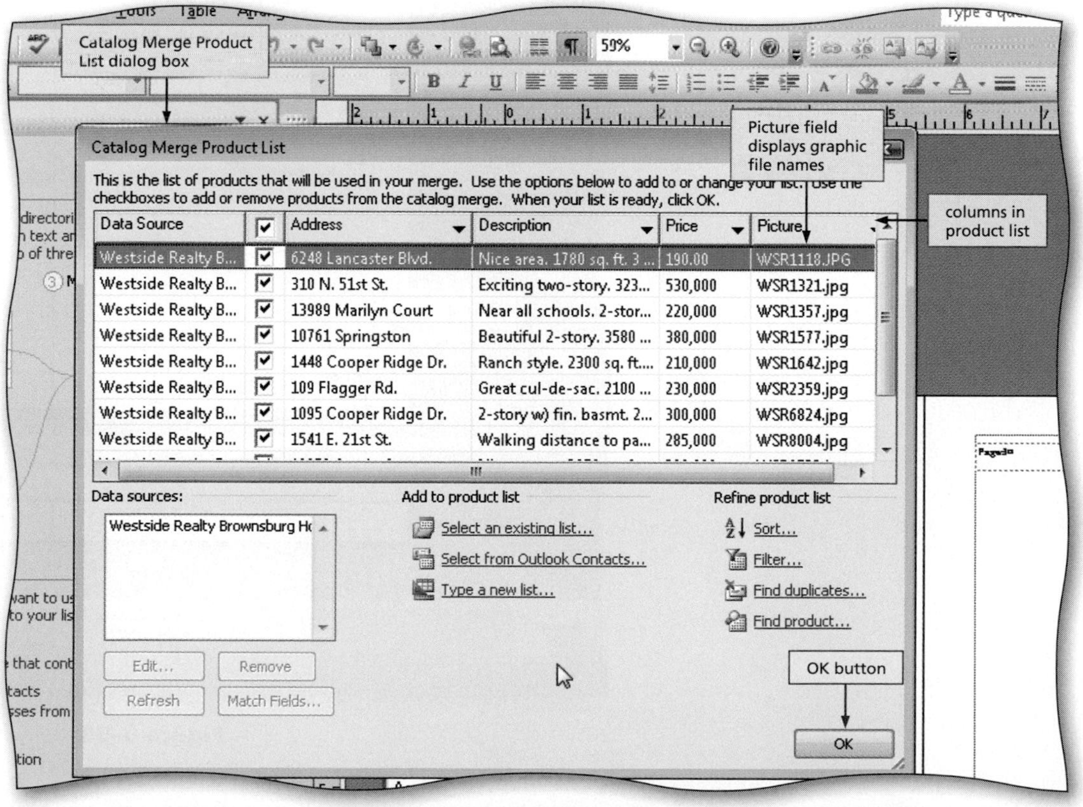

Figure 5–57

Inserting Catalog Fields

When performing a catalog merge, Publisher displays the Catalog Merge Layout toolbar and creates a repeatable area in the publication. The **Catalog Merge Layout toolbar** contains boxes to specify how often the layout of each item repeats and the merge area order.

If you start a catalog merge using any other method besides the Start Catalog Merge link, the catalog merge area will be inserted on the current page in the publication. It is a good idea to create the number of blank pages that you may need, before accessing the catalog merge from the menu or Other Task Panes button.

Using the Catalog Merge Layout Toolbar

The following step creates a grid of 2 × 10 in the catalog, using the catalog merge layout toolbar.

1

• In the Catalog Merge Layout toolbar, select the text in the Down box. Type 5 to replace the text.

• If necessary, replace the text in the Across box with the number 1. If necessary, click the Merge Area Order box arrow and then click Down, then across in the list (Figure 5–58).

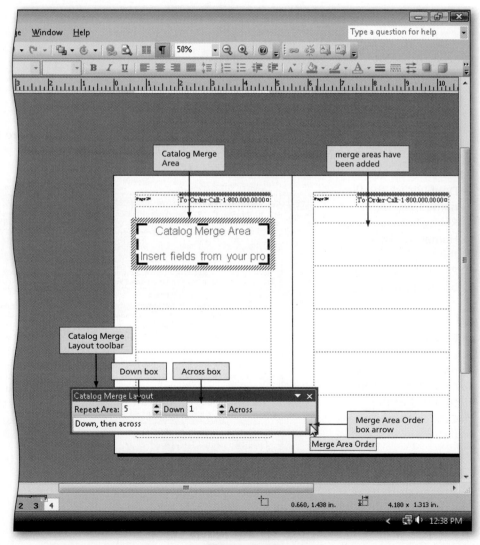

Figure 5–58

Inserting Fields into the Catalog Merge Area

The following steps insert the fields from the data source or product list into the catalog merge area. Fields or objects inserted in the catalog merge area will repeat for each record in the data source. Objects outside the area will not repeat. You can resize and reposition objects in the catalog merge area.

1

- Zoom to 100%.

- With the Prepare your publication step still displayed in the Catalog Merge task pane, click the Product Picture link in the task pane to display the Insert Picture field dialog box.

- If necessary, select the Picture field (Figure 5–59).

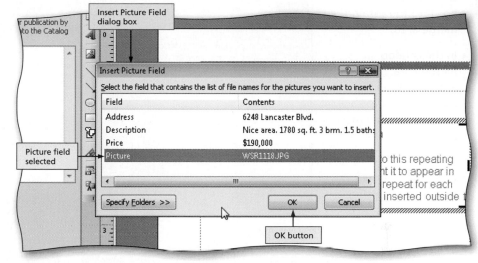

Figure 5–59

2

- Click the OK button to insert the picture into the catalog merge area.

- Point to the border of the inserted Picture box. When the mouse pointer changes to a four-headed arrow, drag the Picture box to the upper-left corner of the catalog merge area.

Q&A

Can I just click the Picture field in the list of fields rather than the link?

No, the Picture field contains only the location of the picture file. The Product Picture link actually goes to the location and then retrieves the picture for inclusion in the catalog.

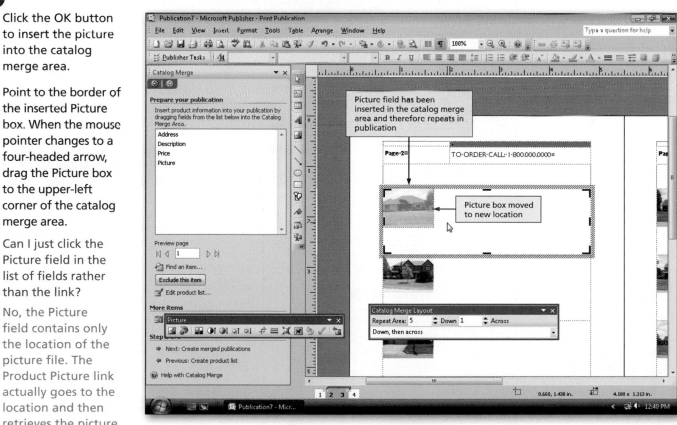

Figure 5–60

- Click the catalog merge area outside of the Picture box to deselect it (Figure 5–60).

3

- In the upper part of the task pane, click Address in the list of fields to insert the Address text box into the catalog merge area.

- In the catalog merge area, resize and reposition the Address text box in the space below the picture, as shown in Figure 5–61.

- Click the catalog merge area outside of the Address text box to deselect it.

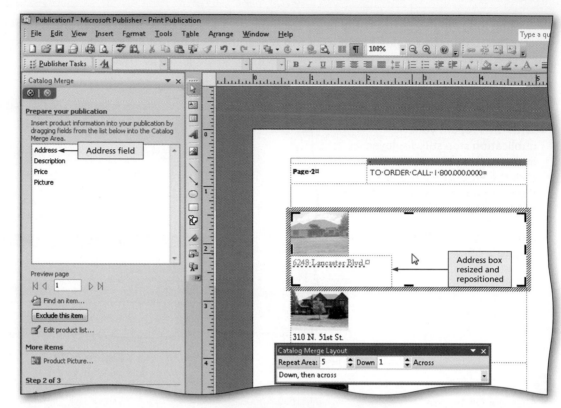

Figure 5–61

4

- In the upper part of the task pane, click Description in the list of fields to insert the Description text box into the catalog merge area.

- In the catalog merge area, resize and reposition the Description text box to fit in the space to the right of the picture, as shown in Figure 5–62.

- Click the catalog merge area outside of the Description text box to deselect it.

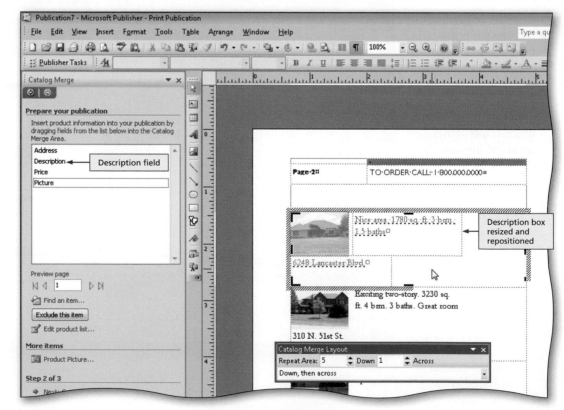

Figure 5–62

5

- In the upper part of the task pane, click Price in the list of fields to insert the Price text box into the catalog merge area.
- In the catalog merge area, drag the border of the Price text box to move it to the upper-right corner of the catalog merge area, as shown in Figure 5–63.
- Click the catalog merge area outside of the Price text box to deselect it.

6

- In the task pane, click the 'Next: Create merged publications' link.

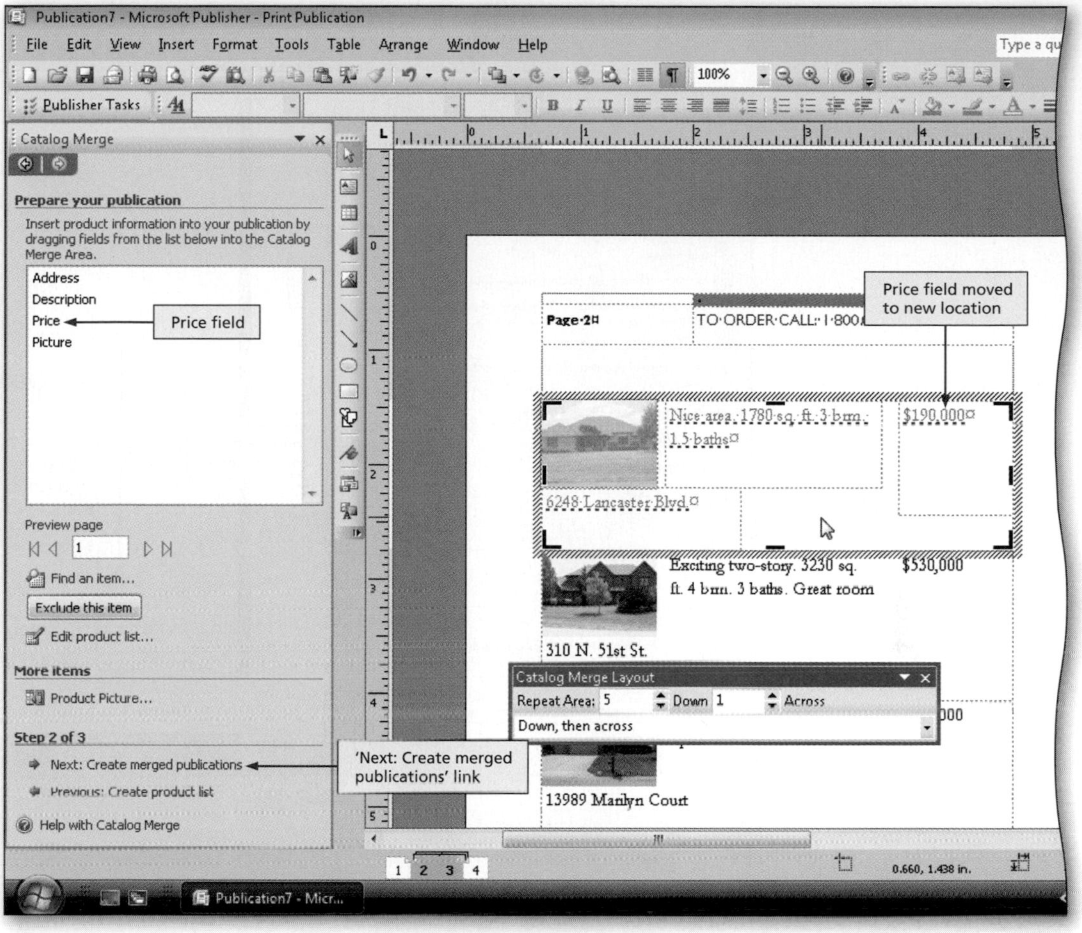

Figure 5–63

Other Ways
1. Drag field from Catalog Merge task pane into publication

To Finish Editing the Catalog Text Boxes

1. On page 2 of the catalog, select all of the text in the TO ORDER text box at the top of the page. On the Formatting toolbar, click the Font size box arrow, and then click 12 in the list. Type `Call Westside Realty at (317) 555-7226` to replace the text.
2. On page 4 of the catalog, zoom and scroll as necessary to replace the address text with `4700 Chesterfield Drive, Brownsburg, IN 46112`.
3. Replace the phone/fax/e-mail text with `Phone: (317) 555-7226; Fax: (317) 555-7220; E-mail: NewHome@Westside.com`.
4. On page 4, delete the organization logo (Figure 5–64 on the next page).

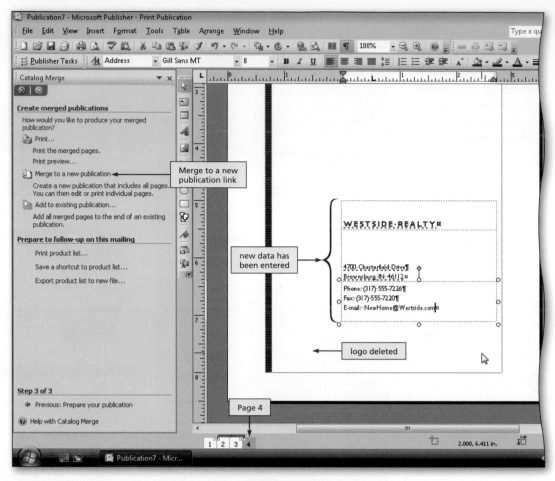

Figure 5–64

Saving a Merged File

Because your catalog file and data source file must be in the same folder location on the same storage device, you may want to save the merged publication so that you do not have to find and merge them again. This method is appropriate for a small file like the Westside Realty catalog. For larger applications, you would need to edit the address list and include the entire path to the permanent location of the pictures on your system, and then remerge each time you print the catalog.

To Save the Merged File

The following steps merge the data source and the main publication into a new publication and save it with the file name, Westside Realty June Catalog. It is best to display the catalog merge area while performing this final step of the merge. On some systems, depending on the printer's available print area, an extra page may be added in preparation for more merged records. In the following steps, if your system displays that blank page, you will delete it.

 With a USB flash drive connected to one of the computer's USB ports, navigate to page 2 of the publication. Click the 'Merge to a new publication' link in the Catalog Merge task pane.

 When Publisher finishes merging the catalog, if your system displays five pages, navigate to the blank page. Right-click the page sorter for the fifth page, and then click Delete Page on the shortcut menu.

③ Click Save on the Standard toolbar to display the Save As dialog box.

④ Type `Westside Realty June Catalog` in the File name text box to change the file name. Do not press the ENTER key.

⑤ Navigate to your USB flash drive.

⑥ Click the Save button in the Save As dialog box to save the publication on the USB flash drive. Do not close the catalog publication.

⑦ Close the task pane.

Calendars

The next series of steps will create a calendar on the back page of the catalog. A **calendar** is a specialized table that Publisher can format with any month and year. Calendar cells, like table cells, can be formatted with color, borders, text, and styles. Calendars are a part of some templates but also can be inserted from the Design Gallery. Publisher 2007 calendar options allow you to customize a calendar to include date ranges from 1900 to 2200, and also to show either one month or an entire year on a page.

Including calendars in a publication dates the material, because the publication may not be useful after the calendar date is over. Companies should take careful consideration when inserting calendars in publications.

Inserting a Calendar

The following steps insert a calendar on page 4 of the Westside Realty June Catalog.

To Insert a Calendar

1

• On the page sorter, click Page 4. Zoom to 100% and scroll to the upper portion of the page (Figure 5–65).

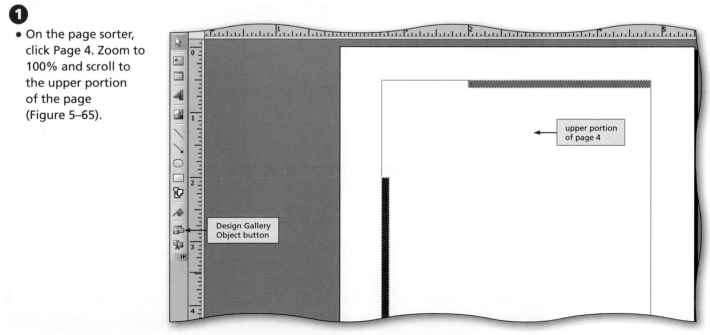

Figure 5–65

2

• On the Objects toolbar, click the Design Gallery Object button to display the Design Gallery window.

• Click the Calendars button in the list on the left side of the window to display the calendar previews (Figure 5–66).

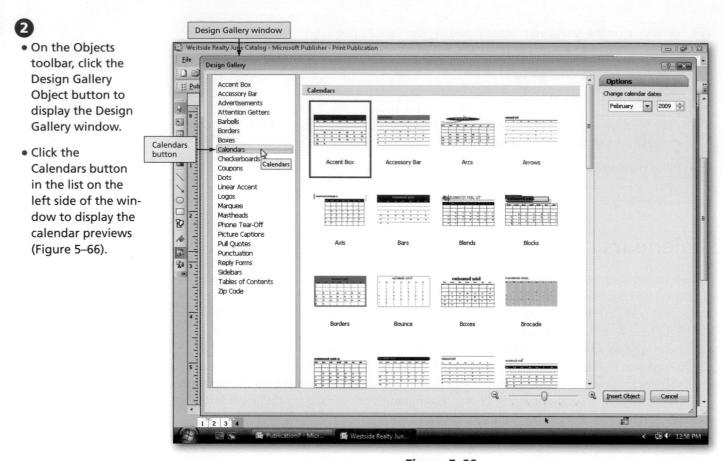

Figure 5–66

3

• Click the Blocks preview.

• In the Options area, click the Month box arrow and then click June in the list.

• Click the up or down button on the Year box to select 2009 (Figure 5–67).

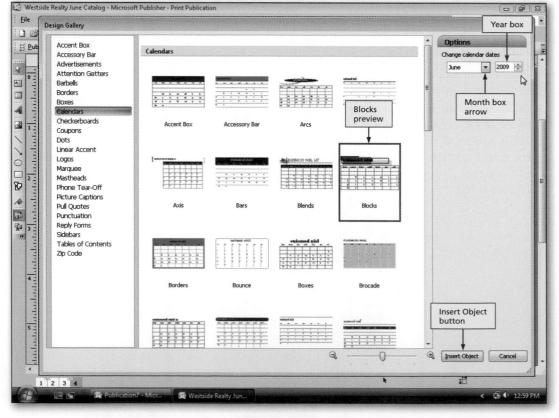

Figure 5–67

4
- Click the Insert Object button to display the calendar (Figure 5–68).

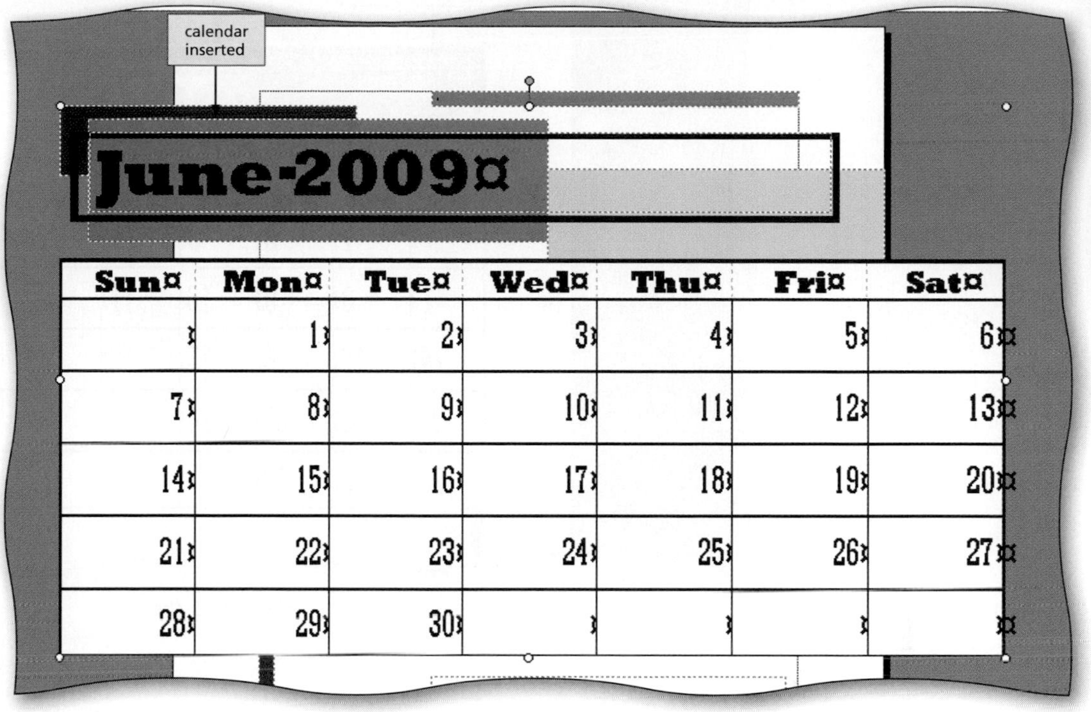

Figure 5–68

Other Ways

1. On Insert menu, click Design Gallery Object, select object, click Insert Object button

Resizing the Calendar and Entering Text

The next steps in formatting the calendar include resizing the calendar and then inserting text in various cells of the calendar table.

To Position and Resize the Calendar

1 If necessary, click the calendar to select it.

2 Drag the border of the calendar until the top-left corner snaps to the top-left margin.

3 Drag the lower-right sizing handle until the calendar fits in the area between the margins (Figure 5–69 on the next page).

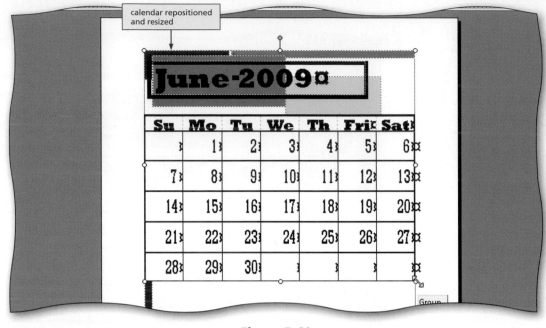

Figure 5–69

To Edit the Calendar

The final steps in completing the calendar are to add asterisks on the dates of the open houses sponsored by the realty office, and to add a reference to the open house below the calendar.

1

- Click the cell containing June 6 to position the insertion point before the number 6.

- Click the Font Color box arrow, and then click Accent 2 in the list.

- Type * to insert an orange asterisk in the cell (Figure 5–70).

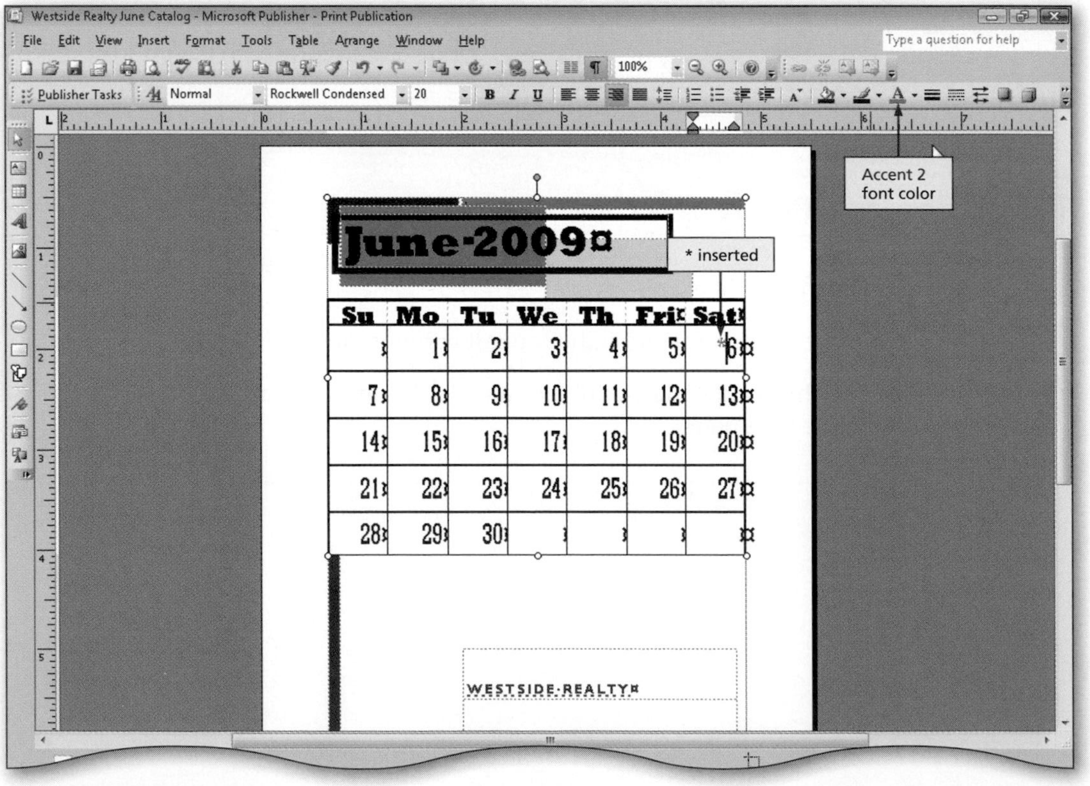

Figure 5–70

2

- Repeat Step 1 for the dates June 14, 20, and 28 (Figure 5–71).

an * has been added to three dates

Figure 5–71

3

- On the Objects toolbar, click the Text Box button.

- Drag a text box below the calendar, approximately 3.5 inches wide and .5 inches tall.

- In the text box, type * Indicates open houses at all locations in this catalog.

- Select the * in the new text box, and change its font color to Accent 2 (Figure 5–72).

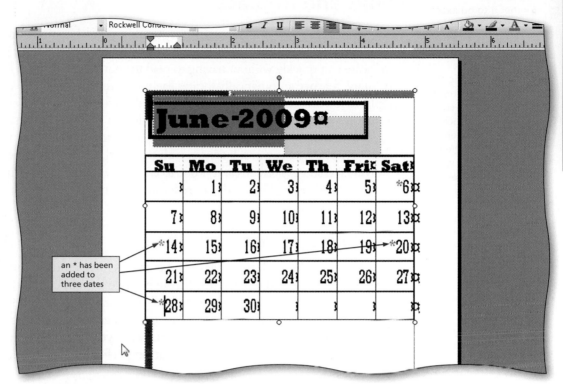

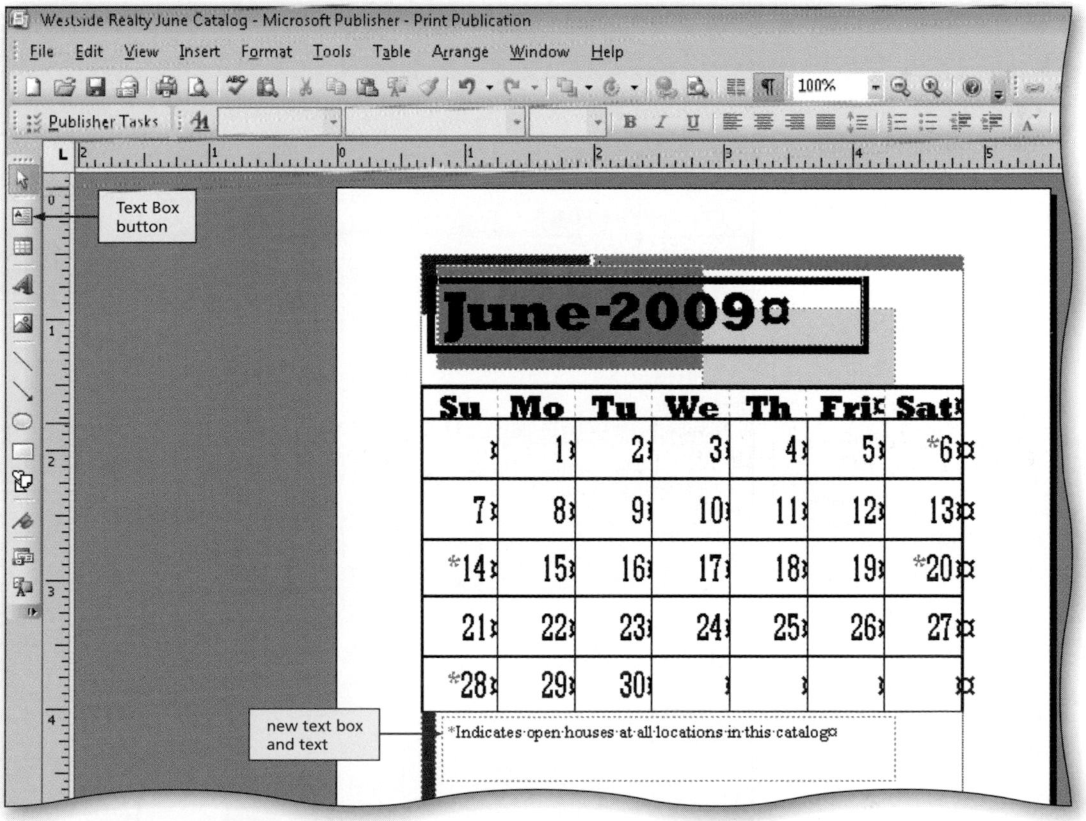

Text Box button

new text box and text

Figure 5–72

BTW

Replace All
You need to be exact with your find and replace text, especially when using the Replace All feature. For example, globally changing the numbers in an area code might also have changed the same sequence of numbers in a street address. Using the Find Next feature, as well as using parentheses in the search text, help you to replace only the appropriate text. The Find options also help narrow the search parameters.

Find and Replace

Sometimes you need to find text in a large publication or to find and replace a piece of data, words, or numbers globally across an entire publication. Publisher's **Find feature** allows you to locate text quickly without having to read the entire publication. Publisher's **Find and Replace feature** automatically locates each occurrence of a specified word or phrase and then replaces it with specified text, consistently and correctly across the entire publication. For example, while proofreading you might decide that an abbreviation used in multiple places really should be spelled out. Or, you might decide to use a different word in your publication, such as replacing the word, business, with the word, company. In these cases, making each individual change is tedious and prone to error — you might miss an occurrence or make a typographical error. The Find feature locates each occurrence.

Finding and Replacing Text

The Find and Replace task pane contains boxes and buttons to help you search for text or search and replace text throughout your publication. In the Westside Realty Catalog, you will replace the area code — a common task to perform in publications as cities increase the number of telephone exchanges and add new area codes. The Find Next button locates individual occurrences, allowing you to review the change before clicking the Replace button. The Replace All button performs a global change.

To Find and Replace Text

Perform the following steps to use the Find and Replace task pane to replace text in the publication.

1
- Click Edit on the menu bar and then click Find to display the Find and Replace task pane.

- In the task pane, click the Replace option button.

- Click the Find what box. Type (317) to enter the search text.

- Click the Replace with box. Type (765) to enter the replacement text (Figure 5–73).

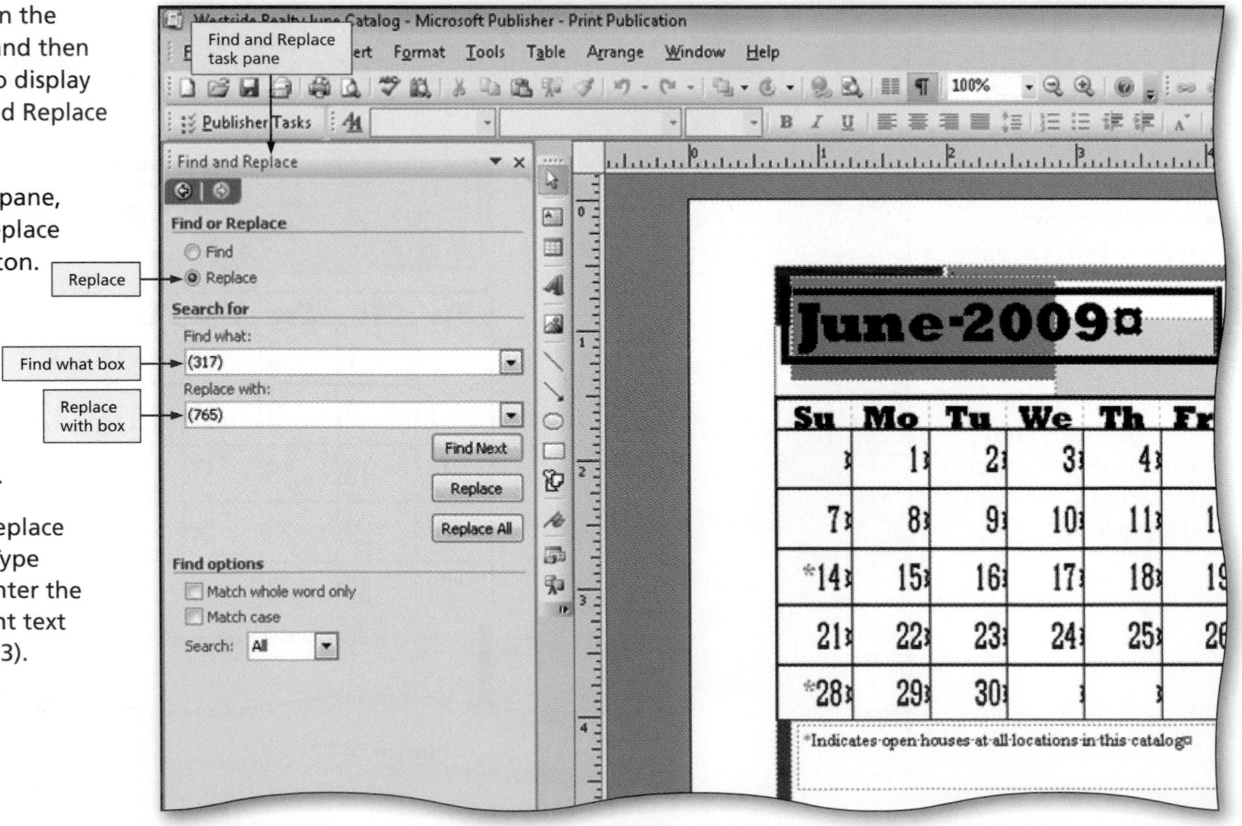

Figure 5–73

2
- Click the Find Next
button to locate
the first occurrence
of the text, (317)
(Figure 5–74).

Q&A Why did Publisher
locate the text on
page 2 first?

The default Search
option, All, searches
the current text box
and then continues
with all other text
boxes in the
publication,
beginning on
page 1 and ending
on the last master
page. When using
the Find feature, you
can click the Search
box arrow and then
click Up or Down to
focus the direction
of the search. The
Up option is not
available with the
Replace feature.

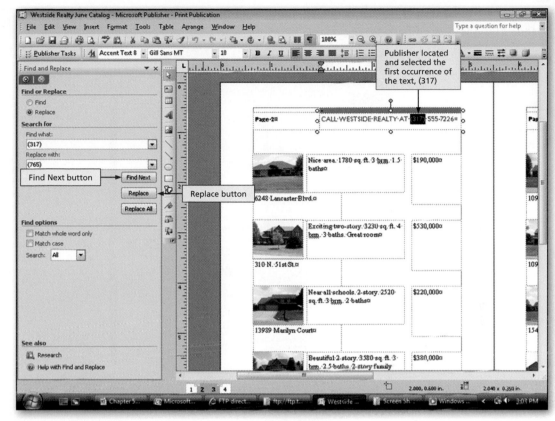

Figure 5–74

3
- Click the Replace
button to replace the
text (Figure 5–75).

Q&A Why did Publisher
move to page 3?

Page 3 originally
contained an
occurrence of (317)
in the Call Westside
Realty text box.
However, since the
text box was a
synchronized
element, the
text changed
automatically.

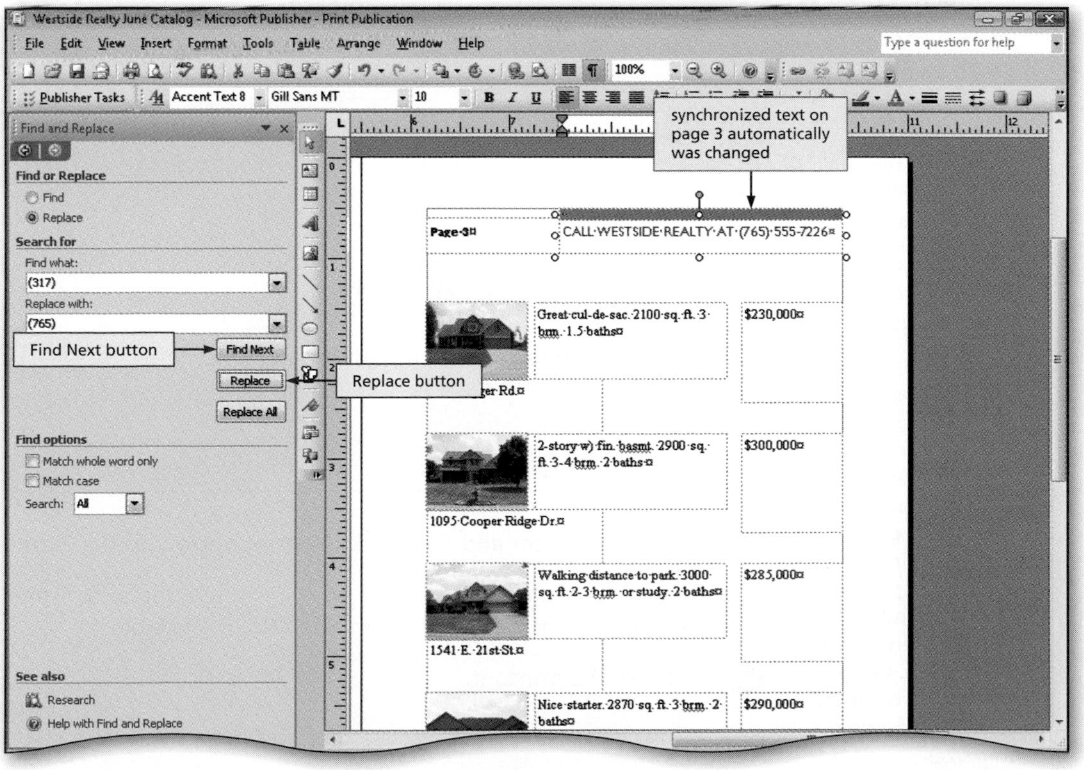

Figure 5–75

4

- Click the Find Next button to find the next occurrence of the search text (Figure 5–76).

5

- Click the Replace button to replace the text and move to the next occurrence of the search text.

- Continue searching and replacing each remaining occurrence of (317) with (765). When finished, click the OK button.

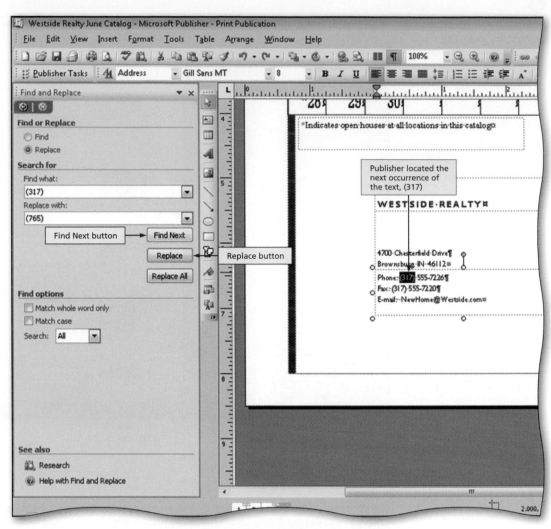

Figure 5–76

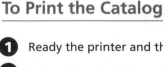

Other Ways

1. Press CTRL+F, select find or replace features
2. Click Other Task Panes button, click Find and Replace, select find or replace features

Printing the Catalog

The following steps print a copy of the catalog.

To Print the Catalog

1 Ready the printer and then click the Print button on the Standard toolbar.

2 In the Print dialog box for your printer, choose duplex printing, if available. Accept the default settings for booklet and side fold, if available.

3 Retrieve the printout.

BTW

Printing a Custom-Size Publication
If you are working on a network printer, choosing a custom-size publication may cause the printer to pause, waiting for custom-size paper. Many labs have a hands-off policy on loading printer paper yourself. Check with your instructor on the best way to print custom sizes.

Saving the Catalog and Quitting Publisher

The following steps save the catalog and then quit Publisher.

To Save the Catalog and Quit Publisher

1 Click the Save button on the Standard toolbar.

2 Click the Close button on the title bar of all open Publisher windows.

3 If Publisher displays a dialog box reminding you to save the document, click the No button.

Chapter Summary

In this chapter you have learned how to merge data files with publications. First, you created a form letter with a drop cap and special character formatting in the letterhead. Then, you created a Publisher address list, customizing the fields and filtering the data. Next, you merged the form letter with the address list, inserting field codes and using tabs and markers. You created merged mailing labels for the form letter envelopes. Finally, you created a catalog and used the catalog merge features of Publisher to embed pictures and data from a catalog data source. You formatted the catalog's merge area and inserted a calendar from the Design Gallery. The items listed below include all the new Publisher skills you have learned in this chapter.

1. Edit the Letterhead Text Boxes (PUB 318)
2. Create and Format a Drop Cap (PUB 320)
3. Track Characters (PUB 323)
4. Kern Character Pairs (PUB 324)
5. Create the Address List (PUB 326)
6. Customize Address List Columns (PUB 327)
7. Enter Data into the Address List (PUB 330)
8. Create New Entries in the Address List (PUB 331)
9. Save the Address List (PUB 332)
10. Start the Form Letter (PUB 333)
11. Connect the Address List (PUB 335)
12. Filter Recipients (PUB 337)
13. Insert Grouped Field Codes (PUB 339)
14. Insert Individual Field Codes (PUB 342)
15. Insert a Tab Stop (PUB 345)
16. Enter Tabbed Text (PUB 346)
17. Print Merged Pages (PUB 349)
18. Change the Print Settings and Print Labels (PUB 353)
19. Create and Print Merged Envelopes (PUB 354)
20. Start the Catalog Merge (PUB 358)
21. Connect to a Catalog Data Source (PUB 359)
22. Insert a Calendar (PUB 365)
23. Edit the Calendar (PUB 368)
24. Find and Replace Text (PUB 370)

Learn It Online

Test your knowledge of chapter content and key terms.

Instructions: To complete the Learn It Online exercises, start your browser, click the Address bar, and then enter the Web address scsite.com/pub2007/learn. When the Office 2007 Learn It Online page is displayed, click the link for the exercise you want to complete and then read the instructions.

Chapter Reinforcement TF, MC, and SA

A series of true/false, multiple choice, and short answer questions that test your knowledge of the chapter content.

Flash Cards

An interactive learning environment where you identify chapter key terms associated with displayed definitions.

Practice Test

A series of multiple choice questions that test your knowledge of chapter content and key terms.

Who Wants To Be a Computer Genius?

An interactive game that challenges your knowledge of chapter content in the style of a television quiz show.

Wheel of Terms

An interactive game that challenges your knowledge of chapter key terms in the style of the television show *Wheel of Fortune*.

Crossword Puzzle Challenge

A crossword puzzle that challenges your knowledge of key terms presented in the chapter.

Apply Your Knowledge

Reinforce the skills and apply the concepts you learned in this chapter.

Creating a Merged Invoice

Instructions: Start Publisher. Download the publication, Apply 5-1 Lawn Care Invoice, and the data file, Chapter 5 Address List, from the Data Files for Students to the same storage location and folder. See the inside back cover of this book for instructions on downloading the Data Files for Students, or contact your instructor for information about accessing the required files.

The publication is a monthly statement that needs to be merged with the address list to produce current billing information. You are to insert a drop cap, edit the address list, and then merge and print. A sample statement is shown in Figure 5–77.

Perform the following tasks:

1. Open the publication, Apply 5-1 Lawn Care Invoice. Save the publication with the name Apply 5-1 Lawn Care Invoice Modified.

2. Click to position the insertion point before the word, Invoice. Click Format on the menu bar and then click Drop Cap. Choose an appropriate style from the Available drop caps list. Click the Custom Drop Cap tab and then type 2 in the Size of letters box.

3. Click the text box for Invoice Date, Customer ID, and Due Date. Press CTRL+A to select all of the text. Click the 1" mark on the horizontal ruler to set a tab. Enter Aug. 3, 2009 at the tab stop for Invoice Date. Enter Sept. 1, 2009 at the tab stop for Due Date.

4. On the Tools menu, point to Mailings and Catalogs, and then click Mail Merge.

5. In the Mail Merge task pane, click the 'Use an existing link' option button, then click Next: Create or connect to a recipient list. Navigate to the Chapter 5 Address List file.

6. In the Mail Merge Recipients dialog box, locate the Data Sources box. Select the file name in the box, and then click the Edit button to display the Edit Data Source dialog box.

7. Click the New Entry button and enter your name and address as new data. Create a fictitious description and dollar amount. Click the OK button.

8. When Publisher asks if you want to update and save the address list, click the Yes button. When the Mail Merge Recipients dialog box again is displayed, click the OK button.

9. In the publication, select the text in the Mailing Address text box. In the Mail Merge task pane, select the grouped field named Address block and choose an appropriate address style.

10. In the Invoice Date text box, click to the right of the words, Customer ID. Press the tab key to move to the tab stop. Insert the Customer ID field from the Mail Merge task pane.

11. Click in the table cell below the word, Description. Insert the Description field from the Mail Merge task pane.

12. Click the table cell below the word, Amount Due. Type $ to begin the entry. Insert the Amount Due field from the Mail Merge task pane. Type .00 to finish the entry.

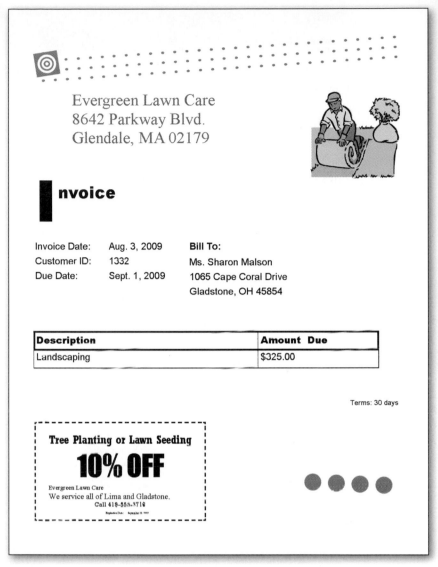

Figure 5–77

13. Use the Design Gallery to insert a coupon in the lower portion of the publication. Change the text in the text boxes to read:

```
Tree Planting or Lawn Seeding
10% OFF
Evergreen Lawn Care
We service all of Lima and Gladstone.
Call 419-555-3716
Expiration Date: September 30, 2009
```

14. Click the Spelling button on the Standard toolbar to check spelling. Correct any spelling errors. Click Tools on the menu bar, and then click Design Checker. Correct any design errors.

15. Save the publication again, using the same name, on your storage device.

16. Print hard copies of the merged publication. Submit the copies to your instructor.

Extend Your Knowledge

Extend the skills you learned in this chapter and experiment with new skills. You may need to use Help to complete the assignment.

Sorting an Address List

Instructions: Start Publisher. Open the publication, Extend 5-1 First America Bank Envelope, from the Data Files for Students. See the inside back cover of this book for instructions on downloading the Data Files for Students, or contact your instructor for more information about accessing the required files.

In this assignment you will filter an address list for persons living in two specific cities. Then, you will sort the list by last name and then first name to create an alphabetical listing. Finally, you will apply the merged address block to an envelope publication.

Perform the following tasks:

1. Save the publication with the name, Extend 5-1 First America Bank Envelope Modified.
2. Access the Mail Merge task pane. Use the existing address list named Chapter 5 Address List.
3. In the Mail Merge Recipients List dialog box, click the Filter link. Choose to filter the list with City equal to Lima. Click the Or button to add a second filter with City equal to Gladstone.
4. In the Mail Merge Recipients dialog box, click the Sort link. Sort the list alphabetically first by last name and then by first name, in ascending order (Figure 5–78).

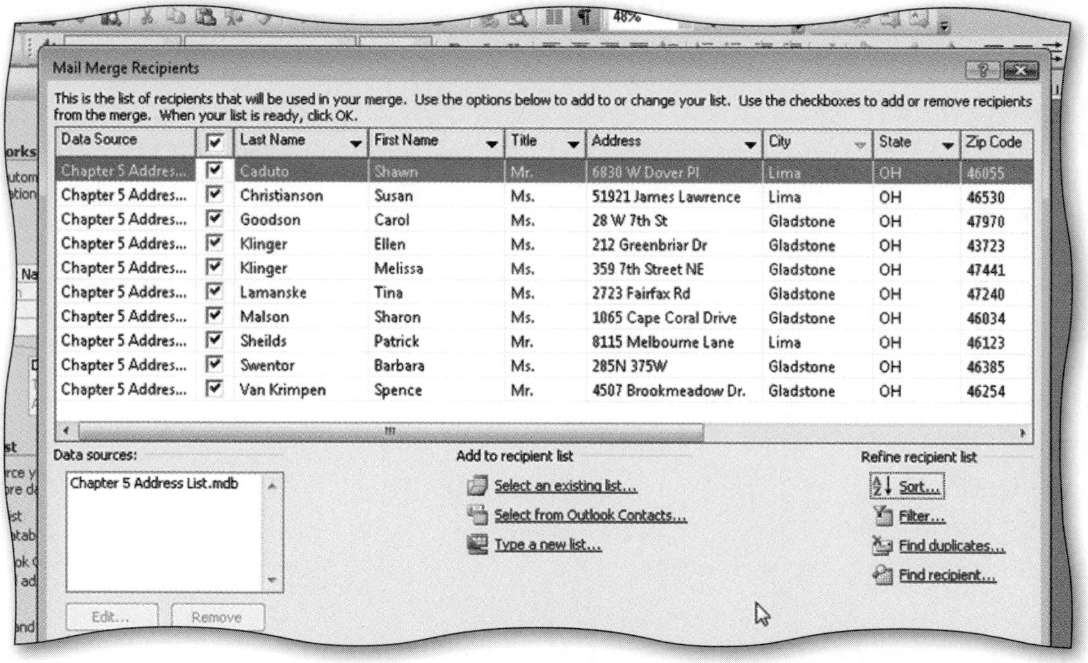

Figure 5–78

5. In the Mail Merge task pane, select the grouped field named Address block and choose an appropriate address style. When Publisher displays the text box, autofit, resize, and reposition the text box so it creates an appropriate envelope address.
6. Return to the Mail Merge task pane and create the merged publication. Click the 'Export recipient list to a new file' link, and save the filtered list with the file name, Lima and Gladstone Residents.
7. Click the 'Print a Recipient list' link and include only the name and address fields. Submit the copies to your instructor.

Make It Right

Analyze a publication and correct all errors and/or improve the design.

Correcting Character and Field Spacing

Instructions: Start Publisher. Open the publication, Make It Right 5-1 Golf Course Label, from the Data Files for Students. See the inside back cover of this book for instructions on downloading the Data Files for Students, or contact your instructor for more information about accessing the required files.

The publication is a large mailing label with tracking and spacing errors, a drop cap error, and errors in the formatting of the field codes, as shown in Figure 5–79. You are to correct the errors.

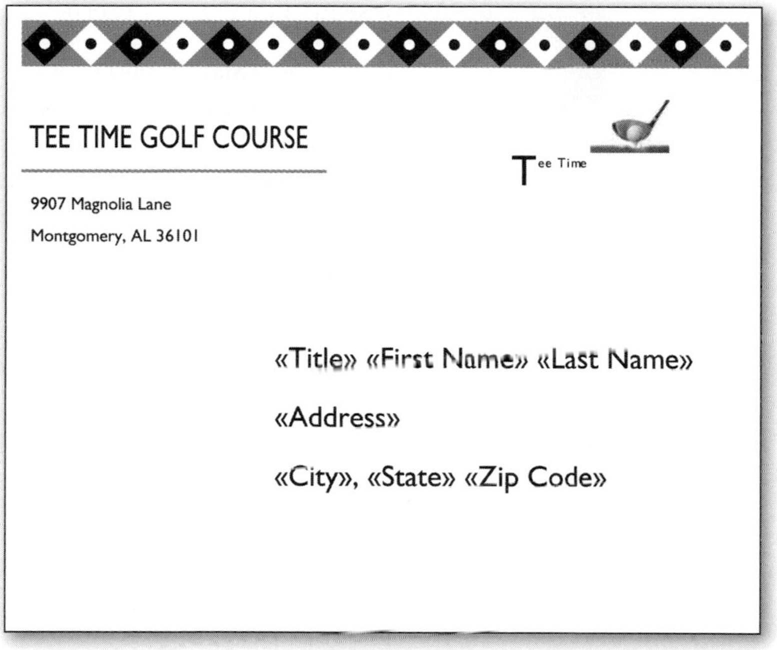

TEE TIME GOLF COURSE

T^{ee Time}

9907 Magnolia Lane
Montgomery, AL 36101

«Title» «First Name» «Last Name»

«Address»

«City», «State» «Zip Code»

Figure 5–79

Perform the following steps:

1. Select the text, Tee Time Golf Course. On the Measurement toolbar, track the text more loosely.

2. Select the return address text. Access the Measurement toolbar and increase the line spacing.

3. Select all the text below the golf logo. Left-justify the text by pressing CTRL+L. Change the font size by typing a 5 in the Font size box on the Formatting toolbar.

4. Select the T drop cap below the golf logo. Access the Drop Cap dialog box. On the Drop Cap tab, choose a non-script T in the Available drop caps list. On the Custom Drop Cap tab, click Dropped. In the Lines box, enter 0. In the Size of letters box, enter 2.

5. Kern the letters T and e in the word, Tee, below the golf logo.

6. Kern the letters m and e in the word, Time, below the golf logo.

7. In the address field codes, insert spaces between each field code. Insert a comma after the field code, City.

8. Save the publication with the file name, Make It Right 5-1 Golf Course Label Revised. Send an electronic copy of the file to your instructor via e-mail.

STUDENT ASSIGNMENTS

Local Pride — Global Knowledge

Prairie University

October 15, 2008

Mr. Dang Chou
764 Clay Street
Lincoln, NE 68504

Dear Mr. Chou,

Thank you for your interest in attending Prairie University. We are extremely happy to supply you with more information about our campus and its programs.

Fully accredited, we offer 43 different undergraduate programs, 9 different Master's degrees and 3 programs of study for the Ph.D. degree. The enclosed brochure outlines our degree options and provides information about admission requirements, required coursework, and plans of study.

We also are happy to be sending you information about scholarship. Nearly 60% of our students receive funding. Our campus is proud to sponsor internships and work-study programs with the community, as well.

Please feel free to contact the specific department of your choice for more information and an application packet.

Again we want to thank you for your interest in Prairie. If I can be of any further assistance to you, please do not hesitate to contact me.

Sincerely,

Gregg Saffell
University Ombudsperson

Office of the Ombudsperson   *425 Woody Hall*
(785) 555-2371   *Goodland, KS 67735*

Figure 5–80

Design and/or create a publication using the guidelines, concepts, and skills presented in this chapter. Labs are listed in order of increasing difficulty.

Lab 1: Creating a Form Letter

Problem: A university has received an address list of interested students from local high school guidance counselors. The admissions department would like to send out a letter to prospective students.

Instructions: Start Publisher and perform the following tasks to create the letter shown in Figure 5–80.

1. Choose a letterhead similar to the one shown in Figure 5–80. On the tools menu, point to Mailings and Catalogs and then click Mail Merge. When the Mail Merge task pane is displayed, choose the 'Type a new list' link.

2. When the New Address List dialog box is displayed, enter the data from Table 5–7. Enter your name as a fifth record to the address list. When Publisher asks you to name the address list, navigate to your storage device and save the file with the name, Lab 5-1 Prairie Address List.

3. In the publication, change the business name, tag line or motto, and address boxes to match Figure 5–80.

Table 5–7 Prairie Address List

Title	First Name	Last Name	Address	City	State	Zip Code
Mr.	Dang	Chou	764 Clay Street	Colby	KS	67701
Ms.	Michelle	Knight	267 Green Way	Scott City	KS	67871
Mr.	Raphael	Garcia	345 Norton Ave.	Goodland	KS	67735
Mr.	Patrick	See	1422 88th St.	Hays	KS	67601

4. Create a large text box to hold the letter. In the text box, insert the current date and then press the ENTER key twice.

5. In the Mail Merge task pane, proceed to the Prepare your publication step. Insert the grouped field named Address block. Choose an appropriate style. Press the ENTER key twice.

6. Insert the grouped field named Greeting Line. Choose an appropriate style. Press the ENTER key twice.

7. Click Insert on the menu bar and then click Text File. Navigate to the Data Files for Students. See the inside back cover of this book for instructions on downloading the Data Files for Students, or contact your instructor for information about accessing the required files. Select the Microsoft Word file named, Prairie University Letter, and insert it as the body of the letter.

8. On the File menu, click Save As. Save the publication using the file name, Lab 5-1 Prairie Form Letter.

9. In the Mail Merge task pane, navigate to your name in the address list. Then, click the 'Next: Create merged publications' link.

10. In the Mail Merge task pane, click the Print preview link.

11. Print a copy of the letter with your name, and submit it to your instructor.

In the Lab

Lab 2: Creating a Catalog

Problem: You are to use a catalog template to design a catalog that will display pictures and descriptions of cacti for a park district publication.

Instructions: Start Publisher. Download the folder named, Cacti, from the Data Files for Students. See the inside back cover of this book for instructions on downloading the Data Files for Students, or contact your instructor for more information about accessing the required files. The folder contains pictures of various cacti and a data source file with the names and descriptions of the pictures. A sample catalog is displayed in Figure 5–81 on the next page.

1. Start Publisher. Choose to display the catalog templates. Select the Studio template with the default size of 5.5 3 8.5, the Studio font scheme, and Desert color scheme, if you would like to match the figure.

2. When the publication is displayed in the workspace, do not close the task pane. Delete all but the front and back pages.

3. On page 1:

   a. In the Catalog Subtitle text box, enter Your guide to identifying the host of the desert.

   b. In the Catalog Title text box, enter Cactus Calling.

   c. Replace the picture with the file named, Front Cover Cactus, located in the Cacti folder of the Data Files for Students.

Continued >

In the Lab *continued*

Figure 5–81

    d. In the bulleted list, enter the following:

       `Inside`

       • `Pictures and descriptions of the most popular cacti`

       • `Size and genus`

       • `Find out which cacti are edible`

       • `Calendar of Events`

    e. In the Business Name text box, enter `Tucson Park District`.

    f. In the Date text box, type `Summer 2009` to complete the entries on page 1.

4. In the Format Publication task pane, choose Start Catalog Merge. When the Catalog Merge task pane is displayed, click to navigate to the next step, which is to connect to a data source.

5. In the Select Data Source task pane, navigate to the location of the Data Files for Students. In the Cacti folder, select the file named Cactus Address List. When the list is displayed, click the OK button to display the catalog merge area on page 2.

6. In the task pane, click the Product Picture link to insert the picture field into the catalog merge area. Position the picture box in the upper-left corner of the catalog merge area.

7. Create a table inside the catalog merge area that fills the empty space beside the picture. When the Create Table dialog box is displayed, choose 4 rows and 2 columns, with no formatting.

8. In the first column of the table, enter the following row headings, Name:, Genus:, Size:, and Food use:. From the task pane, enter the corresponding field codes in the second column.

9. On page 4:

   a. Delete the organization logo.

   b. Insert a calendar for June 2009. When the calendar is displayed, select the weekday cells and then use the Fill Color button on the Formatting toolbar to fill the cells with Accent 2 from the color scheme. Fill the weekend cells with the Accent 3 color.

   c. Below the calendar, create a rectangle approximately .5 inches square. Fill the rectangle with the Accent 2 color. Create a text box next to the rectangle approximately 3 inches wide and .5 inches tall. Using a font of size 10 or larger, type Open from 10 a.m. to 7 p.m. in the text box.

   d. Below the previous rectangle and text box, create another similar rectangle, filled with the Accent 3 color. Create a similar text box. Using a font of size 10 or larger, enter Open from 10 a.m. to 10 p.m. in the text box.

   e. In the address text box, enter:

   5200 Park Drive

   Tucson, AZ 85719

   f. In the phone text box, enter:

   Phone: 520-555-4800

   Fax: 520-555-4801

10. Save the publication with the name, Lab 5-2 Cactus Catalog.

11. Navigate to page 2. In the task pane, click the link to proceed with the merge. Choose to merge to a new publication. If the new publication has a blank page, delete it.

12. Run the spell checker and design checker, fixing any errors. Save the new publication with the name, Lab 5-2 Cactus Catalog Merged.

13. Print the merged file and send a copy to your instructor.

In the Lab

Lab 3: Create a Set of Play Tickets

Problem: A local theater company needs tickets that are individualized for seat assignments as shown in Figure 5-82 on the next page.

Instructions: Publisher's merge feature is often used with an Excel spreadsheet to track customers through mailing labels, coupons, gift certificates, and promotional marketing pieces. Tracking the success of marketing efforts helps determine what marketing tactics are effective for which customers. Tracking, recording, and categorizing customer responses helps a company plan future marketing strategies. Individualized tracking numbers also can be used for generating tickets, as you will do in this exercise. In the steps on the next page, you will create the ticket and then merge it with an Excel spreadsheet that contains the seat numbers. The spreadsheet is located in the Data Files for Students. See the inside back cover of this book for instructions on downloading the Data Files for Students, or contact your instructor for information about accessing the required files.

Continued >

In the Lab *continued*

Figure 5–82

1. Start Publisher. Click Blank Publications in the catalog. At the top of the catalog, click Business Cards.

2. Select a blank template with a size of 3.5 × 2 inches. Select the Redwood color scheme and the Metro font scheme.

3. In the publication, draw a text box approximately 3 × .5 inches. Position it in the upper center of the card. Change the font size to 26. Type A KING'S RANSOM in the text box.

4. Draw a text box approximately 2.1 × .4 inches. Position it right-aligned with the previous text box. Change the font size to 18. Type A play in three acts in the text box.

5. Draw another text box approximately 2.1 × .4 inches. Position it right-aligned with the previous text box. Change the font size to 7.4. Double-click the status bar to display the Measurement toolbar. Decrease the line spacing to .69. Type Friday, October 9, 2009 at 7:30 p.m. and then press the ENTER key. Type Stellar Auditorium — 303 Main Street to complete the text.

6. Click the Table button on the Objects toolbar. Drag in the publication to create a table located below the previous text box, right-justified and approximately 2.1 × .3 inches. When Publisher displays the Create Table dialog box, select 1 row, 6 columns, and the Checkerboard! Format. Select the entire table and then set the font size to 6. Type Section in the first cell, Row in the third cell, and Seat in the fifth cell.

7. Access the Clip Art task pane. Search using the keyword, king. Insert a picture similar to the one shown in Figure 5–82. Position the picture in the lower-left corner of the publication.

8. To create the border, click the Rectangle tool and then draw a rectangle around all of the objects. Right-click the rectangle, and then click Format AutoShape on the shortcut menu. In the Format AutoShape dialog box, click the BorderArt button and select a border similar to the one shown in Figure 5–82.

9. Access the Mail Merge task pane. Choose to use an existing list. When Publisher displays the Select Data Source dialog box, click the All Data Source button and then click Excel Files in the list. Navigate to the Data Files for Students and select the file named Ticket Seat Numbers. Do not filter or sort the data.

10. In the Mail Merge task pane, choose to prepare your publication. Click the second cell in the table, and then click Section in the list of fields shown in the task pane. Click the fourth cell in the table, and then click Row in the list of fields. Click the sixth cell in the table, and then click Seat in the list of fields.

11. Save the publication on your storage device with the name, Lab 5-3 Play Tickets.

12. In the Mail Merge task pane, choose to create the merged publication. Click the Print link to display the Print dialog box. On the Publication and Paper Settings tab, select Multiple pages per sheet. Click the Print preview button to see the various tickets, tracked by seat number. Close the Print preview screen.

13. Choose to print entries 1–8, which will print the first page of tickets. Submit the printout to your instructor.

Cases and Places

Apply your creative thinking and problem solving skills to design and implement a solution.

● EASIER ●● MORE DIFFICULT

● 1: Merging a Form Letter and Address List

You are activities chairperson for the Summer Day Camp at your place of worship. Letters must be sent to all parents informing them of the rules for the event. Create a form letter using the following information: First United Church; 6100 Ridge Road; Allegria, NM, 87501; Telephone: (505) 555-4700; Fax: (505) 555-4701. Create the address list shown in Table 5–8. Customize the columns as necessary. Use the name and address field codes for the first part of the address. Then enter the same city, state, and zip code for all letters: Allegria, NM, 87501. The first paragraph of the body of the letter will include the Child Gender field code and should say: Summer Day Camp is scheduled from July 23 through July 27 at the church outdoor shelter. Camp will be from 9:00 a.m. until 3:00 p.m. each day. Your <<Child Gender>> should bring the following items, labeled with the child's name, in a backpack: extra socks and shoes, sweatshirts, raincoat, water bottle, insect repellent, mess kit, and sit-upon. The next paragraph should say, If you have any questions, please contact Donna at 555-4700. Use your name in the signature block. Create address labels for the same list.

Table 5–8 Data for Summer Day Camp Address List

Title	First Name	Last Name	Address Line 1	Address Line 2	Relationship
Mrs.	Lourdes	Nunez	1567 Katuche		Son
Ms.	Juanita	Espinoza	1145 Santa Fe Drive		Daughter
Dr.	Raymond	Enderly	1235 Main St.	Suite 102	Daughter
Mr.	Michael	Louks	9876 Desert Road	Apt. 107	Son
Mr.	Mohammed	Al-Ghizzawi	509 NE 81st Terr.		Son

● 2: Create a Movie Logo

Create a one-page flyer from scratch, advertising your favorite movie. Design a text-based logo for the title of the movie. Use a font that goes with the theme of the movie. For example, a comedy movie might use the Joker, Jokewood, or Comic Sans fonts; a classic movie might use a serif font; or a horror movie might use the Showcard Gothic or the Chiller font. Use the Character Spacing dialog box (accessed via the Format menu) or the Measurement toolbar to edit the character spacing. Use a font size of at least 48. Scale the first letter of each word to give your text logo its own special character. Kern at least one character pair to improve the logo. Change the tracking on all of the characters. If your logo is two lines of text, experiment with the line spacing to add more visual contrast to the logo.

●● 3: Create a Visitor Catalog

Using a digital camera, take pictures of at least eight different locations of interest in your city. Record the locations of the buildings and their significance to the community. Create a new folder on your storage device and store the eight pictures in that folder. Open a catalog template in Publisher, and delete all but the first and last pages. Use the 'Create an address list' command to create a new data source. Customize the columns and include fields such as building name, location, description, and picture. In the picture field, enter the names of the digital files. Choose to store the address list in the

Continued >

same folder as the pictures. Use the Catalog Merge task pane to merge the data from your address list in a 4 × 2 catalog merge area. Save the merged publication in the same folder as the pictures and address list.

•• 4: Sending Out Your Resume and Cover Letter

Make It Personal

You currently are seeking employment in your field of study. You already have prepared a resume and would like to send it to a group of potential employers. You decide to design a cover letter to send with the resume. Obtain a recent newspaper and cut out five classified advertisements pertaining to your field of study. Create the cover letter for your resume as a main publication to merge with a data source. Be sure the cover letter has an attractive letterhead containing your name, address, and telephone number. Use the information in the classified ads for the address list. Insert the personal information components as the inside mailing address underneath the letterhead. Create a large text box for the body of your letter. Merge the letter with the address list and print all five copies. Turn in the classified ads with your printouts.

•• 5: Creating a Class Mailing List

Working Together

Individually, create a large mailing label using a label template. Choose an appropriate font scheme. Use the Mail Merge task pane to create an address list of the students in your class. Insert data into the fields for first name and e-mail address. Create a new field called Year in School, in which you will enter freshman, sophomore, junior, or senior. If your instructor permits you to do so, go from one computer station to the next, inserting your personal data. On your computer, in the label's address text box, select the text. Use the Mail Merge task pane to insert the four fields. Print multiple labels on the page.

6 | Creating an Interactive Web Site

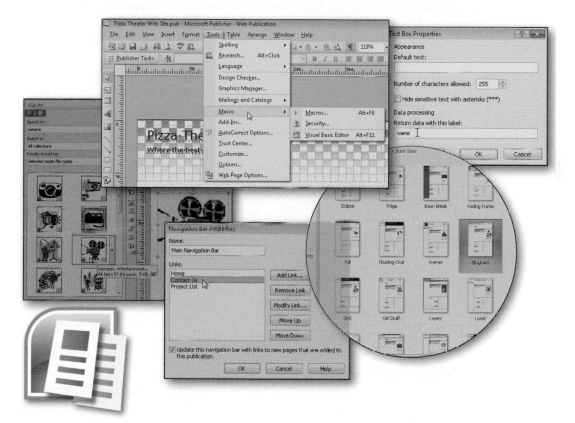

Objectives

You will have mastered the material in this chapter when you can:

- Select Web site template options
- Edit the navigation bar
- Create and use a bookmark
- Insert an animated graphic and alternative text
- Use an empty picture frame
- Set Web page options
- Insert a background sound
- Create a Web page from scratch

- Insert form controls
- Set form control properties
- Set form properties
- Use return data values
- Add a hot spot
- Create an HTML code fragment
- Use VBA to create a message box
- Set the security level in Publisher

6 | Creating an Interactive Web Site

Introduction

Interactive Web sites are Web sites that allow visitors to enter information or interact with the Web site. They are used to get feedback from visitors, to allow visitors to navigate and view more features of the Web site, or to accommodate e-commerce. **E-commerce**, or **electronic commerce**, has established itself in the business world as an inexpensive and efficient way to increase visibility and, therefore, sales. Customers visit, browse, make purchases, and ask for assistance at a Web site, just as they would at a physical location. Using server tools or through direct communication, visitor information may be passed to the server for processing in order to store, confirm, or respond to an inquiry.

An **electronic form** is used on a Web page to request and collect information, comments, or survey data, and to conduct business transactions. An electronic form is made up of a collection of **form controls**, which are the individual buttons, boxes, and hyperlinks that let Web site visitors communicate with Web site owners. Electronic forms must include a submit button; otherwise, Web site visitors cannot return their form data to the Web site owner.

Publisher's Design Gallery contains many Web-based objects including mastheads, navigation bars, buttons, and forms — all designed to look good and load quickly on the Web. Additionally, the Form Control button menu contains many features to assist in designing forms from scratch. Most desktop publishers use a combination of rapid form development techniques, such as the use of templates, Web controls, or Design Gallery objects, to tailor their Web site to suit their needs.

In both Web and print publications, when you issue an instruction to Publisher by clicking a button or command, Publisher follows a prewritten, step-by-step set of instructions to accomplish the task. For example, when you click the Print button on the Standard toolbar, Publisher follows a precise set of steps to print your publication. In Publisher, this series of instructions is called a **procedure**. A procedure also is referred to as a **program** or **code**.

The process of writing a procedure is called **computer programming**. Every Publisher command on a menu, and every button on a toolbar, has a corresponding procedure that executes when you click the command or button. **Execute** means that the computer carries out the step-by-step instructions. In a Windows environment, an event causes the instructions associated with a task to be executed. An **event** is an action such as clicking a button, clicking a command, dragging a scroll box, or right-clicking selected text.

Although Publisher has many toolbar buttons and menu commands, it does not include a command or button for every possible task. Thus, Microsoft has included with Publisher a powerful programming language called Visual Basic for Applications. The **Visual Basic for Applications (VBA)** programming language allows you to customize and extend the capabilities of Publisher to suit your own needs.

Project — Interactive Web Site

To illustrate some of the Web site features of Microsoft Publisher, this chapter presents a series of steps to create an interactive Web site for a pizzeria named Pizza Theater. Figure 6–1a shows the home page for the site, and Figure 6–1b shows a Web form created for the site. This chapter also demonstrates the use of a VBA-generated message box to remind the designer to upload the most recent copy of the publication to the Web (Figure 6–1c).

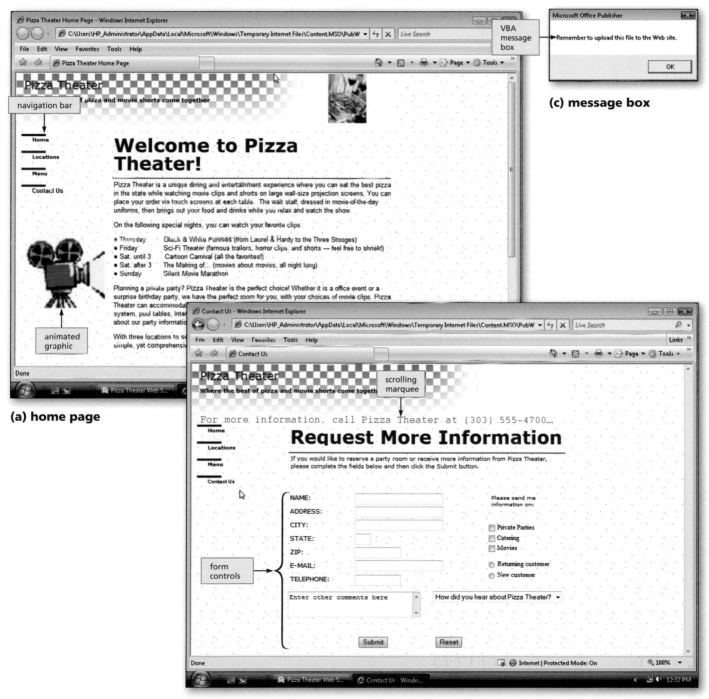

(c) message box

(a) home page

(b) Web form

Figure 6–1

The project in this chapter shows you how to create an interactive Web site that sends data to its owner; the Web site comes complete with a navigation bar, animated graphics, a background sound, form controls, and HTML code. Additionally, you will learn how to program a message box that is displayed when you close the publication.

Overview

As you read through this chapter, you will learn how to create the Web site publications shown in Figure 6–1 on the previous page by performing these general tasks:

- Select a Web site template and specify the options
- Create and use a bookmark
- Add a sound, animated graphics, and alternative text to a Web site
- Insert a new Web page in the site, created from scratch
- Insert form controls and set their properties
- Create a hot spot and a scrolling marquee
- Use VBA to create a message box

<table>
<tr>
<td>

Plan Ahead

</td>
<td>

General Project Guidelines

When creating a Publisher publication, the actions you perform and decisions you make will affect the appearance and characteristics of the finished publication. As you create an interactive Web site, such as the one shown in Figure 6–1, you should follow these general guidelines:

1. **Design navigation in your Web site.** The most important feature of a Web site is its navigation capabilities. Visitors need to be able to find information easily. They expect a navigation bar with links to other pages in your site. Use a logical order to present the pages, and create a navigation bar that is almost identical on all pages.

2. **Design and create a functional form.** Design a well-thought-out draft of the form — being sure to include all essential form elements. Sketch the form on paper first, to view the overall affect and placement of the objects before creating the elements on the computer screen. Essential elements include the form's title, text and graphics, data entry fields, and data entry instructions. A form control or data entry field is a placeholder for data that a user enters in the form.

3. **Determine how the form data will be analyzed.** If the data entered in the form will be analyzed by a program other than Publisher, create the data entry fields so that the entries are stored in separate fields that can be shared with other programs, and therefore filtered, sorted, and exported easily.

4. **Test the form.** Be sure that the form works as you intended. Fill in the form as if you were a user. Have others fill in the form and provide feedback to you as to whether the form is organized in a logical manner, is easy to understand, and complete. If any errors or weaknesses in the form are identified, correct them and test the form again.

5. **Add macros to automate tasks.** In Publisher, a macro consists of VBA code. To add macros, you do not need a computer programming background. To write advanced VBA code, however, you should be familiar with computer programming.

6. **Incorporate security in a publication.** Publisher provides several tools that allow you to secure your publications. For example, you can add a digital signature, set the security level, and save with a backup or versions.

When necessary, more specific details concerning the above guidelines are presented at appropriate points in the chapter. The chapter also will identify the actions performed and decisions made regarding these guidelines during the creation of the Web site in this chapter.

</td>
</tr>
</table>

To Start Publisher

If you are using a computer to step through the project in this chapter and you want your screens to match the figures in this book, you should change your computer's resolution to 1024 × 768. For information about how to change a computer's resolution, read Appendix D.

The following steps, which assume Windows is running, start Publisher based on a typical installation. You may need to ask your instructor how to start Publisher for your computer.

Note: If you are using Windows XP, see Appendix F for alternate steps.

1 Click the Start button on the Windows Vista taskbar to display the Start menu, and then click All Programs at the bottom of the left pane on the Start menu to display the All Programs list.

2 Click Microsoft Office in the All Programs list to display the Microsoft Office list, and then click Microsoft Office Publisher 2007 to start Publisher and display the Getting Started with Microsoft Office Publisher 2007 catalog.

3 If the Publisher window is not maximized, click the Maximize button next to the Close button on its title bar to maximize the window.

Creating a Web Site

Publisher's Web site templates offer many advantages over other Web page creation programs and authoring tools. The templates automatically include mastheads, animated graphics, hyperlinks, and text boxes. They also give you the ability to add new pages easily with navigation bars that are updated automatically. A **navigation bar** is a set of buttons or hyperlinks that allows visitors to move to any page within the Web site. Navigation bars may be placed on a page vertically, horizontally, along the top, along the bottom, or down the side. Additionally, navigation bars can be duplicated in multiple places on the page for easy access while scrolling through the page.

Web site templates provide a variety of home page, navigation bar, and secondary page styles. A **home page** is the opening page or main document that displays when you visit a Web site. Typically, the home page welcomes you and introduces the purpose of the site and the sponsoring business. Home pages commonly provide links to the **secondary pages** or lower-level pages in the site. Publisher provides a list of common secondary page types, such as a contact page or about page, from which you may choose.

Whether you use a template or design a Web site from scratch, you do not need extensive knowledge of HTML. HTML, which stands for Hypertext Markup Language, is a special formatting language that programmers use to format documents for display on the Web. Publisher provides user-friendly tools and controls to make it easy for even beginners to design interactive and highly effective Web sites.

BTW

XML
Publisher does not support all implementations of XML-related Web site development. For example, Publisher does not support content that is database-driven, as is the case with shopping cart technology. In addition, third-party credit card verification programs might not work properly with Publisher data, and Publisher might not be the best tool if you expect to edit raw HTML code after you create your Web site.

To Select Web Site Template Options

You will use a Web site template from the catalog, for the first three pages of the Web site. The following steps choose a template, a font scheme, a color scheme, and navigation bar options for the Web site.

1

- With the catalog displayed, click the Web Sites button in the list of Publication Types to display the Web site templates.

- At the top of the catalog click Classic Designs, and then scroll as necessary to click the Gingham preview.

- In the Customize area, select the Garnet color scheme and the Online font scheme (Figure 6–2).

Figure 6–2

2

- In the Options area, click the Navigation bar box arrow and then click Vertical Only in the list to specify a vertical navigation bar.

- If necessary, click the Use Easy Web Wizard check box so that it displays a check mark (Figure 6–3).

Q&A

What is the Easy Web Wizard?

The **Easy Web Wizard** will display choices for secondary pages after you click the Create button.

3

- Click the Create button to display the Easy Web Site Builder dialog box.

Experiment

- One at a time, click the various check boxes on the left side of the Easy Web Site Builder dialog box to display the visual hierarchy of pages in the Web site. The visual hierarchy helps you understand how many pages will be added to the Web site.

- Click so that check marks display only in the 'Tell customers how to contact us' and 'Display a list of projects or activities' check boxes (Figure 6–4).

Figure 6–3

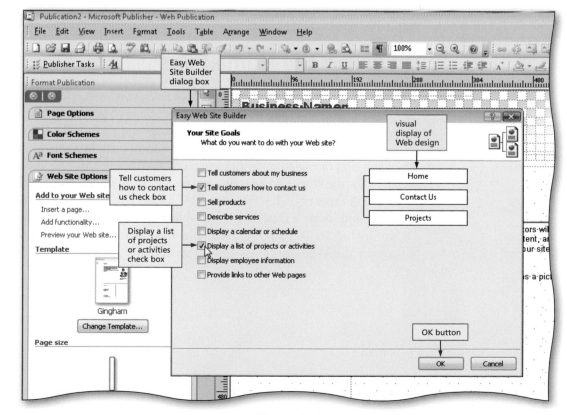

Figure 6–4

4

- Click the OK button to create the Web site with the selected secondary pages. A working box will display while the additional Web pages are created.

- When the publication is displayed, close the task pane. If the Special Characters button on the Standard toolbar is not selected already, click it to display formatting marks on the screen. Your title bar may display a different publication number (Figure 6–5).

- If the Web Tools toolbar is displayed, click its Close button.

Figure 6–5

Editing the Home Page

When using a Publisher Web site template, you must edit template objects and insert content specific to the business, purpose, or Web site owner. The home page is the first page that Web site visitors will see, so it should explain the site's purpose, content, and layout. The home page should contain appropriate information in the masthead and navigation bar so that visitors can navigate the site and find key information.

In the steps on the following pages, you will edit the masthead and navigation bar that will repeat on all pages in the Web site. You also will edit the heading and the main story, and insert a Design Gallery object unique to page 1 of the publication. Finally, you will include both a static graphic and an animated graphic on the home page to help convey the Web site's message and style.

To Edit the Masthead and Heading

The following steps edit the masthead and heading text boxes on the home page of the Web site. The masthead text boxes are synchronized elements; therefore, editing the text once will change each instance of the masthead in the Web site. Heading text boxes on each page are independent of one another.

1

- Zoom to Page Width.

- Select the text in the Business Name text box and then type `Pizza Theater` to replace the text.

- Select the text in the tag line text box and then type `Where the best of pizza and movie shorts come together` to replace the text (Figure 6–6).

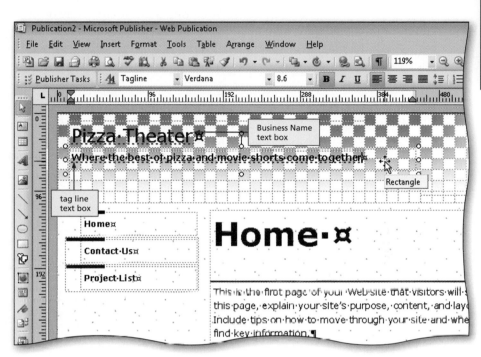

Figure 6–6

2

- Select the word Home in the heading text box. Type `Welcome to Pizza Theater!` to replace the text (Figure 6–7).

Q&A Why did my font size change?

The heading text box in the template is set to copyfit the text automatically. Recall that Publisher's AutoFit feature copyfits the font size to be as large as possible to fit the space in the text box.

Figure 6–7

Editing the Navigation Bar

The navigation bars that come with the Web site templates, and those inserted using the Design Gallery, are grouped objects. Navigation bars include hyperlinks to the other pages in the Web site, text to guide the Web site visitors, and graphical shapes unique to each template or Design Gallery object. You can change the components in a navigation bar by editing them individually or by using the Navigation Bar Properties dialog box. The **page title**, which displays in the browser title bar, also is edited via the Navigation Bar Properties dialog box. Because the navigation bar is a synchronized object, changing it on one page of the Web site changes it on all pages.

Plan Ahead

Design navigation in your Web site.
Publisher has navigation bars in its Design Gallery and templates. Make sure you edit the bars appropriately, and use terms that are common to most Web sites. For instance, visitors expect links such as Locations, Contact Us, and About.

To Edit the Navigation Bar

The following steps edit the navigation bar's text and its accompanying page title.

1

- Select the navigation bar, and then click the button below the navigation bar that displays a magic wand symbol to display the Navigation Bar Properties dialog box.

- In the Links area, click Contact Us to select the link (Figure 6–8).

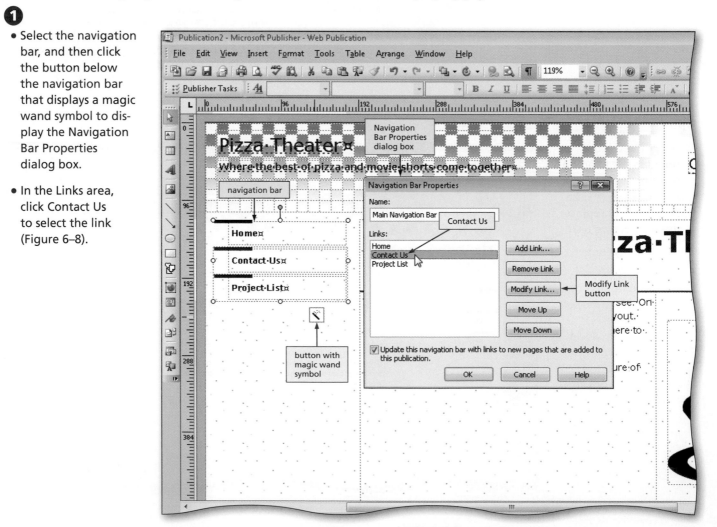

Figure 6–8

2

- Click the Modify Link button to display the Modify Link - Main Navigation Bar dialog box.

- Select the text in the Text to display box, and then type Locations to replace the text (Figure 6–9).

Q&A Where will the new text display in the Web page?

Text entered in the Text to display box will display in the navigation bar itself.

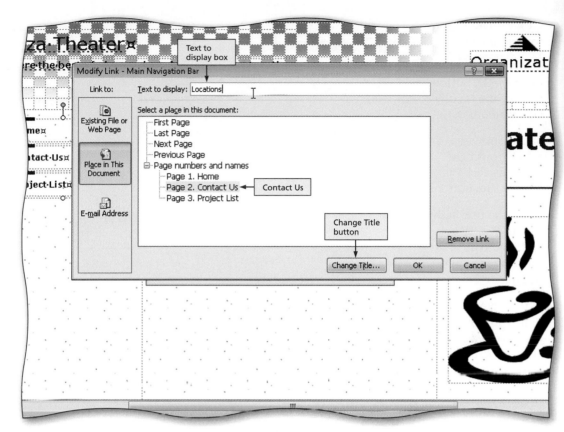

Figure 6–9

3

- Click the Change Title button to display the Enter Text dialog box.

- Select, if necessary, the text in the Page title box and then type Pizza Theater Locations to replace the text (Figure 6–10).

Q&A Where will the title display in the Web page?

The title will display in the Web browser's title bar when the Web page is viewed. The title also is displayed in a ScreenTip when you point to the page icon on the page sorter, located on the Publisher status bar.

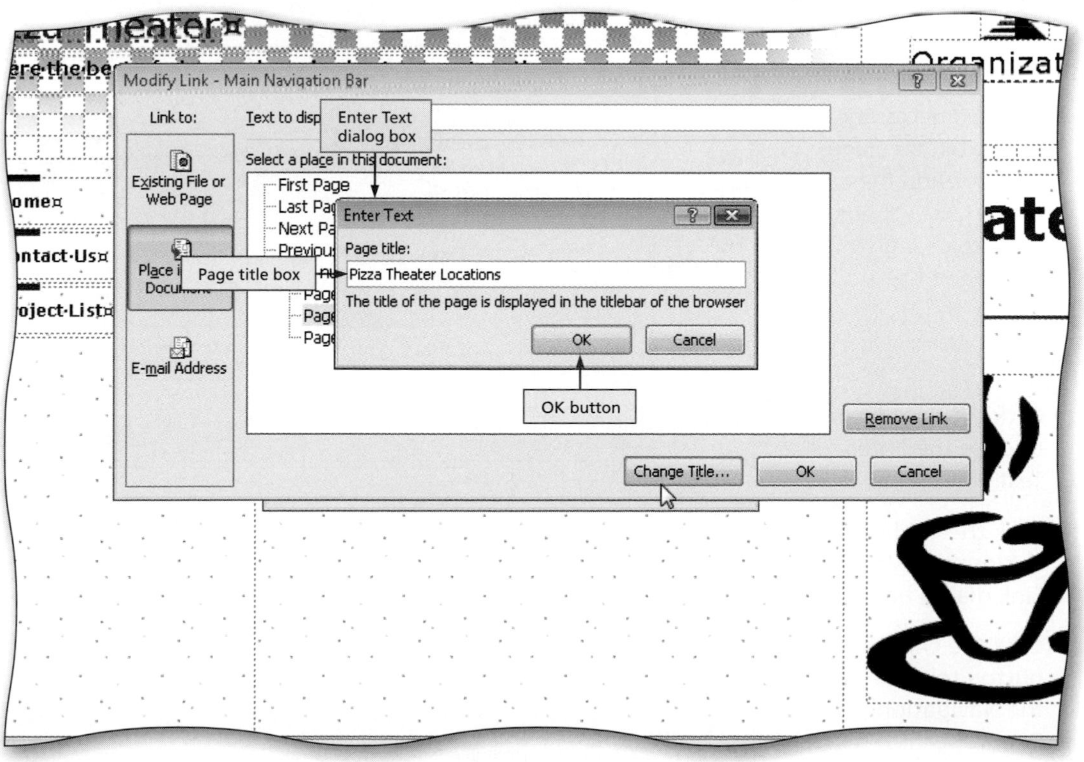

Figure 6–10

4

- Click the OK button to close the Enter Text dialog box.

- Click the OK button to close the Modify Link dialog box.

- In the Links area, select Project List and then click the Modify Link button.

- Select the text in the Text to display box, and then type Menu to change the navigation bar text.

- In the 'Select a place in this document' area, click Page 3. Project List to select it (Figure 6–11).

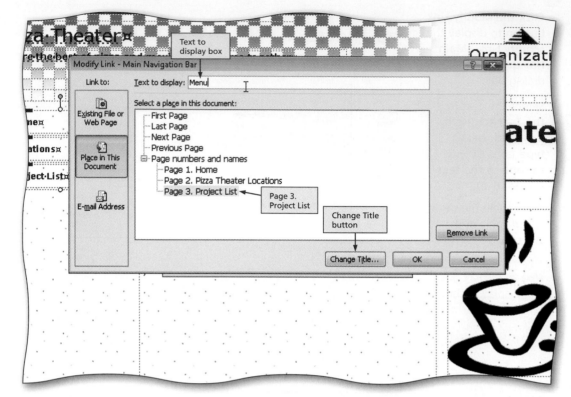

Figure 6–11

5

- Click the Change Title button to display the Enter Text dialog box.

- Select, if necessary, the text in the Page Title box and then type Pizza Theater Menu to change the page title (Figure 6–12).

6

- Click the OK button to close the Enter Text dialog box.

- Click the OK button to close the Modify Link dialog box.

- Click the OK button to close the Navigation Bar Properties dialog box.

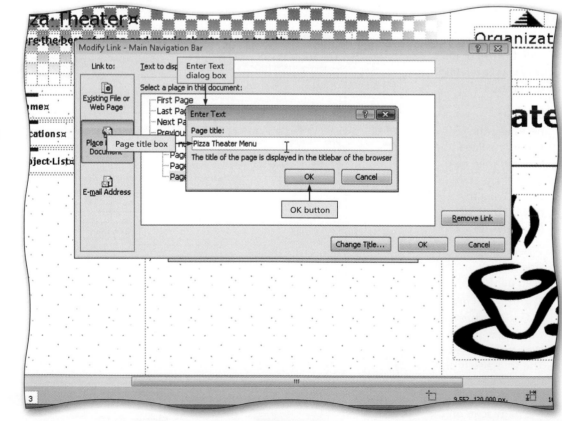

Figure 6–12

To Edit Other Objects on the Home Page

The following steps delete, reposition, and resize other objects on the page.

1 Delete the organization logo in the upper-right corner of the page.

2 Scroll as necessary, and then delete the Caption text box below the graphic of the coffee cup.

3 Move the coffee cup graphic to a location approximately 100 pixels below the navigation bar.

4 Select the main story text box. Double-click the status bar to reveal the Measurement toolbar. Change the width to 567 pixels. Change the height to 387 pixels.

5 Close the Measurement toolbar (Figure 6–13).

Figure 6–13

To Import the Main Story

With the main story text box resized, the following steps import the text for the story from a Word document included in the Data Files for Students. See the inside back cover of this book for instructions on downloading the Data Files for Students, or contact your instructor for more information about accessing the required files.

Note: If you are using Windows XP, see Appendix F for alternate steps.

1 Right-click the default text in the main story text box to display the shortcut menu. Point to Change Text, and then click Text File to display the Insert Text dialog box.

2 Navigate to the Data Files for Students and then double-click the file, Pizza Theater Text, to insert the text file (Figure 6–14 on the next page). A Converting box will display while the text is being inserted.

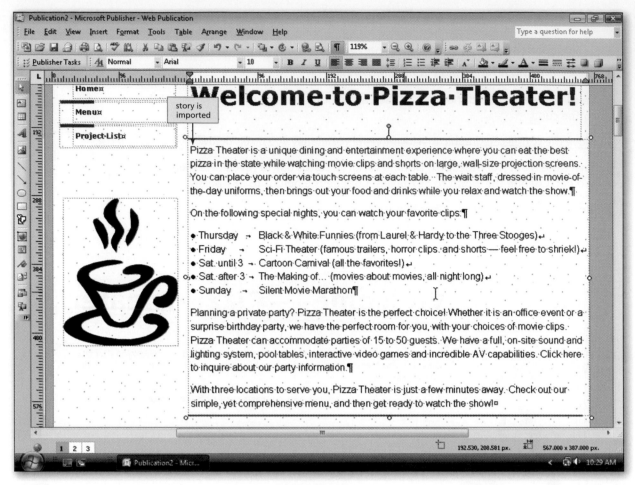

Figure 6–14

To Edit the Contact Information

The following steps edit the contact information text boxes that repeat on all pages of the Web site.

1 Scroll down to display the contact information text boxes.

2 Select the text in the address text box and then type `Pizza Theater Downtown` and press the ENTER key. Type `4700 Main Street` and then press the ENTER key. Type `Denver, CO 80012` to finish the address.

3 Select the text in the phone/fax/e-mail text box and then type `Phone: (303) 555-4700` and press the ENTER key. Type `Fax: (303) 555-4705` and then press the ENTER key. Type `E-mail: theboss@pizzatheater.biz` to finish the address (Figure 6–15).

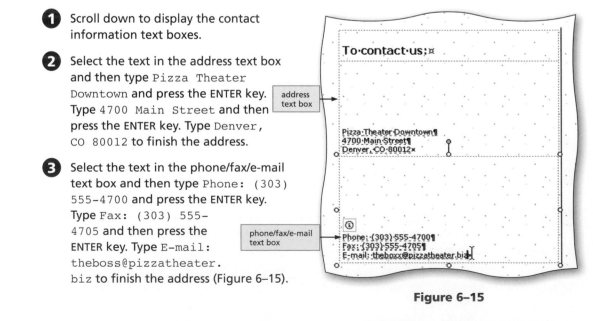

Figure 6–15

To Insert a Design Gallery Object

The following steps insert an object from the Design Gallery and edit its text to display the business hours of Pizza Theater.

1 On the Objects toolbar, click the Design Gallery Object button to display the Design Gallery window.

2 In the list of objects on the left, click the Pull Quotes button, and then double-click the Punctuation pull quote to insert the Design Gallery object into the publication.

3 Drag the pull quote to a location right of the contact information. Resize the pull quote to approximately 220 × 137 pixels. Select the text and then type `All of our locations open every day at 11:00 a.m. We close at 10:00 p.m. Sunday through Thursday and midnight on Friday and Saturday.` to replace the text (Figure 6–16).

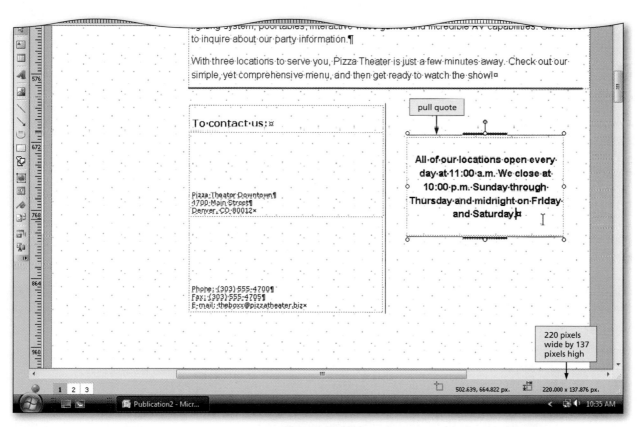

Figure 6–16

Bookmarks

A **bookmark** is a location in a publication that you name for reference purposes as you design a publication. Bookmarks display as small flags in page layout only. They do not print in print publications, and they do not display in browsers when visitors are viewing a Web site. Bookmarks are saved, however, when the publication is saved.

Bookmarks are used to organize large or multi-page publications and to locate objects that you want to revise at a later time. Instead of scrolling through the publication pages to locate an object or text, a named bookmark allows you to go to it quickly, using the Bookmark dialog box.

Inserting a Bookmark

To create a bookmark, you click the **Bookmark button** on the Objects toolbar. Publisher then displays a Bookmark dialog box in which you give the bookmark a name. Using the dialog box, you also can add, delete, sort, or go to bookmarks. Once a bookmark is created, you can drag it to any location on the page.

In the following steps, you will create a bookmark next to the pull quote so that you can find it quickly later in the chapter without jumping to the page or scrolling.

To Insert a Bookmark

1

- Deselect the pull quote.

- Click the Bookmark button on the Objects toolbar to display the Bookmark dialog box.

- In the Bookmark name box, type `pull quote` to enter a name for the bookmark (Figure 6–17).

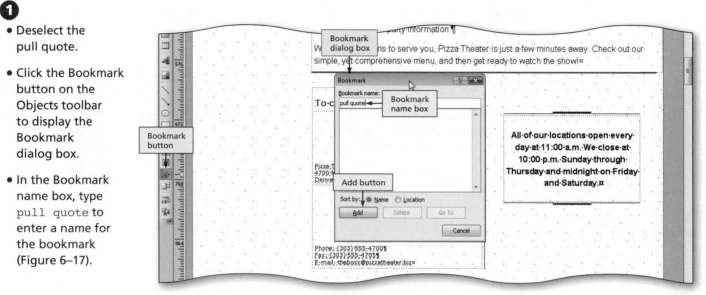

Figure 6–17

2

- Click the Add button to create the bookmark.

- Drag the bookmark to a location near the pull quote (Figure 6–18).

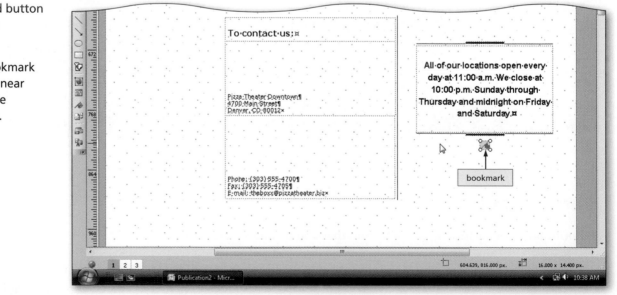

Figure 6–18

Other Ways

1. On Insert menu, click Bookmark

Web Graphics

When using graphics on Web pages, you must take into consideration visual appeal, download time, resolution, and purpose. Unless the home page is a picture gallery, two or three graphics is enough to create visual appeal and catch the visitor's eye. Keep in mind that each image added to a Web page increases the amount of time it takes to download the page. In addition, some people browse the Web with images turned off in order to speed up the process; others turn off graphics to make the page more accessible.

Even though the computer screen is lower in resolution than most printed pages, Web graphics easily can rival the quality of color images printed on paper. **Resolution** refers to the number of horizontal and vertical pixels in a display device or the sharpness and clarity of an image. A high resolution graphic makes a Web page more visually appealing, but increases the download time.

Purpose may be the most important consideration in using Web graphics; they should help convey the Web site's message, not clutter the layout. The graphics should add interest or color, brand a company, draw attention, show relationships, or simplify complex information.

The number and type of graphics you use on your page will be a compromise between what is appealing visually and what makes the best sense for your target audience.

BTW

Changing Pages
Another way to jump to specific locations is to use the **Go To Page feature**. Pressing the F5 key displays the Go To Page dialog box, allowing you to jump quickly to any page in the publication.

Inserting an Animated Graphic

An **animated graphic** is a picture that displays animation when viewed in a Web browser. While too much animation may distract users, a subtle animation may convey the Web site owner's message or style. The following steps preview an animated graphic.

To Preview an Animated Graphic

1

- Scroll to the upper portion of the home page. Double-click the coffee cup graphic to display the Clip Art task pane.

- In the Clip Art task pane, type camera in the Search for box.

- Click the Search in box arrow, and then click the Everywhere check box so that it displays a check mark.

- Click the Results should be box arrow, and then click the Movies check box so that it displays a check mark. Click to remove any other check marks.

- Click the Go button to perform the search (Figure 6–19).

Q&A How do I know if the clip art is animated?

Animated clip art or movies display a star in the lower-right corner of the preview in the task pane. You will not see the animation until you view the publication in a browser.

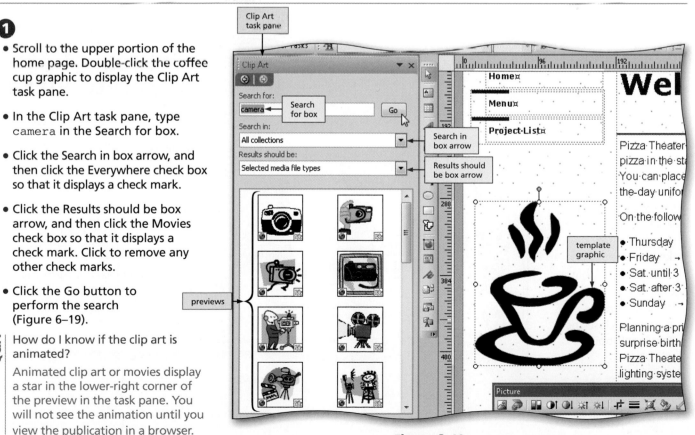

Figure 6–19

2

- Click the button on any preview to display its menu (Figure 6–20).

Q&A What are some of the other commands on the button menu?

The Make Available Offline command gives you the opportunity to save the graphic on your computer system. The Edit Keywords command displays a dialog box where you can edit searchable keywords in order to find clip art more easily.

Figure 6–20

3

- Click Preview/ Properties to display the Preview/ Properties dialog box (Figure 6–21).

🔍 **Experiment**

- Click the Next or Previous button several times to view the animation for each of the graphics found in the keyword search.

4

- Click the Close button to close the Preview/Properties dialog box.

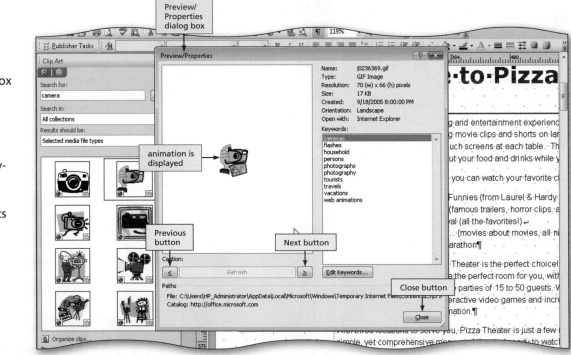

Figure 6–21

To Insert a Graphic

The following steps insert the animated graphic on the home page.

1 In the Clip Art task pane, click a graphic similar to the one shown in Figure 6–22 to insert it into the publication.

2 Close the Clip Art task pane.

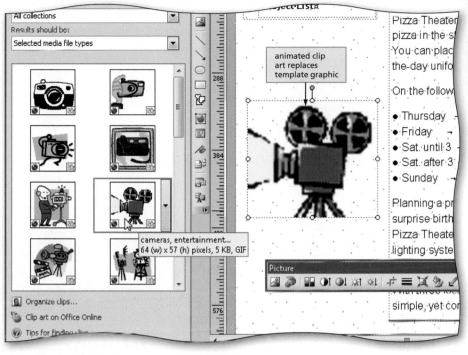

Figure 6–22

To Flip a Graphic

The next step flips the graphic so it faces to the right.

1 Click Arrange on the menu bar, point to Rotate or Flip, and then click Flip Horizontal (Figure 6–23).

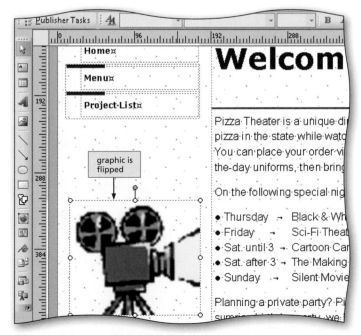

Figure 6–23

Using Empty Picture Frames

A **static graphic** does not display animation; the picture stays the same when viewed in a Web browser. In the following steps, you first will create an empty picture frame and then you will insert a static graphic that is a photograph of a pizza. Using an **empty picture frame** rather than inserting directly from the Clip Art task pane will size the desired graphic automatically.

To Create an Empty Picture Frame

- Scroll to display the upper portion of the Web page.

- On the Objects toolbar, click the Picture Frame button to display the Picture Frame menu (Figure 6–24).

Figure 6–24

②

- Click the Empty Picture Frame command.

- Drag to create an empty picture frame in the upper-right corner of the Web page (Figure 6–25).

Figure 6–25

Other Ways

1. On Insert menu, point to Picture, click Empty Picture Frame

To Insert a Static Graphic

The following steps fill the empty picture frame with a picture from the Clip Art task pane.

 Right-click the empty picture frame. On the shortcut menu, point to Change Picture, and then click Clip Art to display the Clip Art task pane.

 Search for photographs of a pizza.

3 Select a graphic similar to the one shown in Figure 6–26.

4 Close the task pane.

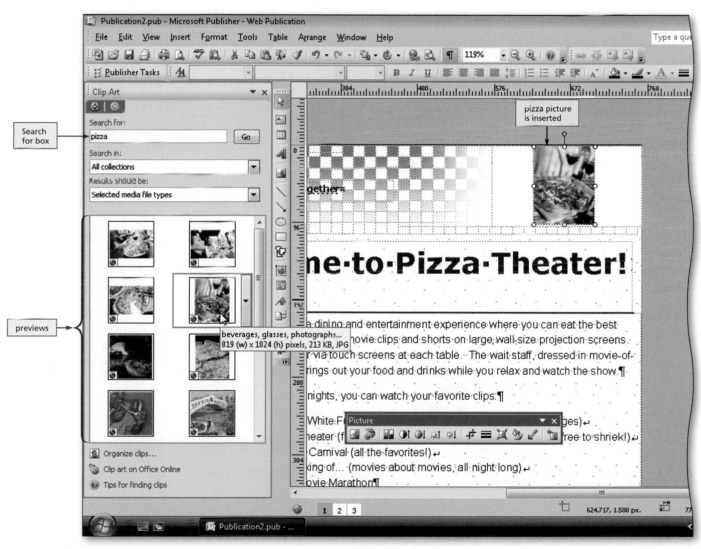

Figure 6–26

Alternative Text

A special consideration when using graphics on the Web is the issue of accessibility. Screen readers that read Web pages for people with disabilities can provide feedback about pictures, but only if the picture has alternative text. **Alternative text** is descriptive text that appears as an alternative to a graphic image on Web pages. Graphics without alternative text are not usable by screen readers. Web browsers may display alternative text when graphics are loading or when graphics are missing. Screen readers read the alternative text.

In the following steps, you will insert alternative text for the two graphics on the home page.

To Add Alternative Text

1

- Right-click the photograph of the pizza, and then click Format Picture on the shortcut menu. When the Format Picture dialog box is displayed, click the Web tab.

- Type A picture of a pizza displays on a table at the Pizza Theater restaurant. in the Alternative text box (Figure 6–27).

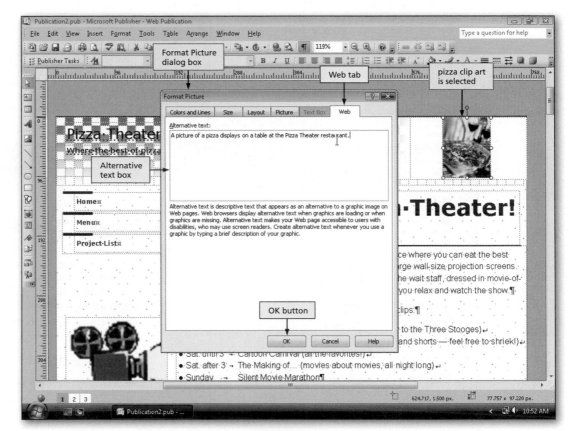

Figure 6–27

2

- Click the OK button to close the dialog box.

- Right-click the photograph of the camera, and then click Format Picture on the shortcut menu. When the Format Picture dialog box is displayed, click the Web tab.

- Type An animated graphic displays a picture of a movie camera with rotating film reels and flashing projection. in the Alternative text box (Figure 6–28).

3

- Click the OK button to close the dialog box.

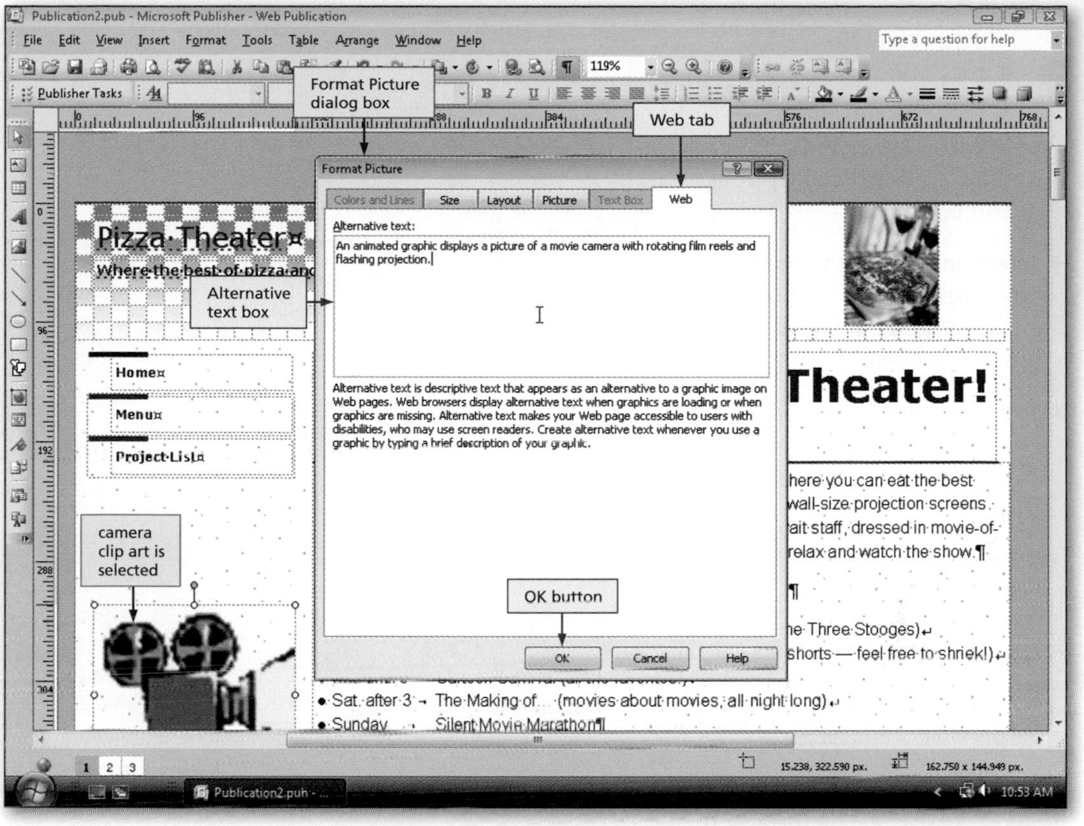

Figure 6–28

Other Ways

1. On Format menu, click Picture, click Web tab

Setting Web Page Options

Publisher's **Web page options** allow you to customize the way the Web page displays and how it works on the Web. You can edit the page title, the file name, search engine information, and the background sound. Recall that the page title is the text that will display in the browser's title bar. The file name is the name of the individual Web page as it is stored on a server.

The search engine information, such as description and keywords, creates **meta tags** in Web publications; these tags are HTML specification tags that tell search engines what data to use. The **description** is a sentence or phrase that you create about your Web site. The description is displayed in most search engine results pages. The description should encourage people to click the link to your Web site. The **keywords** are a list of words or phrases that some search engines may use to locate your page. While keywords are used less frequently than they once were, you still should insert them and make sure they accurately reflect the content of the Web page for effective searching.

The Web Page Options command on the Tools menu displays a dialog box where you can edit the various options, as shown in the steps on the next page. The Web Page Options command displays only when you are working with Web publications in Publisher.

To Edit Web Page Options

The following steps edit Web page options for the Pizza Theater Web site.

1

- Click Tools on the menu bar, and then click Web Page Options to display the Web Page Options dialog box.

- Select any text in the Page title box if necessary, and then type `Pizza Theater Home Page` to replace the text.

- Select any text in the File name box if necessary, and then type `index` to replace the text (Figure 6–29).

Q&A Why is the home page named index?

It is standard practice to name the main page of any Web site or directory, index. Web servers recognize index as the main page and thus do not require visitors to type the file name at the end of the URL when navigating to the page.

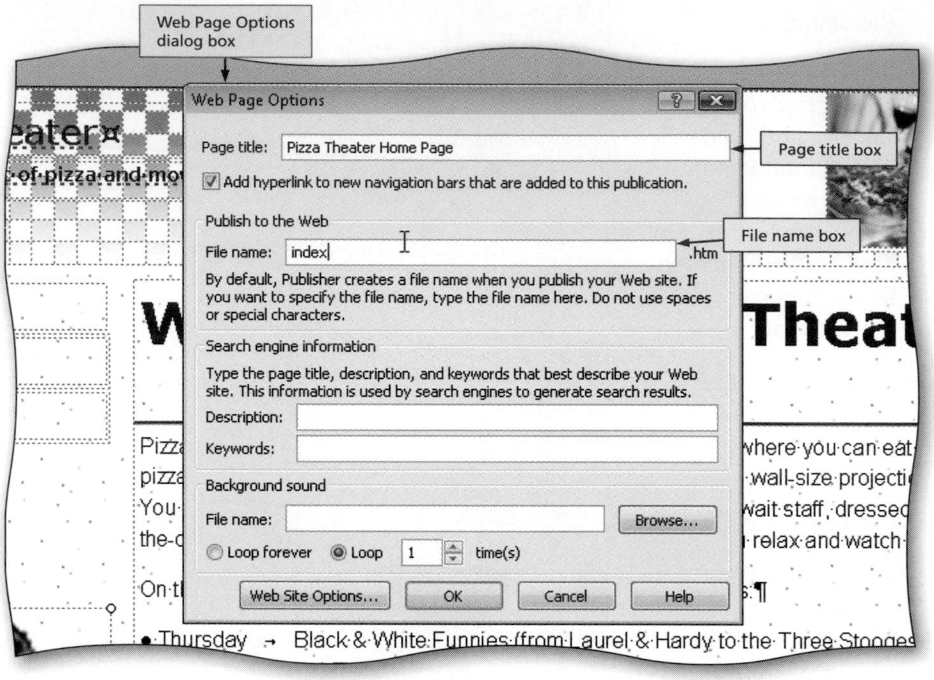

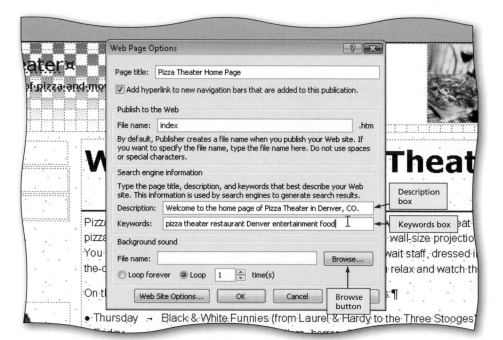

Figure 6–29

2

- In the Description box, type `Welcome to the home page of Pizza Theater in Denver, CO.` to describe the Web site.

- In the Keywords box, type `pizza theater restaurant Denver entertainment food` to create the keywords list (Figure 6–30).

Q&A Do I need to type commas between the keywords?

It is not necessary to type commas between each keyword. The search engines that still use keyword meta tags can accept the data either way.

Figure 6–30

Other Ways

1. In Background task pane, click Background sound, enter options

6 Chapter Publisher (1st) C6156 41289 Page 408 08/07/07—ALL

Background Sound

When you add a **background sound** to a Web publication, the sound plays when you view the Web page in a browser. The following steps insert a background sound from the sounds that come with an initial installation of Publisher. This location of the sound clip art commonly is C:\Program Files\Microsoft Office\CLIPART\PUB60COR. Your instructor may specify a different location for your sound clip art.

BTW

Background Sound
Adding sound generates interest, attracts attention, and can add a certain style to your Web site. Disadvantages of adding sound include additional download time and visitors who navigate away from the Web site because they may not want to listen. You should use sound only to enhance the site and do so only in appropriate amounts.

To Insert a Background Sound

1

- With the Web Page Options dialog box still displayed, click the Browse button to display the Background Sound dialog box.

- If necessary, navigate to the location of sound clip art on your system (Figure 6–31).

Q&A | Can I hear the sound before I choose it?

Yes, on most systems, you can right-click a sound file and the shortcut menu will contain a Play command. Check with your instructor about sound and speakers in lab situations.

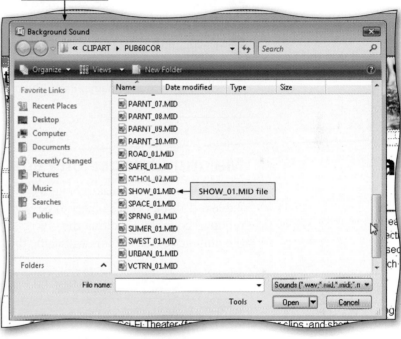

Figure 6–31

2

- Double-click the SHOW_01.MID file or other sound file on your system (Figure 6–32).

Q&A | What does the extension MID mean?

The MID or MIDI (pronounced middy) stands for musical instrument digital interface and is a protocol designed for recording and playing back music using synthesizers and other input devices. The MID extension is supported by most computer sound cards.

3

- Click the OK button to close the Web Page Options dialog box.

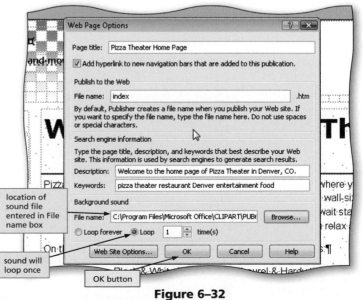

Figure 6–32

Saving the Web Site

With the home page complete it is a good time to save the publication, as shown in the following steps. Later in the chapter you will publish the file to the Web and then save it in HTML format.

To Save the Web Publication

1 With a USB flash drive connected to one of the computer's USB ports, click the Save button on the Standard toolbar.

2 Type Pizza Theater Web Site in the File name box to change the file name. Do not press the ENTER key.

3 Navigate to your USB flash drive.

4 Click the Save button in the Save As dialog box to save the publication on the USB flash drive with the file name, Pizza Theater Web Site.

Making Changes on Page 2 of the Web Site

The next steps make changes on the Locations page for the Pizza Theater Web site. Table 6–1 displays each object to be edited, the current text or setting, and the new text or required edits. After editing the objects, you then will go to a bookmark and copy and paste the pull quote. Finally, you will name the file using the Web Page Options dialog box.

Table 6–1 Page 2 Edits		
Object	**Current Text (or Setting)**	**New Text (or Edits)**
Heading text box	Contact Us	Locations
Subheading text box	Heading	Three locations to serve you
Main story text box	(default text)	Pizza Theater North in Arvada 1352 Elgin Road Phone: (303) 555 1352 Pizza Theater Downtown 4700 Main Street Phone: (303) 555-4700 Pizza Theater South in Littleton 9916 Mountain Ave. Phone: (303) 555-9916
Company text box	Company or Organization Name	(delete text box)
Street address	Your street address or the name of your neighborhood	(delete text box)
Logo	Organization	(delete object)
Map graphic	(default picture)	(delete object)

To Edit Objects on Page 2

1 Navigate to page 2. Individually, select the objects in Table 6–1 and edit them as directed in the table.

2 In the main story text box, select the middle three lines of text, representing the address of the downtown location. On the Formatting toolbar, click the Bold button. Click the Font Color button, and then click Accent 2 in the list. Deselect the text to view the color (Figure 6–33).

3 If instructed by your professor, insert a graphic of a map or a hyperlink to a map Web site.

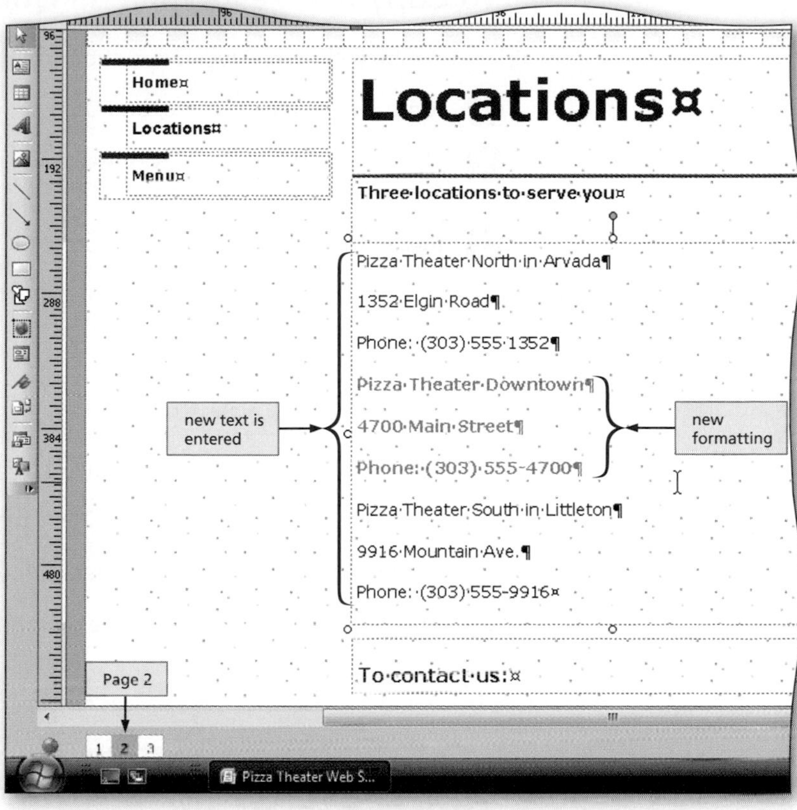

Figure 6–33

To Go to a Bookmark

The following steps go to the previously named bookmark.

1

- On the Objects toolbar, click the Bookmark button to display the Bookmark dialog box (Figure 6–34).

2

- If necessary, select the pull quote bookmark and then click the Go To button.

- Close the Bookmark dialog box by clicking the Close button in the title bar.

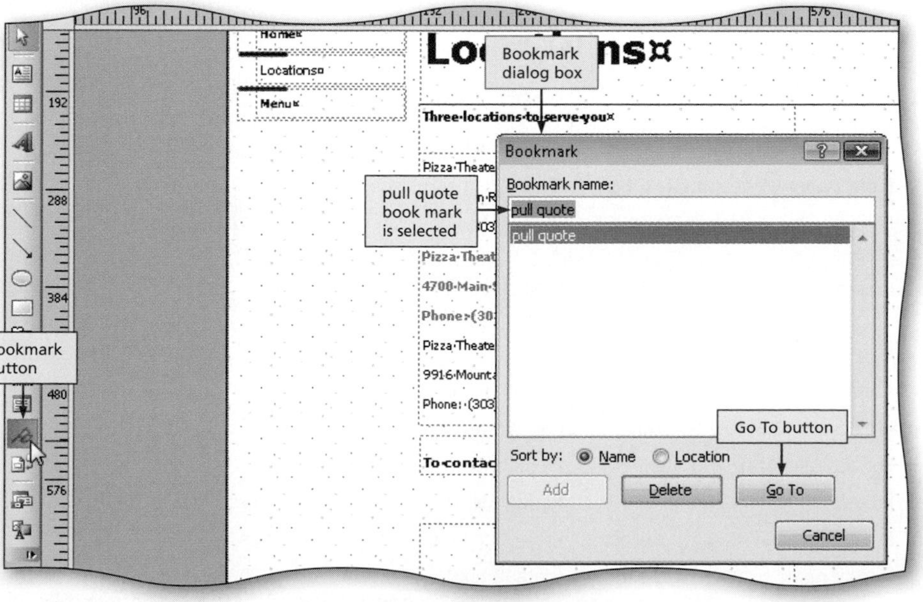

Figure 6–34

To Copy and Paste the Pull Quote

The following steps copy the pull quote and paste it on page 2.

1 Right-click the pull quote, and then click Copy on the shortcut menu.

2 Navigate back to page 2, right-click an empty portion of the page layout, and then click Paste on the shortcut menu.

3 Resize the pull quote as necessary.

To Name the Web Page File

The following steps name the Web page file for page 2 of the Web site.

1 Click Web Page Options on the Tools menu to display the Web Page Options dialog box.

2 In the File name box, type `locations` to name the file.

3 Click the OK button to close the dialog box.

Making Changes on Page 3 of the Web Site

The next steps make changes on the Menu page of the template for the Pizza Theater Web site. Table 6–2 displays the object to be edited, the current text or settings, and the new text or required edits. You will name the Web page file using the Web Page Options dialog box.

Table 6–2 Page 3 Edits		
Object	**Current text (or Setting)**	**New Text (or edits)**
Logo	Organization	(delete object)
Heading text box	Project List	Menu
Main story text box	(default text)	Our simple menu makes it easy to order using the touch screen pad at each table. All of our items are available in small, medium, and large sizes.
Project name 1 heading text box	Project name 1	Pizza
Project name 1 story text box	(default text)	Our famous crust and sauce comes with a thick layer of cheese and your choice of toppings.
Project name 2 heading text box	Project name 2	Salads
Project name 2 story text box	(default text)	Tossed or Caesar with your choice of dressings and toppings, including grilled chicken
Project name 3 heading text box	Project name 3	Sides
Project name 3 story text box	(default text)	Breadsticks, fried mushrooms, nachos, fried zucchinis
Project name 4 heading text box	Project name 4	Drinks
Project name 4 story text box	(default text)	Your favorite soft drinks and classic adult beverages
Project name 5 heading text box	Project name 5	Desserts
Project name 5 story text box	(default text)	Pizza Theater's famous sundae — offered every day of the week!
All more details text boxes	More details	(delete object)
Default graphics	(default pictures)	(replace with appropriate graphics)

To Edit Objects on Page 3

 Navigate to page 3.

2 Individually, select the text-based objects in Table 6–2 and edit them as directed in the table.

3 For each of the graphics, use the Clip Art task pane to find appropriate graphics to match the text.

4 To add alternative text to each graphic individually, right-click the graphic, and then click Format Picture. On the Web tab, enter an appropriate, short description (Figure 6–35).

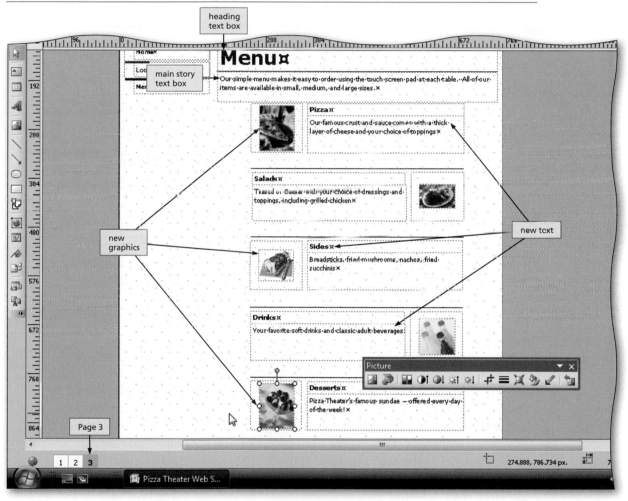

Figure 6–35

To Name the Web Page File for Page 3

The following steps name the Web page file for page 3 of the Web site.

1 Click Web Page Options on the Tools menu to display the Web Page Options dialog box.

2 In the File name box, type menu to name the file.

3 Click the OK button to close the dialog box.

To Save the Heading and Main Story in the Content Library

Because you will want to use a heading and main story on a new page later in the chapter, the following steps store the objects in the Content Library.

1 Click the border of the heading text box that displays the text, Menu, in order to select the text box. Shift-click to add the decorative line below the heading to the selection. Shift-click to add the main story text box below the decorative line to the selection.

2 Right-click the selected objects and then click Group on the shortcut menu to group the objects.

3 Right-click the selection to display the shortcut menu. Click the Add to Content Library command to add the selected objects to the Content Library.

4 Click the OK button to close the Add Item to Content Library dialog box.

5 Close the Content Library task pane.

Saving the Web Site Again

With pages 2 and 3 complete, it is a good time to save the Web site again, as shown in the following step.

To Save a Publication with the Same Name

1 With a USB flash drive connected to one of the computer's USB ports, click the Save button on the Standard toolbar to save the publication again with the same name.

Creating a Web Page from Scratch

Pizza Theater would like a Web page created from **scratch**, which means beginning with a blank page rather than a Web page template. The Web page should contain a way for customers to provide contact information and party preferences to Pizza Theater.

When beginning with a blank Web page, desktop publishers may set font and color schemes and then insert text and appropriate electronic form controls graphics and sounds. A variety of objects is available to create pages, including design sets with mastheads, color schemes, font schemes, backgrounds, and navigation bars.

Inserting a New Page in a Web Publication

The following steps insert a new page. Publisher's **Insert Page command** copies the basic color and font schemes of the other pages in the Web site as well as the masthead to jump start the creation process.

To Insert a New Page in a Web Publication

1

- Right-click the Page 3 icon in the page sorter to display the shortcut menu (Figure 6–36).

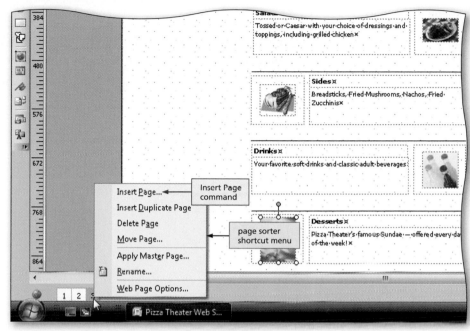

Figure 6–36

2

- Click Insert Page on the shortcut menu to display the Insert Web Page dialog box.

🔍 **Experiment**

- Click several of the page types in the 'Select a page type' area to view what kind of preformatted pages are available.

- In the 'Select a page type' area, click Blank to select it (Figure 6–37).

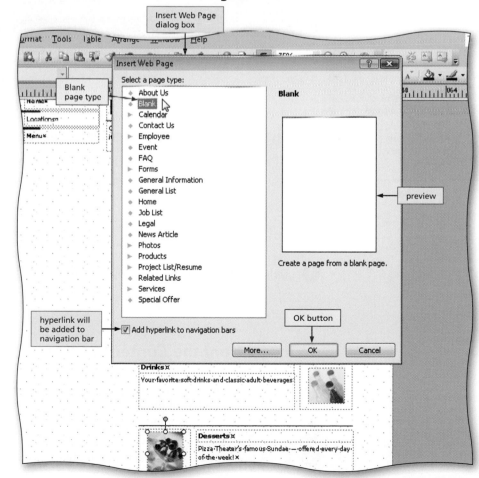

Figure 6–37

3
- Click the OK button to display the new page. Your logo may differ.

- Zoom to page width (Figure 6–38).

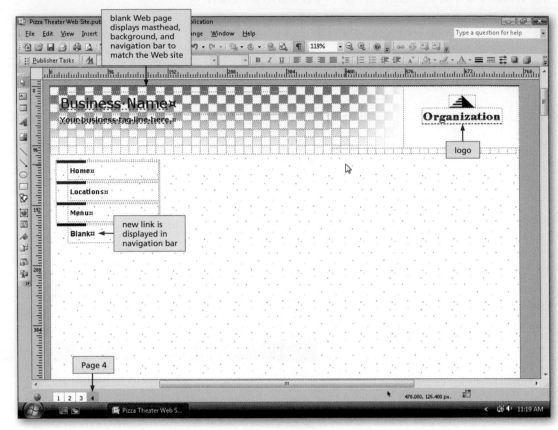

Figure 6–38

Other Ways

1. On Insert menu, click Page, select a page type, click OK
2. Press CTRL+SHIFT+N, select a page type, click OK

Editing Objects on the New Web Page

The following steps delete the logo, insert the grouped heading from the Content Library, edit the inserted text boxes, and rename the page.

To Delete the Logo

1 Delete the logo in the upper-right corner of the Web page.

To Insert from the Content Library

1 With no other object selected on the page, click the 'Item from Content Library' button on the Objects toolbar to display the Content Library task pane.

2 In the Content Library area, double-click the previous stored, grouped object in the list.

3 In the publication, drag the grouped object to a location right of the navigation bar.

4 Close the task pane.

To Edit the Text Boxes

1 Double-click the text, Menu. Type `Request More Information` to replace the text.

2 Select the text in the main story heading and then type `If you would like to reserve a party room or receive more information from Pizza Theater, please complete the fields below and then click the Submit button.` to replace the text.

3 In the masthead, select the text in the Business Name text box and then type `Pizza Theater` to replace the text. Select the text in the tag line text box and then type `Where the best of pizza and movie shorts come together` to replace the text.

4 In the navigation bar, double-click the word, Blank, and then type `Contact Us` to replace the text. If necessary, select the text and change the font to Verdana and the font size to 7.7 to match the other navigation bar text boxes (Figure 6–39).

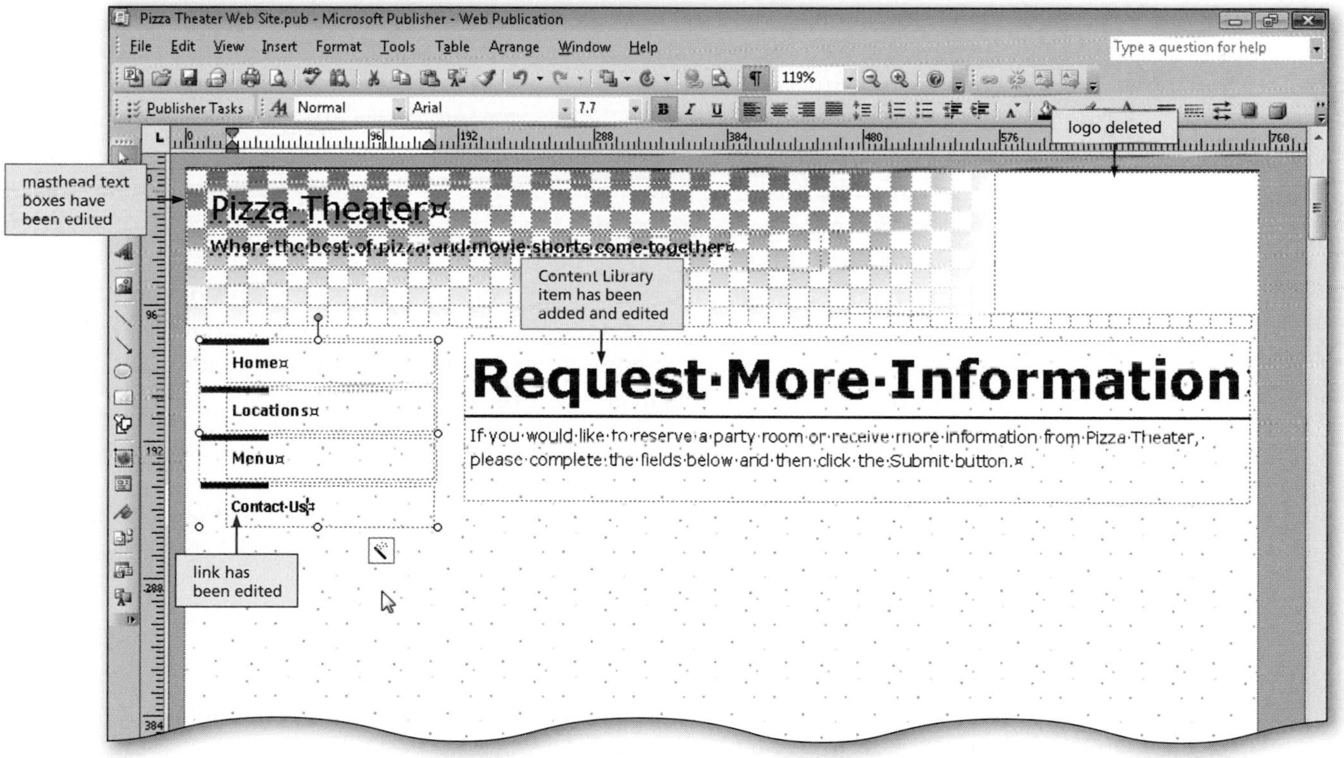

Figure 6–39

To Rename the Page

1 To display the Web Page Options dialog box, click Web Page Options on the Tools menu.

2 In the Page title box, type `Contact Us` to rename the page.

3 In the File name box, type `contact` to name the file.

4 Click the OK button to close the Web Page Options dialog box.

BTW

Forms
When creating a standard business form, it is easier to edit one of Publisher's nine different reply forms from the Design Gallery or to select a Form page when inserting a new page into your Web site than it is to start one from scratch. The check boxes on Publisher forms are combinations of small rectangles and text boxes permanently grouped together. The text boxes, tables, and lines in other parts of the forms are preformatted to display and print correctly.

Form Controls

Recall that form controls are the individual boxes and buttons used by Web site visitors to enter data. Each form control has editable properties and values that change its appearance and functionality. The data from a form control is transmitted from the visitor to the site owner via a submit button. Publisher supports six types of form controls.

A **checkbox form control** is a square box that presents a yes/no choice. It displays a check mark or X when selected. Several checkboxes function as a group of related but independent choices. An **option button form control** is a round button that presents one choice. When it is selected, an option button circle is filled in. When grouped, option buttons function like multiple-choice questions. The difference between an option button and a checkbox is that users can select only one option button within a group, but any number of checkboxes. Checkboxes and option buttons both display a label you can edit. Furthermore, you can choose to display either control as selected or not selected at startup.

A **list box form control** presents a group of items in a list. Visitors can scroll to select from one or any number of choices in the list box. You determine the available choices and the number that may be selected when you set list box properties.

If you want Web visitors to type information in a text box, you insert a **textbox form control.** Sensitive information, such as credit card information or passwords, can be displayed as asterisks or bullets. Textbox form controls are different from regular text box controls that display text entered during the design process. Textbox form controls are displayed as white boxes, with an insertion point for data entry by the Web user. Many times a textbox form control is accompanied by a regular text box that serves as a label to help users identify the information.

A **text area form control**, or multi-line text box, provides a means of entering information by making available to the visitor a larger text box with multiple blank lines. Most Web sites include regular text boxes as instruction labels next to textbox and text area form controls to assist visitors in entering the correct information.

Plan Ahead

> **Design and create a functional form.**
> Arrange data entry fields in logical groups on the form and in an order that users would expect. Data entry instructions should be succinct and easy to understand. Ensure that users can change and enter data only in designated areas of the form.

You must include a **submit button** on every form. This button allows visitors to send you their form data. A **reset button** can be created using a second submit button with different properties. Reset buttons are optional, but provide a simple way to clear form data and allow the Web visitor to start over. A submit button can display any words in its visible label, such as Send or Clear.

Each form control has a set of **properties** or attributes, such as a return data label, text, width, or other settings. These properties change the appearance and functionality of the form control. To edit the properties of a form control, you double-click the control.

Form controls each have a logical **internal data label**, also called a **return data label**. This return data label references and identifies the visitor-supplied information when submitted to the Web site owner. For instance, a return data label with the word, Course#, could accompany a user-supplied course number in an e-mail submission. Without a return data label, a random number in the e-mail might be hard to decipher.

Table 6–3 displays the controls you will use in the Pizza Theater Web site. Note that the List Box grouping in the table has blank rows, because all of the values will be inserted into one form control.

Table 6–3 Pizza Theater Form Controls

Form Control	Return Data Label	Value
Textbox	name	(none)
Textbox	address	(none)
Textbox	city	(none)
Textbox	state	(none)
Textbox	zip	(none)
Textbox	email	(none)
Textbox	telephone	(none)
Text area	comments	(none)
Checkbox	parties	Yes
Checkbox	catering	Yes
Checkbox	movies	Yes
Option button	customer_type	returning
Option button	customer_type	new
List Box	media_type	none
		on the radio
		in the newspaper
		from a friend
		on the Web
		other
Submit	(none)	submit
Submit	(none)	reset

Labels

Some Publisher form controls do not include text to prompt the Web user for specific kinds of data entry. In these cases, it is appropriate to use a text box, placed close to the form control, as a label. A **label** is an instructive word or words directing the user to enter suitable data. Because the Pizza Theater Web form will collect seven pieces of individual information entered by the user, each one needs to be labeled to instruct and assist the user in filling out the form.

A guide can help align labels and form controls so they display in a professional-looking manner on the Web page. The following steps create guides to help align the labels and form controls.

To Create Guides

1 Drag from the horizontal ruler to create a guide at approximately the 260 pixels measurement on the vertical ruler.

2 Drag from the vertical ruler to create a guide at approximately the 192 pixels measurement on the horizontal ruler.

To Create Labels

The first items in the feedback Web page form are text boxes, which will serve as labels for the form control text boxes. The following steps create a label and then copy it six times on the form.

1

- Click the Text Box button on the Objects toolbar and then drag a text box, beginning at the intersection of the guides, down and right to create a text box approximately 125 pixels wide and 25 pixels high.

- Click in the text box and then click the Font Size box on the Formatting toolbar. Type 10 as the new font size.

- Press CTRL+C to copy the label (Figure 6–40).

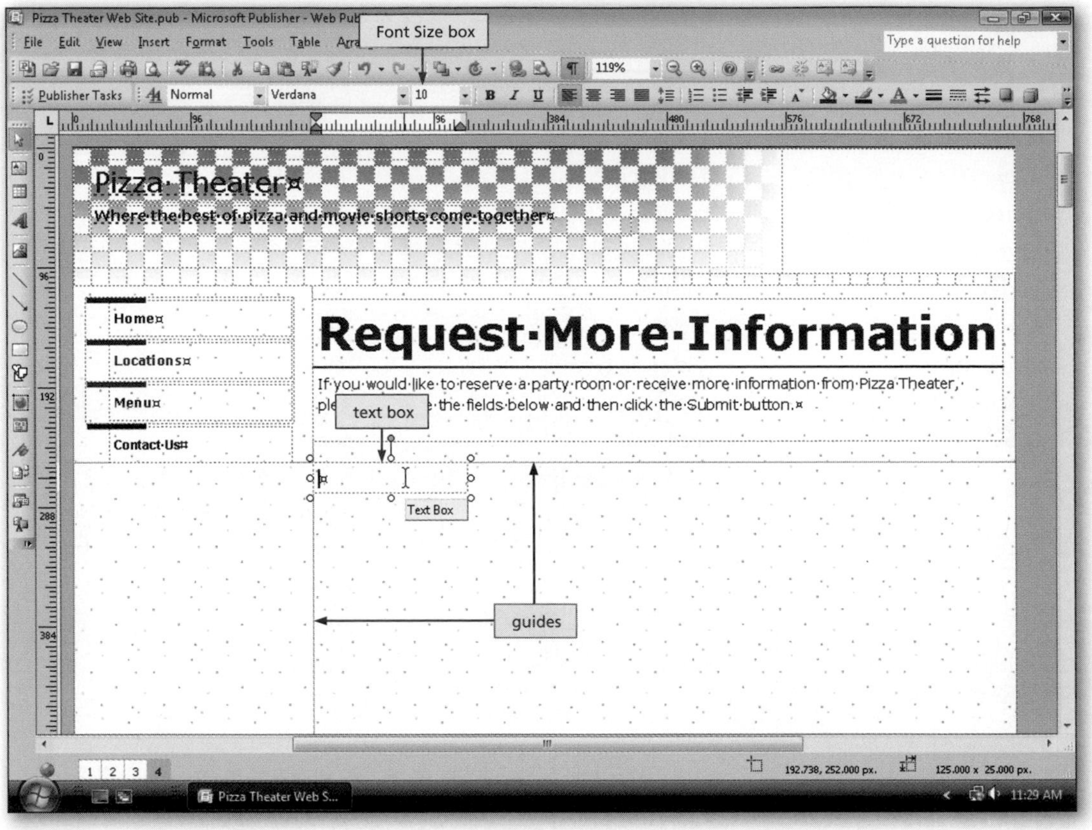

Figure 6–40

2

- Press CTRL+V to paste a copy of the label. Drag the copy below the original so that it snaps to the guide (Figure 6–41)

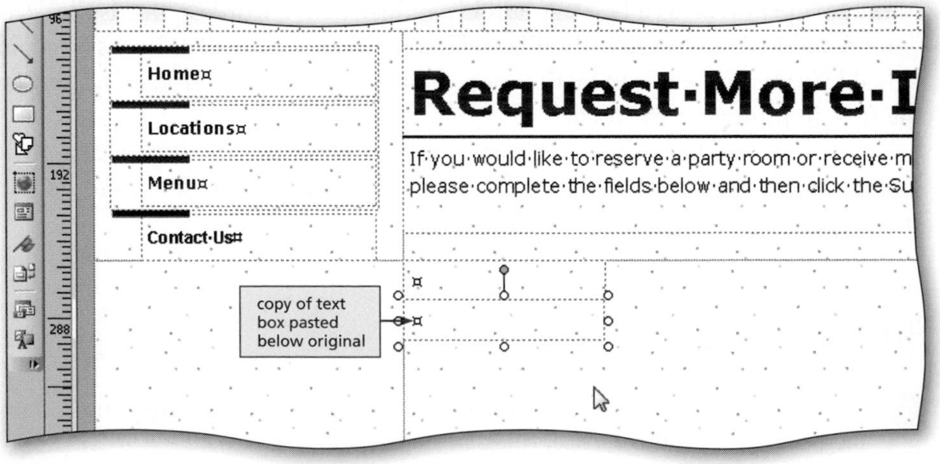

Figure 6–41

3

- Repeat Step 2 to create a total of seven labels, positioning them below each other (Figure 6–42).

4

- If necessary, select all seven text boxes. On the Arrange menu, point to Align or Distribute, and then click Distribute Vertically.

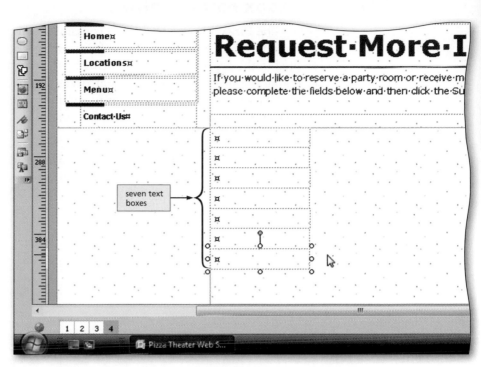

Figure 6–42

To Complete the Labels

To complete the labels, you will enter text in each of the text boxes as shown in the following steps:

1 Click inside the first text box and type NAME: to enter the text.

2 One at a time, select each of the remaining text boxes. Type the new label for each, as shown in Figure 6–43.

Figure 6–43

Textbox Form Controls

The Pizza Theater Web form contains seven textbox form controls to collect information from customers. These form controls correspond with the seven labels created in the previous steps. By placing textbox form controls close to their labels and changing the size or width of the controls to approximate the amount of data expected from the user, you can help the user to enter information correctly. Later, you will set properties to provide additional help for users.

Plan Ahead

Determine how the form data will be analyzed.
Make sure your form controls are the correct type for each piece of data. Determine the properties for each control, such as its return data type, and then make a list of possible values that it can contain.

To Insert Textbox Form Controls

1

• Click the Form Control button on the Objects toolbar to display the Form Control menu (Figure 6–44).

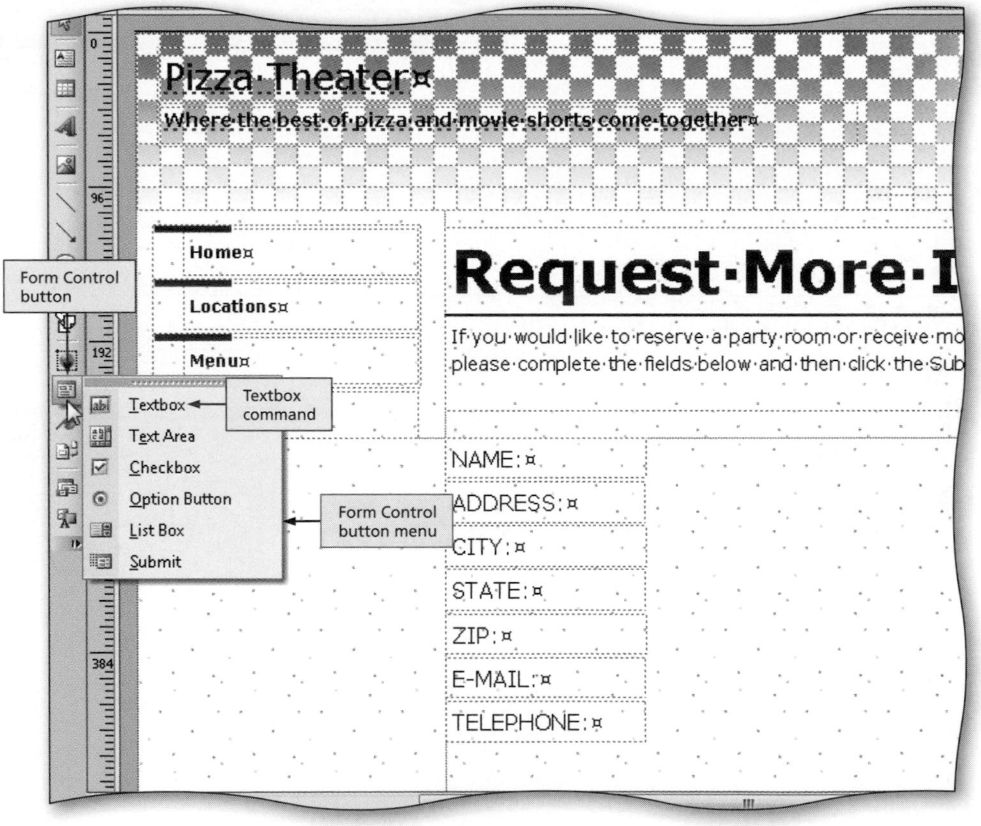

Figure 6–44

2

- Click Textbox to place a textbox form control in the publication.

- Drag the middle-right handle of the textbox form control to create a box that is approximately 200 pixels wide.

- Drag the textbox form control to the right of the name label.

- Press CTRL+C to copy the control. (Figure 6–45).

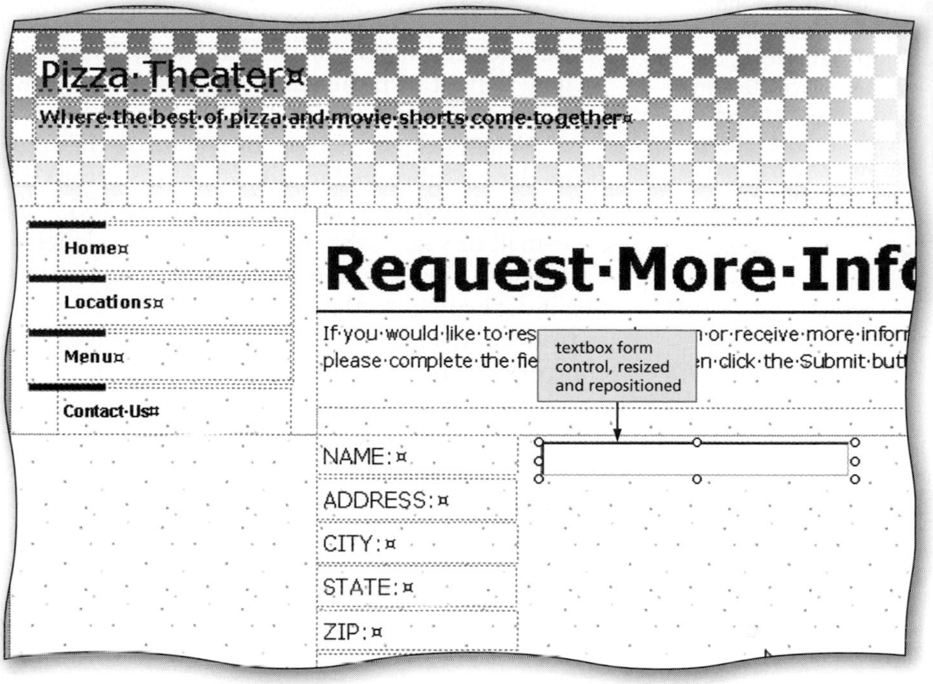

Figure 6–45

3

- Press CTRL+V six times to create a total of seven textbox form controls, dragging each copy to the right of a label.

- Resize the textbox form controls to approximate the data they will contain from the user. You do not have to be exact.

- Align and distribute the controls as necessary (Figure 6–46).

Figure 6–46

Other Ways

1. On Insert menu, point to Form Control, click Textbox

BTW

Return Data Labels
If you plan on using multiple words in your return data labels, do not use spaces. Use an underscore between words, such as return_ customer, or use initial caps on each word with no spaces, such as ReturnCustomer. Some database programs will not accept spaces in field names; consequently, upon submission, Publisher might generate an error if a space were included. If you are using a previously created database, check with the database administrator for the exact spelling of field names.

Textbox Form Control Properties

Recall that each form control has a set of properties or attributes that change the appearance and functionality of the form control. **Textbox form control properties** include default text, the number of characters or width, the ability to hide information with asterisks, and a return data label.

When using a textbox form control, the return data label is an important property. If the data is submitted to a database, the return data label must match the database field exactly for the data to be stored correctly. If the data is submitted to the Web site owner via e-mail or some other tool, a return data label helps differentiate among the various data fields. The data label accompanies user input when the form is submitted. For example, if data comes to the Web site owner via e-mail, the user input will have the field name in front of it, so that the owner will recognize that piece of data. Setting each textbox form control's return data label will help the Web site owner identify the source of the data.

The following steps edit the properties of the textbox form controls by assigning return data labels and setting field widths. The width of a textbox form control keeps the user from entering too much information. For example, the width of a zip code should be less than 10, even if the user enters the four-digit zip code extension and a dash. Limiting the user to 10 characters will help assure that he or she is entering the correct data in the correct box. Textbox form controls allow users to enter a maximum of 255 characters, no matter how wide the visible box is on the form.

To Edit Textbox Form Control Properties

1

- Double-click the textbox form control located to the right of the name label to display the Text Box Properties dialog box.

- Select the text in the 'Return data with this label' box, and then type name to replace the text (Figure 6–47).

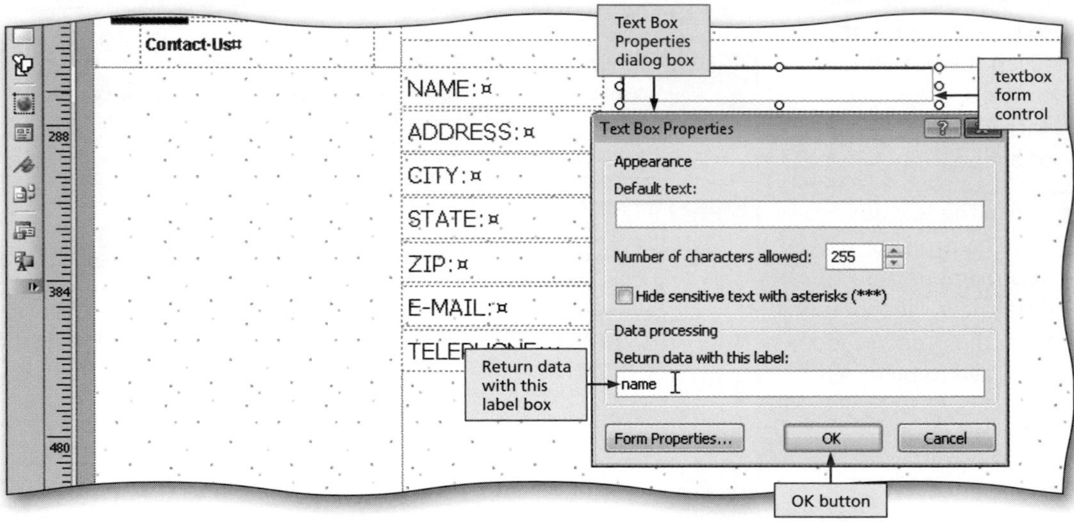

Q&A

When would I enter a default text value?

Default text appears inside the form control itself, such as, Please enter your name here. Because labels have been created for each textbox form control on this form, default text is unnecessary.

Figure 6–47

2

- Click the OK button to close the dialog box.

- Repeat Steps 1 and 2 for the other textbox form controls. Use the return data labels listed in Table 6–3 on page PUB 419. Allow only 2 characters for the state, 10 characters for the zip code, and 14 characters for the telephone.

Other Ways
1. On shortcut menu, click Format Form Properties
2. On Format menu, click Form Properties

Text Area Form Controls

A text area form control allows users to enter multiple lines of text. On the Web, the scroll bar and scroll arrows become active when the text area begins to fill. The Pizza Theater Web site form will use a text area form control to allow users to enter additional comments, such as the number of people in their party or reservation dates.

The following step creates a text area for the form.

BTW

Sensitive Data
The **'Hide sensitive text with asterisks'** check box should be checked if the user is entering a password, social security number, credit card number, or other sensitive data. That way, the user's information is replaced with asterisks as he or she types, so others cannot see the data.

To Insert a Text Area Form Control

1

- Click the Form Control button on the Objects toolbar, and then click Text Area.

- Drag the Text Area form control to a location below the telephone label and form control, as shown in Figure 6–48.

- Resize the text area to approximately 275 × 75 pixels.

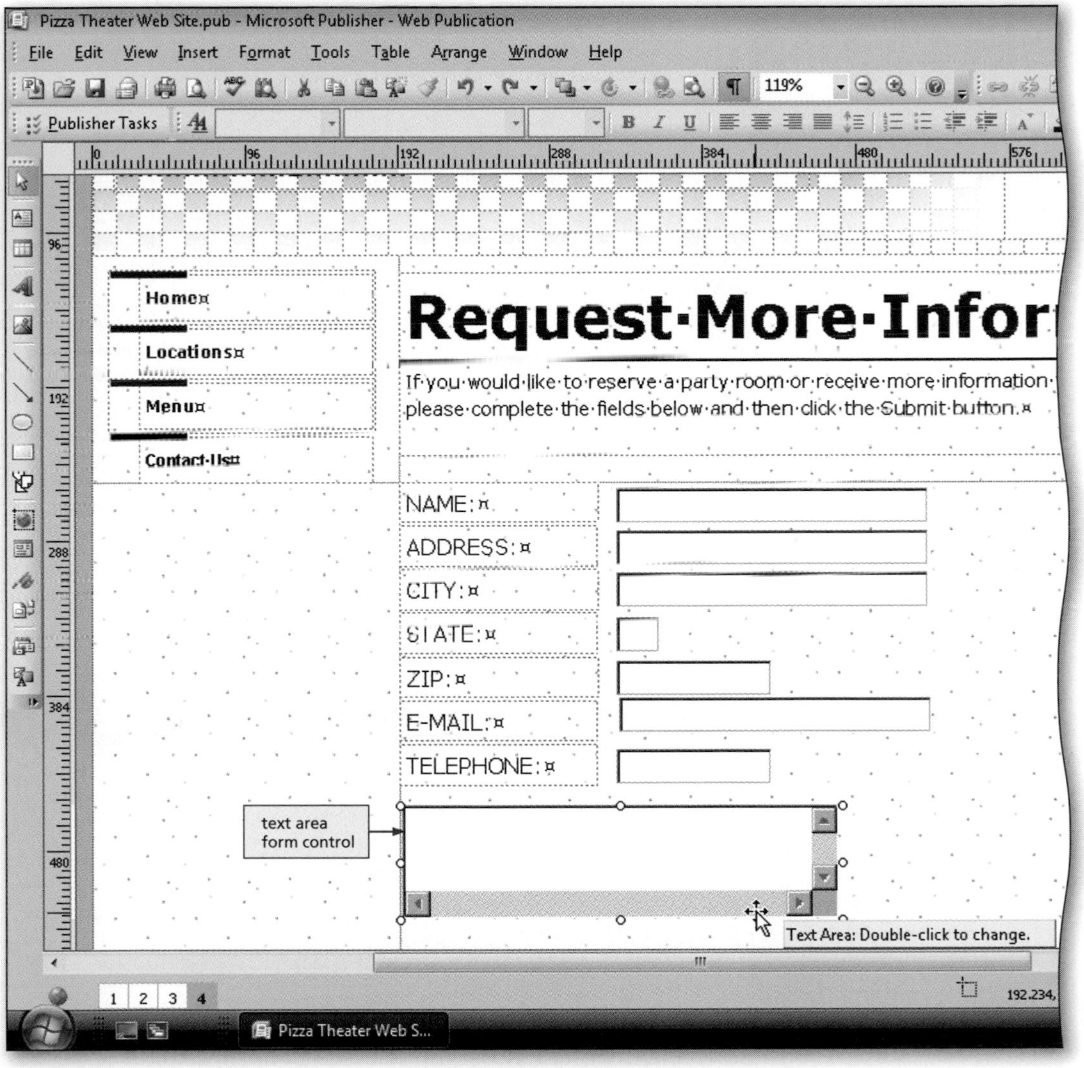

Figure 6–48

Text Area Form Control Properties

Text area form control properties include default text and a return data label. For the Pizza Theater Web site form, instructions will appear in the default text, as shown in the steps on the next page.

To Edit Text Area Form Control Properties

1

- Double-click the text area form control to display the Text Area Properties dialog box.
- In the Default text box, type `Enter other comments here` as the new text.
- Select the text in the 'Return data with this label' box and then type `comments` to replace the text (Figure 6–49).

2

- Click the OK button to close the dialog box.

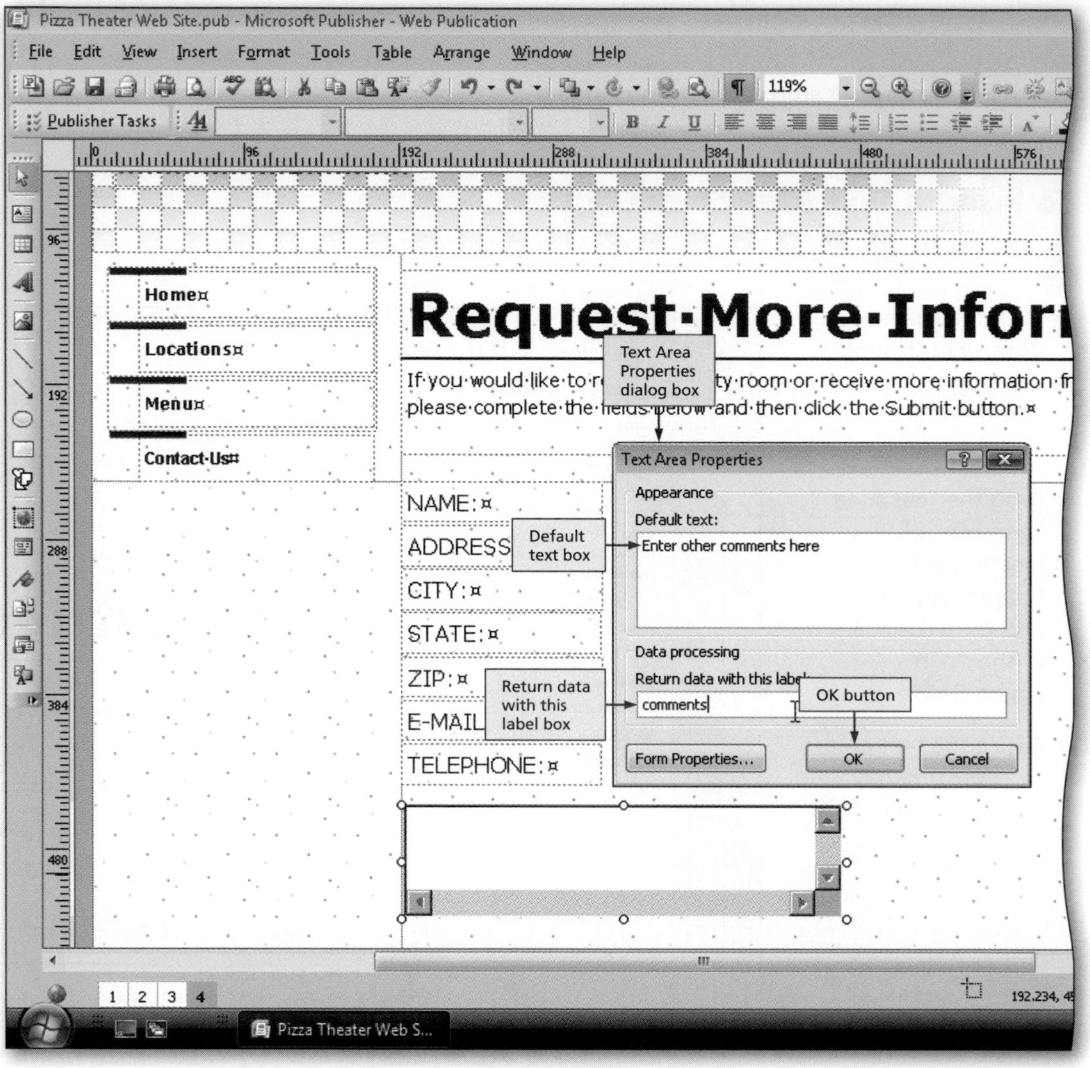

Figure 6–49

Other Ways

1. On shortcut menu, click Format Form Properties
2. On Format menu, click Form Properties

To Create Another Label

Before creating a group of checkbox form controls, the following steps create a text box label instructing users to select the appropriate check boxes.

1. Click the Text Box button on the Objects toolbar.
2. At a location to the right of the other form controls, and near the horizontal guide, drag a check box approximately 125 × 50 pixels.
3. In the text box, type `Please send me information on:` to complete the label (Figure 6–50).

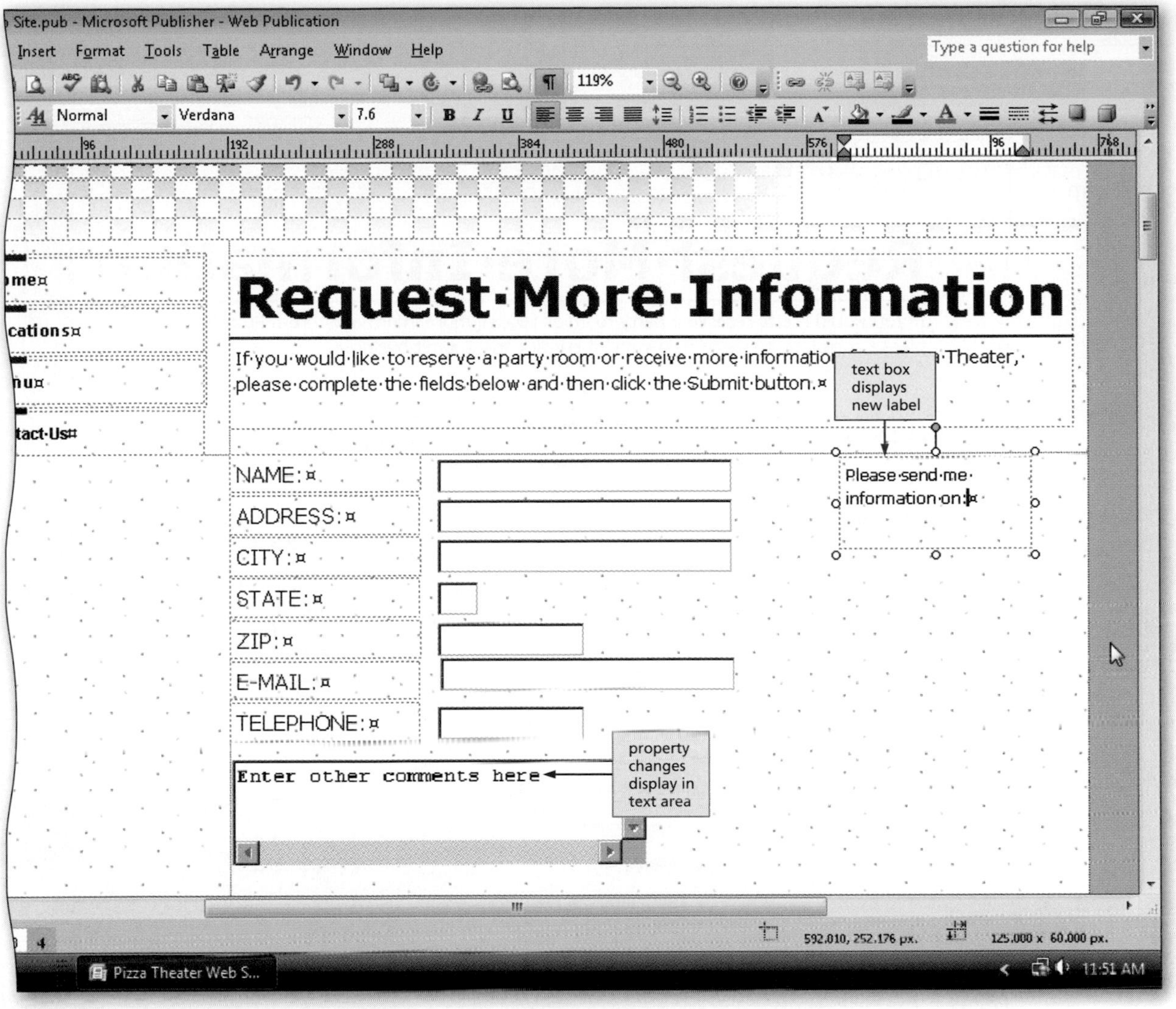

Figure 6–50

Checkbox Form Controls

Publisher provides checkbox form controls to allow users to submit yes and no responses without having to type the words into a text box. Unlike textbox form controls, checkbox form controls come with their own labels. When clicked, the checkbox form control displays a check mark.

The steps on the next page create three check boxes for Web site visitors to request information about catering, parties, or movies.

To Insert Checkbox Form Controls

1

- With no other object selected on the page, click the Form Control button on the Objects toolbar and then click Checkbox to insert a checkbox form control in the publication.

- Drag the checkbox form control to a location below the instruction label.

- Click to select the text beside the check box.

- Type `Private Parties` to replace the text (Figure 6–51).

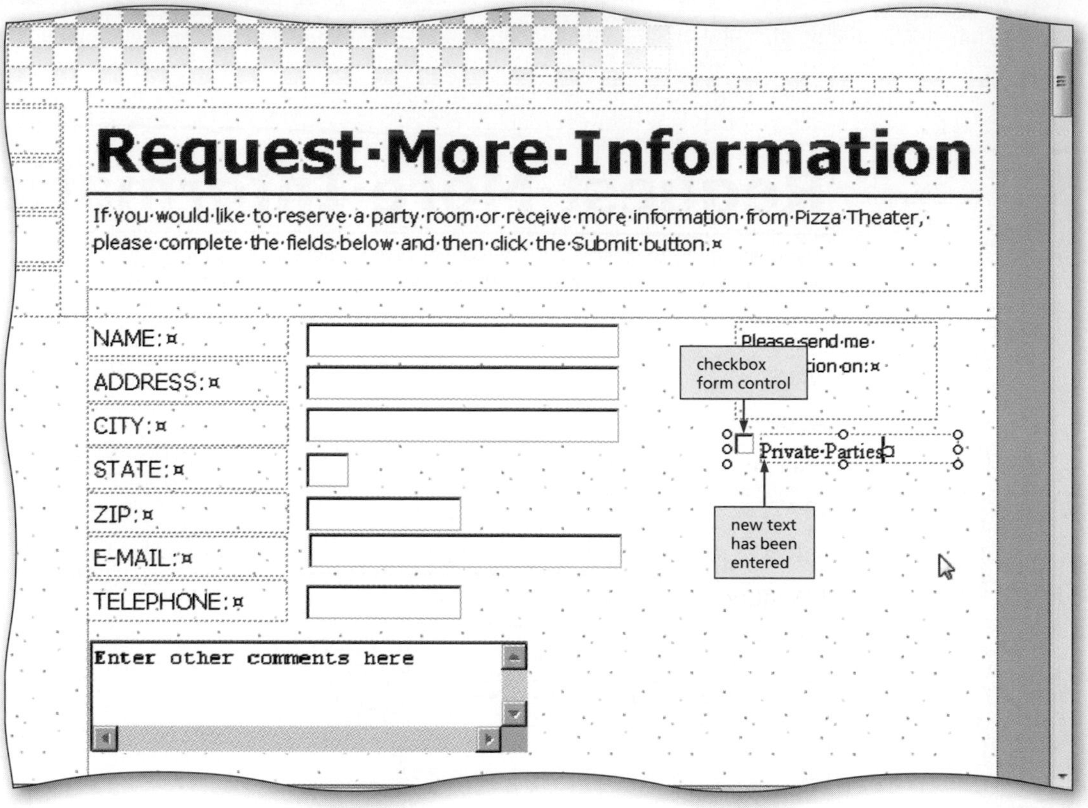

Figure 6–51

2

- Repeat Steps 1 and 2 to create two more checkbox form controls with the words `Catering` and `Movies`.

- Position the checkbox form controls below each other. Align and distribute as necessary (Figure 6–52).

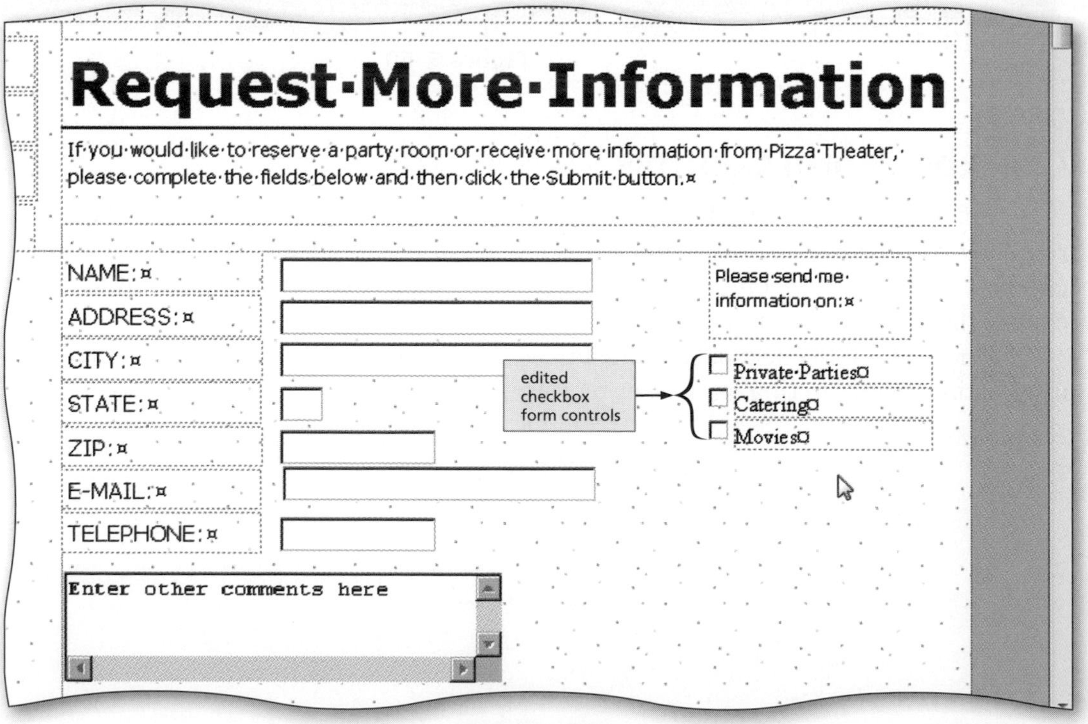

Figure 6–52

Checkbox Form Control Properties

Checkbox form control properties include the ability to display the check box as selected or not selected, a return data label, and a checkbox value. The checkbox value accompanies the return data label when the form is submitted. By specifying a value such as checked, true, or yes, the Web site owner knows the information is from the checkbox form control and whether or not it has been checked.

Checkbox form controls are grouped objects in Publisher, consisting of a box that can be clicked and a label. Therefore, when editing the properties, you must double-click the box portion of the control rather than the label to display the Checkbox Properties dialog box. The following steps edit the checkbox form control properties.

BTW

Checkbox Properties
Text in the **Checkbox value box** will display in submitted data. For example, in an e-mail the Web site owner would see the return data label, parties, followed by the word, Yes, and thus know to send information about parties to the customer.

To Edit Checkbox Form Control Properties

1

• Select the Private Parties checkbox form control. Double-click the small check box to display the Checkbox Properties dialog box.

• Select the text in the 'Return data with this label' box, and then type parties to replace the text (Figure 6–53).

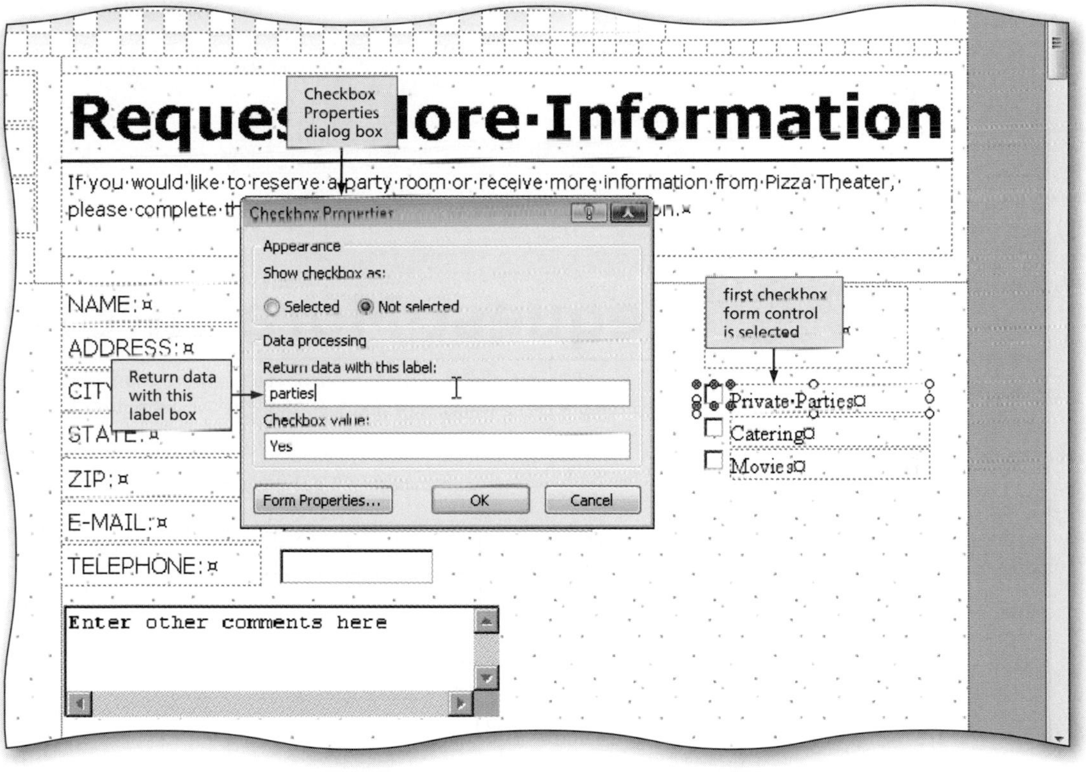

Q&A When would it be appropriate to choose Selected?

The **Selected option button** is used to display a check mark in the check box when Web site visitors first view the form. You might want to display a selected check box to encourage visitors to inquire about specific options or if it is the owner's practice to include information by default.

Figure 6–53

2

• Click the OK button to close the dialog box.

• Repeat Steps 1 and 2 for the other checkbox form controls. Use the return data labels listed in Table 6–3 on page PUB 419 and the value, Yes, for each of the controls.

Other Ways

1. On shortcut menu, click Format Form Properties

2. On Format menu, click Form Properties

BTW

Check Boxes and Option Buttons
Check boxes and option buttons are grouped objects in Publisher; that is, the physical box or button is grouped with an accompanying text box label. To ungroup or regroup them, select them and then press CTRL+SHIFT+G.

Option Button Form Controls

Publisher provides option button form controls to allow users to make one choice from a group of options. Like checkbox form controls, option button form controls come with their own labels. When selected, the option button form control displays a filled-in circle or bullet.

Multiple option button form controls are grouped automatically so that users may select only one. For example, Pizza Theater customers can specify that they are returning customers or nonreturning customers, but not both.

The following steps show how to create two option buttons that will be used to indicate whether the user is a returning customer.

To Insert Option Button Form Controls

1

• Click the Form Control button on the Objects toolbar, and then click Option Button.

• When the Option Button form control is inserted in the publication, drag it to the right of the e-mail textbox form control, aligned under the Movies check box.

• Click the label text and then type Returning customer to replace the text. (Figure 6–54).

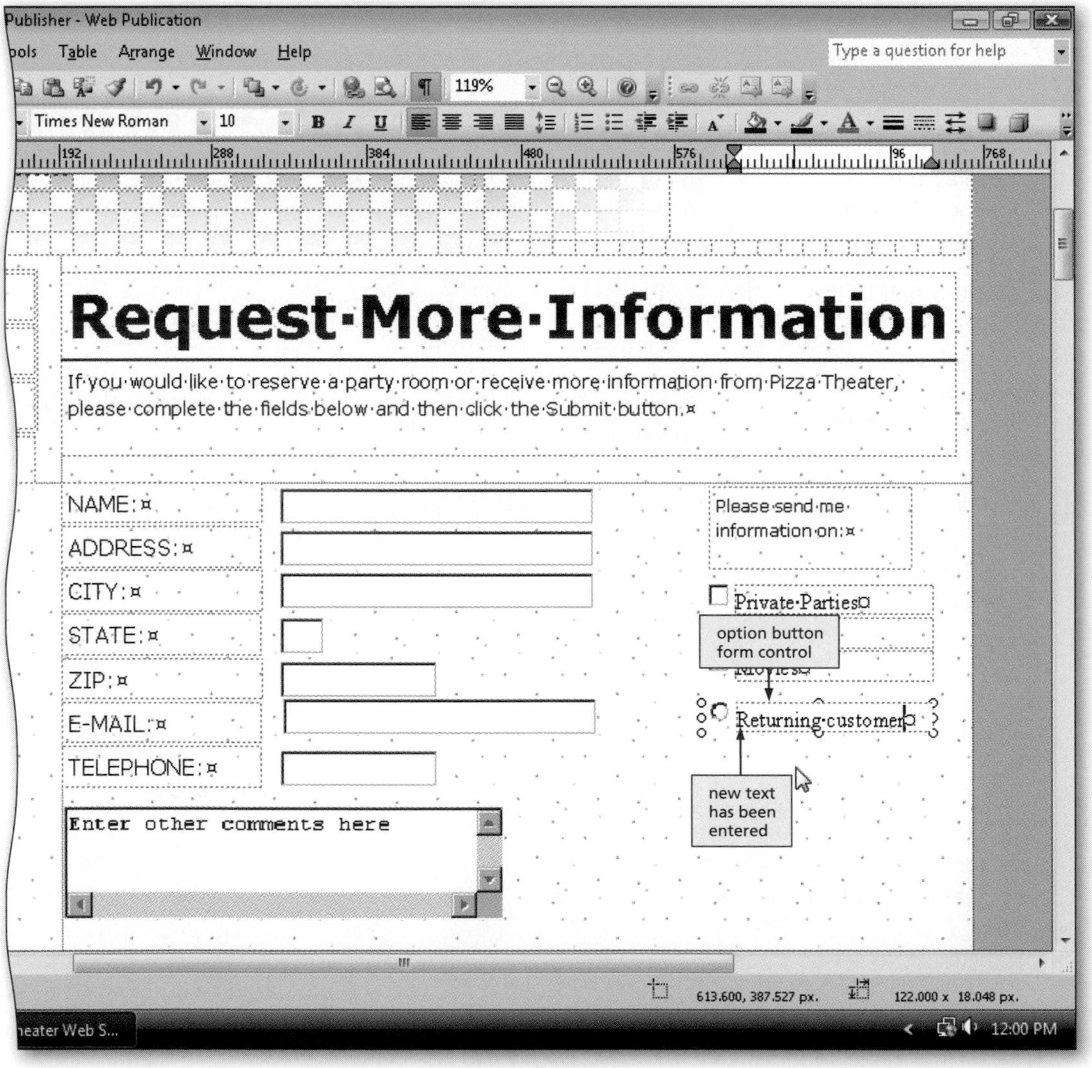

Figure 6–54

- Create another option button form control just below the first one. Use the words New customer as the label (Figure 6–55).

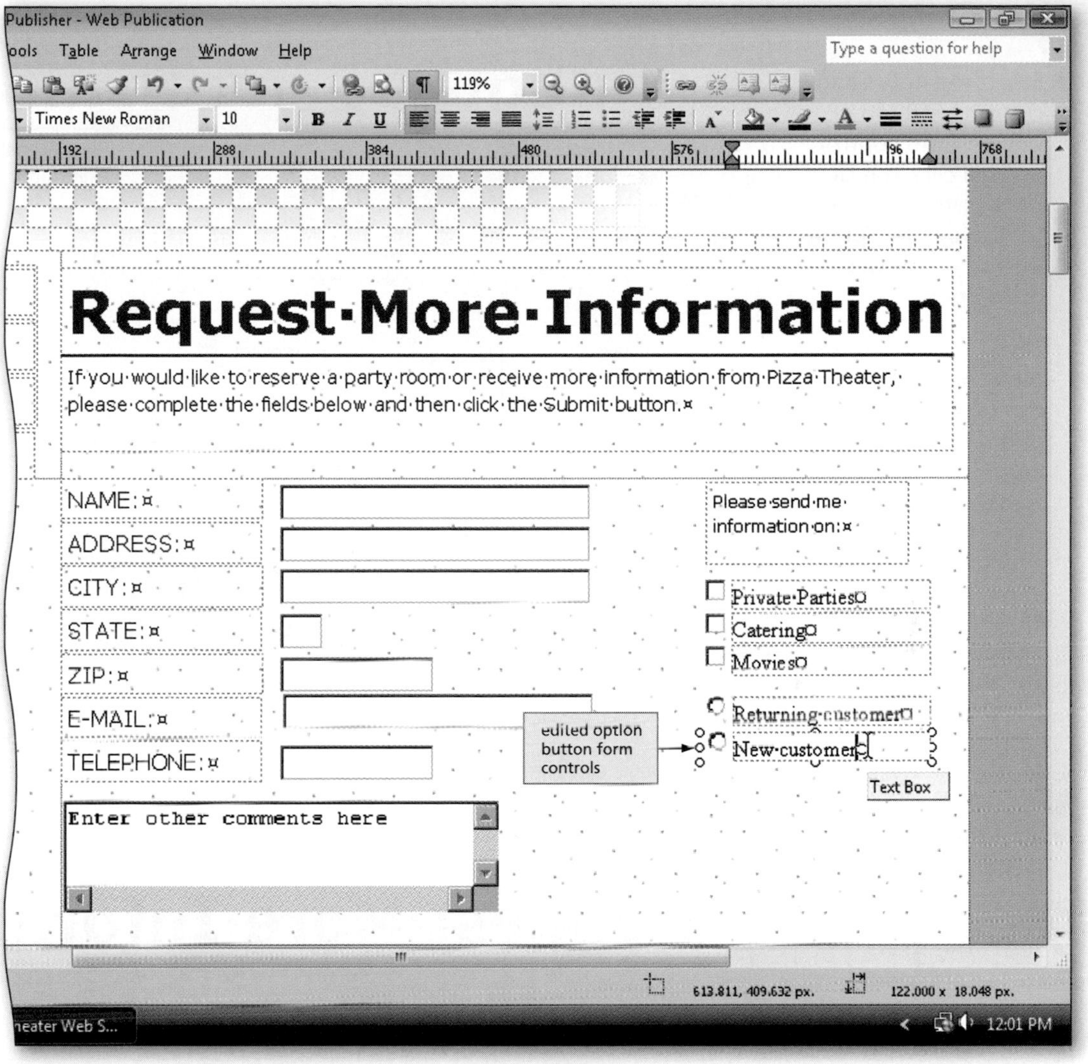

Figure 6–55

Option Button Form Control Properties

Option button form control properties include the ability to display the option button as selected or not selected, a return data label, and an option button value.

A special consideration with option button form controls is their logical grouping. Sometimes you may want to use multiple groups of option buttons. For example, a Web site that sells t-shirts might need option button groupings for size, color, and neckline. Because option buttons are mutually exclusive, selecting a color could turn off a previously selected size, unless you specify the logical grouping. To group the buttons logically, Publisher requires that you use the same return data label for each member within a group. The option button value identifies the member in the group and accompanies the return data label when the form is submitted. Typically the option button value is a descriptive word to describe the selected option button.

To edit the option button form control properties, you double-click the option button, as shown in the steps on the next page.

To Edit Option Button Form Control Properties

❶

- Select the Returning customer option button form control. Double-click the circular option button to display the Option Button Properties dialog box.

- Select the text in the 'Return data with this label' box, and then type `customer_type` to replace the text.

- Select the text in the Option button value box, and then type `returning` to replace the text (Figure 6–56).

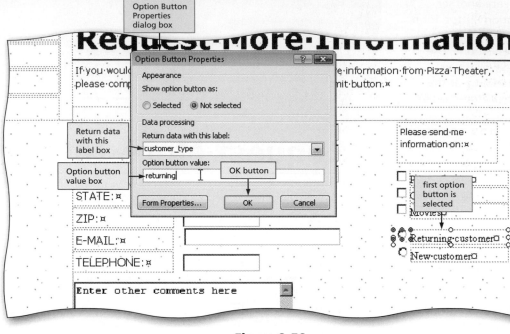

Figure 6–56

❷

- Click the OK button to close the dialog box.

- Select the New customer option button form control. Double-click the circular option button to display the Option Button Properties dialog box.

- Click the 'Return data with this label' box arrow, and then click customer_type in the list.

- Select the text in the Option button value box, and then type `new` to replace the text (Figure 6–57).

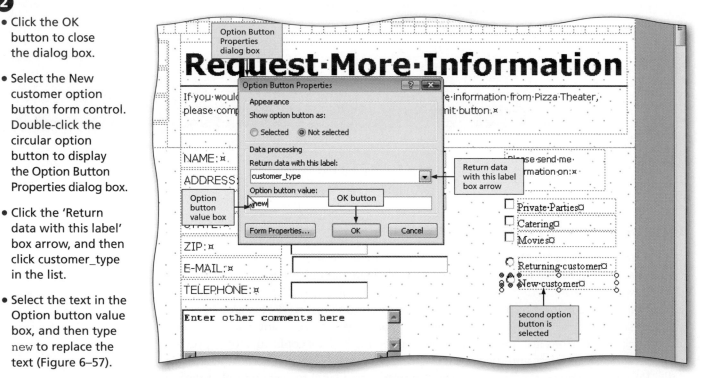

Figure 6–57

❸

- Click the OK button to close the dialog box.

Other Ways	
1. On shortcut menu, click Format Form Properties	2. On Format menu, click Form Properties

List Box Form Controls

A list box form control offers users one or more specific choices displayed in a boxed area. Designers use a list box rather than grouped option buttons when the choices are related closely, such as a list of quantities; when the list is long, such as a list of states; or when users may choose more than one from the list. List boxes can be customized with item text, initial selections, and return values that can be updated and reordered easily. List boxes can display multiple, possible choices, or they can become drop-down list boxes with a box arrow, by resizing to display only one choice.

The Pizza Theater Web form will use a list box with a box arrow to gather information from users about how they heard about the restaurant, as shown in the following step.

BTW

Updating Databases
The return data for option buttons is sent back to the database as alphabetic data. The database field must be formatted to accept alphabetic or **string** data. Checkboxes can return either alphabetic or numeric data, typically 0 for off and 1 for on, when the check box data is transferred to a database.

To Insert a List Box Form Control

1

- Click the Form Control button on the Objects toolbar, and then click List Box to create a list box on the page.

- Drag the list box form control to a location right of the text area.

- Drag the lower-center handle until the list box form control displays only Item One to create a drop-down list (Figure 6–58).

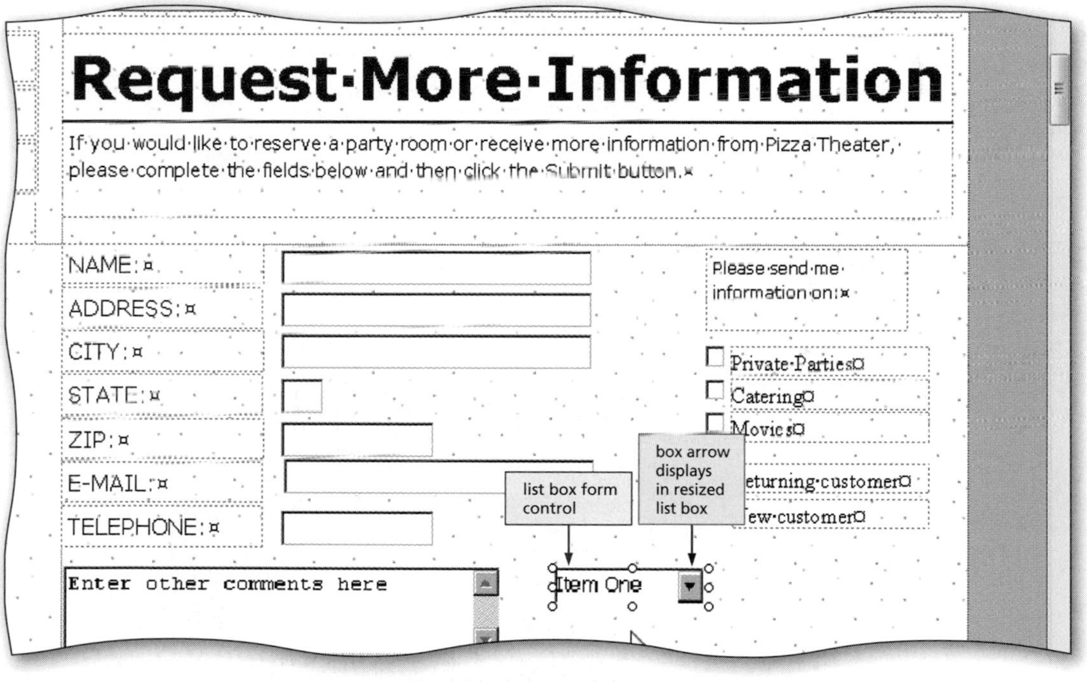

Figure 6–58

List Box Form Control Properties

List box form control properties include the return data label, the ability to choose more than one item in the list, and several appearance options, including the ability to edit the choices, create new choices, and move the choices in the list. The width of the list box form control is generated to accommodate the longest entry in the list.

Like option buttons, the return data label is the same for all items in the list. When the form is submitted, the Web site owner can determine which item was chosen by looking at the item value. The item value may be unique text or the text from the item itself. You also can decide if individual items should be displayed as selected.

The steps on the next page edit the list box form control properties.

BTW

List Boxes
If you resize your list box form control to display only one item, the item will always be the original Item One from your list, even if you rearrange the items. If you no longer want the item to display first, delete it and add another one. Then click the Move Up button to position the new item at the top.

To Edit List Box Form Control Properties

1

- Double-click the list box to display the List Box Properties dialog box.

- Select the text in the 'Return data with this label' box, and then type `media_type` to replace the text.

- In the Appearance area, select Item One (Figure 6–59).

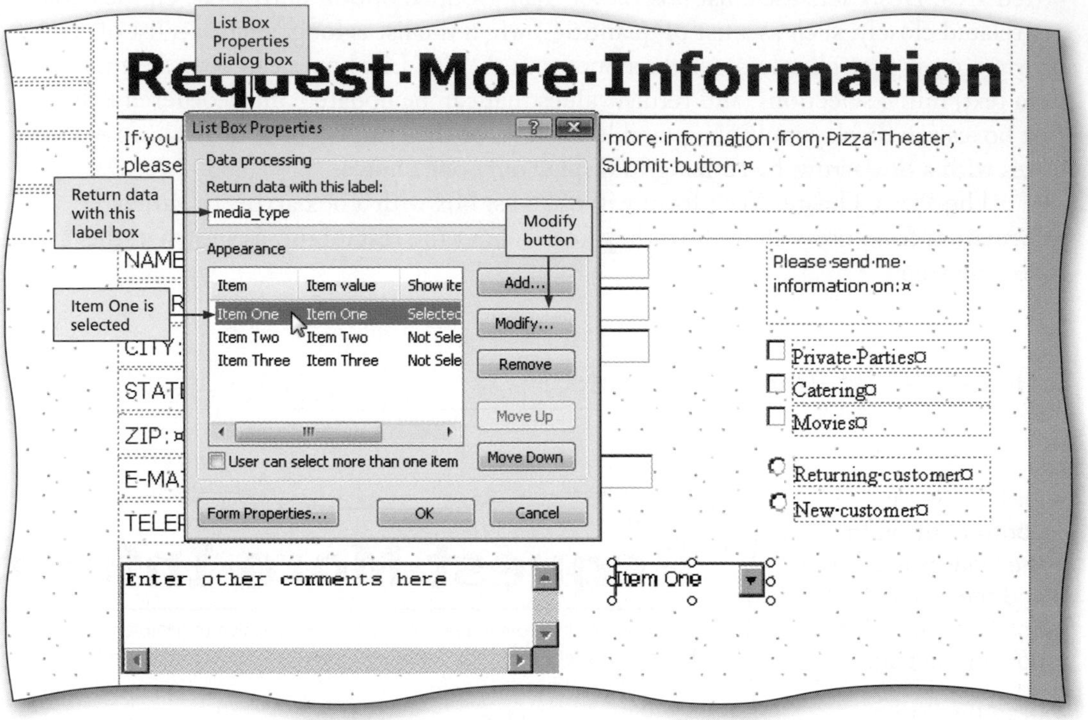

Figure 6–59

2

- Click the Modify button to display the Add/Modify List Box Item dialog box.

- In the Item box, type `How did you hear about Pizza Theater?` to replace the text (Figure 6–60).

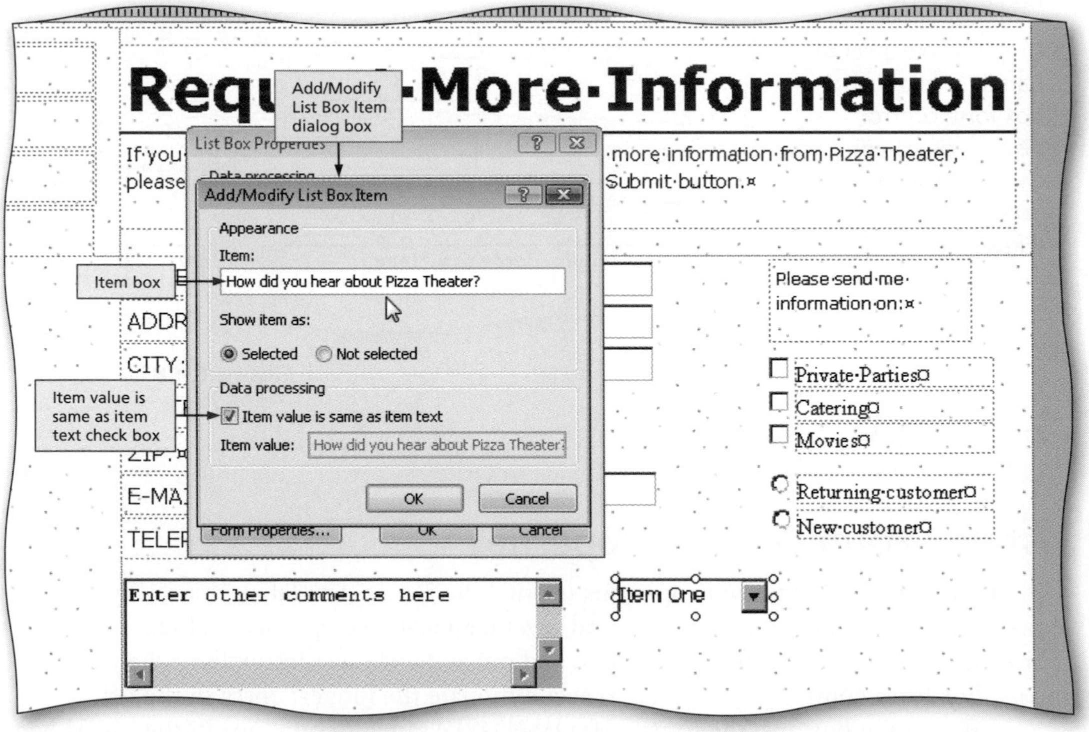

Q&A

Why am I including directions or instructions in the list of media?

Using instructions as the first item in the list will cause the instructions to display on the Web site, even if a person does not click the list button. The Web site owner will be able to tell if the visitor answered the question or left it at the default value.

Figure 6–60

3

- Click to remove the check mark in the 'Item value is same as item text' check box.

- Select the text in the Item value box if necessary, and then type none to replace the text (Figure 6–61).

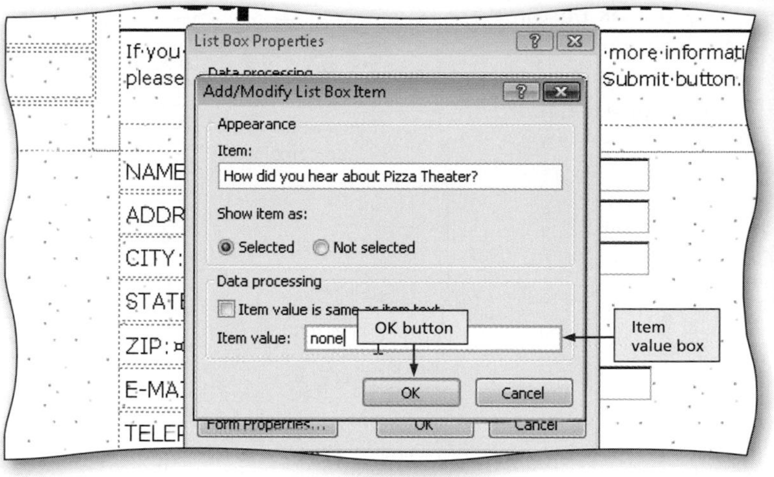

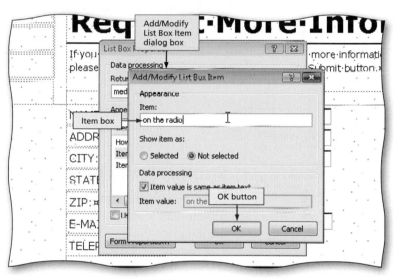

Figure 6–61

4

- Click the OK button to close the Add/Modify List Box Item dialog box.

- In the Appearance area, select Item Two and then click the Modify button to display the Add/Modify List Box Item dialog box.

- In the Item box, type on the radio to replace the text. Do not change the Item value box (Figure 6–62).

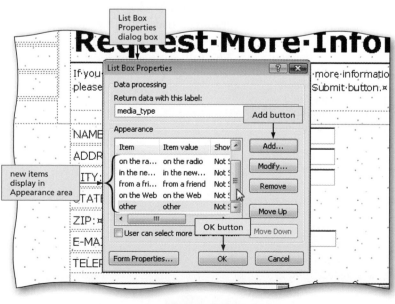

Figure 6–62

5

- Repeat Step 4 to modify Item Three using the words, in the newspaper, in the item box.

- In the List Box Properties dialog box, click the Add button to add additional items with the words, from a friend, on the Web, and other (Figure 6–63).

Figure 6–63

6
• Click the OK button to close the List Box Properties dialog box (Figure 6–64).

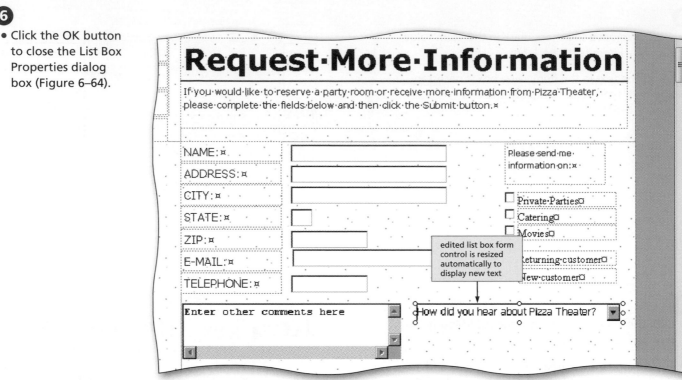

Request·More·Information

If·you·would·like·to·reserve·a·party·room·or·receive·more·information·from·Pizza·Theater, please·complete·the·fields·below·and·then·click·the·Submit·button.¤

NAME:¤

ADDRESS:¤

CITY:¤

STATE:¤

ZIP:¤

E-MAIL:¤

TELEPHONE:¤

Please·send·me· information·on:¤

☐ Private·Parties☐

☐ Catering☐

☐ Movies☐

edited list box form control is resized automatically to display new text

Returning·customer☐

New·customer☐

Enter other comments here

How did you hear about Pizza Theater?

Figure 6–64

BTW

Connecting to a Database
If you plan to save the data in a file, the file must be created and uploaded to the Web server. It should be organized with the same fields and return data types as are included on your form. When you select the 'Use a program from my ISP' option button in the Form Properties dialog box, your Web server must have a special program or script to update from a Web submission.

Submit Form Controls

A **submit form control** creates a Submit button, which is clicked by the user to submit data from all controls on the form. Three kinds of submission are available: saving the data in a file on the Web server, sending the data via e-mail, and using a special program provided by an Internet service provider.

The owner of the Pizza Theater Web form wants the data sent via e-mail, and wants a second button labeled Reset, which will allow users to clear previous entries. The submit button form control is a special kind of command button used to issue commands in a graphical user interface. You can tailor the button by changing its caption and its type or purpose. The two available types of command buttons in Publisher are Submit and Reset. The following steps create these two buttons.

To Insert Submit Form Controls

1

- Click the Form Control button on the Objects toolbar, and then click Submit to display the Command Button Properties dialog box.

- If necessary, click the Submit option button to select it (Figure 6–65).

Q&A Can I add a picture to the button?

Yes, if you click the Image check box, you can browse to select a picture file that becomes a clickable button when displayed in a browser. You cannot combine words and pictures on a button unless the picture file already contains the words. Pictures or graphics with plain backgrounds and distinctive shapes work best. You may need to resize the graphic once it is inserted into the publication.

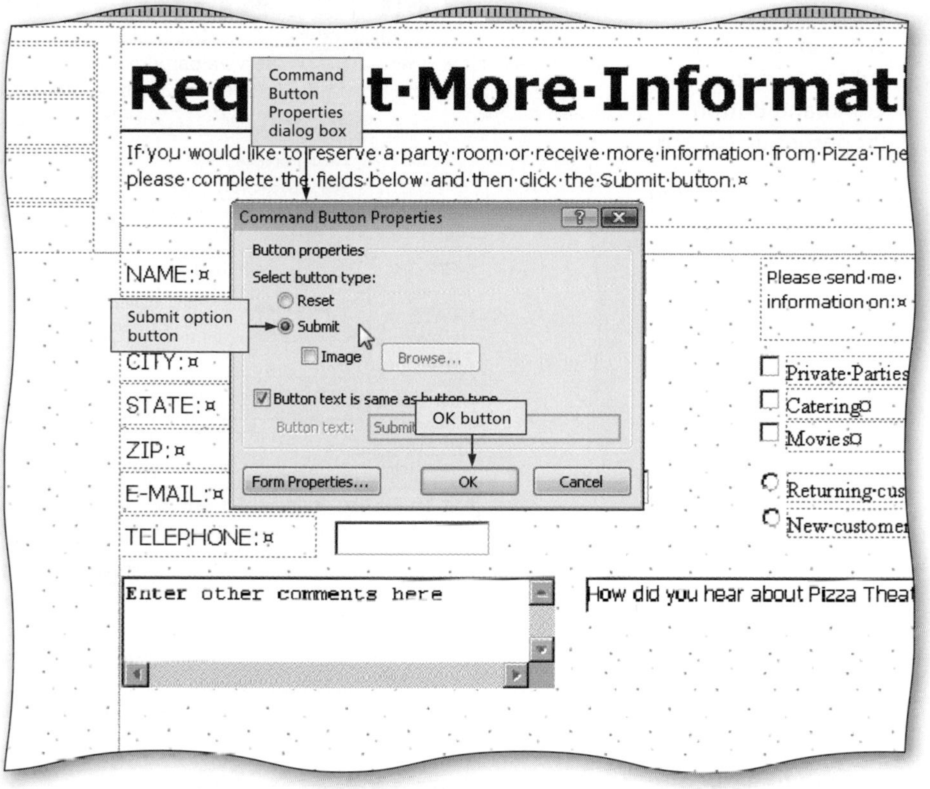

Figure 6–65

2

- Click the OK button to place the control on the page.

- Drag to reposition the Submit button to a location below the text area, as shown in Figure 6–66.

Q&A Can I change the words on the button?

Yes, if you remove the check mark in the 'Button text is same as button type' check box, you can type new text in the Button text box.

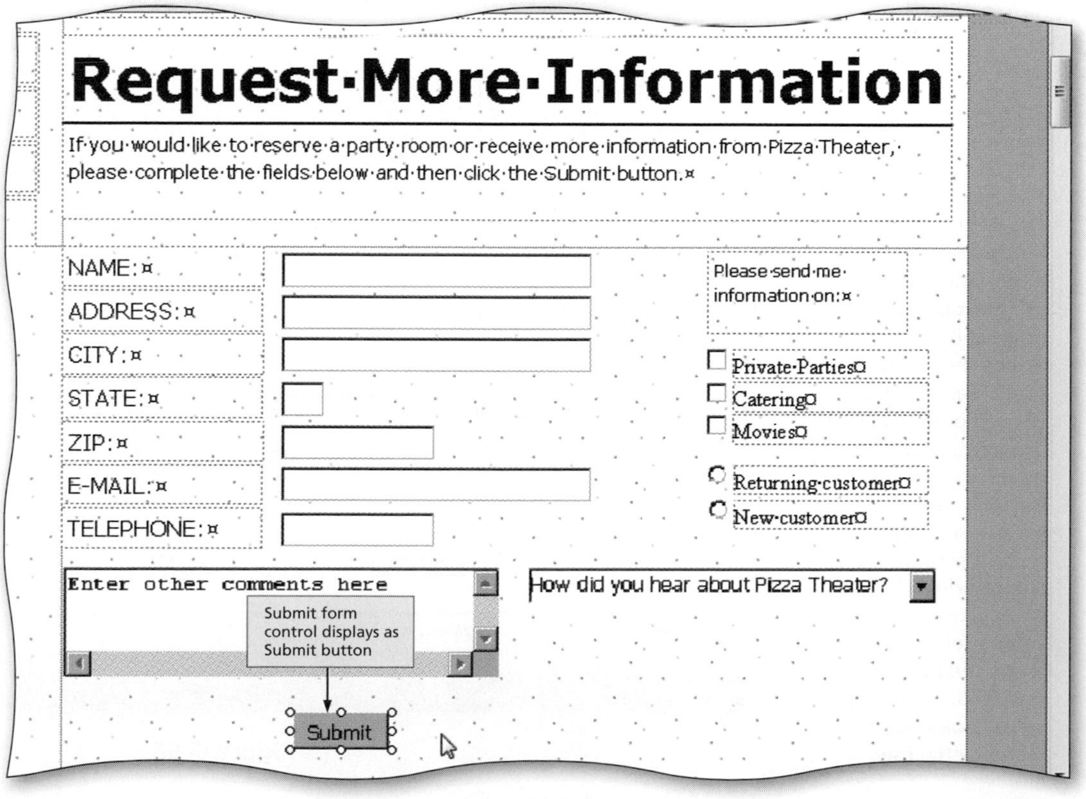

Figure 6–66

3

- Click the Form Control button on the Objects toolbar, and then click Submit to display the Command Button Properties dialog box.

- Click the Reset option button to select it (Figure 6–67).

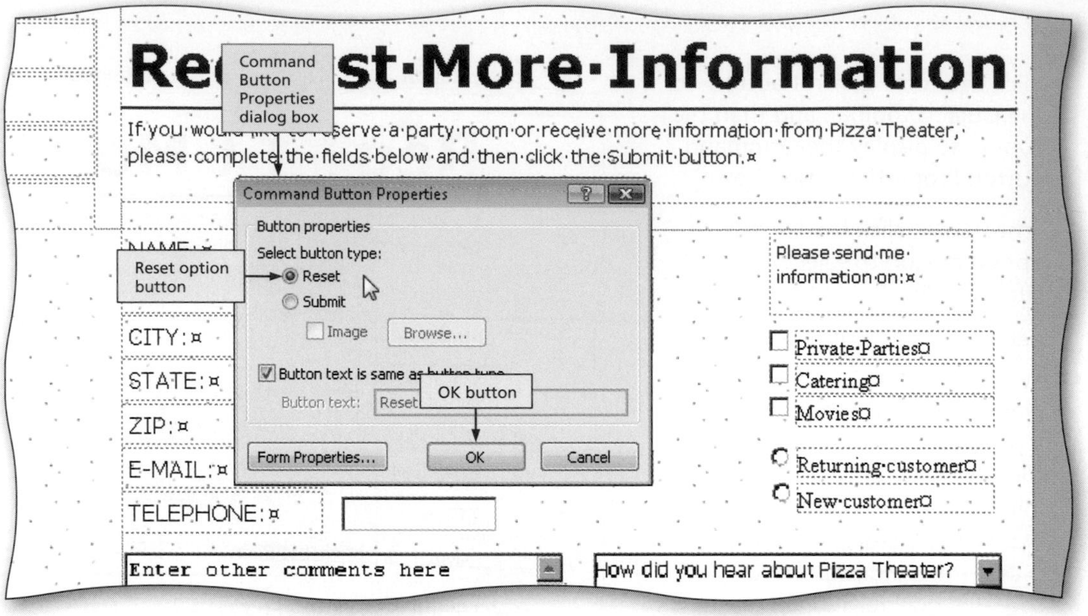

Figure 6–67

4

- Click the OK button to place the control on the page.

- Drag to reposition the Reset button to a location below the list box, as shown in Figure 6–68.

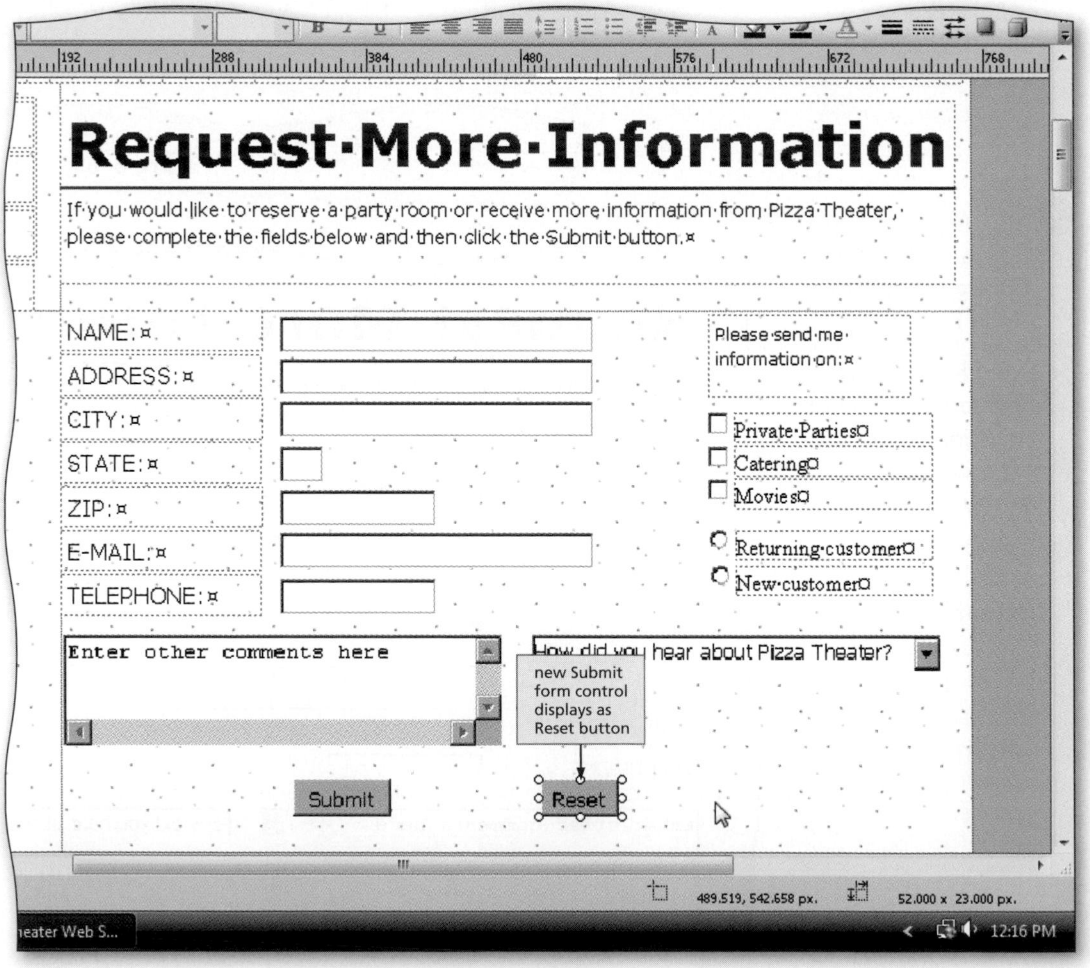

BTW

The Reset Button
The Reset command button in Publisher automatically restores all controls back to their original or default values. Text boxes and text areas either are cleared or display their default text; check boxes and option buttons are reset; and list boxes display their default setting. If a choice originally was set to display as selected, it will be selected again when the Reset button is clicked, no matter what choices were made by the user.

Figure 6–68

Form Properties

Form properties include specifying the data retrieval method and entering data retrieval information, as shown in the following steps.

To Edit Form Properties

1

- Double-click the Submit button to display the Command Button Properties dialog box.

- Click the Form Properties button to display the Form Properties dialog box.

🔍 **Experiment**

- Click each of the option buttons to view what type of data is needed for each of the retrieval methods.

- Select the 'Send data to me in e-mail' option button.

- Select the text in the 'Send data to this e-mail address' box, and then type theboss@pizzatheater.biz to replace the text (Figure 6–69).

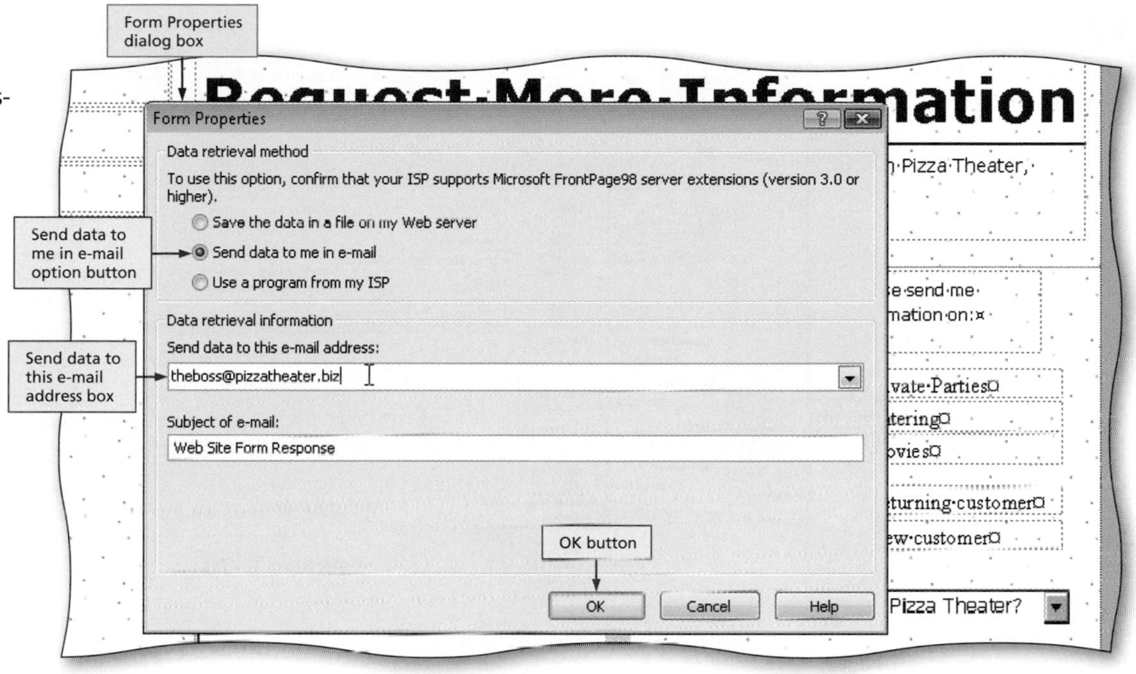

Figure 6–69

2

- Click the OK button to close the Form Properties dialog box.

- Click the OK button to close the Command Button Properties dialog box.

Other Ways

1. From any properties dialog box, click the Form Properties button, choose data retrieval method, enter data

Hot Spots

To facilitate interaction, Web pages also may contain hot spots or area hyperlinks. Recall that text hyperlinks are colored and underlined text that you click to go to a file, an address, or another HTML page on the Web. A **hot spot** is a location other than text that contains a hyperlink, typically a graphic, picture, or other discernable area. Users may click the hot spot in the same way they click other hyperlinks.

When viewing a Web page with a browser, the mouse pointer changes to a hand when positioned on a text or picture hyperlink. The change in the mouse pointer icon is called a **mouse-over event**. Events are an integral part of the object-oriented concepts used in Web technology. Even the click of a hyperlink or button is considered an event.

Creating a Hot Spot

The following steps create a hot spot for the Pizza Theater masthead at the top of the page. Users of the form will be able to click the masthead to send an e-mail to the company.

To Insert a Hot Spot

1

- Scroll to the top of the page layout.

- On the Objects toolbar, click the Hot Spot button and then drag a rectangle that includes the entire masthead.

- When the Insert Hyperlink dialog box is displayed, click E-mail Address in the Link to bar.

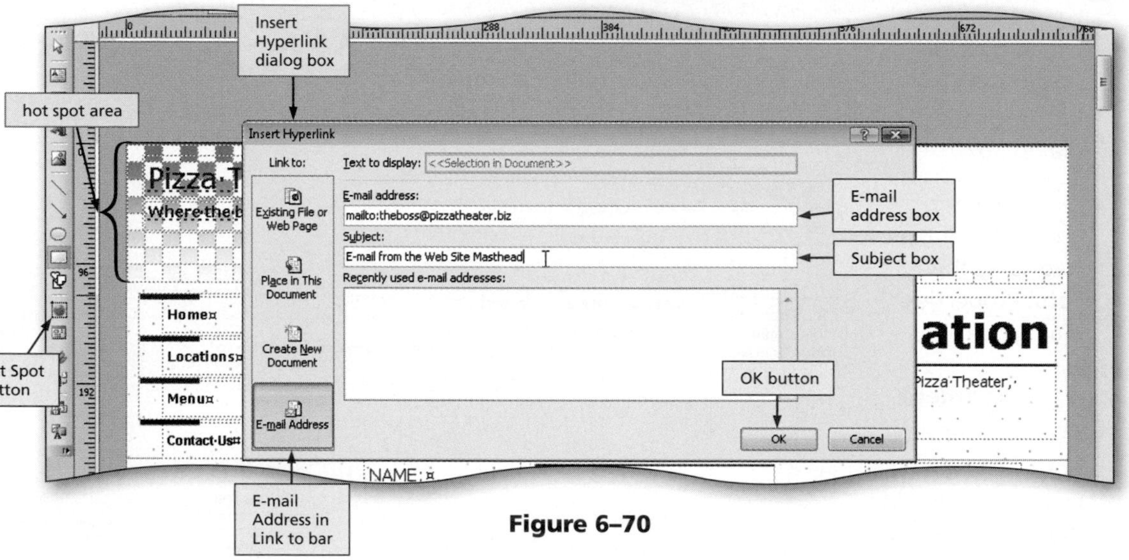

Figure 6–70

- Type `theboss@pizzatheater.biz` in the E-mail address text box.

- Press the TAB key and then type `E-mail from the Web Site Masthead` in the Subject text box (Figure 6–70).

2

- Click the OK button to close the dialog box.

Other Ways

1. Select graphic, click Insert Hyperlink button
2. Select graphic, on Insert menu click Hyperlink
3. Select graphic, press CTRL+K

HTML Code Fragments

An **HTML code fragment** is code that you add to your Web page to create features such as a counter, a scrolling marquee, or advanced data collection objects. Publisher does not supply HTML code fragments. You must have the correct HTML code to insert into the HTML code fragment object once it is inserted on the Web page.

BTW

Editing Raw HTML
Microsoft warns against trying to edit the Publisher-generated HTML that is created when you save a publication for the Web. Because of the heavy reliance on XML technology, editing the file in a text-editing program, or in an application other than Publisher, might produce undesirable effects.

Creating a Scrolling Marquee

The owner of the Pizza Theater wants a scrolling message to remind customers of the pizzeria's telephone number, but with a limited number of scrolls so that it does not become annoying. Using HTML code, the following steps insert an HTML code fragment to create a scrolling marquee. A **scrolling marquee** is an animation technique that displays text that scrolls across the screen.

HTML code fragments appear as code in a frame on the Web page. The result of the HTML code appears when you preview or publish your Web page, as shown in the following steps. The text will scroll from the right side of the screen to the left, displaying in the width of the HTML Code Fragment box.

The HTML code lines and their purposes are listed in Table 6–4.

Table 6–4 HTML Code

HTML Code	Purpose
`<font size="5" face="courier" color=red>`	Opens font tag and sets face and color
`<marquee behavior=scroll loop=3>`	Opens marquee tag and sets behavior
`For more information, call Pizza Theater at (303) 555-4700…`	Sets text
`</marquee></font>`	Closes settings

The following steps insert an HTML code fragment to display a scrolling marquee across the top of the Pizza Theater Web page.

To Insert an HTML Code Fragment

- Click the HTML Code Fragment button on the Objects toolbar to display the Edit HTML Code Fragment dialog box.

- Enter the code that is displayed in the first column of Table 6–4 (Figure 6–71).

Q&A

Can I copy HTML code from the Web?

Yes, many Web sites offer free code fragments for a variety of purposes. Make sure you understand what the code is doing and that it is from a trusted site. Also make sure there are no copyright restrictions on the code.

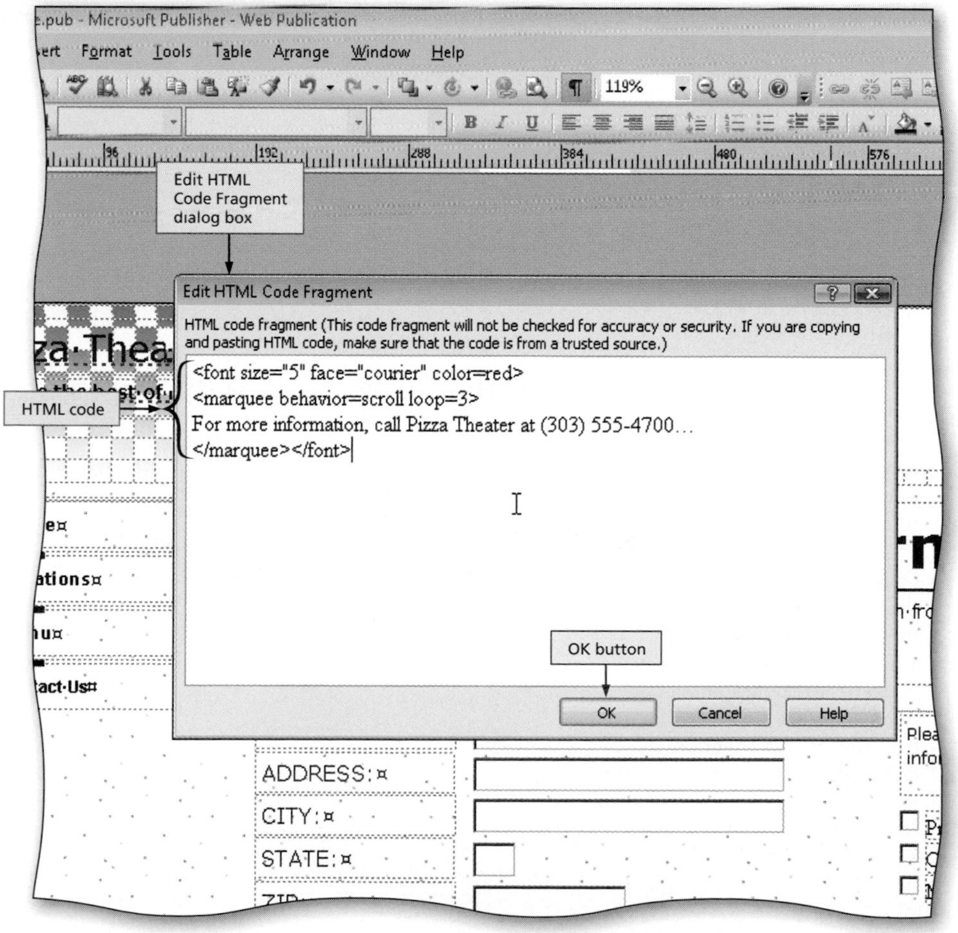

Figure 6–71

2

- Click the OK button to close the dialog box.

- Drag the HTML Code Fragment object to a location above the navigation bar. Resize the HTML Code Fragment object to stretch across the page and fit the area between the masthead and the navigation bar, as shown in Figure 6–72.

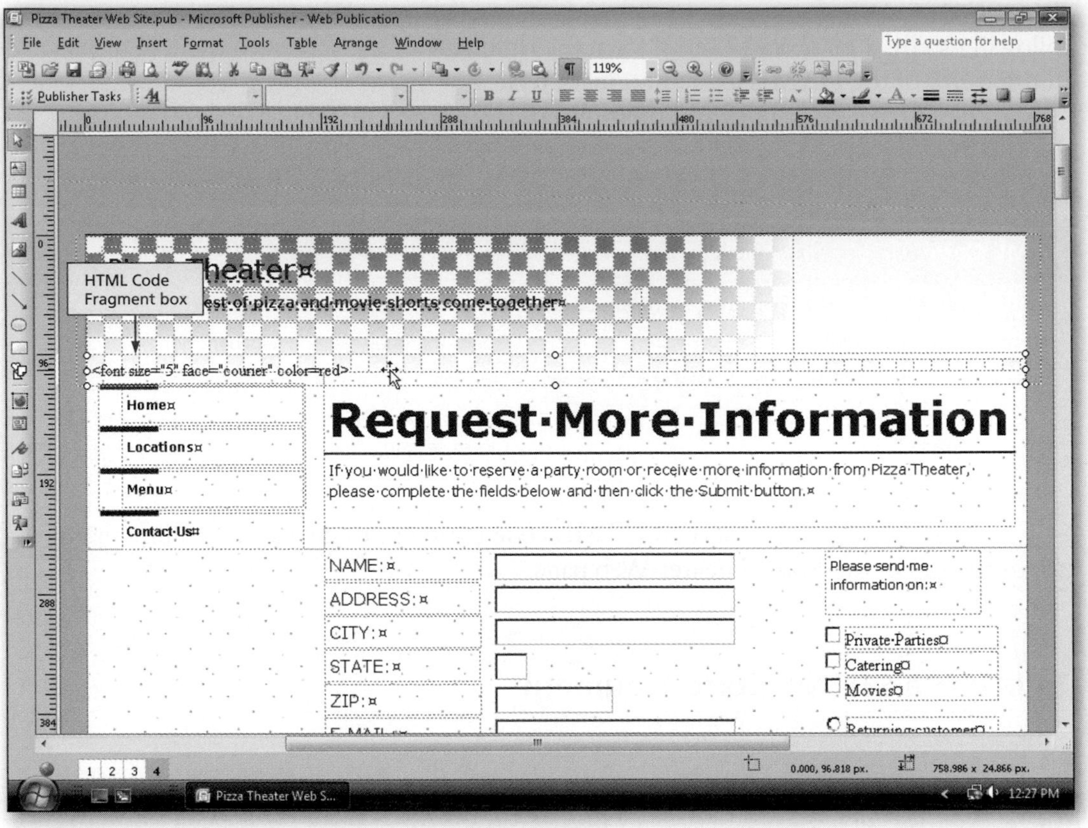

Q&A

What if I make a mistake in the HTML?

Errors in HTML code fragments may cause performance or security problems for your Web site. Publisher does not verify HTML code fragments for accuracy or security. You can always double-click the control and fix your errors.

Figure 6–72

Other Ways

1. On Insert menu, click HTML Code Fragment

BTW

Visitor Counters
With your own HTML code, you can add other Web objects, such as counters, to your Web site. Simply click the HTML Code Fragment button on the Objects toolbar and then insert the HTML code. You will need to check your HTML code fragment to make sure it is correct, however, as Publisher does not verify it.

To Save the Publication with Completed Form Controls

Now that the form is complete, it is a good time to save the publication again, as shown in the following step.

1 With a USB flash drive connected to one of the computer's USB ports, click the Save button on the Standard toolbar to save the publication again with the same name.

To Preview and Test the Web Site

In the following steps, you will preview the Web site. You will view the animation, listen to the background sound if your system has speakers, test the navigation bar, view all the pages, enter data into the Web form, check the scrolling marquee, and test the hot spot and Reset button.

Test the form.
Be sure that the form works as you intended. Fill in the form as if you are a user. Have others fill in the form to be sure it is organized in a logical manner and is easy to understand and complete. If any errors or weaknesses in the form are identified, correct them and test the form again. Finally, publish the form on the Web.

Plan Ahead

1

- Navigate to page 1 of the publication.

- Click the Web Page Preview button on the Standard toolbar to display the Web site in a browser (Figure 6–73).

Experiment

- Scroll as necessary to view the page.

Q&A Why is the URL different in my browser?

Publisher uses a temporary location to hold the Web page file while you are viewing it. Your location might be different depending upon the way you are logged into your system or network.

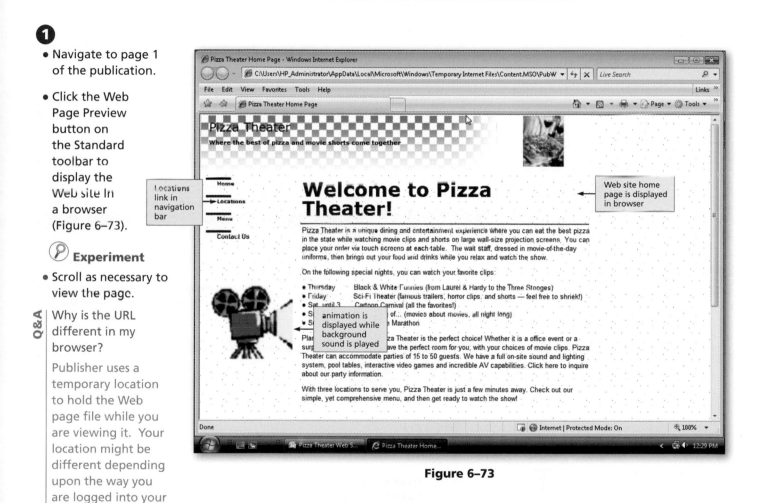

Figure 6–73

2

- Click Locations in the navigation bar to display the Locations page (Figure 6–74).

Experiment

- Scroll as necessary to view the page.

Q&A

Why is the menu missing in my browser?

Some newer browsers do not display the menu bar automatically. In most browsers, you can right-click the toolbar area and then click Menu in the list to display the menu bar.

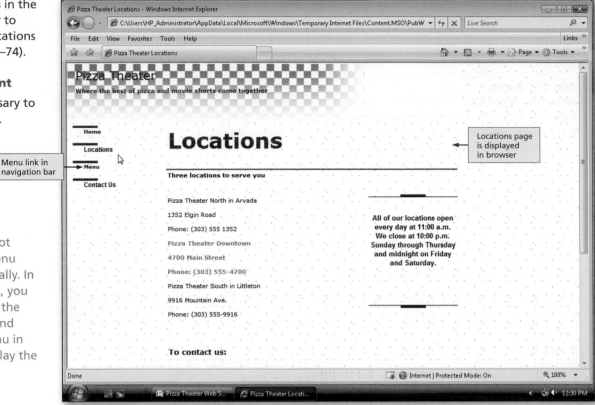

Figure 6–74

3

- Click Menu in the navigation bar to display the Menu page (Figure 6–75).

Experiment

- Scroll as necessary to view the page.

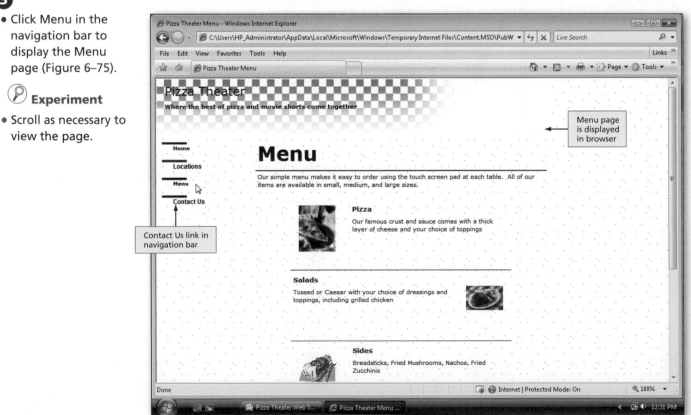

Figure 6–75

4

- Click Contact Us in the navigation bar to display the Contact Us page (Figure 6–76).

Q&A Why does my marquee display incorrectly?

If you do not see the scrolling text or if it is displayed incorrectly, there are several possible reasons. You may have made errors in typing the HTML code, or the HTML code fragment might overlap another object. Additionally, different browsers interpret HTML in different ways, with potentially varying results.

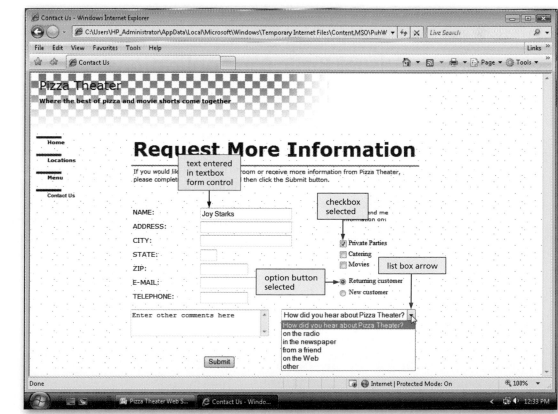

Figure 6–76

5

- Enter your name in the Name box.

- Click a check box, select an option, and click the list box arrow (Figure 6–77).

Q&A Will the Submit button work?

It is possible to enter text, make choices, and click the Reset button in the Web page preview; however, the Submit button will not work until the Web page is uploaded to an appropriate server.

Figure 6–77

6

Experiment

- Select options and fill in boxes. Point to the masthead to see the mouse pointer change to a hand over the hot spot.

- Click the Reset button to reset all of the form controls (Figure 6–78).

7

- Click the Close button in the browser title bar to close the window.

Figure 6–78

Visual Basic for Applications

Visual Basic for Applications (VBA) is a powerful tool to program how Publisher and other applications perform while creating documents. In Publisher, VBA includes the ability to run macros, write procedures, and create new menus and buttons.

A **macro** is a procedure made up of VBA code. Recall that a procedure is a precise, step-by-step series of instructions. In some applications, you can create new macros by recording keystrokes of common tasks that you wish to automate. In Publisher, you can run macros recorded elsewhere or program the macros yourself.

Publisher has seven prenamed macros, called **document events**, which execute automatically when a certain event occurs. Table 6–5 lists the name and function of these document events.

Table 6–5 Document Events

Macro Name	Runs
BeforeClose	Immediately before any open publication closes.
ShapesAdded	When one or more new shapes are added to a publication. This event occurs whether shapes are added manually or programmatically.
Undo	When a user undoes the last action performed.
Redo	When reversing the last action that was undone.
Open	When you open a publication containing the macro.
ShapesRemoved	When a shape is deleted from a publication.
WizardAfterChange	After the user chooses an option in the wizard pane that changes any of the following settings in the publication: page layout (page size, fold type, orientation, label product); print setup (paper size or print tiling); adding or deleting objects; adding or deleting pages; or object or page formatting (size, position, fill, border, background, default text, text formatting).

The name you use for an automatic macro depends on when you want certain actions to occur. In this project, when a Publisher user exits the Web Order Form publication, you want a message box to be displayed, reminding the user to upload the appropriate files to the Web. Thus, you will see how to create a BeforeClose macro using the Visual Basic Editor.

Add macros to automate tasks.
A macro is a shortcut to a more complicated task. Using VBA, a powerful programming language included with Publisher, you can customize and extend the capabilities of Publisher. Add macros for repetitive tasks or to automate procedures and results.

**Plan
Ahead**

Using the Visual Basic Editor

The **Visual Basic Editor** is a full-screen editor that allows you to enter a procedure by typing lines of VBA code as if you were using word processing software. VBA displays a **code window** in which you may choose document events and type code.

Because the code window is similar to a text box or word processor window, at the end of a line, you press the ENTER key or use the down arrow key to move to the next line. If you make a mistake in a code statement, you can use the ARROW keys and the DELETE or BACKSPACE keys to correct it. You also can move the insertion point to lines requiring corrections.

The steps on the next page open the VBA coding window. The document event will apply only to the current publication. Other publications will not have access to the macro created in this publication.

To Open the VBA Code Window

1

- Click Tools on the menu bar, and then point to Macro to display the Macro submenu (Figure 6–79).

Figure 6–79

2

- Click Visual Basic Editor to open the Microsoft Visual Basic window.

- If necessary, double-click the Microsoft Visual Basic title bar to maximize the window.

- If the Project window is not displayed, click View on the menu bar and then click Project Explorer.

- In the Project window, if a plus sign is displayed next to Project (Pizza Theater Web Site.pub), click the plus sign.

- If a plus sign is displayed next to Microsoft Office Publisher Objects, click the plus sign.

- Double-click ThisDocument to open the code window (Figure 6–80).

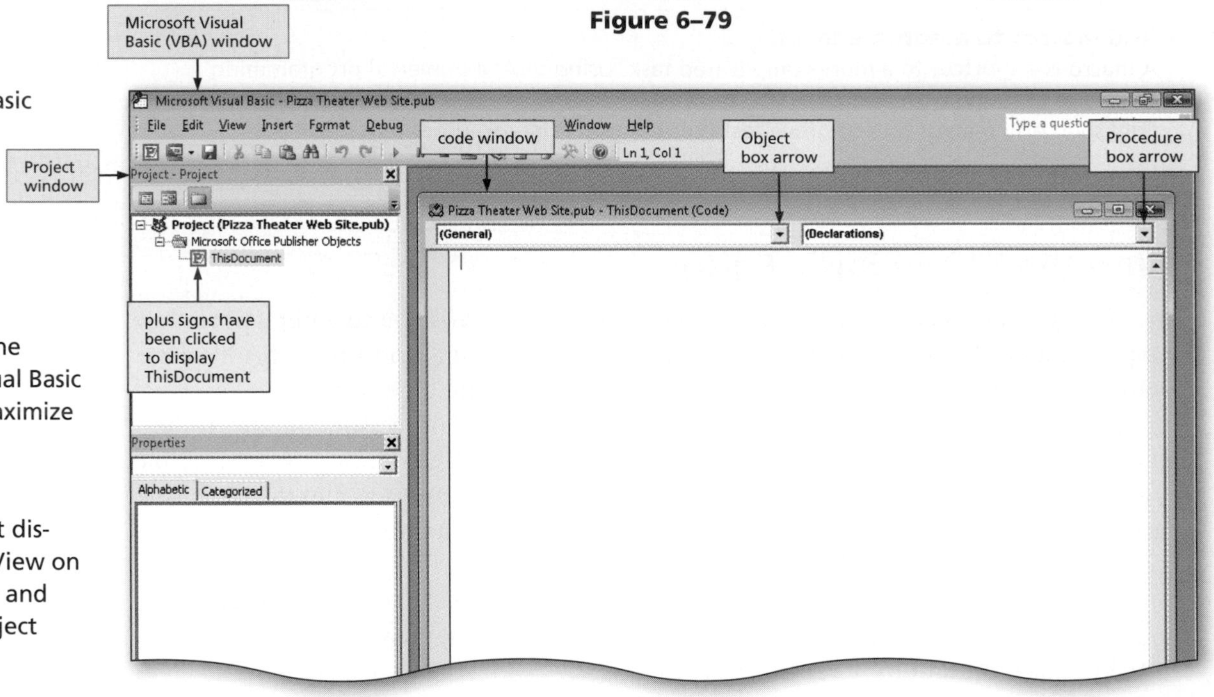

Figure 6–80

Other Ways

1. Press ALT+F11

Entering Code Statements and Comments

The BeforeClose event in the Pizza Theater Web Order Form publication includes a code statement that calls a function named MsgBox. A **function** is a keyword, already programmed in VBA, which activates a procedure. The **MsgBox function** displays a message in a dialog box and then waits for the user to click a button. In its simplest forms, the code statement includes the function keyword, MsgBox, and the text that will be displayed in the message box enclosed in quotation marks. VBA programmers use a message box to display copyright information about a publication, remind users to save publications in a certain location, or let Web users know their submission was complete.

Adding comments before and within a procedure helps you remember the purpose of the macro and its code statements later. **Comments** begin with the keyword, Rem, or an apostrophe (') and are displayed in green in the code window. Comments have no effect on the execution of a procedure; they simply provide information about the procedure, such as its name and description.

The following steps show how to write a comment and code statement in the BeforeClose event. VBA provides beginning and ending code statements for document event procedures. It is common practice to indent comments and code within these statements.

BTW

Message Boxes
VBA offers several intrinsic constant keywords to assist you with the buttons in message boxes. These include vbOKOnly, vbOKCancel, vbYesNo, vbYesNoCancel, vbRetryCancel, and vbAbortRetryIgnore. To use these constant keywords, type a comma after the MsgBox prompt and then type the keyword.

BTW

The VBA Editor
The VBA editor uses AutoComplete boxes as you type the code. When you type the beginning of a command, the VBA editor displays a prompt to help you construct the remainder of the command, complete with the type of data it expects, or a list of valid constant keywords from which you may choose.

To Program the BeforeClose Event

1

- In the ThisDocument (Code) window, click the Object box arrow and then click Document in the list to choose the object.

- Click the Procedure box arrow and then click BeforeClose in the list to choose the procedure to code (Figure 6–81).

Q&A

Why did Publisher create two procedures?

The beginning and ending code statements for the BeforeClose and Open procedures are displayed. Publisher automatically displays the Open procedure, but it will have no effect on this publication.

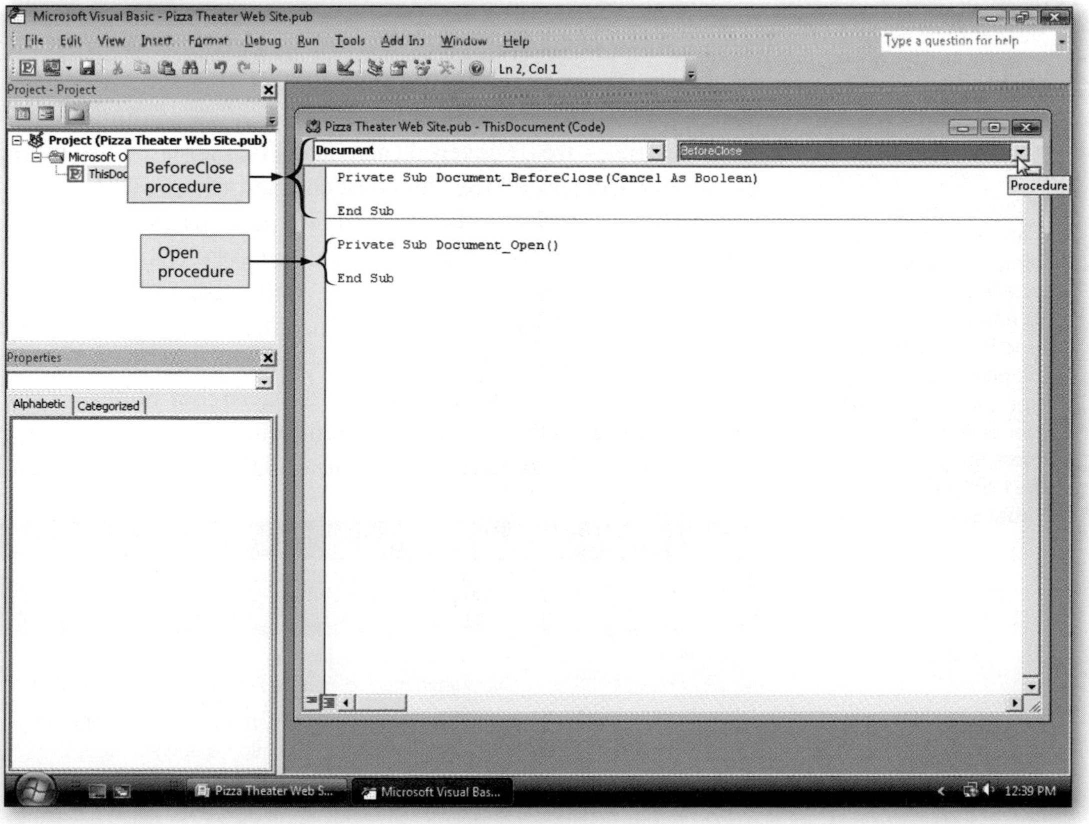

Figure 6–81

2

- Press the TAB key. Type 'When the publication closes, a reminder message box will be displayed. and then press the ENTER key to enter the comment line.

- Type MsgBox "Remember to upload this file to the Web site." to complete the code (Figure 6–82).

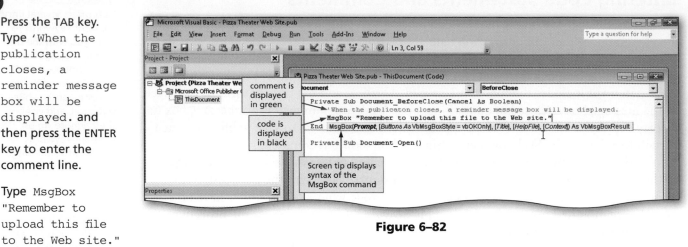

Figure 6–82

Q&A

Why did I press the TAB key?

Pressing the TAB key indents the lines of code. The TAB key has no effect on how the code is executed; it merely aids in readability.

3

- Click the Close button on the Microsoft Visual Basic title bar to close the VBA window.

BTW

Other Macros
You can modify the procedure or event associated with any command on Publisher's menu bar or toolbar, and you can create custom toolbars, menu bars, and shortcut menus using VBA. VBA is an extensive programming language with a detailed Help library. To find out more about functions you can use in document events, type the text, document events, in the 'Type a question for help' box on the right of the Microsoft Visual Basic menu bar.

Security Levels

A **computer virus** is a potentially damaging computer program designed to affect, or infect, your computer negatively by altering the way it works without your knowledge or permission. Currently, more than 80,000 known computer viruses exist, and an estimated six new viruses are discovered each day. The increased use of networks, the Internet, and e-mail has accelerated the spread of computer viruses.

To combat this problem, most computer users run antivirus programs that search for viruses and destroy them before they ever have a chance to infect the computer. Macros are a known carrier of viruses because of the ease with which a person can write code for a macro. For this reason, you can reduce the chance your computer will be infected with a macro virus by setting a **security level** in Publisher. Security levels allow you to enable or disable macros. An **enabled macro** is a macro that Publisher will execute, and a **disabled macro** is a macro that is unavailable to Publisher.

Table 6–6 summarizes the four available security levels in Publisher.

Table 6–6 Publisher Security Levels	
Security Level	**Condition**
Very High	Publisher will execute only macros installed in trusted locations. All other signed and unsigned macros are disabled when the publication is opened.
High	Publisher will execute only macros that are digitally signed. All other macros are disabled when the publication is opened.
Medium	Upon opening a publication that contains macros from an unknown source, Publisher displays a dialog box asking if you wish to enable the macros.
Low	Publisher turns off macro virus protection. The publication is opened with all macros enabled, including those from unknown sources.

**Plan
Ahead**

Incorporate security in a publication.
Digital signatures and security levels are two ways that Publisher helps you secure your publications. Be sure to notify all parties who open your publication or publish your Web pages that you have implemented security features.

Setting Security Levels in Publisher

If Publisher security is set to very high or high and you attach a macro to a publication, Publisher will disable the macro when you open the publication. Because macros are created in this chapter, you should ensure that your security level is set to medium. Thus, each time you open this Publisher publication or any other document that contains a macro from an unknown source, Publisher displays a dialog box warning that a macro is attached and allows you to enable or disable the macros. If you are confident of the source (author) of the publication and macros, you should click the Enable button in the dialog box. If you are uncertain about the reliability of the source of the publication and macros, you should click the Disable button.

The following steps set Publisher's security level.

To Set a Security Level in Publisher

1

- Click Tools on the menu bar, point to Macro, and then click Security to display the Trust Center dialog box.

- If necessary, click the Macro Settings button to display the macro options.

- If necessary, click the 'Disable all macros with notification' option button (Figure 6–83).

2

- Click the OK button to close the Trust Center dialog box.

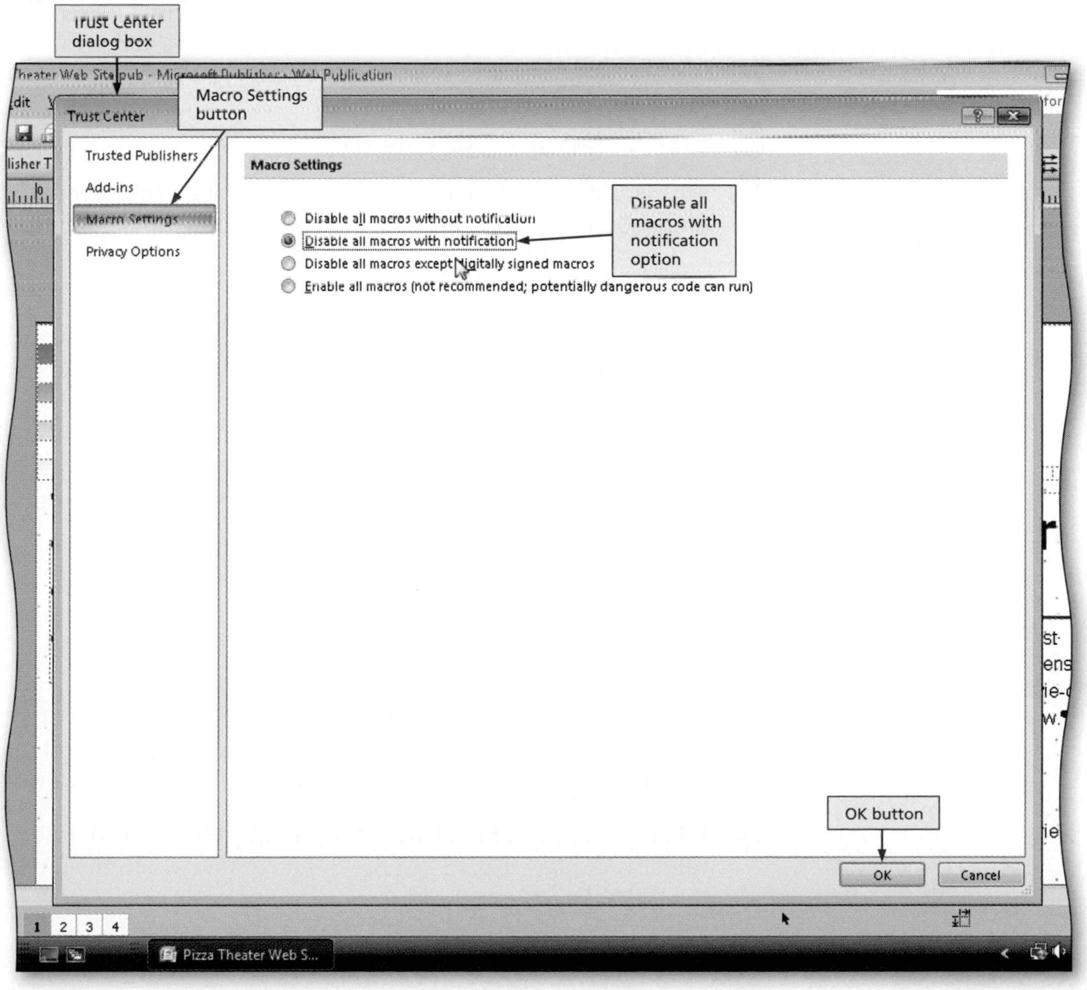

Figure 6–83

BTW

Security
The next time you open a publication that contains a macro from an unauthorized source, Publisher will ask if you wish to enable or disable the macro.

BTW

Digital Signatures
Several companies provide authenticated, certified digital signatures via the Web. When you attach a digital signature to a macro project, Publisher will display the digital signature when the user of the file is asked to enable macros.

Checking and Saving the Publication

To complete the Web order form, the final tasks are to check for spelling and design errors, save the publication as both a Publisher publication and as a Web file, and then test the macro.

Checking for Spelling and Design Errors

Recall that Publisher's Design Checker scans the publication for overlapping errors and large graphics that may prevent the page from loading quickly on the Web.

The following steps show how to check for spelling errors, run the Design Checker, and save the publication with the same file name.

To Check the Publication and Save Again

1 Click the Spelling button on the Standard toolbar. If Publisher flags any words that are misspelled, fix them.

2 When Publisher asks to check the entire publication, click the Yes button.

3 Fix any other errors.

4 Click Tools on the menu bar, and then click Design Checker. If the Design Checker identifies any errors, fix them as necessary.

5 Ignore any messages regarding transparency, line, or fill errors.

6 Close the Design Checker task pane.

7 With a USB flash drive connected to one of the computer's USB ports, click the Save button on the Standard toolbar to save the publication again with the same name.

Saving the Web Files

Saving the Web order form involves using Publisher's Publish to the Web command. Recall that this command saves the publication as a filtered Web page ready for uploading. The following steps show how to publish to the Web, creating a new folder to hold the Web site.

To Publish to the Web in a New Folder

1 With a USB flash drive connected to one of the computer's USB ports, click File on the menu bar and then click Publish to the Web. If a Microsoft Publisher dialog box is displayed, reminding you about Web hosting services, click the OK button.

2 When the Save As dialog box is displayed, click the New Folder button. When the new folder is displayed, type Pizza Theater Web Site to name the folder and then press the ENTER key.

3 If necessary, type index in the File name text box.

4 Click the Save button in the Publish to the Web dialog box. If a Microsoft Publisher dialog box is displayed, reminding you about filtered HTML, click the OK button.

Testing the Web Site

After you have published to the Web, you should test your electronic form to make sure it functions as you intended and returns the form data to you. The following steps illustrate this procedure. To receive results, change the e-mail address to your own in the Form Properties dialog box (Figure 6–70 on page PUB 440).

To Check Form Controls for Accuracy

1. Use a browser to locate your Web site on the Web.

2. Enter information into several of the text boxes and click one of the option buttons.

3. Click the Reset button.

4. Complete the electronic form. As you use the form, make sure the controls work as you intended.

5. Click the Submit button.

6. Verify that you received the data you entered. If you did not, contact your Internet service provider and ask about their ability to support Microsoft Office Publisher 2007 files.

7. Check the data to make sure you understand the format in which the responses were returned to you.

BTW

Servers
Talk to your instructor about making this Web site available to others on your network, intranet, or the World Wide Web (see Appendix C). The **server**, or hosting computer system, on which you store e-commerce Web pages must support Microsoft Front Page extensions, a common format for Web transactions.

Testing the Macro and Quitting Publisher

To test the automatic macro, you activate the event that causes the macro to execute. For example, the BeforeClose macro runs whenever you exit the Publisher publication. The following steps show the reminder message box that is displayed when the user quits Publisher.

To Test the Macro and Quit Publisher

1
• Click the Close button on the Publisher title bar to display the message box created by the macro (Figure 6–84).

2
• Click the OK button to close the message box.

Figure 6–84

Other Ways
1. On File menu click Exit, click OK
2. Press ALT+F4, click OK

Chapter Summary

Chapter 6 introduced you to Web forms in Publisher. First, you created a Web site using a template. It included a navigation bar, an animated graphic, and alternative text. Then, you created a blank Web page, set Web page options, and inserted, edited and aligned form controls. You learned that each form control should have a unique name and a return value for submission purposes. Text boxes, text areas, check boxes, option buttons, list boxes, and command buttons were added to the interface. Then, a hot spot and scrolling marquee were added. Finally, a message box was programmed in the publication itself, using Visual Basic for Applications. When the publication closes, the message box reminds users to upload the latest version of the Web page.

1. Select Web Site Template Options (PUB 390)
2. Edit the Masthead and Heading (PUB 393)
3. Edit the Navigation Bar (PUB 394)
4. Insert a Static Graphic (PUB 405)
5. Edit Web Page Options (PUB 408)
6. Insert a Background Sound (PUB 409)
7. Go to a Bookmark (PUB 411)
8. Name the Web Page File (PUB 412)
9. Insert a New Page in a Web Publication (PUB 415)
10. Insert Textbox Form Controls (PUB 422)
11. Edit Textbox Form Control Properties (PUB 424)
12. Insert a Text Area Form Control (PUB 425)
13. Edit Text Area Form Control Properties (PUB 426)
14. Insert Checkbox Form Controls (PUB 428)
15. Edit Checkbox Form Control Properties (PUB 429)
16. Insert Option Button Form Controls (PUB 430)
17. Edit Option Button Form Control Properties (PUB 432)
18. Insert a List Box Form Control (PUB 433)
19. Edit List Box Form Control Properties (PUB 434)
20. Insert Submit Form Controls (PUB 437)
21. Edit Form Properties (PUB 439)
22. Insert a Hot Spot (PUB 440)
23. Insert an HTML Code Fragment (PUB 441)
24. Preview and Test the Web Site (PUB 443)
25. Open the VBA Code Window (PUB 448)
26. Program the BeforeClose Event (PUB 449)
27. Set a Security Level in Publisher (PUB 451)
28. Test the Macro and Quit Publisher (PUB 453)

Learn It Online

Test your knowledge of chapter content and key terms.

Instructions: To complete the Learn It Online exercises, start your browser, click the Address bar, and then enter the Web address scsite.com/pub2007/learn. When the Office 2007 Learn It Online page is displayed, click the link for the exercise you want to complete and then read the instructions.

Chapter Reinforcement TF, MC, and SA

A series of true/false, multiple choice, and short answer questions that test your knowledge of the chapter content.

Flash Cards

An interactive learning environment where you identify chapter key terms associated with displayed definitions.

Practice Test

A series of multiple choice questions that test your knowledge of chapter content and key terms.

Who Wants To Be a Computer Genius?

An interactive game that challenges your knowledge of chapter content in the style of a television quiz show.

Wheel of Terms

An interactive game that challenges your knowledge of chapter key terms in the style of the television show *Wheel of Fortune*.

Crossword Puzzle Challenge

A crossword puzzle that challenges your knowledge of key terms presented in the chapter.

Apply Your Knowledge

Reinforce the skills and apply the concepts you learned in this chapter.

Working with Form Controls

Instructions: Start Publisher. Open the publication, Apply 6-1 Pool Store Web Site, from the Data Files for Students. See the inside back cover of this book for instructions on downloading the Data Files for Students, or contact your instructor for more information about accessing the required files. The publication is a Web page order form for a swimming pool store. You are to insert a masthead, a graphic with a picture hyperlink and alternative text, and form controls as described below to create an electronic form. The completed form is shown in Figure 6–85.

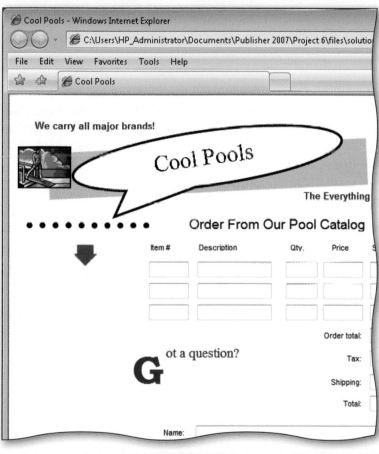

Figure 6–85

Perform the following tasks:

1. Click the Design Gallery Object button on the Objects toolbar. Click Page Headers in the Categories list, and then insert the Bubbles header at the top of the publication. Edit each text box in the masthead individually to match Figure 6–85.

2. Ungroup the masthead by pressing CTRL+SHIFT+G. Delete the graphic. Use the Insert Clip Art task pane to insert a new animated graphic similar to the one in Figure 6–85. Insert another graphic of your choice lower on the page.

3. Right-click the graphic and then click Format Picture. On the Web tab, insert alternative text describing the picture. Do the same for the graphic in the lower portion of the page.

4. Create a hot spot around the graphic in the lower portion of the page so that users who click the area can send an e-mail to webmaster@coolpools.com. Type E-mail from the Web order form as the subject of the e-mail.

5. Double-click the Credit Card # textbox form control. When the Properties dialog box is displayed, click to select the check box that hides sensitive text with asterisks. Do the same for the expiration date.

6. Use the Form Control button on the Objects toolbar to insert a Submit button and a Reset button at the bottom of the page. Double-click the Submit button and then click the Form Properties button. Have the data sent to the same e-mail address and use the same subject line as the hot spot created in Step 4.

Continued >

Apply Your Knowledge *continued*

7. Use the Align or Distribute command on the Arrange menu to align controls as necessary.

8. Run the Design Checker and check the spelling. Fix any errors.

9. Test the Web page by previewing it and clicking all links.

10. On your storage device, create a folder named Pool Store Web Site. Save the publication in the new folder with the name Pool Store Web Site Modified.

11. Use the Publish to the Web command and save the resulting files in the new folder.

12. Submit the publication in the format specified by your instructor.

Extend Your Knowledge

Extend the skills you learned in this chapter and experiment with new skills. You may need to use Help to complete the assignment.

Editing Graphics

Instructions: Start Publisher. Open the publication, Extend 6-1 Photo Gallery Web Site, from the Data Files for Students. See the inside back cover of this book for instructions on downloading the Data Files for Students, or contact your instructor for more information about accessing the required files. The file contains a home page photo gallery with eight additional pages containing full-size images.

You will edit the Web site shown in Figure 6–86 so it displays compressed, thumbnail pictures for each photo. The first thumbnail is displayed for you.

Perform the following tasks:

1. Use Help to learn more about thumbnail images and reducing download times.

2. Browse the pages in the publication to become familiar with the page names, layout, and photographs.

3. For each photo:

   a. Navigate to the page and copy the photo. Paste the photo into the workspace.

   b. Navigate back to page 1. Resize the photo to create a thumbnail image that fits in the area below its caption.

   c. Compress the photo for the Web.

   d. Create a hyperlink or hot spot to link the thumbnail to the appropriate Web page in the site.

Figure 6–86

4. Navigate to page 2. Create an empty picture frame to the left of the photo. Search for a clip art image of a Back button and insert it into the empty picture frame.

5. Press CTRL+K to create a hyperlink back to page 1.

6. Below the back button, create a label that says Return to Photo Gallery.

7. Select both the Back button and the label. Copy and paste them on pages 3 through 9.

8. Navigate to page 1. Below the photo gallery, create a Web form to collect the visitor's name and e-mail address.

9. Below the Web form, create a scrolling marquee that says Thank you for visiting my Web page.

10. Change the publication properties, as specified by your instructor.

11. On your storage device, create a folder named Photo Gallery Web Site. Save the publication in the new folder with the name Photo Gallery Web Site Modified.

12. Test the Web page by previewing it and clicking each photo.

13. Use the Publish to the Web command and save the resulting files in the new folder.

14. Submit the publication in the format specified by your instructor.

Make It Right

Analyze a publication and correct all errors and/or improve the design.

Correcting Page Titles and File Names

Instructions: Start Publisher. Open the publication, Make It Right 6-1 Financial Services Web Site, from the Data Files for Students. See the inside back cover of this book for instructions on downloading the Data Files for Students, or contact your instructor for more information about accessing the required files.

The publication shown in Figure 6–87 is a prototype Web site for a financial services company. The navigation bar needs to be updated to reflect the three products offered by the company. The pages need to be titled and named. The headings on page 1 need to be linked to the appropriate pages, as well. The company will update the content at a later time.

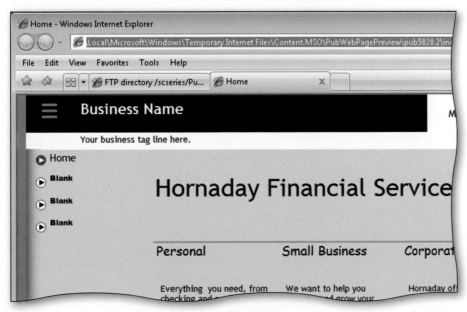

Figure 6–87

Perform the following tasks:

1. Edit the navigation bar text boxes to say, Home Page, Personal, Small Business, and Corporate.

2. Navigate to page 2. Edit the Web page options so the page title is Personal and the page name is personal.

Continued >

Make It Right *continued*

3. Navigate to page 3. Edit the Web page options so the page title is Small Business and the page name is small_business.

4. Navigate to page 4. Edit the Web page options so the page title is Corporate and the page name is corporate.

5. Navigate to page 1. Edit the Web page options so the page title is Financial Services Corporation and the page name is index. Include appropriate keywords and a description.

6. Create hot spots surrounding each column in the main story. Link the hot spots to the appropriate pages for Personal, Small Business, and Corporate.

7. Preview the publication and check all of the links. Modify the file as necessary so every link works and every page title displays correctly in the browser title bar.

8. On your storage device, create a folder named Financial Services Web Site.

9. Save the publication in the new folder with the name Financial Services Web Site Modified.

10. Use the Publish to the Web command and save the resulting files in the new folder.

11. Submit the publication in the format specified by your instructor.

In the Lab

Design and/or create a publication using the guidelines, concepts, and skills presented in this chapter. Labs are listed in order of increasing difficulty.

Lab 1: Creating a Web Order Form

Problem: The Textbook Connection is a bookstore located on a local college campus. They would like a Web order form for students to order textbooks online, as shown in Figure 6–88. Data should be collected about the student, including name, address, telephone number, and credit card information. Also include option buttons for delivery or pick-up and a text area where students can list their course numbers or the names of the books they wish to purchase.

Instructions: Perform the following tasks:

1. Start Publisher and choose Web Sites in the catalog. Select the Crisscross template, the Waterfall color scheme, and the Impact font scheme. Choose not to display a navigation bar. Do not insert any additional pages in the Web site.

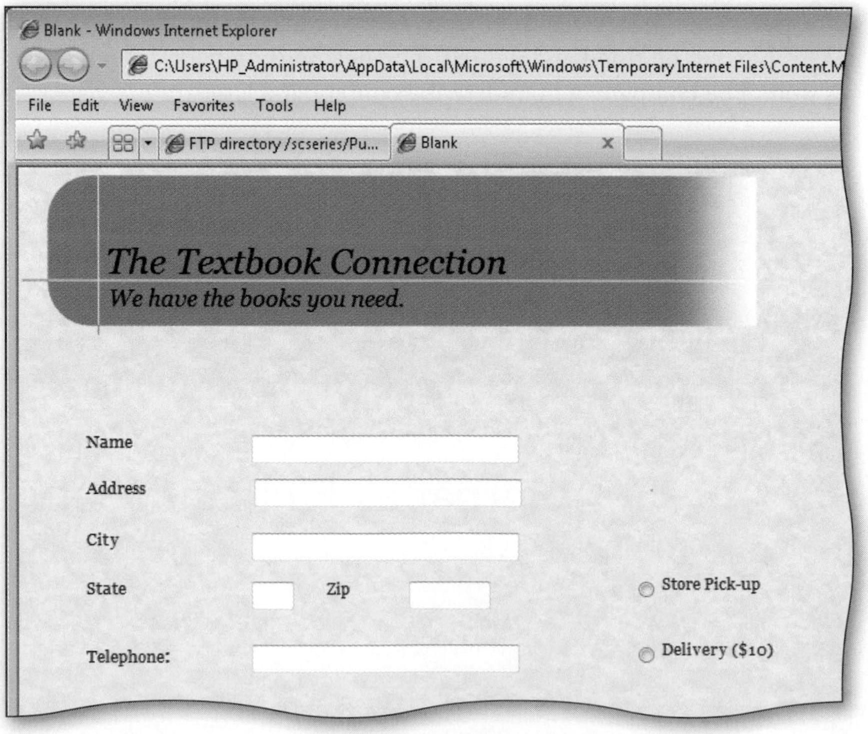

Figure 6–88

2. In the task pane, click Page Content and then click Background fill and sound.

3. In the background previews, click the Parchment preview or a similar preview.

4. In the masthead, click the text in the Business Name text box and then type The Textbook Connection to replace the text.

5. Select the text in the tag line text box and then type We have the books you need. as the new tag line.

6 Right-click the logo and then click Delete Object on the shortcut menu. Click Insert on the menu bar, point to Picture, and then click Clip Art. When the Clip Art task pane is displayed, type book in the Search for box. Click the Results should be box arrow and select only the Movies. Click the Go button. Choose a graphic similar to the one shown in Figure 6–88.

7. In the upper half of the Web page, create text box labels for Name, Address, City, State, Zip, and Telephone. Position them as shown in Figure 6–88. Create a textbox form control to accompany each of the labels. Resize the form controls and place them appropriately. Double-click each form control and set the return data label to be the same as the accompanying label. Align and distribute the controls as necessary.

8. To the right of the labels and form controls, create two option buttons. Change the label text on the first option button to read Store Pick-up. Change the label text on the second option button to Delivery ($10). Double-click each option button and set the return data label to the word service. Set the option button value to be the same as the accompanying label. Align and distribute the controls as necessary.

9. Below the previously inserted form controls, create a text box with the words Please list your course numbers or the book titles and authors. and then position and resize as necessary. Create a text area form control. Move it to the location shown in Figure 6–88 and resize as necessary. Double-click the text area, and set the return data label to book_ information.

10. Below the previously inserted form controls, create a text box with the words, Method of Payment. Create another text box with the words, This credit card information may be sent to an unsecured site and may be visible to others.

11. Next, create five option buttons with the following labels: Check, Bill Me, American Express, Visa, and MasterCard. Double-click each option button and set the return data label to the word payment. Set the option button value to be the same as the accompanying label. Align and distribute the controls as necessary.

12. Create two more text boxes with the words, Credit Card #: and Exp. Date:. Create accompanying textbox form controls. Double-click each control and enter return data labels that match the labels. Choose to hide sensitive data. Move, resize, align, and distribute as necessary.

13. Finally, create a Submit button that sends data to your e-mail address, and a working Reset button.

14. Check the publication for spelling and design errors. Preview the publication using the Web Page Preview button on the Standard toolbar.

15. Save the publication with the file name, Lab 6-1 Textbook Connection Web Site, in a new folder. Print a copy for your instructor. Publish the files to the Web.

In the Lab

Lab 2: Creating a Web Page with Picture Hyperlinks and HTML Code Fragments

Problem: Your friend, Fred Jones, has asked you to make a family home page for him, as shown in Figure 6–89. He wants to include pictures of his wife and children, a background sound, and a scrolling marquee at the top. He has friends and co-workers who routinely use screen readers, so he also has asked you to include alternative text.

Figure 6–89

The hyperlink information, alternative text, and caption are displayed in Table 6–7.

Table 6–7 Data for Picture Hyperlinks and Alternative Text			
Picture	**Hyperlink Information**	**Alternative Text**	**Caption**
baby	http://www.jonesfamily.com/~deanna	This is a picture of baby Deanna. Click here to see more.	Click Deanna's picture to see more cute poses.
corn	http://www.jonesfamily.com/~paul	This is a picture of 5-year-old Paul in the cornfield. Click here to see more.	Paul can attest to last year's bumper crop. Click the picture to see more.
fish	helen@jonesfamily.com	This is a picture of Helen holding a fish. Click here to send her an e-mail.	Click the picture to send Helen your own fish stories.

Instructions: Perform the following tasks:

1. Start Publisher. In the catalog, select Web Sites, and then scroll to select a blank Web publication 760 × 4608 pixels. Choose an appropriate color and font scheme.

2. Click the Other Task Panes button on the title bar of the task pane, and then click Background in the list. Select the Canvas preview.

3. On the Tools menu, click Web Page Options to display the dialog box. Type The Jones Family Home Page in the Page title box. Type index in the File name box. Type This is the home page of the Jones family. in the Description box. Type Helen Paul Deanna Fredrick Jones Des Moines Iowa in the Keywords box.

4. Click the Browse button and then select the SWEST_01.MID sound file or other suitable sound on your system. Click the OK button to close the Web Page Options dialog box.

5. Click the HTML Code Fragment button on the Objects toolbar. When the Edit HTML Code Fragment window opens, type the following code:

```
<font face="Comic Sans MS, Arial, Helvetica">

<p align="left"><b>

<font color="#9933CC" size="6">

<marquee>Thanks for keeping up with the Jones!

</marquee></font></b></p>
```

6. Click the OK button and then drag the HTML Code Fragment object to the top of the page, approximately ¼ inch from the top. Drag the left handle to approximately ½ inch from the left side of the page. Drag the right handle to approximately ½ inch from the right side of the page.

7. Click Insert on the menu bar, point to Picture, and then click Clip Art. Search for a photograph of a baby similar to the one shown in Figure 6–89. Drag the picture to just below the HTML Code Fragment, and align it on the left side.

8. Click the publication so the picture is not selected, and then scroll to select another picture in the Clip Art task pane, similar to the picture of the boy holding corn shown in Figure 6–89. Drag the picture to the center of the publication, approximately ½ inch below the HTML Code Fragment.

9. Click the publication so the picture is not selected, and then scroll to select another picture in the Clip Art task pane, similar to the picture of the fish in Figure 6–89. Drag the picture to the right side of the publication, directly below the HTML Code Fragment.

10. Individually, select each picture and press CTRL+K to create a picture hyperlink. Enter the information from Table 6–7.

11. Individually, right-click each picture and then click Format Picture. Click the Web tab and then enter the alternative text from Table 6–7.

12. Check the publication for spelling and design errors. Preview the publication using the Web Page Preview button.

13. Save the publication with the file name, Lab 6-2 Jones Family Web site, and then print a copy.

14. Publish the publication to the Web.

In the Lab

Lab 3: Adding VBA Procedures to a Publication

Problem: The Pizza Theater restaurant would like to add a copyright notice to its previous Web site publication. The owner now has asked you to insert a copyright message box each time the publication is opened, as shown in Figure 6–90a. The message box should display the information icon that is represented in VBA by the code, vbInformation. The title bar of the message should contain the name of the business. Table 6–8 lists the code and its purpose to create a copyright message box.

She also wants to warn any employees who edit the publication of accidental deletions (Figure 6–90b). Table 6–9 displays the code and its purpose to create a message box that will be displayed when an object in the publication is deleted.

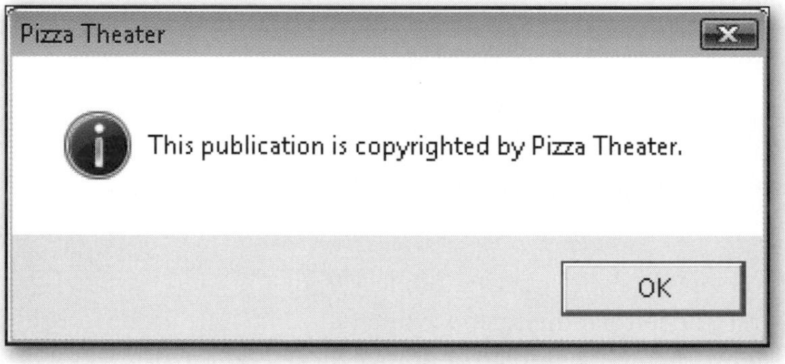

(a) copyright message box

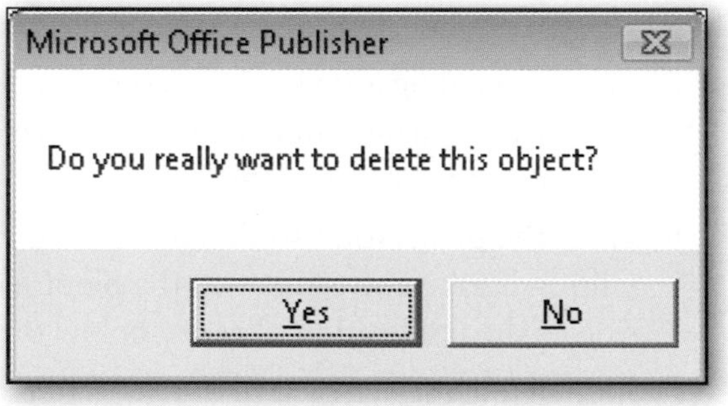

(b) warning message box

Figure 6–90

Table 6–8 VBA Code for a Copyright Message Box	
VBA Code	**Purpose**
'When the publication opens, a copyright message box will be displayed.	Comment
MsgBox "This publication is copyrighted by Pizza Theater.", vbInformation, "Pizza Theater"	Function to display message box prompt, icon, title bar caption

Table 6–9 VBA Code for a Warning Message Box

VBA Code	Purpose
'When a user deletes an object in the publication, a confirmation message box will be displayed.	Comment
Dim intResponse As Integer	Declares a storage location for the user's response
intResponse = MsgBox("Do you really want to delete this object?", vbYesNo)	Function to display message box prompt and two command buttons
If intResponse = vbNo Then Publisher.ActiveDocument.Undo	Tests to see if the user clicked the No button and then calls the Undo button procedure

Instructions: Perform the following tasks with a computer:

1. Start Publisher and open the Pizza Theater Web Site or any of your previous publications.

2. Press ALT+F11 to open the Visual Basic Editor window.

3. If necessary, click the plus sign next to Project (Pizza Theater Web Site) and then click the plus sign next to Microsoft Office Publisher Objects. Double-click ThisDocument.

4. Click the Object box arrow and then click Document in the list. Click the Procedure box arrow and then click Open. Enter the code from Table 6–8, pressing the TAB key at the beginning of each line.

5. Click the Procedure box arrow and then click ShapesRemoved. Enter the code from Table 6–9, pressing the TAB key at the beginning of each line.

6. Click File on the menu bar and then click Print. Retrieve the printout and check your code for accuracy.

7. Click the Close button in the Microsoft Visual Basic window.

8. Click Tools on the menu bar, point to Macro, and then click Security. When the Security dialog box is displayed, if necessary, click Disable all macros with notification, and then click the OK button.

9. Save the publication with the file name, Lab 6-3 VBA Procedures. Test the two macro events by quitting Publisher and reopening the publication. When the Microsoft Office Publisher dialog box is displayed warning you of possible macro viruses, click the Enable button. When Publisher displays the information dialog box, click the OK button.

10. Delete an object in the publication. When Publisher displays the message box, click the No button.

11. Close the publication. Submit the printout created in Step 6 to your instructor.

Cases and Places

Apply your creative thinking and problem-solving skills to design and implement a solution.

• Easier •• More Difficult

• 1: Visitors to the Web Site

You decide to use Publisher to create form controls to collect information about people who have visited your Web site. Create a Web page using a template of your choice; a scrolling marquee that reads, Welcome to My Home Page; and an animated graphic with alternative text. Include Textbox form controls for the visitor's name and e-mail address. Make sure to set the return data labels for the textboxes. Include a Submit button that sends data to you in an e-mail and a Reset button.

• 2: Creating a Macro

Choose any publication you previously have created from scratch and add a message box when the publication opens. Use Visual Basic for Applications to program a MsgBox function for the Open document event. Code the message box to say, This publication was created by, and then insert your name. Be sure to include a comment in the code.

• 3: Feedback Web site

Craig Poff is the city planner for Albany. A new city growth plan has been announced, and pro- and anti-plan groups have flooded his office with responses. Craig wants an online form that people can fill out and submit with their views on specific topics. Specifically, Craig wants sets of grouped option buttons so once a choice is made on one topic the others are closed, thus giving a clear-cut response. Create a set named Schools that includes options to use existing schools, expand existing schools, or build new schools. Create a set named Economics that includes options to build new strip malls, build individual businesses, or no new buildings. Create a set named Parks that includes options to build new parks, expand existing parks, or no expansion of parks. Make sure to use appropriate data return labels. Include a Submit button.

•• 4: T-Shirt E-Commerce Site

Crossing Our Tees is an online vendor of customized t-shirts. Its owner would like you to design a Web order form. You will need to create textbox form controls and labels for customer name, address, telephone, and credit card number. Make sure the credit card number displays with asterisks. Use a list box for sizes of youth, small, medium, large, and extra-large. Use option buttons for mailing preferences of overnight, express, or regular mail. Use a text area form control for the customer to include information about the desired customization.

•• 5: Exploring Commercial Printing

Working Together

Microsoft Publisher is a popular solution to desktop publishing needs. Other software is available, however, for preparing everything from greeting cards to book publication film. Other desktop publishing products include QuarkXPress, Adobe InDesign, and Corel Ventura. Other Web authoring tools, such as Dreamweaver, Microsoft Expression Web, Microsoft Silverlight, and the .Net environment, create interactive kiosks and Web pages. Have each member of your group research a Web authoring software package by looking for examples, tutorials, and screenshots on the Web. Compare Publisher's Web form controls to those of the other software. Bring your findings back to the group and create a table of features and products.

Integration Feature

Object Linking and Embedding

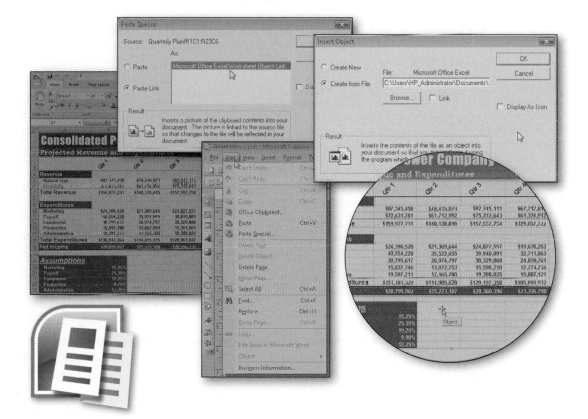

Objectives

You will have mastered the material in this project when you can:

- Understand Object Linking and Embedding (OLE)
- Embed an Excel worksheet in a Publisher publication

- Edit an embedded worksheet
- Link an Excel worksheet to a Publisher publication
- Edit a linked worksheet

Introduction

With Microsoft Office 2007, you can incorporate parts of files or entire files as objects from one application to another application. Copying specific objects between applications can be accomplished in one of three ways: (1) copy and paste, (2) copy and embed, and (3) copy and link. All Microsoft Office 2007 applications allow you to use these three methods to copy objects between applications; however, the latter two methods enable you to use the embedded application's tools to edit the object. The concept of creating or editing an object in this manner is called **Object Linking and Embedding** (**OLE**). With OLE, the application copied from is called the **source**. The application into which the object is copied is called the **destination**.

Project – Object Linking and Embedding

In Chapter 2, you learned how to edit a story using Microsoft Word from within Publisher. This Integration Feature shows how to use a worksheet created in Excel within a Publisher publication. A **worksheet** is the primary document used by Excel to store data. A worksheet consists of cells that are organized into columns and rows; many worksheets can be stored in a **workbook**. Figure1a shows the Publisher publication destination document. Figure 1b shows the Excel worksheet source document. The combined document is displayed in Figure 1c.

You would use copy and paste when you want a static, or unchanging, copy of an object in two different documents. For example, a pie chart of last year's sales probably is not going to change; thus, if you paste it into a Publisher brochure about the company's sales history, it will look the same each time you open the publication. Copy and paste is easy to do across Microsoft Office 2007 applications, using the Copy and Paste commands.

You would use the copy and embed method when you want the ability to edit the object in its destination location. For example, if someone sends you a table of figures that you would like to use in an expense report created with Publisher, you can embed it into Publisher, retaining the ability to edit some of the numbers and recalculate the totals. When you edit an embedded object, the source application software allows you to use its features; however, when you save the file, the changes are reflected in the destination publication only. The copy and embed method typically uses the Insert menu to insert an object.

You would use the copy and link method over the other two methods when an object is likely to change, and you want to make sure the object in the destination file reflects the changes made in the source file. For example, suppose you link a portion or all of an Excel worksheet to a Publisher investment statement and update the worksheet quarterly in Excel. With linked documents, any time you open the investment statement in Publisher, the latest update of the worksheet will be displayed as part of the investment statement; in other words, you always show the latest data in the statement. You also might use the copy and link method when the copied object is large, such as a video clip or sound clip, because only one copy of the object is stored on disk when you link. The copy and link method typically uses the Paste Special command.

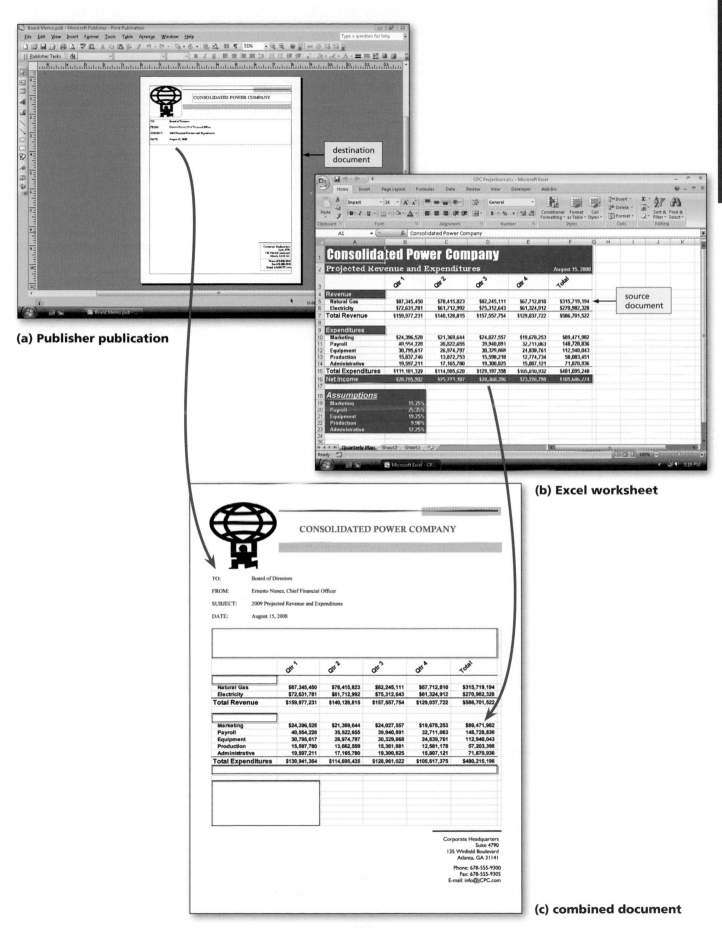

(a) Publisher publication

(b) Excel worksheet

(c) combined document

Figure 1

Table 1 summarizes the differences between the three methods.

Table 1 Copying between Applications	
Method	**Characteristics**
Copy and paste	Source data becomes part of destination document. Object can be edited, but the editing features are limited to those in the destination application. An Excel worksheet becomes a Publisher table. If changes are made to values in the Publisher table, any original Excel formulas are not recalculated. Publisher objects become pictures when pasted into Excel worksheets.
Copy and embed	Source data becomes part of the destination document. Object can be edited in destination application using source-editing features. An Excel worksheet remains a worksheet in Publisher. If changes are made to values on the worksheet within Publisher, Excel formulas will be recalculated, but the changes are not updated in the Excel source workbook. If you use Excel to change values on the worksheet, the changes will not show in the Publisher publication the next time you open it.
Copy and link	Source data does not become part of destination document even though it is displayed. Rather, a link is established between the two publications so that when you open the Publisher publication, the worksheet is displayed as part of it. When you attempt to edit a linked worksheet in Publisher, the system activates Excel and opens the original workbook. If you change the worksheet in Excel, the changes will show in the Publisher publication the next time you open it. When copying from Publisher to Excel, a link becomes an icon on the worksheet.

BTW

Using Linked Objects
When you open a publication that contains linked objects, Publisher displays a dialog box asking if you want to update the Publisher publication with data from the linked file. Click the Yes button only if you are certain the linked file is from a trusted source; that is, you should be confident that the source file does not contain a virus or other potentially harmful program before you instruct Publisher to link the source document to the destination document.

In Publisher, objects from Word become text boxes; objects from Excel and Access become tables. Objects from other applications may become pictures or graphics. Moving objects from Publisher into other applications, on the other hand, deserves special consideration. Because Publisher is commonly a mixture of text, tables, and graphics, other applications typically display the embedded or linked object as a clickable icon. The copy and paste method sometimes is a better alternative to display Publisher objects within other applications, even though you lose the OLE capabilities.

Overview

As you read through this feature, you will learn how to create the integration project shown in Figure 1 on the previous page by performing these general tasks:

- Open a publication and a worksheet
- Embed a worksheet into a publication
- Edit the embedded worksheet from within the publication
- Link a worksheet to a publication
- Edit the linked worksheet from within the publication

Plan Ahead

General Project Guidelines
When creating a Publisher publication that contains an object created in another Office program, the actions you perform and decisions you make will affect the appearance and characteristics of the finished publication. When you create a document that will contain another Office program's object, such as the project shown in Figure 1, you should follow these general guidelines:

1. **Determine how to copy the object.** You can copy and paste, embed, or link an object created in another Office program to the Publisher publication.
   - If you simply want to use the object's data and have no desire to use the object in its source program, then copy and paste the object.

(continued)

Plan Ahead

(continued)

- If you want to use the object in the source program, but you want the object's data to remain static if it changes in the source document, then embed the object.
- If you want to ensure that the most current version of the object appears in the destination document, then link the object. If the source file is large, such as a video clip or a sound clip, link the object to keep the size of the destination publication smaller.

2. **Be certain files from others are virus free.** When using objects created by others, do not use the source document until you are certain it does not contain a virus or other malicious program. Use an antivirus program to verify that any files you use are free of viruses and other potentially harmful programs.

Starting Publisher

The first step in embedding the Excel worksheet in the Publisher publication is to open the publication in Publisher, as shown in the following steps. The file is included in the Data Files for Students. See the inside back cover of this book for instructions on downloading the Data Files for Students, or contact your instructor for more information about accessing the required files.

To Start Publisher and Open a File

1. Start Publisher for your system.
2. With your USB flash drive connected to one of the computer's USB ports, click File on the menu bar and then click Open. Navigate to the Data Files for Students.
3. Double-click the file named Board Memo.
4. If the Publisher window is not maximized, click the Maximize button on its title bar to maximize the window. Close the task pane (Figure 2).

Other Ways

1. In Windows Explorer window, double-click file name

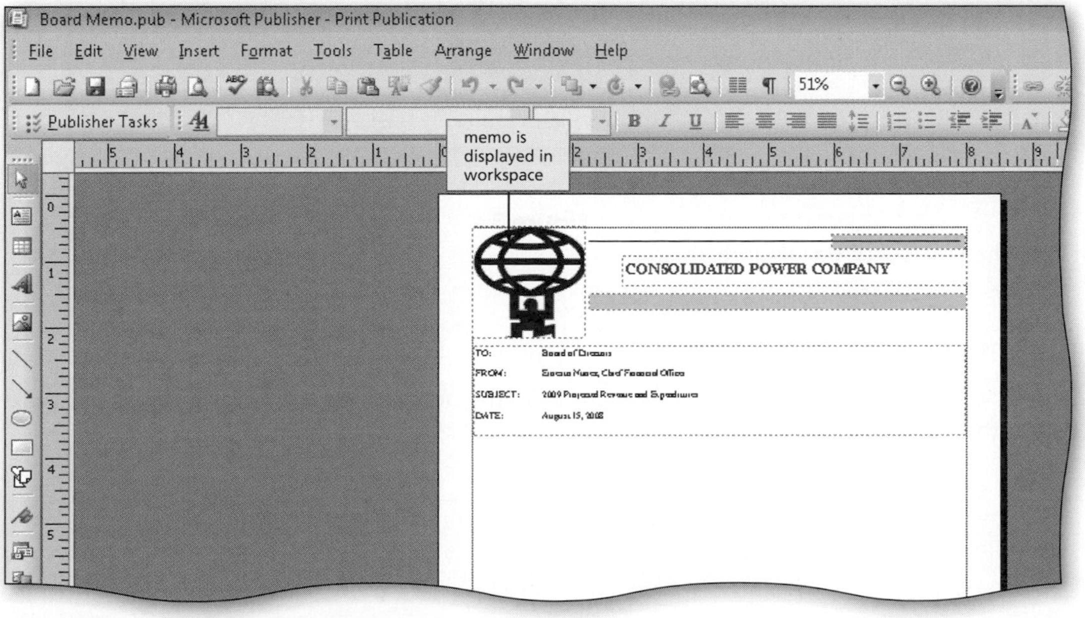

Figure 2

Embedding an Excel Worksheet in a Publisher Publication

Embedding means using a copy of a source document in a destination document without establishing a permanent link. Embedded objects can be edited; however, changes do not affect the source document. For example, if a business embeds an Excel worksheet into its Publisher electronic newsletter that contains a what-if template, users viewing the publication in Publisher could enter their personal data into the embedded table and calculate totals. Those users would not need access to the original Excel worksheet.

Embedding an Excel Worksheet

The next steps embed the Excel worksheet.

To Embed an Excel Worksheet in a Publisher Publication

1

- In Publisher, click Insert on the menu bar and then click Object.

- When the Insert Object dialog box is displayed, click Create from File, and then click the Browse button.

- When Publisher displays the Browse dialog box, if necessary, navigate to the Data File for Students. Double-click the Excel workbook file named CPC Projections.

- When the Insert Object dialog box again is displayed, do not click the Link check box (Figure 3).

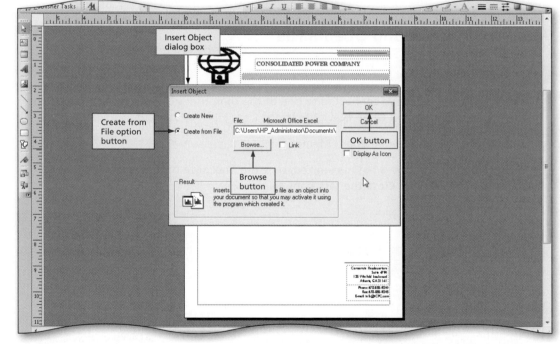

Figure 3

2

- Click the OK button to embed the worksheet.

- When Publisher displays the worksheet in the publication, if necessary, drag the boundary of the worksheet so that the worksheet is centered between the margins and does not obscure other parts of the memo.

Other Ways
1. Open Excel file, copy worksheet cells, use Paste Special command in Publisher, do not click Link check box

Editing an Embedded Worksheet

Double-clicking most embedded objects does not start the source application; rather, it activates a subset of the source application — usually a toolbar, buttons, or ribbons — which display in the destination application. The embedded features allow you to edit the object. Editing the object in Publisher does not change any saved files in the source application.

The following steps show how to edit the embedded projections worksheet for Consolidated Power Company. The Excel cell references in the following steps represent the intersection of the column (indicated by a capital letter) and the row (indicated by a number).

To Edit an Embedded Worksheet

1

- Zoom to 100% magnification.

- Double-click the embedded worksheet.

- Scroll in the worksheet to display the Assumptions area (Figure 4).

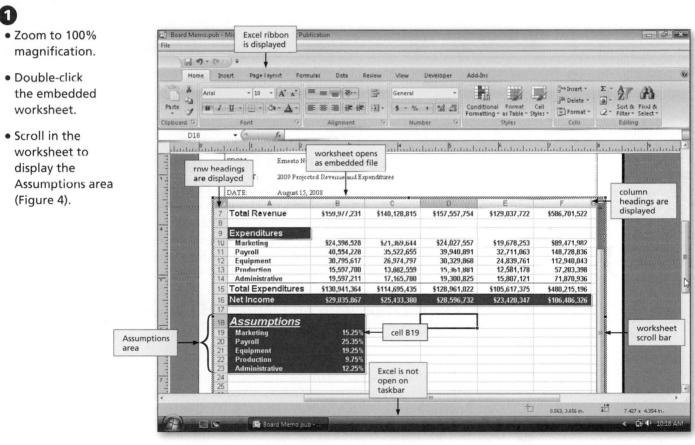

Figure 4

2

- Click the cell containing the Marketing assumption percentage (cell B19).

- Type 16 and then press the ENTER key to change the value (Figure 5).

Q&A Why did the cell highlight on my system move to B20?

Your installation of Excel may automatically move down or across when users press the ENTER key.

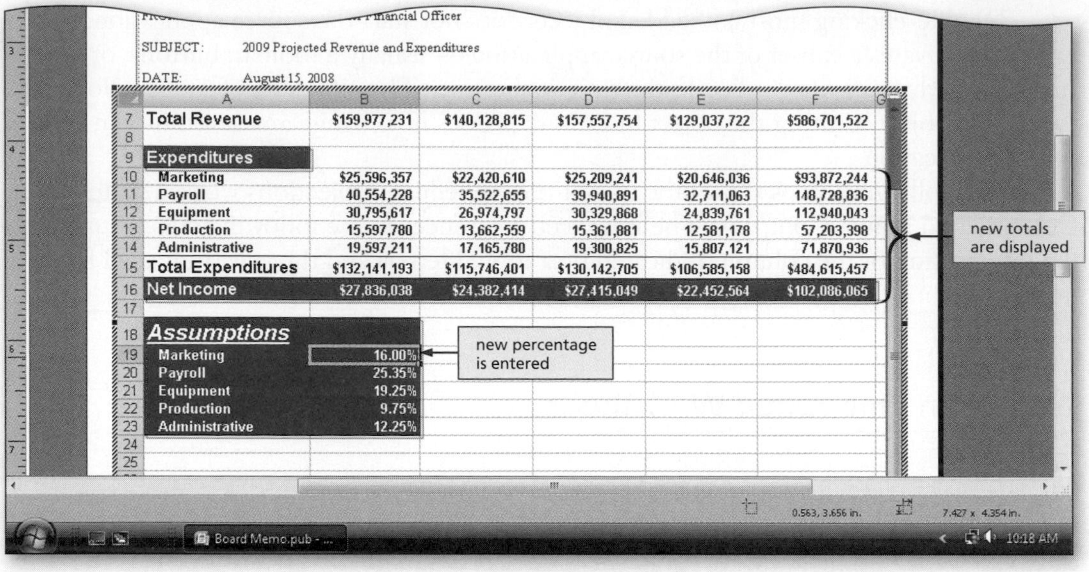

Figure 5

Other Ways

1. On Edit menu, point to Microsoft Office Excel Worksheet Object, click Edit

---

BTW

Embedding for the Web
When you edit an embedded object, you do not have to have the source application installed on your system. This is a tremendous advantage for Web-based publications, as users have the ability to do what-if calculations without installing Excel.

Saving a Publication with an Embedded Worksheet

The next steps save the Publisher publication containing the embedded worksheet with the file name, Board Memo Embedded. The steps also quit Publisher. If you reopen Board Memo Embedded, the worksheet will be displayed in the publication even though Excel is not running. Because Publisher supports Object Linking and Embedding (OLE), it can display the embedded portion of the Excel worksheet without launching Excel.

To Save a Publication with an Embedded File and Quit Publisher

1 Click the publication outside of the worksheet to deselect it.

2 With a USB flash drive connected to one of the computer's USB ports, click File on the menu bar and then click Save As. When the Save As dialog box is displayed, type the file name Board Memo Embedded in the File name box. Click the Save button in the Save As dialog box.

3 Click the Close button on the title bar.

Starting Publisher and Excel

In preparation for linking the Excel worksheet to the Publisher publication, the following steps open both files in their respective applications. The files are included in the Data Files for Students. See the inside back cover of this book for instructions on downloading the Data Files for Students, or contact your instructor for more information about accessing the required files.

With both Publisher and Excel in main memory, you can switch between the applications by clicking the appropriate button on the taskbar.

To Open a Publisher Publication and an Excel Workbook

1

- Start Publisher.
- With your USB flash drive connected to one of the computer's USB ports, click File on the menu bar and then click Open. Navigate to the Data Files for Students.
- Double-click the file named Board Memo (Figure 6).

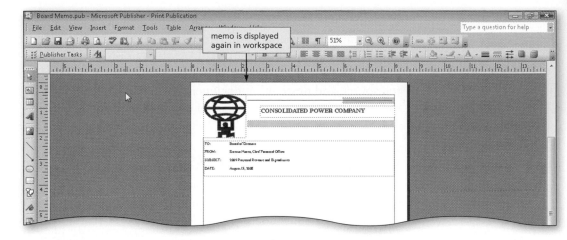

Figure 6

2

- Click the Start button on the Windows taskbar to display the Start menu.
- Point to All Programs on the Start menu, and then click Microsoft Office on the All Programs submenu to display the Microsoft Office submenu.
- Click Microsoft Office Excel 2007 on the Microsoft Office submenu to start Excel.
- Click the Office Button in the upper-left corner of the Excel window, and then click Open.
- When the Open dialog box is displayed, navigate to the Data Files for Students.
- Double-click the workbook file named CPC Projections.
- If the Excel window is not maximized, click the Maximize button on its title bar to maximize the window (Figure 7).

Figure 7

Other Ways

1. In Windows Explorer window, double-click file name

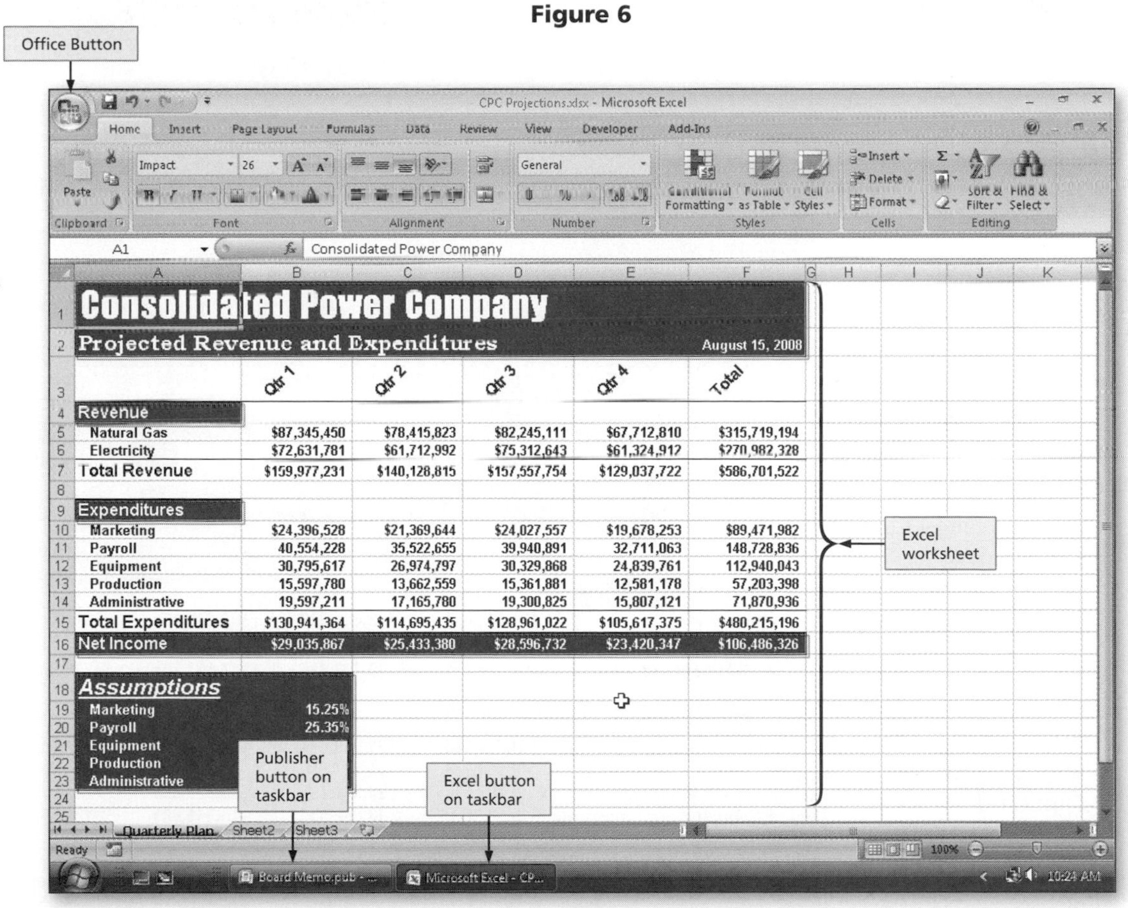

Linking an Excel Worksheet to a Publisher Publication

Linking means pasting a copy of a source document into a destination document, establishing a permanent and interactive link. When linked objects are edited, changes affect both documents. A linked object does not become a part of the destination document even though it appears to be part of it. Rather, a connection is established between the source and destination documents so that when you open the destination document, the linked object appears as part of it.

Linking an Excel Worksheet

The CPC Projections worksheet needs to be linked to the Board Memo. With both applications running, the next step in this Integration Feature links the Excel worksheet to the Publisher publication.

To Link an Excel Worksheet to a Publisher Publication

1

- With the Excel window active, drag the Zoom slider to 100% if necessary.

- Drag through the range from cell A1 through cell F23 to select it.

- Click the Copy button on the Home tab of the Ribbon to place the selected range on the Office Clipboard (Figure 8).

Q&A
What is the dotted line around the selected cells?

Excel surrounds copied cells with a moving marquee to help you visually identify the copied cells.

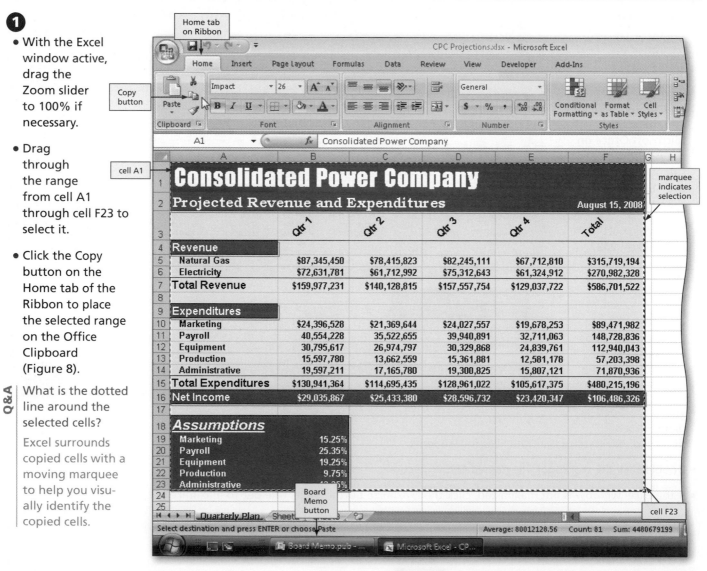

Figure 8

2

- Click the Board Memo button on the taskbar to activate the Publisher window.

- Click Edit on the menu bar (Figure 9).

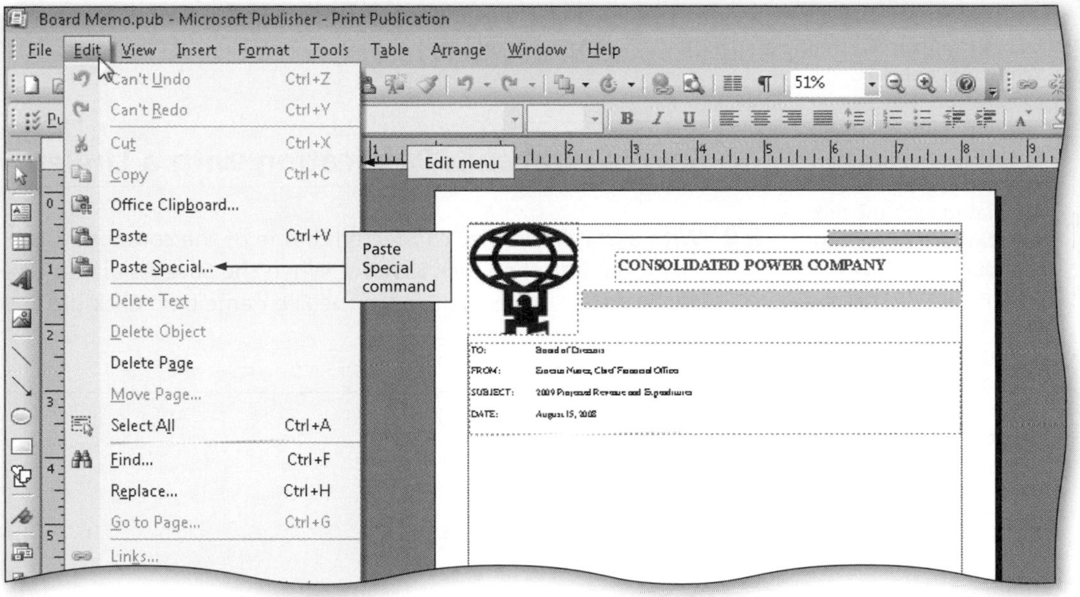

Figure 9

3

- Click Paste Special.

- When the Paste Special dialog box is displayed, click Paste Link. If necessary, click Microsoft Office Excel Worksheet Object Link in the As box (Figure 10). The name of your object and your list of objects may differ.

Q&A

What does the Paste option button do?

The Paste option inserts the contents of the clipboard as a new object rather than a linked one.

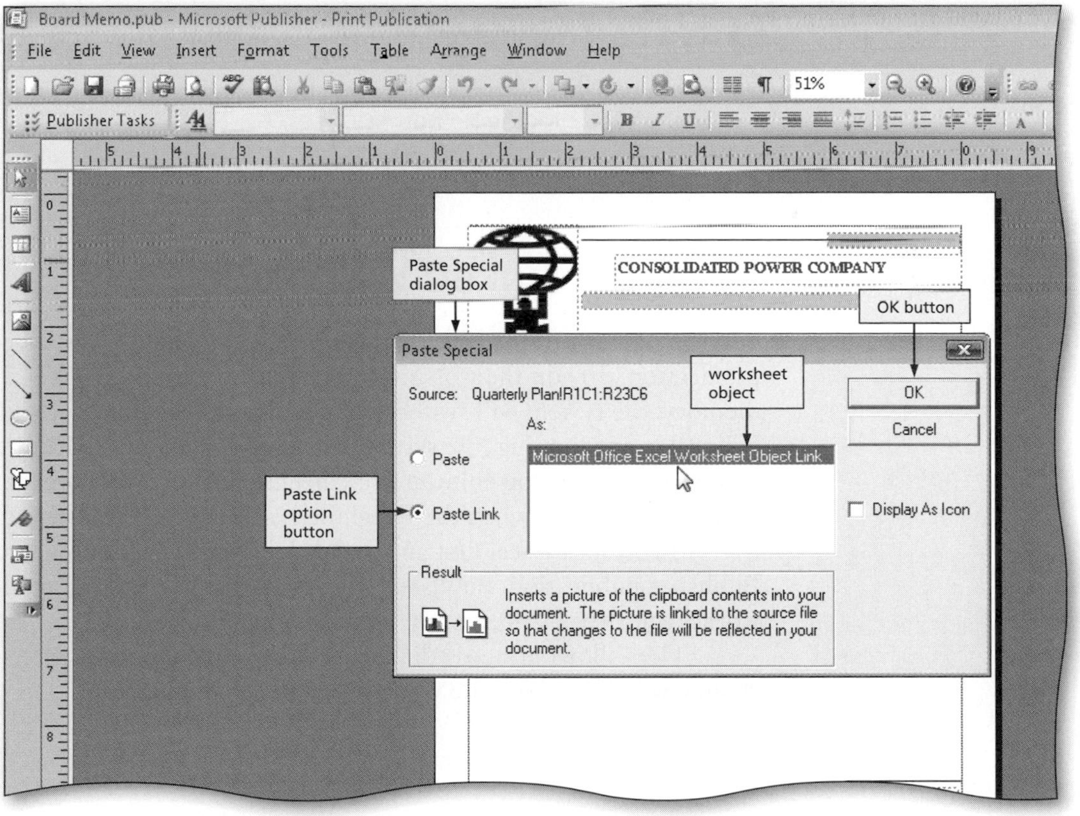

4

- Click the OK button.

- If necessary, when the worksheet is inserted, drag the boundary of the worksheet to a location that does not obscure any of the memo.

Figure 10

Other Ways

1. On Insert menu, click Object, click Create from File, click Link, browse to file, click OK

Saving a Publication with a Linked Worksheet

The next step saves the Publisher publication containing the linked worksheet with the file name, Board Memo Linked.

BTW

Locating Source Files
When you open a publication that contains a linked object, Publisher attempts to locate the source file associated with the link. If Publisher cannot find the source file, click Edit on the bar, and then click Links to display the Links dialog box. Next, select the appropriate source document in the list, click the Change Source button, locate the source file and then click the Open button.

To Save a Publisher Publication with a Linked Worksheet

1 With a USB flash drive connected to one of the computer's USB ports, click File on the menu bar and then click Save As. When the Save As dialog box is displayed, type the file name `Board Memo Linked` in the File name box. Click the Save button in the Save As dialog box.

Quitting Excel

The next steps quit Excel.

To Quit Excel

1 Click the Microsoft Excel button on the taskbar.

2 Click the Close button on the Excel title bar. If Excel asks if you want to save the worksheet, click the No button.

Editing a Linked Worksheet

You can edit any of the cells on the worksheet while it is displayed as part of the Publisher publication. To edit the worksheet in Publisher, double-click it. If Excel is running in main memory, the system will switch to it and display the linked workbook and its worksheet. If Excel is not running, the system will start Excel automatically and display the linked worksheet. Then, you edit the worksheet. The edited changes to the linked worksheet became permanent when the Excel file is saved. Excel transfers you back to Publisher.

If you start Excel first and make changes, the next time you open the linked Publisher publication, Publisher will verify that you wish to update the link to the Excel worksheet, thereby presenting the most current data.

The following steps edit the production assumption percentage (cell B22). The change will affect both the worksheet and the publication.

To Edit a Linked Worksheet

1

- With the Publisher window and the Board Memo Linked publication active, zoom to 100% magnification.

- Double-click the worksheet table.

- When the Excel window becomes active, if necessary, double-click the title bar of the worksheet to maximize the worksheet in the Excel window.

- Click cell B22, type 9.9, and then press the ENTER key (Figure 11).

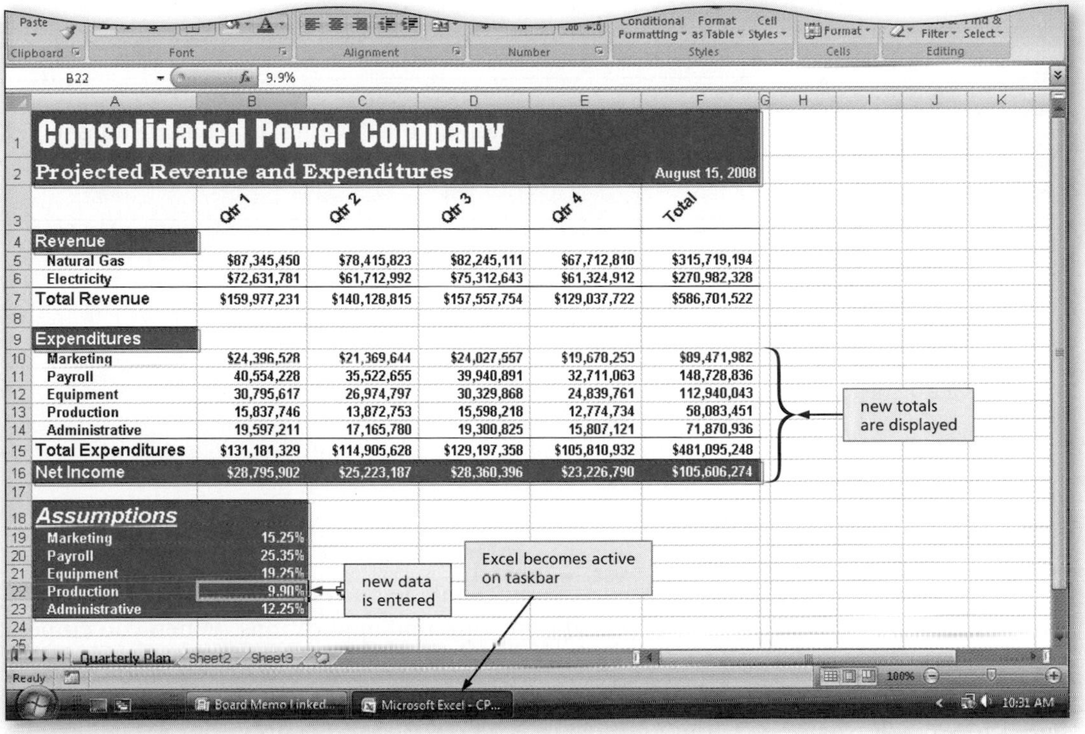

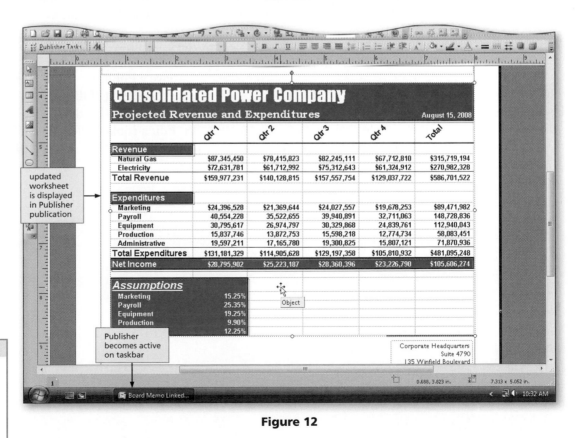

Figure 11

2

- Click the Close button on the Excel window's title bar. When the Excel dialog box is displayed asking if you want to save the changes, click the Yes button (Figure 12).

Other Ways

1. On Edit menu, point to Microsoft Office Excel Worksheet Object, click Open

2. On Edit menu, click Links, click object, click Open Source

Figure 12

BTW

Editing in the Application
When linking, double-click a linked object when you want to edit it. Windows will activate the application and display the worksheet or document from which the object originated. You then can edit the object and return to the destination application. Any changes made to the object will be displayed in the destination publication. While editing the object in the source application, you cannot edit it in the destination publication.

Quitting Publisher and Saving the Publication

The next step quits Publisher and saves the publication.

To Quit Publisher and Save

1 Click the Close button on the Publisher title bar. If Publisher asks if you want to save the publication, click the Yes button.

Feature Summary

This Integration Feature introduced you to object linking and embedding (OLE). OLE allows you to bring together data and information that has been created using different applications. When you embed an object in a publication, the changes you make to that object appear only in the publication. Double-clicking an embedded object causes a subset of editing commands from the destination application to display in Publisher. When you link an object to a publication and save it, only a link to the object is saved with the publication. You edit a linked object by double-clicking it. The system activates the application and opens the file in which the object was created. If you change any part of the object and then return to the destination publication, the updated object will display.

1. Start Publisher and Open a File (PUB 469)
2. Embed an Excel Worksheet in a Publisher Publication (PUB 470)
3. Edit an Embedded Worksheet (PUB 471)
4. Save a Publication with an Embedded File and Quit Publisher (PUB 472)
5. Open a Publisher Publication and an Excel Workbook (PUB 473)
6. Link an Excel Worksheet to a Publisher Publication (PUB 474)
7. Save a Publisher Publication with a Linked Worksheet (PUB 476)
8. Quit Excel (PUB 476)
9. Edit a Linked Worksheet (PUB 477)
10. Quit Publisher and Save (PUB 478)

In the Lab

Design and/or create a publication using the guidelines, concepts, and skills presented in this chapter. Labs are listed in order of increasing difficulty.

Lab 1: Linking an Investment Statement to a Report

Problem: Monisha Lukatou is director of personnel resources for Natural Life. She sends out a memo (Figure 13a) to all employees in the retirement program showing changes in fund balance reserves for the previous quarter. You have been asked to simplify her task by linking the balance sheet (Figure 13b) to the quarterly report memo.

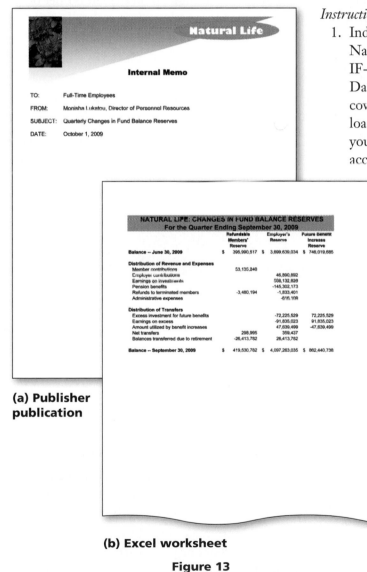

(a) Publisher publication

(b) Excel worksheet

Figure 13

Instructions:

1. Individually, open the publication Lab IF-1 Natural Life Memo and the workbook Lab IF-1 Natural Life Quarterly Reserves from the Data Files for Students. See the inside back cover of this book for instructions on downloading the Data Files for Students, or contact your instructor for more information about accessing the required files.

2. In preparation for linking, use the Save As command on the File menu to save the Publisher publication with the file name Lab IF-1 Natural Life Linked Memo on your USB flash drive. Save the Excel worksheet with the file name Lab IF-1 Natural Life Updated Quarterly Reserves on your USB flash drive.

3. With the Excel window active, copy the range A3 through D21 from the Excel worksheet.

4. Click the Publisher button on the taskbar. Use the Paste Special command on the Edit menu to link the copied range to the bottom of the Natural Life Linked Memo publication. Resize as necessary to fit the linked worksheet into the open space in the memo.

5. Print the publication.

6. Double-click the linked worksheet and use the keyboard to increase the Member contributions value from 52,451,478 to 53,135,246.

7. Close the Excel window. If Excel asks if you want to save the workbook, click the Yes button.

8. Click the Publisher button on the taskbar again to activate Publisher, and print the publication with the new values. Save and close the publication.

In the Lab

Lab 2: Pasting a Publication into a Worksheet

Problem: Monisha Lukatou now has asked you to paste the Publisher publication into the Excel worksheet, rather than linking the Excel worksheet to the Publisher publication as was done in Exercise 1.

Instructions:
1. Individually, open the publication Lab IF-1 Natural Life Memo and the workbook Lab IF-1 Natural Life Quarterly Reserves from the Data Files for Students. See the inside back cover of this book for instructions on downloading the Data Files for Students, or contact your instructor for more information about accessing the required files.

2. With the Excel window active, drag through the row numbers 1 through 20 on the left border of the worksheet to select 20 rows. Click the Insert button on the Home tab, and then click Insert Sheet Rows. When the blank rows display, click cell A1.

3. Click the Publisher button on the taskbar. Click Select All on the Edit menu. Click the Copy button on Publisher's Standard toolbar to copy the selected objects.

4. Click the Excel button on the taskbar. On the Edit menu, click Paste Special. When the Paste Special dialog box is displayed, click Picture (Enhanced Metafile), and then click the OK button.

5. When the publication object is displayed, drag the picture to the upper-left corner of the worksheet and resize as necessary.

6. Save the worksheet with the file name, Lab IF-1 Quarterly Reserves with Memo. Print a copy. Quit Excel. Quit Publisher without saving the publication or the Clipboard contents.

In the Lab

Lab 3: Embedding a Worksheet

Problem: Monisha Lukatou now has asked you to embed the Excel worksheet into the Publisher publication, rather than linking it as you did before.

Instructions:
1. Individually, open the publication Lab IF-1 Natural Life Memo and the workbook Lab IF-1 Natural Life Quarterly Reserves from the Data Files for Students. See the inside back cover of this book for instructions on downloading the Data Files for Students, or contact your instructor for more information about accessing the required files.

2. With the Excel worksheet active, copy the range A3 through D21 from the Excel worksheet.

3. Click the Publisher button on the taskbar. On the Edit menu, click Paste Special. When the Paste Special dialog box is displayed, click the Paste option button to embed the worksheet rather than link it. Click Microsoft Office Excel Worksheet Object in the As box. Click the OK button.

4. When the worksheet range is displayed as a table in the publication, double-click it. Notice that Excel is not linked or activated. Rather, row and column borders are displayed around the table.

5. Save the publication as Lab IF-1 Natural Life Embedded Report, and then quit Publisher and quit Excel.

Appendix A
Project Planning Guidelines

Using Project Planning Guidelines

The process of communicating specific information to others is a learned, rational skill. Computers and software, especially Microsoft Office 2007, can help you develop ideas and present detailed information to a particular audience.

Using Microsoft Office 2007, you can create projects such as Word documents, Excel spreadsheets, Access databases, and PowerPoint presentations. Computer hardware and productivity software such as Microsoft Office 2007 minimizes much of the laborious work of drafting and revising projects. Some communicators handwrite ideas in notebooks, others compose directly on the computer, and others have developed unique strategies that work for their own particular thinking and writing styles.

No matter what method you use to plan a project, follow specific guidelines to arrive at a final product that presents information correctly and effectively (Figure A–1). Use some aspects of these guidelines every time you undertake a project, and others as needed in specific instances. For example, in determining content for a project, you may decide that a bar chart communicates trends more effectively than a paragraph of text. If so, you would create this graphical element and insert it in an Excel spreadsheet, a Word document, or a PowerPoint slide.

Determine the Project's Purpose

Begin by clearly defining why you are undertaking this assignment. For example, you may want to track monetary donations collected for your club's fundraising drive. Alternatively, you may be urging students to vote for a particular candidate in the next election. Once you clearly understand the purpose of your task, begin to draft ideas of how best to communicate this information.

Analyze Your Audience

Learn about the people who will read, analyze, or view your work. Where are they employed? What are their educational backgrounds? What are their expectations? What questions do they have?

PROJECT PLANNING GUIDELINES

1. DETERMINE THE PROJECT'S PURPOSE
Why are you undertaking the project?

2. ANALYZE YOUR AUDIENCE
Who are the people who will use your work?

3. GATHER POSSIBLE CONTENT
What information exists, and in what forms?

4. DETERMINE WHAT CONTENT TO PRESENT TO YOUR AUDIENCE
What information will best communicate the project's purpose to your audience?

Figure A–1

Design experts suggest drawing a mental picture of these people or finding photographs of people who fit this profile so that you can develop a project with the audience in mind.

By knowing your audience members, you can tailor a project to meet their interests and needs. You will not present them with information they already possess, and you will not omit the information they need to know.

Example: Your assignment is to raise the profile of your college's nursing program in the community. How much do they know about your college and the nursing curriculum? What are the admission requirements? How many of the applicants admitted complete the program? What percent pass the state Boards?

Gather Possible Content

Rarely are you in a position to develop all the material for a project. Typically, you would begin by gathering existing information that may reside in spreadsheets or databases. Web sites, pamphlets, magazine and newspaper articles, and books could provide insights of how others have approached your topic. Personal interviews often provide perspectives not available by any other means. Consider video and audio clips as potential sources for material that might complement or support the factual data you uncover.

Determine What Content to Present to Your Audience

Experienced designers recommend writing three or four major ideas you want an audience member to remember after reading or viewing your project. It also is helpful to envision your project's endpoint, the key fact you wish to emphasize. All project elements should lead to this ending point.

As you make content decisions, you also need to think about other factors. Presentation of the project content is an important consideration. For example, will your brochure be printed on thick, colored paper or transparencies? Will your PowerPoint presentation be viewed in a classroom with excellent lighting and a bright projector, or will it be viewed on a notebook computer monitor? Determine relevant time factors, such as the length of time to develop the project, how long readers will spend reviewing your project, or the amount of time allocated for your speaking engagement. Your project will need to accommodate all of these constraints.

Decide whether a graph, photograph, or artistic element can express or emphasize a particular concept. The right hemisphere of the brain processes images by attaching an emotion to them, so audience members are more apt to recall these graphics long term rather than just reading text.

As you select content, be mindful of the order in which you plan to present information. Readers and audience members generally remember the first and last pieces of information they see and hear, so you should put the most important information at the top or bottom of the page.

Summary

When creating a project, it is beneficial to follow some basic guidelines from the outset. By taking some time at the beginning of the process to determine the project's purpose, analyze the audience, gather possible content, and determine what content to present to the audience, you can produce a project that is informative, relevant, and effective.

Appendix B

Introduction to Microsoft Office 2007

What Is Microsoft Office 2007?

Microsoft Office 2007 is a collection of the more popular Microsoft application software. It is available in Basic, Home and Student, Standard, Small Business, Professional, Ultimate, Professional Plus, and Enterprise editions. Each edition consists of a group of programs, collectively called a suite. Table B-1 lists the suites and their components. **Microsoft Office Professional Edition 2007** includes these six programs: Microsoft Office Word 2007, Microsoft Office Excel 2007, Microsoft Office Access 2007, Microsoft Office PowerPoint 2007, Microsoft Office Publisher 2007, and Microsoft Office Outlook 2007. The programs in the Office suite allow you to work efficiently, communicate effectively, and improve the appearance of the projects you create.

Table B–1

	Microsoft Office Basic 2007	Microsoft Office Home & Student 2007	Microsoft Office Standard 2007	Microsoft Office Small Business 2007	Microsoft Office Professional 2007	Microsoft Office Ultimate 2007	Microsoft Office Professional Plus 2007	Microsoft Office Enterprise 2007
Microsoft Office Word 2007	✓	✓	✓	✓	✓	✓	✓	✓
Microsoft Office Excel 2007	✓	✓	✓	✓	✓	✓	✓	✓
Microsoft Office Access 2007					✓	✓	✓	✓
Microsoft Office PowerPoint 2007		✓	✓	✓	✓	✓	✓	✓
Microsoft Office Publisher 2007				✓	✓	✓	✓	✓
Microsoft Office Outlook 2007	✓		✓				✓	✓
Microsoft Office OneNote 2007		✓				✓		
Microsoft Office Outlook 2007 with Business Contact Manager				✓	✓	✓		
Microsoft Office InfoPath 2007						✓	✓	✓
Integrated Enterprise Content Management						✓	✓	✓
Electronic Forms						✓	✓	✓
Advanced Information Rights Management and Policy Capabilities						✓	✓	✓
Microsoft Office Communicator 2007							✓	✓
Microsoft Office Groove 2007						✓		✓

Microsoft has bundled additional programs in some versions of Office 2007, in addition to the main group of Office programs. Table B–1 on the previous page lists the components of the various Office suites.

In addition to the Office 2007 programs noted previously, Office 2007 suites can contain other programs. Microsoft Office OneNote 2007 is a digital notebook program that allows you to gather and share various types of media, such as text, graphics, video, audio, and digital handwriting. Microsoft Office InfoPath 2007 is a program that allows you to create and use electronic forms to gather information. Microsoft Office Groove 2007 provides collaborative workspaces in real time. Additional services that are oriented toward the enterprise solution also are available.

Office 2007 and the Internet, World Wide Web, and Intranets

Office 2007 allows you to take advantage of the Internet, the World Wide Web, and intranets. The Microsoft Windows operating system includes a **browser**, which is a program that allows you to locate and view a Web page. The Windows browser is called Internet Explorer.

One method of viewing a Web page is to use the browser to enter the Web address for the Web page. Another method of viewing a Web page is clicking a hyperlink. A **hyperlink** is colored or underlined text or a graphic that, when clicked, connects to another Web page. Hyperlinks placed in Office 2007 documents allow for direct access to a Web site of interest.

An **intranet** is a private network, such as a network used within a company or organization for internal communication. Like the Internet, hyperlinks are used within an intranet to access documents, pages, and other destinations on the intranet. Unlike the Internet, the materials on the network are available only for those who are part of the private network.

Online Collaboration Using Office

Organizations that, in the past, were able to make important information available only to a select few, now can make their information accessible to a wider range of individuals who use programs such as Office 2007 and Internet Explorer. Office 2007 allows colleagues to use the Internet or an intranet as a central location to view documents, manage files, and work together.

Each of the Office 2007 programs makes publishing documents on a Web server as simple as saving a file on a hard disk. Once placed on the Web server, users can view and edit the documents and conduct Web discussions and live online meetings.

Using Microsoft Office 2007

The various Microsoft Office 2007 programs each specialize in a particular task. This section describes the general functions of the more widely used Office 2007 programs, along with how they are used to access the Internet or an intranet.

Microsoft Office Word 2007

Microsoft Office Word 2007 is a full-featured word processing program that allows you to create many types of personal and business documents, including flyers, letters, resumes, business documents, and academic reports.

Word's AutoCorrect, spelling, and grammar features help you proofread documents for errors in spelling and grammar by identifying the errors and offering suggestions for corrections as you type. The live word count feature provides you with a constantly updating word count as you enter and edit text. To assist with creating specific documents, such as a business letter or resume, Word provides templates, which provide a formatted document before you type the text of the document. Quick Styles provide a live preview of styles from the Style gallery, allowing you to preview styles in the document before actually applying them.

Word automates many often-used tasks and provides you with powerful desktop publishing tools to use as you create professional looking brochures, advertisements, and newsletters. SmartArt allows you to insert interpretive graphics based on document content.

Word makes it easier for you to share documents for collaboration. The Send feature opens an e-mail window with the active document attached. The Compare Documents feature allows you easily to identify changes when comparing different document versions.

Word 2007 and the Internet   Word makes it possible to design and publish Web pages on the Internet or an intranet, insert a hyperlink to a Web page in a word processing document, as well as access and search the content of other Web pages.

Microsoft Office Excel 2007

Microsoft Office Excel 2007 is a spreadsheet program that allows you to organize data, complete calculations, graph data, develop professional looking reports, publish organized data to the Web, and access real time data from Web sites.

In addition to its mathematical functionality, Excel 2007 provides tools for visually comparing data. For instance, when comparing a group of values in cells, you can set cell backgrounds with bars proportional to the value of the data in the cell. You can also set cell backgrounds with full-color backgrounds, or use a color scale to facilitate interpretation of data values.

Excel 2007 provides strong formatting support for tables with the new Style Preview gallery.

Excel 2007 and the Internet   Using Excel 2007, you can create hyperlinks within a worksheet to access other Office documents on the network or on the Internet. Worksheets saved as static, or unchanging Web pages can be viewed using a browser. The person viewing static Web pages cannot change them.

In addition, you can create and run queries that retrieve information from a Web page and insert the information directly into a worksheet.

Microsoft Office Access 2007

Microsoft Office Access 2007 is a comprehensive database management system (DBMS). A **database** is a collection of data organized in a manner that allows access, retrieval, and use of that data. Access 2007 allows you to create a database; add, change, and delete data in the database; sort data in the database; retrieve data from the database; and create forms and reports using the data in the database.

Access 2007 and the Internet   Access 2007 lets you generate reports, which are summaries that show only certain data from the database, based on user requirements.

Microsoft Office PowerPoint 2007

Microsoft Office PowerPoint 2007 is a complete presentation graphics program that allows you to produce professional looking presentations. With PowerPoint 2007, you can create informal presentations using overhead transparencies, electronic presentations using a projection device attached to a personal computer, formal presentations using 35mm slides or a CD, or you can run virtual presentations on the Internet.

PowerPoint 2007 and the Internet PowerPoint 2007 allows you to publish presentations on the Internet or other networks.

Microsoft Office Publisher 2007

Microsoft Office Publisher 2007 is a desktop publishing program (DTP) that allows you to design and produce professional quality documents (newsletters, flyers, brochures, business cards, Web sites, and so on) that combine text, graphics, and photographs. Desktop publishing software provides a variety of tools, including design templates, graphic manipulation tools, color schemes or libraries, and various page wizards and templates. For large jobs, businesses use desktop publishing software to design publications that are **camera ready**, which means the files are suitable for production by outside commercial printers. Publisher 2007 also allows you to locate commercial printers, service bureaus, and copy shops willing to accept customer files created in Publisher.

Publisher 2007 allows you to design a unique image, or logo, using one of more than 45 master design sets. This, in turn, permits you to use the same design for all your printed documents (letters, business cards, brochures, and advertisements) and Web pages. Publisher includes 70 coordinated color schemes; 30 font schemes; more than 10,000 high-quality clip art images; 1,500 photographs; 1,000 Web-art graphics; 340 animated graphics; and hundreds of unique Design Gallery elements (quotations, sidebars, and so on). If you wish, you also can download additional images from the Microsoft Office Online Web page on the Microsoft Web site.

Publisher 2007 and the Internet Publisher 2007 allows you easily to create a multipage Web site with custom color schemes, photographic images, animated images, and sounds.

Microsoft Office Outlook 2007

Microsoft Office Outlook 2007 is a powerful communications and scheduling program that helps you communicate with others, keep track of your contacts, and organize your schedule. Outlook 2007 allows you to view a To-Do bar containing tasks and appointments from your Outlook calendar. Outlook 2007 allows you to send and receive electronic mail (e-mail) and permits you to engage in real-time communication with family, friends, or coworkers using instant messaging. Outlook 2007 also provides you with the means to organize your contacts, and you can track e-mail messages, meetings, and notes with a particular contact. Outlook's Calendar, Contacts, Tasks, and Notes components aid in this organization. Contact information is available from the Outlook Calendar, Mail, Contacts, and Task components by accessing the Find a Contact feature. **Personal information management (PIM)** programs such as Outlook provide a way for individuals and workgroups to organize, find, view, and share information easily.

Microsoft Office 2007 Help

At any time while you are using one of the Office programs, you can interact with **Microsoft Office 2007 Help** for that program and display information about any topic associated with the program. Several categories of help are available. In all programs, you can access Help by pressing the F1 key on the keyboard. In Publisher 2007 and Outlook 2007, the Help window can be opened by clicking the Help menu and then selecting Microsoft Office Publisher or Outlook Help command, or by entering search text in the 'Type a question for help' text box in the upper-right corner of the program window. In the other Office programs, clicking the Microsoft Office Help button near the upper-right corner of the program window opens the program Help window.

The Help window in all programs provides several methods for accessing help about a particular topic, and has tools for navigating around Help. Appendix C contains detailed instructions for using Help.

Collaboration and SharePoint

While not part of the Microsoft Office 2007 suites, SharePoint is a Microsoft tool that allows Office 2007 users to share data using collaborative tools that are integrated into the main Office programs. SharePoint consists of Windows SharePoint Services, Office SharePoint Server 2007, and, optionally, Office SharePoint Designer 2007.

Windows SharePoint Services provides the platform for collaboration programs and services. Office SharePoint Server 2007 is built on top of Windows SharePoint Services. The result of these two products is the ability to create SharePoint sites. A SharePoint site is a Web site that provides users with a virtual place for collaborating and communicating with their colleagues while working together on projects, documents, ideas, and information. Each member of a group with access to the SharePoint site has the ability to contribute to the material stored there. The basic building blocks of SharePoint sites are lists and libraries. Lists contain collections of information, such as calendar items, discussion points, contacts, and links. Lists can be edited to add or delete information. Libraries are similar to lists, but include both files and information about files. Types of libraries include document, picture, and forms libraries.

The most basic type of SharePoint site is called a Workspace, which is used primarily for collaboration. Different types of Workspaces can be created using SharePoint to suit different needs. SharePoint provides templates, or outlines of these Workspaces, that can be filled in to create the Workspace. Each of the different types of Workspace templates contain a different collection of lists and libraries, reflecting the purpose of the Workspace. You can create a Document Workspace to facilitate collaboration on documents. A Document Workspace contains a document library for documents and supporting files, a Links list that allows you to maintain relevant resource links for the document, a Tasks list for listing and assigning To-Do items to team members, and other links as needed. Meeting Workspaces allow users to plan and organize a meeting, with components such as Attendees, Agenda, and a Document Library. Social Meeting Workspaces provide a place to plan social events, with lists and libraries such as Attendees, Directions, Image/Logo, Things To Bring, Discussions, and Picture Library. A Decision Meeting Workspace is a Meeting Workspace with a focus on review and decision-making, with lists and libraries such as Objectives, Attendees, Agenda, Document Library, Tasks, and Decisions.

Users also can create a SharePoint site called a WebParts page, which is built from modules called WebParts. WebParts are modular units of information that contain a title bar and content that reflects the type of WebPart. For instance, an image WebPart would contain a title bar and an image. WebParts allow you quickly to create and modify a SharePoint site, and allow for the creation of a unique site that can allow users to access and make changes to information stored on the site.

Large SharePoint sites that include multiple pages can be created using templates as well. Groups needing more refined and targeted sharing options than those available with SharePoint Server 2007 and Windows SharePoint Services can add SharePoint Designer 2007 to create a site that meets their specific needs.

Depending on which components have been selected for inclusion on the site, users can view a team calendar, view links, read announcements, and view and edit group documents and projects. SharePoint sites can be set up so that documents are checked in and out, much like a library, to prevent multiple users from making changes simultaneously. Once a SharePoint site is set up, Office programs are used to perform maintenance of the site. For example, changes in the team calendar are updated using Outlook 2007, and changes that users make in Outlook 2007 are reflected on the SharePoint site. Office 2007 programs include a Publish feature that allows users easily to save file updates to a SharePoint site. Team members can be notified about changes made to material on the site either by e-mail or by a news feed, meaning that users do not have to go to the site to check to see if anything has been updated since they last viewed or worked on it. The search feature in SharePoint allows users quickly to find information on a large site.

Appendix C
Microsoft Office Publisher 2007 Help

Using Microsoft Office Publisher Help

This appendix shows how to use Microsoft Office Publisher Help. At any time while you are using one of the Microsoft Office 2007 programs, you can use Office Help to display information about all topics associated with the program. To illustrate the use of Office Help, this appendix uses Microsoft Office Publisher 2007. Help in other Office 2007 programs responds in a similar fashion.

In Office 2007, Help is presented in a window that has Web browser-style navigation buttons. Each Office 2007 program has its own Help home page, which is the starting Help page that is displayed in the Help window. If your computer is connected to the Internet, the contents of the Help page reflect both the local help files installed on the computer and material from Microsoft's Web site. As shown in Figure C–1, four methods for accessing Publisher's Help are available:

1. Microsoft Office Publisher 'Type a question for help' text box near the upper-right corner of the Publisher window
2. Microsoft Office Publisher Help button on the Standard toolbar
3. Microsoft Office Publisher Help command on the Help menu
4. Function key F1 on the keyboard

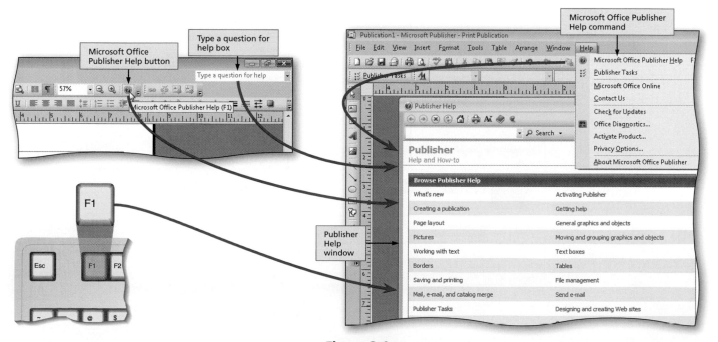

Figure C–1

To Open the Publisher Help Window

The following steps open the Publisher Help window and maximize the window.

1

• Start Microsoft Publisher, if necessary. Press F1 to open the Publisher Help window (Figure C–2).

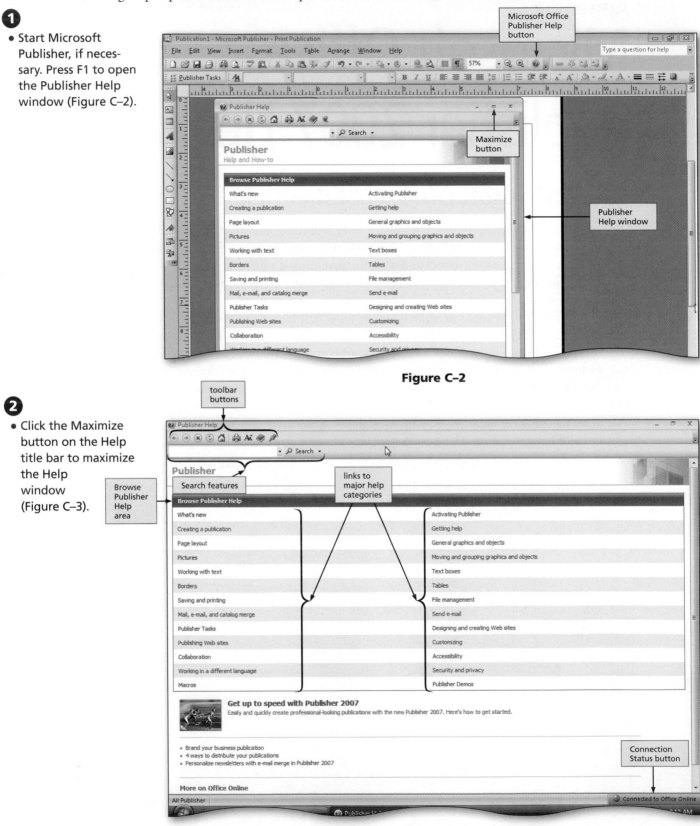

Figure C–2

2

• Click the Maximize button on the Help title bar to maximize the Help window (Figure C–3).

Figure C–3

The Publisher Help Window

The Publisher Help window provides several methods for accessing help about a particular topic, and also has tools for navigating around Help. Methods for accessing Help include searching the help content installed with Publisher, or searching the online Office content maintained by Microsoft.

Figure C–3 shows the main Publisher Help window. To navigate Help, the Publisher Help window includes search features that allow you to search on a word or phrase about which you want help; the Connection Status button, which allows you to control where Publisher Help searches for content; toolbar buttons; and links to major Help categories.

Search Features

You can perform Help searches on words or phrases to find information about any Publisher feature using the 'Type words to search for' text box and the Search button (Figure C–4a).

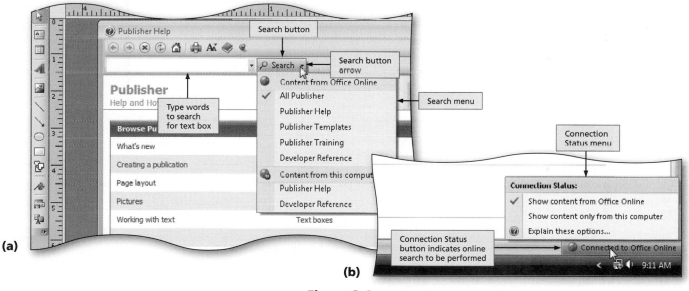

Figure C–4

Publisher Help offers the user the option of searching the online Help Web pages maintained by Microsoft or the offline Help files placed on your computer when you install Publisher. You can specify whether Publisher Help should search online or offline from two places: the Connection Status button on the status bar of the Publisher Help window, or the Search button arrow on the toolbar. The Connection Status button indicates whether Help currently is set up to work with online or offline information sources. Clicking the Connection Status button provides a menu with commands for selecting online or offline searches (Figure C–4b). The Connection Status menu allows the user to select whether Help searches will return content only from the computer (offline), or content from the computer and from Office Online (online).

Clicking the Search button arrow also provides a menu with commands for an online or offline search (Figure C–4a). These commands determine the source of information that Help searches for during the current Help session only. For example, assume that your preferred search is an offline search because you often do not have Internet access. You would set Connection Status to 'Show content only from this computer'. When you have Internet access, you can select an online search from the Search menu to search Office Online for information for your current search session only. Your search will use the Office Online resources until you quit Help. The next time you start Help, the Connection Status once again will be offline. In addition to setting the source of information that Help searches for during the current Help session, you can use the Search menu to further target the current search to one of four subcategories of online Help: Publisher Help, Publisher Templates, Publisher Training, and Developer Reference. The local search further can target one subcategory, Developer Reference.

In addition to searching for a word or string of text, you can use the links provided on the Browse Publisher Help area (Figure C–3 on page APP 10) to search for help on a topic. These links direct you to major help categories. From each major category, subcategories are available to further refine your search.

Finally, you can use the Table of Contents for Publisher Help to search for a topic the same way you would in a hard copy book. The Table of Contents is accessed via a toolbar button.

Toolbar Buttons

You can use toolbar buttons to navigate through the results of your search. The toolbar buttons are located on the toolbar near the top of the Help Window (Figure C–5). The toolbar buttons contain navigation buttons as well as buttons that perform other useful and common tasks in Publisher Help, such as printing.

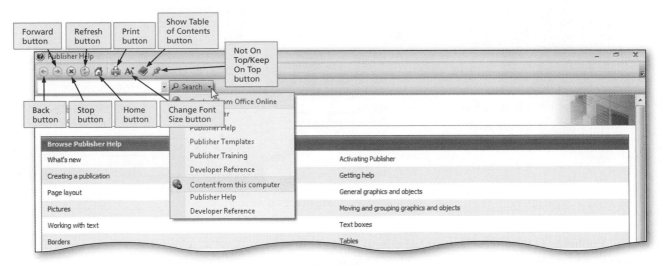

Figure C–5

The Publisher Help navigation buttons are the Back, Forward, Stop, Refresh, and Home buttons. These five buttons behave like the navigation buttons in a Web browser window. You can use the Back button to go back one window, the Forward button to go forward one window, the Stop button to stop loading the current page, and the Home button to redisplay the Help home page in the Help window. Use the Refresh button to reload the information requested into the Help window from its original source. When getting Help information online, this button provides the most current information from the Microsoft Help Web site.

The buttons located to the right of the navigation buttons — Print, Change Font Size, Show Table of Contents, and Not On Top — provide you with access to useful and common commands. The Print button prints the contents of the open Help window. The Change Font Size button customizes the Help window by increasing or decreasing the size of its text. The Show Table of Contents button opens a pane on the left side of the Help window that shows the Table of Contents for Publisher Help. You can use the Table of Contents for Publisher Help to navigate through the contents of Publisher Help much as you would use the Table of Contents in a book to search for a topic. The Not On Top button is an example of a toggle button, which is a button that can be switched back and forth between two states. It determines how the Publisher Help window behaves relative to other windows. When clicked, the Not On Top button changes to Keep On Top. In this state, it does not allow other windows from Publisher or other programs to cover the Publisher Help window when those windows are the active windows. When in the Not On Top state, the button allows other windows to be opened or moved on top of the Publisher Help window.

You can customize the size and placement of the Help window. Resize the window using the Maximize and Restore buttons, or by dragging the window to a desired size. Relocate the Help window by dragging the title bar to a new location on the screen.

Searching Publisher Help

Once the Publisher Help window is open, several methods exist for navigating Publisher Help. You can search for help by using any of the three following methods from the Help window:

1. Enter search text in the 'Type words to search for' text box
2. Click the links in the Help window
3. Use the Table of Contents

To Obtain Help Using the Type words to search for Text Box

Assume for the following example that you want to know more about symbols. The following steps use the 'Type words to search for' text box to obtain useful information about symbols by entering the word, symbol, as search text. The steps also navigate in the Publisher Help window.

- Type `symbol` in the 'Type words to search for' text box at the top of the Publisher Help window.

- Click the Search button arrow to display the Search menu (Figure C–6).

- If it is not selected already, click All Publisher on the Search menu to select the command. If All Publisher is already selected, click the Search button arrow again to close the Search menu.

Q&A

Why select All Publisher on the Search menu?

Selecting All Publisher on the Search menu ensures that Publisher Help will search all possible sources for information on your search term. It will produce the most complete search results.

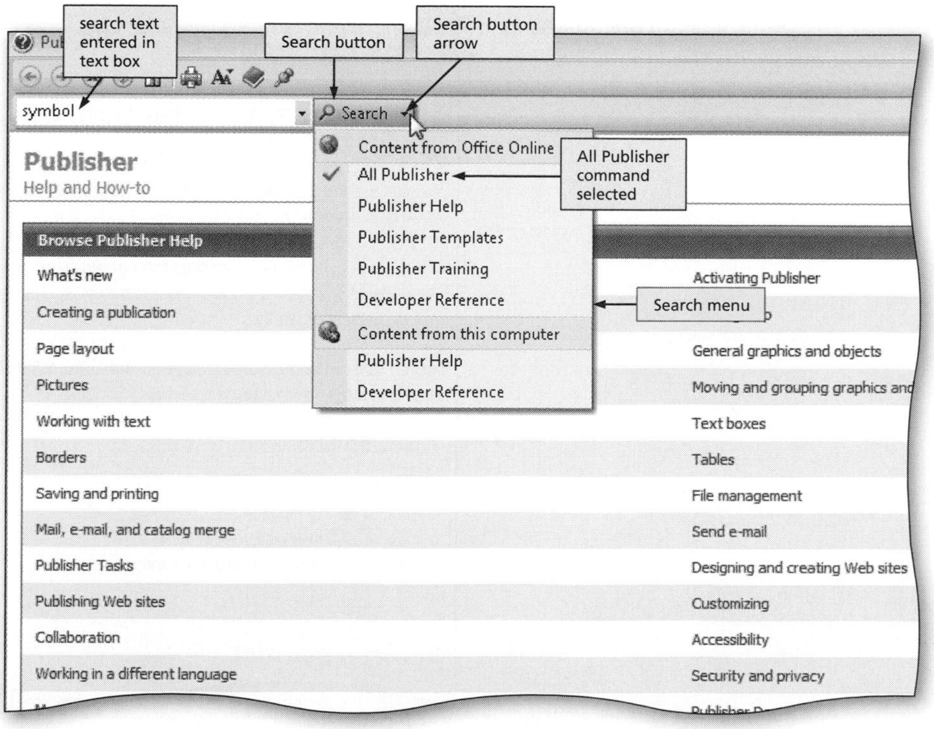

Figure C–6

2

- Click the Search button to display the search results (Figure C–7).

Q&A

Why do my results differ?

If you do not have an Internet connection, your results will reflect only the content of the Help files on your computer. When searching for help online, results also can change as material is added, deleted, and updated on the online Help Web pages maintained by Microsoft.

Q&A

Why were my search results not very helpful?

When initiating a search, keep in mind to check the spelling of the search text and to keep your search very specific, with fewer than seven words, to return the most accurate results.

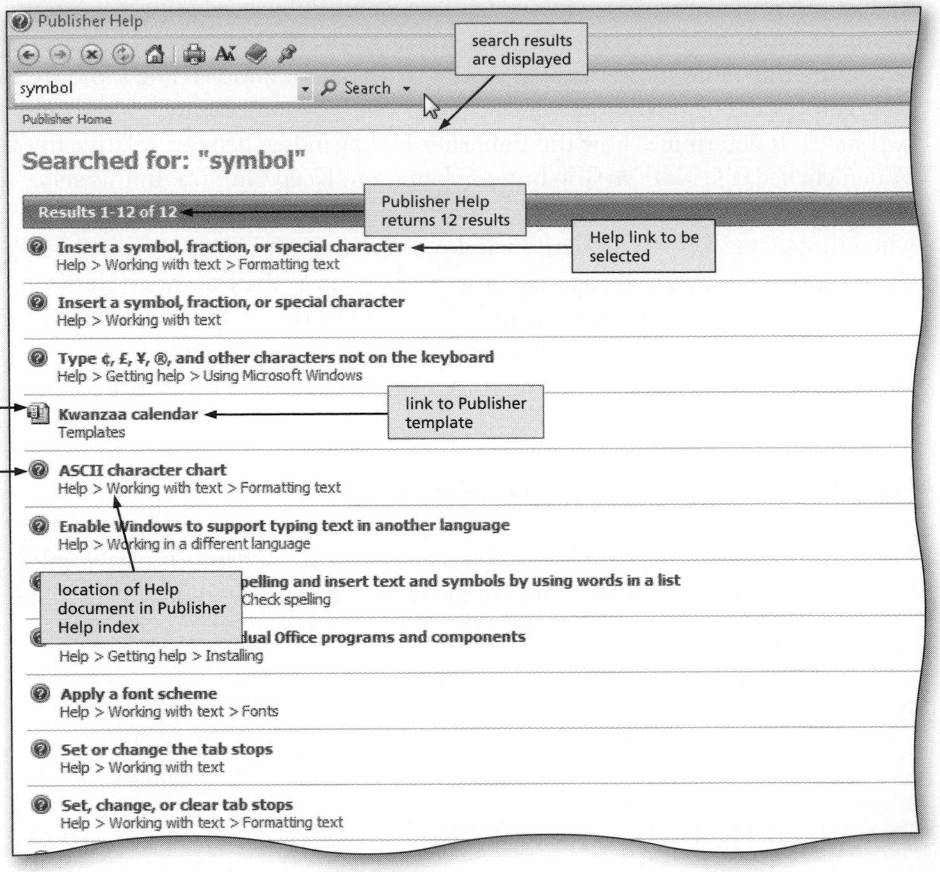

Figure C–7

3

- Click the 'Insert a symbol, fraction, or special character' link to open the Help document associated with the link in the Help window (Figure C–8).

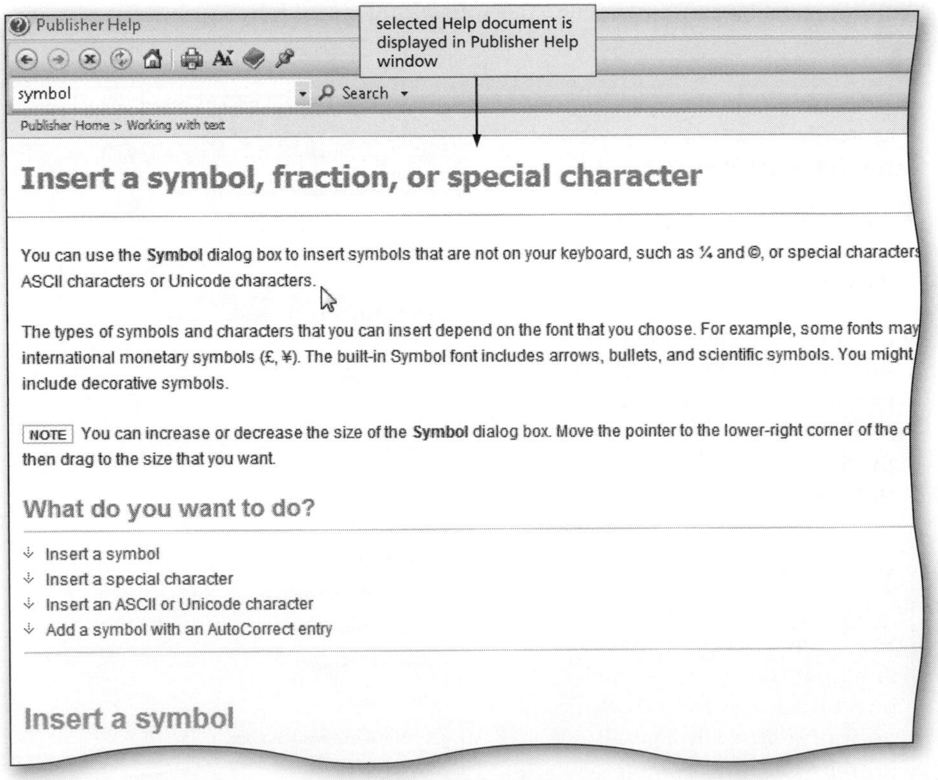

Figure C–8

4

- Click the Home button on the taskbar to clear the search results and redisplay the Publisher Help home page (Figure C–9).

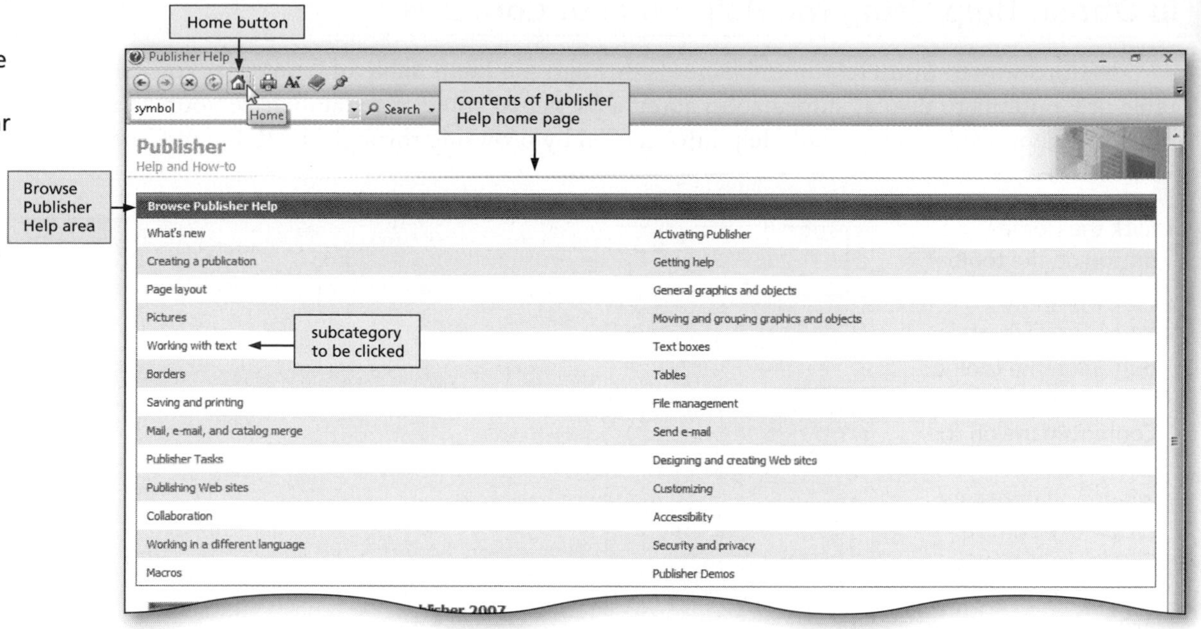

Figure C–9

To Obtain Help Using the Help Links

If your topic of interest is listed in the Browse Publisher Help area, you can click the link to begin browsing Publisher Help categories instead of entering search text. You browse Publisher Help just like you would browse a Web site. If you know in which category to find your Help information, you may wish to use these links. The following steps find the symbol Help information using the category links from the Publisher Help home page.

1

- Click the 'Working with text' link to open the 'Working with text' page.

- Click the 'Insert a symbol, fraction, or special character' link to open the Help document associated with the link (Figure C–10).

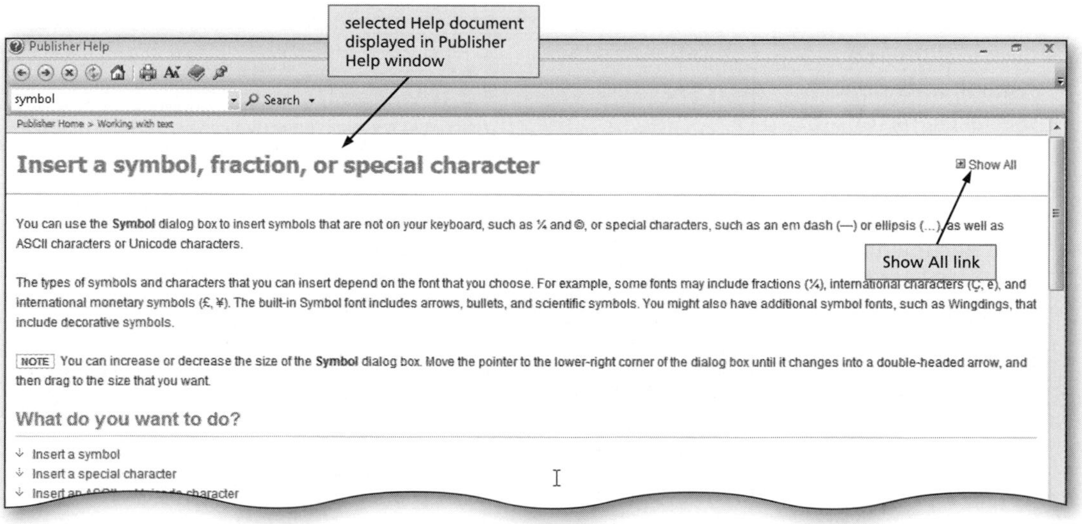

Q&A

What does the Show All link do?

In many Help documents, additional

Figure C–10

information about terms and features is available by clicking a link in the document to display additional information in the Help document. Clicking the Show All link opens all the links in the Help document that expand to additional text.

To Obtain Help Using the Help Table of Contents

A third way to find Help in Publisher is through the Help Table of Contents. You can browse through the Table of Contents to display information about a particular topic or to familiarize yourself with Publisher. The following steps access the symbol Help information by browsing through the Table of Contents.

1

- Click the Home button on the toolbar.

- Click the Show Table of Contents button on the toolbar to open the Table of Contents pane on the left side of the Help window. If necessary, click the Maximize button on the Help title bar to maximize the window (Figure C–11).

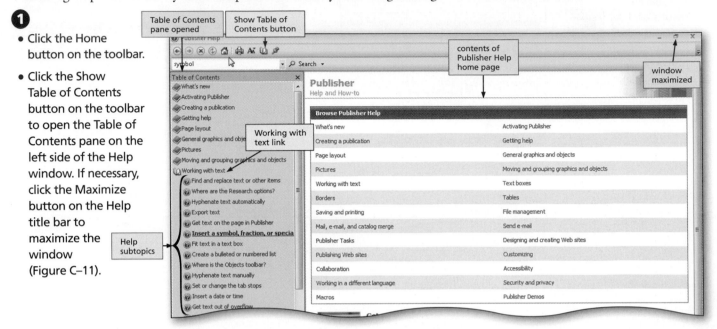

Figure C–11

2

- Click the 'Working with text' link in the Table of Contents pane to view a list of Help subtopics.

- Click the 'Insert a symbol, fraction, or special character' link in the Table of Contents pane to view the selected Help document in the right pane (Figure C–12).

Q&A How do I remove the Table of Contents pane when I am finished with it?

The Show Table of Contents button acts as a toggle switch. When the Table of Contents pane is visible, the button changes to Hide Table of Contents. Clicking it hides the Table of Contents pane and changes the button to Show Table of Contents.

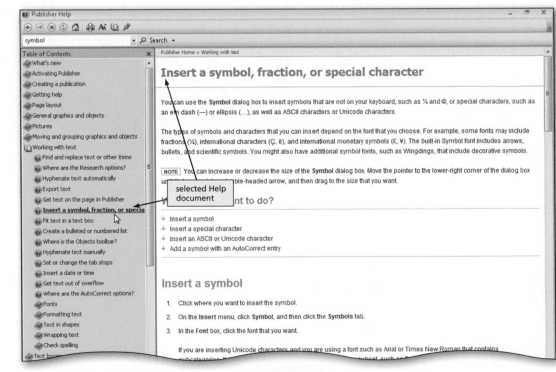

Figure C–12

Obtaining Help while Working in Publisher

Often you may need help while working on a document without already having the Help window open. For example, you may be unsure about how a particular command works, or you may be presented with a dialog box that you are not sure how to use. Rather than opening the Help window and initiating a search, Publisher Help provides you with the ability to search directly for help.

Figure C–13 shows a dialog box with a Help button in it. Pressing the F1 key or clicking the Help button in the title bar while the dialog box is displayed opens a Help window. The Help window contains help about that dialog box, if available. If no help file is available for that particular dialog box, then the main Help window opens.

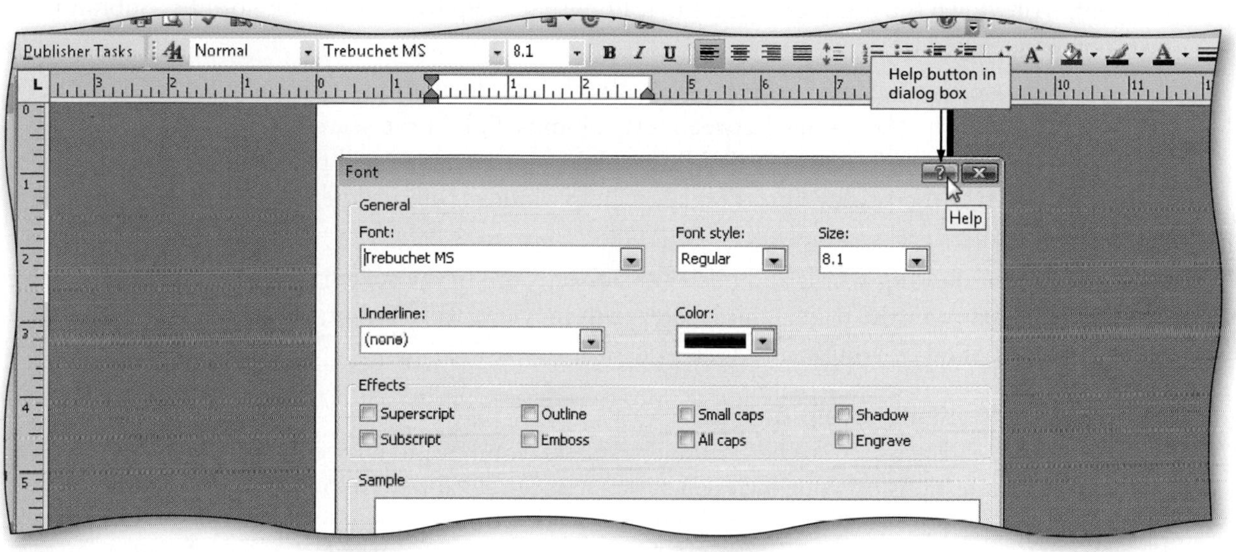

Figure C–13

STUDENT ASSIGNMENTS

Use Help

1 Obtaining Help Using Search Text

Instructions: Perform the following tasks using Publisher Help.

1. Use the 'Type words to search for' text box to obtain help about crop marks. Use the Connection Status menu to search online help if you have an Internet connection.

2. Click Print crop marks in the list of links in the search results. Double-click the Microsoft Office Publisher Help window title bar to maximize it. Read and print the information. At the top of the printout, write down the number of links Publisher Help found.

3. Use the Search menu to search for help offline. Repeat the search from Step 1. At the top of the printout, write down the number of links that Publisher Help found searching offline. Submit the printouts as specified by your instructor.

4. Use the 'Type words to search for' text box to search for information online about adjusting line spacing. Click the 'Add a line between text columns' link in the search results. If necessary, maximize the Microsoft Office 2007 Publisher Help window. Read and print the contents of the window. Close the Microsoft Office Publisher Help window. Submit the printouts as specified by your instructor.

5. For each of the following words and phrases, click one link in the search results, click the Show All link, and then print the page: tables; date; print preview; word count; and borders. Submit the printouts as specified by your instructor.

2 Expanding on Publisher Help Basics

Instructions: Use Publisher Help to better understand its features and answer the questions listed below. Answer the questions on your own paper, or submit the printed Help information as specified by your instructor.

1. Use Help to find out how to customize the Help window. Change the font size to the smallest option and then print the contents of the Microsoft Office Publisher Help window. Change the font size back to its original setting. Close the window.

2. Press the F1 key. Search for information about charts, restricting the search results to Publisher Templates. Print the first page of the Search results.

3. Search for information about charts, restricting the search results to Publisher Help files. Print the first page of the Search results.

4. Use Publisher Help to find out what happened to the Office Assistant, a feature in the previous version of Publisher. Print out the Help document that contains the answer.

Appendix D

Publishing Office 2007 Web Pages to a Web Server

With the Office 2007 programs, you use the Save As command on the Office Button menu or the Save As command on the File menu in Publisher to save a Web page to a Web server using one of two techniques: Web folders or File Transfer Protocol. A **Web folder** is an Office shortcut to a Web server. **File Transfer Protocol (FTP)** is an Internet standard that allows computers to exchange files with other computers on the Internet.

You should contact your network system administrator or technical support staff at your Internet access provider to determine if their Web server supports Web folders, FTP, or both, and to obtain necessary permissions to access the Web server. If you decide to publish Web pages using a Web folder, you must have the Office Server Extensions (OSE) installed on your computer.

Using Web Folders to Publish Office 2007 Web Pages

When publishing to a Web folder, someone first must create the Web folder before you can save to it. If you are granted permission to create a Web folder, you must obtain the Web address of the Web server, a user name, and possibly a password that allows you to access the Web server. You also must decide on a name for the Web folder. Table D–1 explains how to create a Web folder.

Office 2007 adds the name of the Web folder to the list of current Web folders. You can save to this folder, open files in the folder, rename the folder, or perform any operations you would to a folder on your hard disk. You can use your Office 2007 program or Windows Explorer to access this folder. Table D–2 explains how to save to a Web folder.

Table D–1 Creating a Web Folder
1. In applications with ribbons, click the Office Button and then click Save As or Open. In applications with menus, click Save As or Open on the File menu.
2. When the Save As dialog box (or Open dialog box) appears, click the Tools button arrow, and then click Map Network Drive... When the Map Network Drive dialog box is displayed, click the 'Connect to a Web site that you can use to store your documents and pictures' link.
3. When the Add Network Location Wizard dialog box appears, click the Next button. If necessary, click Choose a custom network location. Click the Next button. Click the View examples link, type the Internet or network address, and then click the Next button. Click 'Log on anonymously' to deselect the check box, type your user name in the User name text box, and then click the Next button. Enter the name you want to call this network place and then click the Next button. Click to deselect the 'Open this network location when I click Finish' check box, and then click the Finish button.

Table D–2 Saving to a Web Folder
1. In applications with ribbons, click the Office Button, click Save As. In applications with menus, click Save As on the File menu.
2. When the Save As dialog box is displayed, type the Web page file name in the File name text box. Do not press the ENTER key.
3. Click the Save as type box arrow and then click Web Page to select the Web Page format.
4. Click Computer in the Navigation pane.
5. Double-click the Web folder name in the Network Location list.
6. If the Enter Network Password dialog box appears, type the user name and password in the respective text boxes and then click the OK button.
7. Click the Save button in the Save As dialog box.

Using FTP to Publish Office 2007 Web Pages

When publishing a Web page using FTP, you first must add the FTP location to your computer before you can save to it. An FTP location, also called an **FTP site**, is a collection of files that reside on an FTP server. In this case, the FTP server is the Web server.

To add an FTP location, you must obtain the name of the FTP site, which usually is the address (URL) of the FTP server, and a user name and a password that allows you to access the FTP server. You save and open the Web pages on the FTP server using the name of the FTP site. Table D–3 explains how to add an FTP site.

Office 2007 adds the name of the FTP site to the FTP locations list in the Save As and Open dialog boxes. You can open and save files using this list. Table D–4 explains how to save to an FTP location.

Table D–3 Adding an FTP Location
1. In applications with ribbons, click the Office Button and then click Save As or Open. In applications with menus, click Save As or Open on the File menu.
2. When the Save As dialog box (or Open dialog box) appears, click the Tools button arrow, and then click Map Network Drive... When the Map Network Drive dialog box is displayed, click the 'Connect to a Web site that you can use to store your documents and pictures' link.
3. When the Add Network Location Wizard dialog box appears, click the Next button. If necessary, click Choose a custom network location. Click the Next button. Click the View examples link, type the Internet or network address, and then click the Next button. If you have a user name for the site, click to deselect 'Log on anonymously' and type your user name in the User name text box, and then click Next. If the site allows anonymous logon, click Next. Type a name for the location, click Next, click to deselect the 'Open this network location when I click Finish' check box, and click Finish. Click the OK button.
4. Close the Save As or the Open dialog box.

Table D–4 Saving to an FTP Location
1. In applications with ribbons, click the Office Button and then click Save As. In applications with menus, click Save As on the File menu.
2. When the Save As dialog box is displayed, type the Web page file name in the File name text box. Do not press the ENTER key.
3. Click the Save as type box arrow and then click Web Page to select the Web Page format.
4. Click Computer in the Navigation pane.
5. Double-click the name of the FTP site in the Network Location list.
6. When the FTP Log On dialog box appears, enter your user name and password and then click the OK button.
7. Click the Save button in the Save As dialog box.

Appendix E
Customizing Microsoft Office Publisher 2007

This appendix explains how to change the screen resolution in Windows Vista to the resolution used in this book. It also describes how to customize the Publisher toolbars and menus.

Changing Screen Resolution

Screen resolution indicates the number of pixels (dots) that the computer uses to display the letters, numbers, graphics, and background you see on the screen. When you increase the screen resolution, Windows displays more information on the screen, but the information decreases in size. The reverse also is true: as you decrease the screen resolution, Windows displays less information on the screen, but the information increases in size.

The screen resolution usually is stated as the product of two numbers, such as 1024×768 (pronounced "ten twenty-four by seven sixty-eight"). A 1024×768 screen resolution results in a display of 1,024 distinct pixels on each of 768 lines, or about 786,432 pixels. The figures in this book were created using a screen resolution of 1024×768.

The screen resolutions most commonly used today are 800×600 and 1024×768, although some Office specialists set their computers at a much higher screen resolution, such as 2048×1536.

To Change the Screen Resolution

The following steps change the screen resolution to 1024×768 to match the figures in this book.

1

- If necessary, minimize all programs so that the Windows Vista desktop appears.

- Right-click the Windows Vista desktop to display the Windows Vista desktop shortcut menu (Figure E–1).

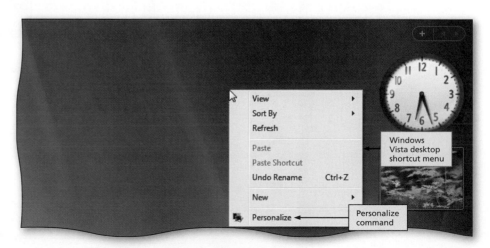

Figure E–1

2

- Click Personalize on the shortcut menu to open the Personalization window.

- Click Display Settings in the Personalization window to display the Display Settings dialog box (Figure E–2).

Personalization window

Display Settings dialog box

Control Panel ▸ Appearance and Personalization ▸ Personalization

Search

Personalize appearance and

Display Settings

Monitor

Window Color and Appearanc
Fine tune the color and style o

Desktop Background
Choose from available backgr

Screen Saver
Change your screen saver or a
your screen and appears when

Sounds
Change which sounds a
Bin.

Resolution area

Mouse Pointers
Pick a different mouse pointer
as clicking and selecting.

Theme
Chan   hemes ca
inclu   nce of m
mouse pointers.

Display Settings link

Display Settings
Adjust your monitor resolution
can also control monitor flicke

1

fault Monitor) on VMware SVGA II

current settings – your display may differ

slider

Resolution:

Low   High

1280 by 1024 pixels

Colors:
Highest (32 bit)

How do I get the best display?

Advanced Settings...

OK   Cancel   Apply

Figure E–2

3

- If necessary, drag the slider in the Resolution area so that the screen resolution is set to 1024 × 768 (Figure E–3).

▸ Appearance and Personalization ▸ Personalization

Search

Personalize appearance and

Display Settings

Monitor

Window Color and Appearanc
Fine tune the color and style o

Desktop Background
Choose from available backgr

Screen Saver
Change your screen saver or a
your screen and appears when

Sounds
Change which sounds are hea
Bin.

Mouse Pointers
Pick a different mouse pointer
as clicking and selecting.

Theme
Change the theme. Ther
including the appearanc
mouse pointers.

screen resolution set to 1024 × 768

Display Settings
Adjust your monitor resolution
can also control monitor flicke

1

(Default Monitor) on VMware SVGA II

Resolution:

Low   High

Colors:
Highest (32 bit)

1024 by 768 pixels

OK button

How do I get the best display?

Advanced Settings...

OK   Cancel   Apply

Figure E–3

4

- Click the OK button to set the screen resolution to 1024 × 768 (Figure E–4).

5

- Click the Yes button in the Display Settings dialog box to accept the new screen resolution.

- Click the Close button to close the Personalization Window.

Figure E–4

Customizing the Publisher Toolbars and Menus

Publisher customization capabilities allow you to reset toolbars and menus, create custom toolbars by adding and deleting buttons, and personalize menus based on their usage. Each time you start Publisher, the toolbars and menus display using the same settings as the last time you used it. The figures in this book were created with the Publisher toolbars and menus set to the original, or installation, settings.

Resetting the Publisher Toolbars

If in the past, buttons or commands were added or removed on any Publisher toolbars, you quickly can restore the original settings. The following steps reset the six toolbars that initially display in Publisher. The six toolbars include the following:

- Standard toolbar
- Formatting toolbar
- Connect Text Boxes toolbar
- Menu Bar
- Objects toolbar
- Publisher Tasks toolbar

To Reset the Publisher Toolbars

1

- If necessary, start Publisher for your system as described in Project 1.

- Open any recent publication, blank publication, or template.

- Click Tools on the menu bar to display the Tools menu (Figure E–5).

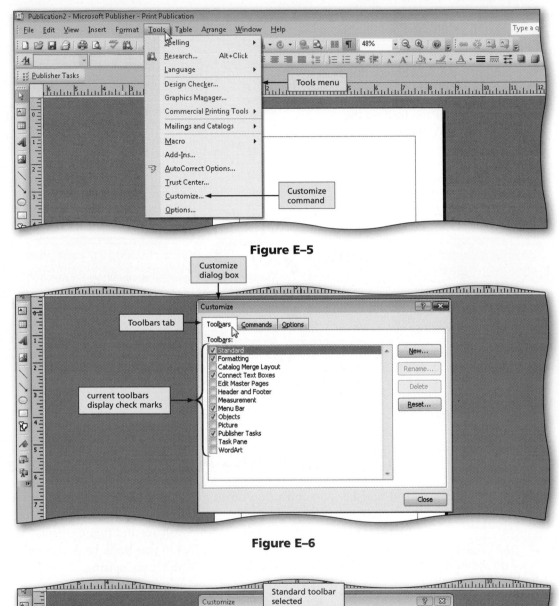

Figure E–5

2

- Click Customize to display the Customize dialog box.

- In the Customize dialog box, click the Toolbars tab, if necessary. (Figure E–6).

3

- In the Toolbars list, if necessary, click Standard to select it.

- Click the Reset button to reset the toolbar (Figure E–7).

- Click the OK button in the Microsoft Office Publisher dialog box to confirm the changes.

Figure E–6

4

- Follow steps 1 through 3 to reset each of the other toolbars that display a check mark in the list.

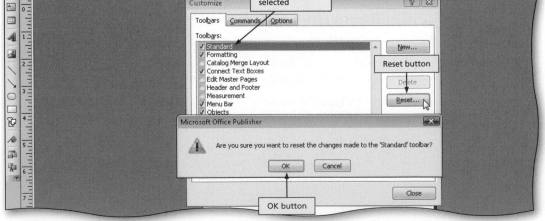

Figure E–7

Editing Toolbars

You can add, delete, or rearrange the commands and buttons on Publisher toolbars. You might want to promote commands that you use frequently to a higher position in the menu. Or you might want to move a button from one toolbar to another to facilitate your use of the button. You even can create new toolbars and menus and populate them with buttons from the list or buttons that you create using macros. On the Commands sheet in the Customize dialog box, the commands are grouped by category or purpose on the left and listed individually on the right.

Another way to edit toolbars is to change the way the buttons look or behave. For example, you can create a button that automatically opens a browser and goes to a specific Web address.

BTW

New Toolbars
If you want to create a new toolbar, click the New button (shown in Figure E–7) to display a dialog box where you can name the new toolbar. Once the new toolbar is created, you can use the Commands sheet to add or remove buttons on the new toolbar.

To Edit Toolbars

The following steps rearrange commands on the File menu and then reset them back to the default order.

1

- With the Customize dialog box still displayed, click the Commands tab.

- If necessary, click File in the Categories list (Figure E–8).

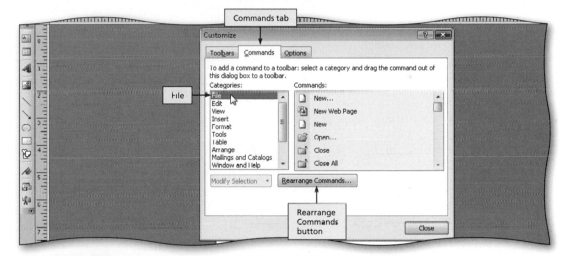

Figure E–8

2

- Click the Rearrange Commands button to display the Rearrange Commands dialog box (Figure E–9).

Q&A

How do I rearrange other menus or toolbars?

At the top of the Rearrange Commands dialog box, you can select Menu Bar or Toolbar by clicking the desired option button. You then can choose a specific menu or toolbar by clicking the box arrow. Publisher will change the list of Controls based on your choices.

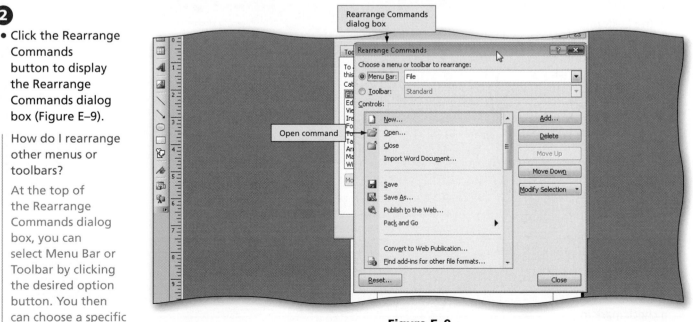

Figure E–9

3

- Click Open in the Controls list and then click the Move Up button to rearrange the commands (Figure E–10).

Q&A

What does the Modify Selection button do?

The Modify Selection button offers you many choices to edit each button and menu command. You can choose a different name, image, or text; edit, copy, or paste images; insert a new separator line to begin a group; or assign a hyperlink. If you change the name or assign a hyperlink, the screen-tip also changes.

Figure E–10

4

- Click the Close button in the Rearrange Commands dialog box and then click File on the Publisher menu bar to view the rearrangement (Figure E–11).

5

- In the Customize dialog box, click the Rearrange Commands button again, and then click the Reset button to restore the original order.

- When Publisher displays the Microsoft Office Publisher dialog box, click the OK button to confirm the changes.

- Click the Close button in the Rearrange Commands dialog box.

Figure E–11

Resetting the Publisher Menu Usage

On an initial installation, Publisher displays the entire menu when you click a menu command. You can customize or personalize the menus to display the more popular menu commands or recently used commands in a short menu; a More Commands button allows you access to the longer menu. You can reset the short menu and toolbar usage, and you can choose to display the Standard and Formatting toolbars on one row or two.

BTW

Adding New Commands
Using the **Commands sheet** in the Customize dialog box, you can add buttons to toolbars and commands to menus. To add buttons, click a category name in the Categories list and then drag the command name in the Commands list to a toolbar. To add menu commands, click a category name in the Categories list, drag the command name in the Commands list to a menu name and then to the desired location in the menu.

To Reset the Publisher Menu Usage

The following steps reset the menu or toolbar usage.

1
- With the Customize dialog box still displayed, click the Options tab (Figure E–12).

2
- Click the Reset menu and toolbar usage data button. If Publisher displays a dialog box asking you to confirm the reset, click the Yes button.

3
- Click the Close button in the Customize dialog box.

Options tab

Reset menu and toolbar usage data button

Close button

Figure E–12

Other Ways

1. On toolbar, click Toolbar Options button, point to Add or Remove Buttons, click Customize, on Options sheet click Reset menu and toolbar usage data, click Yes.

2. Right-click toolbar, click Customize, on Toolbars sheet click Reset menu and toolbar usage data, click Yes.

BTW

Short Menus
If you choose to display short menus, Publisher retains a record of the commands that you select on menus and toolbars. When you click a command on a menu or a button on a toolbar, the Microsoft Office program records your action and makes the command or button always visible to you. The More Commands button at the bottom of menus, and the Toolbar Options button at the end of toolbars display commands and buttons used less frequently. As you choose the less frequently used commands or buttons, Publisher promotes them to the short menu or to the toolbar display.

Appendix F

Steps for the Windows XP User

For the XP User of this Book

For most tasks, no differences exist between using Office 2007 under the Windows Vista operating system and using an Office 2007 program under the Windows XP operating system. With some tasks, however, you will see some differences, or need to complete the tasks using different steps. This appendix shows how to start Publisher, save a publication, open a publication, insert pictures and text, import a Word Document, and publish to the Web, while using Microsoft Office under Windows XP.

To Start Publisher

The following steps, which assume Windows is running, start Publisher based on a typical installation. You may need to ask your instructor how to start Publisher for your computer.

1

- Click the Start button on the Windows taskbar to display the Start menu.

- Point to All Programs on the Start menu to display the All Programs submenu.

- Point to Microsoft Office on the All Programs submenu to display the Microsoft Office submenu (Figure F–1).

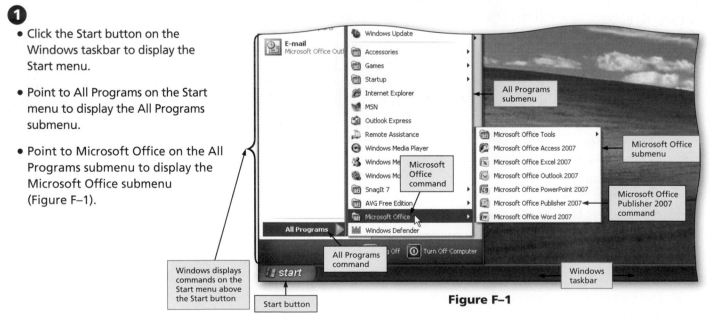

Figure F–1

2

- Click Microsoft Office Publisher 2007 to start Publisher and display the catalog (Figure F–2).

- If the Publisher window is not maximized, click the Maximize button next to the Close button on its title bar to maximize the window.

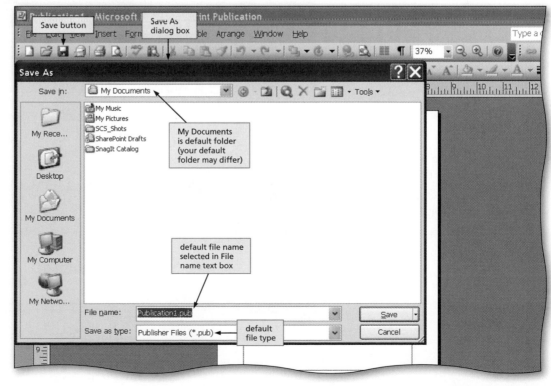

Figure F–2

Other Ways
1. Double-click Publisher icon on desktop, if one is present   2. Click Microsoft Office Publisher 2007 on Start menu

To Save a Document

After editing, you should save the document. The following steps save a document on a USB flash drive using the file name, Horseback Riding Lessons Flyer.

1

- With a USB flash drive connected to one of the computer's USB ports, click the Save button on the Standard Toolbar to display the Save As dialog box (Figure F–3).

Q&A

Do I have to save to a USB flash drive?

No. You can save to any device or folder. A **folder** is a specific location on a storage medium. You can save to the default folder or a different folder. You also can create your own folders, which is explained later in this book.

Figure F–3

2

- Type the name of your file (Horseback Riding Lessons Flyer in this example) in the File name text box to change the file name. Do not press the ENTER key after typing the file name (Figure F–4).

Q&A What characters can I use in a file name?

A file name can have a maximum of 255 characters, including spaces. The only invalid characters are the backslash (\), slash (/), colon (:), asterisk (*), question mark (?), quotation mark ("), less than symbol (<), greater than symbol (>), and vertical bar (|).

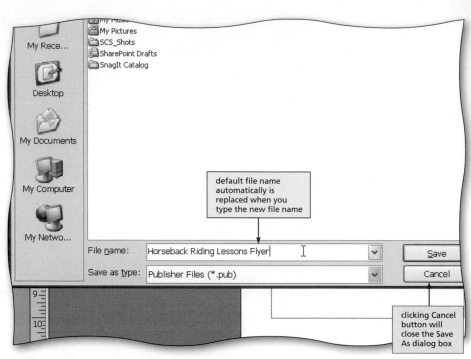

Figure F–4

3

- Click the Save in box arrow to display a list of available drives and folders (Figure F–5).

Q&A Why is my list of files, folders, and drives arranged and named differently from those shown in the figure?

Your computer's configuration determines how the list of files and folders is displayed and how drives are named. You can change the save location by clicking shortcuts on the **My Places bar**.

Q&A How do I save the file if I am not using a USB flash drive?

Use the same process, but be certain to select your device in the Save in list.

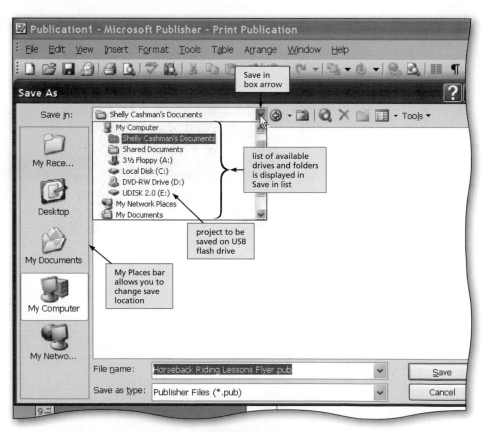

Figure F–5

4

- Click UDISK 2.0 (E:) in the Save in list to select the USB flash drive, Drive E in this case, as the new save location (Figure F–6).

- Click the Save button to save the document.

Q&A

What if my USB flash drive has a different name or letter?

It is very likely that your USB flash drive will have a different name and drive letter and be connected to a different port. Verify the device in your Save in list is correct.

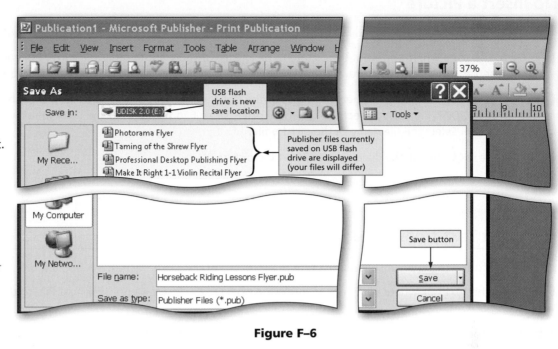

Figure F–6

Other Ways
1. On File menu, click Save, type file name, select drive or folder, click Save button   2. Press CTRL+S, type file name, select drive or folder, click Save button

To Open a Publication

The following steps open the Horseback Riding Lessons Flyer file from the USB flash drive.

1

- With your USB flash drive connected to one of the computer's USB ports, click File on the menu bar to display the File menu.

- Click Open on the File menu to display the Open Publication dialog box.

- If necessary, click the Look in box arrow and then click UDISK 2.0 (E:) to select the USB flash drive, Drive E in this case, in the Look in list as the new open location.

- Click Horseback Riding Lessons Flyer to select the file name (Figure F–7).

- Click the Open button to open the document.

Q&A

How do I open the file if I am not using a USB flash drive?

Use the same process, but be certain to select your device in the Look in list.

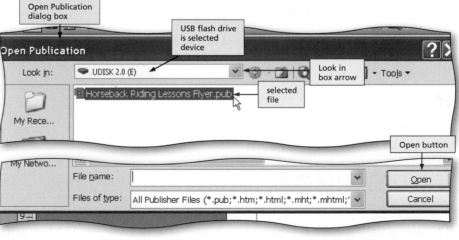

Figure F–7

Other Ways
1. On File menu, click file name in Recent Documents list
2. Press CTRL+O, select file name, press ENTER

To Insert a Picture

The following steps insert a picture, which, in this example, is located on a USB flash drive.

1 Go to the page where you want the picture to be located. If you want to replace a current picture, select the picture. On the Insert menu, point to Picture, and then click From File to display the Insert Picture dialog box.

2 With your USB flash drive connected to one of the computer's USB ports, if necessary, click the Look in box arrow and then click UDISK 2.0 (E:) to select the USB flash drive, Drive E in this case, in the Look in list as the device that contains the picture. Select the file name of the picture file.

3 Click the OK button in the dialog box to insert the picture.

To Insert Text from a File

The following steps insert text from a file located on the USB flash drive.

1 Select the text box where you want to insert the text. On the Insert menu, click Text File to display the Insert Text dialog box.

2 With your USB flash drive connected to one of the computer's USB ports, if necessary, click the Look in box arrow and then click UDISK 2.0 (E:) to select the USB flash drive, Drive E in this case, in the Look in list as the device that contains the file. Click to select the file name.

3 Click the OK button in the dialog box to insert the text.

To Import a Word Document

The following steps import a Word document from a file located on the USB flash drive.

1 Select the text box where you want to display the Word document. On the File menu, click Import Word Document to display the Import Word document dialog box.

2 With your USB flash drive connected to one of the computer's USB ports, if necessary, click the Look in box arrow and then click UDISK 2.0 (E:) to select the USB flash drive, Drive E in this case, in the Look in list as the device that contains the file. Click to select the file name.

3 Click the OK button to import the Word file into the selected text box.

To Publish to the Web

The following steps publish the current publication to the Web.

1 With a Web publication open in the Publisher workspace, on the File menu, click Publish to the Web to begin the process. If Publisher displays an information dialog box about Web hosting, click the OK button to display the Publish to the Web dialog box.

2 If necessary, click the Save in box arrow and then click My Network Places in the Save in list as the new open location.

3 Double-click the Web folder name in the Network Location list. If the Enter Network Password dialog box appears, type the user name and password in the respective text boxes and then click the OK button.

4 Click the Save button in the Publish to the Web dialog box.

Index

' (apostrophe), PUB 449
@ (at sign), PUB 49
* (asterisk), APP 30, PUB 32, PUB 425
\ (backslash), APP 30, PUB 32
: (colon), APP 30, PUB 32
" (double quotes), APP 30, PUB 32, PUB 164
... (ellipsis), PUB 16, PUB 43
/ (forward slash), APP 30, PUB 32
> (greater than symbol), APP 30, PUB 32
- (hyphen), PUB 164, PUB 236
< (less than symbol), APP 30, PUB 32
. (period), PUB 49
? (question mark), APP 30, PUB 32
" (quotation mark), PUB 32
| (vertical bar), APP 30, PUB 32

A

Access (Microsoft)
  described, **APP 5**
  Merge features and, PUB 325
additions, **PUB 44**
address lists, PUB 376, PUB 383
  connecting, to form letters, PUB 335–336
  described, PUB 325–332
Adobe Photoshop, PUB 184
Align or Distribute command, PUB 255
alignment, of text, PUB 46, PUB 47–48, PUB 180
alternative text, **PUB 406–407**
animated GIF, PUB 264, PUB 401–404
apostrophe ('), PUB 449
Apply Master Page task pane, PUB 198
asterisk (*), APP 30, PUB 32, PUB 425
at sign (@), PUB 49
Author text box, PUB 39
autoCorrect options, **PUB 164–167**
AutoCorrect Options button, PUB 164, PUB 165–166
AutoFit, **PUB 193**
autoflow
  described, **PUB 92**
  newsletters and, PUB 92–95
autoformatting, **PUB 164**
AutoRecover feature, PUB 157

AutoShapes
  business information sets and, PUB 264
  described, **PUB 187**, PUB 190–193
  editing, PUB 268–273
AutoShapes button, PUB 188
AutoShapes check box, PUB 187

B

Back button, PUB 16
background(s)
  described, **PUB 235**
  for e-mail, PUB 235–236
  sounds, **PUB 409**
backslash (\), APP 30, PUB 32
baseline guides, **PUB 14**, PUB 180
BeforeClose event, PUB 449–450
Best Fit option, PUB 193
bitmap format, **PUB 183**. *See also* graphics
blank publications
  business information sets and, PUB 246–247
  described, **PUB 246–247**
boldface text, PUB 46, PUB 173–274. *See also* fonts
bookmarks
  described, **PUB 399–400**
  going to, PUB 411
Bookmarks button, PUB 400
border styles, PUB 272
BorderArt button, PUB 272
Both Pages option, PUB 84
boundaries
  described, **PUB 14**
  hiding/displaying, PUB 14
brightness, **PUB 261**
brochure(s)
  AutoCorrect options, PUB 164–167
  benefits of, PUB 148–149
  checking, PUB 204
  described, **PUB 146**
  Format Painter and, PUB 167–169
  logos and, PUB 187–195
  mediums for, PUB 148–150
  options, PUB 150–152
  paragraphs in, formatting, PUB 180–182

photographs in, PUB 183–186
  publishing, PUB 145–224
  replacing text in, PUB 157–161
  saving, PUB 157, PUB 204
  sign-up forms, PUB 178–180
  templates, PUB 150, PUB 152, PUB 158–161
  two-page view, PUB 205
  watermarks and, PUB 196–198
browsers
  described, **APP 4**, PUB 53
  e-mail and, PUB 235
  previewing Web publications in, PUB 57
Bullet button, PUB 114
bulleted lists. *See also* lists
  described, **PUB 26–27**
  editing, PUB 114
  flyers and, PUB 26–27
  newsletters and, PUB 114
Bullets button, **PUB 26**
business cards, PUB 295–298, PUB 309–310
  described, **PUB 295**
  saving, PUB 300
  templates, PUB 295
business information set(s)
  automatic dates and, PUB 279–282
  creating, PUB 247–250
  Content Library and, PUB 282–284
  deleting, PUB 301–302
  described, **PUB 242–245**
  editing, PUB 247–250
  guidelines, PUB 244
  letterhead and, PUB 242–243, PUB 245–246, PUB 279–282, PUB 285, PUB 309–310
  multiple, PUB 250
  overview, PUB 241–312
  saving, PUB 250

C

calendars
  described, **PUB 365**
  inserting, PUB 365–367
  Merge features and, PUB 365–373
  resizing, PUB 367–369
Cancel button, PUB 41

Caption text box, PUB 109
captions
  deleting, PUB 108
  editing, PUB 106–110
catalog(s). *See also* catalog merge
  data sources, connecting to, PUB 258–259
  fields, PUB 360, PUB 261–262
  printing, PUB 372
  saving, PUB 373
catalog merge, PUB 314–315, PUB 372–373, PUB 379–380, PUB 383
  area, **PUB 358**
  described, **PUB 354–364**
  templates, **PUB 354–358**
Catalog Merge Layout toolbar, **PUB 260**
cell(s)
  calendars and, PUB 365–366
  described, **PUB 286–287**
  diagonals, **PUB 290–292**
  formatting, PUB 289–280
  merging, **PUB 290–292**
Center button, PUB 47, PUB 48
Change Page Size button, PUB 230
Change Picture command, PUB 107
Change Source button, PUB 476
character spacing, PUB 322–324, PUB 377
checkbox form control, **PUB 418**, PUB 419, PUB 427–430
clip(s). *See also* clip art; graphics
  collections, **PUB 34**
  described, **PUB 34**
clip art. *See also* clips; graphics
  brochures and, PUB 184
  described, **PUB 34**
  flyers and, PUB 34–37
  inserting, PUB 34–37, PUB 110–111, PUB 261
  Merge features and, PUB 320
  moving, PUB 112
  newsletters and, PUB 76, PUB 105–112
  resizing, PUB 109, 112
  ungrouping, PUB 265–266

Clip Art task pane, PUB 34–37, PUB 107, PUB 110–112, PUB 184, PUB 186, PUB 260, PUB 262–263, PUB 320
Clip Organizer, PUB 37
Clipboard (Office), PUB 95, **PUB 116**. *See also* Office
Clipboard (Windows system), **PUB 116**
Clipboard task pane; @ Paste Special command
Close button, PUB 5, PUB 16, PUB 17, PUB 41, PUB 43, PUB 52, PUB 57, PUB 156, PUB 205
Close command, PUB 41
Close Master View button, PUB 202
CMYK color model, **PUB 208–209**, PUB 215
code
  comments, PUB 449
  described, **PUB 386**
  statements, entering, PUB 449–450
  window, **PUB 447–450**
colon (:), APP 30, PUB 32
color. *See also* color schemes
  accent, PUB 154–155
  brochures and, PUB 152–157, PUB 187, PUB 190–191, PUB 193, PUB 201, PUB 207–208, PUB 218–219
  business information sets and, PUB 260
  CMYK, **PUB 208–209**, PUB 215
  digitizing, PUB 183
  fill, PUB 187, PUB 189–190, PUB 268, PUB 269–271
  font, PUB 174, PUB 193, PUB 277
  line, PUB 190–191, PUB 271–272
  logos and, PUB 187, PUB 189–190
  main, **PUB 153**
  -matching libraries, PUB 207, PUB 208, PUB 209
  models, PUB 208–209
  palettes, PUB 154–155, PUB 277
  Pantone, PUB 154, PUB 155, **PUB 208**
  printing, PUB 207–208
  RGB, PUB 155, PUB 207
  separations, PUB 208

shadow, PUB 273–274
  spot, PUB 208, PUB 218–219
  WordArt and, PUB 201
Color dialog box, PUB 155
Color Printing dialog box, PUB 209
color schemes. *See also* color
  brochures and, PUB 152–157, PUB 224
  business information sets and, PUB 250
  custom, PUB 152–157, PUB 224
  flyers and, PUB 6, PUB 9–10, PUB 63–64
  interactive Web sites and, PUB 390
  newsletters and, PUB 78–79, PUB 102
  saving, PUB 156–157
Colors and Lines tab, PUB 187
columns
  described, **PUB 325**
  Merge features and, PUB 325, PUB 327–329
Command sheet, **APP 27**
comments, **PUB 449**
Comments box, PUB 39
components
  data for, PUB 248
  described, **PUB 247**
  inserting/positioning, PUB 256–258
computer programming, **PUB 386**
Connect Frames toolbar, PUB 15
Connect Text Boxes toolbar, **PUB 16**
Connection Status button, APP 11–12
contact information, PUB 6, PUB 398
Content Library, PUB 298–298, PUB 414, PUB 416
  deleting content from, PUB 300–302
  described, **PUB 282–284**
continued notices
  described, **PUB 95–97**
  inserting, PUB 139–140
contrast, **PUB 261**
Convert to Web Publication command, PUB 51, PUB 53
copy and embed, PUB 468
copy and link, PUB 468
copy and paste
  described, **PUB 116**, PUB 119–120
  OLE and, PUB 468

Copy button, PUB 119
Create button, PUB 12, PUB 152
Create New Color dialog box,
    PUB 153–154
cropping, **PUB 262–264**
Custom tab, PUB 39
Customize dialog box, APP 24–27
cutting, **PUB 116**

D

Dash Style button, PUB 272
data
  labels, return, PUB 424
  merging, PUB 313–384
  sources, PUB 324, PUB 325,
    PUB 348
databases
  described, **APP 5**
  flyers and, PUB 18
  interactive Web sites and, PUB 436
  Merge features and, PUB 324
Date and Time dialog box,
    PUB 279–282
dates
  automatic, PUB 279–282
  for newsletters, PUB 87
DBMSs (database management
    systems), APP 5. *See also* databases
decimal tabs, **PUB 343–344**
Delete Object command, PUB 45,
    PUB 103, PUB 115
Delete Page dialog box, PUB 84
descriptions, **PUB 407**
Design Checker
  brochures and, PUB 204
  described, **PUB 51–53**
  e-mail and, PUB 236
  interactive Web sites and, PUB 452
  newsletters and, PUB 108, PUB 129
  running, PUB 51–52
Design Checker command, PUB 52
Design Checker task pane, PUB 52
Design Gallery, APP 6, PUB 187
  described, **PUB 116**
  forms and, PUB 418
  inserting pull quotes from,
    PUB 116–121

interactive Web sites and, PUB 386,
    PUB 392, PUB 394
  objects, inserting, PUB 399
Design Gallery Object button,
    PUB 116
desktop publishing. *See* DTP (desktop
    publishing programs)
destination, **PUB 466**
dictionary, PUB 29, PUB 30,
    PUB 126–129. *See also* spell
    checking
digital
  cameras, PUB 107
  printing, **PUB 208**
  signatures, PUB 452
digitizing, use of the term, **PUB 183**
dimmed commands, **PUB 16**
distribute alignment, of text, PUB 180
Do Not AutoFit option, PUB 193
document events, **PUB 446–447**
dotted lines, beneath text, PUB 20
double quotes ("), APP 30, PUB 32,
    PUB 164
drag-and-drop editing, **PUB 121–123**
drive(s). *See also* USB flash drives
  letters, PUB 33
  ports, PUB 33
drop caps, **PUB 320–322**
DTP (desktop publishing programs),
    APP 6, PUB 2, **PUB 74**. *See
    also* Microsoft Office Publisher
    (Microsoft)
duplex printing, **PUB 134–135**. *See
    also* printing

E

e-commerce
  described, **PUB 386**
  interactive Web sites and, PUB 386,
    PUB 464
electronic forms. *See* forms
ellipsis (...), **PUB 16**, PUB 43
embedding. *See also* OLE (object
    linking and embedding)
  described, **PUB 470–472**, PUB 480
  for the Web, PUB 472
e-mail
  attachments, **PUB 226**
  backgrounds, **PUB 235–236**

greetings, PUB 231
  headings, PUB 231
  hyperlinks and, PUB 48, PUB 49–50,
    PUB 233–234, PUB 237
  hyphenation, PUB 236
  marketing, **PUB 226**
  merge, **PUB 226**
  messages, creating, PUB 229–240
  newsletters, PUB 238–239, PUB 240
  overview, PUB 225–240
  page size, PUB 230
  saving, PUB 236
  sending, PUB 236–239
  templates, PUB 228–230
  text, editing, PUB 231–232
  transmitting print publications as,
    PUB 238–239
empty picture frame, **PUB 404**
end of field markers, PUB 24
Enter Network Password dialog box,
    APP 32
envelopes, PUB 351, PUB 353–354
EPS (Encapsulated PostScript) format,
    PUB 261
errors. *See also* Design Checker; spell
    checking
  brochures and, PUB 204, PUB 217
  business information sets and,
    PUB 294
  e-mail and, PUB 236
  flyers and, PUB 44–45
  interactive Web sites and, PUB 452
  newsletters and, PUB 76,
    PUB 126–129
event(s)
  BeforeClose event, PUB 449–450
  described, PUB 386
  document, **PUB 446–447**
  mouse-over, **PUB 439–440**
Excel (Microsoft). *See also* worksheets
  described, APP 5
  Merge features and, PUB 325
  OLE and, PUB 466–467,
    PUB 474–475, PUB 480
  starting, PUB 472–473
execute, use of the term, **PUB 386**
extensions, **PUB 183**
Extra Content task pane, **PUB 239**

F

Favorite Links section
  flyers and, PUB 32, PUB 41, PUB 52
  newsletters and, PUB 91
field(s)
  codes, inserting, PUB 338–343,
    PUB 351–352
  empty, PUB 343
  inserting, PUB 261–262, PUB 360
  spacing, PUB 377
file(s). *See also* file names
  described, **PUB 31**
  opening, APP 31
  read-only files, PUB 284
  saving, APP 29–31, PUB 31–33
file name(s)
  brochures and, PUB 157
  character restrictions for, APP 30,
    PUB 32
  described, **PUB 31**
  extensions, PUB 31
  interactive Web sites and,
    PUB 457–458
  newsletters and, PUB 104, PUB 132
  saving existing publications with the
    same, PUB 40
  Web pages and, PUB 412, PUB 413
fill
  color, PUB 187, PUB 189–190,
    PUB 268, PUB 269–271
  described, **PUB 268**
  effects, **PUB 268**
filters, **PUB 183**, PUB 337–338
Find and Replace feature,
    PUB 370–372
Find feature, **PUB 370–372**
flyer(s). *See also* tear-offs
  converting, to Web pages, PUB 51–57
  correcting errors in, PUB 44–45
  deleting elements of, PUB 28–29,
    PUB 44–45
  entering text in, PUB 18, PUB 19–20
  graphics and, PUB 28–29,
    PUB 34–37, PUB 65–68
  headlines, PUB 18–19, PUB 30
  hyperlinks in, PUB 49–50
  opening, PUB 41–43
  printing, PUB 6, PUB 13, PUB 40

publishing, PUB 3–72
  saving, PUB 31, PUB 40, PUB 52
  special characters and, PUB 24
Flyers button, PUB 7
folders. *See also* Web folders
  described, **APP 29**, PUB 31, PUB 55
  interactive Web sites and,
    PUB 452–453
  saving files in, APP 29–31,
    PUB 31–33
Folders list, PUB 31, PUB 42
font(s). *See also* font schemes;
    styles; text
  brochures and, PUB 151,
    PUB 162–164, PUB 169–178,
    PUB 210
  changing, PUB 46
  character spacing and, PUB 322–324
  color, PUB 174, PUB 193, PUB 277
  effects, **PUB 176–178**
  embedding, **PUB 210–212**, PUB 323
  flyers and, PUB 6, PUB 46–48,
    PUB 63–64
  formatting, PUB 176–180
  Merge features and, PUB 352
  newsletters and, PUB 86, PUB 96,
    PUB 99
  printing and, PUB 210
  size, PUB 46–48, PUB 63–64,
    PUB 101, PUB 174
  Word and, PUB 99
Font button, PUB 174
Font dialog box, PUB 174
font scheme(s). *See also* fonts
  brochures and, PUB 151,
    PUB 162–163, PUB 169
  business information sets and,
    PUB 250
  described, **PUB 9**, PUB 390
  newsletters and, PUB 80
  options, PUB 169
  selecting, PUB 10–11
Font Size button, PUB 48
Font Size box, PUB 47–48, PUB 101
form(s). *See also* form controls
  described, **PUB 386**
  options, **PUB 150**
  Order, **PUB 150**

properties, **PUB 439**
  Response, **PUB 150**
  sign-up, PUB 178–180
  testing, PUB 443–446, PUB 453
form control(s). *See also* fonts
  described, **PUB 386**
  overview, PUB 418–419
  properties, **PUB 418**, PUB 424–427,
    PUB 429–436
  saving publications with completed,
    PUB 442
  working with, PUB 455–456
form letters. *See also* letterhead
  connecting address lists to,
    PUB 335–336
  creating, PUB 333–334
  described, **PUB 314**
  Merge features and, PUB 378–379,
    PUB 383
  printing and, PUB 348–350
  saving, PUB 347
Format Painter
  described, **PUB 167**
  brochures and, PUB 167–169
Format Painter button, PUB 168
Format Publication task pane,
    PUB 16–17, PUB 82, PUB 153–154,
    PUB 156, PUB 230
Format Text Box dialog box, PUB 96
Format WordArt dialog box, PUB 202
formatting marks. *See also* special
    characters
  described, PUB 24
  displaying, PUB 24, PUB 81
  hiding/displaying, PUB 99, PUB 229
  newsletters and, PUB 81, PUB 99
  Word and, PUB 99
Formatting toolbar, PUB 16,
    PUB 47–48
forward slash (/), APP 30, PUB 32
Forward button, PUB 16
Fox Pro (Microsoft), PUB 325
FTP (File Transfer Protocol)
  described, **APP 19**
  sites, APP 20
  using, APP 20
functions, **PUB 449**

G

animated GIFs, PUB 264,
   PUB 401–404
Go button, PUB 37, PUB 184,
   PUB 186
Go To Page feature, **PUB 401**
gradient fill, PUB 274–277
grammar checkers, PUB 98
graphic(s). *See also* logos; photographs
 animated GIFs, PUB 264,
   PUB 401–404
 brochures and, PUB 183–195
 business information sets and,
   PUB 245, PUB 248–249,
   PUB 262–268
 creating, PUB 187–195
 cropping, PUB 262–264
 deleting, PUB 28–29, PUB 103,
   PUB 268
 editing, PUB 260–261, PUB 306
 e-mail and, PUB 227, PUB 234–235
 finding appropriate, PUB 34
 flipping, PUB 403
 flyers and, PUB 28–29, PUB 34–37,
   PUB 65–68
 formats, PUB 183
 in headers and footers, PUB 125
 importing, PUB 106–109
 inserting, APP 32, PUB 184
 interactive Web sites and,
   PUB 401–405, PUB 456–457
 moving, PUB 112
 newsletters and, PUB 103–112
 outlines, **PUB 264**
 re-coloring, **PUB 260–261**
 rectangular, PUB 274–277
 replacing, PUB 106–109, PUB 186
 resizing, PUB 35, PUB 108,
   PUB 112, PUB 263
 saving, PUB 267–268
 selecting, PUB 104
 static, **PUB 404–405**
 wrapping text around, PUB 185
Graphics Manager command,
   PUB 107
Graphics Manager task pane,
   PUB 107

gray lines, display of, instead of text,
   PUB 101
greater than symbol (>), APP 30,
   PUB 32
gridlines, **PUB 292**
Group Objects button, PUB 296
guide(s)
 creating, PUB 419
 grid, **PUB 14**
 hiding/displaying, PUB 14
 -lines, overview, APP 1–2
 types of, **PUB 14**

H

hard copy, PUB 40. *See also* printing
headers and footers
 accessing, PUB 125
 described, **PUB 124–125**
 newsletters and, PUB 124–125
headings
 editing, PUB 393
 for e-mail, PUB 231
 interactive Web sites and, PUB 393,
   PUB 410, PUB 414
headlines
 described, **PUB 19**, PUB 89
 editing, PUB 89–91
 replacing, PUB 97
 spell checking, PUB 30
help. *See also* Help window
 accessing, APP 10–11, APP 17,
   PUB 58
 described, **APP 7**, APP 9–18,
   PUB 58–60
 links, APP 15
 search features, APP 11–18
 Table of Contents, APP 13, APP 16
 toolbar buttons, APP 12–13
Help window, **APP 7**, APP 10–17,
   PUB 58–60. *See also* help
hide sensitive text with asterisks
   option, PUB 425
home pages. *See also* Web pages;
   Web sites
 described, **PUB 389**
 editing, PUB 392–399
Home button, APP 15, APP 16

hot spots, PUB 439–440
HTML (HyperText Markup
   Language). *See also* Web pages;
   Web sites
 code fragments, **PUB 440–442**,
   PUB 460–461
 described, **PUB 55**, PUB 389
 -enabled e-mail, **PUB 226**
 format, **PUB 55**, PUB 410
 hot spots and, PUB 439–440
 interactive Web sites and,
   PUB 388–389, PUB 407, PUB 410,
   PUB 440–446, PUB 460–461
 publishing to the Web and,
   PUB 55–56
 raw, editing, PUB 440
 testing, PUB 443–446
hyperlinks. *See also* URLs (Uniform
   Resource Locators)
 creating, PUB 233–234
 described, PUB 49
 editing, PUB 233–234
 e-mail and, PUB 233–234, PUB 237
 inserting, PUB 49–50
 interactive Web sites and,
   PUB 460–461
 testing, PUB 443–446
hyphen (-), PUB 164, PUB 236
Hyphenation dialog box, PUB 236

I

Ignore button, PUB 127
Ignore Master Page command,
   PUB 196
illustration software, PUB 184
image setters, PUB 208
images. *See* graphics
importing
 described, **PUB 89**, PUB 325
 graphics, PUB 106–109
 newsletter text, PUB 88–89,
   PUB 92–95, PUB 97
indent(s)
 described, **PUB 180**, PUB 343
 hanging, PUB 347
 Merge features and, PUB 343–347
Insert Hyperlink button, PUB 50,
   PUB 233

Insert Hyperlink dialog box, **PUB 49–50**, PUB 233
Insert Object button, PUB 118
Insert Page command, PUB 414–415
Insert Picture dialog box, APP 32
Insert Table button, PUB 286
insertion points
  deleting text and, PUB 85
  described, **PUB 18**
  flyers and, PUB 18, PUB 24
  word wrap and, PUB 24
interactive Web sites. *See also*
    Web sites
  contact information for, PUB 398
  created from scratch, PUB 414–416
  described, **PUB 386**
  guidelines, **PUB 388**
  options, setting, PUB 407–409
  overview, PUB 385–464
  previewing, PUB 443–446
  saving, PUB 410, PUB 452
  testing, PUB 443–446, PUB 453
internal data labels, **PUB 418**
Internet Explorer (Microsoft),
    PUB 55. *See also* browsers
intranets, **APP 4**
ISPs (Internet Service Providers),
    PUB 436
italicized text, PUB 46, PUB 175. *See
    also* fonts

J

JPEG (Joint Photographic Expert
    Group) file format, PUB 183. *See
    also* graphics; photographs
jump lines
  described, **PUB 92**
  newsletters and, PUB 92, PUB 97
justified alignment, of text, PUB 180

K

Keep Text Only command, PUB 120
kerning, **PUB 322–324**
keyboard shortcuts, **PUB 16**
keyword(s)
  described, **PUB 38**, PUB 407–408

meta tags and, PUB 407–408
  properties and, **PUB 38**, PUB 39
Keywords text box, PUB 39

L

labels
  creating, PUB 350–352
  described, **PUB 419–421**
  interactive Web sites and,
    PUB 419–421
  printing, PUB 352–353
  templates, PUB 351
landscape orientation, **PUB 109**
layering, PUB 278–279
layout
  business cards and, PUB 295–296
  business information sets and,
    PUB 251–254, PUB 295–296
  described, **PUB 295**
  guides, **PUB 14**
leader tabs, **PUB 344**
less than symbol (<), APP 30, PUB 32
letterhead. *See also* form letters
  business information sets and,
    PUB 242–246, PUB 279–282,
    PUB 285, PUB 309–310
  described, **PUB 245**
  Merge features and, PUB 317
  saving, PUB 282
  templates, PUB 317
  text boxes and, PUB 318–319
  using, PUB 285
letters. *See* form letters; letterhead
libraries, color, PUB 207, PUB 208,
    PUB 209
line(s)
  border styles, PUB 272–273
  color, **PUB 271–272**
  dotted, beneath text, PUB 20
  editing, PUB 190–192
  gray, display of, instead of text,
    PUB 101
  inserting blank, PUB 25
  jump, PUB 92, PUB 97
  logos and, PUB 190–192
  selecting, PUB 104
  spacing, **PUB 180–182**
  WordArt and, PUB 201

Line Spacing button, PUB 180
Line/Border button, **PUB 272**
linking. *See also* hyperlinks; OLE
    (object linking and embedding)
  described, PUB 474
  worksheets and publications,
    PUB 474–475
links. *See* hyperlinks
list box form controls, **PUB 418–419**,
    PUB 433–436
List Builder (Microsoft), PUB 325
lists, PUB 18, PUB 26–27. *See also*
    bulleted lists; list box form controls
logo(s). *See also* graphics
  brochures and, PUB 156,
    PUB 187–189, PUB 195, PUB 224
  business information sets and,
    PUB 248–249
  copying, PUB 194
  creating, PUB 187–195
  deleting, PUB 28–29, PUB 416
  described, **PUB 187**, PUB 234
  e-mail and, PUB 227, PUB 234–235
  editing, PUB 234
  formatting, PUB 187
  interactive Web sites and, PUB 416
  newsletters and, PUB 103
  positioning, PUB 195
  resizing, PUB 195
  shapes for, PUB 187–189

M

Macintosh, PUB 212
macros, PUB 453, PUB 464
  described, **PUB 446–447**
  enabled/disabled, **PUB 450–451**
Mail Merge task pane, **PUB 335–336**,
    PUB 349
margin(s)
  business information sets and,
    PUB 250–254, PUB 259
  changing, PUB 251–252
  e-mail and, PUB 238–239
  guides, **PUB 14**
  word wrap and, PUB 24–27
markers
  described, **PUB 343**
  Merge features and, PUB 343–347

master pages
  accessing, PUB 196–198
  closing, PUB 202
  described, **PUB 196**
  multiple, PUB 198
mastheads, PUB 85–88, PUB 139–140,
    PUB 393
  creating, PUB 141
  described, **PUB 85**
Maximize button, PUB 5, PUB 41
memory
  brochures and, PUB 206
  newsletters and, PUB 98, PUB 101
  printer, PUB 206
menu(s)
  bars, **PUB 15–16**
  customizing, APP 23–24
  described, **PUB 16**
  names, **PUB 16**
  resetting, APP 27, PUB 16
  short, displaying, APP 27
  sub-, **PUB 16**
Merge features. *See also* merging
  address lists and, PUB 325–332,
    PUB 335–336, PUB 376, PUB 383
  calendars and, PUB 365–373
  catalogs and, PUB 314–315,
    PUB 354–364, PUB 372–373,
    PUB 379–380, PUB 383
  field codes and, PUB 338–343
  guidelines, PUB 316
  labels and, PUB 350–352
  overview, PUB 313–384
  printing documents and,
    PUB 348–350
  saving merged files and,
    PUB 364–365
merging. *See also* Merge features
  data into publications, PUB 324–343
  described, **PUB 324**
message boxes, PUB 449
Measurement toolbar, **PUB 298–299**
meta tags, **PUB 407–409**
metadata, **PUB 38**
Microsoft Access
  described, **APP 5**
  Merge features and, PUB 325
Microsoft Excel. *See also* worksheets
  described, **APP 5**
  Merge features and, PUB 325

OLE and, PUB 466–467,
    PUB 474–475, PUB 480
  starting, PUB 472–473
Microsoft Internet Explorer, PUB 55.
    See also browsers
Microsoft Office 2007. *See also specific
    applications*
  described, **APP 3–8**
  collaboration with, APP 4, APP 7–8
  Professional Edition, **APP 3**
Microsoft Office Publisher
    (Microsoft). *See also specific topics*
  described, **APP 6**, PUB 2
  quitting, PUB 41, PUB 60, PUB 135
  starting, PUB 4–5, PUB 6
  workspace, **PUB 13–15**
Microsoft Outlook
  described, **APP 6**
  Merge features and, PUB 325
Microsoft Office Online Web page,
    APP 6, PUB 9, PUB 37, PUB 183
Microsoft PowerPoint, **APP 6**
Microsoft SharePoint, **APP 7–8**
Microsoft SharePoint Server, APP 7
Microsoft SharePoint Services, APP 7
Microsoft Visual Basic for Applications
    (VBA), **PUB 386**, PUB 446–451,
    PUB 462–463
Microsoft Windows Vista, APP 21–22,
    APP 28–32
  quitting Publisher with, PUB 41,
    PUB 60, PUB 135
  starting Publisher with, PUB 4–5,
    PUB 6, PUB 41–43
  Web folders and, PUB 55
Microsoft Windows XP, APP 28–32
  opening files with, APP 31
  saving files with, APP 29–31
Microsoft Word
  described, **APP 4–5**
  documents, importing, APP 32
  interactive Web sites and,
    PUB 397–398
  Merge features and, PUB 325
  newsletters and, PUB 89,
    PUB 98–101
monospacing, **PUB 322–323**
mouse pointers
  described, **PUB 18**
  saving files and, PUB 33

mouse-over events, **PUB 439–440**
MsgBox function, **PUB 449**

N

navigation bars
  described, PUB 389
  editing, PUB 394–396
  flyers and, PUB 54
Navigation pane, PUB 31
New Publication task pane, PUB 41
newsletter(s)
  analysis, PUB 142
  benefits of, PUB 77
  continued notices and, PUB 95–97
  described, **PUB 74**
  designing, PUB 73–144
  drafts, PUB 76, PUB 106
  editing, PUB 82–88
  graphics and, PUB 103–112
  importing text for, PUB 88–89
  mastheads, PUB 85–88
  moving text in, PUB 121–123
  pagination, PUB 82–85
  saving, PUB 104–105
  selecting text or objects in, PUB 104
  two-sided, PUB 134–135
Newsletter Date text box, PUB 87
newspaper advertisements, PUB 70
None wrapping style, **PUB 185**
nonprinting characters. *See*
    formatting marks
Notepad, PUB 325
notices, continued
  described, **PUB 95–97**
  inserting, PUB 139–140

O

object(s). *See also* OLE (object linking
    and embedding)
  brochures and, PUB 157, PUB 196,
    PUB 198–199, PUB 216
  deleting, PUB 28–29, PUB 115,
    PUB 157, PUB 297
  described, **PUB 15**
  editing, PUB 410–413, PUB 416
  flyers and, PUB 15, PUB 28–29
  handles, **PUB 15**
  inserting, PUB 198–199, PUB 399
  margins and, PUB 253

moving, PUB 111–115, PUB 196

nudging, **PUB 196**

positioning, PUB 299

resizing, PUB 15, PUB 111–115, PUB 397

rotating/flipping, **PUB 265–266**

selecting, PUB 15, PUB 104, PUB 296–298

ungrouping, PUB 108

Object Position box, **PUB 15**

Object Size box, **PUB 15**

Objects toolbar, **PUB 16**, PUB 45, PUB 46

OCR (optical character recognition)
address fonts, PUB 352

described, **PUB 352**

Office Clipboard, PUB 95, **PUB 116**. *See also* Office Clipboard task pane

Office Clipboard task pane. *See also* Office Clipboard
described, **PUB 116**

moving text and, PUB 121–123

OLE (object linking and embedding). *See also* objects
described, **PUB 466**

guidelines, PUB 468–469

overview, PUB 465–480

Open button, APP 31, PUB 43

Open command, PUB 42

Open Publication dialog box, APP 31

option button form control, PUB 418–419, PUB 430–432

Order command, PUB 278

order forms, PUB 150, PUB 459–450. *See also* forms

ordering, **PUB 278–279**

orphans, **PUB 183**

OSE (Office Server Extensions), APP 19

Other Task Panes button, PUB 16

outlines, for graphics, **PUB 264**

Outlook (Microsoft)
described, **APP 6**

Merge features and, PUB 325

overflow area, PUB 95

P

Pack and Go Wizard, PUB 129, **PUB 210–212**, PUB 224

page(s)
changing, PUB 83–84

continuing newsletter stories across, PUB 92–97

deleting, PUB 83–84, PUB 356

inserting, PUB 85

layout, **PUB 13–14**

master, PUB 196–198, PUB 202

numbers, PUB 124–125

renaming, PUB 83

size, PUB 149, **PUB 150**, PUB 230, PUB 238–239

sorter, **PUB 15**

titles, PUB 394, PUB 457–458

Page command, PUB 85

Page Options button, PUB 121

Page Setup dialog box, PUB 251–252

Page Up button, PUB 205

pamphlets. *See* brochures

Pantone color system, PUB 154, PUB 155, **PUB 208**

paper
blade-coated, **PUB 207**

glossy, **PUB 207**

linen, **PUB 207**

stock, PUB 224

20 lb. bond, **PUB 207**

types of, PUB 207

paragraph(s). *See also* text
beginning new, PUB 24

bulleted lists and, PUB 26–27

described, **PUB 180**

formatting, PUB 180–182

marks, PUB 24, PUB 229

orphans and, PUB 183

selecting, PUB 104

spacing, PUB 180–181

widows and, PUB 183

Paragraph dialog box, PUB 183

passwords, APP 32, PUB 425

Paste button, PUB 119

Paste Options button, PUB 116, PUB 117–121, PUB 120

Paste Special command, PUB 466, PUB 475, PUB 480

pasting, **PUB 116**

path, **PUB 355**

patterns, **PUB 268**

PDF (Portable Document Format), PUB 229

period (.), PUB 49

Personalization window, APP 22

photographs, PUB 183–186. *See also* graphics

Photoshop (Adobe), PUB 184

picture
frames, **PUB 34**

fills, **PUB 268**

PIM (personal information management) programs, **APP 6**

pixels, PUB 272

placeholder text, PUB 19, PUB 22, PUB 86. *See also* text
brochures and, PUB 156–161

newsletters and, PUB 89–91

plagiarism, PUB 88

PNG (Portable Network Graphics), PUB 267

points, **PUB 47**

portrait orientation, **PUB 109**

PostScript
described, **PUB 212**

dumps (Encapsulated PostScript), PUB 212

PowerPoint (Microsoft), **APP 6**

PPD (PostScript printer drivers), **PUB 212**

preflight checks, **PUB 212**

prepress tasks, **PUB 212**

Print button, PUB 40, PUB 134

Print command, PUB 135

Print dialog box, PUB 206

Print Preview button, PUB 205

print publications, converting, to Web publications, PUB 53–54

Print Setup dialog box, **PUB 352–353**

printer(s). *See also* printing
commercial, PUB 224

drivers, PUB 212

orientation settings, PUB 109

PostScript and, PUB 212

printing. *See also* printers
area, **PUB 250–251**

black-and-white, **PUB 208**

brochures and, PUB 148–149, PUB 154, PUB 205–212, PUB 224

business cards, PUB 300

catalogs, PUB 372
commercial, PUB 224, PUB 464
considerations, PUB 206–208
digital, **PUB 208**
envelopes, PUB 353–354
flyers, PUB 6, PUB 13, PUB 40
fonts and, PUB 323
four-color, **PUB 208**
graphics, PUB 261
letters, PUB 294
Merge features and, PUB 348–350,
    PUB 352–353, PUB 372
multiple copies, PUB 40
newsletters, PUB 76, PUB 78,
    PUB 134–135
offset, PUB 208
overview, PUB 206–209
Pantone color system and, PUB 154
plates, PUB 208
previewing before, PUB 205
process-color, **PUB 208**
services, packaging publications for,
    PUB 210–212
tools, choosing, PUB 208–209
printouts, **PUB 40**. *See also* printing
programs, **PUB 386**
project planning
  brochures, PUB 147–148
  flyers and, PUB 2–PUB 4
  overview, APP 1–2
  newsletters and, PUB 76
proofreading, PUB 40, PUB 126–129
  brochures and, PUB 148, PUB 196
  described, **PUB 126**
  newsletters and, PUB 76, PUB 126
properties. *See also* tags
  automatically updated, **PUB 38**
  changing, PUB 38–39
  described, **PUB 18**, PUB 38–39
  flyers and, PUB 18, PUB 32,
    PUB 38–39
  form control, PUB 418,
    PUB 424–427, PUB 429–436
  newsletters and, PUB 131–132
  standard, **PUB 38**
Properties dialog box, PUB 38–39
proportional spacing, **PUB 322–323**
.pub file extension, PUB 31

publication(s). *See also* Web
    publications
  closing, PUB 57
  main, **PUB 324**
  merging, PUB 313–384
  opening, PUB 41–43, PUB 285
  options, PUB 9–13
  packaging, for printing services,
    PUB 210–212
  properties, **PUB 38–39**
  saving, PUB 31–33, PUB 40
  setting up, for printing,
    PUB 206–208
  types, **PUB 6**
Publish to Web feature, APP 19–20,
    APP 32, **PUB 55–56**, PUB 452
Publisher (Microsoft). *See* Microsoft
    Office Publisher (Microsoft)
Publisher Tasks task pane,
    PUB 129–132
Publisher Tasks toolbar, **PUB 16**
Publisher window, **PUB 13–16**
pull quotes, **PUB 105**, PUB 116–121,
    PUB 411–412
Pull Quotes button, PUB 117

Q

question mark (?), APP 30, PUB 32
quitting Publisher, PUB 41, PUB 60,
    PUB 135, PUB 284
quotes
  double ("), APP 30, PUB 32,
    PUB 164
  smart, PUB 164

R

raised dot, PUB 24
read-only files, PUB 284
Rearrange Commands dialog box,
    APP 25–26
refresh rates, PUB 101
Rename command, PUB 83
Rename Master Page button, PUB 198
repeatable area, PUB 358
reset button, **PUB 418**, PUB 438
resolution
  of graphics, PUB 272–273, PUB 401
  screen, APP 21–23, PUB 4, PUB 15,
    PUB 78, PUB 149

Response forms, **PUB 150**
resumes, PUB 384
return data labels, **PUB 418**
revision tracking, PUB 98
RGB (red green blue) color model,
    PUB 155, PUB 207
ruler guides
  business information sets and,
    PUB 250–254
  described, **PUB 253–254**
rulers, **PUB 14**

S

sans serif font, **PUB 323**
Save As command, PUB 33, PUB 157
  e-mail and, PUB 236
  flyers and, PUB 31, PUB 32–33,
    PUB 40, PUB 52
  newsletters and, PUB 104–105
Save button, APP 32, PUB 31,
    PUB 33, PUB 40, PUB 52,
    PUB 105, PUB 133, PUB 156,
    PUB 157, PUB 236
scaling, **PUB 322–323**, PUB 260
scanners, PUB 34, PUB 107
scratch
  area, **PUB 187**
  creating Web pages from,
    PUB 414–416
screen resolution, APP 21–23, PUB 4,
    PUB 15, PUB 78, PUB 149
ScreenTips, **PUB 16**, PUB 43
scroll bars, **PUB 14**
scroll boxes, **PUB 14**
scrolling marquees, **PUB 440–441**
Search button, APP 11–12, APP 14
secondary pages, **PUB 389**
security
  interactive Web sites and, PUB 388,
    PUB 425, PUB 450–451
  levels, PUB 450–451
  passwords, APP 32, PUB 425
Select Objects button, **PUB 296–298**
Send E-Mail command, PUB 236–237
serif font, **PUB 323**
servers, APP 7, APP 19–20, PUB 453
shades, **PUB 268**
shadows, **PUB 273–274**
SharePoint (Microsoft), **APP 7–8**

SharePoint Server (Microsoft), APP 7

SharePoint Services (Microsoft), APP 7

shortcut menus, PUB 18

Show/Hide button, PUB 99

Shrink Text On Overflow option, PUB 193

sidebar(s)
deleting, PUB 115
described, **PUB 105**
editing, PUB 113–114
tables, PUB 115

sign-up forms, **PUB 150**, PUB 178–180

smart
quotes, PUB 164
tags, PUB 20, PUB 87

snapping, **PUB 255–256**

sounds, background, PUB 409

source files, locating, PUB 476

special characters. *See also* formatting marks; special characters (listed by name)
file names and, APP 30, PUB 32
hiding/displaying, PUB 24, PUB 99
newsletters and, PUB 81

special characters (listed by name). *See also* special characters
' (apostrophe), PUB 449
* (asterisk), APP 30, PUB 32, PUB 425
@ (at sign), PUB 49
\ (backslash), APP 30, PUB 32
: (colon), APP 30, PUB 32
" (double quotes), APP 30, PUB 32, PUB 164
... (ellipsis), PUB 16, PUB 43
/ (forward slash), APP 30, PUB 32
> (greater than symbol), APP 30, PUB 32
- (hyphen), PUB 164, PUB 236
< (less than symbol), APP 30, PUB 32
. (period), PUB 49
? (question mark), APP 30, PUB 32
" (quotation mark), PUB 32
| (vertical bar), APP 30, PUB 32

Special Characters button, PUB 24, PUB 81, PUB 153

Special Paper command, PUB 13

spell checking, PUB 307, PUB 452. *See also* errors
brochures and, PUB 199, PUB 204
described, **PUB 29–30**
e-mail and, PUB 236
flyers and, PUB 20, PUB 29–30, PUB 66–67
newsletters and, PUB 126–129
WordArt and, PUB 199

Spelling button, PUB 127, PUB 204, PUB 236

Spelling command, PUB 127

Spelling Options dialog box, PUB 30

Square wrapping style, **PUB 185**

Standard toolbar, PUB 15, **PUB 16**, PUB 40, PUB 81

Start button, PUB 5, PUB 41

starting Publisher, APP 28–32, PUB 4–5, PUB 6, PUB 41–43

status bar, **PUB 15**

story, use of the term, **PUB 89**

straight quotes, PUB 164

styles. *See also* fonts
applying, PUB 162–164, PUB 167, PUB 175
borders and, PUB 272
brochures and, PUB 162–164, PUB 167–175
creating, PUB 169–175
custom, PUB 169–175
described, **PUB 162**
wrapping, **PUB 185**

Styles task pane, PUB 171–172

Subject text box, PUB 39, PUB 50

Submit button, **PUB 418–419**, PUB 436–438, PUB 445

submit form control, **PUB 436–448**

subscripts, **PUB 176**

superscripts, **PUB 176**

synchronization, PUB 27, PUB 158, PUB 161

T

tab(s)
described, **PUB 343**
Merge features and, PUB 343–347
selectors, **PUB 343**
stop(s), PUB 345
stop markers, **PUB 343–347**

table(s)
creating, PUB 286–287
described, **PUB 286–287**
editing, PUB 304–305
entering data in, PUB 292–293
formatting, PUB 289–280
Merge features and, PUB 325
selecting within, PUB 287–288

tags. *See also* HTML (HyperText Markup Language)
described, **PUB 32**, PUB 131
newsletters and, PUB 131–133
smart, PUB 20, PUB 87

task panes. *See also specific task panes*
closing, PUB 17–18
described, **PUB 16–17**

Tasks and Formatting toolbar, PUB 15

tear-offs, PUB 3, PUB 11–12
deleting, PUB 44–45
described, **PUB 27**
entering text for, PUB 18, PUB 27–28

template(s)
brochures and, PUB 150, PUB 152, PUB 158–161
business card, PUB 295
catalog merge, PUB 354–358
choosing, PUB 78–81
clip art and, PUB 34–37
creating, PUB 129–133
described, **PUB 6–8**
downloading, PUB 9
e-mail and, PUB 228–230, PUB 238
editing, PUB 82–85, PUB 113–114
flyers and, PUB 3–4, PUB 6–8, PUB 11–12, PUB 19–20, PUB 34–37
label, PUB 351
letterhead, PUB 317
newsletters and, PUB 74–81, PUB 113–114, PUB 129–133, PUB 141
options, PUB 6–8
previewing, PUB 7–8
types of text in, PUB 19–20
Web site, PUB 390–382

text. *See also* fonts; styles; text boxes
aligning, PUB 46, PUB 47–48, PUB 180
alternative, PUB 406–407

area form control, **PUB 418**,
  PUB 425–427
AutoShapes and, PUB 192–193
captions, PUB 106–110
character spacing and, PUB 322–324,
  PUB 377
deleting, PUB 28–29
deselecting, PUB 123
entering, PUB 18–20, PUB 25,
  APP 32
finding and replacing, PUB 370–372
headlines, PUB 19, PUB 30,
  PUB 89–91, PUB 97
importing, PUB 88–89, PUB 92–95,
  PUB 97
moving, PUB 121–123
replacing, PUB 157–161
selecting, PUB 104
word wrap, PUB 24–27, PUB 108,
  PUB 185
text box(s). *See also* textbox form
  controls
brochures and, PUB 158–163,
  PUB 166, PUB 178–179, PUB 204
creating, PUB 166
deleting, PUB 178–179
described, **PUB 18**, PUB 419
editing, PUB 318–319, PUB 417
e-mail and, PUB 232
flyers and, PUB 18–20, PUB 59–60
help resources for, APP 13–15,
  PUB 59–60
inserting/positioning, PUB 45–48,
  PUB 162–163, PUB 256–259
interactive Web sites and,
  PUB 397–398, PUB 417
linked, **PUB 89**, PUB 93–95
Merge features and, PUB 318–319,
  PUB 357, PUB 363
notices and, PUB 96–97
transparent, PUB 204
using, PUB 18–20
Text Box button, **PUB 45–46**,
  PUB 162, PUB 166
Text Box tab, PUB 96
textbox form controls. *See also*
  text boxes
described, **PUB 418**
inserting, PUB 422–423
Text Overflow symbol, **PUB 95**

Text Wrapping button, PUB 185
textures
  business information sets and,
    PUB 268, PUB 277
  described, **PUB 268**
Through wrapping style, **PUB 185**
tints, **PUB 268**
toggle, **PUB 89**
toolbar(s). *See also specific toolbars*
  buttons, PUB 15, PUB 260
  creating, APP 25
  customizing, APP 23–24, PUB 15
  described, **PUB 15–16**
  docked, **PUB 16**
  editing, APP 25–26
  floating, **PUB 16**
  hiding, PUB 255
  resetting, PUB 16, APP 23–24
  rows, PUB 15
Toolbar Options button, PUB 15
Top and bottom wrapping style,
  PUB 185
track kerning, **PUB 322–323**
tracking, **PUB 322–323**
t-shirts, printing, PUB 208

U

underlined text, PUB 29, PUB 46
Undo Automatic Capitalization
  option, PUB 166
Undo button, PUB 84, PUB 123,
  PUB 161
Undo Font Schemes option, PUB 161
Undo Update Fields button, PUB 161
Ungroup Objects button, PUB 108
URLs (Uniform Resource Locators),
  PUB 165–166, PUB 443–446. *See
  also* hyperlinks
USB flash drives. *See also* drives
  brochures and, PUB 157,
    PUB 210–212
  e-mail and, PUB 236
  flyers and, PUB 31–33, PUB 42,
    PUB 52, PUB 55
  newsletters and, PUB 91, PUB 93,
    PUB 104–105, PUB 131
  Windows XP and, APP 29–32
user names, APP 32

V

variables, PUB 324
VBA (Visual Basic for Applications),
  PUB 386, PUB 446–451,
  PUB 462–463
VBA Code Window, PUB 447–450
vertical bar (|), APP 30, PUB 32
viruses, **PUB 34**, PUB 450
visitor counters, PUB 442
Visual Basic Editor, **PUB 447–450**
Visual Basic for Applications
  (Microsoft), **PUB 386**,
  PUB 446–451, PUB 462–463

W

watermarks
  creating, PUB 196–198
  described, **PUB 196**
  removing, PUB 203
Web folders. *See also* folders
  creating, APP 19
  described, **APP 19**, PUB 55
  flyers and, PUB 55–56
  publishing Web pages with,
    APP 19–20
  saving to, APP 19
  Windows XP and, APP 32
Web mail, **PUB 238**
Web mode, **PUB 53**
Web offset printing, **PUB 208**
Web page(s). *See also* Web
  publications; Web sites
  converting flyers to, PUB 51–57
  creating, PUB 51–57
  file names and, PUB 412, PUB 413
  inserting new, PUB 414–416
  options, PUB 407–409
  publishing, APP 19–20, APP 32,
    PUB 55–56, PUB 452
  renaming, PUB 417
Web Page Preview button, PUB 57
Web publications. *See also*
  publications; Web pages
  described, **PUB 53**
  converting print publications to,
    PUB 53
  previewing, PUB 55–57
  publishing, PUB 55–57
  Windows XP and, APP 32

Web servers, APP 19–20. *See also* servers

Web site(s). interactive Web sites; Web pages

navigation, designing, PUB 394–396

previewing, PUB 443–446

saving, PUB 452

templates, PUB 390–382

testing, PUB 443–446, PUB 453

WebParts page, APP 7–8

widows, **PUB 183**

windows, maximized, PUB 5, PUB 41

Windows Vista (Microsoft), APP 21–22, APP 28–32

quitting Publisher with, PUB 41, PUB 60, PUB 135

starting Publisher with, PUB 4–5, PUB 6, PUB 41–43

Web folders and, PUB 55

Windows XP (Microsoft), APP 28–32

opening files with, APP 31

saving files with, APP 29–31

Word (Microsoft)

described, APP 4–5

documents, importing, APP 32

interactive Web sites and, PUB 397–398

Merge features and, PUB 325

newsletters and, PUB 89, PUB 98–101

word wrap, PUB 24–27, PUB 108, PUB 185

WordArt

described, **PUB 198–205**, PUB 264

formatting, PUB 187

objects, inserting, PUB 198–199

t-shirts and, PUB 208

workbooks. *See also* worksheets

described, **PUB 466**

OLE and, PUB 473

worksheets. *See also* workbooks

described, PUB 466

editing, PUB 476–477

OLE and, PUB 467–468, PUB 470–475, PUB 480

workspace

described, **PUB 13–15**

using the, PUB 286

wrapping

points, PUB 264–265

styles, **PUB 185**

X

XML (eXtensible Markup Language), **PUB 389**, PUB 440

XPS files, PUB 229

Z

zero point, **PUB 344**

Zoom box, PUB 21, PUB 23

Zoom In button, PUB 21

zooming

brochures and, PUB 167, PUB 171, PUB 175, PUB 188, PUB 189

e-mail and, PUB 230

flyers and, PUB 8, PUB 21–23, PUB 25, PUB 35

methods, PUB 21–23

newsletters and, PUB 89

template previews and, PUB 8

Quick Reference Summary

In the Microsoft Office Publisher 2007 program, you can accomplish a task in a number of ways. The following table provides a quick reference to each task presented in this textbook. The first column identifies the task. The second column indicates the page number on which the task is discussed in the book. The subsequent four columns list the different ways the task in column one can be carried out.

Microsoft Publisher 2007 Quick Reference Summary

Task	Page Number	Mouse	Menu Bar	Shortcut Menu	Keyboard Shortcut
Add Text	PUB 194			Add text	
Address List Columns, Customize	PUB 327	Customize Columns button in New Address List dialog box	Tools | Mailings and Catalogs | Edit Address List		
Address List, Connect to Main Publication	PUB 335		Tools | Mailings and Catalogs | Mail Merge		
Address List, Create	PUB 326		Tools | Mailings and Catalogs | Create Address List		
Address List, Create New Row	PUB 331	New Entry button in New Address List dialog box			
Alternative Text	PUB 406		Format | Picture | Web tab	Format Picture | Web tab	
Animated Graphic, Preview	PUB 401	In Clip Art task pane, click graphic button, click Preview/Properties			
AutoCorrect Options	PUB 166	Point to smart tag, click AutoCorrect Options button			
AutoFit Text	PUB 18, 319		Format | AutoFit Text	ChangeText | AutoFit Text	
AutoShape	PUB 269	Fill Color button arrow on Standard toolbar	Format | AutoShape | Colors and Lines tab	Format AutoShape | Colors and Lines tab	
AutoShapes, Fill	PUB 269	AutoShapes button on Objects toolbar	Insert | Picture | AutoShapes		
Automatic Saving	PUB 158		Tools | Options | Save tab		
Background Sound	PUB 409	Browse button in Web Page Options dialog box			

Microsoft Publisher 2007 Quick Reference Summary *(continued)*

Task	Page Number	Mouse	Menu Bar	Shortcut Menu	Keyboard Shortcut
Backgrounds	PUB 235	Apply a Background in Background task pane	Format	Background		
Best Fit	PUB 195			Change Text	AutoFit Text	Best Fit	
Bookmark, Create	PUB 400	Bookmark button on Objects toolbar	Insert	Bookmark		
Bookmark, Go To	PUB 411	Bookmark button on Objects toolbar			
Brightness, Decrease for Picture	PUB 260	Less Brightness button on Picture toolbar	Format	Picture	Picture tab	Format Picture	Picture tab	
Brightness, Increase for Picture	PUB 260	More Brightness button on Picture toolbar	Format	Picture	Picture tab	Format Picture	Picture tab	
Bullets	PUB 26, PUB 114	Bullets button on Standard toolbar	Format	Bullets and Numbering		
Business Information Set Components	PUB 256	Other task panes button on task pane title bar	Business Information	Insert	Business Information		
Business Information Set, Create	PUB 248		Edit	Business Information		
Business Information Set, Delete	PUB 301		Edit	Business Information		
Business Information Set, Update	PUB 250	Smart tag button	Edit Business Information	enter data	Update Publication	Edit	Business Information	enter data	Update Publication		
Calendar	PUB 365	Design Gallery Object button on Objects toolbar	Insert	Design Gallery Object		
Catalog Merge	PUB 358	Start Catalog Merge link in Format Publication task pane	Tools	Mailings and Catalogs	Catalog Merge		
Cell Diagonal, Create	PUB 291		Table	Cell Diagonals	Change Table	Cell Diagonals	
Cell, Select	PUB 287	Triple-click cell	Table	Select	Cell		
Center	PUB 48	Center button on Formatting toolbar	Format	Paragraph	Change Text	Paragraph	CTRL+E
Change Pages	PUB 83	Page icon on status bar	Edit	Go to Page		CTRL+G
Checkbox Form Control Properties	PUB 429	Double-click form control	Format	Form Properties	Format Form Properties	
Checkbox Form Controls	PUB 428	Form Control button on Objects toolbar	Checkbox	Insert	Form Control	Checkbox		
Clip Art	PUB 261	Picture Frame button on Objects toolbar	Insert	Picture	Clip Art		
Clip Art, Ungrouping	PUB 265		Arrange	Ungroup		CTRL+SHIFT+G
Close Task Pane	PUB 17	Close button on task pane title bar			
Close Publication	PUB 284	Close button on title bar	File	Close		CTRL+F4

Microsoft Publisher 2007 Quick Reference Summary *(continued)*

Task	Page Number	Mouse	Menu Bar	Shortcut Menu	Keyboard Shortcut
Color Effects, Select for Picture	PUB 260	Color button on Picture toolbar	Format | Picture | Picture tab	Format Picture | Picture tab	
Color Scheme	PUB 9	Color scheme box arrow in Customize area	Format | Color Schemes		
Column, Resize	PUB 292	Point to column border | drag border			
Column, Select	PUB 287	Point to top of column | when pointer becomes a downward pointing arrow, click	Table | Select | Column		
Commercial Printing Tool	PUB 211		Tools | Commercial Printing Tools		
Compress Pictures	PUB 260	Compress Pictures button on Picture toolbar	Format | Picture | Picture tab	Format Picture | Picture tab	
Connect to Catalog Data Source	PUB 359	Use an existing list option button in Catalog Merge task pane | Next: Create or connect to a product list link			
Content Library, Add to	PUB 283	Add selected items to Content Library in Content Library task pane	Insert | Add to Content Library	Add to Content Library	
Content Library, Delete from	PUB 300	Content button in Content Library task pane | Delete			
Content Library, Insert from	PUB 297	Item from Content Library button on Objects toolbar	Insert | Item from Content Library		CTRL+SHIFT+E
Contiguous Cells, Rows, or Columns	PUB 287	Drag through cells, rows, or columns.			
Continued Notices	PUB 95	Double-click text box | Text Box tab	Format | Text Box | Text Box tab	Format Text Box | Text Box tab	
Contrast, Decrease for Picture	PUB 260	Less Contrast button on Picture toolbar	Format | Picture | Picture tab	Format Picture | Picture tab	
Contrast, Increase for Picture	PUB 260	More Contrast button on Picture toolbar	Format | Picture | Picture tab	Format Picture | Picture tab	
Convert to Web Publication	PUB 53		File | Convert to Web Publication		
Copy	PUB 119	Copy button on Standard toolbar	Edit | Copy	Copy	CTRL+C
Crop Picture	PUB 260, 262	Crop button on Picture toolbar	Format | Picture | Picture tab	Format Picture | Picture tab	
Crop to a Nonrectangular Shape	PUB 264		Arrange | Text Wrapping | Edit Wrap Points		
Custom Color Schemes	PUB 154	Create new color scheme link in Format Publication task pane	Format | Color Schemes | Create new color scheme link		
Date and Time	PUB 280		Insert | Date and Time		

Microsoft Publisher 2007 Quick Reference Summary *(continued)*

Task	Page Number	Mouse	Menu Bar	Shortcut Menu	Keyboard Shortcut
Delete Objects	PUB 28, PUB 158		Edit | Delete Object	Delete Object	DELETE
Delete Pages	PUB 83		Edit | Delete Page	Delete Page	
Design Checker	PUB 51		Tools | Design Checker		
Design Gallery Objects	PUB 117	Design Gallery Object button on Objects toolbar	Insert | Design Gallery Object		
Drop Cap, Create and Format	PUB 320		Format | Drop Cap	Change Text | Drop Cap	
Edit Story in Microsoft Word	PUB 98		Edit | Edit Story in Microsoft Word	Change Text | Edit Story in Microsoft Word	
Empty Picture Frame	PUB 404	Picture Frame button on Objects toolbar | Empty Picture Frame	Insert | Picture | Empty Picture Frame		
Fill Color	PUB 191	Fill Color button on Formatting toolbar		Format AutoShape | Colors and Lines tab	
Find and Replace Text	PUB 370	Other Task Panes Button | Find and Replace	Edit | Find		CTRL+F
First-line Indent Marker	PUB 345	Drag to desired location	Format | Tabs		
Font Color	PUB 102	Font Color button arrow on Formatting toolbar			
Font Effect	PUB 178		Format | Font	Change Text | Font	
Font Scheme	PUB 163	Style box arrow on Formatting toolbar	Format | Font Schemes	Change Text | Font	
Font Size	PUB 47	Font Size box arrow on Formatting toolbar	Format | Font	Change Text | Font	
Form Properties	PUB 439	Double-click form control			
Format Painter	PUB 169	Format Painter button on Standard toolbar			
Format Picture	PUB 260	Format Picture button on Picture toolbar	Format | Picture	Format Picture	
Formatting Marks	PUB 24, PUB 81	Special Characters button on Standard toolbar	View | Special Characters		CTRL+SHIFT+Y
Go To Feature	PUB 401				F5
Gradient Fill Effect, Create	PUB 275	Fill Color button arrow on Formatting toolbar | Fill Effects	Format | AutoShape | Colors and Lines tab	Format AutoShape | Colors and Lines tab	
Graphic	PUB 403	Click graphic in Clip Art task pane			
Graphic, Flip	PUB 403		Arrange | Rotate or Flip		
Grouped Field Codes	PUB 339	Display second step of Mail Merge task pane | click appropriate link			
Help	PUB 58	Microsoft Office Publisher Help button on Standard toolbar	Help | Microsoft Office Publisher Help		F1

Microsoft Publisher 2007 Quick Reference Summary *(continued)*

Task	Page Number	Mouse	Menu Bar	Shortcut Menu	Keyboard Shortcut
Horizontal Ruler Guide, Create	PUB 254	Drag horizontal ruler	Arrange | Ruler Guides | Add Horizontal Ruler Guide		
Hot Spot	PUB 440	Hot Spot button on Objects toolbar	Insert | Hyperlink		CTRL+K
HTML Code Fragment	PUB 441	HTML Code Fragment button on Objects toolbar	Insert | HTML Code Fragment		
Import Text	PUB 89, PUB 92		Insert | Text File	Change Text | Text File	
Individual Field Codes	PUB 342	Display second step of Mail Merge task pane | click appropriate link			
Insert a New Page	PUB 415		Insert | Page	Insert Page	CTRL+SHIFT+N
Insert Fields	PUB 361	Display first step of Catalog Merge task pane, click appropriate link			
Insert Graphic	PUB 110	Picture Frame button on Objects toolbar | Clip Art	Insert | Picture | Clip Art		
Insert Hyperlink	PUB 49, PUB 233	Insert Hyperlink button on Standard toolbar	Insert | Hyperlink	Hyperlink	CTRL+K
Insert Page Numbers	PUB 124	Insert Page Number button on Header and Footer toolbar	Insert | Page Numbers		
Insert Picture	PUB 260	Insert Picture button on Picture toolbar	Insert | Picture		
Insert Picture from Scanner or Camera	PUB 260	Insert Picture from Scanner or Camera button on Picture toolbar	Insert | Picture | From Scanner or Camera		
Kern Character Pairs	PUB 324	Double-click status bar | change value in Kerning box	Format | Character Spacing	Change Text | Character Spacing	CTRL+SHIFT+] CTRL+SHIFT+[
Labels, Print	PUB 353	Print link in Mail Merge task pane			
Left Indent Marker	PUB 345	Drag to desired location	Format | Tabs		
Line/Border Style, Change	PUB 260, 272	Line/Border Style button on Picture toolbar	Format | Picture | Colors and Lines	Format Picture | Colors and Lines	
Line/Border Style, Select	PUB 272	Line/Border Style button Formatting toolbar	Format | Picture | Colors and Lines	Format Picture | Colors and Lines	
Line Color	PUB 192	Line Color button on Formatting toolbar		Format AutoShape | Colors and Lines tab	
Line Color, Select	PUB 271	Line Color button arrow on Formatting toolbar	Format | AutoShape | Colors and Lines tab	Format AutoShape | Colors and Lines tab	
Line Spacing	PUB 181	Line Spacing button on Formatting toolbar	Format | Paragraph	Change Text | Paragraph	
Line/Border Style	PUB 192	Line/Border Style button on Formatting toolbar		Format AutoShape | Colors and Lines tab	
List Box Form Control	PUB 433	Form Control button on Objects toolbar | List Box	Insert | Form Control | List Box		

Microsoft Publisher 2007 Quick Reference Summary *(continued)*

Task	Page Number	Mouse	Menu Bar	Shortcut Menu	Keyboard Shortcut
List Box Form Control Properties	PUB 434	Double-click form control	Format | Form Properties	Format Form Properties	
Margin Guides, Display	PUB 251		View | Boundaries and Guides		CTRL+SHIFT+O
Margin Guides, Edit	PUB 251		File | Page Setup		
Master Page	PUB 198	View master pages link in Apply Master Page task pane	View | Master Page		CTRL+M
Master Page, Ignore	PUB 205		View | Ignore Master Page		
Measurement Toolbar, Position Objects with	PUB 299	Double-click Object Size box on status bar	View | Toolbars | Measurement		
Merged Pages, Print	PUB 349	Print button on Standard toolbar	Tools | Mailings and Catalogs | Mail Merge		
Move	PUB 122	Point to border and drag			Select object | ARROW KEY
Move Both Markers	PUB 345	Drag to desired location	Format | Tabs		
Move to Next Cell	PUB 287				TAB
Move to Previous Cell	PUB 287				SHIFT+TAB
Navigation Bar Properties	PUB 394	Select Navigation bar, click displayed button			
Nudge	PUB 122		Arrange | Nudge		Select object | ALT+ARROW KEY
Object, Flip	PUB 266		Arrange | Rotate or Flip	Format Picture | Size tab	
Object Margins, Set	PUB 345		Format | Text Box | Size tab	Format Text Box	
Open Publication	PUB 42	Open button on Standard toolbar	File | Open		CTRL+O
Option Button Form Control Properties	PUB 432	Double-click form control	Format | Form Properties	Format Form Properties	
Option Button Form Controls	PUB 430	Form Control button on Objects toolbar | Option Button	Insert | Form Control | Option Button		
Order, Change	PUB 278		Arrange | Order	Order	ALT+F6; ALT+SHIFT+F6
Pack and Go Wizard	PUB 212		File | Pack and Go | Take to a Commercial Printing Service		
Page Options	PUB 82	Page Options in Format Publication task pane			
Page Size	PUB 238	Change Page Size button in Format Publication task pane	File | Page Setup		
Paste	PUB 119	Paste button on Standard toolbar	Edit | Paste	Paste	CTRL+V
Picture Toolbar	PUB 187		View | Toolbars | Picture	Show Picture Toolbar	
Picture, Reset	PUB 260	Reset Picture button on Picture toolbar	Format | Picture | Picture tab	Format Picture | Picture tab	
Print	PUB 40, PUB 134	Print button on Standard toolbar	File | Print		CTRL+P

Microsoft Publisher 2007 Quick Reference Summary (continued)

Task	Page Number	Mouse	Menu Bar	Shortcut Menu	Keyboard Shortcut
Print Preview	PUB 207	Print Preview button on Standard toolbar	File | Print Preview		
Publication Properties	PUB 38		File | Properties		
Publish to the Web	PUB 55		File | Publish to the Web		
Publication, New	PUB 247	New button on Standard toolbar	File | New		CTRL+N
Publisher Tasks	PUB 130	Publisher Tasks button on Standard toolbar			
Quit Publisher	PUB 41	Close button on Publisher title bar	File | Exit	Microsoft Publisher button on Windows taskbar | Close	ALT+F4
Recipients, Filter	PUB 337	Filter link in Mail Merge Recipients dialog box			
Replace Graphic	PUB 34	Picture Frame button on Objects toolbar	Insert | Picture | Clip Art	Change Picture | Clip Art	
Resize Graphic	PUB 112, PUB 197	Format Picture button on Picture toolbar | Picture tab	Format | Picture | Picture tab	Format Picture | Picture tab	Drag handle
Right Indent Marker	PUB 345	Drag to desired location			
Row, Resize	PUB 292	Point to row border | drag border			
Save	PUB 40	Save button on Standard toolbar	File | Save		CTRL+S
Save As	PUB 31, PUB 52		File | Save As		CTRL+S
Security Level	PUB 435		Tools | Macro | Security		
Select All	PUB 20, PUB 86		Edit | Select All		CTRL+A
Select Characters	PUB 104	Drag character(s)			SHIFT+ARROW KEY
Select Graphic	PUB 104	Click graphic			
Select Multiple Objects	PUB 296	SHIFT+click each object			
Select Paragraph	PUB 104	Triple-click paragraph or double-click left margin			
Select Paragraphs	PUB 104	Drag left margin			
Select Picture within Grouped Object	PUB 104	Click picture | Click picture again			
Select Row	PUB 104	Click left of row in table	Table | Select | Row		
Select Rows	PUB 104	Drag left of rows in table or triple-click left of table			
Select Sentence	PUB 104	Drag text			
Select Text	PUB 22				Click beginning, SHIFT+click end
Select Word	PUB 104	Double-click word			
Select Words	PUB 104	Drag words			

Microsoft Publisher 2007 Quick Reference Summary *(continued)*

Task	Page Number	Mouse	Menu Bar	Shortcut Menu	Keyboard Shortcut
Send Publication via E-Mail	PUB 237		File | Send E-mail		
Shadow, Add	PUB 274	Shadow Style button on Formatting toolbar			
Shape	PUB 190	AutoShapes button on Objects toolbar	Insert | Picture | Autoshapes		
Snap to Guides	PUB 255		Arrange | Snap | To Guides		CTRL+SHIFT+W
Snapping, Turn on	PUB 255		Arrange | Snap		
Special Characters	PUB 247	Special Characters button on Standard toolbar	View | Special Characters		CTRL+SHIFT+Y
Spell Check	PUB 30, PUB 127	Spelling button on Standard toolbar	Tools | Spelling | Spelling	Proofing Tools | Spelling	F7
Style, Apply	PUB 176	Styles box arrow on Formatting toolbar			
Style, New	PUB 174	New Style button in Styles task pane			
Styles	PUB 172	Styles button on Formatting toolbar	Format | Styles		
Submit Form Controls	PUB 437	Form Control button on Objects toolbar | Submit	Insert | Form Control | Submit		
Tab Selector	PUB 345	Tab Selector box at left end of horizontal ruler			
Tab Stop Marker	PUB 345	Click ruler to create; drag to move	Format | Tabs		
Table, Create	PUB 286	Insert Table button on Objects toolbar	Table | Insert | Table		
Table, Deselect	PUB 287	Click outside of table			
Table, Format	PUB 289		Format | Table |	Format Table	
Table, Resize	PUB 292	Drag sizing handle			
Table, Select	PUB 287	Click table border	Table | Select | Table		
Template	PUB 7, PUB 150	Click template preview in catalog			
Text Area Form Control	PUB 425	Form Control button on Objects toolbar | Text Area	Insert | Form Control | Text Area		
Text Area Form Control Properties	PUB 426	Double-click form control	Format | Form Properties	Format Form Properties	
Text Box	PUB 46, 333	Text Box button on Objects toolbar	Insert | Text Box		
Text Box, Position Relative to Margins	PUB 259		Arrange | Align or Distribute | Relative to Margin Guides		
Text, Convert to Plain Text	PUB 318	Point to Business Information text | click smart tag | Convert to Plain Text			

Microsoft Publisher 2007 Quick Reference Summary *(continued)*

Task	Page Number	Mouse	Menu Bar	Shortcut Menu	Keyboard Shortcut
Text Wrap	PUB 187	Text Wrapping button on Picture toolbar			
Textbox Form Control Properties	PUB 424	Double-click form control	Format | Form Properties	Format Form Properties	
Textbox Form Controls	PUB 422	Form Control button on Objects toolbar | Textbox	Insert | Form Control | Textbox		
Track Characters	PUB 323	Double-click status bar | change value in Tracking box	Format | Character Spacing	Change Text | Character Spacing	
Transparent Color, Set	PUB 260	Set Transparent Color button on Picture toolbar			
Transparent Object	PUB 187, PUB 206				CTRL+T
VBA Code Window, Open	PUB 448		Tools | Macro | Visual Basic Editor		ALT+F11
Web Site, Preview and Test	PUB 443	Web Page Preview button on Standard toolbar	File | Web Page Preview		
Web Page Options, Edit	PUB 408		Tools | Web Page Options		
Web Page Preview	PUB 57	Web Page Preview button on Standard toolbar	File | Web Page Preview		
WordArt, Format	PUB 202	WordArt Shape button on WordArt toolbar			
WordArt, Insert	PUB 201	Insert WordArt button on Objects toolbar			
Wrap Text	PUB 260	Text Wrapping button on Picture toolbar	Format | Picture | Layout tab	Format Picture | Layout tab	
Zoom	PUB 8	Zoom Out or Zoom In button on Standard toolbar	View | Zoom	Zoom	F9